THE SOLDIER IN RUSSIAN POLITICS

Robert V. Barylski

THE SOLDIER IN RUSSIAN POLITICS

Duty, Dictatorship, and Democracy Under Gorbachev and Yeltsin

Transaction Publishers
New Brunswick (U.S.A.) and London (U.K.)

This book is printed on acid-free paper that meets the American National Standard for Permanence of Paper for Printed Library Materials.

Library of Congress Catalog Number: 97-51704
ISBN: 1-56000-335-9
Printed in the United States of America

Library of Congress Cataloging-in-Publication Data

Barylski, Robert V.
    The soldier in Russian politics : duty, dictatorship and democracy under Gorbachev and Yeltsin / Robert V. Barylski.
        p. cm.
    Includes bibliographical references (p.   ) and index.
    ISBN 1-56000-335-9 (alk. paper)
    1. Civil-military relations—Russia (Federation). 2. Russia (Federation)—Politics and government—1991– 3. Civil-military relations—Soviety Union. 4. Soviet Union—Politics and government—1985–1991. I. Title.
JN6693.5.C58B37   1998
322'.5'094709048—dc21   97-51704
                                                                            CIP

This book is dedicated to my wife Irene, my son Alexander, and my daughter Natasha.

Contents

Preface

I wish to thank the colleagues on the administration, faculty, and staff of the University of South Florida for providing a supportive environment and thoughtful assistance as I completed the research and writing of this book over the past six years. Without major public universities that nurture independent research and strong teaching America would be poorer intellectually and less well served by its academic intellectuals.

I wish to thank Transaction Publishers and Irving Louis Horowitz for editing and publishing this book. Without a large number of competitive presses, American society would be weaker, less adaptive, and less free.

Although we compete and debate freely, we tend to move in patterns as a community of scholars influenced by prevailing ideological and methodological preferences. The Cold War produced its dominant schools and the post-Cold War is already encouraging some lines of inquiry and discouraging others. I have tried to leave the Cold War behind without being swept up in the new intellectual stampede. Nevertheless, it is difficult to study post-Soviet Russian society and politics without being drawn into the new dominant trend that insists upon giving the Russians advice about building a better society. But to promote objectivity over advocacy I regularly asked myself questions such as these: What are we *supposed* to be saying about the Russians now and why? What are Russian colleagues saying about themselves and why? What does the accumulated body of social science have to offer? Is it Western bourgeois thinking or is it universal science? Why is there such ambiguity about the most important terms such as the *state*, *politics*, and *society*? Why are coercion and armed forces part of building, rebuilding, and maintaining states? How do military functions change as societies change their political and economic systems?

But there are more questions than can be answered in one book and history moves on. Social scientists found themselves trying to explain events before the political historians established what actually happened. The general public, business leaders, and politicians wanted simple, clear answers about the direction of change in the former Soviet Union. They had a preferred, positive interpretation for what was taking place. At first Gorbachev was their hero; then he became their favorite failed hero. Then Yeltsin took up the mantle. But he failed to deliver on his promise, the economy was still in deep recession, and the state could not meet its obligations. Who would straighten it out? The rising class of financial entrepreneurs? The armed forces? An alliance of new money and old arms? What happened to the invisible hand—the promised miracle of competitive politics and economics?

During the late 1980s and 1990s I discussed such questions with colleagues from Russia, Ukraine, and Azerbaijan. I was interested in how fellow professionals struggled to deal constructively and progressively with systemic reform. From the outset, their perceptions did not match the prevailing Western views. They were more pessimistic about systemic breakdown and prospects for organizing political and economic life in a way that would convert ordinary human venality into prosperity and freedom. Civilian leaders were swept up in the great post-Soviet rush to privatization and ethno-national sovereignty. The Soviet defense system did not escape the political knife that cut the unitary Soviet Union into some fifteen sovereign states. This left military leaders bewildered and wondering what happened to the greater national interest and the state's ability to maintain basic functional viability.

Military reporters, analysts, and accountable officers faced two major strategic intellectual problems. First they had to change the way the armed forces news was reported and discussed. They provided more and better information about military affairs, they expanded the public debate about defense policy, and they began the long task of revising political history. Second, they tried to support progressive reform and to find a fair balance between military corporate interests and the public interest in cutting and controlling defense spending. Although some Russian military professionals were able to analyze the dilemmas of political, economic, and military reform in keeping with the best international standards, it was extremely difficult to translate such theory into successful political practice. Some Soviet colleagues used to joke about the problem and to recommend that Gorbachev put up a "Closed for Renovations" sign at every border crossing. But history does not stop for societal repairs.

This book has several basic goals. I wanted to leave a detailed narrative of the military's role in the politics that brought down the Soviet state and began its reconstruction. Therefore I produced a work of current history. But I also wanted to explain the events as examples of universal political and sociological processes and thereby mixed political science and political sociology into the historical narrative. The central idea is that complex, modern societies cannot survive without viable states to make and enforce authoritative decisions. The state needs an effective political system to make and enforce the general operating rules or authoritative decisions which nurture overall societal cohesion and sustain high levels of complex economic activity. Armed forces are essential to the state's political functions. Military forces defend the state against external threats. Police forces enforce laws and maintain domestic order. Military and police functions fuse during periods of chronic and major domestic instability. When political breakdown threatens the state's ability to support the armed forces adequately, military leaders are drawn into politics in search of allies capable of restoring state viability.

This book also invites readers to explore political-cultural differences between Western and Russo-Soviet thinking about military participation in political life and societal governance of defense affairs. Those explorations suggest that we need to expand our discussion beyond the standard focus on civilian control into the realm of democratic governance of defense affairs.

A Note on Transliteration and Translation

Over the decades scholars have developed various systems for spelling Russian names and terms in the Latin alphabet. These vary from country to country and change over time. The predominant American system was established by the Library of Congress and is normally used by American scholars. That system has strengths and weaknesses. Its main strength is consistency in letter by letter transliteration. Its main weaknesses is that it does not convey the sound of Russian to non-Russian speakers. I follow the Library of Congress system but adapt it for non-Russian speakers who need to know the sound of Russian in order to pronounce family names and concept terms properly. The current president of Russia is "Yeltsin" in the American press and in this book's text but "El'tsin" in the Library of Congress system. The Russian family name equivalent to "Smith" is rendered "Kovalev" in the Library of Congress system and "Kovalyev" in my system. The astute reader will thereby learn to stress the final syllable "yev" and to pronounce the name properly. The Defense Ministry's daily paper, *Red Star*, is *Krasnaia zvezda* in the Library of Congress system and *Krasnaya zvezda* in my text. However, I have generally followed the Library of Congress system in the bibliography in order to assist researchers who need to locate materials.

There are serious translation problems which have not been resolved. One of the most important involves the meaning of the word, Russian. The English language has only one word but the Russian language has two words and two different ideas. When Russians wish to describe the inhabitants of Russia—all the citizens without regard to ethnic background, they use the plural noun *Rossiyane* and the adjective *Rossiiskiye*. But when they want to describe the ethnic Russians among the *Rossiyane,* they use the plural noun *Russkiye*. The ethnic Russian nouns and adjectives are neither used to describe the state of Russia (*Rossiiskaya Federatsiya*) nor its departments of government. Thus, the armed forces are called the *Rossiiskiye Vooruzhennye Sily*—the Rossiyan Armed Forces, not the *Russkiye Vooruzhennye Sil*—the Russian Armed Forces. Since American translations of Yeltsin's speeches and other Russian language materials fail to convey these distinctions, Americans are given the impression that Yeltsin and others are speaking like ethno-Russian nationalists when they are actually doing the opposite and using the ethnically neutral words *Rossiyane* and *Rossiiskiye*.

We really need to add the word "Rossiyan" to the English language and to learn to make the same distinctions that Russian speakers have to make when they discuss their country's ethnic and political issues. However, since we do not have two words, I have started using "ethno-Russian" to designate the ethnic Russian idea and to render *Russkiye* in English. I use "Russian" for the ethnically neutral or geopolitical designation *Rossiyane*. All students of Russian politics should take note of this problem and realize that many translations of remarks made by Russian political leaders are faulty. On the whole, our translations make them sound like ethno-Russian nationalists when they are actually trying to avoid sounding like ethno-Russian nationalists.

Introduction

The Soldier in Russian Politics examines military dimensions of contemporary Russian politics. It is both a political history and a political-sociological analysis. As political history it is a study of the military's role in the events that brought the Soviet state down, removed Mikhail Gorbachev from power, and consolidated Boris Yeltsin's position as the primary civilian leader responsible for Russia's reconstruction. As political-sociological analysis it is a modest revision of the Cold War's intellectual legacy, an effort to adapt the study of civil-military relations to new political and intellectual conditions. It develops concepts and paradigms that explain problems Russia experienced as it attempted to democratize political control over military affairs while giving the military an active voice in the national political debate.

The book is chronological, analytical, and theoretical. Each chapter describes what happened and explains events in terms of general political processes that are not unique to Russia. It assumes that Russian politics are understandable to all students of politics and do not represent some esoteric field of inquiry. The book is divided into three parts. The first part opens with an essay on the evolution of Western ideas about civil-military relations in the Soviet Union, sketches a brief political history of the Russian military in the twentieth century, discusses Mikhail Gorbachev's increasingly troubled relationship with the armed forces, analyzes the military's involvement in the coups of August 1991, and describes the military's contribution to the peaceful dissolution of the Soviet Union in December 1991.

The second part examines the military's role in post-Soviet reconstruction, the new Russian state's struggle to achieve viability, and the effort to build a Commonwealth of Independent States centered on Russia. The evidence shows that military political life operated on three levels and involved three related sets of interests: the individual officer with personal and career interests, the military institutions with their institutional interests, and the state with its national interests. The book discusses the interaction between individuals, institutions, and society as a whole. Although modernization theory, systems analysis, and organization theory help explain general trends, individuals still shape the outcome of political conflicts. Consequently, the book is about people as well as institutions.

Marshal Dmitry Yazov is remembered as the minister of defense who joined the failed coup against his commander-in-chief, Soviet President Mikhail

1

Gorbachev in August 1991. Yazov's personal, professional, and national patriotic dilemmas reflected those faced by the Soviet military as a whole. He is the Soviet minister of defense who implemented Gorbachev's reforms, retired the more conservative senior generation of military leaders, put leading Soviet officers in contact with foreign counterparts in the advanced democratic states, and gave officers expanded opportunities to discuss national policy, military policy, and professional issues. Although Yazov used lethal force to defend the Soviet state in Georgia, Azerbaijan, and Lithuania and joined the coup against Gorbachev in August 1991, it was also Yazov who refused to turn Soviet military guns on the Soviet people, pulled the military out of the coup, and thereby doomed it to failure on the night of August 20–21, 1991.

Yazov's successor, Soviet Defense Minister Yevgeny Shaposhnikov emerges as a more positive figure. During the critical months following the August 1991 coup, he immersed himself in politics and kept the Soviet military sufficiently cohesive and politically reliable to prevent civil war. At first, Shaposhnikov found himself in the position of reporting to two presidents simultaneously, Gorbachev and Yeltsin. He abandoned Gorbachev before Gorbachev had officially released him and before Gorbachev formally closed the presidency of the Soviet Union. Once Gorbachev fully understood that the military had rejected him in favor of Yeltsin, he had little choice but to resign. Although the military rejected Gorbachev's weak leadership, it was uncomfortable with Yeltsin's cycles of manic and depressive behavior. Yeltsin demanded immediate breakthroughs; Shaposhnikov urged restraint. Yeltsin decided to nationalize the bulk of the Soviet military machine in the name of sovereign Russia and to divide the rest with the republics. Shaposhnikov tried but failed to mobilize enough civilian and military political support to build a strong collective security alliance based upon a strong Commonwealth of Independent States (CIS). After making an enormous contribution to the relatively peaceful transition from a Union of Soviet Socialist Republics to a weak CIS, Shaposhnikov lost favor and his collective security project lost ground to a Russocentric agenda.

Yeltsin passed over Shaposhnikov and chose General Pavel Grachev to serve as post-Soviet Russia's first minister of defense. Grachev had to lead the military through reconstruction while coping with enormous financial and political difficulties. But the Yeltsin administration did not govern effectively. The president competed with Parliament and Moscow competed with the regions. Yeltsin decided that he needed a bold political breakthrough to resolve the political impasse. Senior military leaders reluctantly supported his presidential putsch of September-October 1993. Even though the military as a whole shared the growing national disillusionment with the Yeltsin administration's performance, senior officers supported state-strengthening policies, including the putsch for two reasons. Military corporate interests and national security interests were compatible with Yeltsin's new *statist* ideology and Yeltsin was their legal commander-in-chief. Tanks and commandos conquered Parliament for Yeltsin on 4 October 1993. Nevertheless, senior military leaders deeply resented such breakdowns in civilian leadership coherence, actively tried to discourage Parliament from resisting, warned Parliament that a military attack was coming, and controlled the final assault in a manner that protected the lives of the rebellion's leaders.

The book's third part describes the military's response to Russia's deepening economic and political instability during the three years following the October 1993 presidential *putsch*. Individual chapters examine the Chechen war, the Duma elections of 1993 and 1995, and the presidential elections of 1996. They discuss the military's adaptation to competitive elections, civil liberties, and a lively mass media. The facts support the thesis that changes in national political structures encourage new types of military political behavior. But they also demonstrate that adaptation is an eclectic process in which seemingly incompatible habits coexist. Civilian leaders combined new democratic formalities with old Soviet authoritarian habits. So did the military. Personal loyalty systems, informal civil-military bonding, disrespect for the letter of the law, and administrative highhandedness—such old habits persisted and sometimes actually helped the military to cope with change. One new habit—the political outspokenness or *glasnost* that sprouted under Gorbachev continued into the reconstruction era. Military officers spoke out on political questions, ran for office, and engaged in duels with the press, with each other, and with civilian leaders. Both military cohesion and civilian control weakened.

The Russian military initially supported *perestroika* because civilian leaders ordered them to, enough senior military leaders understood the theoretical relationship between market competition, technological innovation, and defense modernization, and many had become familiar with Western models of military professionalism and were attracted to them. But post-Soviet Russia wasn't France, Germany, Great Britain or the United States of America where a healthy economy and a strong defense lobby sustained high levels of defense spending. The Russian military was confronted by a national consensus that believed defense spending had been too high and had to be slashed and a faltering economy that deprived the Kremlin treasury of the funds needed to support military reform properly.

Russia's democratic reformers alienated the national defense constituency, imposed huge defense spending and personnel cuts in the 1992 budget, and stuck to them. Therefore, in the Duma elections of 1993, military personnel voted primarily for opposition candidates, nationalists and former Communists who promised to use state power to rebuild Russian political, economic, and military might. The opposition won far more votes than the pro-administration party. However, once elected, the opposition had more constituencies to satisfy than resources available and did not raise military spending. Military discontent increased and more military officers ran for Duma seats in 1995 than in 1993. Some officers predicted that new national leaders capable of leading Russia out of crisis would emerge from military circles. Others argued that most officers were not prepared to serve as effective civilian leaders. The book examines that debate and describes the more prominent military politicians who ran for office and how they fared. A prominent Chechen war hero, Lt. General Lev Rokhlin, was elected on the pro-administration ticket although he was critical of administration policies. Rokhlin became head of the Duma's defense committee. But he faced the same resistance to defense spending and the same grim news from the Kremlin treasury.

The book analyzes the presidential elections of 1996, the first major test of Russian democracy and new example of the Russian military's propensity to invade civilian political space. It explains how Lt. General (Ret.) Aleksandr Lebed used his national standing and influence with voters to breach the Kremlin political walls and to forge a highly controversial, short-lived, political alliance with Yeltsin. Russian politicians were learning to compete in democratic elections and engaging in political behavior typical of politicians in countries with democratic political cultures. But they were also engaging in Kremlin factional intrigue and there were disturbing signs that the emerging financial elite was less committed to the democratic process than to consolidating its new power and position.

Yeltsin's staff studied public opinion as a whole, in various regions, and in various sectors of the electorate and planned the president's campaign strategy and tactics accordingly. Yeltsin's senior civilian advisers gave lectures on politics to senior military leaders, a move that resembled the former Communist Party dictatorship's practices. Senior officers were reminded that the president was their commander-in-chief and had the power to appoint and remove them. The Defense Ministry ordered all military personnel to study Yeltsin's key policy document and instructed the military press and media to propagate it throughout the armed forces. Yeltsin also promised to improve support to the military, to move more rapidly towards an all-professional military system, and to increase benefits to military personnel. He responded to military criticisms of the Chechen war and to the general public's concerns about the draft. He let the military attack the main rebel bases and he pledged to stop sending draftees to Chechnya—except those who volunteer, and to end the draft by the year 2000. To demonstrate that he really wanted peace, he met the Chechen rebel leader in the Kremlin. He courted the military-industrial complex vote by increasing the federal defense procurement order and by pledging to provide financial relief to the enterprises. He also created a new Ministry of Defense Industry. But Yeltsin still felt insecure about the military vote and he forged an electoral alliance with Aleksandr Lebed, a deal that put Yeltsin over the 50 percent mark but which precipitated a wave of top level changes in national military and security leadership including Pavel Grachev's resignation.

The deals and the changes were a reminder that the senior military and security appointments were in the political domain and part of the spoils of political combat. The Yeltsin-Lebed alliance was reminiscent of the proverbial Russian hunter locked in an embrace with a bear. Yeltsin tried to contain the ambitious Lebed while still advancing the national interest and protecting his personal political power. Yet, Yeltsin was in poor health and the military was angry with the civilian leadership's failure to resolve basic national economic and political problems.

The fact that Yeltsin selected Rodionov to lead the military during his second administration brought military-political history full circle. It was Col. General Rodionov who emerged as the first controversial *political* general of the Gorbachev era. Rodionov took personal command of the military-police operation against Georgian civilian demonstrators that resulted in the death of women and children in April 1989. General Rodionov was also an elected deputy to the Soviet parliament who stood his ground, defended his men, and criticized the civilian leaders for mismanaging domestic politics and causing soldiers to kill fellow citizens. At the time some progressives read into his remarks a military threat to civilian rule but he was trying to focus attention upon due process, competency, and accountability issues.

Yeltsin appointed Col. General Rodionov to serve as defense minister in July 1996 and then promoted him to the highest military rank, army general. Rodionov was emerging as Yeltsin's primary military statesman. Yeltsin needed such an ally because the military was warning that the army, the economy, and the state were in danger of collapse. In December 1996, Yeltsin asked Rodionov to resign from the military but to continue serving Russia as defense minister. This act made Igor Rodionov post-Soviet Russia's first, *civilian* Defense Minister. Yeltsin explained that he wanted to demonstrate that civilians controlled the military. However, Yeltsin's relationship with Rodionov soured quickly and Yeltsin fired him in May 1997 for openly challenging the administration's optimistic statements about defense reforma nd defense system reliability. Yeltsin named a military commander, Igor Rodionov to succeed Rodionov but also promulgated a new State Military Inspectorate headed by civilians to monitor the armed forces. The book's final chapter evaluates those events and raises basic questions about the difference between civilian control in Yeltsin's presidential state and democratic governance of military affairs.

This book is neither pro- nor antimilitary. Its main goal is to describe what happened fairly and objectively. It is a political history of the military's role in the events that ended the Soviet dictatorship and changed world history. It is dedicated to the progressive officers, soldiers, and politicians who made the professional and personal decisions that prevented bloodshed and civil war at critical turning points and which helped limit and stop such conflicts when prevention eluded them. But it is also a warning that when civilian political institutions fail to cope with basic developmental tasks, the use of coercion to settle domestic political conflicts tends to increase and so does the military's participation in domestic political life. In 1985 when the civilian oligarchy was cohesive and effective, there were no civil wars inside the Soviet Union and the military was under reliable civilian control. By 1995–1996, civilian leadership cohesion and effectiveness had both declined, civil war had broken out in various parts of the former Soviet Union, including Russia, and the military had become more involved in politics. That pattern confirms the validity of the general body of theory that predicts increases in military political activity when civilian institutions founder and, more hopefully, a retreat from politics if and when national political institutions perform more effectively.

The social scientist can describe and explain the institutional settings in which the game of Russian politics is played and can sketch several likely futures. But we cannot predict the precise outcomes which still depend upon the will, intelligence, and energy of the players. In writing this book I gained a deep appreciation for the enormous effort and dedication it takes to move the Russian reform enterprise forward and of the mixture of idealism and venality embedded in post-Soviet political culture. It is easy to criticize bold leaders such as Gorbachev and Yeltsin for lacking the political sophistication required to design political institutions and to set political precedents that would speed the institutionalization of effective democratic government. Yet it is precisely the real political actors who combine idealism and venality who make history and for whom institutions need to be designed. The best political institutions are structured in ways that encourage normal human beings to produce better politics than they would otherwise produce. My research found that some military political analysts made similar comments after every major domestic political crisis, a fact that inspires hope if not absolute confidence in the eventual success of the democratic enterprise.

Part I

The Military and the End of the Soviet State

1

Thinking About Civil-Military Relations in Russia

For decades, Western thinking about civil-military relations in Russia has trailed behind Russian politics. One school of analysis followed another as Western scholars competed to bring their models of Soviet politics into alignment with changing Soviet political realities. This chapter traces the evolution of Western thinking about Russia's political system and the military's place within it. It opens with a brief discussion of the Yeltsin administration's efforts to explain its position in political history as Russia approached the presidential elections of 1996. This is followed by a brief discussion of modernization theory for two reasons. First, it was influential in post-Soviet, Russian political science and among highly placed Russian political advisers to the Gorbachev and Yeltsin administrations. Second, it helps explain the general direction of Russian political change. The chapter then discusses the succession of Western schools, beginning with the totalitarian school and ending with state-building and democratic transition studies, and describes each school's influence on the study of the Russian military's role in politics.

The Political Use of History and Social Science

Russia is rediscovering and rebuilding its national history. On 23 February 1996, President Boris Yeltsin invoked the lessons of history in his annual message to the Federal Assembly. Yeltsin said, "I am categorically against the conclusions drawn by some theorists that Russia is virtually fated by tradition to be a dictatorship."[1] Yeltsin urged Russians to break with the old political culture's authoritarianism and radical utopianism. He described Russia as a country engaged in a complex struggle with its own bad habits: "No one has the power to help Russia and to lift Russia except us. We have to fight our own barbarism, disorder, poverty, laziness, and lack of culture."[2] He urged fellow citizens to persevere with reform and to build a democratic government as the only viable alternative to dictatorship and anarchy.

National history is part of national political culture and it shapes present and future political behavior. The same holds true for military history. What soldiers believe about the past will influence their current political behavior. Did the military make a positive contribution to Russia's development or was it primarily a burden? Is the military naturally allied to Russian authoritarianism or can it prosper under a more open, competitive political system? Can the military trust civilian politicians? Yeltsin's comments on the relationship between Soviet military-industrial power and the Soviet dictatorship described the military-industrial complex as an enormous engine that devoured national wealth, one not justified by Russia's true security needs. Although Yeltsin did not blame the military itself for that situation, he gave the armed forces no hope of ever returning to the high levels of defense spending and staffing that prevailed before 1991.

The Yeltsin administration rejected the Soviet dictatorship's ambitious international policies and high levels of defense spending. Yeltsin explained, "The attempt to maintain military parity with the *capitalist world* and to help the countries of the *socialist camp* and all *progressive forces* had sucked the last juices from the economy and destroyed civilian consumption."[3] Yeltsin's remarks confirmed that his economic strategy was based upon a firm belief that defense spending had to be cut and kept at levels far lower than those maintained during the Soviet period. The military supported political and economic reforms because the military wanted a more dynamic economy, one capable of supplying the armed forces with leading-edge, military technology. But things developed very differently. The reform movement expanded into a rebellion against the Soviet dictatorship and Soviet militarism. Yeltsin's 1996 message to the Federal Assembly confirmed that linkage.

But Yeltsin still argued for basic economic reform and insisted that the new competitive economic system would eventually produce an abundance of new technology. He repeated the standard Western criticisms of the Soviet model: The Soviet system could not respond to the demands of modernization that hit with full power at the end of the twentieth century—the scientific and technological revolution, the information revolution, the emerging globalization of world economy. Totalitarian control stifles economic and technological dynamism and cannot harness the new technologies. The dictatorship's need for strict political control prevented science and technology from developing their full potential. Any return to state-driven models of development would be counterproductive: "Now at the end of the twentieth century, it is clear that states based on rule by fear are doomed. History has pronounced its judgment."[4]

Key ideas in Yeltsin's message should be familiar to Western readers because they are based upon a combination of modernization theory and complex systems analysis not Marxism-Leninism or some particularistic, postcommunist, Russian social science. They also draw upon basic concepts in political sociology such as *political culture*. Such ideas moved into political life through the political scientists and sociologists who served as political consultants and staff members inside the Gorbachev and Yeltsin administrations. Today Russian scholars and their Western colleagues are working from a similar base of social science principles and concepts. The more intellectually inclined and thoughtful civilian and military leaders are likewise becoming assimilated into the universal body of knowledge related to their professions. They see themselves in two ways. On the one hand they are rational political actors who are changing history. On the other hand, they are being pushed by forces beyond their control, a mixture of old habits and new interest groups that make it extremely difficult for the Kremlin to reform Russia successfully.

Not even the Communist opposition has been immune to these trends. However, the Communists adopted a Burkean or conservative line. They argued that national traditions and political culture require Russia to modernize within tradition in order to be successful. They criticized the Yeltsin administration and the Western modernization paradigm for having underestimated the role that a strong Russian state and socialist traditions can and must play in societal reconstruction. They ridiculed Yeltsin's attempts to lay the main blame for Russia's economic and military decline on the Soviet regime in general, Gorbachev in particular, and radical democrats—his own political appointees! The Communists argued for a directed modernization strategy in keeping with Russian tradition; their program had considerable appeal.

In order to drive a wedge between the Communists and the military, the Yeltsin campaign invoked history. Yeltsin sent his chief of staff, Nikolai Yegorov, to lecture the senior military officers on reasons to reject the Communists who were using nationalist and patriotic appeals to attract military voters.[5] Yegorov's talk was designed to damage the Communist Party's patriotic and nationalist appeal. Yegorov reminded officers that it was the Communist Party that had undermined military cohesion, encouraged soldiers to kill officers, and destroyed Russia's democratic reform movement in 1917. The Communists plunged the country into civil war and destroyed the 1000-year-old Russian state.[6] But Yegorov also agreed with military complaints that in recent years it was the democratic reformers not the Communists who imposed radical changes on the country such as deep cuts in national defense. Yegorov noted that similarly immature reformers in the tsarist Duma had refused to fund tsarist military reforms properly. This damaged the Russian state's military capability and contributed to the political collapse that led to revolution and civil war.[7] Yegorov insisted that Yeltsin was aware of his responsibilities as head of state and supreme commander of the armed forces and had already rejected the antimilitary line popular in some democratic circles. Yegorov said, "It is above all to the credit of the President of the Russian Federation that we broke that negative trend and adopted a realistic, truly statist ideology and policy for military development."[8]

The debate about what went wrong, whom should be held accountable, and what should be done was a healthy development, a sign that Russia's political culture was changing. Politicians were competing for public support and the debate was producing ideas about how to improve the general political economy without reverting to Soviet dictatorship. Modernization—the institutionalization of political and economic competition, had broad support. The theory had won but the practice—the shift from the unitary state and planned economy into fifteen sovereign republics and a mixed economic system, had encountered major problems which no political party could resolve easily. Instead of giving the military a new powerful economy, the changes produced a collapsing economy and an ineffective state administrative system that could not collect enough revenue to support national defense responsibly even at greatly reduced levels.

Modernization Theory

What was driving the Soviet political system towards the radical reforms that took place under Gorbachev and Yeltsin? Why did the Soviet military accept those changes instead of insisting upon a more conservative approach to reform? Is there a general theory that can identify and explain the process that took place within the Soviet system and that convinced civilian and military leaders to support deep political and economic reforms? Western modernization theory describes political changes associated with the transition from agricultural to industrial society and predicts that all societies that make that transition will end up having some features in common. It predicted that tension would grow between Stalinist dictatorship and the new Soviet professional elites. It argued that Stalin's success at building an industrial society in the former Russian empire would eventually create new groups and values that were incompatible with totalitarian dictatorship.

The political sociology of modern industrial society identified a basic contradiction between Stalin's totalitarian aspirations and the aspirations of Soviet professionals and technocrats. Stalin created large bureaucracies to plan and manage the Soviet economy. Stalin and those who studied Stalinism's operating systems noticed that local and middle-level managers and political bosses *naturally* tend to seek ways of protecting themselves from sometimes incompetent and even lethal meddling by higher authorities. Stalin used political terror and personal insecurity to keep the massive bureaucratic system responsive to central control. However, astute observers noticed that Soviet professionals resented political meddling and longed for a more, stable, rational administrative system. If so, Soviet society was naturally creating resistance to totalitarian politics and evolving towards more rational authoritarian administration.

In 1954, Barrington Moore, Jr. identified these trends in his classic study, *Terror and Progress: USSR.*:

> Perhaps the Soviet system is suffering from the disease of creeping rationality, much as some think ours is suffering from creeping socialism. Beneath the turmoil of the purges, demotions, and meteoric promotions that constitute such a

prominent feature in the Soviet political landscape one may detect throughout the history of the regime a steady lumbering movement in the direction of the clearer allocation of responsibility. It is worth while, therefore, to explore what might happen if this trend should display still greater strength with the passage of time.[9]

Moore predicted the decline of Stalinist terror and the emergence of a new type of Soviet politics, one in which the professional experts or *technocrats* would have increased opportunity to shape policy. He wrote, "The end result can be imagined as a technocracy—the rule of the technically competent. By definition, such a development would imply a heavy reduction of emphasis on the power of the dictator and its replacement by technical and rational criteria of behavior and organization. The share in power and prestige held by the instruments of violence and persuasion, the secret police would decline. That of the industrial manager, the engineer, and the technical administrator would rise."[10]

Moore's writings were somewhat controversial because he was predicting the clash between modern industrial values and Stalinism at the height of the Cold War, a time when the national political climate favored more pessimistic assessments of the Soviet threat. Moore identified the essential tension between Stalinist dictatorship and modern efficiency. He predicted the general direction of change. The Soviet Union would try to transform itself into a rationally managed authoritarian state. After Stalin's death, this actually became the Communist Party's official view of itself especially under Leonid Brezhnev's administration (1964–1982).

Moore also noted that the Soviet Union had inherited from the tsarist system a preindustrial, political-administrative culture that bred inefficiency and corruption. In 1950 he described Stalin's highly centralized dictatorial methods as the state's response to traditional Russian inefficiency and corruption. Moore raised serious questions about Russian political culture which are still relevant today.[11] The Party claimed to be the bearer of what Moore called "machine civilization and the qualities that by necessity accompany it."[12] However, the Party leadership knew that the country's managerial elite fell short of the efficient, professional ideal. All Soviet leaders have complained about the gap between modern, rational efficiency and Russian managerial habits. Corruption and inefficiency survived; the Soviet authoritarian dictatorship actually perpetuated such preindustrial attitudes instead of eradicating them.

It was Gorbachev who pushed official Soviet political thought to a higher level by directly confronting basic structural issues. Why did the Western model for modernization produce better politics and better economics than the neo-Stalinist, Soviet model? Gorbachev's answers were based upon a combination of modernization theory and systems analysis. The West had built political and economic competition into its basic political and economic operating systems. Periodic elections and constant economic competition promoted renewal and change better than authoritarian dictatorship. When

Gorbachev tried to infuse such dynamics into the Soviet system, he lost control and the new forces he had released destroyed the highly centralized Soviet state. The state's collapse inevitably produced huge economic disruptions as the Soviet common market divided into fifteen sovereign political economies—one for each republic, and managers began breaking economic contracts with impunity. Nevertheless, the Yeltsin administration continued to subscribe to modernization theory; however, after initially trying to introduce Westernization rapidly, it had to make policy concessions to conservatives who argued for slower change under tighter governmental control. The need to win elections forced the Yeltsin administration to coopt parts of the conservative reform agenda that the Communist opposition was promoting and that had broad popular appeal.

Modernization theory explains the long-term process at work in the former Soviet Union but it cannot predict the precise manner in which democratization takes place, the exact timing of key political events, nor the number of democratic take-offs and authoritarian landings that may be required before Russia develops stable democratic political institutions. Barrington Moore's analysis withstood the greatest test of social science theory, the ability to predict future developments. The second generation of Soviet professionals changed the Soviet political system from a totalitarian to a rational authoritarian regime. But what pushed the second and third generations into democratization and market reforms? According to Gorbachev's own accounts, it was a combination of internal and external influences.

Tsars and general secretaries had to assess strategic threats to their regimes and to adopt practical responses to them. Military threats—the development of advanced weapons systems that could tip the military balance against the Soviet Union, could not be ignored. The gap between Soviet and Western economic and military performance, already noticed in the 1970s, became pronounced during the 1980s. The West's audacious demonstration of new military technology and military science during Operation Desert Storm helped to convince Soviet military leaders that major reforms had to be undertaken. The Soviet Union tried to import Western political and economic technology.

The Schools

Over the decades Soviet area experts have created at least six schools in their search for the best models of the Soviet political system and the military's place within it: the totalitarian school, the conflict school, the symbiotic school, the eclectic school, the democratic transitions school, and the state-building school. The schools changed as the Soviet Union evolved from totalitarian socialism under Stalin to social-democratic reformism under Gorbachev. And when the Soviet state collapsed and divided into fifteen new states, problems of state-building became paramount.

Stalin used extreme methods to postpone the Soviet political system's evolution into a complex network of bureaucracies that resisted central control. Our *totalitarian* models described Stalin's system for building and controlling the vast Soviet administrative machine, imposing deep social and economic changes, and preserving his personal power. Under Stalin the military was extremely tightly supervised by political officers and security agents and subjected to ruthless purges. When Stalin died and his successors rejected systematic terror, the Soviet political process changed and so did our models. We became more aware of political competition among the great bureaucracies for resources. Khrushchev's memoirs confirmed that thesis and described the senior military leadership as one of the major competitors. This gave rise to the so-called *conflict school* to explain civil military relations. It assumed that civilian leaders had to work hard at keeping the military in check. After Khrushchev's fall from power, the Brezhnev regime stressed rational dictatorship and cooperation between the Soviet Union's leading technocrats. This shift in Soviet domestic political behavior gave rise to the *symbiotic* model for civil-military relations. During the early Brezhnev years, the military had a closer, more positive relationship with the general secretary and defense spending steadily increased. However, during the later Brezhnev years, the Soviet economy began to stagnate, competition for resources heated up, and the conflict model became fashionable again. The next logical step in Western thinking was to combine the conflict and symbiotic schools into a more complex model of Soviet reality which allowed for both conflict and cooperation. The *participatory model* created such a paradigm.

But scholarly trends were broadening rapidly and more and more work was being done on the maturing Soviet socialist dictatorship by researchers who drew upon and tested concepts originally developed outside the Soviet field. I call this period the *eclectic school* because Soviet-area specialists were drawing upon various bodies of theory ranging from organizational behavior to systems analysis and discovering more and more analogies between political behavior in the Soviet Union and other countries. This was a healthy development that coincided with the decline of the Cold War. But even before we completed the process of understanding how the mature authoritarian system operated and closing the gap between Soviet-area specialists and mainstream social science, the Soviet Union plunged into a new round of reforms. A new *democratic transitions school* was born as political scientists began studying the transition from Soviet dictatorship to democracy and from state-controlled socialism to market economics. However, when the Soviet state broke into fifteen sovereign states all with different levels of state viability, the *state-building school* appeared and began to compete with the *democratic transitions school* for primacy.

TABLE 1.1
Leadership Periods & Civil-Military Relations Schools

1. Stalin:	1928–1953	Totalitarian School
2. Khrushchev:	1953–1964	Conflict School
3. Brezhnev (early):	1964–1971	Symbiotic School
4. Late Brezhnev/Early Gorbachev	1972–1988	Eclectic School
5. Late Gorbachev/ Early Yeltsin	1988–1996	Democratic Transitions and State-Building

The Totalitarian School

Stalin saw himself as a socialist modernizer who used dictatorship to mobilize human and material resources and to keep himself in power. After the Second World War, Western observers began calling the Stalinist mobilization regime *totalitarian* in keeping with the *totalitarian model* developed by Carl Friederich, Zbigniew Brzezinski, and others. Their model described the political machinery of Stalin's revolutionary, socialist, modernizing dictatorship. The totalitarian school identified tensions within the system. The rivalry between the autocratic leader and other aspirants to power, the damage that excessive terror and dictatorship did to the professions and rational management, the tendency for the regions to resist the center, and the natural resistance huge bureaucracies develop to innovation and change. Western analysts predicted that the totalitarian system could not endure unless it periodically renewed the ideology of struggle and imposed new rounds of terror. Brzezinski and others reasoned that a *permanent purge* would be required to keep it going. Stalin's behavior in the 1930s, late 1940s and the early 1950s inspired that point of view. But it also predicted Mao's Great Proletarian Cultural Revolution in the second half of the 1960s and Pol Pot's slaughterhouse in Cambodia.

The totalitarian school produced a number of classic studies on Soviet politics in general and on the military in particular that have withstood the test of time. The most enduring works are rich political histories that provide a wealth of information. D. Fedotoff-White's 1944 study, *The Growth of the Red Army* is a pretotalitarian work is less systematic and rather naive about Soviet politics compared to the totalitarian classics that were written after the war. Yet, its somewhat naive discussion of Stalin's military modernization program captures some of the perverse, positive flavor of Soviet totalitarianism, its ability recruit and train able youth for new and exciting careers even while subjecting huge numbers of people to nightmarish abuse. Merle Fainsod's *How Russia Is Ruled* (1953) and Leonard Shapiro's *The Commu-*

nist Party of the Soviet Union (1960) describe the Red Army's political history within their excellent general political histories of the Soviet state. John Erickson's *The Soviet High Command* (1962) provides a detailed study of the Red Army's development through 1941–42 and demonstrates the progress scholars made in understanding the complex politics of military modernization under Stalinist dictatorship. It covered the same period treated by D. Fedotoff-White but with much greater methodological and intellectual sophistication.

In the totalitarian school, the central military themes are somewhat contradictory. On the one hand, Stalin purged the Soviet officer corps ruthlessly between 1937 and 1940 and is remembered as a tyrant who abused and murdered outstanding military professionals. On the other hand, during the war he nurtured and promoted an impressive array of military leaders, defense industrialists, and weapons designers, and is remembered for his victory over Hitler.[13] Stalin studied foreign military developments carefully and tried to obtain the latest technology. He cooperated with postwar Germany's defense industrialists and military leadership until Hitler took power and canceled the program in 1933. In violation of the Treaty of Versailles, for a decade Germans produced and tested weapons in the Soviet Union. Under Stalin, professionals worked under a capricious dictatorship but one oriented towards rapid industrialization and general modernization. Stalin combined personal despotism with a progressive agenda, a perversion of Western modernization. The proof is the modern military technology that the Stalinist defense industries created before the Nazi invasion, developed and improved during the war, and that moved into the nuclear and space ages after the war.

Stalinism raised excruciating moral and professional questions. How should military professionals behave when their commander in chief is an abusive tyrant? Should the professional soldier initiate a corrective political coup, actively defend the leader, remain on the sidelines? These are difficult moral and political questions because military professionals understand that the obligation to obey orders is the central rule, the habit that guarantees military cohesion and reliability. Yet, under Stalin, loyal professional service did not guarantee either personal or professional survival. Stalinism also confirmed the thesis that external developments that affect military balances cannot be ignored. He was importing Western manufacturing technology but not Western political technology.

The Conflict School

There are two ways to view the military's role in the transition from Stalinism to Khrushchevism. The first view is positive and emphasizes the military's contribution to several peaceful transfers of power including the corrective political coup that destroyed Stalin's henchman, Lavrenty Beria in

1953 and the conspiracy that forced Khrushchev into retirement in October 1964. The second is more negative and emphasizes rivalry between civilian and military leaders. It portrays the military as a threat to civilian political dominance. Western scholarship tended to emphasize the negative side of the coin. Therefore, it was unprepared for the military's positive contribution to the transfer of political power from Gorbachev to Yeltsin and to the relatively peaceful dismantling of the Soviet Union in 1991.

The key political event took place in July 1953 and was based upon a conspiratorial agreement between senior military leaders and Nikita Khrushchev. Marshal Zhukov, the World War II hero, and Col. General Moskalenko, the commander of the Moscow military district were enlisted in the Kremlin coup against Lavrenty Beria. They flew in naval special forces to disarm and replace Beria's NKVD troops who guarded the Kremlin, the seat of Soviet political power. They brought the Kantemir tank division into Moscow to demonstrate that they had the firepower and political determination to smash resistance. They dispatched special forces to all key NKVD facilities. Some of Beria's deputies got on the anti-Beria bandwagon early and saved their jobs temporarily. No open resistance was reported.[14] The specific pivot was 1:00 PM on 26 July 1953 when five top military officers, led by Zhukov and Moskalenko, burst into a Politburo meeting and arrested Beria. They kept him under tight control in the Kremlin until midnight and then whisked him away to a secure place of confinement.[15]

Zhukov and Moskalenko brought the Red Army into the plot against Beria and supported the post-Stalinist reforms that ended the Stalinist system of terror. Because they moved in concert with the Party majority at the request of civilians, their participation in the corrective coup should not be considered military intervention in civilian affairs. Military professionals and Soviet professionals as a whole resented Stalin's dictatorship and terror and welcomed Khrushchev's reforms. However, they soon discovered that Khrushchev was determined to dictate national defense policy and would demote senior officers who appeared to challenge that authority.

The military saved Khrushchev a second time in June 1957 when civilian rivals tried to oust him. The generals refused to recognize the coup's legitimacy and flew Khrushchev's supporters to Moscow for an official vote on his Party leadership in keeping with formal Party regulations. However, several months after this incident, Khrushchev forced Marshal Zhukov to resign his position as minister of defense. Khrushchev claimed to have received negative reports from the security services and from the Party's political officers inside the military about what Zhukov was saying to his colleagues. Khrushchev explained, "We received information that Zhukov was indeed voicing Bonapartist aspirations in his conversations with military commanders. We couldn't let Zhukov stage a South American-style military take-over in our country."[16] Khrushchev describes it as a matter of principle: "It was a struggle between my head and my heart. In my heart I was all in favor of Zhukov, but in my head I knew we had to part company with him." He replaced Zhukov with First Deputy Minister of Defense, Marshal Rodion Y. Malinovsky who served as minister of defense from 1957 to 1967.

When he fired Zhukov, Khrushchev reinforced his personal political position, the office of the general secretary, and civilian control over the military. Khrushchev needed competent, and assertive military leaders but neither *too* strong nor *too* assertive. He chose Malinovsky over Marshal Ivan S. Konev because the latter was too headstrong. Khrushchev's political antennae picked up political warning signals: "Frankly, Konev made us very uneasy. We were afraid his attitude toward the government and the Party leadership was similar to Zhukov's."[17] Nevertheless, Konev remained the Soviet Union's commander of Warsaw Pact armed forces and deputy minister of defense. Konev should have made Khrushchev nervous. It was Konev who presided over the military tribunal that tried and sentenced Lavrenty Beria in December 1953. And Konev commanded the Soviet military forces that crushed the Hungarian revolution in 1956.[18]

After some eleven years of erratic domestic and foreign policy, Khrushchev had alienated enough civilian and military leaders for a successful conspiracy to form against him. With military backing, civilian leaders carried out a corrective political coup against him on 22 October 1964. The military decided to stop obeying Khrushchev even before he had resigned. Two weeks after Khrushchev had been forced to retire, while imbibing during celebrations marking the anniversary of the Bolshevik revolution, Defense Minister Malinovsky told China's Premier Zhou Enlai: "Let's drink to Sino-Soviet friendship. Now that we've kicked out our Nikita why don't you do the same to your Mao Zedong?"[19] Khrushchev's retirement ushered in a rather quiet time in Soviet political history during which General Secretary Brezhnev tried to run a rational authoritarian regime that rewarded its supporters with long tenure in office and access to a privileged lifestyle. But it took Western scholars several years to notice the shift in the Soviet political system. They continued to emphasize conflict.

The colorful Malinovsky served as Brezhnev's minister of defense until March 1967 when he died in office. Malinovsky was followed by his own first deputy minister of defense, Marshal Andrei A. Grechko another war hero who had been serving as supreme commander of the Warsaw Pact military forces. Grechko led the Ministry of Defense for ten years until his death in April 1976.

Modernization theory predicted that political competition would inevitably develop between the technocrats and professionals who sought increased autonomy and the general secretary and the politician generalists who strove to maintain overall policymaking control. As information about such political "conflict" became available, political scientists began to revise their totalitarian model. They were impressed by the competition for resources and power among the key bureaucracies in the Soviet system. In *Khrushchev and the Soviet Leadership* (1966) Carl Linden demonstrated that without Stalin's use of terror the struggle for power at the top of the Soviet political system became a series of shifting alliances involving personal and bureaucratic interests. H. Gordon Skilling began testing the hypothesis that interest groups competed for resources in the Soviet Union in ways that had enough in common with Western politics to be understandable in Western terms with some adjustments for the Soviet context.[20]

In 1967, Roman Kolkowicz published a major work that earned him the reputation of being the founder of the conflict school of civil-military relations, *The Soviet Military and the Communist Party*.[21] Kolkowicz identified the central trend in Soviet political evolution, the growing tension between the political dictatorship and military professionalism and he provided reasonable estimates about the future: "In effect the Party has three options: It can acknowledge that the military must be spared oppressive controls and constant indoctrination if it is to be highly effective; it can reduce those of its political objectives that necessitate the use of the military; it can reorganize and thereby reduce the military establishment to the point where it ceases to be a significant factor in Soviet politics."[22]

Soviet history vindicated Kolkowicz because the three options he identified actually became Soviet policy. Gorbachev reduced political interference in military professional life, he changed Soviet doctrine in order to justify a smaller military, and he began cutting the armed forces and Soviet defense expenditures. Boris Yeltsin intensified those changes. The Soviet military and the Soviet military-industrial complex as a whole found themselves in a weakened political position once the traditional one-party dictatorship had been dismantled.

In 1978, a decade after "founding" the conflict school, Kolkowicz was still pointing to the "perpetual tension" in the military's relationship with the Party; but he had also noticed the military's odd political position in Soviet society as a whole: "The military has a limited national 'constituency,' therefore, except for certain circles in the Party and in the managerial-technocratic circles connected to defense industries. Only as the protector of the country from external threats does it gain support and respect from society."[23] Kolkowicz predicted that the Soviet military could quickly find itself isolated politically if Soviet society moved towards major revisions of the authoritarian political system: "In sum, the military differs profoundly from those interest groups in Soviet society whose particular interests and visions are also the larger objectives or hopes of people seeking urgent changes in the social, political, and philosophical realities of an authoritarian system."[24]

Thus, although Kolkowicz had been criticized for holding on to the conflict model for too long, some of his ideas were amazingly prescient and are important insights into the changes which took place after 1991. The big Soviet defense establishment found itself without much popular support. The rebellion against Soviet dictatorship had a powerful antimilitary component. The Soviet public resented the huge investment that Soviet society had been forced to make in order to maintain an enormous defense establishment that had been justified on the basis of a false picture of international realities. All this suggested that senior civilian and military Communist leaders shared a common interest in keeping the Soviet system afloat. The Soviet military faced a dilemma. There were signs that it supported general societal modernization including more authority for professionals as opposed to politicians. But the military sensed that political liberalization could threaten its funding and the stability of the Soviet state. Therefore, Kolkowicz decided that the military probably would play its political cards conservatively.[25]

The Symbiotic Model

It was an American *military* intellectual, Lt. General William Odom who argued for a richer and more complex model of civil-military relations than either the totalitarian or the conflict school provided.[26] General Odom reminded the civilian academic community that Soviet military officers were Communists much as their civilian counterparts and seemed to be patriotic and supportive of the Soviet system as a whole. His point of view came to be called the "symbiotic" model of civil-military relations in the Soviet Union. General Odom's analysis forced Western students of Soviet civil-military relations to notice the existence of more normal bureaucratic politics such as competition for resources and rivalries *within* the Soviet one-party system. Further, he reminded non-Soviet analysts that Soviet officers who were involved in such competition and who were asserting military interests did not perceive themselves as being either anti-Soviet or anti-Communist. They were patriotic Soviet officers engaged in the normal competition for resources. They were members of the Communist Party and made their careers in the military as military professionals and Communists.

The Cold War's political noise about conflict between the Party and the professions had obscured the fact that the Party had become what might be called the Soviet Union's "union" of professionals.[27] The Communists whom I came to know during the last decade of Soviet power were mainly professionals, leaders and managers in their respective fields. Some were politicians or people who spent their time resolving the competition for resources and making the authoritative decisions in formal and informal ways. In the military, virtually all high-ranking officers were Communists but most of these were engaged in military professional work not political activity.[28] Thus, I found Odom's approach well-suited to the task of breaking down Cold War, stereotypical thinking.

By reminding readers that officers were professionals who had much in common with civilian colleagues, Odom made it more likely that we would begin to notice and to understand civil-military cooperation in support of reform: "Finally, *de-Stalinization* is an issue that cuts across the Party-military boundary. Like many Party *apparatchiki* senior Soviet military officers value the insurance against blood purges that de-Stalinization provides." Odom predicted that senior Party and military figures would have common concerns about the breakdown in the values that gave Soviet society cohesion: "At the same time, the denigration of the Soviet system that has to some extent been implicit in de-Stalinization has evoked ambivalent and cautious reactions in both Party and military circles."[29]

The Eclectic School

The notion that Kolkowicz and Odom represented two extremes on an analytical spectrum bounded by conflict and cooperation became widespread. Although it was unfair to both authors, this dialectical scheme was a useful heuristic device, an effective way to remind scholars that Soviet civil-military relations had been characterized by both conflict and cooperation. The scheme took hold and was often repeated in academic discussions of the field's evolution.[30]

Timothy Colton proposed a *participatory model* which was a synthesis of the conflict and symbiotic schools because the evidence from the Soviet Union could not be satisfactorily explained by either extreme model. He argued that we needed to give more attention to basic politics. He produced a complex, eclectic study which did not fit the dominant paradigms. It rejected the totalitarian and the conflict schools and began the search for more normal studies of politics and political processes. Colton argued that the Soviet military was like most militaries rather conservative in its political views and unlikely to challenge the Soviet system. The idea that the Soviet military might serve as the mid-wife for radical political change seemed truly remote in 1979.[31]

What I have called the *eclectic school* was the beginning of the merger of Soviet area studies with the social sciences in general. It also included the emergence of normal social science in the former Soviet Union. Western observers were learning to see competition for resources as a normal part of the Soviet policy making process. Soviet observers were becoming familiar with the international political science and noticing that the Soviet Union could be understood in terms of modernization theory, systems theory, political development, and so on. Western experts on the Soviet Union were studying the writings of Soviet experts on the West and vice versa.[32] Politics operated differently in the Soviet Union but not so differently as to make Soviet politics a unique field of study. The Soviet cases could be treated as an example of universal processes. Rising scholars—the post-totalitarian generation, produced dozens of new studies and a gave us a richer understanding of Soviet politics in general and civil-military relations in particular.[33] As a result, we could describe and explain the Red Army's overall organizational structure and operational habits, its internal sociology, and its general involvement in defense policymaking. But these studies neither prepared us for the extremely rapid dismantling of the Soviet empire in Eastern Europe nor the fragmentation of the Soviet Union.

As a result, the scholarly community was criticized for trailing behind events rather than predicting them. Within academia, the old tension between the main disciplines and regional specialists revived. The area specialists lost prestige when the Soviet threat dissolved and the Soviet state fell apart. Some political scientists claimed that the work of the area specialists had not been scientific.[34] However, if the central test of the scientific worth of academic scholarship is its ability to predict the future, then it is legitimate to ask the main line political scientists why they hadn't predicted Gorbachev's radical reforms and their impact on the Soviet system. And what about Gorbachev himself? What explains his miscalculations? Clearly, the scientific problem is larger than the purported weaknesses in area studies. Neither the mainline Western social sciences nor the Soviet Union's chief statesmen seemed to know what lay ahead. Nonetheless, as this chapter demonstrated, Soviet-area studies made substantial progress since the Second World War.

Western political science had discovered the primary trends in Soviet development but it did not know how or when the final denouement would take place. It knew that the mature Soviet authoritarian socialist system was having difficulty achieving satisfactory levels of economic growth, was facing demographic imbalances that had ethno-political implications, and was deeply concerned about the developing technology gap between it and the advanced industrial states. We knew that Soviet elites were debating the merits of various reform strategies even as they competed for power. But neither we nor they knew how fast and how far the reform process would go. Neither were we prepared to predict that the Soviet military-industrial complex would permit civilian politicians to divide the Soviet Union into fifteen independent states each with its own army. Nevertheless, after an initial period of confusion, the area specialists began to rebuild. Instead of knocking Soviet studies onto the scrap heap of academic history, the Soviet Union's collapse spawned a new generation of nationality studies, state-building studies, and democratic transitions studies.

Nationality Studies, Transition, and State-Building Models

Area experts quickly recovered and began to find new patrons and audiences. Experts were needed on each republic and its ethnic groups. Scholars once considered somewhat peripheral and esoteric suddenly found themselves at the cutting edge of the field. Estonian, Latvian, Lithuanian, Belarussian, Ukrainian, Moldovan, Georgian, Armenian, Azeri, Turkmen, Uzbek, Tajik, Kyrgyz, and Kazakh experts began to chide their Russian-speaking colleagues about their inability to read the new literature published in the native languages of the fourteen non-Russian, newly independent states. On the one hand, Soviet studies began to fragment into smaller parts. On the other, new thematic and comparative studies began to appear, efforts to understand how the post-Soviet space would develop as a whole. Further, anti-Russianism started to replace the anti-Sovietism of the former Cold War literature. The heroic struggle of the little republics against Russian neo-imperialism become a popular theme.[35] Orest Subtelny offered the *imperial model* as a substitute for the fallen totalitarian model because it focused on a central concern of Soviet politics, the preservation of the Union. From this vantage point, the Soviet state had been a continuation of the old Russian empire in a new form.[36]

There are now fifteen armed forces and fifteen ministries of defense on the territory that used to be defended by one military organization, the Soviet Armed Forces. Scholars are producing books and articles about all of them.[37] To one extent or another, they all address military development as part of political development and general state-building. They are also producing a new type of regional studies, the analysis of new regional groupings of states.[38] The primary issue is the Russian state's security relations with the other former Soviet republics, what Kremlin policymakers call the *near-abroad.* In *Commonwealth or Empire,* Odom and Dujarric argue that the new Russian state will strive to dominate the *near-abroad.*[39] Russian policy makers view the new world order as a set of regional systems led by major powers. They regard Russia as the natural leader of a Eurasian regional system composed of most of the former Soviet republics. I have argued that it is possible to describe and to some extent predict how Russia and the states on its periphery are likely to behave according to a *near-abroad syndrome.*[40]

The new Russian empire hypothesis points to a key question in post-Soviet studies. How deep and permanent were the changes that took place 1991 and 1992? The initial rush to reaffirm that most if not all the former Soviet republics were led by political elites who intended to build viable democratic states with market-oriented economies has given way to a more realistic, scientific, and differentiated approach. It is particularly difficult to assess the current status and future potential of the Russian military-industrial complex and military system. Some argue that Russia's dismal performance in the Chechen conflict proved that the once-mighty Soviet military system had degenerated to the point where it could not fight a local war. Others warn that the Russian state can rebuild and reassert its military and political power quickly. Richard F. Starr dedicated a book to the debate about the extent of change in the Russian military system. In an analysis structured around ten myths about the new Russian military, Starr warned against simplistic thinking about Russia's post-Soviet political and military development.[41]

Early in the debate about how much change the military would tolerate and whether the military would serve as a conservative force in post-Soviet politics, Tom Nichols described the Soviet officer corps as the carriers of Marxist-Leninist world views and values and a threat to the deep detente which the democratic reformers used to justify deep cuts in military spending. In *The Sacred Cause*, Nichols described the military as an *ideologically indoctrinated officer corps* that was pitted against an *increasingly pragmatic Party elite*.[42] In 1990, when Nichols was completing *The Sacred Cause*, disgruntled military officers—especially political officers, were providing plenty of grist for the mill. Their comments suggested that a significant part of the armed forces would be ready to support the restoration of the Soviet Union under a new modernizing dictatorship. His book reflects that pivotal moment in the reform process when the defense establishment complained but failed to take effective action to prevent the changes that severely damaged its immediate interests.

I agree that the military longed for strong, effective civilian leadership, a government capable of rebuilding the economy and maintaining domestic stability. But it also wanted a dynamic economic system capable of furnishing it with the latest weapons and a substantially higher standard of professional support. The military was caught in an approach-avoidance conflict. On the one hand, it was attracted to Western economic dynamism and Western-style military professionalism. On the other hand, it feared Soviet economic and political collapse but it refused to make war against its own people to save the Soviet regime. In August 1991, Boris Yeltsin offered the military a way out of this dilemma by promising to lead the country decisively into the Western model while avoiding civil war. He also appealed to military professionals who hoped to be rid of Communist political commissars and the old political control system.

However, during Yeltsin's first administration, a wide gap opened between the armed forces and Russia's democratic reformers for three reasons. First, they cut military spending sharply and destroyed hundreds of thousands of military professional careers and threatened the scientific and economic viability of Russia's defense industries. Second, during their watch the Russian economy plunged into deep recession, revenues, fell, and the Russian government could not finance national defense properly. Third, Yeltsin ordered the military to use armed force to settle two major domestic political conflicts: the struggle between Parliament and the presidency in October 1993, and the Chechen rebellion against the federal government from 1994–1996.

Military Intervention and Military Participation Models

There is a rich literature on civil-military relations readily available to students of Soviet government and politics. Soviet scholars were familiar with this literature and began debating its implications for Russia's future during the last years of the Gorbachev administration. They invited prominent Western military sociologists such as Charles Moskos into the search for new directions in civil-military relations.[43] The Party also held special workshops on conflict resolution in society at which some argued that the military had to be prepared to join police forces in domestic peacekeeping activities and others insisted that the military be prohibited from taking on such domestic policing functions.[44] In summer 1991, I participated in a seminar on that subject at the Central Committee's Academy of Social Sciences. The discussion turned to the role authoritarian regimes can play in political transitions from authoritarianism to democracy and the new literature on that topic.[45]

The political processes at work in the Soviet Union can be better understood by drawing upon the accumulated knowledge of praetorianism and its relationship to political instability. Although much of the literature is based upon the analysis of the political history of Latin America and Iberian Europe, the body of knowledge has far wider application.

In *The Military and Politics in Modern Times,* Amos Perlmutter summarized the wisdom gleaned from decades of research into civil-military relations in Europe, Asia, Africa, and the Americas. The general consensus is that the military is more likely to intervene in politics when civilian leadership is ineffective and fragmented, there is a sense of national crisis, the military is still cohesive, and leading officers have values that justify such intervention.[46] The Russian military was cohesive and it was convinced that the country was in crisis. However, it did not see itself as the appropriate force to take control over the Russian political system though it understood that the armed forces guaranteed Russia's basic security and domestic political stability. Military professionals hoped that responsible and competent civilian political professionals would take command of the situation and lead Russia through political and economic reconstruction.

Alfred Stepan has reviewed decades of his own work and that of colleagues interested in Latin American military regimes. In *Rethinking Military Politics*, he develops an analytical system for placing civil-military relations along a spectrum running from a low likelihood and capacity to a high probability for military intervention in the domestic political system. The low end is defined by a military with few political prerogatives and a small number of grievances or "contestations" against civilian leadership.[47]

Even a cursory knowledge of Russian political life since 1988 suggests that the military's level of discontent has grown, civilian leadership's demonstrated capacity for effective leadership has declined, and Russian soldiers have become more active politically. Borrowing and adapting concepts from Latin American studies, civil-military relations, and political development to the study of Soviet politics is a natural scholarly response to the political changes that have taken place in the former Soviet Union and a natural extension of the field of comparative politics. Although there are major social, political, and economic differences between the regions, similar political processes operate in diverse cultural-historical settings. Latin America's experience is instructive though not definitive for Russia and other former Soviet republics. The political history of Latin America demonstrates that some societies can sustain both democratic and authoritarian potential and can move between democratic and authoritarian forms of government in recurring patterns.[48]

Is Russia an Exceptional Case?

Although Russian military analysts are generally familiar with the Latin American praetorian model, in personal conversations Russian colleagues argue that the Russian case is different. The Latin American model doesn't fit Russia. The Russian revolutionary tradition—the socialist-revolutionary ideal, may be closer to the Israeli tradition in which soldiers are supposed to be citizens and great soldiers are expected to be politically aware and capable of moving in and out of political life.[49] If the military is part of society's political life; it is neither outside society nor outside politics. Consequently, it can participate in and influence the political sphere without invading it.[50] Military participation influences the political process as a normal part of politics and may even tip the scales in a major election or a party caucus. Russian generals show up in various political movements, serve as mayors and governors, and sit in parliaments; but the military as a whole is unlikely to take over government. It is more likely to participate in some civilian takeover as part of a coalition.

The Russian revolution's legacy gave the soldier a claim to full political citizenship including the right to run for and to serve in office at all levels of government. However, some Russian commentators have argued that officers' rights are traced to Peter the Great's reforms which gave officers landed estates, incomes, and political responsibilities and thereby confirmed their special position in Russia's governing elite.[51] From this perspective, the Russian revolution of 1917 expanded military participation by giving all soldiers full citizenship. Officers and enlisted personnel became equals temporarily. Traditional military ranks were abolished. Civilian and military roles were interchangeable and leaders such as Leon Trotsky and Joseph Stalin alternated between them. Modernization's demands for professionalism and differentiation of functions won in the longer run. Officers once again became the more important citizens, a part of the Soviet political elite, when Stalin restored ranks and privileges in the 1930s. Nevertheless, the Party still taught officers that the "Army and the People are One," made them attend Party conferences and congresses along with their civilian counterparts, and regularly assigned soldiers nonmilitary tasks ranging from road building to harvesting potatoes.

Under the Communist Party dictatorship military participation was routine and highly ritualized. Military leaders could challenge civilian leaders during policy debates affecting national defense but only within strict limits which normally precluded public disclosure of their disagreements; and, the civilians made the final decisions. The democratization of Soviet civil-military relations strengthened the military's political voice by removing the Party civilian dictatorship. This left the border between military and civilian spheres of life quite porous and disorderly when compared with the dominant Western models of civil-military relations.

In 1996, some five years after the end of the Communist dictatorship, Russian paratroopers on special assignment from their normal military duties were still harvesting potatoes in the Moscow region. However, military reformers and President Yeltsin were formally committed to the professionalization of Russian military life along Western lines. During the 1996 election campaign Yeltsin called for an all-professional, volunteer army by the year 2000. That goal was popular with the military and with Russian society. It reflected society's deep alienation from the military draft system and the military's alienation from the populist socialist military service model. The military advocated the Western models which promised higher standards of living and better all-round support for professional soldiers. This suggests that Russians were not committed to their indigenous political culture's populist values in civil-military relations and were eager to modernize along Western lines.

Conclusion

During the twentieth century, the Russian political system was a moving target which refused to remain stable long enough to be thoroughly understood. The former Russian empire was a complex, unstable, developing political system. When the Russian state entered the twentieth century, its political system was adapting to pressures for democratic reform while trying to prevent democratization from destroying the empire's political integrity. Eighty years later as Russia prepared to enter the twenty-first century, it was still trying to build effective democratic institutions. During most of the twentieth century, the Russian state was a one-party dictatorship. Soviet dictatorship was sandwiched between two periods of unstable democratic reform.

Therefore, we need developmental models to explain Russia's long term evolution and these need to account for both democratic and authoritarian tendencies in society. We need to explain continuity and change and cannot be satisfied with sweeping generalities such as the claim that Russian political culture was, is, and always will be Eurasian and despotic. We need to wrestle with the difficult question of how and why political culture changes.[52] Totalitarian socialist society became authoritarian socialist society and then attempted to transform itself into a democratic social-market economy. The military system evolved similarly and moved from being the obedient tool of the Stalin's totalitarian dictatorship to serving Gorbachev and Yeltsin as a stabilizing force in a democratizing society. Stalinism prolonged the Russian empire's political life but political liberalization killed it. Russian politics and the military's participation in political life differed during each of the five stages through which the Russian state moved: tsarist reforms, the revolutionary period, Stalinist totalitarianism, authoritarian socialism, and post-Soviet democratization. Yet, all five stages are part of a longer process through which the tsarist empire modernized. Further, modernization did not take place evenly throughout the empire and the different former Soviet republics will necessarily have different domestic political systems.

The military and military issues were involved in every major turn in Russia's twentieth-century political development. Civilian leaders enlisted military support to force the tsar to abdicate in March 1917, to win the civil war and to establish a viable Soviet dictatorship, to prevent Lavrenty Beria from taking power after Stalin's death in 1953, to keep Khrushchev from being toppled in June 1957, to force Khrushchev to retire in October 1964, to secure Yeltsin's victory over the both the right-wing coup and Gorbachev in August 1991, and to implement Yeltsin's dissolution of the Russian Parliament in October 1993. Military issues will be an essential part of state-building in the fifteen former Soviet republics and a major element in the political relationships between them.

The parade of schools, models, and paradigms described in this chapter had three causes. First, the Russian political system was changing and new models were required after each major change. Second, scholars were competing for places at the cutting edge of the discipline and this competition promoted innovation. Third, as the body of knowledge about political processes increased, Soviet-area specialists drew upon that knowledge and applied it to Russian area studies. The Soviet Union's fragmentation will produce more models and paradigms as we seek to understand the relationships within and among the new states and their neighbors.

If we sort all the models and changes into three levels, a definite order comes into view. The primary or highest level identifies the long-range trend, modernization's impact upon the tsarist empire. It identifies the types of problems that the political system will have to solve at each stage in the broad developmental process. Next come the secondary models and studies. These describe the larger institutional operations at each stage, how the military participated in politics under totalitarianism, authoritarian socialism, and in post-Soviet Russia. Lastly, there are tertiary studies which focus on the details of military institutional life and civil-military relations. The primary trend should set the overall context for larger institutional development which should in turn inform the operational details. Thus, for example, the primary shift from authoritarian to democratic socialism, requires that society make the state and its military accountable to the people. Different types of institutional arrangements encourage and discourage different types of political behavior.

Gorbachev's reforms caused primary changes in the political system and in the military system that supported it. The Yeltsin years should confirm the basic paradigm shift and reveal changes in military institutions and in the civil-military interface, basic shifts appropriate to the end of the mature authoritarian socialist system and the beginning of a democratic socialist system. This book tests that hypothesis as it writes a political history of the period, one that focuses on the military's role in the momentous changes that took place.

Western writing assumes that democratic *civilian* control is the same as control by duly elected officials. It assumes that military leaders and individual officers will engage in politics obliquely and conduct themselves differently from civilians who have special civilian interests to represent. Military leaders are expected to be more private than public, to work through departmental channels or civilian legislators who take sides on issues instead of speaking publicly for themselves. In post-Soviet Russia a different tradition began to develop. Some military officers were duly elected officials. Others were appointed to major administrative positions. Ministers of defense gave interviews and took positions on controversial issues. Such practices raised questions about the military's proper role in Russian political life. Should military participation in politics be regularized or prohibited? Does the military have a direct, positive contribution to make to national policy debate or should its voice be muffled? The West has grown used to leaving those who know the most about defense out of the public debates on defense. The Russians are still wrestling with the issue.

Notes

1. Boris Yeltsin, "President of the Russian Federation's Annual Message to the Federal Assembly, 23 February 1996" (in Russian); official text published in *Krasnaya zvezda*, 11 March 1996. My translation.
2. *Ibid.*
3. *Ibid.*
4. *Ibid.*
5. The presidential administration includes over 1,000 professional employees housed in the office complex formerly used by the Central Committee of the Communist Party of the Soviet Union (CPSU).
6. See N. D. Yegorov, chief of the president's administration, "Velikoi Rossii nuzhna sil'naya armiya" (Great Russia needs a powerful army); *Krasnaya zvezda*, 20 April 1996.
7. See *Ibid.*
8. *Ibid.*
9. Barrington Moore, Jr. *Terror and Progress: USSR (Some Sources of Change and Stability in the Soviet Dictatorship)* (Cambridge, Mass.: Harvard University Press, 1954), p. 159.
10. *Ibid.* p. 189.

11. See chapter 12, "The Bureaucratic State," in Barrington Moore, Jr., *Soviet Politics—The Dilemma of Power: The Role of Ideas in Social Change* (New York: Harper & Row, 1965 [reprint of 1950 edition]). Also note Yeltsin's references to Russian cultural deficiencies in his 1996 Message to the Federal Assembly.

12. *Ibid.*, p. 297.

13. See Harold Shukman ed., *Stalin's Generals* (New York: Grove Press, 1993).

14. See chapter 7, "The Succession: Contention and Conspiracy," in Roy Medvedev's *Khrushchev: A Biography* (New York: Anchor/Doubleday, 1983).

15. See John Erickson, "Kirill Semenovich Moskalenko," pp. 137–53, in Harold Shukman, ed., *Stalin's Generals.* A military tribunal judged Beria and a military execution squad killed him.

16. Nikita S. Khrushchev, *Khrushchev Remembers: The Last Testament* (Boston: Little, Brown and Co., 1974), p. 14. Notice that Khrushchev did not actually claim that the reports were true or that Zhukov actually had higher political aspirations. Zhukov denied such allegations. The better explanation is that Khrushchev was politically uncomfortable with such as strong leader at the head of defense.

17. *Ibid.*, p. 17.

18. See Oleg Rzheshevsky, "Ivan Stepanovich Konev," pp. 91–107 in Shukman, *Stalin's Generals.*

19. Cited by Georgi Arbatov, p. 109 in *The System: An Insider's Life in Soviet Politics* (New York: Random House, 1993). Arbatov calls Khrushchev's ouster "the palace coup of 1964."

20. See H. Gordon Skilling, "Interest Groups and Communist Politics," *World Politics*, no. 18, 1966, pp. 435–51; and H. G. Skilling and Franklyn Griffiths, eds., *Interest Groups in Soviet Politics* (Princeton, N.J.: Princeton University Press, 1971).

21. See Roman Kolkowicz, *The Soviet Military and the Communist Party* (Princeton, N.J.: Princeton University Press, 1967).

22. *Ibid.*, p. 342.

23. Roman Kolkowicz, "Interest Groups in Soviet Politics: The Case of the Military," in Dale R. Herspring, and Ivan Volgyes, eds., *Civil-Military Relations in Communist Systems* (Boulder, Colo.: Westview Press, 1978), p. 24.

24. *Ibid.*, p. 24.

25. See Roman Kolkowicz, "The Military," chapter 5 in Skilling and Griffiths, *Interest Groups.*

26. See for example, Lt. General William E. Odom's "The Party-Military Connection: A Critique," in Dale R. Herspring and Ivan Volgyes, eds., *Civil-Military Relations in Communist Systems.*

27. Jerry F. Hough studied Soviet political careers in detail and when he revised Merle Fainsod's classic, he described the new political class. See *How the Soviet Union is Governed* (Cambridge, Mass: Harvard University Press, 1979). Hough knew that different generations of military leaders had different political tendencies and applied this insight to explain the outcome of the August 1991 coup. See his, "Assessing the Coup," *Current History*, vol. 90, no. 558, October 1991, pp. 305 ff.

28. See chapters 2 and 7 below.

29. William E. Odom, "The Party-Military Connection: A Critique," p. 33.

30. See for example pp. 24–32 in Timothy J. Colton and Thane Gustafson, eds., *Soldiers and the Soviet State: Civil-Military Relations from Brezhnev to Gorbachev* (Princeton, N.J.: Princeton University Press, 1990); pp. 11–14, in Dale R. Herspring, *The Soviet High Command, 1967–1989* (Princeton, N.J.:

32   The Soldier in Russian Politics

Princeton University Press, 1990); and pp. 24–32, in Thomas M. Nichols, *The Sacred Cause: Civil-Military Conflict Over Soviet National Security, 1917–1992* (Ithaca, N.Y.: Cornell University Press, 1993).

31. See Timothy J. Colton, *Commissars, Commanders, and Civilian Authority: The Structure of Soviet Military Politics* (Cambridge, Mass.: Harvard University Press, 1979).
32. See chapter 10, "The Institute: How We 'Discovered' America," in Georgi Arbatov, *The System: An Insider's Life in Soviet Politics* (New York: Random House, 1993).
33. See for example, Ellen Jones, *Red Army and Society: A Sociology of the Soviet Military* (Boston: Allen & Unwin, 1985); Dale R. Herspring, *The Soviet High Command, 1967–1989* (Princeton, N.J.: Princeton University Press, 1990); Timothy J. Colton and Thane Gustafson, eds. *Soldiers and the Soviet State: Civil-Military Relations from Brezhnev to Gorbachev* (Princeton, N.J.: Princeton University Press, 1990); Kimberly Marten Zisk, *Engaging the Enemy: Organization Theory and Soviet Military Innovation, 1955–1991* (Princeton, N.J.: Princeton University Press, 1993); and James M. Goldgeier, *Leadership Style and Soviet Foreign Policy: Stalin, Khrushchev, Brezhnev, Gorbachev* (Baltimore, Md.: Johns Hopkins University Press, 1994).
34. See Robert H. Bates, "Letter from the President" in the *Newsletter of the APSA Organized Section in Comparative Politics*, vol. 7, no. 1, 1996.
35. See for example Ian Bremmer and Ray Tarras, eds., *Nations & Politics in the Soviet Successor States* (Cambridge: Cambridge University Press, 1993).
36. See Orest Subtelny's "American Sovietology's Great Blunder: The Marginalization of the Nationality Issue," *Nationalities Papers*, vol. 22, no. 1, 1994: 141–55.
37. See Bruce Parrot, ed., *State Building and Military Power in Russia and the New States of Eurasia* (Armonk, N.Y.: M. E. Sharpe, 1995); Mark Galeotti, *The Age of Anxiety: Security and Politics in Soviet and Post-Soviet Russia* (New York: Longman, 1995); William E. Odom and Robert Dujarric, *Commonwealth of Empire? Russia, Central Asia, and the Transcaucasus* (Indianapolis, Ind.: The Hudson Institute, 1995); Constantine P. Danopoulos and Daniel Zirker, eds., *Civil-Military Relations in the Soviet and Yugoslav Successor States* (Boulder, Colo.: Westview Press, 1996); and Richard F. Starr, *The New Military in Russia: Ten Myths That Shape the Image* (Annapolis, Md.: Naval Institute Press, 1996).
38. Thus, for example, there was a rush to study the republics of Islamic heritage and their relationships with Russia, one another, and with the greater Islamic community of states. The three Slavic republics—Belarus, Russia, and Ukraine, also emerged as a special set.
39. See William E. Odom and Robert Dujarric, *Commonwealth of Empire?*; Mark Galeotti, *The Age of Anxiety*; Constantine P. Danopoulos and Daniel G. Zirker, eds., *Civil-Military Relations in Soviet and Yugoslav Successor States*; and Bruce Parrot, ed., *State Building and Military Power.*
40. See Robert V. Barylski, "The Caucasus, Central Asia, and the Near-Abroad Syndrome," *Central Asia Monitor*, vol. 2, no. 5: 31–37, and no. 6: 21–28.
41. See Richard F. Starr, *The New Military in Russia.*
42. Thomas M. Nichols, *The Sacred Cause*, p. ix.
43. See General N. A. Chaldymov and A. I. Cherkasenko ed. *Armiya i obshchestvo* (Army and society) (Moscow: Progress, 1990).
44. See V.I. Zhukov, V.M. Safronova, and V.V. Serebryannikov, eds. *Grazhdanskii mir i soglasie: Mirnoe rezreshenie konfliktov v obshchestve* (Civil peace and

accord: The peaceful resolution of societal conflict) (Moscow: Moscow Higher Party School Press, 1991).

45. See, for example, Guillermo O'Donnell, Phillip C. Schmitter, Laurence White-head, eds., *Transitions from Authoritarian Rule: Prospects for Democracy* (Baltimore, Md.: Johns Hopkins University Press, 1986).

46. See Amos Perlmutter, *The Military and Politics in Modern Times* (New Haven, Conn.: Yale University Press, 1977). Also see Samuel P. Huntington, *Political Order in Changing Societies* (New Haven, Conn.: Yale University Press, 1968).

47. See Alfred Stepan, *Rethinking Military Politics: Brazil and the Southern Cone* (Princeton, N.J.: Princeton University Press, 1988).

48. See Robert V. Barylski, "Explaining the Soviet *Junta* of August 1991: Latin American and Soviet Eurasian Political Instability," paper presented at the 23rd National Convention of the American Association for the Advancement of Slavic Studies, November 22–25, 1991, Miami, Florida. Soviet colleagues who attended this panel agreed that there were similarities but warned against mechanically transferring ideas.

49. See for example, Rebecca L. Schiff, "Civil-Military relations Reconsidered: A Theory of Concordance," *Armed Forces & Society*, vol. 22, no. 1, Fall 1995, pp. 7–24.

50. See Perlmutter, *Military and Politics,* chap. 9, "Israel: The Routinized Revolutionary Army."

51. See Lt. Col. Aleksandr Bat'kovskii, Col. Yevgeny Khrustalev, Capt. Sergei Balychev, "Detonator sotsial'nogo vzryva" (The social explosion's detonator), *Krasnaya zvezda,* 5 October 1996.

52. See Frederick J. Fleron Jr.'s "Post-Soviet Political Culture in Russia: An Assessment of Recent Empirical Investigations." *Europe-Asia Studies*, vol. 48, no. 2, 1996, 225–60, for a frank and intellectually sophisticated discussion of the use and abuse of the concept.

2

Gorbachev's Reforms:
Political Change and Civilian Control

This chapter raises general questions about political change, examines the specic circumstances that brought Gorbachev to power, and analyzes how Gorbachev's reforms unleashed forces that destroyed the administrative chain of command the Kremlin needed to govern the Soviet Union effectively. After introducing several major questions about modernization which the entire book will continue to discuss, the chapter focuses on four key political institutions—the office of the general secretary, the Ministry of Defense, the Main Political Administration, and the Soviets. By changing them, Gorbachev undermined his ability to command and control the Soviet Union's civilian and military bureaucracies. He made himself politically ineffective and thereby undermined his personal political legitimacy.

Gorbachev used a military metaphor to describe his final political dead end: "Imagine a commander surrounded by a staff, marshals, and generals, but not having army units at his disposal."[1] He had the proper titles—president, general secretary, and supreme commander and he sat in the right Kremlin offices. He even had the infamous nuclear button in his possession. But the vast army of civilian administrators and managers was beginning to look around for new leadership and starting to fend for itself by developing new political alliances and ways of conducting business without Gorbachev and the Union state. In the end, that staff—his very cabinet, conspired against him and launched an abortive coup in a short-lived attempt to save its power and the Union.

But the country did not degenerate into large scale civil war. The military remained sufficiently disciplined and cohesive to steer itself through a very complex series of changes in political direction without degenerating into warring factions associated with different political tendencies. Gorbachev and military leaders had been more cautious and conservative with military reform than with civilian leaders had been with civilian institutional changes. The Ministry of Defense came through perestroika relatively intact. Military reform lagged behind civilian institutional change and this gap helped to stabilize society.

Accidental Revolutionary or Systematic Reformer?

In March 1985 when the civilian political oligarchy elevated Mikhail Gorbachev to serve as its leader, the Soviet Union appeared stable, Soviet armed forces were firmly entrenched in Central and Eastern Europe, and the Soviet military was under reliable civilian control. In March 1990, only five years later, the Soviet political and military system was in deep crisis. The three Baltic republics were demanding complete independence. Illegal, anti-Russian armed forces were appearing in the Baltic region, Western Ukraine, and the Caucasus. And Moscow was under great pressure to liquidate Soviet military and political positions in Central and Eastern Europe where all the Communist regimes had recently been overthrown.

By late summer 1990 there were unmistakable signals that important segments in the Soviet military no longer supported Gorbachev because his reforms had damaged their professional and institutional interests and undermined Soviet state viability. Military officers who under normal circumstances would not have dared to criticize their supreme commander became vocal, sometimes rude critics of Gorbachev. Traditional deference gave way to behavior bordering on insubordination. The Soviet military's political activity increased, a trend that confirms the axiom that the armed forces are more likely to become involved in politics when civilian leadership is divided and civilian political institutions lose their effectiveness. But instead of attempting to silence his military critics by using the powers available to him as supreme commander—denying promotions to some and forcing others to retire, Gorbachev permitted military critics to air their grievances in public in a manner that diminished his office's authority.

Three facts raise major questions about the relationship between conscious political leadership and deeper systemic forces. Gorbachev destroyed the political institutional links that Soviet general secretaries needed in order to function as effective dictators. Gorbachev neither intended to make himself ineffective nor to undermine the Soviet Union's political viability. The *system* failed to defend itself against Gorbachev's mistakes even though key military and security leaders correctly analyzed the general situation and predicted that it was headed for ruin. Was the Russian revolution of 1988–1991 the result of a series of political blunders or the triumph of deliberate, brilliant thinking based upon modernization theory? Was the system carrying the politicians along or were the politicians in control of destiny? How could a social system that was supposed to be inherently authoritarian—one based on 1,000 years of Eurasian despotism, produce a democratic breakthrough?

By investing Gorbachev with dictatorial powers in March 1985, the Soviet system made a strategic mistake. More specifically, the top dozen leaders in the Soviet oligarchy—the Politburo, picked the wrong person to lead the reform process. They entrusted supreme political power to a person who made changes which undermined the Soviet state's basic operating systems and destroyed its viability without intending to do so. If there had been a systemic wisdom embedded in the Soviet political system and the 18,000,000 members of the Communist Party, it should have prevented Gorbachev from taking power and removed him when he began to threaten its viability. Or, is there a higher wisdom which propels human institutions towards disruptive changes which enhance *long-term* viability at the expense of *short-term* viability? Was *greater Russia* transforming itself by shedding old institutional patterns in order to grow into new, more advanced forms of political, economic, and social organization?

There is broad agreement all across the Russian political spectrum that the *system* had to adapt to new imperatives. Even the coup plotters who tried to depose Gorbachev in August 1991 and Boris Yeltsin who successfully deposed him and officially dissolved the Soviet state in December 1991 accepted the modernization imperative. So did the military, the domestic police, and the security services—the so-called power ministries. They criticized Gorbachev for the manner in which he implemented change but not for having placed structural change on the national political agenda.

The Last General Secretary: Gorbachev's Rise to Power

The general secretaries of the Communist Party of the Soviet Union were political *generalissimos* in the Soviet system. The word "general" in the title "general secretary" was appropriate because the individual holding the office had overall policymaking authority and commanded the area-specific secretaries who monitored all key areas of Soviet society through the departments in the Central Committee of the Communist Party. Central Committee staff worked for the general secretary. Central Committee cadre departments had to clear all top managerial appointments throughout the Soviet Union. This power to appoint, to promote, and to dismiss was the key to the general secretary's power and what made the 18,000,000 Communists into a cohesive administrative system.[2]

General Secretaries Stalin, Khrushchev, Brezhnev, and Gorbachev were powerful dictators who appointed and dismissed all top civilian administrators and military officers. They also had the final word over national policy and spending priorities. In effect, they were the commanders in chief over the Soviet state's civilian and military bureaucracies. In the civilian sector, the basic operating principle that kept the pyramid of power viable was called *democratic centralism*. In the military sector, it was called *unity of command*. As long as the military and civilian chains of command remained cohesive, competent, and loyal, the general secretary governed effectively.

By tradition, the great Soviet political leaders were expected to understand and to direct national defense and military affairs. Stalin, Khrushchev, and Brezhnev established that expectation. However, the next three general secretaries—Yury Andropov, Konstantin Chernenko, and Mikhail Gorbachev, could not match their experience in defense affairs. Before becoming general secretary, Gorbachev had neither served in the armed forces nor handled any important Soviet defense or industrial managerial portfolio. Further, his main rivals, two well-entrenched Communist bosses—Grigory Romanov and Viktor Grishin, had close ties to the Soviet military-industrial complex. Romanov ran the Leningrad region and Grishin managed greater Moscow's affairs.[3]

Gorbachev tried to improve his prospects for promotion by cultivating a relationship with the Soviet Union's top defense administrator but he never broke into defense-industrial circles. Instead of forming a working political alliance with the military-industrial complex, Gorbachev came to resent it. This resentment persisted even after Gorbachev won the main political prize. But Gorbachev wasn't an isolated case, the emerging cohort of radical political and economic reformers had an anti-defense bias. Defense's very success at consuming a lion's share of resources and preventing other interest groups from invading its domain developed into a political liability. When the Soviet Union began to reform under Gorbachev, defense lacked broad political support among the general population.

Gorbachev's account of the competition for the general secretariat is revealing. Gorbachev needed and wanted a close relationship with the Soviet Union's last imposing Minister of Defense, Dmitry F. Ustinov. general secretary Brezhnev gave high priority to military and agricultural affairs.[4] Since Gorbachev was in charge of Soviet agriculture, he had half the portfolio needed to succeed Brezhnev. He therefore astutely cultivated a good relationship with Ustinov who was the most influential figure on the Politburo. Gorbachev mentions discussions in which he, Brezhnev, and Ustinov engaged in friendly debates about whether it should be *"Defense and Bread"* or *"Bread and Defense."*[5] In practice, *Defense* took priority and military spending was growing twice as fast as the Soviet GNP. In Gorbachev's words, "This Moloch devoured the fruits of hard labor and mercilessly exploited the industrial plant.... Worst of all, the problem could not even be analyzed. All statistics concerning the military-industrial complex were top secret, inaccessible even to members of the Politburo."[6] Without Ustinov and the defense *Moloch*, Gorbachev could not expect to advance towards the coveted top position. Gorbachev put it candidly: "No-one in the Politburo dared to stand up to him."[7]

Brezhnev died in late 1982 and the Politburo had to select a new general secretary. At that time, Gorbachev lobbied for Ustinov even though he was aging and in poor health. However, former KGB boss, Yury Andropov won the competition and took the helm. Andropov, brought Grigory Romanov to Moscow to work with the ailing Ustinov on defense affairs. Gorbachev describes this rival, Romanov, as "a narrow-minded and insidious man with dictatorial ways."[8]

Nevertheless, Andropov mentored Gorbachev and tried to prepare him for higher levels of responsibility by assigning him tasks that added breadth to his leadership experience; but rivals kept Gorbachev out of defense and military affairs. Andropov launched programs to reduce corruption and to increase accountability and Gorbachev supported him. Andropov relied upon Gorbachev as his primary assistant for general Party work. In effect, Gorbachev had become the junior general secretary and he expected to succeed Andropov who died in early 1984. However, a coalition with more conservative views blocked him. Gorbachev once again lobbied for Ustinov who was already seventy-five years old and quite ill. In turn, Ustinov supported Gorbachev but the other seniors leaders still thought him too young and inexperienced for the job. The elders—Andrei Gromyko, Nikolai Tikhonov, and Dmitry Ustinov put their peer, the ailing Konstantin Chernenko into the general secretary's chair in a transitional arrangement that lasted just over a year.[9] Chernenko made Gorbachev his primary assistant, the person who managed the daily flow of information and policy papers in the Central Committee.[10]

Minister of Defense Ustinov died in December 1984. general secretary Chernenko died three months later in March 1985 and the oligarchy faced another succession crisis. Gorbachev won this round because his main rivals—Grishin and Romanov, canceled each other out. He emerged as the unity candidate who was supposed to engage in reform in a responsible manner. Foreign Minister Andrei Gromyko, the senior leader on the Politburo, mediated among the factions, arranged Gorbachev's nomination, and presented him to the Central Committee as the Politburo's unanimous choice.

The military remained stable and outside of politics during the transitions from Brezhnev to Andropov, from Andropov to Chernenko, and from Chernenko to Gorbachev. They flew senior Party bosses to Moscow from the provinces and republics to attend the Central Committee meetings which endorsed the leadership changes which the Politburo had already agreed upon. The armed forces performed their usual security functions and the Union's political life functioned smoothly in spite of the instability at the top from 1982 to 1985. It was not the type of instability that required military intervention or involvement. No faction needed to arrest any other or seems to have considered such options. The oligarchy functioned reasonably well. The senior generation passed the baton to a new generation in its fifties with Gorbachev at its head. Neither the military nor the military-industrial complex sensed any major threat to its interests in those changes. Instead, the overall mood was positive. The top leadership position had been renewed without major incident.

The Soviet system appeared to be adapting reasonably well. Ten years later Gorbachev described the situation negatively, "The very system was dying away; its sluggish senile blood no longer contained any vital juices."[11] However, in March 1985, he saw himself more positively. He was supposed to be the new, vital juice and he was excited about having been chosen to play that role in Soviet history. His pledged to increase the velocity of policy change and to renew the political and economic system. His acceptance speech was replete with references to change, new directions, increased authority and accountability for enterprises, and democratization.[12] Other leaders had said similar things; but he was in his mid-fifties and the generation that was leaving power was in its mid-seventies. He was determined to make an impact on the system and immediately began to promote changes.

Disrupting the Soviet Political Contract

When Gorbachev took office, the national leadership system needed renewal. Brezhnev had allowed too many civilian and military leaders to enjoy a long, comfortable tenure in office. This produced an overall climate which Gorbachev called "stagnation." Andropov had started forcing corrupt and incompetent civilian bosses into retirement. The process slowed under Chernenko and speeded up again under Gorbachev. He spent his first two years (1985–86) working within the Soviet system and made no systemic changes in basic operating rules. He launched an ill-conceived war on alcoholism, promoted new work-team incentive plans in industry, and inched towards market reforms. But the overall results were disappointing. His third year (1987) was a transition period during which he became convinced that the Soviet system needed changes in basic operating rules and institutions. Gorbachev began searching for ways to reconstruct the Soviet political system in order to take advantage of the competitive forces that seemed to keep Western society constantly changing and adapting to new ideas and inventions.

For the seventieth anniversary of the revolution of 1917, Gorbachev issued a bold call to democratize the political system and to push the economy into profit and loss accounting and market-driven relationships. He boasted that this radical reconstruction program—perestroika, would be the most important policy shift since the revolution of 1917. Lenin and Stalin created the Soviet system and, for better and worse, led the country through rapid, radical policy shifts. Khrushchev tried to reform Stalinism but failed to achieve a major breakthrough. Now, he, Gorbachev, would be bolder than Khrushchev and would implement deep changes rapidly, changes that could not be turned back by some conservative reaction. Instead of condemning competitive elections and markets, he praised them as universally recognized human achievements that were compatible with socialist ideals.[13] Nevertheless, he intended to preserve one-party rule, a strong state role in economic affairs, and a unified Soviet Union.

In summer 1988, Gorbachev decided to impose competitive elections on the Soviet political system. He convened a national conference of Party leaders at the end of May 1988 and televised its proceedings live to the Soviet public. He encouraged delegates to criticize the Soviet system constructively and to endorse changes in the Party rules and in the Soviet Constitution. The main idea was to introduce competitive elections while retaining the one-party system.[14] Gorbachev wanted to push the reform process beyond the point of no return lest conservative forces reverse perestroika.[15] Although it is fashionable to criticize him for imposing a flawed political modernization plan on the Soviet state, he was trying to solve an extremely difficult problem. The basic operating system, one-party dictatorship, had functioned for seventy years. Gorbachev reasoned that the country needed a transitional period between one-party dictatorship and multiparty democracy. Therefore, he decided to create a hybrid system, a one-party state with competitive electoral features. But instead of introducing competition at lower levels of government and working step by step over a number of years to the top, he rushed matters and wanted elections at all levels within a year's time. He brushed aside conservatives who urged him to adopt a slower strategy, called them "enemies of perestroika," and encouraged bold reformers to come forward.

In September 1988, he summoned the Soviet parliament into session and obtained parliamentary approval for the required constitutional changes in a hastily convened session that also elected him chairman of the Supreme Soviet which entitled him to be called president of the Soviet Union. The entire affair took about forty-five minutes. Then he ordered the Communist Party's regional leaders to organize national debates about electoral reforms. He also pressed senior Communist political bosses to retire and to make room for younger leaders at all levels. In November 1988, the Soviet parliament approved constitutional amendments that established a new all-Union legislature or Congress with 2250 members. Two-thirds were to be elected directly while one-third of the seats were to be elected at conventions held by listed, all-union public organizations such as the Communist Party, the Communist Youth League, the official women's organizations, veterans organizations, and so on.

The republican, regional, and local bodies of government were also supposed to democratize, a process that moved forward unevenly since each republic retained some power to control the amendment of its own constitution and in some republics the dominant political elites believed that Gorbachev's reforms threatened their personal interests and general societal stability. Gorbachev stirred up grass roots support for change and permitted popular fronts to develop—movements that rapidly turned into anti-Communist rebellions in the Baltic republics, the and Caucasus, and Western Ukraine. As he toured the country and the world in late 1988 and early 1989, he described his strategy as a political vice. He was squeezing from the top and the popular fronts were squeezing from the bottom. Together they would crush the conservative bureaucracy. And, that is precisely what happened but not with the result he hoped for. The vice destroyed the middle levels of Soviet political administration.

Some parts of the USSR democratized fully over the next two years; others never made the transition. The three Baltic republics democratized rapidly and soon demanded independence from the Soviet Union. The five Central Asian republics moved very cautiously and resisted Gorbachev's reforms. The three Caucasian republics followed three different reform paths. After two years of such differentiated political change, the Soviet state had lost its political integrity. The Russian republic's democratization gave Boris Yeltsin a chance to stand for election and to build an independent Russian power base from which to challenge Gorbachev and the Union state. And, democratization within Russia created conditions that would eventually produce the Chechen secessionist movement and civil war.

Gorbachev's electoral reforms broke the *political contract* between the general secretary and the regional bosses. Elections released forces that chewed apart the hierarchical relationship between the general secretary in Moscow and local and regional political leaders.[16] The general secretary depended upon regional party bosses and the heads of the Party organizations in the fifteen republics to enforce Union political decisions consistently throughout the country. The general secretaries reserved the right to fire any regional boss at any time. It was this power that kept the political-administrative system cohesive. When Gorbachev told the middle-level bosses that they would have to run for office in honest competitive elections in order to retain their power, he destroyed the long-standing political contract that had kept them loyal to previous general secretaries. This act disrupted the system which gave the general secretary the ability to command the 18,000,000 members of the Communist Party, the Soviet Union's managerial class. The grand Soviet political deal used to be an exchange of obedience for power and privilege. The local bosses habitually obeyed Moscow which in turn permitted them to live as local potentates. If the power to hold office came from the people through regular, competitive elections, instead of the from Communist Party bosses and their general secretary in Moscow, then the Soviet dictatorship was over.

Political markets quickly developed in a differentiated manner all across the Soviet Union. In some markets anti-Communism and secession became popular. Candidates who appealed to nationalism won and those who didn't lost in the three Baltic republics. In December 1988, the Lithuanian Communist Party met and divided into pro-Union and pro-independence factions. The latter survived and won votes and seats in the democratic parliament. The former lost. The new electoral system gave radical democrats and nationalists access to political power but this rising group did not become Gorbachev's political allies. He found himself in the unenviable position of being resented by the traditional Communist managerial class and being mistrusted by rising non-Communists. Gorbachev became a politician without a solid political base of his own. Politicians interested in their personal survival turned away from him and found new sources of influence. Gorbachev became a political general without officers to enforce his orders. The Soviet political contract was incompatible with the doctrine of popular sovereignty. In the new electoral system power was derived from the people through the ballot box not from the general secretary and the Central Committee.

Preserving the Military's Unity of Command

The military remained comparatively well-disciplined and cohesive even as the Soviet, civilian political-administrative chain of command began to disintegrate. Gorbachev's military reforms were supposed to improve discipline and to raise professional standards. Military reformers disliked perestroika's instability and radicalism but were attracted to the idea of bringing Soviet military professionalism closer to the highest standards set in the advanced industrial states. By late 1988, the Soviet military system began to understand that the manner in which reforms were being handled was placing the entire reform operation at risk. The armed forces began to experience the negative impact of changes working their way through the civilian governance system. Military leaders understood that military cohesion was threatened by civilian institutional breakdown. They also sensed a rising antimilitary theme in the very societal forces who were most enthusiastic about basic political and economic change.

The Soviet military's relationship with Gorbachev followed a pattern similar to his changing relationship with the Soviet Union's traditional civilian political elite. The first stage was positive and hopeful. The second stage was disruptive and strained. However, by remaining cohesive, the Soviet military saved the country from civil war. There were two reasons for this positive phenomenon. First, military professional values stressed cohesion and the military was deeply aware of what civil war in a multinational nuclear state could mean. Second, Gorbachev tried to improve military discipline and to strengthen it even while encouraging more open discussion of professional reform issues by officers. His approach to military institutional reform was quite conservative even though he intended to cut defense spending and to reduce the size of the armed forces.

In January 1987, Gorbachev convened a special Central Committee plenum on military discipline. A year later in February 1988, all commanders were required to report to the Ministry of Defense's senior officers on progress they had made implementing perestroika's main goal, a drastic reduction in the incidence of conduct in violation of Soviet military codes.[17] On 13 October 1988 at a special meeting of the Politburo, General Secretary Gorbachev heard and discussed a report on disciplinary problems in the Soviet Armed Forces. He ordered the military to take action immediately to effect a dramatic reduction in code violations.[18] In November 1988, all military commanders from the divisional level and higher were assembled in Moscow and told that they would be held personally accountable for improving military discipline. This was the first time in Soviet history that all the commanders had ever assembled in one place. The meeting was intended to impress them with the importance of improving discipline.[19]

Gorbachev did not democratize the armed forces and *unity of command* remained the military's fundamental operating rule. However, he encouraged officers to use their civil liberties including their right to run for elective office and to serve if elected without resigning from the armed forces. Further, to build support for military reform from the bottom-up, Gorbachev encouraged military *glasnost'* or speaking out in favor of constructive change. Soldiers could not elect their generals but they could compete against them in local, regional, republic, and union elections. Officers were still required to obey orders from their commanders but they were encouraged to discuss military professional issues in Officer's Assemblies. Gorbachev wanted Soviet military officers to remain in the Communist Party and the vast majority did. He used military Communist Party organizations to help keep military *glasnost'* within bounds. Initially, this approach served his interests well; however, by mid-1990 a cluster of military Communist leaders began demanding that he take stronger measures to restore the Soviet state's political integrity. (See my discussion of the MPA below.)

The Issue of Democratic Civilian Control

Did officers and soldiers owe their loyalty to a person, a party, or to an office? And what makes that claim upon their loyalty legitimate? According to Soviet tradition, the supreme national political leader controlled the armed forces. Legitimacy was associated with the person and the Party rather than the Constitution. Nevertheless, Soviet dictators traditionally made certain that their puppet legislatures actually passed and registered the bills and resolutions required to make them the legal leaders of the armed forces.

According to the Soviet Constitution, the power to command the armed forces was derived from the Union legislature or Congress. It created a smaller standing body called the Presidium of the Supreme Soviet and this body named a national Defense Council to supervise military affairs. The Defense Council had the power to appoint and dismiss the high command of the Armed Forces of the USSR (1987 Constitution, Article 121, paragraph 14). The Constitution (Article 6) gave the Communist Party the leading role in Soviet society which amounted to a firm political monopoly. The Party ran the parliament and the general secretary dictated Party policy. Soviet general secretaries arranged to have themselves named chairmen of the Defense Council and were not concerned about the national parliament's constitutional authority to serve as a check on their personal control over the military. Since they dictated to the parliament, it could not check their power.

Stalin set the precedents that persisted into the post-Soviet era. Stalin commanded from behind the scenes except during the war when he presented himself as the formal, uniformed supreme commander. All subsequent Soviet leaders derived some of their stature from the awesome Comrade Stalin, the *Generalissimo* or general of generals. After Stalin's death, the power relationships were unclear. Khrushchev reaffirmed the principle that the head of the Party was always to be invested with the powers of the supreme commander of the Soviet armed forces. However, that decision was never formally announced. Khrushchev remembers it this way: "This was a strictly internal decision. We did not publicize the decision and made no mention of it in the press. As for the top officers of our armed forces, they certainly knew who their commander in chief was without having to read an announcement in the newspaper."[20] Later Khrushchev made himself both head of party and head of state. Brezhnev likewise made himself head of party, head of state, and chairman of the Defense Council. So did Gorbachev although from 1985 to 1988, he was head of party and chairman of the Defense Council but not head of State. (He became head of state in September 1988 when veteran diplomat Andrei Gromyko resigned in his favor.) Then, when the first reform Congress met in May-June 1989, it elected Gorbachev head of state for a second time.

In March 1990, the Soviet Congress revised the Constitution and changed the Soviet political system into a multiparty democracy with a popularly elected president as chief of state and supreme commander of the Soviet Armed Forces. But, these reforms neither enhanced Gorbachev's political legitimacy nor increased his effectiveness as supreme commander for three reasons. First, although Congress reaffirmed the idea that presidents derive their power directly from the people through democratic elections, Gorbachev never stood for election. Congress granted him an exception but only for one term. Therefore, Gorbachev's legitimacy was somewhat tainted, a weakness that Yeltsin and other opponents could exploit. Second, Congress itself was politically divided between the new *demokraty*, a moderate conservative but disoriented majority, and a vocal *statist* minority. Gorbachev found himself under attack from the two extremes. Democrats from the Baltic republics and the big cities demanded deeper and faster reforms. Conservatives accused him of lacking the will to make and enforce the hard decisions required to save the Soviet state. Third, soldiers who served as elected deputies in Congress participated in these debates and established the precedent that people in uniform had the right to criticize their supreme commander's policies and to reprimand him in public and on record.

The Ministry of Defense: Historic Background

The Soviet general secretaries exercised their power as commanders in chief directly through the minister of defense. They kept a close eye on the Ministry of Defense and made certain that its senior officers were politically reliable. They also introduced special Party and security structures into the military system in order to create additional channels of information beyond the normal military chain of command. Stalin personally interviewed all senior officers before confirming their appointments to the top several dozen military positions in the country. He changed leaders if he distrusted them or was dissatisfied with their performance. Khrushchev did the same but used retirement rather than executions to keep senior officers in line.[21] Under normal circumstances, Soviet ministers of defense maintained a very low political profile; they *never* criticized the general secretary in public; they did not give press conferences; they did not travel outside the socialist camp without the general secretary; they rarely published anything except material endorsing the policy line set by the general secretary. In private they could argue policy and budgets with the general secretary but once a decision was taken, *democratic centralism* and the *unity of command* demanded that they implement it with integrity and professionalism.[22]

The Soviet Ministry of Defense was the institutional descendent of the tsarist and Provisional Government ministries of war. The Imperial Russian Ministry of War survived the Russian revolution and entered the Soviet political system under a new name, the People's Commissariat of War. Leon Trotsky put it this way: "After the October revolution, the old Ministry of War was formally transformed into the People's Commissariat for Military Affairs. But this Commissariat actually relied, and could not but rely, upon the military organism which had been inherited from the previous epoch."[23]

The Bolsheviks captured, reformed and moved the Provisional Government's Ministry of War from Petrograd to Moscow. They gave it a terrible fright but they could not afford to destroy it since the Soviet state, like the Russian states before it, needed a professional military service to defend itself against foreign states and domestic insurrection. Its personnel changed, sometimes drastically and sometimes more slowly and systematically; but the *institution* continued to perform essential professional military functions from one Russian state to the next. It maintained military organizational cohesion by keeping the armed forces structured in a disciplined, hierarchical command and control system.[24] It assessed security threats and made national security assessments and recommendations to the country's civilian leadership. It studied warfare, trained for war, and waged war as directed by the country's civilian leadership.

The Soviet minister of defense functioned as a minister of Soviet Military Forces. (See Table 2.1.) The minister was the nation's top general, the commander who made certain that the military was combat ready and obedient to its commanders and the general secretary.[25] There were additional ministers— civilian administrators in other ministries who were primarily responsible for the development of Soviet defense industry. This pattern was interrupted for eight years when Leonid Brezhnev made the Soviet Union's leading civilian defense industrialist, Dmitry F. Ustinov, his minister of defense after Marshal Grechko's death in 1976. From 1976 to 1984, under Ustinov, the Soviet regime had an exceptionally strong, well-coordinated military-industrial complex leadership system. Marshal Viktor Kulikov remembers the 1970s as the time when the Soviet military flourished, made substantial progress in technological modernization, and permitted the USSR to serve as an enormous stabilizing force in world affairs. His views reflect veteran military nostalgia for the Soviet system.[26] After Ustinov's death in 1984, the Ministry of Defense reverted to more narrowly defined, military responsibilities under a career soldier, Marshal S. L. Sokolov.

Gorbachev and the Ministry of Defense

After Gorbachev became Soviet dictator, Marshal Sokolov continued as minister of defense until May 1987 when the Mathias Rust incident provided Gorbachev with a convenient if extremely embarrassing excuse to replace him and other top military leaders.[27] Instead of breaking with Russian and Soviet tradition and appointing a civilian to succeed Sokolov, Gorbachev appointed Col. General Dmitry T. Yazov. Sokolov was seventy-six when he retired. Yazov was sixty-four when Gorbachev appointed him. Although Yazov eventually betrayed Gorbachev, the two worked well together for three critical years. In his *Memoirs,* Gorbachev praised Yazov for his contribution to perestroika and expressed surprise and shock over his betrayal.[28] In 1987, Gorbachev and Yazov began a two-pronged attack on stagnation in military leadership circles. They replaced older military managers with younger ones and Moscow-bred professional administrators with people with stronger combat and field experience.

Dmitry Yazov was a soldier's soldier who had risen through the ranks to become the commander of the Far Eastern military district. In 1941, Yazov volunteered to fight the Nazis even though, at seventeen, he was under legal age. He survived the war and then worked his way up, step by step, until he was among the top thirty or so military officers in the Soviet Army. He had a good reputation as a solid commander and honest administrator. He was neither a strategic thinker nor a political general. He was neither a Napoleon Bonaparte nor a Charles de Gaulle. Yazov was a professional soldier who would have been content with a low political profile. But, as fate would have it, his commander in chief, Mikhail Gorbachev, plunged ahead with radical reforms that undermined Soviet state viability. Yazov urged Gorbachev to deal harshly with regional separatists in order to save the Union and he allowed military conservatives to criticize Gorbachev harshly and publicly beginning in summer 1990. He joined the conspiracy to oust Gorbachev but abandoned the August 1991 coup on its third day. Although the latter decision probably saved the country from serious bloodshed and certainly gave the collapsing coup a soft political landing, Yazov lost his job and was arrested. He had, after all, joined an unconstitutional coup against his commander in chief and had to be punished.

The changes Gorbachev made in military leadership from 1985–1990 contributed to his success at overall societal reform as well as to his ultimate failure. As a new general secretary, Gorbachev had to demonstrate that he was indeed the commander in chief and the best way to do this convincingly was to purge the military leadership and he did so. As a reformer, he quickly learned that it was easier to change people than to change the minds and habits of the old guard. Since Gorbachev wanted to promote a new managerial climate, he needed new military managers. Further, the Sokolov generation had been blocking promotions throughout the Soviet military system by holding on to its offices and privileges beyond retirement age. Gorbachev reports that he and Yazov retired some 1,200 generals.[29] By moving them into retirement, Gorbachev increased his popularity with younger officers and contributed to his image as a young, vigorous reformer. Gorbachev really believed that the Ministry's managerial group had become dominated by Moscow-bred generals who were better at office and departmental politics than at promoting military reform, high levels of combat readiness, and overall discipline.

The basic military political handbook for officers published by the Ministry of Defense in 1989 reported that about 50 percent of the managerial personnel in the Ministry of Defense had been changed between 1987 and 1989. Yazov's appointment set the trend. Military commanders who had direct experience with the problems of running major military districts and branches of the armed forces replaced military managers who had made their careers primarily in central office jobs.[30] Under Brezhnev there had been little turnover in top positions. Under Gorbachev, the velocity of change increased dramatically. RAND political scientist Sergei Zamascikov reported that during the 1970s and 1980s prior to Gorbachev's taking power, on average about ten top commanders were replaced each year. The rate increased to fifteen in 1985–86 and twenty in 1987–88. By examining age data, he confirmed that Gorbachev had moved a younger generation into military leadership positions and also made room for the Afghan war generation to advance.[31] Thus, General Secretary Gorbachev demonstrated his political control over the military, his ability to determine who gets what position when, where, and why. Gorbachev's success reaffirmed the tradition of civilian control. It was also part of his overall reform program for Soviet society. The new general secretary had set the new policy line for Soviet society as a whole and it was being applied in both military and civilian spheres.

The Main Political Administration: Background

The Russian military has participated in all the major changes in the Russian political system beginning with the coup against Tsar Nicholas II in Feb-

TABLE 2.1
Soviet Political and Military Leaders: 1945–1991[*]

Paramount Civilian Leaders	Ministers of Defense	Chiefs of General Staff	MPA Chief
J. V. Stalin ('28 3/53)	J. V. Stalin (2/46–3/47) N. A. Bulganin (3/47–3/49) A. M. Vasilevsky-army (4/49–3/53) N. G. Kuznetsov-navy (4/49–3/53)	A. I. Antonov (1945–3/46) A. M. Vasilevsky (3/46–11/48) S. M. Shtemenko (11/48–5/52) V. D. Sokolovsky (6/52–1/60)	I. V. Shikin ('46–'49) F.F. Kuznetsov ('49–'53)
N. S. Khrushchev (3/53–10/64)	N. A. Bulganin ('53–'55) G. K. Zhukov ('55–'57) R. Y. Malinovsky ('57–'67)	V. D. Sokolovsky V. D. Sokolovsky V. D. Sokolovsky M.V. Zakharov ('60–63) S. S. Biryuzov ('63–'64; died 10/ 64) M.V. Zakharov ('64–71)	A. S. Zheltov (4/53–58) F. I. Golikov ('58–'62) A. I. Yepishev ('62–'85)
L. I. Brezhnev (10/64–11/82)	R. Y. Malinovsky (died 3/.67) A. Grechko ('67–'76; died 4/24/76) D. F. Ustinov ('76–'84)	M V. Zakharov ('64–'71) M. V. Zakharov (died 1/72) V. G. Kulikov ('71–77) N. V. Ogarkov (1/77–9/84)	A. I. Yepishev
Y. V. Andropov (11/82–2/84)	D. F. Ustinov	N. V. Ogarkov	A. I. Yepishev
K. U. Chernenko (2/84–3/85)	D.F. Ustinov (died in office 12/20/84) S. L. Sokolov (12/84....)	N. V. Ogarkov N. V. Ogarkov S. F. Akhromeyev (9/84–12/88)	A. I. Yepishev ('62–'85) (died in office)
M. S. Gorbachev (3/85–12/25/91)	S. L. Sokolov (...5/ 87) D. T. Yazov (5/.87–8/21/91) M. A. Moiseyev (12/84–8/91) M. Moiseyev (8/21/ 91) Y. I. Shaposhnikov (8/21/91–12/21/91)	S. F. Akhromeyev S. F. Akhromeyev N. A. Shlyaga (7/90–8/91) V. N. Lobov (8/91–12/8/91) V. N. Samsonov (12/8/91–12/21/91)	A. D. Lizichev (7/85–7/90) *MPA abolished 30/8/91*

* Main sources: M. V. Zakharov ed., *50 Let vooruzhennykh sil SSSR* (50 Years of the Armed Forces of the USSR). Moscow: *Voennoye izdatel'srvo*, 1968; and Marshal Sergei F. Akhromeyev ed. *Voennoe izdateicheskii Slovar'* (Military Encyclopedic Dictionary). Moscow: *Voennoe izdatel'srvo* (The Military Press), 1986.

ruary-March 1917 and ending with Boris Yeltsin's decision to overthrow the Russian parliament in summer-fall 1993. Russia's top soldiers have always been political figures to one extent or another. The civilian leadership demanded that the country's national military leaders be proficient in military affairs and loyal to them politically. Soviet tradition rejected the idea that the armed forces should be outside of politics. The general secretaries wanted to know precisely where the senior military officers stood and to keep them in their camp. What Trotsky said in 1918 continued to be repeated in one form or another for the rest of the century: "Where and when did any army stay out of politics? Let our know-alls tell us, we are listening?"[32]

Since the Party leadership regarded the military as a highly important political tool, it embraced it with an iron grip. Official Soviet military-political literature constantly reaffirmed the Party's leading role in military affairs. The Party's top civilian leaders made the basic policy decisions about national defense. Such decisions were made by the general secretary and the political oligarchy in their Kremlin suites not by the minister of defense and the military officers in the Ministry of Defense building on the Frunze embankment. The general secretary held the minister of defense and the chief of the General Staff accountable for implementing military policy through the military chain of command. The Communist Party organizations within the Ministry of Defense played a secondary and supportive role in policy implementation. They did not make policy either. They took their orders from above and these also came from the general secretary's designates in the Central Committee's Main Political Administration (MPA).

Not all military Communists were on the MPA's staff. Not all Soviet military officers were MPA officers. At the close of the Soviet era, in August 1991, there were 92,500 military personnel on the MPA's staff.[33] By contrast, there were about 1,000,000 Communist Party members in the Soviet armed forces at that time, and about 80 percent of the entire officer corps were members of the Communist Party. The figure was 100 percent for the higher ranks.[34] Military officers could not advance through the ranks without demonstrating their political reliability and the standard way to do so was to participate in Communist Party life as well as to cooperate with the KGB's information gathering operations. The MPA staff and the regular military commanders followed different career lines. Special political leadership academies were set up to train Soviet political officers. A person could become a general in the MPA by doing only political work.[35]

When the civilian Party leadership embarked upon some new policy in any field, the MPA had to confirm that it had explained the policy to the troops and the officers, that people had attended meetings, and that concrete actions had been taken where appropriate. When Stalin ordered the liquidation of the kulaks, military Party workers discussed the policy and trained draftees to become new village leaders. When Stalin signed a nonaggression treaty with Hitler, the MPA personnel described it as a brilliant diplomatic victory and the army carried Soviet power into the Baltic states, Eastern Poland, and Romanian provinces. When Hitler perfidiously broke it and invaded the Soviet Union, the MPA cadres rallied the soldiers to the Great Patriotic War. When Khrushchev proclaimed that the Soviet Union would catch up to and surpass the United States in some types of production, the political officers made certain the military expressed enthusiasm for his program. And so on down through the years until Gorbachev launched perestroika, glasnost', and New Political Thinking. His MPA team explained those policy shifts and began to apply them in the armed forces.

The MPA Chiefs

The MPA played an important role in military political indoctrination; but the MPA chiefs did not become major national political leaders. They were far less significant than the ministers of defense in the postwar period. The MPA played the supporting roles in Soviet military life not the leading roles. The MPA directed thousands of journalists and political lecturers, not tank divisions and crack special forces. When the national political elite needed the military's assistance at a critical turning point, the military commanders were the key players under the leadership of the minister of defense and the chief of the General Staff. Later, after the real power brokers had completed their work, the MPA could write about it and explain it to the troops.

From 1946 to 1991, there were only seven MPA chiefs and one of them, Army General Aleksei I. Epishev, served for twenty-three years from 1962 to 1985. Epishev's tenure even surpassed that of Leonid Brezhnev who was general secretary for eighteen years. Khrushchev appointed Epishev in 1962 when he needed a reliable political ally to remind the officer corps that once the general secretary made a policy decision, they were to carry it out without criticism. Epishev ran the MPA so well that he served under five general secretaries: Khrushchev, Brezhnev, Andropov, Chernenko, and Gorbachev. Epishev guaranteed that the officer corps heard, understood, and expressed support for all key Soviet military and defense policy decisions from the Cuban missile crisis to the invasions of Czechoslovakia and Afghanistan. Epishev died shortly after Gorbachev came to power.

Gorbachev and the MPA: The Military Speaks Out

Epishev's death gave Gorbachev an opportunity to select a new top political officer, someone younger and ready to implement change, someone with major administrative experience but who had been serving outside the Moscow establishment. He tapped General Aleksei D. Lizichev who headed MPA operations among the some 500,000 Soviet military personnel stationed in the German

Democratic Republic. Lizichev supported military reform, particularly Gorbachev's emphasis upon fighting corruption and raising professional expectations for all officers. However, Gorbachev replaced Lizichev during the Twenty-Eighth Party Congress in July 1990 because too many Communist soldier-deputies had made too many highly charged, negative comments about Gorbachev's domestic and foreign policy at open sessions. They were even more aggressive at policy workshops which were closed to the press. Their main target was Gorbachev's foreign policy which they regarded as reckless, a total defeat in the Cold War. The officers made devastating criticisms of the Gorbachev-Shevardnadze policies in international defense affairs. While most military complaints focused on policy, Lt. General Aleksandr Lebed attacked the administration's integrity and was so outrageously impudent that Gorbachev tried to rebuke him. Gorbachev challenged Lebed with a stern "What did you say?" but Lebed started in again and precipitated five to seven minutes of shouting and general mayhem. Lebed in effect accused the Gorbachev team of brazen hypocrisy and caused Gorbachev's leading political adviser, his main target, Aleksandr Yakovlev, to quit the hall.[36]

Lt. General I. Mikulin ridiculed Gorbachev's so-called "defensive" military doctrine which pledged that the Soviet Union would not launch either nuclear or conventional preemptive strikes beyond its borders. He charged the Soviet Union was being pushed out of Europe by NATO and that Gorbachev and Shevardnadze were making 80 percent of the compromises according to American assessments of their negotiating skills. Colonel Alksnis described Gorbachev's concept of replacing the Union of Soviet Socialist Republics with a Union of Sovereign States as the equivalent of "placing a bomb under the Soviet state" that will explode sooner or later. Colonel General Vladislav Achalov warned that Gorbachev had capitulated to nationalist armed forces in the Caucasus, had failed to enforce the vital principle that kept all armed forces under central control, and claimed there were hundreds of thousands of arms in the hands of irregular armed groups who were ready to turn them on Soviet military. Chief of General Staff, Army General Moiseyev spoke more carefully in keeping with his high-level responsibilities in the Ministry of Defense. However, he did warn that the Soviet Union had to maintain its military spending at levels sufficient to maintain credibility even as it worked for arms reductions and used diplomacy to enhance security. Otherwise, Moiseyev explained, the Soviet Union would be perceived as a declining power. Pacific Fleet Commander Admiral G. Khvatov warned that spending cuts would create strategic and conventional imbalances that would damage Soviet security. Khvatov candidly explained that the USSR could not remain an equal nuclear power in the future unless it rebuilt its strategic naval fleet. He charged that the new "defensive" military doctrine could condemn Soviet forces to wait until the enemy had already delivered a crushing blow. Was the Soviet Union going to wait to be attacked like Stalin in 1941?[37]

Colonel General Albert Makashov became one of Gorbachev's most out-spoken military critics as well as an active participant in two future coup attempts. Makashov rejected Gorbachev's appeals for consolidation around his reform program: "I am entirely for consolidation. But, pardon me, not with those who are against the people, the army, and the Party." [38] The liberal press warned that such talk signaled preparations for a coup and demanded that Gorbachev remove Makashov from his post as commander of the impor-tant Volga-Urals military district. But Gorbachev left him in place until the post-coup purges of August 1991.

The torrent of criticism forced Gorbachev to take some action. He moved against his military political chief—Colonel General Lizichev, even though he was a military progressive who supported perestroika, general moderniza-tion, glasnost', and ethnic affirmative action in the Soviet armed forces. Lizichev often turned to Western models in order to argue that the Soviet military needed to spend more on political indoctrination, civics lessons, and general professional development. In fact, he was taking that progressive line at the XXVIII Party Congress. However, Lizichev had failed at his most im-portant political task, keeping the military lined up in support of the general secretary's policies. Gorbachev replaced Lizichev with Col. General Nikolai Shlyaga who had been Lizichev's deputy. However, Shlyaga turned out to be more conservative than Lizichev and he supported the view that the country was in crisis and needed decisive leadership. Thus, Gorbachev had a serious military, political problem. He had lost the military's confidence and respect and the Communist Party's organizational structures inside the armed forces seemed to be turning on him instead of serving his interests.

After March 1990 when the Soviet parliament amended the Constitution and abrogated the Communist Party's constitutional right to monopolize po-litical life, it was no longer appropriate for the Communist Party or any other political party to maintain a special organization within the armed forces. Gorbachev granted the point in principle but still hoped to use the Party to maintain military loyalty and cohesion during the transition from authoritar-ian to democratic socialism. Therefore, Gorbachev adopted a two-part strat-egy. First, during the coming year, the MPA would be stripped of its partisan political status and be converted into a normal military personnel services operation that would report to the minister of defense. Second, the Commu-nists in the armed forces would form a new Communist Party organization for members of the military. Gorbachev wanted to keep his officers cohesive politically and loyal to him. Therefore, it made sense to pressure them to stay in the party which he led, the Communist Party.

But instead of providing political support, the military Communist organi-zation gave voice to the conservative opposition. In late March 1991 the first All-Army Party Conference (AAPC) assembled in Moscow elected General Mikhail Surkov as its full-time leader. Shortly thereafter, Surkov was named to the Politburo of the civilian Communist Party. The AAPC's first national meeting criticized Gorbachev for being too indecisive and weak in dealing with opposition forces that were actively working to break up the Soviet Union. One speaker mocked him for his "iron restraint." Gorbachev retorted, "If you mean we should return to the old methods of pressure and coercion—I won't go for that." He then lectured the officers on constitutional law, Reds and Whites, the military purges of 1937–38, and the signs that new purges were brewing in 1952–53. Gorbachev insisted that he and the citizenry were demanding a new type of politics: "Further, comrades, when our citizens call for decisive action, they support legality and strict order, not repressions."[39]

Gorbachev engaged in open debates with critics. This political tactic damaged his ability to command obedience as a larger-than-life, presidential figure. By fall 1990, Gorbachev's "iron restraint" had fostered a climate in which officers felt free to criticize their commander in chief openly and even impolitely in public. Was he being too democratic? Do presidents and commanders in chief have to demand a higher degree of respect and deference in order to be effective national leaders?

The Soviets: Citizen-Soldiers and the Unity of Command

The Russian revolutions of 1917 established the soldier's rights to full citizenship. During the revolutionary turmoil, soldiers elected representatives to revolutionary councils or soviets. The council system was formalized in the Soviet constitution which established a democratic assembly form of government on paper. However, the Communist Party imposed monopoly control on politics and its political bosses decided who could run for office and who could not.

From the 1920s to the 1980s the Party bosses made certain that a representative sample of Soviet society was elected to the soviets at all levels: soldiers, intellectuals, men, women, workers, peasants, and diverse ethnic groups. The military was encouraged to stand for election and to serve in legislative bodies and village and town councils. The electoral process was an organized public endorsement of a pre-approved list. Every party boss was responsible for making certain that 98–99 percent of the voters in the district voted. After the elections, the civilian Communists dominated the councils and took responsibility for public administration. Soviet military officers expected to be included in the soviets. Under Stalin it became traditional for lower ranking officers to be elected to lower level soviets and for higher ranking officers to be elected to the higher level soviets. Thus, the senior military leaders in the Ministry of Defense and the senior commanders in the military districts used to be elected to the top Union and Republic legislatures. The military Communists voted obediently for the legislation their Party civilian politicians put before them. They did not debate policy in public. But this changed and the united front of civilian and military leaders under one-party discipline broke down in 1989–90.

In 1989, Col. General Aleksandr Lizichev reported that there were 11,900 active duty military personnel holding elective office in the soviets at all levels.[40] In early 1991, there were 1,004 soldiers holding elective office in the Leningrad region alone.[41] There were fifty-three generals and twenty-eight other military officers among the 2,250 deputies in the Soviet Union's last Congress of Peoples deputies which was elected in 1989 according to a complex election law that was supposed to give Gorbachev a reliable majority.[42]

Soviet political scientists such as Georgi Satarov began studying voting patterns in the Gorbachev Congress. Since most major votes were recorded, analysts could begin sorting and sifting data in order to discover patterns. Not surprisingly, it turned out the fifty-three generals tended to vote more conservatively and with greater consistency than the twenty-eight officers. The generals were older and more conservative than their junior officers. For example, at the Congress which convened in December 1989, the generals overwhelmingly voted against the motion introduced by radical democrats to place a proposal to end the Communist Party's monopoly on the agenda. However, the junior officers divided on that issue. All but one general voted against democratization while some two-thirds of the officers supported it.[43] The one general that voted to debate the Communist Party's special powers was Col. General Igor Rodionov, the soldier who had commanded the Soviet forces in Afghanistan, who became the focus of political controversy after the Tbilisi incident of April 1989, and who would reemerge as Boris Yeltsin's minister of defense in July 1996. General Rodionov's maverick vote was a warning to the Party elite that officers were beginning to liberate themselves psychologically from traditional Soviet habits of obedience to capricious Party rule. However, it did not mean that officers were ready to embrace the democratic liberal politicians either (see chapter 3 below).

The younger and middle-level officers in Congress represented a variety of political views. Two colonels—V. I. Alksnis and N. S. Petrushenko together with a civilian, E. V. Kogan, were the leadership core for a pro-Union faction aptly named *Soyuz* or *Union*. They organized a coalition of civilian and military deputies that pressed Gorbachev to take decisive action to preserve the Union's military and political integrity. They also represented those who complained that Gorbachev's foreign policy had been handled irresponsibly.[44] The *Soyuz* colonels were airing views shared by many senior military officers but who did not dare to criticize their commander in chief, Gorbachev, in full public view. Other officers advocated faster military reform than their seniors in the Ministry of Defense supported. For example, Major V. N. Lopatin and Col. A. V. Tsalko became avid proponents of deeper cuts in the size of the Soviet armed forces, a gradual movement towards an all-professional army, better protection for enlisted personnel and junior officers against abuse by commanders, a ban on all partisan political activity in the armed forces, and some compromises with nationalists in the republics who demanded their own national armed forces to defend their sovereignty against "Moscow." In summer 1990, when Lopatin and Tsalko were insisting that the Communist Party organizations be banned, Gorbachev was still pressing to keep them alive. Senior officers in the Ministry of Defense were furious with Lopatin and Tsalko but the two officers enjoyed political immunity by virtue of their election to Congress and went on pushing their reform agenda.[45]

In constitutional theory, Congress is supposed to be a check on the executive branch, including the Ministry of Defense. However, by allowing generals and officers to be elected to Congress, Soviet practice created conflicts of interest, situations in which military personnel would quite naturally try to influence all legislation affecting national defense affairs. Further, various factions within the armed forces might try to use military deputies to push the president or the minister of defense in one direction or another. Such conflicts of interest became painfully clear in summer-fall 1990 as more and more citizen-soldiers openly criticized Gorbachev's policies and administrative record.

Conclusion

Mikhail Gorbachev disrupted the Soviet state's authoritarian, political and economic operating systems. He tried to infuse new dynamism into political and economic activity by removing authoritarian restraints. He launched competitive elections to make political executives, legislators, and public administrators accountable to the people and he expanded civil liberties to promote debate and criticism in society at large. Gorbachev's reforms unleashed new political forces faster than his political institutional reformation could accommodate them. This created a classical imbalance between rising political demands and institutional capacity to deal with them, a systemic crisis that can lead to states of emergency or temporary political dictatorship. Gorbachev's experience demonstrates how political ineffectiveness undermines political legitimacy.

By mid-1990 there was strong military opposition to Gorbachev's policies and to him as a person. Opponents charged that he was too weak, indecisive, and unreliable to give the Soviet Union effective political leadership. Military critics focused their attacks on Gorbachev's personal leadership abilities and some but not all of his policies. The Brezhnev-Ustinov-Ogarkov national defense affairs leadership team had been more effective than the Gorbachev-Yazov-Moiseyev team. The Brezhnev group's depth of knowledge and breadth of expertise was far greater than the Gorbachev team's. Military critics were dismayed that politics had given dilettantes control over Soviet domestic and foreign policy.

Gorbachev discovered modernization theory on the political battlefields of reform and by comparing the Soviet political economy's performance with that of the advanced, reformed capitalist industrial states. Although he did not anticipate the consequences of his reforms, his moves were deliberate not accidental. Soviet political culture encouraged ideological thinking and Gorbachev was attracted to grand systemic overviews. Modernization theory explained why competitive economic and political systems produced better politics and economic behavior than the Soviet bureaucratic command system. The explanations were compelling. They raised to the level of scientific theory the common sense discoveries that the 18,000,000 members of the ruling Communist Party made on a daily basis as they worked in the huge state bureaucracies.

The theory was relatively easy to grasp. Explaining the general idea— once Gorbachev had become convinced of its validity was also comparatively easy. He used a combination of persuasion and dictatorship to lead his country into the new wilderness. The problem was translating the new theory into practice without undermining the Soviet state's political viability.

Mikhail Gorbachev had dictatorial powers in 1985 because four institutions and two systemic operating rules made him the supreme commander over the Soviet state's civilian and military bureaucracies. The four institutions were the office of the general secretary, the Ministry of Defense, the Main Political Administration, and the Soviets.[46] The systemic operating rules were *democratic centralism* and *unity of command*. The Ministry of Defense and *unity of command* survived through the reform turmoil but the office of the general secretary, *democratic centralism*, and the MPA went into rapid decline. The Soviets survived but changed substantially. They began to assert themselves as a check on the executive branches of government.

Without *democratic centralism* and *unity of command* the highly centralized Soviet state began to lose its political integrity and this damaged its overall viability. Power was moving to middle and lower levels where republic, metropolitan area, and regional political organisms not only retained their vitality but became relatively stronger as the center lost effectiveness. Initially, the center's loss was the region's gain, a process that subsequent chapters discuss in detail.

The military remained cohesive but it distanced itself from Gorbachev, a political shift that none of Gorbachev's successors would have permitted. This development was symptomatic of a larger problem, the general breakdown in Soviet executive power, the Kremlin's declining ability to enforce its decisions throughout the Soviet Union. The armed forces held themselves together while civilian political institutions began to fail. Military institutional values—*the unity of command* and military cohesion, remained strong. The military realized that its institutional interests were threatened by Soviet state breakdown and urged Gorbachev to halt the decline in Soviet political cohesion. In 1990 the Ministry of Defense's top leaders rallied behind this political objective since the vast Soviet military machine had been built and maintained by the very Soviet state that was now beginning to decline. However, some officers began to imagine a different future, one in which there were fifteen ministries of defense instead of one. Dividing the Soviet armed force into separate national armies would create new opportunities for professional advancement particularly for non-Russians.

In 1985, the military knew where policy was made and by whom and to whom officers owed their allegiance and their careers. The general secretary was their undisputed supreme commander and all higher officers had to be members of the Communist Party. By summer 1990 they were less certain about how civilian control over military affairs functioned and less confident in the Soviet state's prospects for survival. The office of the general secretary was only a dim shadow of what it had once been. The office of the presidency of the Soviet Union had only just started building its authority and it faced powerful rivals, the presidents emerging in the fifteen Soviet republics. The Communist Party had lost its legal monopoly on political power and new parties were beginning to develop.

In retrospect, the process seems natural. Gorbachev's belief that he was riding the natural laws of societal development and releasing forces that the bureaucratic command system had created and then restrained for too many years has no major opponents. There is only debate about how fast and how far he tried to go. Gorbachev assisted at the birth of what had been gestating for decades if not centuries. Yet, there were several violent confrontations and there is controversy about Gorbachev's personal responsibility for the use of lethal force against Soviet citizens. Those incidents raised important questions about civilian control over the armed forces and when, if ever, a soldier has the right to disobey orders. The next chapter examines them.

Notes

1. Mikhail S. Gorbachev, *Memoirs* (New York: Doubleday, 1995), p. 323.
2. See Gorbachev, *Memoirs*, pp. 84 ff.
3. Bruce Parrot's "Soviet National Security under Gorbachev" is an excellent analytical political history of Gorbachev's first three years, a major turning point in East-West relations. Policy changes required new ideas—*new thinking (novoye myshlenie)* new people—political victories by Gorbachev's allies: the struggles for personal power and policy fused. Civilian political leaders, military professionals, political commissars, civilian experts, defense industrialists and others participated. *Problems of Communism*, 37 (November-December, 1988): 1–36.
4. See Gorbachev, *Memoirs*, pp. 135 ff.
5. *Ibid.*, p. 136.
6. *Ibid.*
7. *Ibid.*
8. *Ibid.*, p. 143

9. Tikhonov was the elderly prime minister who had supervised industrial affairs for decades. See *Ibid.*, p. 155.

10. Later Yegor Ligachev performed this role for Gorbachev. The two broke over the pace of scope of change. Ligachev's memoirs generally reaffirm Gorbachev's account of the key events of 1983–1985. See Yegor Ligachev's *Inside Gorbachev's Kremlin: The Memoirs of Yegor Ligachev* (New York: Pantheon Books, 1993).

11. Gorbachev, *Memoirs*, p. 168.

12. See M. S. Gorbachev, "Rech' General'nogo sekretarya TsK KPSS," 11 Marta 1985; *Pravda*, 12 March 1985.

13. See Mikhail Gorbachev, *October and Perestroika: The Revolution Continues* (Moscow: Novosti, 1987).

14. The Nineteenth Party Conference of summer 1988 permitted some dissent and debate and was broadcast live by Soviet state television. Gorbachev tried to prevent Boris Yeltsin from getting elected to the conference and from speaking. But Yeltsin outmaneuvered him. Yeltsin criticized Gorbachev for moving too slowly and indecisively. Others warned that Gorbachev had a general theory but no concrete no plan and was exposing the Soviet state to enormous risks. Most endorsed Gorbachev. The transcripts were assembled and printed. See L. F. Dekan', ed., *XIX Vsesoyuznaya konferentsiya kommunisticheskoi partii sovetskogo soyuza. Stenograficheskii otchet,* two vols. (Moscow: Politizdat, 1988).

15. See Gorbachev's opening address to the conference in *Ibid.*, pp. 24–92.

16. See Gorbachev's excellent explanation of the critical role the regional first secretaries played in the Soviet political system's integration (*Memoirs*, pp. 84 ff.).

17. Col. General Aleksandr D. Lizichev, *Put' peremen. Vremya deistvii* (Road to change. Time for action) (Moscow: Voenizdat, 1989). Lizichev was Gorbachev's first military political commissar or chief of the Main Political Administration.

18. *Ibid.*, pp. 141–43.

19. *Ibid.*, p. 252.

20. Nikita Khruschev, *Khrushchev Remembers: The Last Testament* (Boston: Little, Brown and Co., 1974), p. 12.

21. Stalin also stopped the practice of killing senior officers as a routine way of handling personnel affairs after the Second World War.

22. For an excellent, early example of *conflict/interest group* school analysis of the first, public, albeit cautious criticism by a senior military leader of Brezhnev's *Tula* military doctrine, see Jeremy Azrael, *The Soviet Civilian Leadership and the Military High Command, 1976–1986* (Santa Monica, Cal.: RAND, 1987). Marshal Ogarkov's critical thinking and policy debates are more fully developed in Herspring, *The Soviet High Command*.

23. P. 126, "Speech at the section of the All-Russian Central Executive Committee, 22 April 1918," in Leon Trotsky, *How the Revolution Armed*, volume 1 (London: New Park Publications, 1979).

24. The radical socialists, including the Bolsheviks, promoted military democratization during the revolution against the Imperial Russian State and the Provisional Government. After the Bolsheviks had taken power, they reimposed military discipline although they abolished the traditional military ranks and replaced them with a hierarchy of commanders. In 1935, Stalin restored the traditional ranks.

25. Stalin took direct charge of the generals during the war and for a brief period after the war. From 1947 to 1949, he placed a civilian, Nikolai Bulganin, at the head of defense. Then from 1949–1953, Stalin had two ministries, one for the Army and one for the Navy. After his death, the two were combined and placed

under Bulganin. In 1955, Khrushchev replaced Bulganin with Marshal Zhukov. The next two defense ministers were also military professionals, Malinovsky and Grechko. They came the defense industrialist, Ustinov. He was followed by military professionals: Sokolov, Yazov, Moiseyev, Shaposhnikov, and Grachev. See table 2.1.

26. See Marshal (Ret.) Viktor Kulikov's interview by Aleksei Khorev, *Krasnaya zvezda*, 5 July 1996.

27. Rust flew a small plane into the USSR and landed smack on Red Square in Moscow making a mockery of the Soviet air defenses and of Kremlin defense specifically. Gorbachev was in Berlin at a Warsaw pact Summit when the news hit the world press. See Gorbachev, *Memoirs*, pp. 232–33.

28. See *Ibid.*, p. 233.

29. *Ibid.*

30. Lizichev, *Put' peremen*, pp. 75–76.

31. See Alexander R. Alexiev and Robert C. Nurick, *The Soviet Military Under Gorbachev: Report on a RAND Workshop* (Santa Monica, Cal.: RAND Corporation, 1990; and Dale R. Herspring, *The Soviet High Command* (Princeton, N.J.: Princeton University Press, 1990), pp. 265 ff.

32. "A Necessary Explanation, 23 April 1918," Leon Trotsky, *How the Revolution Armed*, p. 185.

33. *Krasnaya zvezda*, 26 September 1991.

34. See Robert V. Barylski, "The Soviet Military Before and After the August Coup," *The Armed Forces & Society*: 10 (1), pp. 27–45; and Lizichev, *Put' peremen*, p. 60.

35. See Timothy J. Colton's *Commissars, Commanders, and Civilian Authority: The Structure of Soviet Military Politics* (Cambridge, Mass.: Harvard University Press, 1979) the last classic on the MPA.

36. See Aleksandr Lebed, *Ya za derzhavu obidno*, Moskovskaya pravda: Moscow, 1995; pp. 321–22.

37. These transcripts were printed in late summer 1990 in the MPA's officer's journal, *Kommunist vooruzhennykh sil*, no. 18, September 1990, pp. 3–20. The editors explained that the general press had failed to cover these sessions properly and they wanted the officers to know what had been said.

38. Colonel General Albert Makashov, cited by *Krasnaya zvezda*, 12 July 1990.

39. Gorbachev's session with the All-Army Party Conference as reported by *Krasnaya zvezda*, 4 April 1991.

40. Lizichev, *Put' peremen*, p. 238.

41. See Major Demin's report in *Krasnaya zvezda*, 31 January 1991.

42. See, INDEM's *Informatsionno-analiticheskii byulleten' No. 1: Vtoroi i tretii syezdy narodnykh deputatov SSSR* (Moscow: Inter-verso, 1990).

43. See *Ibid.*, p. 7.

44. See comments by congressmen Alksnis, Kogan, and Petrushenko at the hearings on Shevardnadze's foreign policy, 15 October 1990. Printed in *Kommunist vooruzhennykh sil*, no. 24, 1990, pp. 28–33. They challenged Shevardnadze to demonstrate that he was defending Soviet rather than American nationalists by evacuating Central Europe and abandoning former allies in the Middle East.

45. See for example, Col. General Vladislav Achalov's attacks on their policy agenda as a preemptive strike against military cohesion and damaging to the army's ability to maintain stability in the Soviet Union during its period of crisis. See Achalov's interview in *Krasnaya zvezda*, 6 September 1990.

46. There is of course a fifth key institution, the KGB and its successors. More on this later.

3

The Military, Domestic Political Violence, and the Gorbachev-Yeltsin Rivalry

This chapter explores three main themes in civil-military relations. The first is the military's classical dilemma during times of domestic instability—its tendency to be attracted to and repulsed by the use of violence to settle political disputes. The second is the military's loss of respect for Gorbachev and its availability for an alliance with Yeltsin. The third is the network of political relationships among senior military officers and civilian politicians. The chapter also identifies officers who began to emerge as leaders in national political life. This group includes two future ministers of defense—Pavel Grachev and Igor Rodionov, the ambitious Aleksander Lebed, and others. It also explains why the elite paratroopers played an important role in conspiratorial plans.

Overview

There is a connection between three bloodsoaked political confrontations—Tbilisi, Baku, and Vilnius, and three major political changes—the August 1991 coup's failure, Gorbachev's fall from power, and the Soviet Union's collapse. The confrontation in Tbilisi took place in April 1989, Baku happened in January 1990, and Vilnius in January 1991. The total number of civilians killed was less than 300. But those 300 deaths produced an outburst of public outrage and debate about the proper relationship between the armed forces, the people, and the state. Instead of pacifying Georgia, Azerbaijan, and Lithuania respectively, the Union's violence strengthened the nationalists in their determination to win independence and to defend it with arms. Instead of preparing the military psychologically to use deadly force against fellow Soviet citizens, the three incidents had quite the opposite affect. To be sure, some leading officers called for tough-minded suppression of the secessionists but others demanded peaceful change. The balance shifted from suppression to accommodation between 1989 and 1991. This shift required a rapprochement between like-minded civilian and military leaders.

Significant changes were taking place in the relationship between the state, the people, and the armed forces. On the one hand, authoritarian patterns were receding and democratic patterns were emerging albeit unevenly. Soldiers and state officials were beginning to learn new ways of behaving towards the media, elected representatives, and the citizenry. On the other hand, the use of violence as a tool in domestic politics was increasing. More precisely, mixed patterns that combined old and new attitudes created confusion, hesitation, and inconsistency in Soviet political life. Responsible officials struggled with very difficult political issues and decisions. Should experienced authorities step down immediately when thousands of protesters demand that they relinquish power to new politicians who lack experience in public administration? Should Union authorities grant independence speedily to any republic where a majority endorses secession in free elections? Should civilian leaders permit the armed forces to question their judgment. Should officers ever disobey orders from commanders?

Tbilisi, Baku, and Vilnius drove a wedge between the Soviet military and Gorbachev and between the military and would-be dictators who intended to use soldiers to preserve the Union. By late summer 1990, military officers were speaking directly to Gorbachev, demanding that he exercise firm leadership, and warning that his personal authority and the Soviet state were at risk. This created the impression that the military was available to be mobilized in support of a suppressive regime; however, matters were more complex. Yeltsin took advantage of Gorbachev's collapsing authority and presented himself as the leader the country needed to restore state viability and to complete the reform program. Eventually, the military moved with Yeltsin but only after having learned from bitter experience that the other alternatives were less acceptable. The military rejected continued drift under Gorbachev and a new dictatorship supported by bayonets. The military supported progressive reform but its conceptual framework and perception of what ailed the country were not the same as the democratic camp's point of view.

The Military and the *Demokraty*

Although the military eventually joined the demokraty to oppose dictatorship, this political cooperation was based upon substantial but far from complete agreement about politics in general. The demokraty focused upon civil liberties and constitutional principles when they criticized the regime's use of military force for domestic political purposes. The demokraty treated the military as part of the guilty state machinery instead of one of the victims. The military complained that civilians were failing to meet their political responsibilities, using the military to bail themselves out, and then turning the military into political scapegoats in order to appease the public. In each case of political violence, the *military* saw its own personnel as the primary victims.

The military became impatient with the demokraty who appeared to believe that citizens in military uniform, especially those with high rank, were the natural allies of would-be dictators. The military wanted effective and unified civilian leadership instead of ineffective and confused governance and it wanted the change from ineffective to effective national leadership to take place without civil war or bloodshed. Both demokraty and military progressives agreed on that much.

Events made the military suspicious of the demokraty and the authoritarians. But when forced to choose between more killing under an authoritarian regime and a chance to have controlled change without bloody repression under a Yeltsin regime, the military moved with Yeltsin. Officers defeated the immediate political threat to their personal dignity and moral consciences by supporting Yeltsin. By August 1991, they knew that the cluster of civilian politicians near Gorbachev had neither the organizational ability nor the political will to impose an authoritarian regime successfully.

The Tbilisi Syndrome

Military officers used the term *Tbilisi syndrome* to express military resentment towards civilian politicians for the way they treated the officers and soldiers who carried out their orders and applied lethal force against civilians. The Tbilisi syndrome has three stages. First, the civilian leaders govern poorly, opposition develops, and things get out of hand. Second, the civilian authorities decide to use coercion and order the armed forces to restore law and order. The military completes the task but not without civilian casualties because the opposition refuses to yield peacefully. Third, democrats and nationalists blame the military for the killings, launch politically manipulated investigations, and castigate individual officers and the "military" as a whole. Meanwhile, the civilian authorities who gave the orders somehow manage to avoid taking responsibility for them

The specific incident that produced the syndrome took place in Tbilisi, the capital of the Georgian republic, in April 1989. Nineteen people, mainly women, were killed in the melee. The victims ranged in age from sixteen to seventy. Civil disobedience that ends in tragedy is not a uniquely Soviet phenomenon. Violent confrontations between civilian dissidents and state authorities take place from time to time even in established democracies. However, the fact that the Tbilisi incident became a major political issue is highly significant. It demonstrates that Soviet society was beginning to wrestle with fundamental questions about the relationship between the citizenry and the state, the armed forces and civilian political leaders, the armed forces and the citizenry, and the Union state and the republics. The fact that a respected senior officer, Col. General Rodionov took personal command of the highly controversial operation instead of putting one of his subordinates on the political firing line is also noteworthy. Although that decision damaged his career in the short run, it raised his prestige among the armed forces and taught him important political lessons which paid off handsomely in the longer run.

The confrontation between anti-Communist nationalists and the old regime in Tbilisi took place shortly after the first Union-wide elections to Gorbachev's first semidemocratic Soviet Congress. The Georgian Communists ran a Soviet-style election in which the candidates had been vetted by the Party machine. The Georgian Communists reported that 97 percent of the people had voted.[1] Ironically, one of the people elected to represent Georgia at the Union Congress was Col. General Igor Rodionov, the commander of the Caucasian Military District, and a resident of Tbilisi. In keeping with Soviet practice, Rodionov was simultaneously a leading military officer, a member of the Communist Party, and an elected representative of the people. He was part of the national and regional political establishment and an ideal citizen and military professional in the Soviet sense of the terms. Prior to taking command of the Caucasian military district, Rodionov served as overall commander of the Soviet forces in Afghanistan, the Fortieth Army. Rodionov did not need to place his professional and personal reputation on the line in Tbilisi but he decided to do so.

Military Participation in Decision Making: Old Rules

The Communist elite was frightened by the rising tide of anti-Communist nationalism. On 4 April 1989, Georgian nationalists launched a political sit-in at the government center in Tbilisi. Rodionov participated in the debates as part of the political elite that made the key decisions at closed door gatherings. Instead of deadly formal and stiff affairs, these had become quite lively as a result of Gorbachev's reforms. After several days of hectic but unproductive discussion, the Party elite decided that it would be driven from power unless it demonstrated the will and ability to defend its authority. During the decision-making process the comrades in Tbilisi telephoned various military and political leaders in Moscow for advice and approval. The comrades in Moscow—key civilian, military, and KGB leaders agreed and supported a firm show of force. The plan was to use mixed armed forces—a combination of military, police, and security professionals to break the peaceful siege. No firearms were to be issued although the troops had clubs, shields, and shovels.

Who were the comrades who made the decisions? They were Communist Party secretaries and top military and security leaders who had never stood for democratic election and who were used to making decisions according to Communist Party rather than Soviet constitutional procedures. The list included people at the all-Union or Moscow and the republic or Georgian levels of power. Soviet Minister of Defense Dmitry Yazov, his Chief of Staff, Mikhail Moiseyev, Gorbachev's chief administrator for Communist Party

Central Committee operations, Yegor Ligachev, KGB Chairman Viktor Chebrikov, and Georgian Party boss Dzhumber Patiashvili, and other Georgian Party officials. Rodionov was against using military troops but the leadership reached a different consensus and he went along with it. The authorities decided to use armed forces to lift the siege and Yazov formally ordered Rodionov to place all key governmental facilities in Tbilisi under his protection and thereby prevent the anti-Communist nationalists from executing a peaceful political revolution against the Soviet authorities.

Yazov issued the orders on 7 April 1989. When that decision was made, President Mikhail Gorbachev and Foreign Minister Eduard Shevardnadze were abroad and were not directly involved in the debate or the decision making. However, they returned to Moscow on 8 April 1989 and had more than enough time to investigate the situation and to reach their own conclusions had they really tried to do so. As soon as their plane landed in Moscow, they asked about the situation and were told that it was being brought under control. Both later claimed that the first they learned that lethal force had been used was the next morning after the tragic events had taken place. When the news broke, they expressed concern and anger and did not rally behind the local Communists or the armed forces.[2]

On the night of 8–9 April 1989, mixed forces consisting of paratroopers who had recently returned from Afghanistan, MVD personnel, and KGB assembled in Tbilisi under Rodionov's command. After some initial confusion, the public announcements were made and the demonstrators were ordered to disperse peacefully; and, when they did not, the armed forces surrounded them and moved in.[3] The confrontation turned brutal. Civilians were beaten, and trampled. Although the number of deaths was relatively small—nineteen victims, the Soviet public was deeply disturbed to learn that the list included women, youngsters, and elderly civilians.

The events strained relations between President Gorbachev, Defense Minister Yazov, and Foreign Minister Shevardnadze. The latter was an ethnic Georgian, the former boss of the Georgian KGB, and the former leader of the republic's Communist Party organization. The very people that Shevardnadze used to lead in Georgia had just mismanaged a major political crisis. He and Gorbachev were infuriated and embarrassed by the killings which pushed the Georgian public into the nationalist, anti-Communist, secessionist camp. (A year later, in September 1990, the nationalists won control over Georgian parliament in the Georgia's first competitive elections, an event which undermined Shevardnadze's political credibility in Moscow.)

The right to gather, to petition, and to demonstrate—these new civil rights came from Gorbachev and Shevardnadze. They were central to perestroika's political reforms and were supposed to renew the Communist Party not destroy it. The fact that Georgian nationalists began using such rights to demand national independence troubled the reformers. The ruling Communist elite tried to decelerate the rate of change and postponed democratic elections in Georgia. At the time of the Tbilisi incident, the Georgian parliament was firmly under Communist control. Therefore, the democratic movement and the Georgian nationalists took their case to the new Union Congress which assembled in Moscow on 25 May 1989, seven weeks after the killings. They demanded that the new Congress reaffirm civil liberties and take measures to prevent Communist bosses from using the Soviet armed forces against Soviet citizens without strictly observing the legal requirements and constitutional processes.

President Gorbachev and General Rodionov

Gorbachev had other priorities at the first Congress. The Soviet Constitution gave the new Union Congress the power to pick the next President of the Soviet Union and Gorbachev intended to have that job. The Congress also had the power to conduct investigations. Gorbachev was anxious to avoid any damaging association with the killings in Tbilisi. Therefore, in April and May 1989 he somehow avoided explaining how and why he failed to take immediate control of events as soon as he landed in Moscow on 8 April 1989. To this day, neither he nor Shevardnadze has really explained what happened.[4] If they truly neglected to check into the details after arriving in Moscow, they were negligent. If they actually knew that the Party and the armed forces were preparing to break up the demonstration and had given either formal or informal approval, they were to some extent responsible for the outcome. If they had been deceived by the military, they failed to exercise proper control over the armed forces and were open to severe criticism. Gorbachev was in a lose/lose situation unless someone else took the fall. General Rodionov made himself a natural candidate for that role.

General Rodionov took a principled stand and defended his actions and the armed forces. He argued that he never intended to use lethal force and accused the demonstrators of deliberately provoking conflict for cynical political reasons. The demokraty accused Rodionov's troops of excessive and wanton violence. Rodionov lost control of the agenda. By making the classical case for authority when confronted by recalcitrant civil disobedience, he appeared stiff and insensitive to the deaths. He insisted that the armed forces had acted under orders and within the standard rules of engagement. He said that civilian authorities and civilian opposition politicians caused the crisis not the military. He claimed that the nationalists deliberately prevented the women from leaving the demonstration area before the confrontation. Defense Minister Yazov and the military supported him but President Gorbachev did not. Gorbachev relieved him of his command. Nevertheless, at the end of the year Gorbachev quietly appointed Rodionov to serve as commandant of the prestigious Academy of the General Staff in Moscow. The military procurator's official investigation cleared Rodionov of all charges.[5] Seven years later, in July 1996 Boris Yeltsin made Rodionov Russia's minister of defense.

New Standards for Constitutional Control

Constitutional control not civilian control was the issue. Rule of law and due process had to replace Party dictatorship. Civilians had controlled the military, the wrong civilians and in the wrong manner. Democratic reformers wanted to emphasize those points. Congress created its own Tbilisi commission and placed a democratic lawyer, Anatoly Sobchak, the mayor of St. Petersburg, at its head. The Sobchak commission's report included a variety of views but on the whole, it tried to be constructive.[6] Sobchak conducted hearings, interviewed participants, and obtained and evaluated the official records from various military and civilian institutions. In addition to establishing a fair record of what happened in Tbilisi, Sobchak was determined to expose problems and to propose solutions aimed at strengthening democratic political practices. His commission tried to improve the constitutional process.[7]

First, the commission's investigation exposed the fact that Gorbachev had difficulty controlling hardliners within the Kremlin elite at the Central Committee and the Ministry of Defense. The fact that like-thinking military and civilian politicians made decisions to use force while Gorbachev and Shevardnadze were out of the country was a very serious affair, a mini-putsch in its own right. Further, their actions demonstrated that some political leaders in Gorbachev's administration had not really accepted the transfer of political power from the Communist Party elite to the elected representatives of the people.

Second, Sobchak and the demokraty targeted problems in military political values and standards of conduct. They wanted to impress upon the officer corps the idea that they could be held accountable for the manner in which they executed their orders. Progressives saw Rodionov as a classical Soviet military professional who was used to taking orders from Communist Party authorities and who did not seem to understand that the military shared responsibility for protecting the civil rights of the country's citizens, including the right to protest peacefully and the right to life. Political liberals wanted the military to learn that it was correct and appropriate to defend the right of the political opposition to protest peacefully. Soldiers had to obey orders but their commanders were supposed to make certain that the orders had come from legitimate authorities according to the new standards of legitimacy. Further, when implementing orders, officers had to understand that they did not have carte blanche to use force and had to anticipate being held accountable for excessive use of force.[8] Two years later, during the August 1991 coup, Yeltsin, Sobchak, and the democratic coalition used these arguments to convince the military to refuse to obey the illegal State of Emergency Regime. Sobchak referred specifically to Rodionov's fate when confronting General Samsonov who had been ordered by the SEC to secure St. Petersburg.[9]

Sobchak's parliamentary commission made four constructive recommendations designed to move the Soviet armed forces closer to Western models of civil-military relations. First, the Soviet state should prohibit the use of military personnel for domestic police and gendarme operations. Second, it should raise the professional standards of domestic police forces and teach them to handle civilian crowds in a humane manner that respects their basic civil rights. Third, it must prevent former Communist Party organizations from issuing orders to the military and other armed forces and firmly establish the new constitutional procedures that will become the foundation for a law-governed Soviet state. Finally, it emphasized that the State leaders in Moscow needed to begin respecting the regional and republican authorities and their rights and responsibilities under the respective Union and Republic constitutions. [10] Some commissioners further argued that the republics needed their own national guards and police forces in order to prevent the Union from dictating from them.

The Military and the *Demokraty* on Tbilisi

The military and the demokraty drew different lessons from Tbilisi. The military learned that it had to exercise extreme caution before agreeing to any actions against Soviet civilians because the politicians who were pushing the military into violent confrontations might not be there to protect the military against retribution by society for the results of those actions. This military distrust applied to demokraty and to authoritarians. The demokraty used Tbilisi to score points about the rule of law and due process. They focused on how the decisions had been made and carried out. They insisted that the military only take orders from legitimate state leaders and that they take extreme care in implementing orders that could lead to violent confrontations with civilians.

The fact that Col. General Rodionov had decided to lead what he knew might become a very controversial operation instead of saddling a lower-ranking officer with the assignment made him popular but damaged his ability to monitor events objectively. His political courage earned him high marks with the soldiers and officers although it was an unwise move from a strictly professional point of view since he became deeply involved psychologically and politically in the denouement. The fact that he steadfastly defended his men when the public and the Kremlin civilian top brass were looking for political scapegoats, added to his popularity among officers.

One of his admirers was Aleksandr Lebed, a colonel in the elite paratroopers whose unit had been flown to Tbilisi to assist with post-crisis stabilization. Lebed followed the affair closely and described it in his own political autobiography.[11] Seven years later in 1996, when Lebed emerged as Yeltsin's top national security adviser, he supported the successful drive to name Col. General Igor Rodionov to serve as Russia's second minister of defense. To officers such as Lebed, Rodionov epitomized military professionalism and patriotism. Demokraty suspected such military officers of giving higher priority to order than to due process and civil rights. Indeed, the military wanted order and to serve a well-ordered state rather than one where established civilian authorities were confused and unable to provide effective leadership. The military criticism applied to Communists and non-Communists alike.

As 1989 progressed, the Soviet military watched as the Communist regimes of Eastern Europe were driven from power by successive peaceful revolutions which often began with civilian demonstrations similar to those that had taken place in Tbilisi. Neither Soviet troops in Eastern Europe nor the armed forces of the Warsaw Pact took action to prevent those revolutions. In the single case where the dictatorship tried to defend itself, Romania, the military overthrew it. The Eastern European example suggested that the military could not be counted upon to save the old guard's power in the Soviet Union either. Although Gorbachev and Shevardnadze abandoned the traditional Communist institutions of Eastern Europe—the dictatorships that made those countries semi-colonies of the Soviet Union, they were more cautious within the Soviet Union.

In May and June when Rodionov defended military action against the Georgian nationalists, he explained the link between rising nationalism in the republics and the potential collapse of the Soviet state. The Union was threatened by democratization which permitted anti-Union forces to organize politically and militarily. By December 1989, the threat had increased and the Soviet Congress which was over 70 percent Communist in terms of party membership was nervous about its future power and the Soviet state's viability. On 24 December 1989, the military procurator came to Congress and presented his analysis and evaluation of the Tbilisi events. He exonerated the military and held the nationalists primarily responsible for the tragedy. Demokraty and congressmen from the nationalist movements protested that the report lacked balance and could legitimize the use of violence against citizens. But, the conservatives and Unionists shouted them down. At this point, Gorbachev counseled Shevardnadze against speaking out. Shevardnadze took his advice but later regretted it.[12]

Baku: January 1990—Saving the Union and Perestroika?

The second armed confrontation between the Soviet state and civilians came in January 1990 in Baku, the capital of the Soviet republic of Azerbaijan. This time Gorbachev took responsibility and observed the required constitutional procedures at the Union level. Although he and his staff worked hard to avoid a final confrontation, in the end they decided to occupy Azerbaijan militarily and to effect a corrective political coup designed to preserve a pro-Union regime. The Union state intervened militarily and politically in Azerbaijan's domestic affairs.

The Union state's problems in Azerbaijan developed as the unanticipated consequences of Gorbachev's political reforms. By ordering local Communist bosses to permit some grass roots political opposition in their republics, Gorbachev created conditions favorable to the revival of ethno-communal feuding and national independence movements that Soviet dictatorship had suppressed but had not resolved. Armenians and Azeris had complex border problems and a deep legacy of distrust.

Armenian nationalists seized the initiative and began to agitate for Armenian political control over an ethnic-Armenian enclave within Azerbaijan, Nagorno-Karabakh. Although only about 120,000 Armenians lived in rural Nagorno-Karabakh—fewer than the number of Armenians living and working in Azerbaijan's main urban centers, nationalists fanned secessionist flames. Further, in Armenia itself, the Armenian national movement began building irregular armed forces. Initially Gorbachev underestimated the depth of feeling involved in these disputes and their ability to destabilize the greater Caucasus. He lost patience with Armenian and Azeri Communist leaders because neither seemed capable of finding ways to reverse the trend. He instructed both sets of leaders about the Soviet commitment to interethnic concord and the need to win popular support by improving the quality of government; he warned them that he would remove them if they failed to keep control but refused to authorize them to suppress their respective nationalists effectively. The policy failed.

By summer 1988, the Armenian nationalists had rudimentary armed forces. These developed into a direct threat to the Soviet state's political integrity. Moscow lost the ability to enforce its policies in some parts of Armenia and Azerbaijan. However, Gorbachev refused to launch a full scale drive to disarm the Armenian nationalists and to arrest their leaders. After several armed confrontations between Armenian nationalists and Soviet military units in 1988 and 1989, the nationalists reached an uneasy truce with Soviet authorities. However, the nationalists kept building their military capability. Further, by late 1989, the tit-for-tat ethnic struggle had created hundreds of thousands of refugees. Gorbachev could not win support in Azerbaijan without alienating Armenia and vice versa. Further, the Armenian cause had broader support in Gorbachev's entourage and among the democratic intelligentsia who had started to associate nationalism in the republics of Islamic heritage with political extremism and brutal killings. But progressives in those republics were convinced that cynical political bosses—so-called "enemies of perestroika," were deliberately provoking ethnic pogroms to foster an anarchic environment favorable to dictatorship since they needed dictatorship to preserve their own power and privileges.

By December 1989, Azerbaijan's Communist government was about to collapse and to surrender to the Popular Front of Azerbaijan, a loose coalition of political groups opposed to Communist dictatorship and Muscovite control over their republic's affairs. The Popular Front had learned to use massive public demonstrations effectively. It also had armed units. The Popular Front subjected the capital city, Baku, to repeated political sieges. During this process, nationalists and Communists began to search for ways to cooperate. Gorbachev was in danger of losing control. In order to keep loyalists in power, Moscow needed either a deal with the Popular Front, Soviet intervention, or some combination of the two. Gorbachev did not trust the Popular Front because it advocated independence for Azerbaijan within a new international balance of power. Gorbachev was particularly disturbed by incidents along the Soviet border with Iran, where Soviet Azeris had torn down fences and demanded the right to commune with Iranian Azeris. Further any major conflict between Armenia and Azerbaijan had the potential to spark a larger regional conflict involving the Soviet Union, Turkey, and Iran.[13]

Gorbachev launched intensive negotiations and tried to demonstrate that he had the "stuff" required to preserve the Union without abandoning reform. But instead of flying to Baku personally, Gorbachev worked through others. Although he had traveled the world since becoming general secretary, Gorbachev had not bothered to visit Azerbaijan. He spent five years manipulating Azeri politics from his Kremlin office. The net result was extremely negative for the Communist Party of Azerbaijan which lost its internal cohesion and ability to govern effectively. Gorbachev sent Yevgeny Primakov to Baku to face the crisis. Having grown up in Tbilisi, studied and served in the greater Middle East, and done high-level intelligence work, Primakov knew the Caucasus well. He tried to salvage the Communist regime and Azerbaijan's allegiance to the Soviet Union. (After the Soviet Union's collapse, Primakov oversaw Russia's Foreign Intelligence Service and in early 1996, he replaced Andrei Kozyrev and became foreign minister of Russia.)

Primakov conducted his negotiations in public and in private. Primakov braved the huge crowds and tried to talk common sense about the Union, the need for peace, and the prospects for reform. He met with all manner of political leaders in order to hammer out a deal that could save the Union, restore the Communist Party's ability to govern effectively, and give Azeri nationalism a positive role in politics. In the end, Union leaders, republican leaders, and military and security officers decided upon a compromise plan that would give Azerbaijan a new government that would remain loyal to the Union but which would coopt much of the Popular Front's Azeri-heritage agenda. Further, in order to satisfy the demands that Azeri refugees from Armenian-held territory were making for housing and to demonstrate "balance" in the ethnic dispute, Gorbachev decided to impose stronger control on Nagorno-Karabakh and to support the civilized deportation/evacuation of tens of thousands of

Armenians from Azerbaijan's urban centers. He also pledged more money from the Union budget for both republics.

Military and Political Intervention: A Constitutional Act?

But Moscow was not confident that it could retain its hold on Azerbaijan without a show of force and a period of emergency rule. The Ministry of Defense, MVD, and KGB prepared plans to increase their presence in Azerbaijan and to put more Soviet armed forces into key urban centers. On 11–12 January 1990, there was an outbreak of killing, looting, and general violence against Armenians in Baku—events which Popular Front progressives insist were inspired by Moscow, the local Communist hardliners and their semicriminal political machines, or some combination of all three. Gorbachev immediately cited such violence against innocent civilians as the primary reason why he had to impose a special state of emergency in Azerbaijan and to use Soviet troops.

Within the Soviet armed forces, political officers quickly organized materials designed to convince military, police, and security forces that they were going to Azerbaijan because Soviet citizens, innocent civilians were being raped and killed. Therefore, the armed forces expected to be welcomed by their fellow citizens in Baku. They were psychologically prepared to maintain order and to assist with evacuations but they were not prepared to face angry crowds and irregular armed forces who decided to stand and fight rather than permit Gorbachev to overthrow their popular rebellion.[14]

In Moscow Gorbachev took the proper formal steps and imposed a temporary emergency regime in keeping with the Soviet Constitution. He also took many of the right informal steps such as consultations, sometimes very frank and strained, with the key Communist leaders of Azerbaijan and Armenia. (He even informed U.S. President George Bush who had just launched an American military political intervention in Panama to overthrow the Noriega dictatorship.) Azeri nationalists claimed that Gorbachev violated the republic's sovereignty by making decisions at the Union level without consulting with the republic's parliament. He brushed aside such criticisms arguing that law and order had already broken down in Azerbaijan. Supreme Commander Gorbachev ordered Soviet military, MVD, and KGB reinforcements into Azerbaijan and prepared to take control of Baku by air, land, and sea. This show of force convinced most Popular Front activists to accept a negotiated settlement, a partial victory. The alternative was civil war and the destruction of Azerbaijan's key cities, oil fields, petrochemical industry, and ecology.

On the night of 19–20 January 1990, Soviet armed forces were ordered to move into Baku and to occupy all key facilities: airports, governmental centers, train stations, police compounds, and the seaport terminals. Some units encountered armed resistance. About 200 people were killed and many more wounded. Things would have been much worse had the Popular Front, the Union government, and local Communist leaders not cooperated to reduce violence. Although Soviet power was formally restored, the Popular Front had not been defeated. It retreated and continued to build its political organizations and some paramilitary forces. The Union state and its local allies had restored Soviet power but only temporarily.

The news that some 200 people had been killed overwhelmed the fact that Gorbachev had successfully negotiated a settlement that was sensitive to the Popular Front and the outgoing Communist leadership. Neither group had to face severe penalties or wholesale retribution. Gorbachev preferred such negotiated political soft landings and hoped that they would encourage compromise and cooperation. But the 200 deaths and show of military force destroyed Gorbachev's political legitimacy in Azerbaijan and dramatically increased support for political independence. Azerbaijan's Popular Front declared the people killed by the Union armed forces heroes and martyrs—*shahids*. Approximately 1,000,000 people attended their funeral at which Islamic, Jewish, and Christian clergy officiated, an event that transformed the hillside park above Baku into a sacred place for Azeri nationalists. Most victims were of Azeri Turkic ethnic extraction and Islamic religious heritage but several Slavs and Jews were also killed in the clashes with Soviet troops. It was a cathartic experience for Azerbaijan. It damaged interethnic relations between the ethnic Russian community in Azerbaijan and the Azeri Turkic majority. The former started leaving the republic as opportunities became available. It destroyed all chances for Armenians in Azerbaijan to live a normal life.

Aleksandr Lebed in Baku

Baku taught Soviet officers and soldiers to be skeptical of civilian explanations of events. Things turned out to be far more complex than the simplistic explanations the political officers had given the troops. Colonel Aleksandr Lebed's experience illustrates the point. Lebed was in charge of three regiments of elite paratroopers from the Kostroma, Ryazan, and Tula divisions. The regiment from Ryazan had to push its way through thirty kilometers of suburban and urban streets from the Baku airport to the city center. Since Baku was a sprawling city of some 1,700,000 this was potentially a very dangerous and destructive operation. The first barricade they encountered consisted of about 100 people; they moved them aside without injury or shooting. But the next twelve barricades offered some armed resistance. Soldiers were upset to be facing their fellow Soviet citizens in the heart of a major Soviet city. They hesitated and asked for advice. Lebed's commander, Col. General Vladislav Achalov first agreed that they should halt but later insisted that they keep moving. Military personnel were not used to such events and found it difficult to use armed force against fellow Soviet citizens.

Another of Lebed's units, soldiers from the Kostroma regiment, were ordered to take the sea port's main terminal on the Caspian shore. The terminal was allegedly serving as an operational center for Popular Front paramilitary groups in Baku. By the time Lebed's troops had reached the terminal, the 150–200 fighters that were supposed to be there were nowhere to be found. Lebed admits that his troops took a few kegs of beer from restaurant stores and relaxed a bit but insists that the officers, soldiers, and restaurant administrators cooperated and there was no major damage to the facility. Nevertheless, immediately after the events, Moscow sent a special investigatory commission of some twenty-nine people to Baku and began pressing for information about the military's conduct, including the restaurant incident. Lebed was infuriated that civilian politicians would harass soldiers over such minor affairs when they had just risked their lives to restore the very order that the politicians had failed to maintain.

Lebed's troops also completed military-political missions outside Baku. Soviet authorities sent them to other Azeri towns and cities where the Popular Front had driven local Communists from power and had refused to retreat. Thus, for example, on 25 January 1990, Col. General Achalov called Lebed and ordered him to fly to Dzhalilabad "where Soviet power had been overthrown" and to restore it. Lebed's paratroopers flew there and were joined by other Soviet armed forces. The Popular Front quickly abandoned its positions and the old Communist administration, "Soviet power," was back in place.[15] That was the typical pattern. The Popular Front did not confront the Soviet military and the two sides quickly learned to coexist. As time went on the Popular Front was primarily interested in obtaining arms and attracting Soviet military personnel to help it to wage war against the Armenians who were tempting and harassing the Soviet military in a similar manner.[16]

The Tbilisi Syndrome and Baku

President Gorbachev's political reaction to the events in Azerbaijan was predictable. As the Soviet Union's leader, he had to express deep regret over the civilian deaths in Baku and to call for a thorough investigation. But this neither satisfied the Azeris nor the Soviet military. Lebed and his fellow officers became angry. Gorbachev and the civilians seemed to be preparing for a repetition of the Tbilisi syndrome and planning to hold the military accountable in the court of public opinion for the loss of life and property damage. Instead of placing failed civilian Communist leaders on trial, the military was being criticized. As a result, Lebed reports that officers all shared the same sentiment, "The devil take all party and state leaders."[17] Lebed and fellow officers remembered and discussed what had happened to Col. General Igor Rodionov after the killings in Tbilisi and were determined to prevent the military from becoming political scapegoats once again.[18] Later, when investigators confronted the Kostroma regiment back at its home base, they received an extremely cold reception and backed off.[19] Instead of charging the military with excessive use of force and marauding in Baku, the Defense Ministry rewarded them. On 17 February 1990, Lebed was promoted to the rank of major general.

Without military, police, and security support from Moscow, the Communist Party regime would have been overthrown and the Popular Front would have taken power in January 1990. Gorbachev's military intervention helped extend the life of the dictatorship which Moscow regarded as a stabilizing force in the frontier region with Turkey and Iran. It settled no major disputes but it prevented them from running out of control. In neighboring Armenia, the Communists lost ground steadily to nationalist politicians and Armenians continued to build their national armed forces in defiance of Moscow. Levon Ter-Petrosian's nationalists took power in fall 1990 and obtained Gorbachev's approval to convert the nationalist irregulars into Armenia's national guard. Thus, Armenia became the first Soviet republic to rid itself of its Communist regime and to arm itself with its own nationalist military. In neighboring Azerbaijan, the reform Communist government led by Ayaz Mutalibov lagged behind Armenia in military development. It lasted until May 1992 when the Popular Front drove it from office for having lost its spring offensive against the Armenians. Thereafter relations with Moscow deteriorated and the Popular Front government demanded that Russian military forces withdraw from Azerbaijan. Armenia played its diplomatic cards quite differently and signed military cooperation and basing agreements with Russia. The Armenian example had positive and negative implications for Moscow. On the one hand, Armenia wanted a firm security relationship with the Soviet state. On the other hand, the Armenians rejected Communist rule, formed their own armed forces, and were using military force to support their nationalist program towards neighboring Azerbaijan. If other republics followed Armenia's example, the Soviet state would spawn fifteen or more national armed forces and a number of regional wars over borders and minority demands for political autonomy.

Azeri nationalists argue that there is a Baku syndrome in which peoples of Islamic heritage get less sympathetic treatment than peoples of Christian heritage from the democratic public and from the Soviet state and its primary successor, the Russian Federation. The Soviet state's military intervention in Baku was far greater than either its intervention in Tbilisi or its confrontation with secessionists in Vilnius. Ten times more people were killed in Islamic-heritage Baku than in Christian-heritage Tbilisi. In the immediate post-Soviet period, the major military conflicts were in Islamic-heritage areas: Abkhazia, Tajikistan, and Chechnya. There are religious-civilizational heritage issues in military affairs and the use of force. The intervention in Baku and the Nagorno-Karabakh problem put them on the military-political agenda.

Generals Lebed and Achalov in Politics

While Col. General Achalov was managing the use of paratroopers in Azerbaijan, he was also thinking about his personal, explicit political activities in two political institutions, the Communist Party and the new Russian parliament. In the Soviet political system Achalov was expected to be in formal political life and he seems to have been attracted to it. Soviet officers had to learn political skills in order to be successful as they rose to higher ranks and Achalov was doing that. Senior military leaders expected the officers just below them to understand and to respond to their political needs with little prodding and Achalov was no exception to the rule. Lebed was also interested in politics but he took on the role of the political maverick within the system.

Col. General Achalov decided that he should be elected to the Russian Federation's parliament and *mentioned* that interest to Lebed while the latter was still completing his mission in Azerbaijan. This turned into an informal assignment for Lebed as Achalov's campaign manager. This was neither unusual nor unexpected. A Soviet officer had to learn to work with civilian leaders in political institutions at all levels. In the past the officers met with civilian politicians, drew up the lists of vetted Communist Party candidates for Soviet-style elections, and got them on the regular civilian ballot. Now they were meeting for post-Soviet candidate selection in a very similar manner. Lebed and civilian political leaders picked a relatively safe race for Achalov, a Tula region district with a block of military voters. They arranged to get civilian and military funding lined up for some public works projects—campaign pledges. They toured the area with Achalov and met the right people; and on election day, 4 March 1990, Col. General Vladislav Achalov was elected to Russia's Congress.[20] A year earlier they had organized a successful campaign for Chief of General Staff Mikhail Moiseyev, who was elected from another Tula district to represent the citizens in the Union Congress.

There had also been politicking to select the delegates to the 28th Congress of the Communist Party of the Soviet Union, an event that Gorbachev had hoped to use to make democratic socialism the official Party ideology. The military Communists of the Tula division had the right to elect two delegates. The "word" from above was that one of the delegates had to be their commander, Achalov. Lebed decided to compete for the second position and he defeated the favored insider, Lt. General Polevik. This put Lebed in position to face Gorbachev and other civilian Party leaders at the forthcoming July 1990 meeting.[21]

Soldiers could be in the field with their officers on a Wednesday, in Moscow for a formal political meeting on a weekend, and back at war immediately thereafter. Col. General Rodionov had done precisely that during the period when he was general commander over Soviet forces in Afghanistan.[22] Formal participation in primarily civilian political institutions was not new but the right to speak out and the willingness to exercise that right even at risk to one's career was new. Thus, during the Afghanistan war, General Rodionov did not publicly criticize the war policy or the civilian leadership that caused it because such conduct was prohibited by powerful informal rules. But in 1989 and 1990 he did criticize policy and the policymaking process in public and with the protection afforded elected deputies. Most senior generals did not dare to be so candid and bold. They were more inclined to speak when their minister of defense and several senior officers in his entourage had signaled that some military political pressure on the president would be appropriate.

Defense Minister Yazov and Col. General Achalov lobbied for a hard line towards all secessionists and irregular armed forces during all of 1990. Lebed seems to have supported that line as well. This military pressure led to the political-military action against the Baltic republics—the Vilnius incident in January and the August coup of 1991. The first two incidents—Tbilisi and Baku, angered the military but did not end support for hard ball politics. The military wanted solid teamwork between determined civilian and military authorities. They also wanted greater authority in defense policy decision making.

Two political trends were developing simultaneously. First, the military and the KGB were pushing Gorbachev towards a semi-authoritarian regime, tighter national political discipline, and a show of force against the secessionists. Second, Yeltsin was emerging as the champion of a softer line, an alternative to military conflict at home, and a potential successor to Gorbachev. After the hardline failed, relationships between Yeltsin and some military leaders began to improve.

The New Military Opposition: Rational Authoritarianism

Military professionals complained that Gorbachev had neglected their interests and professional advice and that he had been more capricious and disruptive to Soviet defense than Soviet dictator Nikita Khrushchev.[23] The Ministry of Defense supported military reform and military professionalization and held up Western models as examples of responsible, steady reform programs.[24] The military was searching for competent, firm, civilian leadership not a return to capricious dictatorship. Even MPA chief Shlyaga praised U.S. military reforms made over a ten-year period after the Vietnam war as an example of responsible management of national military affairs. He complained that it was unreasonable for Gorbachev to expect the Soviet military to do what the U.S. had taken more than ten years to accomplish and with far better financial support at that![25]

Col. General Achalov made the classic case for military professional control over defense policy. He resented "irresponsible" and "incompetent" meddling in military affairs by Russian congressmen, specifically Colonel Vladimir Lopatin and Colonel Aleksandr Tsalko. General Achalov compared them to

Stalin who repeatedly disregarded advice from military professionals. In Congress, Achalov, Lopatin, and Tsalko were all equal, elected congressmen. In the Armed Forces, he was their superior, the second or third most powerful figure in the Ministry of Defense. But they challenged him in Congress and demanded deeper cuts in the armed forces, more rights for military personnel, contract service instead of the military draft, and faster changes than the Ministry of Defense deemed prudent. Achalov insisted that military professionals not such demokraty should set policy: "The history of our country and other states shows that violating that principle leads to dire consequences. We have had examples when composers were told how to write music, writers and poets how to write novels and poetry, and peasants how and when to sow.... To improve our national defense any competent idea should be valued. But this area is primarily a matter for military professionals. The defense of the Fatherland is their direct responsibility."[26]

Achalov resented incompetent interference by politicians but he wasn't an anti-Communist. He vowed to save the Communist Party's organizations in the elite paratrooper forces: "To all Communists of the country and of Russia, I say the Party organizations of the paratrooper forces are strong. We are not preparing to change the Party standard and we will not [applause]." He saw no contradiction between preserving the one-party system and ending capricious interference. He imagined an ideal situation in which the best professionals were Communists who solved the country's problems without *politics*. Achalov further argued that the Soviet Union needed a cohesive military to guarantee society's stability and the country's security during the transitional period from the old to the new domestic and international order. [27]

Dress Rehearsal for a Coup?

Two days after the Defense Ministry published Achalov's statements, the Soviet military flexed its muscles and provoked two months of media debate about its intentions. The elite paratroopers which Achalov commanded conducted battle-gear exercises and deployments that tested their ability to occupy Moscow rapidly. Yazov launched the exercises just as President Gorbachev was preparing for a special summit meeting with President Bush in Helsinki. The summit's main topic was the Persian Gulf crisis, Iraq's invasion of Kuwait, and Soviet military relations with Saddam Hussein.

The demokraty sounded the political alarms and warned that a coup attempt or a rehearsal for one was underway. The free press, led by *Komsomolskaya pravda*, demanded to know what was happening. Yazov disingenuously described the troop movements as nothing other than preparation for the annual military parades in honor of the anniversary of the Bolshevik revolution. The commander of the Moscow Military District, Col. General Kalinin assembled officers and ordered them to answer all inquiries from reporters with the same explanation. He addressed each officer individually and made him give his pledge. Therefore, the military maintained a united front and supported the Defense Minister's line. [28]

According to Aleksander Lebed's account, the military was indeed preparing for action. His Tula paratrooper division was ordered into full combat readiness on 8 September 1990. Troops remained on full combat alert for two days. Lebed had special orders to move equipment and supplies into Moscow itself and he took two regiments into Moscow on the night of 9–10 September 1990 and accomplished that mission.[29] But Lebed claimed that neither he nor his immediate colleagues ever learned precisely what had caused the September alert. Yazov reassured the press that the Soviet military would not take action against the Soviet people and repeated the familiar slogan, *The Army and the people are one!* There were more coup rumors in October, especially when Gorbachev ruled that traditional military parades would indeed be held in the Soviet republics on 7 November. But, Yazov again proclaimed, "The Soviet Armed Forces are part of the Soviet people and they will never take action against it or against its will."[30]

Since the Tula division and other elite mobile forces were supposed to be prepared to secure Moscow on short notice, it was appropriate for them to train for such assignments and they did. Officers were aware of what had happened in China a year earlier. Tank units were familiar with the incident in which one Chinese protester stood in front of a Peoples Liberation Army tank and temporarily blocked an entire military convoy. At one Moscow Military District planning meeting, Lebed asked Commander Kalinin what to do if a Soviet citizen stood in front of a tank. Kalinin told him to shut up and sit down.[31] These were not idle concerns as would be demonstrated in Moscow a year later and in Grozny in 1994.

Yeltsin's Early Approaches to the Military

Yeltsin was elected to Russia's Congress in spring 1990. In May the congress elected him speaker, a position which made him the president of Russia. Thereafter, Yelstin—the president of Russia, competed with Gorbachev—the president of the Soviet Union. At first, the military resented Yeltsin's habit of using every opportunity to undermine Gorbachev's political authority because it damaged Soviet state viability and security and the unitary Soviet military's corporate interests. However, as the months passed, Yeltsin became more successful than Gorbachev at building bridges to the military and cultivating his image as a decisive leader. And, as Gorbachev became less effective, Yeltsin's claim to be the better leader gained credibility. Yeltsin's strategy was transparent. He kept Gorbachev off balance and deprived Gorbachev of the political space needed to form a true centrist political coalition.

For example, in August 1990, Boris Yeltsin announced his intention to place Soviet defense industrial establishments within the Russian Federation under Russian Federation political control, to begin looking into the possibility of building Russian Federation armed forces, and to support legislative action to restrict the Union government's ability to use draftees from Russia in the Union hotbeds of ethno-political conflict.[32] Such anti-Union politicking damaged the military's interests. Gorbachev responded by criticizing *those* who deliberately work to damage the Union's integrity and warned all officials of the Union state that his basic domestic and foreign policies had been approved by the Union Supreme Soviet and were the law of the land.[33]

Boris Yeltsin took note of the criticism and adjusted his approach towards the military. By September he had created an office for coordinating defense and security affairs with the respective Union ministries. This gave him a formal excuse to begin building political relationships with the senior military and KGB personnel. They could turn to Yeltsin if Gorbachev was ignoring their requests since Russia was starting to claim part of the Union defense budget and was willing to find some projects. Instead of threatening the integrity of the Soviet defense system, he presented himself as a politician who really cared about what was happening to the military. Yeltsin knew that military personnel were deeply concerned about their future and felt abandoned by Gorbachev who was sacrificing their careers in order to advance his economic reform agenda. When Gorbachev took office, there were over 4,250,000 authorized positions in the military. In December 1988, he unilaterally announced that he would cut 500,000 positions from the military budget. In fall 1990, Chief of General Staff Moiseyev reported that the Ministry of Defense was planning to reduce military manpower to about 3,000,000 personnel by the year 2000. Further, all Soviet military personnel in Germany, Eastern Europe, and Mongolia—some 750,000 soldiers had to be repatriated.[34] Where would these repatriated officers and their families live? Work? Had they been abandoned by their constitutional supreme commander, Mikhail Gorbachev? Yeltsin reached out to them.

On 2 November 1990, Boris Yeltsin's prime minister, Ivan T. Silayev convened a special session with 570 citizen-soldiers who held elective positions in the Russian Federation to discuss ways the Russian Federation could improve its support to the military. This was an important preemptive political strike by the Yeltsin team against Gorbachev and a pattern that Yeltsin would use again in the future. Yeltsin would either meet with the military or send word that it could count upon his support on the eve of some major political event. During Silayev's meeting with military deputies, some delegates began demanding that Gorbachev also face the military. Some officers demanded to know why the Russian Federation was holding a conference on Union military affairs which heretofore had been primarily the Union's responsibility. Had the republics taken responsibility for the military?[35]

Gorbachev Faces the Citizen Soldiers

Gorbachev agreed to meet with an all-Union assembly of citizen-soldiers. On 12 November 1990 Minister of Defense Yazov assembled 1,100 citizen-soldiers, military officers who had been elected to public office throughout the Soviet Union and held preliminary discussions with them. However, the next day, when Gorbachev faced them, they went on the offensive. The meeting turned into a broad critique of Gorbachev's leadership. The public spectacle of the civilian commander in chief under attack was highly damaging. Gorbachev attempted to make the best of it by holding it up as a demonstration of the new democratic nature of Soviet political life. The meeting was a tactical political mistake but one that could not be avoided after the Russian Federation's conference with its citizen-soldiers. Gorbachev's prestige was damaged as he took one shot of criticism after another. This was a good example of why most democratic political systems prohibit active-duty military officers from holding public office. As elected representatives, the 1,100 military officers had special political rights and responsibilities that do not fit the normal requirements of military discipline and unity of command. Their status as citizen-soldiers gave them the constitutional right to question and criticize their commander in chief. In that arena, he was a public servant and they were the public's representatives.

One of the most telling comments came from V. Ya. Akhalidze, a deputy regimental commander, who said the following:

Mikhail Sergeyevich, I'm one of many people who from 1985–1988 loved you without limit. you were my ideal. Honestly. Everywhere and always ready to become a hero for you. But since 1989, bit by bit, I'm leaving, separating from you. And there are more such people every day. People who were inspired by perestroika are developing an allergy to it.[36]

The speeches from the floor were a torrent of complaints about the breakdown in the Soviet state's authority in the rebellious regions. Instead of hiding them from public view, Defense Minister Yazov had them printed in *Krasnaya zvezda* which could be bought anywhere in the country. Gorbachev was being criticized for failing to take effective action to preserve the political integrity of the Soviet state and for making too many decisions about defense spending cuts and arms agreements too rapidly. Gorbachev made all the right points about perestroika and "new thinking" in foreign policy; he insisted that his broad policy goals were correct but acknowledged that a tactical shift towards more authoritative leadership was now required. But, he did not yield on defense spending. He confirmed that he had decided that defense spending had to be cut and that the Soviet Union could not afford to continue the arms race with the United States. That policy had driven the Soviet state into an "economic dead end." There was no turning back on that policy front. But he pledged to strengthen the state and to take more effective measures to preserve the Union. He concluded: "A government that does not understand the meaning of the Armed Forces and does not demonstrate concern for them does not have the right to exist."[37]

Shortly after Gorbachev's meeting with the 1,100 citizen-soldiers, the Union Congress's standing parliament or Supreme Soviet demanded that he adopt a concrete plan for bringing economic and political reform under control. Col. Viktor Alksnis, one of the three leaders of the Unionist faction, *Soyuz,* bluntly told Gorbachev that his "political credit had run out" and "gave" Gorbachev thirty days to come up with a good emergency plan or Soyuz would introduce motions to impeach him at the full Union Congress in December.[38] Again, the spectacle of a Colonel giving political orders to the commander in chief damaged Gorbachev's political power and the powers of the office of the presidency of the Soviet Union. This overt pressure was combined with private meetings during which Soyuz members convinced Gorbachev to form a new cabinet and to steer a firm course designed to preserve the Union. The Congress gave Gorbachev enhanced executive powers to implement reform. One of the institutional innovations was a new Security Council through which the president was supposed to coordinate foreign and domestic policy. But, instead of gratefully accepting enhanced powers, Gorbachev complained that the Congress had "literally squeezed the proposals out of me."[39] Nevertheless, the Unionists thought they had won a political victory. Col. Alksnis declared that the Union would be preserved and that the armed forces would play a major role in the process."[40] The political shift towards authoritarianism caused Foreign Minister Eduard Shevardnadze to resign and bluntly warn that dictatorship was coming. The Soyuz faction celebrated Shevardnadze's resignation as a victory.

The Soviet press asked Minister of Defense Yazov to express his views on the domestic policy shift. He was characteristically cautious even a bit enigmatic. He repeated his usual statement that the Army cannot be outside of politics because it is an instrument of the state and is "political." He reaffirmed that the army takes its orders from the civilian leadership and would like to keep its involvement in domestic conflict minimal: "The less such tasks are placed on the Army the better." He left the door open to using military forces at home if civilian lives were threatened. Yazov explained, "But if blood were to be shed and the army were to stand aside, then I don't think that would be the best position."[41]

The Military's Rationale for a Show of Force

At the end of December 1990, Yazov was preparing to take action in defense of the Union in general and to intimidate the nationalists in a set of republics. Gorbachev had authorized him to enforce Soviet draft laws and to prevent the formation of nationalist paramilitary organizations. The two phenomena were linked since paramilitary organizations were forming in the same republics and regions that were resisting the draft calls. For example, the fall 1990 military draft compliance rates were as follows for the republics where nationalist resistance to the Soviet state was the strongest: Georgia 10.0 percent, Lithuania 12.5 percent, Estonia 24.5 percent, Latvia 25.3 percent, Armenia 28.1 percent, and Moldova 58.9 percent. These areas plus Western Ukraine were rapidly moving towards the point where only an armed confrontation could restore the Soviet state's authority. Non-Russians were refusing to serve in the Soviet military. The rise of ethnic nationalism was damaging military cohesion and the military's draft program. The Soviet Ministry of Defense reported that the absolute majority of those who reported for military service in those non-Russian republics were ethnic Russians or fluent speakers of Russian.[42]

The Defense Ministry's fundamental analysis was correct. If the nationalists continued to arm and to defy the Soviet military draft, the unitary Soviet state was doomed. However, even the Defense Ministry knew that there was a middle ground between complete national independence and the old unitary Soviet state and it was prepared to make some compromises but not until the Soviet state had demonstrated its political and military muscle.

In anticipation of such measures, Yazov made Col. General Vladislav Achalov his first deputy minister of defense because Achalov was a strong Unionist. Achalov's position as commander of all Soviet paratrooper divisions went to Pavel Grachev. Aleksander Lebed was also promoted and put in charge of all paratrooper training and education.[43] This set up the interpersonal and command relationships that would be so important during the coup attempt of August 1991. The KGB and the Ministry of Defense were working together to preserve the Union and the Ministry of Defense was relying primarily upon the paratroopers for its domestic political actions. If Yeltsin wanted to break that network or to subvert it, he would have to target the paratrooper commanders, particularly Pavel Grachev since Achalov was too close to Yazov. Achalov made public statements to the effect that the military had been authorized to play a more active role in the defense of Soviet state integrity and would soon begin doing so. He said that the Union could be preserved if effective action were taken to implement Gorbachev's decrees beyond the Kremlin's walls. Enforcement was the problem not laws. Achalov predicted, "In 1991, the army's political weight will increase sharply. Now the army is almost the only guarantor the preservation of the integrity of our state. I believe that we must show restraint and patience. Yes, they are hitting us, sometimes hitting us hard. But all will change soon. Right now we have to save the army from splitting. And if we save the army, we'll save the state."[44]

The KGB and the Ministry of Defense were developing plans to put soldiers on the streets of every major city where Soviet political authority was threatened. Gorbachev apparently approved the plans for joint patrols in December 1990 when he authorized KGB Chairman Vladimir Kryuchkov and Defense Minister Dmitry Yazov to make separate television addresses announcing that measures would be taken to preserve law and order in the country. However, it is odd that the formal action, joint order No. 493/513 was issued by Kryuchkov and Yazov on 29 December 1990 rather than by Gorbachev himself. Instead of placing his authority and prestige directly behind the action, Gorbachev decided to put them directly in the line of fire. [45]

Vilnius: A Failed Attempt to Restore State Military Integrity

The KGB and the Army cooperated and took the public lead in demanding strict enforcement of Union laws throughout the country. The KGB organized Unionist political movements in the Baltic republics and these began demanding that Moscow take action to enforce the Union Constitution and Union laws. Military, militia, and KGB officers and veterans took part in the formation of such "Committees of National Salvation." They demanded that Gorbachev fulfill his obligations to defend the Soviet Constitution and impose emergency presidential rule; but Gorbachev hesitated and waited to see how things would develop.

The "spontaneous" citizens actions were timed to coincide with the deployment of special units of Soviet paratroopers which Deputy Minister of Defense Vladislav Achalov personally led. The demonstration of military-political power was supposed to intimidate the Baltic nationalists into cooperating with Soviet draft laws instead of encouraging youth to bear arms in new, independent Baltic home defense forces. But the problem was bigger than the Baltic republics. There were more problem regions and the Ministry of Defense hoped to frighten them all into abandoning their efforts to build independent republican national guards. The Ministry of Defense simultaneously ordered Soviet military commanders in Armenia, Georgia, Moldova, and Western Ukraine to take immediate steps to enforce military conscription.[46] Achalov said that he was willing to negotiate compromises with the nationalists but he made little headway.

In Lithuania, national independence militias took up positions around parliament and the national television and radio center in the capital, Vilnius. The Union forces attacked them with seven tanks, fourteen armored cars, and 190 men and officers. They killed thirteen people and wounded forty-eight according to Soviet Procurator General Nikolai. Trubin's official account.[47] Achalov's paratroopers were not involved but their presence in Lithuania fueled the crisis and gave the impression that larger confrontations could follow.

Where was Commander Gorbachev during these events? Instead of leading, he stayed out of the public eye. Gorbachev made no immediate major addresses to the nation about the crisis. He claimed to have learned of it only the morning after. Later he gave a rather incoherent explanation that blamed Lithuania's pro-independence president, Vitautas Landsbergis, for refusing to engage in a political dialogue and attributed the overall tensions to protests against high prices.[48] It was a terrible political performance which severely damaged Gorbachev's legitimacy all across the Soviet political spectrum. In fact, it was Gorbachev who refused to accept telephone calls from Landsbergis before the killings. Had the two spoken, the crisis might have been diffused. While Gorbachev behaved in an ineffective and confused manner, Yazov came to the political defense of his soldiers. He argued that they had to take action to stop nationalist broadcasts that were calling Lithuanians to war against Soviet authorities.[49] The KGB, MVD, and the military did not have an effective civilian commander in chief. Gorbachev had not stood up for them. Gorbachev's personal collapse left a major political vacuum.

Yeltsin's Drive for Power: Military Aspects

Boris Yeltsin jumped into the leadership vacuum. He flew to nearby Estonia for emergency consultations on the Baltic crisis. Yeltsin condemned the violence and Gorbachev's clumsy handling of the Baltic problem. Yelstin signed several agreements between the Russian Federation and the Baltic republics which he held up as examples of how the Union could be rebuilt, a progressive response to the general crisis. He announced that it was against the law for military service personnel who were citizens of the Russian Federation to be used for political-military interventions outside the Russian Federation. The Russian Federation and most other key republics had passed such resolutions in response to public pressure after the Union State began using Soviet military units in domestic political conflicts. Yeltsin even suggested that the Russian Federation might need its own armed forces to defend itself against illegal actions by the Union. This brought a storm of protest. Yeltsin had made a mistake but he was clearly engaged in a dialogue with the military and that was to his advantage. The protests confirmed that the military saw him as a major leader and wanted him to behave responsibly.

Four marshals of the Soviet Union, one admiral, and ten generals published an open letter that condemned Yeltsin on two counts. First, he seemed to be advocating the fragmentation of the unitary Soviet armed forces. His biggest mistake was to suggest that Russia might create its own military. Second, he had damaged the military's most important operating principle, *the unity of command.* Yeltsin had inserted himself between Commander in Chief Gorbachev and the troops. The letter warned against destroying the army from within and using the armed forces in political games.[50] Another letter signed by some 800 members of the Baltic Fleet accused Yeltsin of exploiting a difficult situation for personal political gain at the expense of Soviet State interests.[51] But, instead of backing down, Boris Yeltsin warned Union Minister of Defense Dmitry Yazov that he could be put on trial in the Russian Federation for violating Russian Federation laws that prohibit the use of Russian servicemen in domestic conflicts. Yeltsin accused Gorbachev of plotting to impose Union presidential dictatorship on all the republics. He defended his mission to the Baltic republics as a clear demonstration of responsible leadership which laid the foundations for a qualitative change in relations between the republics.[52] *Pravda* accused Boris Yeltsin of plotting with Ruslan Khasbulatov to replace the Union government with a Federal Council "where Yeltsin will play first violin."[53] That accusation was prophetic.

The Vilnius killings damaged the reputations of Yazov, Kryuchkov, Pugo, and Gorbachev who, after all, was their civilian commander. Captain V. Gromak made an impressive and bold statement in *Krasnaya zvezda*: "Like it or not, our talk about building a law-governed state will remain empty words until state figures begin accepting personal responsibility for the actions of their subordinates." Gromak and his chief editor, Vyacheslav Lukashevich, were expressing precisely the right ideas for a military that was seeking to enhance its professionalism within a democratic state.[54] A group of Baltic and Leningrad civilian and military Communists conferred to discuss the situation and concluded that "The explanations of the President of the USSR, the Minister of Defense, and the Minister of Internal Affairs of the USSR on the reasons Soviet army units were used in Vilnius have sounded unconvincing. The country has not yet received the clear answer it expected." The Communist regional plenum condemned using the army in nationalist conflicts and criticized nationalist attacks on the role and honor of the armed forces.[55]

The fiasco in Vilnius sealed Gorbachev's fate and taught the military another lesson. There was no easy solution to the secessionist problem. The country was moving towards a redistribution of power between the Union and the republics and the military would certainly be affected by those changes. Yeltsin began to emerge as the most likely successor to Gorbachev.

Yeltsin's Summer Victories over Gorbachev

Gorbachev's ineffectiveness emboldened Yeltsin who began demanding that Gorbachev resign and make way for effective, determined national leadership. Yeltsin supporters held huge rallies in Moscow with crowds estimated at some 200,000. His message was positive. Reform could be saved but this required decisive leadership, new leadership, his leadership.[56] Gorbachev responded by trying to get the conservatives in the Russian republic's Congress to replace Boris Yeltsin with a new Russian president. Congress had the power to do that.

The idea was simple. Congress would assemble in two weeks and the Communist majority would vote to replace Yeltsin. In order to prevent Yeltsin supporters from organizing mass rallies designed to intimidate Communist

Party loyalists, Gorbachev declared a three-week ban on political demonstrations in central Moscow and transferred the capital police force from Russian
Federation to Union control. The ban was to begin on 26 March and to end on
15 April 1991. KGB Chairman Kryuchkov and MVD head Pugo summoned
prominent Yeltsin organizers and warned them not to violate the ban. They
claimed that popular demonstrations were a method of political intimidation
and could not be tolerated.[57] Their goal was to prevent Yeltsin's supporters
from organizing large demonstrations in anticipation of Gorbachev's effort to
unseat him.

On the evening the ban went into effect, Gorbachev made a rambling ninety-
minute televised address. He complained that the city of Moscow had become
hostage to political demonstrations and insisted that democracy would fail unless law and order were restored. He denied that he intended to establish a
dictatorship like General Pinochet's in Chile. But he vowed to provide effective
leadership and confirmed that he had authorized his cabinet to take all action
necessary to provide the secure environment required for the Russian Congress
to do its work.[58]

Gorbachev decided to surround the Kremlin area where the Congress would
meet with troops. On the morning Russia's Congress convened, all adjacent
streets were lined with troops, a spectacle that inspired the delegates to rally
to Yeltsin. Congress assembled, demanded that Gorbachev remove the troops,
and adjourned for the day. More demonstrations were held in the streets but
Yeltsin's people stopped their march several blocks from the Kremlin area
and avoided a confrontation. Gorbachev decided to recall the troops. The
next morning Congress reassembled, defeated efforts to unseat Yeltsin, and
approved his recommendation that Russia institute a popularly and democratically elected presidency. The people of Russia would vote for the candidate and the reform program they wanted. Col. Aleksandr Rutskoi was
instrumental in organizing a group of congressmen called Communists for
Democracy to support Yeltsin against Gorbachev. Rutskoi was a decorated
Afghan war veteran who had political aspirations of his own. His support was
a sign that Yeltsin could appeal to a wide spectrum of voters including military Communists who wanted reform but who believed that Gorbachev had
to be replaced.

After Gorbachev's failures in March, he decided to negotiate a division of
power with Yeltsin, a new Union Treaty that would require the reformation of
the Union's leading political institutions. This deal was struck on 23 April
1991 and became known as the Novo-Ogaryovo accord. From then on the
Soviet government, Gorbachev and his cabinet were lame ducks. Soyuz
damned the political deal as a "velvet" coup against the Union.[59] Gorbachev
assembled the Central Committee to hear his report on plans to reform the
Union by giving increased powers to the republics. The commanders of the
military districts were invited to attend. Gorbachev warned that unless the

Party rallied to these reforms, the last chance to save the Union and to save the reform process peacefully would be lost.[60]

But Yeltsin did his own military-political work and began building political relationships with Pavel Grachev the general commander of the very paratrooper divisions that would have to be used against him should Gorbachev or some other leader try to block his drive for power. On 31 May 1991, presidential candidate Yeltsin toured the Tula region with Grachev and dispensed a mixture of promises and actual gifts such as wrist watches to soldiers he met including drivers. His biggest gift was a promise to fund a new 500 unit apartment complex for the Tula division's officers. The day's political activities culminated in a party of eating and drinking for Yeltsin, his personal security guard, Aleksandr Korzhakov, and some eighteen military officers. It was a chance for political networking and bonding to take place. Yeltsin wanted the elite paratroopers to know him personally and to be prepared to support him politically and otherwise.[61] The message: Gorbachev was aloof and distant but Yeltsin was earthy and close to his people, the real national leader.

Russia's First Presidential Elections

Boris Yeltsin's political gamble won. Russia went to the polls on 12 June 1991 and elected him Russia's first democratically elected president. Yeltsin's running mate was Col. Aleksander Rutskoi. They received 57.3 percent of the popular vote even though they were opposed by five other tickets. The second place ticket also included a civil-military pairing. It consisted of former Soviet prime minister Nikolai Ryzhkov and Col. General Boris Gromov, the soldier who led the Soviet military contingent in Afghanistan during the final stages of the war. The Ryzhkov-Gromov ticket received 16.8 percent of the popular vote. None of the remaining four presidential hopefuls passed the 10 percent mark in the voting. The results for them were as follows: Vladimir Zhirinovsky, 7.8 percent; Aman Tuleyev, 6.8 percent; Col. General Albert Makashov, 3.7 percent; and, MVD Col. Gen. (Ret.) Vadim Bakatin, 3.42 percent.[62] The candidate self-selection process and the ticket strategies suggested that Russian politicians believed that military candidates were attractive additions to their tickets. Soldiers who presented themselves as defenders of the reform process were more popular than those who, like Col. General Makashov, demanded tough measures to save the Union.

On 17 June 1991, KGB Chief Kryuchkov, Minister of Defense Yazov, and MVD head Pugo attempted a Union parliamentary coup against Gorbachev, the passage of special legislation by the lame duck Union Parliament to enhance the powers of Union Prime Minister Pavlov. Gorbachev sped back to Moscow to halt this first mutiny by his cabinet's most powerful officers. He refused to surrender the leadership role to Prime Minister Pavlov even though the three "power" ministers were backing that move. However, Gorbachev did not remove them from office probably because time was running out for them anyway. At his last cabinet session before he left for vacation, they were still insisting that he take firm measures to halt the Union state's disintegration.[63]

On 20 July 1991, President Yeltsin struck a blow against the Communist Party by issuing *ukaz* no. 14 which prohibited partisan political activity in all Russian state institutions, organizations, and agencies. In effect, Yeltsin shut down the Communist Party in all the factories, public administration, and cultural institutions of Russia.[64] The Communist Party had already lost 25 percent of its membership since 1990.[65] Yeltsin's action accelerated the trend. Since the Soviet armed forces were Union not Republic institutions, Yeltsin's ban had no direct, immediate impact upon the Communist structures in the military. However, his move was a clear signal of where he intended to take the country should he come to power.

Military-Political Alliances on the Eve of the August Coup

The elite paratroopers were emerging as that part of the Soviet military that the Soviet state's civilian leaders relied most upon to defend the state's internal political integrity against rising nationalist and secessionist forces. They were also trained and deployed in a manner that made them quickly available for political-military interventions in the Moscow region, a potential made clear in the training exercises held in early September 1990. The paratroopers had become the Soviet state's ultimate political weapon, the political-military tool that any would-be ruler would have to control, neutralize, or defeat. The paratroopers were not the only armed forces available for domestic use but they were the best troops and were ready to back up the MVD's internal armies as necessary.

There were clear signs that Minister of Defense Yazov and First Deputy Minister Achalov were deeply concerned about the Gorbachev administration's ineffective response to serious challenges to the Union state's monopoly on armed force and ability to enforce its decisions uniformly. Achalov became a spokesman for senior military leaders who demanded that the administration govern more effectively and use demonstrations of military power if required to protect the Soviet state's viability. The Ministry of Defense press featured him as such a military leader. Defense Minister Yazov and KGB Chairman Kryuchkov shared the same point of view and pressed Gorbachev to authorize them to use firmer measures.

The attentive military learned three lessons when the Vilnius conspiracy failed. First, and quite obviously, there was a pro-Unionist conspiratorial group with support in high places but a low ability to plan and execute an effective coup. Second, the extremely negative public reaction to the killings in Vilnius confirmed that public opinion did not support sending tanks and troops against Soviet citizens even to prevent Baltic secession. Third, Gorbachev could not be relied upon to support the military in a difficult political crisis. In other words, the Tbilisi syndrome continued to operate and it was better for the military to resist being used for domestic political purposes.

What had Boris Yeltsin learned from the events? He quickly understood that the public and the soldiers were seeking a positive way out of the national crisis and were disillusioned with Gorbachev. He presented himself as the leader who could implement the soft-line skillfully and decisively. Although his sharp condemnation of Yazov's involvement in the affair and threats to take him to court for using Russian citizens for Soviet gendarme work upset the military establishment, he quickly adapted to military criticism and began cultivating his own political relationships with both active-duty and retired officers. He also knew that he needed to bond politically with the paratroopers and several key commanders.

According to Lebed's accounts, Yeltsin developed a political and personal friendship with Pavel Grachev, the general commander of Soviet paratrooper forces. That was a wise choice since Grachev's troops were the military units most likely to be deployed in any political showdown in Moscow. Further, Grachev's political behavior made him more attractive to Yeltsin than either Achalov or Lebed. Grachev was less inclined to perform as a politician and had not drawn much public attention to himself. By contrast, Achalov had taken strong positions in favor of the Communist Party and the Soviet state and Lebed was a political maverick, a military populist who showed little respect for politicos and officers who cultivated relationships with them. This made Grachev the most likely to emerge as Yeltsin's military, political ally.

Conclusion: Progressive, Authoritarian, or Bewildered?

The accumulated theory on civil-military relations predicts that military participation in domestic politics increases when civilian political institutions become unstable, the military retain institutional viability, and the military leadership has the will to intervene in the domestic political game.[66] As Soviet civilian political institutions began to lose their effectiveness, civilian control over the armed forces weakened and the military became more active politically. Thus, Soviet developments broadly fit the pattern observed in other parts of the world. However, Russian analysts warned me not to equate Soviet and Russian civil-military relations with Latin American, Western European, or any other regional experience because Soviet practices mixed democratic, authoritarian, populist, and professional behaviors into a unique Russo-Soviet blend. Nevertheless, I argue that developments in Russia do fit the general rules of political evolution even though there are indeed many interesting, rather quaint and idiosyncratic practices.

Soviet political habits and structures had already put the military in the political sphere. Military personnel did not have to invade the civilian political domain because they were already in it. The Soviet practice was to include military personnel in Soviet political institutions and organizations. Thus, the fact that some 1,100 soldiers held elective office as deputies in local, regional, republic, and Union legislatures and councils was normal in Soviet society. Further, under the old unofficial rules of politics, junior officers were expected to do political work for their senior commanders. Thus, Col. General Achalov expected Lt. General Lebed to arrange his election to the Russian Congress in 1990 much as Lebed had helped to arrange Col. General Moiseyev's election to the Soviet Congress in 1989. Professional soldiers such as Aleksandr Lebed had to keep several dimensions of political work going simultaneously. Thus, while Lebed was still pacifying Baku, he had to start thinking about Achalov's election campaign back in Russia's Tula region. He also had to worry about how his performance in Azerbaijan would be assessed by the press and by civilian leaders. And he had to be militarily and politically effective in Azerbaijan.

Under the old rules, military deputies were supposed to endorse the positions taken by civilian political bosses. Under the new rules junior officers could challenge senior officers in competitive elections and in policy debates and military personnel could criticize civilian leaders, even their president. They had the right to initiate legislation and to criticize current policies. They could defend themselves against civilian critics. Colonel General Rodionov's outspoken defense of the armed forces and sharp criticism of civilian leaders and the media is an outstanding example of this new military political behavior. It caused a stir in 1989 because the public and the political elite had not yet become used to hearing directly from the military. General societal democratization and weak leadership from Supreme Commander Gorbachev gave the military political wiggle room. In retrospect, Rodionov's political message seems responsible and professional especially when compared to some of the extreme nationalism and authoritarianism espoused by generals such as Albert Makashov, the commander of the Volga-Urals military district who ran for president against Yeltsin and who engaged in factional politics within the Communist Party.

Officers were in politics whether they liked it or not. Politics was part of their life. Some branches of the military were more involved in politics than others. The elite paratroopers were political tools par excellence. The Soviet state used them to overthrow the Hungarian leadership in 1956, the Czechoslovakian reformers in 1968, and the Afghan regime in 1979. It sent them to pacify Tbilisi, Baku, and Vilnius and trained them for action in Moscow as well.

Yeltsin took advantage of Gorbachev's inattention to military control and began cultivating relationships with military officers including the elite paratroopers. However, their former commander, First Deputy Minister of Defense Achalov was supporting the Unionist position and found fault with both Yeltsin and Gorbachev. Minister of Defense Yazov and KGB Chairman

Kryuchkov also favored authoritarian measures to prevent the Union's disintegration. It was professionally and politically dangerous for any officer to support Yeltsin openly. This became somewhat easier once Yeltsin had been elected president of Russia in direct competitive elections in June 1991. The fact that his vice president was an Afghan war hero, Colonel Aleksandr Rutskoi, also helped. The Yeltsin-Rutskoi ticket soundly defeated their authoritarian Unionist rivals including Colonel General Albert Makashov.

According to Western modernization theory the authoritarians are doomed by history in the longer run but their near to midterm prospects are more positive. Rumors of impending authoritarian coups were a frequent occurrence after winter 1989–90. Military discontent with Gorbachev's leadership reached unprecedented levels in summer 1990 because the political revolutions in Central and Eastern Europe and the secessionist movements in the Baltic and Caucasian republics were undermining the Soviet defense system's viability. The armed forces had substantial institutional reasons to support the Union's political and security integrity. But the military's experiences in Tbilisi, Baku, and Vilnius had taught officers bitter lessons about the political courage and reliability of civilian leaders who had ordered them into domestic political battle. The Unionists failed to produce a competent leader and Boris Yeltsin began to attract support around a Russocentric solution to the Union's growing political crisis. Yeltsin rejected the hard-line, Unionist thesis and favored major compromises with the republics. The best policy from a military point of view was to remain patient and to prevent the Soviet Union from disintegrating into civil war.

As military leaders made decisions about military participation in short term political crises, they had to consider the longer term consequences of their actions. The Soviet military leadership was statist in its general political orientation and highly sensitive to the requirements of state viability. If the military had set itself against the civilian political leadership or split along factional lines, it would have damaged national political cohesion and its own military corporate interests. Thus, the military tended to be statist and strapped in for the political ride even when civilian political leaders governed ineffectively. The Soviet military was extraordinarily patient but could not remain indifferent since the Soviet state's fate was its fate.

There is a complex, organic relationship between a state's military and political organs and a state's overall viability. State viability requires an internal political system that makes and enforces authoritative decisions over a definite territory. State viability requires political authorities capable of building effective armed forces and maintaining a monopoly on their use. State viability requires territorial integrity which entails demarcation and defense of borders. The state is neither viable nor sovereign unless it has the capacity to defeat internal and external challengers to its authority. The state needs modern armed forces to guarantee its security and the armed forces need an effective political regime to define their mission and to furnish their resources. Without effective civilian, police, and military bureaucracies to enforce decisions, both political effectiveness and stateness weaken. Conversely, when the political regime improves its organizational and administrative capacity, the state strengthens.[67] It follows that responsible military citizenship requires senior officers to support state strengthening and to maintain military organizational discipline in order to avoid civil war and to maintain combat readiness to protect the state against external enemies.

Was the military more inclined towards authoritarian conservative politics or democratic politics? The evidence requires a nuanced answer. The military was naturally inclined towards progressive reform but would have preferred a semi-authoritarian regime, one in which experienced professionals made policy decisions and implemented them efficiently. The military became impatient with the civilian leaders, deeply concerned about the Soviet defense system's future, and individual military careers. Tbilisi, Baku, and Vilnius had made the military suspicious of authoritarian solutions to complex problems and uncomfortable with the demokraty. They were more inclined to pull back from politics than to become actively involved in some new adventure. This mood would make it possible for relatively few military and civilian actors to launch and reverse the August 1991 coup.

Notes

1. For the official elections results, see *Pravda*, 5 April 1989.
2. See Eduard Shevardnadze, *Moi vybor v zashchitu demokratii i svobody!* (My choice in defense of democracy and freedom!) (Moscow: Novosti, 1991), pp. 320–31.
3. See Rodionov's account to the Soviet parliament or Congress of Peoples Deputies at which, as an elected deputy, he debated the issue with Gorbachev presiding. See the stenographic record, First Congress of Peoples Deputies of the USSR, 25 May–9 June 1989 (in Russian); Supreme Soviet: Moscow, 1989; vol. 1, pp. 524 ff.
4. Gorbachev's 700-page *Memoirs* reveal nothing. He only mentions the Tbilisi incident briefly. See pp. 286 and 301.
5. See the Military Procurator's formal report, *Krasnaya zvezda*, 20 March 1991.
6. See the Commission's recommendations, pp. 208–9 in Anatoly Sobchak, *Tbilisskii izlom, ili Krovavoe voskresenye 1989 goda* (Moscow: "Stretenie," 1993).
7. See *Ibid.*
8. See Anatoly Sobchak, *Tbilisskii izlom ili, Krovavoe voskresenye 1989 goda* (Moscow: "Stretenie," 1993).
9. *Ibid.*, p. 193.
10. *Ibid.*, pp. 208–9.
11. See Lebed, *Obidno za derzhavu* (Moscow: Moskovskaya pravda, 1995), pp. 279 ff.
12. See Shevardnadze, *Moi vybor.*
13. See Robert V. Barylski, "The Russian Federation and Eurasia's Islamic Crescent," *Europe-Asia Studies,* vol. 46 (3), 1994, pp. 389–416 for a fuller discussion of these events.

14. See Lebed, *Obidno za derzhavu* (Moscow: Moskovskaya pravda, 1995) p. 298.
15. Lebed, *Obidno,* pp. 303–4.
16. Based on the author's interviews with Popular Front and Communist Party members. in Azerbaijan in summer 1991, 1992, and 1993.
17. Aleksandr Lebed, *Obidno,* pp. 287–88.
18. *Ibid.,* p. 297.
19. *Ibid.,* pp. 298–300.
20. *Ibid.,* pp. 312–13.
21. *Ibid.,* pp. 317 ff.
22. See Aleksander Zhilin, "General Turns His Back on Past," *Moscow News,* 25–31 July 1996.
23. See Oleg Odnokolenko's biting criticism of incompetent civilian dictatorship in national defense affairs, "Lt. General Khrushchev" (in Russian), *Krasnaya zvezda,* 31 August 1990. Odnokolenko revisited the Zhukov affair and used it as an illustration of how civilian dictators had bullied competent military professionals and had damaged national defense. He argued that contemporary military politicization was helping the military to correct its own professional inadequacies.
24. See Anatoly Dokuchayev's three part series on military professionalism in the West; *Krasnaya zvezda,* 26, 28, and 29 August 1990.
25. See his comments in *Krasnaya zvezda,* 4 September 1990.
26. See Col. General Vladislav Achalov in *Ibid.,* 6 September 1990.
27. Vladislav Achalov, *Ibid.*
28. See Lebed, *Obidno,* pp. 343–50.
29. *Ibid.,* p. 384.
30. Defense Minister Yazov as cited by *Krasnaya zvezda,* 20 October 1990.
31. See Lebed, *Obidno,* p. 360.
32. See *Krasnaya zvezda's* report on Yeltsin's remarks at Sverdlovsk; *Ibid.,* 17 August 1990.
33. See M. S. Gorbachev's remarks at the military exercises of the Odessa military District, "Dostoino proiti pereval v istorii," *Ibid.,* 19 August 1990.
34. See Chief of Staff, Army General Mikhail Moiseyev's overview of military reform guidelines from 1990 to 2000 in *Krasnaya zvezda,* 18 November 1990.
35. See Vladimir Urban's report, "Komu reshat' problemy armii," *Krasnaya zvezda,* 3 November 1991. Russian Federation Prime Minister I.S. Silayev led the discussions for Boris Yeltsin.
36. Readers who are not familiar with Russian forms of address should know that it is polite and respectful to address the president by his first name and patronymic. The family name is rarely used in direct address. Thus, instead of "President Gorbachev," they say "Mikhail Sergeyevich. His full name is Mikhail Sergeyevich Gorbachev. "Sergeyevich" means "son of Sergei," his father. The transcript of the dialogue between Gorbachev and the officers is printed in *Krasnaya zvezda,* 15 November 1990.
37. Mikhail S. Gorbachev as cited in *Krasnaya zvezda's* transcript of the meeting of 13 November 1990, *Krasnaya zvezda,* 15 November 1990.
38. Col. Viktor Alksnis as cited by Vladimir Urban in "Sokhranim li my Soyuz? *Krasnaya zvezda,* 18 November 1990.
39. See *Krasnaya zvezda,* 25 December 1990.
40. Col. Viktor Alksnis, "Soyuz budet sokhranen," *Ibid.,* 31 December 1990.
41. See report on Marshal Yazov's press conference, *Ibid.,* 20 December 1990.
42. Reported in *Krasnaya zvezda,* 10 January 1991.
43. See Lebed, *Obidno,* pp. 370–71.

44. Col. General Vladislav Achalov, "Soyuz budet sokhranen" (The Union will be preserved), *Krasnaya zvezda*, 29 December 1990.
45. See the discussion of Joint Order no. 493/513 for joint patrols in the capitals of all Soviet republics starting 1 February 1991 in *Ogonyok*, no. 7, 1991.
46. See Col. A. Oliinik, "Vypolnyaya ukaz Prezidenta," *Krasnaya zvezda*, 10 January 1994.
47. See *Moscow News*, no. 24, 1991.
48. See *Krasnaya zvezda*, 15 January 1991.
49. See *Ibid.*
50. Marshal Nikolai V. Ogarkov et al., "Otkritye pisma B. N. Yeltsinu," *Krasnaya zvezda*, 18 January 1991.
51. See *Ibid.*, 19 January 1991.
52. See *Krasnaya zvezda's* report on Yeltsin's address to the Russian Federation's Supreme Soviet. Delegates applauded when Yeltsin threatened to put Yazov on trial. *Ibid.*, 22 January 1994.
53. See Anatoly Karpichev, "Poslushaite vnimatel'no," *Pravda*, 23 January 1994.
54. Captain V. Gromak, "Togda v Vilniuse," *Krasnaya zvezda*, 11 January 1991.
55. See B. V. Gaspadov's report. *Pravda*, 24 January 1991.
56. See *The New York Times*, 11 March 1991.
57. See *Krasnaya zvezda*, 26 and 29 March 1991.
58. As reported in *Pravda*, 29 March 1991.
59. See *Moscow News*, no. 24, 1991.
60. See *Krasnaya zvezda*, 25 April 1991.
61. See Lebed, *Obidno*, pp. 378–82.
62. Results as reported in *Krasnaya zvezda*, 20 June 1991.
63. The claim was made by Dmitry Steinberg who was defending Army General Varennikov who insisted upon a trial and refused the Duma's amnesty. Steinberg claims the stenographic record of the cabinet meeting indicates that Gorbachev authorized the cabinet to go ahead making plans. He cites Gorbachev as saying: "Tomorrow I'm leaving for vacation, with your approval, to keep from interfering with your work." Petr Karapetyan, "Mikhail Gorbachev govorit' obo vsem i...ni o chem," *Krasnaya zvezda*, 9 July 1994.
64. *Krasnaya zvezda*, 24 June 1991.
65. *Krasnaya zvezda*, 25 June 1991.
66. See Samuel Huntington's classic, *The Soldier and the State* (Cambridge, Mass.: Harvard University Press, 1957), and Amos Perlmutter's *The Military and Politics in Modern Times* (New Haven, Conn.: Yale University Press, 1977).
67. See Robert V. Barylski, "Russian Domestic Politics, Military Power, and the Eurasian State System," in Hafeez Malik, ed., *The United States, Russia, and China in the New World Order* (New York: St. Martins, 1997).

4

The Double Coup of August 1991

The August 1991 coup was a poorly planned and incompetently executed effort by the key members of President Gorbachev's cabinet to save the Union state, the Union institutions they headed, and their personal power and privileges. Minister of Defense Yazov played a central role in launching the coup and in calling it off. His actions brought the military more deeply into domestic politics than any time since the revolutionary period, 1917–1921.

The evidence tends to confirm the thesis that the military becomes more involved in politics when civilian governmental institutions begin to disintegrate. The military is drawn into protracted civilian leadership crises. However, the record also shows that the Russian military, as an institution, did not yet see itself as a viable substitute for civilian public administration. The Soviet military had been indoctrinated to accept civilian political leadership and it continued to do so. In 1991, the military was searching for effective civilians to back; it was not planning to run the country on its own.

Although Gorbachev was the de jure commander in chief, he had lost the military's loyalty because his policies had disrupted military careers, damaged Soviet military institutions, and weakened Soviet state power. The military tried to play a positive role in the national political crisis but there were no easy solutions to the Soviet Union's systemic breakdown. The professional soldiers served the Soviet Union and the Soviet people but their Soviet state was breaking down and some of their peoples were demanding political sovereignty, separate states, and national armies. The obvious solution—a state of emergency that could reverse those trends and save the Union, had some appeal but was fundamentally unsound. The country had to go forward and to adapt to demands for major changes in the division of powers between the Union and the republics.

Boris Yeltsin fought and won two battles in August 1991. He defeated the state of emergency committee and he prevented Gorbachev from restoring his pre-coup powers. Thus, it was a double coup. One coup was launched by the SEC and it failed. Another was launched by Boris Yeltsin and it succeeded. The August events settled the competition for primary leadership over the Soviet Union's reconstruction. Yeltsin won that battle by defeating the

state of emergency committee and Gorbachev. The military's political acquiescence was extremely important to Yeltsin's victory. However, it did not
mean that the military as an institution believed that replacing Gorbachev
with Yeltsin and the demokraty was the ideal solution to the crisis. But given
the choices of August 1991, they were acceptable and offered some hope.

This chapter analyzes Boris Yeltsin's rapprochement with the military before the coup, his intensive, successful campaign to separate the military from
the SEC during the coup, and his generous treatment of the military as the
coup came to a peaceful end. No coup can endure without support from the
armed forces. The evidence shows that the military killed the coup. Minister
of Defense Yazov apparently needed little convincing that he had made a
grave mistake. Yeltsin must have provided Yazov with assurances that the
officers who supported the coup would be treated generously if they withdrew graciously and they did. In this regard, the August coup is a case study
in how would-be civilian victors should approach the military during a major
political crisis.

Yeltsin's Military-Political Ties and the August Coup

In summer 1991 talk of a Unionist coup was rampant in Moscow and in
diplomatic circles. Yeltsin did not ignore it. Yeltsin needed political allies in
the armed forces and had been cultivating them since summer 1990. Yeltsin
enlisted military progressives representing various generations and placed
them on committees that advised him in his capacity as head of the Russian
republic. His senior military adviser was military historian Col. General (Ret.)
Dmitry Volkogonov. His chief liaison to the Soviet Ministry of Defense's
General Staff was Col. General (Ret.) Konstantin Kobets. Since these two
prestigious officers had retired from active duty, they were in a better position to work with Yeltsin than colleagues on active duty for whom President
Gorbachev was still the supreme commander. Yeltsin's vice president was Air
Force Colonel Aleksandr Rutskoi, a highly decorated Afghan War veteran. In
addition to the Russian president's military affairs staff, the Russian parliament had military, security, and internal affairs committees. Some citizen-
soldiers such as Col. Vladimir Lopatin, represented a younger generation of
military dissidents who consistently argued for faster and deeper military reform. In addition to being a member of the Russian parliament, Lopatin became first deputy to General Kobets on Yeltsin's presidential military
committee which was developing into a proto-ministry of defense. The Yeltsin
team had diverse links to the armed forces. It included representatives of
several military generations and a range of views from moderate to radical
reformers. However, it excluded the hard right, professional soldiers who argued that rational, authoritarian dictatorship was in the best interest of the
Soviet peoples.

Some rightists were Yeltsin's political rivals and enemies. Colonel. General Albert Makashov, the commander of the Volga-Urals military district, was among them. He tried to bring the military into an authoritarian drive for power under the banner of a Russian Communist Party. When Rutskoi organized a Communists for Democracy faction, Makashov pressed to expel him from the Party. Makashov ran against Yeltsin in the Russian presidential elections of June 1991 on a pro-Union, pro-Communist platform. During the August 1991 coup Makashov demanded that force be used to arrest Yeltsin. After the coup he continued in his radical ways and tried to overthrow Yeltsin by armed force in September-October 1993.

Because soldiers ran for office, took definite positions on key issues, and were visible, it was relatively easy for civilian politicians to identify potential allies in the armed forces. Civilian democrats and progressives began to develop definite opinions about various military officers. These opinions and relationships helped to determine who got the top jobs after the Yeltsin team defeated the coup in August 1991. Similarly, the radical conservatives knew who their potential friends were and cultivated them.

Boris Yeltsin reports that he had a political understanding with Major General Pavel Grachev, the overall commander of the Soviet state's elite paratrooper forces. However, Grachev was a professional soldier who was busy making a military career rather than running for political office when Yeltsin discovered him. In July 1991 Yeltsin went to the main paratrooper base at Tula to the southwest of Moscow and put the touchstone question to Grachev: "'Pavel Sergeyevich,' I asked him, 'if our lawfully elected government in Russia were ever to be threatened—a terrorist act, a coup, efforts to arrest the leaders—could the military be relied upon, could you be relied upon?'"[1] Grachev gave an affirmative answer, a political promise of support that became vitally important to Yeltsin. This relationship strengthened during and after the coup.

Planning the Coup Against Gorbachev

KGB Chairman Kryuchkov gave the plotters the logistical support and secret meeting places they needed to do their conspiratorial work. Gorbachev left Moscow for vacation on 4 August 1991. The next day at a KGB safe place near Moscow's ring road known as "ABTs." Kryuchkov and Yazov decided to take action.[2] They were rushing to beat a deadline, 20 August 1991, the day Gorbachev would return to Moscow for the signing of the new Union Treaty, an act that doomed them politically because Gorbachev promised Yeltsin that a new government would be formed with new ministers to govern the new Union state based on the new Union treaty. They, the "old" ministers, were lame ducks.[3]

On 12 August 1991 Minister of Defense Yazov assigned Grachev to the inter-agency team of MoD and KGB experts that planned the state of emergency (SEC). Grachev was brought in for two reasons. First, Kryuchkov and Yazov needed professional, technical expertise as they formulated their plans.[4] Second, Grachev commanded the elite paratroopers stationed near Moscow and these military specialists would be needed to seize key installations and to support KGB operations. Grachev was in a very difficult political position. His immediate predecessor, Col. General Achalov, was Yazov's first deputy minister of defense and one of the key players in the coup. Achalov was personally making some of the arrangements required to guarantee paratrooper readiness and loyalty. Grachev had to play his hand very carefully. He was closely watched during the coup and dared not speak openly on his telephones. The third key player from the military was Army General Varennikov who commanded the Soviet land forces. The land forces would have to bear the brunt of the SEC's domestic stabilization operations. Key generals from the land forces were going to be assigned to special committees that monitored and if necessary arrested normal civilian administrators in the towns and cities.

On 16 August 1991 the main conspirators met at the KGB's safe house: KGB Chairman Kryuchkov, Minister of Defense Yazov, Deputy Minister of Defense Col. General Vladislav Achalov, Commander of the Soviet Land Forces, Army General Viktor Varennikov, Prime Minister Valentin Pavlov, Gorbachev's chief of presidential staff Valery Boldin, Gorbachev's top civilian coordinator of Soviet national defense industrial affairs Oleg Baklanov, Gorbachev's top coordinator of Communist Party Central Committee affairs, Oleg Shenin. They decided to impose the SEC plan *with or without* Gorbachev.[5] However, neither Kryuchkov nor Yazov nor any of the civilian conspirators wanted to be identified as the main leader of the coup. They had no real leader and kept trying to make it a collective affair. They wanted Gorbachev to accept their plan and decided to send a delegation to him. They expected to be able to convince him because his entire cabinet was united behind the idea and the Union was really breaking down. Something had to be done. After they picked the delegation that was to confront Gorbachev with the news, the meeting ended. Some stayed for dinner; but Yazov, Achalov, and Varennikov drove off together in the Minister's limo. They talked little but recall that Yazov made several pessimistic comments such as, "Yes, we piled it all up. We managed to wreck it all."[6]

Yevgeny Shaposhnikov, the commander of the Soviet Air Force, had been left out of the inner circle. Yet, the coup required air support to move troops and to transport key coup leaders around the country—to Kiev, Tashkent, Tbilisi, Riga, and Leningrad, cities where the Soviet military had major regional headquarters. On 17 August 1991, Varennikov called Shaposhnikov to request that a special plane be kept ready to fly him at a moment's notice to Kiev for a military inspection mission. Shaposhnikov agreed and made the arrangements. Early Sunday morning, 18 August 1991 Deputy Minister of Defense Achalov began issuing special orders to commanders at certain air bases in the Moscow region without first reporting to Shaposhnikov. When subordinates reported this news, Shaposhnikov reacted angrily and called Minister of Defense Yazov who confirmed that Achalov was acting at his behest, part of the surprise inspection tour program.[7] Since that Sunday was also Soviet Air Power Day, Shaposhnikov was busy with holiday activities and accepted the explanation.

Military Collusion with the KGB: Enemies Lists

Early Sunday morning Yazov held a series of meetings with select groups of Ministry central staff and commanders. At an 8:00 A.M. meeting he revealed that the MoD was ready to support the KGB's plans to arrest prominent democrats and opposition leaders. He ordered Grachev to use elite paratroopers and their facilities to establish a holding area for people whom the KGB would arrest. He said that the KGB had prepared a list of seventy-five people who would be detained. The KGB would be responsible for arresting and bringing the prisoners to the holding center.[8] This detail shows that Yazov had definitely crossed the line between national defense and domestic political warfare. He trusted Grachev to provide important support for a political purge of national leaders and politicians.

The political arrests actually began on Monday 19 August 1991 at around 8:00 A.M. Col. General N. V. Kalinin, the commander of the Moscow Military District, was present at the arrest of Colonel V. G. Urazhtsev—a Russian congressmen and military dissident, and Tel'man Gdlyan—a prosecutor who had aggressively pursued corrupt Communist politicians. Urazhtsev later charged the military with complicity in drawing up the arrest lists. During perestroika Urazhtsev organized an independent trade union for Soviet military personnel, was elected to Congress, and earned a reputation as a thorn in the military establishment's side. In his usual bombastic style, he charged that Achalov wanted to throw him and his union, Shchit, down to the street from their sixth floor offices at the Hotel Rossiya.[9]

Although the political arrests soon lost their momentum, they might have developed into a major operation. Col. General Kalinin's participation raises serious questions about collusion between Yazov and Kryuchkov which were never adequately answered. Yazov had committed the military to support a domestic political purge. This was far more than just keeping the peace and protecting important facilities.

At 9:00 A.M. Yazov held a twenty-five minute meeting with other Ministry staff and told them that things were bad with Gorbachev and that it might be necessary to impose a state of emergency. In that event, the military would have to be used to preserve public order and to protect important institutions. He picked three associates and dispatched them to the Baltic, Leningrad, and Central Asia to explain the situation to the top military commanders in those regions. He emphasized that no actions were to be taken in the districts without specific authorization from his Central Command in Moscow.[10] Later he made personal calls to the commanders of the military districts, and Admiral Chernavin, head of the Soviet navy, and informed them that specific envoys would arrive at a specific time with an important bit of information. The schedule was arranged so that Varennikov would meet with Chernavin and the commanders of the military districts of Ukraine, the North Caucasus, and the Caucasus immediately after the SEC's face to face confrontation with Gorbachev.

The MVD's Late Entry

In the Soviet state, there were three ministries that had major armed forces: the Ministry of Defense, the KGB, and the MVD or Ministry of Internal Affairs. The coup's coercive dimension had been planned by *two sides* of the Soviet power triangle, the MoD and the KGB. MVD chief Boris Pugo did not play an important role and was only brought into the plot on Sunday afternoon, several hours before the SEC's confrontation with Gorbachev. This delay suggests that the KGB and the MVD did not trust the MVD.[11]

Even though its current head, Boris Pugo, was a good Party type, his immediate predecessor, Vadim Bakatin, had pushed perestroika reforms very far and had started giving the republics a stronger role in MVD affairs. Kryuchkov, Yazov, and others insisted that Gorbachev remove Bakatin in late 1990 and he did so. However, from their point of view, enough "damage" had been done so as to make them hesitant to work closely with the MVD until it became absolutely necessary. Vadim Bakatin joined the Yeltsin team during the coup and used his connections with the MVD to help undermine the coup. Kryuchkov and Yazov called Pugo into the Ministry of Defense at 1:00 P.M. on Sunday and told him what was what and obtained his agreement to join the SEC. Pugo warned them that Gorbachev would never agree to the scheme.[12] Pugo fell into a deep depression and committed suicide when the coup failed.

During the coup, Pugo's deputy minister in charge of the MVD's domestic armed forces was Colonel General Boris Gromov, an Afghan veteran and a friend of both Pavel Grachev and Aleksandr Lebed. Their personal relationships helped them to hold their own against pressure from the SEC during the coup. Gromov was well known to the Soviet public as the Soviet commander who led the last contingent of Soviet forces home from Afghanistan. He was featured in all the media and his image became associated with the public's desire to prevent its armed forces from being misused in the future.

The Confrontation with Gorbachev

On Sunday afternoon, the coup plotters sent a delegation to Gorbachev's summer retreat on the Black Sea in the Crimea, a place called Foros some 800 miles south of Moscow. The President was supposed to be protected by special KGB Ninth Directorate detachments who were under strict orders to prevent unannounced and unauthorized guests from entering the presidential compound. But, their commander, General Plekhanov, had joined the conspiracy. He came to Foros and personally ordered the chief of Gorbachev's personal guards back to Moscow and replaced him and some of the guards at the presidential villa with people he could trust. Plekhanov ordered Gorbachev's guards to admit the SEC delegation into the presidential compound and they did.[13] Just prior to giving this command he checked to make certain that Gorbachev's communications to the outside world had been cut off. Gorbachev's telephones including his special nuclear "hot lines" were turned off at 4:50 P.M. on Sunday 18 August 1991. That step was carefully timed to coincide with the SEC delegation's entry into the presidential compound. If fact, the conspirators marched right into Gorbachev's office and summoned him to join them, a gross demonstration of disrespect towards him and the presidency. Gorbachev ordered Plekhanov out of the room and Plekhanov complied although he was the only KGB officer in the group and was probably supposed to report on its conversations with Gorbachev to his boss in Moscow, KGB Chairman Kryuchkov. Gorbachev feared for his life and his family's well-being.[14]

The SEC delegation put the choice to Gorbachev: either join or get out of the way. His political instincts quickly led him to propose a middle position. *Gorbachev rejected the specific process but not the project.* He agreed to support it conditionally. The conditions were designed to give him some political room, a chance to break through the ring that had closed around him. He made procedural and policy demands. First, the procedure must follow the Soviet Constitution which meant that the Soviet parliament or Supreme Soviet should be called into session to discuss the national situation, hammer out a state of emergency plan, and vote for it: "I propose that we call a meeting of the Supreme Soviet and the Congress, and resolve everything there." [15] Second, he insisted that the new powers be used to implement his reform program including cooperation with the West.

General Varennikov demanded that Gorbachev hand in his resignation. Gorbachev described him as the "one who behaved in the crudest manner" and rebuked him saying, "The people are not a battalion of soldiers to whom you can issue the command 'right turn' or 'left turn, march' and they will all do as you tell them. It won't be like that. Just mark my words." Finally, Gorbachev sent them packing with his own barrage of Russian crudities: "And at the end of the conversation, using the strongest language that the Russians always use in such circumstances, I told them where to go."[16]

Meanwhile back in Moscow, the main conspirators gathered in prime minister Pavlov's offices behind the Kremlin walls, the traditional seat of civilian political power, to await news from Foros: Achalov, Kryuchkov,

Pavlov, Pugo, Yanayev, Yazov and Anatoly Lukyanov, speaker of the Union parliament or Supreme Soviet. They brought Lukyanov in because they wanted parliament to legitimize the State of Emergency. Around 6:00 P.M. they received a brief report from Foros and learned that their preferred plan had fallen through. Gorbachev would not proclaim a state of emergency without first having obtained parliamentary approval. At 10:00 P.M. the delegation returned from *Foros* and came to Pavlov's office. The group had to decide what to do next.

Now they began to understand that they had gone too far and could not retreat gracefully. They had committed grave, illegal crimes against the state in the name of saving the state. They had threatened and abused Gorbachev who would certainly demand that they be punished. They had no political alliances with Yeltsin and could expect no help from him.

The Formal Usurpation of Power

They marched into the political abyss. They agreed that they had to proclaim a state of emergency headed by a state of emergency committee led by Vice President Gennady Yanayev. And who would sign the declaration? Three signed: Vice President Yanayev, Prime Minister Pavlov, and Oleg Baklanov, secretary of the Soviet Defense Council and coordinator of defense industrial affairs. Vice President Yanayev signed the decree making himself acting president of the Soviet Union at 11:30 P.M. on Sunday 18 August 1991. Then acting-president Yanayev told Minister of Defense Yazov that troops would have to be brought into Moscow to demonstrate support for the SEC. Yazov asked for formal, legal orders and an official declaration that a special emergency situation exists. Yanayev provided them. Thus, the orders came from an acting president who had usurped Gorbachev's office, a point that would play a critical role in the coup's denouement.

Lukyanov predicted that it would be difficult to get the two-thirds vote which the Constitution required from the Supreme Soviet in order to establish the state of emergency legally. But they went ahead with plans to call the Supreme Soviet into session on 26 August 1991 [17] The people leading the coup were all political bosses of one type or another and they had some influence over the Supreme Soviet deputies. They must have decided among themselves that they could apply enough pressure to get the votes they needed. Further, by arresting opposition leaders prior to the legislative session, they could have a very direct impact on the voting and intimidate others into voting their way. Even Minister of Defense Yazov had a contingent of military deputies. When he met with his commanders on Monday morning, he ordered them to make certain that the military deputies got to Moscow in time for the Supreme Soviet session.[18] However, on Monday and Tuesday, even military deputies in the pro-Union faction, *Soyuz*, were telling Yanayev and

Yazov that the Supreme Soviet was unlikely to support the SEC because its first steps did not inspire confidence.[19]

Monday Morning

In the predawn hours, Minister of Defense Yazov and his staff began their work. At 5:00 A.M., Achalov called Grachev and ordered him to begin moving elements of the Tula elite paratrooper division into Moscow. Yazov ordered Colonel General N. V. Kalinin, the commander of the Moscow Military District, to bring the Taman motorized rifle division and the Kantemir tank division into Moscow and to take up defensive positions at key intersections and institutions. This force amounted to some 4,600 combat troops, more than 300 tanks, some 420 armored vehicles, and 430 specially equipped cars.[20] These forces were already moving into position when Yazov summoned the rest of the military high command to a 6:00 A.M. meeting at the Ministry of Defense. The troops were tired and confused because they had been awakened well before dawn and were told that they were going into the city to help keep public order. When they arrived in town, they didn't see any public disorder and fellow citizens of Moscow began accusing them of seizing power in a military coup about which the typical soldier knew virtually nothing. They had not been prepared psychologically to support a coup.

When the larger military collegium—the top commanders and MoD and General Staff department heads assembled, the coup was already underway and Yazov presented it to them as an accomplished fact. There was no discussion and no voting. Yazov told his top commanders that Gorbachev was in bad shape and could not fulfill his presidential duties. Therefore, in keeping with the Constitution, Vice President Yanayev would govern temporarily along with a state of emergency committee (SEC). He also informed them that Lukyanov had ruled that the new Union Treaty must not be signed without legislative review since it contradicted a March 1991 popular referendum which called for the preservation of the Union. Therefore, the SEC was blocking the Treaty ceremony that had been scheduled for tomorrow, 20 August 1995.

Yazov issued orders without any discussion. He placed the military on special alert and told his commanders that troops were needed in Moscow, Leningrad, and other cities to maintain order. Yazov emphasized the importance of calmness and restraint and insisted *there be no bloodshed*. He announced that Generals Samsonov and Kalinin had been appointed to serve as the SEC's special military commandants for cities of Leningrad and Moscow respectively, a step that signaled that normal city administration was being replaced with something new. The SEC's plans included extraordinary committees that were to stand above and apart from normal public administration and to take immediate action to punish anyone who refused to obey the State of Emergency. A strong, authoritative military presence was necessary on those committees to give them teeth and political clout.

Failure to Arrest Yeltsin

The SEC missed a golden opportunity to arrest Boris Yeltsin who was flying from Alma Ata to Moscow on Sunday. The coup plotters discussed Yeltsin's trip and considered several options. They could try to hold his plane in Kazakhstan or to detain him en route home from the airport in Moscow.[21] But they rejected both options because Yeltsin traveled with armed guards and would not give up easily. They decided to permit him to return to his dacha and to go after him there. Yeltsin returned home safely on Sunday. On Monday morning his telephone links were still operating and he soon learned about the early morning military deployments. He convened a critical meeting at his home early Monday morning. Ruslan Khasbulatov, the speaker of the Russian parliament, Ivan Silayev, the prime minister of Russia, Col. Aleksandr Rutskoi, the vice president of Russia, Anatoly Sobchak, the mayor of Leningrad, and several others had telephone conversations with Yeltsin and then drove to his summer place on Monday morning. They were present when Yeltsin telephoned Major General Pavel Grachev for information about what was happening and to obtain his assurances that he would not use the elite paratroopers against him.[22] They all drove past paratroopers on their way back into Moscow and, in Sobchak's case, to the Moscow airport. None of them was detained.

According to Yeltsin, the KGB observed all this from the woods outside his summer home but took no action. Yeltsin was saved because the KGB's special Alfa commando forces could not believe the orders that their commanders radioed to them. They moved into position near Yeltsin's cottage at 4:00 A.M. on Monday morning without being briefed or prepared for what was to come. Later in the morning, they were radioed orders to arrest the president and the Russian leadership and thereby secure their participation in critical negotiations. Confusion set in and KGB Chairman Kryuchkov scrapped the plan. Kryuchkov was no Beria.[23] Only a fool would have attempted to arrest President Yeltsin on the basis of such obviously illegal orders received over a radio phone system. Further, there would have been an armed confrontation with Yeltsin's own armed guards.

Major General Viktor Karpukhin, the KGB commander in charge of the Alfa forces, gave a somewhat different version of those events. He credits himself with sabotaging the arrests by refusing to order his men to carry out the verbal orders that Kryuchkov personally gave him in KGB headquarters in Moscow during the predawn hours. Karpukhin joined his men in the woods near Yeltsin's dacha, turned off his phones to avoid detection, and became an observer of the morning's events. If Karpukhin had disobeyed Kryuchkov's orders to arrest Yeltsin, why didn't Kryuchkov replace him? Immediately after the coup's defeat, Karpukhin offered the following answer: The Alfa commandos were loyal to Karpukhin and if he were sacked in the middle of the coup, the KGB's special commandos would have thrown their support to Yeltsin.[24] However, Yeltsin never believed this explanation and he had Karpukhin fired after the coup.

Leningrad: Samsonov, Gispadov or Sobchak?

There was neither a clear leader for the coup as a whole nor a definite chain of command for the regional and city SEC committees that were supposed to form all over the former Soviet Union. However, the military was doing more than just participating. The SEC was hoping to use patriotic themes, military uniforms, and military power to convince the general public and the opposition that the State of Emergency was authoritative and effective.

General Samsonov made a radio address at 10:00 A.M. and announced the formation of the Leningrad SEC. Why did a soldier take this political initiative instead of a civilian? Because the old Communist bosses had lost their political legitimacy and they preferred to hide behind the man in uniform. The citizens of Leningrad had broken the Communist Party's grip on city government by electing a non-Communist majority to the city council. If Party boss Boris Gispadov had announced the coup and had made himself highly visible, the general public would have condemned it as a Communist political machine grab for power rather than a patriotic act. Samsonov proclaimed the state of emergency without consulting with the democratically elected mayor, Anatoly Sobchak. The SEC was usurping power in Leningrad while Sobchak was flying home from Moscow. The SEC Moscow leadership wanted the Leningrad MVD and KGB to arrest Sobchak at the airport. However, the Leningrad MVD sabotaged those plans and sent special guards to protect him upon his arrival in Leningrad. Sobchak went directly to Samsonov's Leningrad military district headquarters to confront the general politically.

It is significant that the Leningrad military headquarters rather than city hall was selected as the new locus of SEC political power, another bit of evidence that military institutions were providing general backing for the SEC. When Sobchak arrived, he found the local KGB, military, MVD, and regional border troop commanders there in addition to Boris Gispadov, the boss of the Leningrad Communist Party organization. The Leningrad SEC had also brought over several democrats and was attempting to get them to endorse its policies, a sign that the coup's strategy included co-optation of some reformers. (The SEC probably hoped to do the same with Yeltsin and others in Moscow.)

Sobchak's reformers had trounced Gispadov's Communists in the Leningrad elections. City hall under Sobchak became one of the most progressive political centers in the former Soviet Union and Gispadov was eager to take political vengeance and to recapture power. Gispadov and bureaucratic, authoritarian Communists like him despised Gorbachev's electoral reforms. The SEC was supposed to be their vehicle for recovering power where they had lost it and for preserving it where they still held it. There was a similar situation in Moscow where the demokraty led by Gavril Popov had taken city hall from the Communists and Communist mayor Yury Prokofiev. The SEC was determined to restore Prokofiev and the Communist machine to power. And, Prokofiev was hiding behind General Kalinin's uniform just as Gispadov was using Samsonov as his political shield.

But Sobchak focused on Samsonov, not Gispadov, and warned him that the coup would certainly fail and that any military officers who shed blood would be put on trial for crimes against the people. He gave Samsonov specific, vivid examples of military officers who had been used and abused by failed Communist politicians in recent times. Sobchak knew these cases well since he was a lawyer by training and had conducted special investigations into the Tbilisi (1989) events on behalf of the Soviet Congress. Samsonov did not ignore Sobchak's arguments. He agreed to try to stop the convoys which were already moving towards Leningrad. When Yazov and the coup leaders in Moscow learned of Samsonov's decision, they reacted angrily: "The members of the *junta* were screaming hysterically over the phone that he (Samsonov) had sold out to the democrats." Samsonov held his ground and managed to halt the tanks and to keep them outside the city for the duration of the coup.[25]

Next Sobchak made it to a television studio where he broadcast an appeal to the people. He called for a demonstration of public support. He referred to the SEC in Moscow as the "former" vice president, prime minister, minister of defense, etc. He conjured up images of the first Russian revolutions and urged workers at the industrial establishments that supported the democratic revolution in 1917 to come forward to save democracy in 1991. Huge crowds, larger than Moscow's, gathered on Leningrad's historic Palace Square. The city held against the SEC and the army never occupied it. But Sobchak knew he was vulnerable to a surgical attack by KGB or Ministry of Defense special commandos. He like Yeltsin in Moscow expected the final blow to come on the night of August 20 to 21. At 3:00 A.M. on early Wednesday morning, Sobchak's vice mayor, Rear Admiral Vyacheslav Shcherbakov, a prestigious military officer, informed him that special commandos had indeed occupied city hall. Shcherbakov bluntly explained: "Our whole militia plus all of OMON is no match for these guys; they can polish us off in five minutes."[26] Sobchak took cover in the Kirov factory, the old Putilov works of 1917 revolutionary fame. The final attack never came.

What did the Troops Expect?

The instructions Yazov gave his commanders on early Monday morning were not filled with political invective. They were simplistic and formal.

Gorbachev was ill. The SEC has been formed to govern. The parliament will meet. There could be disorders. You are to take up positions to defend key political and strategic installations in the city. After instructing them, Yazov dismissed the group and gave no opportunity for questions or discussion. Once dismissed, the commanders and department heads left for their respective posts. Shaposhnikov only had a brief word Admiral I. M. Kapitanets who agreed with him that there was something nefarious afoot.[27]

The troops were only told to take up positions to defend the critical institutions and intersections in Moscow. They had no orders to attack any one or to arrest any civilian leaders. They were not psychologically prepared for combat against their peers in the streets of Moscow. No one bothered to read the SEC's main proclamation to them or to explain the general situation. All this suggests that the SEC expected little if any resistance and underestimated Boris Yeltsin's ability to undermine their *corrective* political coup.

The Public Explanation: Fatherland is in Danger!

The SEC plotters told the public that Gorbachev was too ill to fulfill the duties of the presidency. This ploy was used to justify Vice President Yanayev's serving as acting president. This ruse was supposed to move the three "power" ministers, the defense-industrial complex led by Baklanov, and the overall state bureaucracy under Pavlov into position to take quick, effective measures to halt economic and political disintegration. The SEC expected to win broad support among key elites and the general population for its authoritarian program. The SEC's historic Order No. 1 proclaimed the restoration of Soviet state integrity: the Soviet Constitution and Soviet laws were to be enforced strictly and uniformly across the fifteen republics. All irregular armed forces and militias in all republics were to be disarmed or placed under the control of Union MVD, KGB, and MoD officers. The Union would be preserved and the reform process would continue in an orderly *controlled* manner. The overall justification fit the pattern typical of authoritarian coups: the Fatherland is in Danger! Strong leadership is needed. We are providing it and saving the nation from anarchy.

The SEC regime was supposed to stand above and to guide existing institutions of public administration. Order No. 1's first point stated bluntly that all institutions and authorities must obey and execute SEC orders or be replaced by SEC designated substitutes.[28] This key edict could not be implemented unless the SEC gained credibility by arresting opponents or otherwise immobilizing opponents. As noted earlier, arresting prominent dissidents, closing newspapers, taking control over radio stations, and similar acts started early Monday morning. What about the edict that demanded all irregular armed forces to be disarmed immediately? That would have required military coercion on a much larger scale than the skirmishes in Vilnius and Riga and the several hundred deaths in Baku.

The strong leadership theme had a certain appeal because the Union state was disintegrating and people were anxious about the future. But as the day unfolded it was Yeltsin who emerged as the only strong leader capable of rallying the people, not the SEC. The SEC team's civilian core, Vice President Yanayev and Prime Minister Pavlov were not leadership material. They collapsed physically and psychologically under the burdens of the coup by the time of their very first press conference on Monday, 19 August 1991. KGB chairman Kryuchkov was a bureaucrat with no political charisma, a Soviet office type. When the coup collapsed and he was arrested, he wriggled and protested his innocence and claimed that he had never done anything against the national interest. Minister of Defense Yazov was stoic; he simply asked where they wanted him to go. His successor, Yevgeny Shaposhnikov, described him as a typical, competent military district commander of the World War II generation, a person who commanded and pushed his subordinates around in keeping with the *soldatskaya grubost'* or soldier's crudeness which is part of the Bolshevik legacy.[29] Commanders were blunt and strong willed. Subordinates did not debate policy with them and such people made poor national political speakers. They had difficulty expressing their ideas well and diplomatically.

Boris Yeltsin and Military-Political Bandwagoning

At first, the military high command moved with its Minister of Defense and supported the SEC *as ordered.* Many officers were enthusiastic about prospects for bringing a rapid end to national political and economic disintegration. Because the coup failed, information about initial support is not easy to find. But Yeltsin's team later claimed there was enough military support for the SEC to justify retiring 80 percent of the military high command.

The Ministry of Defense appointed military commanders to state of emergency committees in each main administrative division of the Russian Federation and the Baltic Republics. These committees were not to replace regular civilian authorities except where civilians refused to obey Soviet laws, the Soviet Constitution, and SEC decrees. General Kalinin was appointed to the Moscow SEC Committee; General Samsonov to the Leningrad SEC Committee, and so on. However, before this process could move very far, Boris Yeltsin in Moscow and Anatoly Sobchak in Leningrad began leading open resistance to the SEC. World attention focused on Boris Yeltsin who announced that the SEC was illegitimate and would not be obeyed. He forced the SEC to decide between capitulation with or without a blood bath. It was critical to his success that he separate the armed forces from the SEC and give officers a legal foundation to disobey Minister of Defense Yazov and acting president Yanayev. Yeltsin's resistance demonstrates the power individuals have to shape political outcomes.

Yeltsin's most dramatic public condemnation of the coup, the image that captured the popular imagination worldwide was made standing on Tank No. 110, one of the ten tanks of the Taman Division which moved into position outside the Russian Parliament building or White House. Their commander, Major Yevdokimov, accepted the White House point of view, promised to protect Yeltsin, and turned his tanks around so that their guns pointed towards the city. Yeltsin wanted to demonstrate that they were his tanks, military fire-power to defend Russian democracy not to attack the White House. But in addition to public displays of confident resistance, Yeltsin worked the private channels of power intensively. He knew that a few tanks could not save him against a serious assault. He needed to undermine the SEC's authority and to break its hold on the military.

Yeltsin assigned General (Ret) Konstantin Kobets to coordinate relations with the armed forces.[30] Vice President, Col. Aleksandr Rutskoi also played an important part in defeating the coup, but due to their subsequent political falling out, Yeltsin probably gives him less credit than he deserves. So did Yury Skokov who kept in touch with Generals Grachev who controlled the paratroopers, Gromov who controlled elite MVD troops, and others. All these bits and pieces of information describe a key military dimension of Yeltsin's strategy if not a neatly planned and executed game plan. There were so many military contacts that Khasbulatov describes a situation in which "meetings were continually disrupted by solders who were on our side."[31] The Yeltsin team was improvising but doing so with clear aims. The Ministry of Defense's officer's journal, *Armiya* reported that there had been as many as 200 military personnel on Yeltsin's side and in and around the White House as active members of the opposition.[32]

Yeltsin's team began with Ministry of Defense troops that had been sent to secure the White House area. Citizen-soldiers and civilian parliamentarians went out to talk with soldiers and officers and to explain the political situation to them.[33] Yeltsin was on the right track but his strategy still needed something, a powerful legal weapon to disrupt the chain of command running from Yazov to the troops outside the White House. Officers were concerned about legal protection against trial by court-martial for insubordination if they disobeyed *lawful* orders. Therefore, Yeltsin issued an official decree that stated, "As President of Russia in the name of the people who elected me I guarantee your legal defense and moral support."[34] But this still seemed too informal and tentative. Boris Yeltsin credits Lt. General Aleksandr Lebed with the idea that solved the problem.[35] This is politically significant because Lebed was one of the top three or four commanders in charge of the SEC's military operations ostensibly aimed at Yeltsin.

Lebed had official orders and was legally bound to obey them. He and all other officers were trapped in the same situation unless Yeltsin took formal action that either broke or suspended the normal chain of command. Yeltsin had to win the battle for the officers politically because as Lebed told him, "There was no point in talking seriously about defending the White House" from the military firepower available to the SEC. Lebed reminded Yeltsin that the White House defenders were "largely dilettantes and weren't capable of resisting even a small professional military division, although there were already dozens of such divisions in and around Moscow."[36]

Legitimizing Military Disobedience to SEC Orders

Yeltsin's staff immediately drafted, printed, and distributed a formal Presidential *ukaz* bearing the official seal of the Russian Federation, signed by President Yeltsin, and giving the site from which it was issued as the Moscow, the Kremlin. It declared that the SEC was illegal and that Boris Yeltsin, the popularly elected president of the Russian Federation, was taking temporary command of the Union armed forces on the territory of Russia until the legitimate commander in chief, Union President Mikhail Gorbachev could be restored to his office.[37] Yeltsin issued this key decree at 4:40 P.M. on Monday afternoon and struck a brilliant political blow at the SEC's military chain of command.[38] His supporters quickly distributed the official-looking leaflets bearing this critical message:

> Until the USSR Congress of People's Deputies meets for an extraordinary session all organs of executive power of the Soviet Union, including the KGB of the USSR, the MVD of the USSR, and the Ministry of Defense of the USSR, functioning on the territory of the RSFSR, *are subordinated directly to the popularly elected President of the RSFSR.*[39]

Yeltsin further decreed that his Russian federal officials were temporarily functioning in place of the top leaders in the Union's KGB, MVD, and Ministry of Defense who had lost their legitimacy by joining the coup. He further ordered that all citizens and officers of the respective Union institutions were to obey his orders. He declared that the Russian Federation's legal machinery would prosecute anyone who carried out the illegal SEC's orders. In addition to distributing printed leaflets, the White House rigged up a radio station and was sending radio messages to the military, KGB, and the MVD. Each message ended with this phrase: "I believe that in this tragic hour you will make the right choice. The honor and glory of Russian arms will not be stained with the people's blood."[40]

Thus, Boris Yeltsin had given the officers a legal reason to disobey SEC *illegal* orders. There were also powerful psychological reasons why the armed forces sought a way out of the crisis. The SEC began making plans to use armed force to drive Yeltsin from the Russian Federation Parliament building. But the various commanders and officers began warning their superiors and one another that there would be substantial bloodshed and making it clear that at least some of their units would refuse to obey orders to attack. In Grachev's words, "After Tbilisi, Baku, and Vilnius every soldier and officer began feeling particularly responsible for his actions. Further, all the branches understood this well—it was impossible to complete this action without huge human sacrifices. And each certainly asked in the name of what was the blood of peaceful fellow citizens to be shed?"[41]

On Tuesday, 20 August 1991, as news of Yeltsin's formal decree that ordered the military to obey him spread around the armed forces, some commanders who supported the coup began pressing Yazov to take effective measures against Yeltsin. Yeltsin's decree was working and spreading through the military system. Yeltsin was neutralizing if not splitting the armed forces. The ardent Unionist commander of the Volga-Urals military district, Col. General Albert Makashov was insisting that Yeltsin be arrested. Yazov became deeply concerned about military cohesion and insisted that his commanders hold their troops at a high state of combat readiness and prevent outside political agitators and news from the opposition from reaching the troops.[42]

But Yeltsin increased the pressure and issued a second, more specific decree to the military, KGB, and MVD. It included specific orders and named names. For example, Yeltsin sent orders to General Kalinin to withdraw his troops from Moscow's streets and to return them to their barracks and to normal military routine. This put Kalinin in an impossible position. He had two sets of orders. One set from a regime whose legitimacy was in doubt. Another set from a democratically elected leader who claimed new political authority. With respect to Yazov, Yeltsin decreed: "In connection with the involvement of the Minister of Defense D. T. Yazov in the coup d'etat, all orders and other commands issued by him from 18 August 1991 are hereby countermanded. Future orders and other commands signed by D. T. Yazov are not to be executed."[43]

Yeltsin's move would have split the armed forces into three groups. The first group would consist of those who recognized Boris Yeltsin as the legitimate, acting civilian commander in chief. The second group would be those who looked at the two sets of orders and the competing politicians and decided that it was most important for the military to remain strictly neutral and to keep from being dragged into political strife and civil war. The third group sided with Yazov and the SEC idea and demanded Yeltsin's head. This rough analysis must have been made by Yazov as well. Even those who leaned towards the SEC ideology and the dream of imposing order and progress on the Soviet Union came to realize that the SEC was an incompetent lot and that violence could spark civil war and the bloody breakup of the Soviet Union. *Elementary political logic was pushing the middle level and top military leadership towards neutrality if not outright rejection of the SEC.*

On Tuesday, Vadim Bakatin and Yevgeny Primakov, two members of the highest national security policy body of the Soviet state, the Defense Council, condemned the SEC.[44] This news helped undermine the SEC's claim to be a patriotic body acting in the national interest. In Soviet policy making circles, Primakov was known as a realist and a patriot, an authentic expert on domestic and international affairs. He *knew* that bloodshed and civil war would be far more damaging to Soviet national interest than the coup's political defeat and acted accordingly.

Although the political momentum was with Yeltsin and the anti-SEC coalition, Yazov put Achalov to work on plans to storm the White House and to arrest Boris Yeltsin. A combination of Ministry of Defense and Ministry of Internal Affairs troops were supposed to disperse the crowd and clear the path for KGB special forces, the notorious Alfa unit under Major General Karpukhin. Lebed and Gromov warned Achalov that there would be a great deal of bloodshed and resisted the plan. Eventually Achalov decided to have a look for himself and went to the area. He agreed with their assessment and shared it with Yazov. Meanwhile, about 11:00 P.M. on Tuesday night, Lebed, Grachev, and Gromov pledged to one another to refuse to obey any orders to attack. Yazov also wavered back and forth and finally called off the operation some two hours later.[45] Karpukhin confirmed that he had indeed been working with Gromov and Lebed on the coordinated plan. He was also contacted by Yeltsin's team and urged not to obey any orders to attack. Karpukhin, like Gromov and Lebed, advised his superiors against the attacks. However, after the coup he lost his command and was pushed aside by the Yeltsin team instead of being rewarded for his actions.[46]

Shaposhnikov's Motives for Rejecting the Coup

Air Force Chief Yevgeny Shaposhnikov had personal, institutional, and patriotic national interests at stake in the coup. He had only been in office for a little over a year. The conservatives in the Party mistrusted him because he had permitted too many Air Force officers to resign from the Communist Party. Of all the military services, the Air Force had the worst record, from their point of view, on this political front. The fact that he had been kept out of the SEC's inner circle was a warning that a victory by the plotters could mean his downfall. Yet, he did not want to support the new dictatorship by using the Soviet air force against democratically elected officials.

Shaposhnikov hoped for an end to dictatorship by capricious civilian incompetents. He used to think about his predecessors in Soviet Air Force history, the first nine commanders and how the Soviet dictatorship had treated them: K. V. Akashev, A. V. Sergeyev, A. A. Znamenskii, A. P. Rozengol'ts, P. I. Baranov, Ya. I. Alksnis, A. D. Loktionov, Ya. V. Smushkevich, and P. I. Rychagov. Six were executed by Stalin; one died of physical and nervous exhaustion; and two were killed in an air crash. All the political victims were crossed out of official military history until the new Military Encyclopedia of

1986 but even it remained silent about their ultimate fate as if nothing abnormal had ever taken place. After assuming the Air Force command, Shaposhnikov set up a new historical exhibit at Air Force headquarters in Moscow, his personal effort to present the facts.[47] He had a definite sense of history, one that condemned a political system that abused its patriotic military professionals. Could he make a difference?

On Monday morning Shaposhnikov mechanically obeyed Yazov's orders and called all his military district commanders to instruct them personally. They were to remain on alert but under no circumstances were they to accept orders from anyone but him. In other words, they were to be ready to go into action but should take no action without his orders. An Interfaks news agency reporter called Shaposhnikov and asked him to define the Air Force's position on the SEC. Shaposhnikov said that it wasn't worth a single drop of blood but that the reporter shouldn't cite him directly. Thereafter, the media began reporting that the Air Force was not supporting the coup. The next day Leningrad mayor Anatoly Sobchak announced it as fact even though he had not spoken with Shaposhnikov.

Shaposhnikov's first contact with the Yeltsin team came on Monday morning. Yeltsin sent Lt. Col. V. A. Burkov to talk things over with Shaposhnikov at his office in Soviet Air Force headquarters in Moscow. Burkov informed him that Yeltsin would appeal to the people and the armed forces to reject the SEC. Where did Shaposhnikov stand? Shaposhnikov told Burkov that he did not support the coup, that he wasn't alone among the military commanders, and he urged Yeltsin to try to reach as many as possible in order to prevent bloodshed. Burkov and Shaposhnikov also identified ways to keep in touch during the coup even if conditions worsened.[48]

Burkov's visit convinced Shaposhnikov that he could make a difference by delaying if not completely blocking air support for the coup. He even called Achalov and dared to tell him that he insisted upon direct confirmation from Yazov of any orders to transport troops to Moscow. He cut that conversation short as soon as one of his subordinates arrived with a message from Grachev. Achalov was already pressing Grachev to fly more troops into Moscow as soon as possible. Shaposhnikov telephoned Grachev and told him that the "weather" prevented him from giving the planes clearance for take-off. The two were signaling their resistance to the coup without openly saying so because they assumed their lines were bugged.

Burkov returned with another message from Yeltsin. This time Shaposhnikov stated that the Air Force would not move against the people and that he would try to convince the commanders of the other military services to take a similar position. By the next day, Tuesday afternoon, the media began reporting Shaposhnikov's defection from the SEC. Phones starting ringing and some threats were made. Then, the inevitable happened. Minister of Defense Yazov called at 15:00 and summoned Shaposhnikov to his office.

Before leaving for what could have been arrest and imprisonment, Shaposhnikov told his deputies to hold firm, that planes don't fly in reverse, and to uphold Air Force honor. Yazov had a brief private word with Shaposhnikov, a chance to say what he really felt and he used it: "Comrade Minister of Defense, this thing has to be ended." "How?" "Throw out the SEC. Declare it illegal."[49]

Yazov seem to agree but did not say so. However, he protected Shaposhnikov that afternoon from probing questions when Achalov and Chief of Staff Moiseyev joined the meeting. Yazov asked Shaposhnikov to confirm that the Air Force was cohesive and under reliable control, that the stories about its defection from the SEC weren't true. After Shaposhnikov stated as much, Yazov ordered him back to Air Force headquarters thereby preventing Achalov from asking pointed, incriminating questions. Yazov also told him to keep all aircraft under strict control and to make certain that none left any bases without his specific authorization.[50]

Back at Air Force headquarters on Bolshaya Pirogovka No. 23, Shaposhnikov telephoned all his commanders around the Soviet Union to explain what had happened and what he was doing. He gave each a little talk about the country and what it now most needed and issued orders that canceled the special alert and returned the Air Force to normal operations. The majority supported him fully while some grumbled that the country should have been taken under firm control a long time ago. Yet, even these believed it was too late for any SEC to be effective. Shaposhnikov was elated and got in touch with Lt. Col. Burkov again.

Shaposhnikov urged him to exercise maximum restraint and to make certain that Yeltsin's supporters prevented any rash actions that the SEC might seize upon as an excuse to attack. Burkov agreed. Shaposhnikov went home for a brief rest. When he returned to the office, Burkov was on the telephone. The White House expected to be attacked in the early morning hours. Word had reached it that KGB commandos were preparing the assault. Shaposhnikov called Achalov but couldn't get through. Next he tried Grachev who confirmed that plans were being made but that no attack orders had been issued. Grachev said that his paratroopers had strong nerves and that he would get rid of anyone who tried to force him to join any attack. Grachev told Shaposhnikov that he had been talking with Boris Gromov, commander of the MVD's domestic armed forces and that Gromov likewise would refuse to support any attack on Yeltsin.

What if the SEC sent envoys with special attack orders to the units and were prepared to arrest any officer who refused to obey? How could the process be stopped? Grachev and Shaposhnikov came up with the idea of using the Air Force to threaten the SEC. "You have 15 minutes to cancel the orders; otherwise, planes will arrive and bombs could fall."[51] But that plan couldn't work unless Shaposhnikov had made secret arrangements with absolutely trustworthy commanders and pilots.

The White House also wanted more credible plans. Col. Aleksandr Tsalko, another Afghan war veteran on Yeltsin's team, called and Shaposhnikov invited him over. Shaposhnikov drew up special orders and planned to dispatch Tsalko with them to Moscow Military District Air Force Commander General N. T. Antoshkin. If the SEC attacked the White House, Antoshkin was to send jets at the Kremlin as a warning. Yeltsin's team expected to be attacked. They set up a special command bunker in the basement of the White House and took cover there. They made tentative plans to flee in different directions and had made sensitive arrangements with the embassy of the United States of America. But Minister of Defense Yazov made the critical decision to stop the clock. The same Yazov who made the coup possible now undermined it.

The Defenders of the White House

Russian progressives, a diverse assortment of the flower of the cultural, and political elite, had gathered at the White House and offered themselves up as political hostages, people such as the poet Yevgeny Yevtushenko, the cellist Mstislav Rostropovich, and the widow of Andrei Sakharov, Yelena Bonner. Although the crowds outside had dwindled and Rutskoi had even urged them to pull back from the building for security reasons, the fact that people famous throughout the world had stayed on and made themselves hostages weighed heavily upon Yazov who would be held accountable for their deaths.

Yeltsin did have more than poems and leaflets at his disposal. He had enough people under arms to force a fight. According to General Kobets, there were around 1,000 people under arms in the White House: "There were approximately 150 professional officers in the building, about 300 special-purpose MVD troops or OMON under Viktor Barannikov, and about 300 armed deputies. There were another 300 or so reliable trusted men—recent Afghan veterans, the President's body-guards and a few others."[52] The combination of internationally known cultural and political leaders and the White House fighters was a major political-military stumbling block for the SEC. Nevertheless, Yazov kept increasing the pressure on the White House until the first deaths took place at 12:30 A.M. The accidental killings resulted when youths tried to stop a convoy that was advancing towards central Moscow and the White House. The three men killed were Dmitry Komar, Ilya Krichevsky, and Vladimir Usov.[53] This news caused Yazov to act to prevent further bloodshed.

Yazov's Decides against Force

At about 1:30 a.m. on 21 August 1991, Minister of Defense Dmitry Yazov ordered Achalov to halt preparations for the decisive assault on the Russian Parliament.[54] He sent Achalov to inform the SEC leadership group. They argued with Achalov for some two hours, accused the military of betrayal and cowardice, and tried to get him to agree to make Yazov change his mind. But they failed. The military was not going to kill for the SEC. The attack was to have begun at 3:21 A.M. By 4:00 A.M., the White House began to believe that it had really been suspended. Tsalko called Shaposhnikov again to tell him the good news and to let him hear the elated crowd outside the White House chanting its Russia victory slogans.

About 8:00 A.M. Yazov's first deputy minister of defense, Army General Kochetov called Shaposhnikov to a 9:00 meeting of the military collegium at the Ministry of Defense. Achalov and Varennikov met with Yazov in advance but did not stay for the military leadership meeting. Yazov dispatched them to the SEC's Kremlin headquarters as his personal representatives.

Earlier that morning Baklanov, Kryuchkov, Shenin, Prokofiev, and, Tizyakov left the Kremlin and came to see Yazov for face to face talks. They knew that they were lost without the military and they were desperate to get him to change his mind. According to Lt. General Leonid Ivashov's account of the meeting, Yury Prokofiev, the head of the Moscow Communist Party organization became melodramatic and asked for a pistol so that he could shoot himself for having betrayed the Muscovite workers who were ready to support the SEC. But the melodramatic ploys failed and the civilians left without changing Yazov's opinion. He said he would give them his final word after the military collegium met.[55] The soldiers would decide on their own rather than merely be used as pawns by civilian politicians.

At 9:00 A.M. he called the military collegium to order. According to Ministry of Defense tradition, the minister opens the meetings and sets the tone and the theme. Next, those in attendance respond according to rank. This meant that Mikhail Moiseyev, chief of the General Staff and First Deputy Minister Kochetov expected to speak before the service commanders such as Shaposhnikov. Shaposhnikov asked to go first. Moiseyev ignored him and started a rather banal response. Shaposhnikov cut him off. Then Kochetov jumped in and argued that the military should get through to Gorbachev and demonstrate its support immediately. Instead of reacting to Kochetov's position, Yazov asked Shaposhnikov to speak. He repeated the same advice he had given Yazov the day before. Break with the SEC, declare it illegal, throw it out of office.[56] Admiral Chernavin, commander of Soviet Naval Forces and Col. General Maksimov, commander of Soviet Strategic Rocket Forces supported Shaposhnikov.[57]

Yazov understood that it was in the best interests of the military and the country to prevent a bloody conflict over power and accepted the group's recommendation that the troops and tanks be withdrawn from Moscow and Leningrad and that the general military alert be canceled. But he refused to arrest the SEC and decided that he had to stick with it to the end: "But I will not quit the SEC. That is my cross. I will carry it to the end."[58] Yazov called Kryuchkov and said: "I'm not playing this game anymore."[59]

Shaposhnikov urged Yazov to communicate his decision to the Russian Parliament immediately in order to reduce tensions and to help repair the military's image. The Russian Parliament was assembling in the White House which was still surrounded by a motley ring of tanks, barricades, Yeltsin supporters, undercover agents, and reporters. Yazov's official message emphasized that the military collegium had acted to reaffirm the armed forces' loyalty to its constitutional duty and its people. As soon as Shaposhnikov returned to his office, he called the office of Yeltsin's vice president, Col. Aleksander Rutskoi, and instructed Rutskoi's secretary to get the news to the Yeltsin team immediately.

The SEC's top leaders met and decided to fly to Foros for a face-to-face meeting with Gorbachev, an effort to repair the political damage they had done to themselves and to the Union's political institutions. Minister of Defense Yazov and KGB Chairman Kryuchkov were joined by Lukyanov, the speaker of the Union's parliament, and Ivashko, the second in command of the Union's Communist Party organization. Yazov and Kryuchkov still had Gorbachev's official presidential airliner at their disposal and they took off from Moscow at 2:00 P.M. That plane had a special crew and equipment and served as a flying Kremlin for the top leadership. The SEC still had some political life left in it and was hoping to exploit Gorbachev's distrust of Yeltsin. Gorbachev, after all, had told them on Sunday that he was willing to discuss the State of Emergency proposal with the Union's parliament and Lukyanov had already summoned the parliament for a special session scheduled for Monday, 26 August 1991.

Yeltsin was the president of Russia. Gorbachev was the president of the entire Soviet Union. Therefore, Gorbachev's political future was tied to the Union political institutions. Unless Gorbachev could salvage them from the republican onslaught, he would be humiliated and defeated by Yeltsin. Therefore, Gorbachev, Yazov, Kryuchkov, Ivashko, and Lukyanov were in the same, sinking Union political boat. They had a common interest in ending their mutiny and reaching a working agreement against Yeltsin. According to Gorbachev, the SEC tried to get Yeltsin to join them for the trip to Foros but Yeltsin refused and they left without him.[60] Yeltsin had the political momentum and he refused to surrender it to the Unionists.

The Race to Get to Gorbachev First

Yeltsin called Shaposhnikov and urged him to find some way either to prevent or to delay the SEC's arrival at Foros. Yeltsin considered attempting his own flight to Gorbachev but was dissuaded. He would have made a tempting target for the SEC. Therefore, Yeltsin dispatched Rutskoi, Bakatin, and Silayev to bring Gorbachev back to Moscow. Their plane took off after the SEC's departed. Shaposhnikov said it would be nearly impossible to interfere with the official presidential plane carrying the Soviet Union's top military, political, and Communist Party leadership unless either Gorbachev or the senior figure manning the Soviet Union's military headquarters in Moscow during Yazov's absence, Chief of General Staff Moiseyev, issued such orders to the flight crew. Yeltsin asked and Shaposhnikov tried but Moiseyev refused to cooperate and indicated that the people on board were still the Soviet Union's leaders. Moiseyev was not prepared to betray his Minister of Defense. When the SEC team landed at Bilbek, the airport nearest Foros, it was 4:08 P.M. and the field was heavily guarded, completely under the SEC's military control. However, by the time Yeltsin's team landed at 6:45, more than three hours later, a key change had taken place. The SEC had restored Gorbachev's external communications and Gorbachev began to reassert himself as commander in chief. The siege had been lifted.

When Yazov, Kryuchkov, et al. arrived at Gorbachev's villa, instead of barging in on him, they treated him with dignity, obeyed his instructions, and sat waiting in his guest house for hours. Gorbachev refused to allow them to enter his quarters or to talk with them until they restored his external communications. He had become more confident after listening to BBC World Service reports on the short-wave radio. He knew that a group from the Yeltsin team was flying to Foros and he decided to wait for them. Yazov and Kryuchkov obeyed Gorbachev's commands and restored his phones. As soon as his lines had been reconnected, Gorbachev began to function as president again. He called Yeltsin and a host of Soviet and international leaders.

Gorbachev and Yeltsin agreed that there must be no reconciliation with the SEC. They talked about the political situation in the country and Yeltsin insisted that Gorbachev give his presidential approval for the various actions that Yeltsin took during his absence. Gorbachev accepted that proposal without having had a chance to examine the content of Yeltsin's decrees. Yeltsin told Gorbachev that he was sending Col. Rutskoi, Yevgeny Primakov, and Ivan Silayev, and a contingent of thirty-six loyal, armed officers to protect Gorbachev and to take appropriate actions against the SEC members. Gorbachev used his newly restored telephones to order Chief of Staff Moiseyev to permit Rutskoi's plane to land at the Bilbek airfield.[61] He also appointed Moiseyev acting minister of defense and informed him that Yazov was going to be arrested. Gorbachev called the commander of the Kremlin's security forces and ordered him to accept orders from no one but himself.[62]

Rutskoi's special forces escorted Gorbachev back to Moscow on their plane, not the presidential plane. The SEC group was flown to Moscow on the presidential plane and was placed under arrest immediately upon arrival. Rutskoi put Kryuchkov on the same plane used to fly Gorbachev and his family back to Moscow but as a prisoner and a hostage. When Yazov arrived in Moscow about 2:30 A.M., the deputy commander of the KGB's Ninth Directorate met him and escorted him to a room where the procurator general of the *Russian*

Federation placed him under arrest. A similar fate awaited Kryuchkov. There would be no 10:00 A.M. meetings for them with the president. At another part of the airport, a physically and emotionally exhausted Gorbachev faced the press and gave the impression that he believed that he could take up where he had left off before the coup as leader of the Soviet Union.

Arrested in the Name of Russia

Why did Russian Federation rather than Union legal personnel arrest Yazov and Kryuchkov? Because the Union's procurator general, Nikolai Trubin, refused to order their arrest, a step that forced Yeltsin's hand. Yeltsin could not permit Yazov and Kryuchkov to return to their power bases in Moscow as free political actors. Yeltsin used his own, *loyal* legal, security, and military personnel to make the arrests.

The Russian Federation had a minister of internal affairs, Barannikov. He recruited cadets from the MVD's central academies on Wednesday, dressed them in special protective uniforms, and armed them. They took up positions at the Vnukovo Airport in advance of Gorbachev's arrival. The Russian Federation had a minister of state security, Ivanenko. He recruited a special team and pre-positioned it at Vnukovo's special reception rooms in anticipation of the arrests of Yazov, Kryuchkov, and others. The regular Union KGB forces from the Ninth Directorate that always met and guarded the presidential party were also at Vnukovo. But they did not interfere. Barannikov and Ivanenko planned and executed the arrests well and there was no opportunity for Yazov or Kryuchkov to break away or to call for help. The two submitted to arrest by Russia's procurator general, Valentin Stepankov.[63]

By giving the orders, and completing the arrests in the early morning hours of 22 August 1991, Yeltsin demonstrated that he and Russia had the attributes of state power. Russia was beginning to function as a viable state. Russia arrested the Union ministers of defense and state security, a step that clearly demonstrated that the Union state was in decline.

Russia had its own Ministries of Internal Affairs and State Security, two of the three sides of the state-coercion triangle. What was missing? A Russian Ministry of Defense. On the evening of 21 August 1991 while the Gorbachev rescue was still underway, Yeltsin signed special orders appointing Pavel Grachev as Russia's first Minister of Defense and sent Yury Skokov to Grachev with the proposal and the official papers. However, Grachev declined the appointment.[64] Yeltsin decided to hold the position vacant and to refrain from proclaiming the establishment of a Russian Ministry of Defense and Russian Armed Forces. The Soviet military wanted Yeltsin to work for the preservation of its unitary, extraterritorial organizational structure. The Soviet military was against military fragmentation into potentially hostile armed national armed forces. Yeltsin accepted this military corporate policy line as his preferred policy goal but he was convinced that Russia had to be prepared to take over the Soviet Ministry of Defense and to convert it into a Russian state institution if it turned out to be impossible to rebuild the Union state into a viable political organism.

Conclusion

The military abandoned the SEC and switched to Boris Yeltsin for three main reasons. First, Yeltsin offered the military leadership a reasonable way out and did not back the generals into a corner. In any power transition, the winning side must address the military's personal and institutional requirements. Second, the coup's leadership core was ineffective. It was a loose committee rather than a well-organized command under a strong, intelligent leader. Third, the military realized that it was heading for a bloody confrontation with Russia's most respected cultural and political figures and was seeking a way out. If the military continued with the coup, it faced certain humiliation, degradation, and possible dismemberment through civil war. If it withdrew and built its relationships with Boris Yeltsin, it had a better chance to preserve its dignity and to serve the national interest by preventing civil war.

We can argue that history was on Yeltsin's side because he was moving with the deeper trends, the societal pressure for democratization, and that the military was aware of such historical forces and hoped to work with them rather than against them. However, our study of the specific moves which Yeltsin made on the political chess board demonstrates that political talent and boldness determined the confrontation's outcome in August 1991. Yeltsin's team seized the momentum and took control of the political situation by defining the options available to the military. The Yeltsin team made the right political plays faster than the SEC and won the game.

The Soviet state and the one-party dictatorship were in deep political trouble but they probably could have held on longer had it not been for Yeltsin and his team. During the August events he handled the military skillfully and addressed its immediate personal and institutional concerns successfully. He made Gorbachev the political scapegoat for all the military's discontent. He pledged to work to preserve the military's cohesion and unity. He issued official statements that made it legal for the military to support him. He invited a younger generation of military leaders onto his political bandwagon while indicating that he would permit the seniors to retire quietly. The Soviet legacy included military participation in the major turning points in twentieth-century Russia's political history. Yeltsin's political strategy offered the military a positive role, won its support, and achieved victory in the big political competition.

The modernization paradigm explains why the Soviet political system was under stress and indicates the general direction that political change needed to take in order to move towards a better balance between political institutions and the requirements of modern industrial society. The literature also suggests that authoritarian responses to political instability are normal especially in societies that have authoritarian political cultures. What is abnormal is the outcome that Yeltsin achieved, a democratic breakthrough that had military support. Yet, a democratic breakthrough is a beginning not an end. Over the coming months and years, the Yeltsin team struggled with the complex tasks of building a viable, democratic state and a new military system to support it.

Notes

1. Boris Yeltsin, *The Struggle for Russia* (New York: Times Books/Random House, 1994), p.58. Hereafter: Yeltsin, *Struggle*.
2. See Lt. General Leonid Ivashov's account of Yazov's participation in the coup, "Marshal Yazov: Avgust 1991-go," *Krasnaya zvezda*, 21, 22, and 25 August 1992.
3. See Vyacheslav Lukashevich, "Tsiplyat po oseni schitayut" (Counting the fall chicks), *Krasnaya zvezda*, 17 August 1991.
4. Yeltsin, *Struggle*, p. 49.
5. Information was drawn from the transcript of the hearings of the Russian Federation's Commission on the Causes and Circumstances of the State Coup; "GKPCh: Armiya privlekalas', no ne uchastvovala," *Armiya*, nos. 7–8, 1992. Hereafter: *Hearings*.
6. Ivashov, "Marshal Yazov."
7. See Shaposhnikov's *Vybor: Zapiski glavkomanduyushchego* (Moscow: Nezavisimoe Izdatel'stvo), pp. 15–17.
8. *Hearings*, p. 26.
9. See Urazhtsev's complaint that there was a cover-up underway to protect military officers from prosecution for illegal actions during the coup. *Hearings*, p. 30.
10. Ivashov, "Marshal Yazov."
11. The main investigators into the coup support this point of view. See Valentin Stepankov and Yevgeny Lisev, *Kremlevskii zagovor* (The Kremlin conspiracy) (Moscow: Ogonyok), pp. 244 ff.
12. See Ivashov, "Marshal Yazov."
13. Reported by Yan Kasimov, a member of the presidential guards, in "Holiday making in Crimea: The President's Last Summer," *Moscow News*, p. 10, no. 34, 1992.
14. See pp. 18–19, in Mikhail Gorbachev's *The August Coup: The Truth and the Lessons* (New York: Harper Collins, 1991).
15. *Ibid.*, p. 22.
16. *Ibid.*, p. 23. In his prison notes, Varennikov denies Gorbachev's charges and insists that he strongly pressed Gorbachev to disappear or to become conveniently ill for a while. See page 266 in Stepankov and Lisev, *Kremlevskii zagovor*.
17. *Ibid.*
18. Ivashev, "Marshal Yazov," 22 August 1992.
19. See Stepankov and Lisev, *Kremlevskii zagovor*, pp. 162–67.
20. Ivashev, "Marshal Yazov."
21. *Hearings*, p. 25.
22. See pp. 140–41, Ruslan Khasbulatov, *The Struggle for Russia* (London: Routledge, 1993). Hereafter: Khasbulatov, *Struggle*.

23. See Yeltsin, *Struggle*, p. 53.
24. See D. Belovetskii and S. Boguslavskii's interview with Major General Karpukhin, "Tot, kto ne stal palachom" (He didn't become the executioner), *Rossiya, special edition* of 24 August 1991.
25. Anatoly Sobchak, *For a New Russia* (New York: The Free Press, 1992), p. 180.
26. Cited by Sobchak in *Ibid.*, p. 181.
27. See pages 18–19 in Shaposhnikov, *Vybor*.
28. Order No. 1 (*"Postanovlenie* No. 1") was printed in the official press on Tuesday, 20 August 1991.
29. See Shaposhnikov, *Vybor*, pp. 32–35.
30. See pp. 77 ff. in Yeltsin, *Struggle*.
31. P. 147, Khasbulatov, *Struggle*.
32. See *Armiya*, no. 24, 1991, p. 16.
33. See James H. Billington, *Russia Transformed: Breakthrough to Hope* (New York: Macmillan, 1992), pp. 39–40.
34. From Presidential Decree No. 63, issued at 22:39 on 19 August 1991. Text reproduced in Khasbulatov, *Struggle*, p. 148.
35. See Yeltsin, *Struggle*, pp. 86–87.
36. *Ibid.*, p. 87.
37. See *Ibid.*, pp. 86–87. Grachev and Lebed coordinated this highly important political move.
38. Events and times are found in E. Rashivalova and N. Sergin, eds., *Putsch: Khronika trevozhnykh dnei* (Moscow: Progress, 1991).
39. President B. Yeltsin, "UKAZ: Prezidenta Rossiiskoi Sovetskoi Federativnoi Sotsialisticheskoi Respubliki, 19 avgusta 1991 goda, Moskva, Kreml." Personal copy.
40. Cited by Captain 3rd Class, Mikhail Nenashev in "Tri dnya u belogo doma" (Three days at the White House), *Armiya*, no. 24, 1991, p. 18.
41. Commander of the elite paratroopers, Col. General Pavel Grachev as cited by A. Oliinik, "Desantniki protiv naroda ne poshli," *Krasnaya zvezda*, 31 August 1991.
42. Ivashev, "Marshall Yazov," 22 August 1992.
43. Special Decree No. 64's text is reproduced in Khasbulatov, *Struggle*, pp. 156–157.
44. See Yeltsin, *Struggle*, p. 88. Primakov had been through several difficult policy decisions in the Gorbachev administration including the decision to use the military to restore Soviet power in Azerbaijan in January 1990, the most severe use of military power against civilians of the entire Gorbachev era. That decision backfired and drove a wedge between the Azeri people and Moscow.
45. *Hearings*, pp. 24–25.
46. See D. Belovetskii and S. Boguslavskii, "Tot, kto ne stal palachom."
47. See pp. 20–22 in Shaposhnikov, *Vybor.*
48. *Ibid.* pp. 23–24.
49. *Ibid.*, p. 35.
50. Ivashov, "Marshal Yazov," 25 August 1992.
51. Shaposhnikov, *Vybor*, p. 40.
52. Cited by Khasbulatov, *Struggle*, p. 191.
53. Yeltsin, *Struggle,* p. 99.
54. Yeltsin, *Struggle,* p. 80; Stepankov and Lisev, *Kremlevskii zagovor,* pp. 180–197.
55. Ivashov, "Marshal Yazov," 25 August 1992.
56. Shaposhnikov, *Vybor*, p. 45.
57. Ivashov, "Marshal Yazov."

58. Shaposhnikov, *Vybor,* p. 46.
59. Ivashov, "Marshal Yazov."
60. See Gorbachev, *The August Coup,* p. 36.
61. See Stepankov and Lisev, *Kremlevskii zagovor*, pp. 205–8.
62. See Gorbachev's press conference of 22 August 1991 as carried in *Pravda,* 23 August 1991.
63. See Stepankov and Lisev, *Kremlevskii zagovor*, pp. 213–29.
64. See Stepankov and Lisev, *Kremlevskii zagovor*, p. 179.

5

The Dual Presidency

The dual presidency ran from August to December 1991. It began during the August coup when Yeltsin began wielding the key powers that belonged to Gorbachev. After the coup, Yeltsin refused to return them and exercised veto power over important Union-level civilian and military appointments. In effect, the Soviet Armed Forces had two civilian supreme commanders, Boris Yeltsin and Mikhail Gorbachev. Yeltsin's powers at the head of Russian state were increasing and Gorbachev's at the head of the Soviet Union were declining. The dual presidency endured until the Union state was abolished in December 1991, an act that eliminated Gorbachev's position.

The dual presidency was a transitional period in civil-military relations. The power to control the military moved from Gorbachev to Yeltsin. However, all that happened without any solid foundation in any particular constitution. The shift was based upon a combination of formal and informal understandings between Gorbachev, Yeltsin, and the Ministry of Defense leadership. As president of Russia, Boris Yeltsin had no more constitutional right to control the Soviet Armed Forces than the president of Armenia or any other Soviet republic. According to the Soviet Constitution the military were under the Soviet state and their legal supreme commander was Mikhail Gorbachev. Nevertheless, Yeltsin asserted himself and the military accepted his decisions. Strictly speaking, Gorbachev remained the legal supreme commander until December 1991. In practice, Yeltsin was making the important decisions. These formative months left a mixed legacy. Some reforms moved civil-military relations closer to standard democratic models. Others reaffirmed Russo-Soviet traditions.

Yeltsin rebuilt the Soviet high command with military officers acceptable to his team. Consequently, the new appointees and those who survived the house cleaning owed their careers and their loyalty to him. He also accelerated military departization. Yeltsin ended the "Red" political practices that began under Kerensky and Trotsky in 1917 and 1918. He dismantled the MPA and abolished the Communist organization inside the armed forces and insisted that the Ministry of Defense adopt regulations prohibiting any political organization from operating within the armed forces.

But the coup experience did not convince military officers that they were outside of politics. If anything, it confirmed that politics have a profound affect upon personal, institutional, and national security interests. Yeltsin's actions made it clear that those officers who supported him and who stayed loyal to him would be rewarded with promotions. Almost 400 military officers were retired or demoted in the post-coup purge. Yeltsin controlled that process and did not share it with the legislative branch of government. Thus, although he moved civil-military relations closer to the Western model by abolishing the MPA and banning overt partisan political activity in the military, he preserved the backbone of the Russo-Soviet tradition—the military's subordination to the chief executive. Tsars, general secretaries, and presidents jealously guarded the power to appoint and dismiss armed forces officers. Yeltsin clearly intended to command the armed forces without interference from any Congress.

This chapter describes Yeltsin's drive for power and demonstrates how he blended progressive reforms with the Russo-Soviet tradition of strongman rule. It begins with Yeltsin's clever use of the coup to destroy Gorbachev's power and ends with a discussion of Yeltsin's refusal to share power over military personnel decisions with any elective bodies.

Yeltsin's Putsch within the Coup

Although Yeltsin and Gorbachev were allies against the SEC, Yeltsin used the coup to tip the balance of power in his favor. As soon as the coup ended, Yeltsin targeted Gorbachev. Yeltsin set conditions upon Gorbachev's return to the capital. Gorbachev agreed to legitimize the actions that Yeltsin had taken in order to keep the country going during the coup. However, Gorbachev did not know the full extent of Yeltsin's grab for power until he saw the stack of decrees that Yeltsin placed before him on his first working day after the coup, 22 August 1991. During the coup, Yeltsin was preparing for the post-coup battles for power between Gorbachev and himself and between the Union state and the Russian state. Yeltsin tore the guts out of Gorbachev's political machine and the Union state's three main sources of power: the economy, the armed forces, and the administrative elite represented by the Communist Party.

Yeltsin made two key moves on Tuesday, 20 August 1991 and he never retreated from them. While the coup was still in progress and Gorbachev was under house arrest at Foros, Yeltsin issued two decrees which destroyed the Soviet state's viability. Henceforth the Soviet state could not operate without the Russian state's consent.

On 20 August 1991, Yeltsin issued Decree No. 66, "On the Economic Sovereignty of Russia." It gutted the Union government by transferring all the Union's economic assets on the territory of the Russian Federation from Union to Russian Federation control. Further, it set a date certain for the end of

Union state power over the Russian Federation's economic life, 1 January 1992. The Russian Council of Ministers moved swiftly to take control over foreign trade, gold and currency reserves, taxation, mineral rights, and other key sources of revenue without which the Union state's treasury would quickly empty.[1] Without money in the treasury, Gorbachev would have to beg Yeltsin and the other republics for support. That was precisely the position Yeltsin wanted him in. By forcing Gorbachev to accept Decree No. 66, Yeltsin destroyed the Union state's economic feeder bands, its flow of taxes and hard currency revenues from foreign sales.

Yeltsin used this new financial power to increase his influence over Soviet defense affairs. Yeltsin addressed this problem in Decree no. 64 on 20 August 1991: "The Council of Ministers of the RSFSR will take on the payment both monetary and in kind, of the Soviet Armed Forces stationed in the RSFSR." That decree also announced that Russia would form some armed forces of its own: "The Vice President of the RSFSR, A. V. Rutskoi, will draw up proposals for the creation of a national guard for the RSFSR."[2] This indicates that Yeltsin intended to control Soviet military activity on the territory of the Russian Federation after the coup by holding the purse strings. He, not Gorbachev would be making the decisions about what was and wasn't financed in Russia.

The third blow to Gorbachev and the Soviet state came on Thursday, 22 August 1991, when Boris Yeltsin outlawed the Communist Party and seized all its assets in Russia. Since Gorbachev was still relying upon the Communist Party's administrative departments housed in the Central Committee complex on Staraya Ploshchad for key staff support, Yeltsin's decree stripped him of his most important asset. Over the coming year Yeltsin converted the Central Committee into his own staff, the so-called presidential administration. Without money or staff, the Gorbachev presidency withered away.

The Hypothesis: A Yeltsin Deal with the Military

Now that Yeltsin had backed the military into a corner, he had to help them out of it gracefully. The key deal had to have been a promise to limit political witch hunts. On 19 August 1991, his first decrees on military complicity in the coup included threats of criminal prosecution for anyone who obeyed orders from the SEC. His final, long decree, no. 64 of 20 August 1991, does not mention criminal prosecution. It says: "The Vice President of the USSR, the Minister of Defense, the First Deputy Chairman of the Ministry of Defense and other members of the Ministry of Defense have embarked on an unlawful path of forcible change of the Constitution and in so doing have acted outside the law, and thus cannot carry out the duty of running the Armed Forces of the USSR or of the defense of the territorial integrity and sovereignty of the Republics of the USSR as a whole."[3] This is a very mild statement of the facts and contains no threats. Because of what they did, they cannot continue in their positions is what it meant to signal.

What about Yeltsin's pledge to be lenient and, perhaps, to help protect the military from zealous, hostile scrutiny into military complicity in the events? It would have been a wise political move and it is logical to hypothesize that such a pledge was made on 20 or 21 August and included all but the coup's core leadership. Subsequent events support this hypothesis. Gorbachev adopted a similar position and was if anything more inclined than Yeltsin to leave most of the Union's top civilian and military leaders in office in spite of their cooperation with the coup. Gorbachev said that only a limited purge of the most active coup leaders would be appropriate: "One of the main causes for the conspiracy's failure is that those who seized power were unable to use the army against the people. The army generally stayed above it. Therefore, under these circumstances only those who directly prepared the plot and participated in it will be held accountable."[4] Only three senior military leaders were to be arrested: Minister of Defense Dmitry Yazov, Army General Valentin Varennikov, and First Deputy Minister of Defense Vladislav Achalov. They never faced a court-martial and all three were eventually released as were all the civilian SEC leaders in subsequent amnesties which Yeltsin did not try to prevent and did not protest.

There was no general panic in the armed forces when the SEC fell; however, Marshal Akhromeyev, a senior military leader who joined the coup in order to fight for the preservation of the Union and to maintain the unity of the Soviet armed forces, and Boris Pugo, the head of the MVD, killed themselves in desperation. The fact that Yeltsin had backed down from his earlier emphasis on criminal prosecution and Gorbachev was taking a conciliatory position helped keep the military relatively calm as Gorbachev and Yeltsin jockeyed for power.

Chief of General Staff Moiseyev convened the military collegium early on Thursday 22 August 1991 because Gorbachev had instructed him to explain what had happened and to recommend actions later that morning. Moiseyev took the position that the military as an institution should not be held accountable for the coup which was imposed by a small group of conspirators, most of whom were civilians, top officials in the government. He argued that it had not been a military coup because the military did not overthrow anything or use armed force against the people. The entire military leadership should not be blamed for the actions of a few. Since Minister of Defense Yazov joined the coup without first discussing the decision at a military leadership collegium, he was responsible not the military collegium. Officers obeyed him because the law required them to do so. But, in their first official post-coup meeting, they condemned it, denied any culpability, and reaffirmed their obedience to their military oaths, the law, and the Constitution. That was the military high command's line on the coup.[5] The KGB and MVD leadership took similar actions.[6]

Yeltsin's Dominant Role in Military Appointments

The post-coup, Soviet military needed a new Minister of Defense to replace Marshal Dmitry Yazov, who had been arrested and charged with acts of treason by the Russian Federation. (Yeltsin did not entrust the arrest and prosecution of the coup leaders to the Union State's legal institutions. Although they had violated the Union Constitution and were Union officials, they were Yeltsin's political prisoners not Gorbachev's.) Gorbachev did not immediately understand that Yeltsin held veto power over key appoints. On 21 August 1991, a soon as his external communications lines at Foros had been reconnected, Gorbachev began acting as if he were still the president of the Soviet Union. He tried to reassert his personal control over the three power ministries: the Ministry of Defense, the KGB, and the MVD. Gorbachev phoned in orders to replace Yazov with Chief of General Staff Moiseyev. He replaced KGB Chairman Kryuchkov with Leonid Sherbashin; he put V.P. Trushin in Boris Pugo's place at the head of the MVD.

Moiseyev, Sherbashin, and Trushin were second in command in the three power ministries. During the coup they carried out the orders of their immediate bosses, Yazov, Kryuchkov, and Pugo. Why did Gorbachev appoint them instead of taking time to find new people who actively resisted the coup? I believe Gorbachev was in a hurry to fill those positions for two main reasons. First, he acted out of a sense of responsibility for law and order in the country and believed that it was important to keep the three power ministries functioning smoothly. Second, he acted out of personal political interests and rushed to fill the positions before Yeltsin and his rivals could get into the decision-making process.

Yeltsin complained that Gorbachev was breaking the understandings they had reached about key appointments during their talks over the telephone on Wednesday evening as the coup collapsed and Gorbachev waited for Rutskoi and the safe plane back to Moscow: "Despite my urging, Gorbachev made the first personnel appointments on his own...after the news agencies had run the reports of these appointments, I called Gorbachev at night and said: 'Mikhail Sergeyevich, what are you doing?'"[7]

On Thursday 22 August 1991, Gorbachev faced a day of political humiliations that confirmed his new, much reduced political status. He was the figurehead president on a sinking ship of state. Military affairs were too important for a figurehead president such as Gorbachev to lead on his own. Yeltsin remembers it this way: "In his office the next morning, I first demanded that he dismiss Moiseyev immediately. He put up a fight but finally conceded that he had made a mistake. He said, 'I'll think of how I can correct it.' I said: 'No, I won't leave until you do it in my presence. Have Moiseyev come here right away and send him into retirement.'"[8]

While they were debating his fate, Moiseyev's staff was systematically destroying the coup's documentary record, the orders and communications issued and received. This material included choice items such as messages from Army General Varennikov reading, "Procrastination means death. We have agreed that Yeltsin is to be arrested immediately."[9] But someone on Moiseyev's staff sent E-mail to friends outside the Ministry of Defense who immediately contacted Yeltsin's staff with this disturbing news including the name of the lead officer involved and his telephone number. They got that information to Yeltsin while he was arguing with Gorbachev about Moiseyev's future. Yeltsin stopped the meeting, insisted that Gorbachev make the call, confirm the report, and order the work halted.[10] This sealed Moiseyev's fate. He would also be sent into early retirement.

Gorbachev and Yeltsin ended their meeting without reaching conclusion on the key military appointments. They agreed to thrash them out with the State Council, the new ruling oligarchy. This body was meeting and making key decisions even though it had no formal constitutional status. The State Council consisted of the presidents of the nine republics who had been working with Gorbachev since April on a major redistribution of power between the Union state and the republics: Russia, Ukraine, Belarussia, Azerbaijan, Kazakhstan, Kyrgyzstan, Tajikistan, Turkmenistan, and Uzbekistan. The first post-coup, State Council meeting began at 10:00 A.M. on Friday, 23 August 1991. The State Council was made legal on 2 September 1991, some two weeks later!

Around noon, Moiseyev called Shaposhnikov and informed him that Gorbachev wanted to see him immediately. Shaposhnikov broke off a meeting with his own leadership group, the top Air Force commanders and central staff department heads, in order to rush down to the Kremlin. The Air Force had been celebrating the end of the coup; and, with Shaposhnikov taking the lead, the officers were renouncing their membership in the Communist Party. The group gave him a standing ovation with shouts of hurrah when he announced that he had been summoned to the Kremlin and come what may he would insist upon taking the Party and politics out of the armed forces. (Earlier that morning, Shaposhnikov paid a visit to Yeltsin's political headquarteres in the White House and spoke with Rutskoi and others about the general military and political situation.)[11]

Shortly after Shaposhnikov arrived at the Kremlin. While he was. waiting to be invited into the presidential summit, a curious incident took place which could have been a last minute test of Shaposhnikov's political reliability and political alacrity. Yeltsin came out briefly and placed a call to Khasbulatov at the White House and urged him to make certain that the KGB wasn't about to launch a last-ditch attack against him. Shaposhnikov immediately picked up a Kremlin phone and made two calls. The first was to Air Force General Antoshkin, commander of all military airfields in the Moscow region. Shaposhnikov ordered him to put his forces on full combat alert and to be prepared for definite orders to attack if required. The second was to Khasbulatov at the White House, who needed to know that the Air Force was ready to provide support immediately. Shortly thereafter, Shaposhnikov was invited into the summit.[12]

Shaposhnikov Becomes Minister of Defense

Gorbachev was chairing the meeting. Gorbachev put the question to Shaposhnikov: "Tell us what you were doing during those three days." He answered and then began to address a different subject, military departization; but Gorbachev cut him off with the big proposal: "We are of the opinion that you should be designated the Union's minister of defense. What is your view of this?"[13] Shaposhnikov thanked him for the vote of confidence but began talking about remaining in his current post or even considering another position. Gorbachev seized upon this opening to ask the presidents for suggestions but Yeltsin jumped in and settled the matter. He insisted that Shaposhnikov be made minister of defense and that the orders be signed *immediately.* The other presidents supported him and Gorbachev's staff brought in the official orders which had already been prepared in advance.

Instead of accepting quietly, Shaposhnikov felt obliged to inform the group that he had quit the Communist Party that very morning. After a brief hesitation, Gorbachev said, "That's not a disaster." And they went on to fill out the top of the military pyramid—the chief of General Staff and the first deputy minister of defense. Gorbachev proposed Oleg Lobov, the most recent Soviet commander of the Warsaw Pact forces for chief of staff and Pavel Grachev for first deputy minister. Shaposhnikov accepted. It was neither the time nor the place time to argue. The presidents had already agreed to that team. Next Gorbachev instructed Moiseyev to implement the orders immediately and warned him "not to do anything stupid." But he couldn't keep still and had to get a last word in "No, nothing stupid...I'll never leave the Party, not like Shaposhnikov."[14]

Moiseyev was on his way into early retirement while Shaposhnikov and Grachev were being propelled to the top positions where military professionalism and politics overlap. They were taking over the leadership of the second most powerful military force in the world at a time of deep systemic crisis. It was an awesome assignment for which neither had been properly trained. It was the outsider, General Oleg Lobov, the third side of the military leadership triangle, who had the general command experience and the better analytical mind. Oleg Lobov, was a hard-driving, intelligent military professional who, like Marshal Orgakov who served as chief of General Staff from 1977–1984, felt compelled to raise serious policy issues and had a reputation for doing so. He would not be a good partner for either Grachev or Shaposhnikov who were a different type of military professional.

In addition to engineering Shaposhnikov's appointment as Minister of Defense and Grachev's as first deputy minister, Yeltsin prevailed upon

Gorbachev to promote Colonel Rutskoi to the rank of major general and Col. General Kobets to general of the army for their services to the country during the coup. He also insisted that the three youths killed on the night of 20–21 August 1991 be decorated with the nation's highest honor, Hero of the Soviet Union. Later, Yeltsin and Gorbachev went to explain recent developments to the Russian parliament. But instead of letting Supreme Commander Gorbachev explain the promotions and decorations, Yeltsin kept interrupting and adding to Gorbachev's answers to questions from the floor. Once again, Yeltsin was demonstrating who was boss: "See what we have done. I fill in what you, Mikhail Sergeyevich (Gorbachev), sometimes forget to say."[15]

The KGB and the MVD

Just as Yeltsin compelled Gorbachev to back out of the Moiseyev appointment, he made him rescind his first appointments to the top positions in the KGB and the MVD. On Friday 23 August 1991, the Soviet papers announced that M. A. Moiseyev had been appointed acting minister of defense; L. V. Shabarin, acting KGB chairman, and V. P. Trushin, acting minister of internal affairs. The three published decrees bore Gorbachev's signature and were dated 22 August 1991, the Kremlin. On Saturday, 24 August 1991, readers found a new trio in the Soviet press, Ye. I. Shaposhnikov, V. V. Bakatin, and V. P. Barannikov respectively. Bakatin and Barannikov had been with Yeltsin in the White House during the coup and were "his boys." Shaposhnikov was also a Yeltsin ally. Thus, Yeltsin had won a major political victory over Gorbachev and had placed his supporters at the head of the three power ministries: defense, security, and internal affairs.

Yeltsin and the demokraty singled out the KGB for the deepest reformation. The KGB had been their enemy not the military. The KGB had spied on them, harassed them, and arrested them. It was the KGB that had the lists of people to arrest immediately after the coup was launched. Instead of rewarding the leader of the KGB special forces for not attacking him during the coup, Yeltsin had General Karpukhin fired and the new KGB Chairman Bakatin refused to receive him.

From August 1991 to August 1995, the KGB went through serious restructuring, had five top leadership shifts, and four name changes. Yeltsin eventually divided its functions and created five separate Russian agencies where there had only been one powerful KGB in the Soviet system: The Federal Security Service (domestic security), the Federal Counterintelligence Service (foreign security), the Governmental Communications and Information Agency, the Federal Border Service, and the Chief Guards Directorate. In December 1991, he disbanded the Alfa commandos.[16] The progressives also restricted the KGB's operations and imposed new prohibitions against infiltrating social and political organizations for example.

Removing Communist Party Structures from the Military

If Gorbachev had been left to his own devices he would have kept trying to use the Communist Party as a way to mobilize national leadership cadres in all fields including the military professions. He knew that one-party domination of the officer corps was fundamentally incompatible with a multiparty political system. But he moved slowly on the military departization front because he did not want to create a political vacuum in the armed forces, one his political rivals might try to fill. This was a serious problem because the Soviet military was used to handling political indoctrination in certain ways and did not have anything to substitute for the existing Communist Party and its political officers. Shaposhnikov tried to get the military collegium to take positive action at its first, post-coup meeting on 22 August 1991 before he had been made minister of defense. But his colleagues didn't budge. On the one hand, Shlyaga and Moiseyev correctly insisted that such decisions were properly made by their civilian commander in chief. On the other, they feared the change because they associated it with political anarchy inside the armed forces—at least they had been saying as much for the previous eighteen months.

Shaposhnikov wanted the military leadership group to move beyond institutional self-defense into basic reform, specifically departization. In the year before the coup, he allowed Air Force officers to retain their positions and ranks after quitting the Communist Party even though Defense Minister Yazov and his MPA chief Shlyaga were strongly opposed to the practice. The Air Force had the worst record in this regard of all the service branches from Shlyaga's point of view and the most progressive record from Yeltsin's. This also contributed to Shaposhnikov's positive reputation among progressives in civilian and military political leadership in the period leading up to the coup.

Immediately after the coup, when Moiseyev assembled the Military Collegium on early 22 August 1992, Shaposhnikov urged his colleagues to vote for the removal of all political organizations from the armed forces structures. This step would improve military cohesion and the military's ability to build and preserve a high reputation for non-partisan loyalty to the state. Shlyaga balked at the suggestion and belittled Shaposhnikov for being young and rash. After that, no one supported Shaposhnikov. Shlyaga further argued that the matter was not theirs to decide. It was a political decision that belonged to the political domain of the Central Committee and the Politburo. Moiseyev then exercised his authority and adjourned the meeting. [17]

The calm that Moiseyev and Shlyaga displayed and their apparent belief that the Communist Party still had life in it and power over their careers suggests that they had been talking with Gorbachev since these were his positions as well. Gorbachev was still clinging to the Party and wanted good relations with the armed forces as well. Yeltsin's team knew that Gorbachev wanted to preserve the Party and they were determined to shut it down.

Historic Order No. 418

The military officers in Yeltsin's camp supported departization and wanted to use the coup's defeat to force the issue at noon on 22 August 1992. They did this in several steps. First, a small group inside the White House drafted a document and Captain Mikhail Nenashev read it to a big public rally as an appeal to President Yeltsin from those who bore arms to defend democracy and to defeat the coup.[18] Second, later that day when Yeltsin returned to the White House from the Kremlin summit, he endorsed the idea, agreed to place it before the Russian and Union parliaments; and, he also read it to the public rally.

Flanked by military officers and civilian progressives ranging from Father Gleb Yakunin to Edvard Shevardnadze, Yeltsin appeared on the White House balcony during a huge victory rally and read a statement making three demands in the name of the officers who supported democracy: First, the Communist Party's organizations in the Soviet Armed Forces must be liquidated; Second, the generals and admirals who actively supported and encouraged the coup must be retired and replaced; Third, partisan political activity must be prohibited in the armed forces. Yeltsin insisted upon removing what he called the "military bureaucrats" consisting of "the generals, admirals and other highly placed officers who consciously carried out the orders of the SEC." He explained, "The *junta* effected the state betrayal because it relied upon these military bureaucrats dedicated to the Party apparat and not to the people and their military oaths."[19]

Yeltsin supported immediate departization but Gorbachev did not. Yeltsin forced the issue by suspending the activities of the Communist Party inside the Russian Federation and seizing all its properties on Friday 23 August 1991. Gorbachev balked but Yeltsin signed the act at a rowdy session of the Russian parliament during which Gorbachev was subjected to extreme political humiliation In effect, the Party was shut down everywhere including inside the military.

Shaposhnikov and Yeltsin insisted that Gorbachev abolish the MPA and begin the process of rebuilding the military educational and personnel service. Gorbachev consented and on 30 August 1991 he announced that the Soviet institution of political commissars (MPA) had been abolished. Gorbachev, Yeltsin, and Shaposhnikov agreed that a special commission should be established to control the departization process. On 1 September 1991, Minister of Defense Shaposhnikov issued historic Order no. 418 which liquidated the MPA. Col. General Dmitry Volkogonov, Boris Yeltsin's senior military adviser, and Col. Vladimir Lopatin, a younger, more radical military reformer were given overall administrative responsibility to conduct a political and professional evaluation of the 92,500 military political officers and for designing a new military personnel and staff development system free from partisan politics.[20]

Every political officer had to be evaluated individually by a committee. Shaposhnikov issued special guidelines that emphasized fairness and warned against conducting political witch hunts.[21] Shaposhnikov expected some problems since on the whole the commanders deeply resented the Communist Party's political specialists. Political officers deemed competent and loyal were reassigned to new army personnel support positions that reported to the respective general commanders at all levels. The new service retained about half of the MPA's former personnel. It chopped the group of MPA generals down from 345 to about twenty.[22] The overall direction of change fit the modern Western ideal that the military should concentrate upon professional military activities and stay out of partisan politics. This goal was popular with the military but it would be difficult to achieve until post-Soviet civilian political institutions achieved viability.

Shaposhnikov made additional changes in secret military regulations, the "special" military regulations that turned officers into informers on one another and on civilians with whom they worked Shaposhnikov confirmed that the Soviet security service had indeed required military officers to make political reports and announced that he was systematically removing such requirements from the military regulations in keeping with the post-coup, departization policy. [23]

Although Shaposhnikov pushed for and implemented departization, he had mixed emotions about the Party and his membership in it. He remembered that it was natural for him and other ambitious young people who were embarking upon their careers to join the Party because: "It was only there in the Party, from the primary organizations on up to the Politburo that life was at a boil." To have any impact upon society, you had to be in the Party. He was attracted to Party slogans such as: "Communists only have one duty—Be first where things are the worst!" And he had kind words for most military political officers. But times had changed and departization was required because the Soviet Union had become a multi-party system. Military cohesion required the shift.[24]

The MPA's main problem, according to Shaposhnikov's memoirs, was that it had no clear, positive function within the military and created uncertainty and resentment. The Party refused to permit the commanders to nail down the MPA's functions and to fix them as a set of activities clearly linked to building morale, supporting military cohesiveness, and promoting overall combat readiness. Although the MPA claimed to support those goals, it reserved the right to go beyond military work into political activities and to implement Communist Party directives in the armed forces. Periodically the Party would fire up the MPA and turn it into a source of tension for commanders. This happened whenever the national leadership launched a new campaign and insisted that the MPA confirm that all troops and officers had attended the appropriate political information sessions, had passed resolutions in favor of the new program, condemned the old ways, and taken some steps to improve.

At Party meetings all officers were supposed to behave as colleagues and comrades without regard to rank. This in itself created an anomaly inside the military where rank and chain of command were all important. Further, when the Party wanted to humiliate the officers a little in order to bring them down a peg or two, the MPA could institute various internal Party disciplinary hearings with regard to their personal or professional behavior and this was always a source of potential tension. Finally, Shaposhnikov complained that the MPA tended to protect its own and to forgive the indiscretions of political officers while coming down hard on regular military officers. Thus, for example, during the Gorbachev years, the MPA was supposed to be combating unethical and illegal conduct ranging from drunkenness to petty corruption and was under pressure to find and turn offenders over to military legal authorities.

Gorbachev wanted to use the MPA to fight corruption and unprofessional behavior in the armed forces. In order to strengthen the MPA's hand and to effect a careful transition from partisan to nonpartisan armed forces, in early 1991 he divided the MPA into two separate organizations. The first was a partisan, Communist Party organization to which virtually all officers belonged. The second was a set of military educational and personnel officers who were supposed to assist the general commanders with a wide range of personnel operations. Because there was so much civilian political concern about military corruption and conduct unbecoming of officers in violation of the military codes, Gorbachev and some in the Ministry of Defense wanted to give the new MPA officers increased authority and to make them deputy commanders, even first deputy commanders instead of assistants to the commanders for personnel work. Shaposhnikov opposed this move and argued, convincingly, that personnel officers should not be made deputy or first deputy commanders because those high ranks are reserved for military professionals who are capable of taking over the general command in an emergency and personnel officers are not qualifiedfor such command responsibilities.[25]

This debate dragged on even when he was minister of defense and was resolved by making them assistant commanders but not first deputy commanders. The key point is that the coup killed the already withering Bolshevik institution of political commissars in the Soviet armed forces without providing a solid, new system for military personnel work and building strong military morale. The military and political leadership became distracted with other more important problems and tended to underestimate the importance of personnel officers and morale-building activities during times of insecurity, uncertainty, and change.

Written Orders and Accountability

To help protect the military from being given illegal orders in the future, Shaposhnikov ruled that henceforth the documents that authorize the military to take extraordinary actions in domestic emergencies will require the signatures of the chief of staff and the commander in chief. Such orders would have to be sanctioned by the president and the Supreme Soviet in keeping with the law. He also recommended that legislation be passed to prohibit the government from using the military in domestic political conflicts.[26] Shaposhnikov pledged that he would never order his troops to fire on Soviet civilians. He said that he was determined that there would never be such victims again and pledged that "our army will never take arms against its people."[27] Months later as the so-called Red-Browns began organizing massive demonstrations in Moscow to protest Yeltsin's policies, General Kobets was asked point blank by Russian Federation legislators if the military would carry out orders to disperse such crowds. He reaffirmed Marshal Shaposhnikov's determination never to order his troops to kill people for expressing opinions of any color. Shaposhnikov and Kobets wanted a professional military that defended the nation against external enemies, one that was depoliticized not repoliticized to serve partisan political goals.[28]

Shaposhnikov's professional instincts were excellent but perhaps too strong for his alliance with Boris Yeltsin to endure. Shaposhnikov had sworn that as long as he headed the military, soldiers would not fire on Soviet citizens or be used in partisan domestic political conflicts. He also insisted that the military be given written orders before engaging in military action. He accepted civilian control but demanded that civilian leaders accept responsibility for the orders they give. He also made himself available to the press and expanded the public dialogue about defense affairs.

Yeltsin Creates the Yeltsin High Command

The Military Collegium of the Soviet Ministry of Defense immediately understood that Boris Yeltsin would want his own military high command. Yeltsin, Grachev, and Shaposhnikov would sweep through the high command and through the military political commissariat and replace those whom they decided should be replaced. Minister of Defense Shaposhnikov announced that there would be an 80 percent purge of the Military Collegium but that there would be no "witch hunts."[29] By moving a senior group of officers aside and into retirement without public disgrace, Boris Yeltsin made room for a somewhat younger generation including many officers who had fought the long war in Afghanistan, the so-called *Afghantsy* typified by Pavel Grachev, Aleksandr Lebed, and Boris Gromov.

Soon after the coup, Western observers such as Jerry Hough noticed that the military of the past was being pushed aside to make room for the military of the future.[30] Boris Yeltsin referred to the Gorbachev military team as "kitchen generals" because they had made their military careers in comfortable military offices rather than in combat operations.[31] There were changes in the

Ministry of Defense's relationships with society as a whole, an increased will-ingness to enter into dialogue with various groups. Shaposhnikov probably consulted more widely, spoke to more groups, gave more candid interviews, and relied more upon persuasion to achieve his aims than any of his predeces-sors since the 1920s.

Nevertheless, Yeltsin's inner circle kept the investigations into the military's involvement in the coup under tight control and did not permit the press or the radical democrats to turn the process into a political circus. On 5 Septem-ber 1991, Shaposhnikov seized the initiative and created his own special com-mission and named General Kobets to lead it. Kobets and Shaposhnikov agreed that mere formal compliance with orders issued by the SEC did not deserve punishment. He and Kobets met twice daily on the matter and reviewed each case. They moved rapidly in order to repair military cohesion and command and control as quickly as possible. They could not afford to leave the com-manders in suspense for long at a time when the country's civilian leadership was still unstable. On 5 November 1991, Shaposhnikov declared that investi-gation and evaluation of the commanders had been completed and formally closed the process. Shaposhnikov had restructured the military high com-mand in two months time. [32]

The Kobets commission identified thirty generals from the high command: nine deputy ministers of defense, ten military district and fleet commanders, eight heads of major MoD departments, and three other lower-ranking com-manders, and 316 additional generals who actively supported and promoted the coup. These individuals were moved into retirement without public scan-dal or public disgrace except for the most active plotters such as Minister of Defense Yazov, Deputy Minister Achalov, and Commander of Soviet Land Forces Varennikov. [33]

In some cases, officers who had been demoted were later reassigned to re-sponsible leadership positions. The entire episode remains somewhat obscure. Some of the more radical democrats in the Russian parliament organized their own commission of inquiry. They complained that Kobets and Shaposhnikov had been too lenient, that military involvement and support for the coup had been more extensive than the official military report had shown. They were trying to set an important precedent in the struggle to establish a strong role for parliament in civilian control over defense affairs. However, Boris Yeltsin con-sidered civilian control to be primarily the responsibility of the executive branch of government and the Ministry of Defense went along with him.

The Public Hearings

On 18 February 18, 1992, the Russian parliament held public hearings into the work of the Kobets commission. Deputy L. A. Ponomarev chaired the session. [34] Kobets and Shaposhnikov made reports and deputies questioned them and added material for parliament's record. Parliament was trying to assert itself in military affairs which had been tightly controlled by the executive branch. It made some, but not much headway. Yeltsin was dominating military affairs and was not permitting parliament much voice. This had advantages and disadvantages for civil-military relations. On the one hand, Yeltsin could make and implement key personnel decisions efficiently and confidentially. This made is easier to keep the military cohesive and under civilian control. On the other hand, democratic reformers resented being excluded and developed negative attitudes towards the Ministry of Defense. This damaged the military's ability to find support in parliament on key issues such as the national defense budget. The gap between the demokraty and the armed forces might have been closed had Yeltsin handled military affairs differently.

Was Shaposhnikov one of the demokraty? He saw himself as a progressive and a reformer rather than part of the group that pushed the Soviet Union towards its collapse. He admitted that as late as March 1991 he still had authoritarian impulses. At that time he joined his colleagues from the Military Collegium and voted to send an urgent request to Gorbachev to address them in person and to explain how he planned to handle the general political crisis. They indeed sent a letter to Gorbachev strongly advising him to impose a state of emergency on the country in accordance with Soviet law.[35]

It was quite predictable that independent, radical military reformers such as V. G. Urazhtsev would complain about Yeltsin's cautious approach towards the military. For example, the reader will recall that the SEC appointed Col. General Kalinin to serve on the SEC's committee for governing the Moscow region. In that capacity, Kalinin supported the KGB as it moved to arrest political activists and was actually present for some arrests, including the arrests of several military dissidents, including Urazhtsev and other deputies. Kalinin had violated the fundamental principle of political immunity for elected deputies. This complicity between top military officers and the KGB in political arrests infuriated democrats in Yeltsin's camp. They were upset when they learned that Shaposhnikov and Kobets allowed Kalinin to retain his military rank and reassigned him to serve as the commandant of the main academy for training higher tank and heavy artillery force commanders. [36]

Colonel Vladimir Lopatin, one of the organizers of the White House's defense during the coup, complained that Yeltsin had taken control over military affairs and was refusing to give parliament any real voice in military restructuring. Lopatin claimed to have plenty of information from inside the armed forces about commanders who greeted the coup with joy, adopted resolutions in support of it, and even threatened anyone who criticized it. He was particularly interested in those cases where commanders had gone beyond formal compliance with orders and had demonstrated personal support for the coup and its aims. Lopatin put his concerns in writing and submitted them to the Kobets commission and read them into the record at the parliamentary hearings. Lopatin concluded: "In spite of the available evidence on the actions of more than 50 generals and admirals during the state coup, all of them have either retained or strengthened their positions. The commission finished its work per your orders. As a result, the best cadres are leaving the army or are being made to leave." [37]

Lopatin pointed out that political activity was continuing inside the armed forces and that officers assemblies were meeting and taking positions on political decisions. Father Gleb Yakunin said that the democrats were pleased that active proponents of Red-Brown dictatorship such as former Col. General Albert Makashov had been sent into retirement. However, he pointed out that there was still support for dictatorship in the armed forces and that retirees such as Makashov had not retired from politics. Father Gleb argued that Russia needed democratic armed forces to defend democratic institutions.[38]

Col. Sergei Yushenkov explained the Russian Parliament's constitutional predicament. From August 1991 to May 1992, there were no Russian armed forces. The Russian state was being protected by a military machine that was in transition from the unitary Soviet military system into some new combination of republic and unified armed forces. He said that the former Soviet military machine constituted a military republic, another entity beyond the fifteen former Soviet republics. Who was in charge of this military machine? He urged Boris Yeltsin to get on with the formation of Russian armed forces under the Russian state and its Constitution.[39]

Lopatin compared Yeltsin's handling of military affairs to Gorbachev's. Yeltsin was following Soviet tradition in which the political boss made the key decisions with a small group in the executive branch. Further, instead of relying on a combination of military and civilian experts to design and implement reforms, the military continued to handle military affairs as a closed professional domain.[40]

Boris Yeltsin was not willing to give the Russian legislature much voice in military personnel policy. He deliberately held up legislation that would have required consultation on top Ministry of Defense appointments until after he had fully staffed the new Russian Ministry of Defense. In principle, President Yeltsin supported military reform and effective civilian control over the armed forces, including parliamentary participation in the formation of national defense policy and budgets. In practice, he held that power closely within the executive branch of government.

Conclusion

Yeltsin's first moves in military reform were rather progressive: the decision to abolish the last remnants of the Bolshevik political commissars, to ban the Communist Party and all parties from operating inside the armed forces, and the pledge to protect the military from political witch-hunts. They could have been predicted by modernization theory. The system seemed to be moving towards the "universal" model patterned after Western experience, a more "civilized" form of civil-military relations and part of the general effort to build a more "civilized" political culture. Shaposhnikov hoped to prevent any repetition of the ugly confrontations between members of the armed forces and civilians such as had taken place in Tbilisi, Baku, and Vilnius in 1989, 1990, and 1991. He pledged that he would never use the military against unarmed citizens and that he would insist upon receiving legal written orders before deploying military forces. Progressive and democratic ideals were driving such reforms.

Ambition also entered the picture. At some point it became clear to officers that a Yeltsin victory would mean career demotion for those top officers who actively supported the SEC and career advancement for those who resisted the SEC and helped swing support to Yeltsin. By linking these personnel changes to a broader policy shift that abolished the political commissars and demanded that the military be insulated from partisan political struggles, Yeltsin promoted the new generation of military leaders under the banner of progressive reform and societal democratization. The two factors, ambition and progressive reform, combined nicely.

A third critical element was political skill and Yeltsin demonstrated such abilities by engineering an honorable retreat for most officers who had been implicated in the coup. Yeltsin had to shield the military from prosecution for its participation in the August coup and to protect it from the demokraty who wanted to press for radical military reforms, including a greater measure of civilian control and influence over military and national security policy. Yeltsin wanted to secure the military's loyalty, to strap it in for the next political ride. He needed the military and the military needed a strong civilian leader, a figure that could begin to restore military morale and confidence in the future. Yeltsin presented himself as just such a leader. Yeltsin offered a measure of hope that the Soviet Union could escape civil war. By swinging to Boris Yeltsin, the military hoped to close the book on the loss of its positions in Eastern Europe, etc. and to open a new chapter in its history. Gorbachev was the required political scapegoat.

Military leaders placed a high value on military cohesion and control and they cooperated with Yeltsin during the transition from Union to something else. Yeltsin loyalists controlled the two committees that evaluated the officer corps for political and professional suitablilty. General Kobets evaluated the role of the commanders during the coup and General Volkogonov and Colonel Lopatin revetted every political officer. Therefore, during the two months immediately following the coup, all top commanders and all political officers felt the political presence of Boris Yeltsin's appointees. Those who retained their commands and their careers owed something to Yeltsin.

At the very top, Pavel Grachev played the role of bridge between the Soviet military and the what would become the Russian Armed Forces. Grachev was first deputy minister of defense under Shaposhnikov and Yeltsin's designated representative of the Russian Federation within the Soviet Ministry of Defense. Yeltsin was hedging his bets. If it became necessary to take the bulk of the Soviet armed forces under his wing and to form the armed forces of the Russian Federation. Grachev would be ready to lead that effort. If it turned out that the various republics would be willing to accept a strong collective security system and various types of unified armed forces, Shaposhnikov would play the more important role. The model gave Shaposhnikov a stronger personal interest in the preservation of unified armed forces than people who hoped to make their careers in the new Russian Federation military and the high commands and ministries of defense of the fifteen republics.

Yeltsin won the summer political games of August 1991 and imposed a "dual presidency" on the Soviet Union. The military withdrew from the coup and accepted Yeltsin as the best choice among the three contenders for their support: Yeltsin, Gorbachev, and the SEC. Yeltsin put his personal imprint on the post-coup, Soviet high command and selected the people who controlled the political investigations into the military's role in the coup. He took personal control over military personnel policy. Although Yeltsin described himself as a democratic reformer, he preserved the strongman tradition in civil-military relations and refused to share power over military appointments with any elective body. Civil control over defense affairs had been democratized but only in the narrowest sense of the term. It had passed into the hands of a democratically elected president. The doctrine of popular sovereignty legitimized that power but it did not rest on any democratically adopted constitution. The very essence of the Western model is constitutionally based authority and shared authority between several branches of government. Yeltsin was still operating within the Russo-Soviet tradition and behaving more like an elected general secretary than a democratic. law-governed president.

Postscript on the August Coup as Treason

In February 1994 the Russian parliament or Duma amnestied all people arrested for crimes against the state during the August 1991 coup. All agreed except Army General Varennikov who argued that he could not sign the documents to secure his amnesty because he had never committed any crime against the state. He insisted upon a trial because he wanted his and the SEC's point of view put before the public *one more time*. He also wanted to charge Gorbachev with crimes against the Soviet state and to implicate him in the August 1991 coup.

Varennikov's attorney insisted that the official records of Gorbachev's cabinet meetings show that emergency measures were discussed on 3 August 1991.

Gorbachev said: "Tomorrow I go on vacation with your approval so as not to keep you from working." Varennikov was promoting the idea that Gorbachev knew the state of emergency was coming and deliberately stepped into vacation in order to put himself in a win/win situation. If the coup collapsed, he could condemn it and return to Moscow as a hero. If the coup were successful, he could join it and give it legitimacy. This conspiratorial hypothesis had been circulating since August 1991 and remains popular. The fact that on 18 August 1991 Gorbachev agreed to support a state of emergency regime if the Soviet Parliament endorsed it, makes it difficult to put Varennikov's charges to rest.

Varennikov insisted that Gorbachev violated his Soviet presidential oath of office to defend and enforce the Soviet Constitution and the peoples will as expressed in the March 1991 referendum which endorsed the preservation of a reformed Union when he agreed to a new Union Treaty which gutted the Union's powers. Gorbachev planned to sign the new treaty on 20 August 1991 without first placing it before the Soviet parliament. The Unionists regarded such politics as conspiracy against the Union and were delighted to have one more chance to read their point of view into the record.

Vladimir Kryuchkov, Oleg Shenin, and Gennady Yanayev came to court to hear Varennikov's final statement. General Varennikov explained that in August 1941 he swore an oath to serve his country the Soviet Union and went to war to defend it against foreign enemies. He said that in August 1991, exactly fifty years later he had to go to its defense again, this time against internal enemies who were destroying the Soviet state. He argued that his participation in the SEC was honorable and correct and necessary for the country's sake. He declared that he did nothing illegal: "Neither physically nor morally was I even a criminal nor could I ever have been." He insisted that those who destroyed the Soviet Union should be put on the bench, not those who tried to defend it.[41] On 11 August 1994, the Military Collegium of the Supreme Court of the Russian Federation rendered its verdict: General Varennikov is not guilty of treason since the state in question no longer exists.[42]

Army General Varennikov had a point. Gorbachev had indeed violated his oath to uphold the Union and the Union Constitution by agreeing to sign a new Union Treaty that gutted the Union state without first taking the issue to the Union Congress. The Soviet Union's political system can be described as an oligarchy in which formal law and regulations were used to manage routine affairs but in which the oligarchs reserved the right to take major political decisions without being bound by the law and constitutional procedures. The military was used to operating with such double standards. On the one hand, there were the laws of the Soviet Union and the military codes. On the other hand, the oligarchy had to be obeyed. Under such conditions, instability in the oligarchy is a serious threat to military cohesion. In order to avoid military system breakdown, key military leaders moved their support to Yeltsin even before Yeltsin completed the process of rebuilding the constitutional and legal foundations for his authority over the armed forces. Even so, prominent military leaders such as Yevgeny Shaposhnikov were aware that their country's practices fell short of law-governed ideals and called for progressive reform. Hardliners such as Varennikov were also cognizant of such problems. Although they were raised in the Soviet system, they were able to imagine a better system. The problem with Soviet political culture wasn't that it prevented professionals from learning about the basic principles of liberal societal organization or from imagining how much better life could be. The problem was that of mixing legalism and *personalismo* was too deeply ingrained. Although Yeltsin claimed to be more progressive than Gorbachev, his political style was steeped in *personalismo*. He gave too little attention to formal legal and constitutional procedures in his confrontation with Gorbachev and after. The Law was more a political tool than an end in itself.

Notes

1. Decree no. 66 is reproduced on pp. 158–60, in Khasbulatov, *The Struggle for Russia* (London: Routledge, 1993).
2. Decree no. 64 of 20 August 1991 is reproduced in Khasbulatov, *Struggle,* pp. 156–57.
3. *Ibid.*, p. 156.
4. M. S. Gorbachev, "Armiya okazalas' v tselom na vysote," *Krasnaya zvezda,* 29 August 1994.
5. See Shaposhnikov, *Vybor: Zapiski glavkomanduyushego* (Moscow: Nezavisimoe Izdatel'stvo, 1981), p. 54. The text of the Declaration which the military collegium adopted on 22 August 1991 was printed in *Krasnaya zvezda* 23 August 1991.
6. The KGB leadership collegium met on 22 August 1991 and adopted a declaration that condemned the coup and reaffirmed its support for the laws and the Constitution. The text is in *Ibid.*
7. Yeltsin, *The Struggle for Russia* (New York: Times Books/Random House, 1994), p. 106.
8. *Ibid.*
9. See Aleksandr Fyodorov, "Half an hour: the story of a telephone call from President Gorbachev to Sr. Lieutenant Skorodumov," *Moscow News,* nos. 34–35, 1991, p. 7.
10. See Yeltsin, *Struggle,* p. 107.
11. See Shaposhnikov, *Vybor,* p. 61.
12. *Ibid.,* pp. 62–63.
13. *Ibid.*, p. 63.
14. *Ibid.* pp. 63–64.
15. Boris Yeltsin at the meeting of the Supreme Soviet of the RSFSR on 23 August 1991. Transcript excerpts in Khasbulatov, *Struggle,* p. 175.
16. See Vitaly Strugovets, "Terrorizm nachinayet i vyigrivaet ili Chem FSB slabee KGB" (Terrorism starts and wins or How the FSF is weaker than the KGB), *Krasnaya zvezda,* 9 August 1995. Also see Mark Galeotti, *The Age of Anxiety* (London: Longman, 1994), pp. 163–66.
17. See Shaposhnikov, *Vybor,* pp. 54–55.

18. See Captain 3rd Class Mikhail Nenashev, "Tri dnya u Belogo Doma" (Three days at the white house), *Armiya*, no. 24, 1991, pp. 16–23.
19. Boris Yeltsin as cited by *Krasnaya zvezda*, 23 August 1991.
20. See *Krasnaya zvezda*, 14 September 1991.
21. See Shaposhnikov, *Vybor*, p. 98.
22. See Col. O. Valdykin, ""Iz Moskvy: Komissiya zavershaet rabotu" (Moscow: Commission completing work), *Krasnaya zvezda*, 20 November 1991.
23. *Armiya*, no. 6, 1991, p. 17.
24. Shaposhnikov, *Vybor*, p. 56.
25. Shaposhnikov, *Vybor*, pp. 98–99.
26. Marshal Yevgeny Shaposhnikov's comments at Russian Federation hearings on the military's participation in the August 1991 coup, *Armiya*, no. 6, 1992, pp. 16–17.
27. Marshal Yevgeny Shaposhnikov, "Obrashchenie Ministra Oborony SSSR," *Krasnaya zvezda*, 31 August 1991.
28. Kobets in *Armiya*, no. 6, 1992, p.28.
29. See *Krasnaya zvezda*, 27 August 1991.
30. See Jerry F. Hough, "Assessing the Coup," *Current History*, vol. 90, no. 558, October 1991, pp. 305. ff.
31. See Yeltsin, *Struggle*, p. 59.
32. See Marshal Shaposhnikov's report to the Russian parliament's hearings on the military's participation in the coup, "On the Military Leadership's Participation in the State Coup of 19–21 August 1995" (in Russian), *Armiya*, no. 6, 1992. Hereafter: *Hearings*.
33. See General Kobets's report, *Hearings, Ibid.*, p. 24.
34. The transcripts were edited and printed in *Armiya*, nos., 6 and 7–8, 1992.
35. See Shaposhnikov, *Vybor*, p. 31.
36. See V. G. Urazhtsev's comments at the Russian Federation parliament's *Hearings* into the military leadership's participation in the August 1991 coup; *Armiya*, nos. 8–12, 1992, pp. 30–31.
37. See Vladimir Lopatin's comments in *Ibid.*
38. See Father Gleb Yakunin's comments, *Hearings, Armiya*, no. 6, 1992, p. 18.
39. See Yushenkov's comments, *Hearings, Armiya*. nos. 7–8, 1992, pp. 37–38.
40. See Lopatin's comments, *Hearings, Armiya* nos. 7–8, 1992, pp. 33–36.
41. Boris Soldatenko, "Den' pobedy Valentina Varennikova" (Valentine Varennikov's victory day), *Krasnaya zvezda*, 12 August 1994.
42. See Sr. Lieutenant of Justice, Vadim Neustroyev, "Opravdatel'nyi prigovor Valentinu Varennikovu" (Acquittal for Valentine Varennikov), *Ibid.*, 12 August 1994.

6

From Union to Commonwealth

National sovereignty and democracy have military dimensions. Who commands the armed forces and how they are commanded have an immediate bearing upon national independence and general societal democracy. This chapter focuses on problems of national sovereignty and command and control from August 1991 through December 1991, the period when the Soviet Union divided into fifteen sovereign states. As long as the fifteen Soviet republics were under one common dictator—the general secretary of the Communist Party, command and control functions were neatly structured under a pyramidal structure. Under the Soviet system the civilian heads of the fifteen republics were deprived of the power to command and control the armed forces within their borders. Without such power, they could not function as sovereign heads of independent states. Without their own armed forces, they were subjects of the Soviet state not sovereign leaders.

The rise of Russia under Boris Yeltsin's leadership destroyed that structure and replaced it with fifteen pyramids of power in which the Russian state stood out as the largest and dominant element in the set. The second largest and most important from a military-strategic point of view was Ukraine. The third was Kazakhstan. Therefore, the key military-political relationship to examine is that which developed between the Russian and Ukrainian proto-states. Once Boris Yeltsin and Leonid Kravchuk, the presidents of Russia and Ukraine, fully understood that their decisions could make or break the Union and any other post-Union forms of economic, political, or military cooperation, Gorbachev became a spectator to the contests that settled his fate and that of the Union state. Although this chapter gives primary attention to the Russo-Ukrainian relationship, it also touches upon Kazakhstan's inability to get itself accepted as an equal member of a strategic triangle consisting of Russia, Ukraine, and Kazakhstan.

Since the primary political game was the competition between the Soviet state, Russia, and Ukraine, there should have been three sets of actors—a president and a minister of defense for the Union state, Russia, and Ukraine. However, Boris Yeltsin decided that it was in his best political interests to play the game somewhat differently. Yeltsin's game plan was to control the Soviet Ministry of Defense as long as that institution remained viable and to nationalize it in the name of Russia if and when that became necessary or expedient. The Union state's team consisted of President Mikhail Gorbachev and Minister of Defense Yevgeny Shaposhnikov; Ukraine's team was headed by Leonid Kravchuk and Konstantin Morozov; Russia's was headed by Boris Yeltsin and Pavel Grachev who served as Shaposhnikov's first deputy minister of defense and was the political-military bridge between the set of political elites grouped around Boris Yeltsin and the Soviet Ministry of Defense. This political arrangement put Yevgeny Shaposhnikov in an unenviable position. On the one hand, he was expected to represent the interests of the unitary Soviet military machine and according to the law, he reported to Mikhail Gorbachev. On the other hand, he was close to Yeltsin and knew that without Russia the Soviet military machine could not survive. He therefore had to take his main political cues from Boris Yeltsin.

The mighty Soviet military machine was unitary, multinational, and extra-territorial. It embraced and defended the entire Soviet Union and drew its resources from its vast population and economy. It provided a level of defense capability that no single or small group of republics could replicate. The Soviet Ministry of Defense had a direct institutional interest in promoting close military, economic, and political; cooperation among the fifteen republics. As the last Soviet minister of defense, Yevgeny Shaposhnikov presented all the right arguments in support of the common defense in a timely manner to the loose oligarchy of ruling presidents. But he was fighting a losing battle against deeper systemic change driven by a combination of ethnic nationalism and civilian elite self-preservation.

Events were moving rapidly but there were definite patterns that Shaposhnikov and the Soviet officer corps could not but notice. Boris Yeltsin was controlling military developments and his people were deciding which officers were promoted and which were forced into retirement in the wake of the August coup. Yeltsin also controlled the biggest part of the defense budget and this meant that Soviet military personnel who expected to save their military careers needed to get on the Russian ship of state as rapidly as possible since the Union state was sinking. The next best place to serve would be Ukraine and so on down to the smallest republics but even these offered new opportunities for rapid promotion especially to those of the right ethnicity. Thus, the typical mid-career military officer faced major choices, a mixed bag of threats and opportunities. In this whirlwind of change, it was extremely difficult for Shaposhnikov to get the civilian leaders to adopt any firm, mid-range plans for military reform. He had to concentrate upon short-term survival and control. Indeed, he will be remembered for guiding the military through those extremely difficult times.

The Big Russia Problem

As long as the Soviet state survived, the main problem was sovereign Russia's relationship with it. As soon as the Soviet state fell, the main problem became big Russia's relations with the smaller republics as a whole and with the second most powerful and important republic, Ukraine. The natural successor to the Soviet Union was a Russocentric system. No Russian leader could accept a collective security system in which a cluster of small, less developed states could dictate policy to big Russia.

By August 1991, it was clear that a strong Russia, united behind Boris Yeltsin, a popularly elected president, could dictate policy to the nominal head of the Union state, Mikhail Gorbachev. When politicians began working on designs for a new unifying political structure to replace the Soviet Union, they kept running into the big Russia problem. The small states realized that they would have little real power against big Russia and Russian politicians did not wish to be constrained by little states such as Moldova and Georgia. Why should big Russia permit every former Soviet republic an equal vote? After all, Russia alone had 150,000,000 people and more than half the Soviet Union's industrial, scientific, and natural resources. The "natural" arrangement would be a Russian sphere of influence rather than a new political body in which all fifteen former Soviet republics had an equal vote.

At first it was possible to see the problem as a clash of personalities. But as time went on, Yeltsin's treatment of Gorbachev had to be seen differently, big Russia was demanding veto power over all key Union state policies and personnel appointments. The same would apply to any federation, confederation, or commonwealth. By virtue of its size and resources Russia would treat the new political constellation as a Russian sphere of influence, a *near-abroad* system.[1]

The previous chapter revealed that Yeltsin made the key moves against Gorbachev and the Union state while Gorbachev was still under SEC house arrest in the Crimea. Yeltsin nationalized the Union state's economic assets within the borders of Russia. That nationalization was permanent and it deprived the Union state of its economic lifeblood, control over revenues and economic activity. Yeltsin also declared himself to be the commander in chief of all Soviet armed forces within the borders of Russia. This was a temporary measure meant to endure until the emergency ended. However, without Russia's contribution, the Soviet state could not amass the funds to finance the huge Soviet defense budget. Therefore, as long as Yeltsin controlled the Russian economy, he had economic veto power over all major State activities. Russia held the purse strings to more than 50 percent of the Soviet state's revenues and economic power.

Ukraine's Lessons on Sovereignty and Armed Forces

Ukraine learned that the ultimate test of national independence is the power to control armed forces and to defend one's institutions and territory. Until Ukraine had demonstrated the ability to raise, maintain, and command its own armed forces, it would remain a proto-state. The August coup provoked

Ukraine into declaring its sovereignty, demanding its own armed forces, and holding an historic election to determine who would serve as Ukraine's first democratically president and whether Ukraine would become an independent state. The Unionist politicians who led the August coup from Moscow were ethnic Russians who demonstrated the typical imperial myopia about which the non-Russian republics had long complained. The state of emergency (SEC) was a Muscovite and a Russian affair. The key political battles were for control over the two most important Russian cities, Moscow and St. Petersburg. The SEC assumed that the rest of the Soviet Union would "naturally" fall into line when and if the two main Russian metropoli had been pacified. Without their own armed forces, even large republics such as Ukraine which had a population of some 52,000,000 felt acutely defenseless. At the time of the coup, there were over 700,000 Soviet military personnel in Ukraine and many were of Ukrainian ethnicity but the president of Ukraine was not their commander in chief and Ukraine had no Ministry of Defense of its own.

Soviet Minister of Defense Yazov dispatched Army General Varennikov to Kiev on Monday 19 August 1991 to instruct Ukraine's civilian leadership about what the SEC expected from it. At 9:00 A.M. he entered Kravchuk's offices and began explaining how things were going to change now that the "decisive and brave" have taken charge in Moscow. He ordered Kravchuk to suspend normal government in Ukraine's Western districts and to place them under emergency rule. The Communist Party was to be restored to power and all the non-Communist political movements, their offices, their news papers, etc. were to be shut down immediately. No strikes were to be permitted and all protest meetings were to be broken up. He indicated that Kravchuk had better demonstrate cooperation with the SEC by taking extreme measures in support of its program. At 10:45 A.M. Varennikov wired Moscow that Kravchuk and his colleagues had reacted negatively and that he, Varennikov, had to turn the heat up a bit. When they hesitated and insisted that Soviet and Ukrainian laws required parliamentary approval, Varennikov insisted that it was too late for such legalistic scruples since the state of emergency had already been imposed.[2] After the coup, Kravchuk told investigators that Varennikov had indeed come to Kiev to press them but that Ukraine's civilian leaders did not agree to implement the SEC's orders. Kravchuk complained that Varennikov had treated Ukraine's civilian leadership like *junior officers* until Kravchuk reminded him that he was in the office of the Chairman of Ukraine's Supreme Soviet not at Kiev military district headquarters. During Varennikov's visit, Kravchuk placed a call to KGB Chairman Kryuchkov and told him that he was running into some resistance.[3]

In addition to Kravchuk and Varennikov, there were three others present: S. Gurko, head of the Ukrainian Communist Party; General Viktor Chechevatov, Soviet commander of the Kiev Military District; and K. Masik, Ukraine's acting prime minister. This fit the SEC's pattern of bringing Communist bosses and military commanders together to form the core for administrative teams that were to supervise local administrators and to make certain that they obeyed the state of emergency. Chechevatov confirmed Varennikov's claim that Kravchuk seemed to be cooperating, albeit reluctantly, because Kravchuk agreed to form a commission of responsible civilian, KGB, MVD, and military leaders to monitor events in Ukraine.[4] However, Kravchuk never proclaimed a state of emergency in Ukraine and insisted that the matter be placed before parliament.[5]

There was an ethnic dimension to the confrontation between the Muscovite coup leaders and Ukraine's civilian leaders. Minister of Defense Yazov and KGB Chairman Kryuchkov were both ethnic Russians. So was Army General Varennikov. Further, the commander of the Kiev military district, Chechevatov, was also Russian. Thus, the Union's military and security affairs were under ethnic Russian control and ethnic Russians were bullying Ukrainian leaders in the name of the Union state. Such facts led Ukrainian nationalists to demand that Ukraine have its own armed forces led by Ukrainian officers sworn to defend Ukraine

After the August coup, Ukraine's parliament or Rada met on 25 August 1991, declared independence, and proclaimed that Ukraine had legal authority over all Soviet military, police, and security forces within its borders. Ukraine decided to take operational control over the armed forces on its territory and to name expert committees and a minister of defense to negotiate systematically with the respective Union ministries. Kravchuk told the Rada that his views differed from Yeltsin's about future political bonds between Ukraine and Russia. Yeltsin wanted a tight federation; Kravchuk supported a loose confederation between the republics. The Rada announced that a referendum on national independence would be held on 1 December 1991 in order to remove all doubts concerning the peoples attitude towards the issue.[6]

Yeltsin and Shaposhnikov on the Republics

Boris Yeltsin, Mikhail Gorbachev, and Yevgeny Shaposhnikov were all ethnic Russians. They adopted a common stand on the Soviet military system. It was a compromise with the republics. They opposed efforts to split the Soviet defense system but they agreed that each republic, including Russia, could establish republican national guards, relatively small military formations to maintain domestic order, to respond to emergencies, and to protect key installations. Yeltsin admitted that the coup had convinced every republic's government that it needed some self-defense forces. But the main forces, the most powerful and important Soviet military assets had to be preserved. Yeltsin was emphatic: "I firmly declare that along with these formations, unified Union Armed Forces must exist.... Any division of strategic arms among the republics is completely out of the question."[7]

Republican guards could be seen as a positive, professional development. The military resented having been used by politicians in Tbilisi, Baku, Vilnius, and Moscow to impose their will or to restore domestic order after civilians had failed to do their jobs properly. Such domestic police functions were alien to the military's patriotic mission: defending the state against foreign enemies. Each incident damaged the military's pride and dignity and contributed to the military's alienation from moderate nationalists in the republics and from the demokraty in general. Therefore, Shaposhnikov accepted republican guards, as small forces that kept order within the republic and which would immediately be placed under Union military commanders in the advent of war.

Shaposhnikov argued that every republic needed the common nuclear umbrella, air defense systems, and border protection provided by unified armed forces. He wanted to retain a common defense space embracing the complete territory of the former USSR.[8] Shaposhnikov was convinced that he was right and had the best interests of the military and the Soviet peoples in mind. On 31 August 1991, he sent his reform plan Gorbachev and the heads of state of all fifteen republics in advance of their summit.[9] However, before the summit met to consider his proposals, the standing committee or Presidium of Ukraine's Rada appointed Soviet Air Force General Konstantin Morozov, its first Minister of Defense on 3 September 1991. It also authorized the government to draft legislation to create the legal foundations for Ukraine's armed forces.[10] Kiev was going for more than the limited national guards favored by Gorbachev, Yeltsin, and Shaposhnikov. It laid claim to the three Soviet military districts on Ukrainian territory plus the Black Sea Fleet and its Ukrainian ports and support facilities.

The State Council met in Moscow on 6 September 1991. The meeting confirmed that the Soviet Union's future was in the hands of an unstable oligarchy composed of up to twelve heads of state plus Gorbachev who chaired the meetings but did not even set the agenda. The State Council's main task was to manage the political transition from the dying Union to some new form of interrepublican cooperation. The State Council listened to Shaposhnikov's ideas on military reform, unified armed forces, and national guards. Although the State Council did not endorse his reform strategy, it took two steps that pleased Shaposhnikov. First, it authorized Gorbachev to create a special committee on military reform. Second, it voted a substantial increase in military salaries.

The State Council took a third step which can be seen as the first official action dividing the formerly unified Soviet armed forces. It recognized the three Baltic republics as independent states outside the Union. This step forced Shaposhnikov to enter into negotiations with Estonia, Latvia, and Estonia as independent, sovereign states. By giving up its claims on the Baltic states, the State Council made Soviet military personnel, dependents, retirees, and facilities in the Baltic into a foreign army of occupation. Subsequent actions by

Gorbachev confirmed this. On 19 September 1991, he ordered Minister of Defense Shaposhnikov to discharge from the Soviet armed forces all draftees from Estonia, Latvia, and Lithuania since they were now independent states and the Soviet military had no right to hold them.[11]

Who Divided Ukraine and Russia?

There are two main schools of thought. The Moscow school makes Ukraine the key actor and culprit, the agent that split the unitary Soviet Armed forces into separate national armies and then steadfastly prevented Moscow from gathering the national armies into an effective military alliance. This Moscow school tends to blame Ukrainian nationalists, particularly those whose political bases are in the Western districts that Stalin annexed from Poland in 1939. The Kiev school argues that the Soviet state had already collapsed by the time Ukraine declared its intention to build its own armed forces; therefore, Ukraine's role was constructive not destructive. Ukraine's civilian and military leadership took control of a potentially explosive situation, gave clear direction to a disoriented military, and laid the legal foundations for new civil-military relations appropriate to an emerging democracy.

The August coup was the catalyst that precipitated the military's division for political reasons. General Varennikov's efforts to bully Ukraine's civilian leaders into submission was the immediate cause but the deeper causes were rooted in a thousand years of history, all the factors that gave Ukrainians a distinct national identify and a desire for national independence. People remembered that Ukraine's first twentieth-century drive for independence had been crushed by the Red Army in the civil war of 1917–1921. A decade later came Stalin's ruthless persecution of Ukrainian nationalists, including Communists, and the dreadful famine and deportations that killed some 8 million Ukrainians—the result of Stalinist policies which Moscow imposed on Ukraine more ruthlessly than elsewhere. These memories were still alive when the Chernobyl nuclear accident of 1986 revived Ukrainian resentment of Great Russian domination. Brezhnev had imposed nuclear power on Ukraine instead of permitting Ukrainians to burn Soviet oil and natural gas because Brezhnev preferred to sell the oil to the West. After the accident, Gorbachev and the "Russians" in Moscow first concealed the extent of damage and never came through with the type of aid which Ukraine felt it deserved. All this convinced Ukrainians that they needed to take control over their own economic, political, and military affairs.

But the legacy of history is more complex than the typical Ukrainian nationalist litany's content. History both united and divided Ukraine and Russia. In traditional Russian usage, Ukraine was called "little Russia." Russians and Ukrainians jointly composed the backbone of the Soviet officer corps. Ethnic Ukrainians comprised about 30 percent of the Soviet officer corps.

Ethnic Russians were some 15–20 percent of Ukraine's total population. Ukraine's managerial, political, scientific, and cultural elites were fluent in Russian. There were important Soviet defense plants in Ukraine's main industrial centers. Russians viewed some areas inside Ukraine's political borders, the Crimea for example, as historically Russian, important attributes of Russian state power. Russian tsars conquered the Black Sea coast from Turkey and opened it to Ukrainian settlement in the eighteenth century. The port and naval yards at Sevastopol were a special administrative district and closed to the general public during Soviet times. The Soviet strategic defense system had land based nuclear missiles, strategic bombers and warheads, and nuclear submarines in Ukraine.

Russia with a population of 150,000,000 wanted a close alliance with Ukraine which had population of 52,000,000 and stood between Russia and Europe. The loss of Ukraine, Belarus, and the Baltic states would push Russia into the Eurasian heartland, deeper into Asia and its problems. The world powers were primarily interested in the Soviet nuclear arsenals and supported Shaposhnikov's drive to keep them under reliable control. However, the world powers were ready to accept the fifteen republics as independent states and did not press them to sign tight military alliances with Russia.

Although we can name specific politicians and events that split Ukraine from Russia, the best explanations are systemic. In this model, three related political systems operated to weaken the alliance between Moscow and Kiev. First, the international community of states, not just the West but the South and the East as well, supported developments which reduced the "Russian" state to a more manageable, less threatening size. The international environment was favorable to a loosening of Moscow's influence over Kiev. Second, the Soviet regional system also contributed to the break . The Union state had no real power to make and enforce decisions. It was drifting and that political drift encouraged Kiev to reach for independence and viability. (Chronic political instability and a declining economy in Russia had the same affect.) Third, Ukraine's domestic political system also pulled against the Moscow-Kiev alliance. Former Communist bosses such as Leonid Kravchuk faced elections and needed to convince voters that they were patriotic. An easy way to do that was to engage in Moscow-bashing. Although Ukraine's Western regions were more "anti-Russian" than the Southeastern regions where some 10 million ethnic Russians lived, the country's majority definitely favored independence.

Shaposhnikov and Morozov

The first stages of the military divorce between the Russian-dominated Soviet military and Ukraine were tense but they were kept under control. The two ministers of defense worked hard to restrain the more radical and recalcitrant elements in their respective camps. They discouraged ethno-national emotionalism and concentrated upon procedural and legal development. Yevgeny Shaposhnikov and Konstantin Morozov had strong Soviet internationalist values and families of mixed ethnicity. Morozov saw no contradiction between national armed forces and active discouragement of ethnic extremism. He did his best to lay the legal foundations for Ukraine's national armed forces and keep ethnic tensions under control. As people began to realize that military funding would be cut all across the former Soviet Union, competition for positions increased and this added to the problems Morozov and his counterparts would have to face.

Shaposhnikov's chief of General Staff, Army General V. N. Lobov estimated that about 33 percent of all Soviet officers were of Ukrainian ethnicity, far more than Ukraine could ever afford to employ in its national armed forces.[12] They were a stabilizing influence during the split because they were Soviet professionals who spoke Russian fluently and had been indoctrinated to resist radical nationalism. They worked with their Russian colleagues to prevent political differences between Russia, the dying Union state, and Ukraine from erupting into armed conflict. Soviet officers helped maintain military cohesion and generally prevented the Soviet armed forces from being dragged into civil war all across the former Soviet Union.

Marshal Shaposhnikov felt very strongly about this point and vowed to prevent the armed forces from being used against the people or from being dragged into political conflicts.[13] Since he had risen above common nationalism and fully appreciated the significance of the vast, Soviet strategic defense system, he expected responsible civilian politicians to understand military assets and to do their best to preserve them. From his perspective, it all seemed terribly rational and simple. But the civilian politicians kept behaving contrary to their higher interests. Shaposhnikov fundamentally disagreed with Ukraine's decision to build comprehensive national armed forces because it diminished Russian and Ukrainian security and raised the cost of defense to both countries. He argued against it and Ukraine moved carefully on the military front from August to December 1991. But the direction was clear, towards independent, comprehensive armed forces.

Konstantin Morozov, Ukraine's minister of defense was well suited to the task of managing the sensitive relationship with Shaposhnikov. Like Shaposhnikov he was a Soviet Air Force officer, a military professional and an internationalist in the best sense of the term. Morozov had a Ukrainian mother and a Russian father. His father had a full career as a Soviet military professional. I asked Morozov about his entry into high military politics, his selection as Ukraine's first minister of defense, and his relationship with Moscow. He told me that the civilians came to him and recruited him for the job because they knew his political and professional values: he supported democratic and peaceful development and an independent Ukraine. Civilian demokraty proposed his name to Kravchuk who nominated him to the Rada's

Presidium which endorsed the appointment on 3 September 1991. They gave him the task of building a Ukrainian Ministry of Defense and of keeping it under firm, reliable control.[14]

Morozov viewed Shaposhnikov positively and believed they shared similar progressive values even though they had to build different institutions. Shaposhnikov had to work for a strong unified military model, one in which the joint forces and central institutions were the most important. Morozov had to build the military forces required to guarantee Ukraine's sovereignty. Both worked to prevent tensions over the Black Sea Fleet and other issues from becoming unmanageable. Shaposhnikov and Morozov cooperated to keep the extremists in their respective camps from inciting violence.

Military professionals such as Shaposhnikov and Morozov were buffeted by civilian leadership instability as they tried to steer a reasonable, rational course. They were more than military professionals, they were statesman. Morozov believed that Shaposhnikov had the more difficult task. He had to face fifteen different proto-ministries of defense who were responsible to fifteen different civilian governments all of which were somewhat unstable. It was easier for Morozov to lay the foundations for one, Ukrainian national army than for Shaposhnikov to design a structure capable of holding from six to twelve armies together under a committee of from six to twelve heads of state. Morozov served a definite state, Ukraine with one civilian leader, Leonid Kravchuk. Shaposhnikov served a shifting, unstable coalition of states, the largest of which, Russia, was considering following Ukraine's example.

In October 1991, the Ukrainian Rada defined the size of Ukraine's future army at 400,000 positions or a bit less than 1 percent of the population, and its military budget as 2.8 percent of the GNP. The Rada also endorsed Ukraine's denuclearization, a step that enhanced U.S. support for Ukrainian independence. Further, in order to demonstrate that Ukraine was sovereign and that Leonid Kravchuk was the legal commander in chief of its sovereign armed forces, Konstantin Morozov swore a new military oath to Ukraine before the Rada and Kravchuk promoted him to the rank of Colonel General. However, neither Kravchuk nor Morozov were ready to order the Soviet military in Ukraine to transfer their allegiance to them. That move would come several months later in January. Special expert teams were planning that shift carefully in order to prevent radical opponents from provoking conflict. Morozov was steady, professional, and deliberately reassuring in his public remarks addressed to the Soviet military.[15] There was no turning back but Morozov was determined to effect the shift responsibly.

Russia Begins to Take Charge of Military Reform

The vast Soviet military machine was rapidly becoming stateless. More precisely, it was being pulled in several directions by a cluster of competing entities. Soviet political culture saved Eurasia from civil war. The fact that Soviet military and political leaders were used to working without legal formalities was positive because the legal-institutional side of civilian control over the vast Soviet defense system was in a shambles. No one had taken comprehensive responsibility for the 1992 Soviet military budget. The Union state was sinking and no effective substitute could be built rapidly enough to give the military formal, law-governed leadership. Shaposhnikov had to play it by ear. Commanders obeyed him because they accepted responsibility for war and peace in the former Soviet Union. Similarly, Shaposhnikov worked with Gorbachev, Yeltsin, and the other presidents in an ad hoc but highly responsible manner.

In early October 1991, Shaposhnikov warned the State Council that it was becoming increasingly difficult to maintain military cohesion and he recited the litany of reasons why the heads of state should draft and sign a defense alliance immediately.[16] At the State Council's November 4 meeting, he cautioned that unilateral actions by the republics were destabilizing the armed forces and urged the presidents to adopt a five-year plan to govern military reform and reconstruction. Although Yeltsin and Gorbachev endorsed his rational thinking and the State Council understood the case for unified defense, it refused to take action. Nevertheless, Yeltsin and Gorbachev instructed Shaposhnikov to continue giving all republics assistance with the tasks of building their own ministries of defense. They also authorized an interrepublican committee to coordinate military budgets but only seven republics sent representatives and even these had little authority.[17]

Yeltsin and the big-Russia syndrome had destroyed Gorbachev and the Union. The Soviet military began to accept Yeltsin as the key to its future, the only prominent civilian leader with the power base necessary to give the armed forces reliable support. Yeltsin's man inside the Soviet Ministry of Defense, Army General Pavel Grachev was making public statements to the effect that Russia supported unitary armed forces and would not be the one to provoke their division. But, if things go differently, Russia will establish its army quite easily.[18] Russia would have to be the center of any new alliance system and the leader of Russia would be responsible for building it. Ever since the August coup, Yeltsin was calling the shots in military policy and appointments. He became bolder and started representing Russia internationally.

Germany, Russia, and Ukraine Precipitate the Union's End

Just prior to Gorbachev's last Novo-Ogaryovo summit, Yeltsin made a state visit to Germany and a visit to the Soviet military forces and related personnel stationed there, the so-called, Western Group of Forces. Yeltsin behaved as if he were their commander in chief, not Gorbachev. He had to say something because the officers were extremely concerned about their futures.

They knew that they had to be repatriated but to which country? They went to Germany as representatives of the Soviet Union but the Soviet state was melting away? Who was responsible for them now and who would be responsible for them in the future? Someone had to give that answer and Yeltsin was the only civilian leader who really counted. Therefore, he stated flatly that he and the Russian republic took full responsibility for the Soviet forces in Germany, in Russia, and in all the former Soviet republics. Germany's foreign minister, H. D. Genscher, joined Yeltsin for the tour of Soviet military installations. The two spoke about future relations between Germany and Russia and announced that a major treaty was being prepared. Since Russia was now entering into treaty relations with Europe's greatest power, there was no longer any major role for Gorbachev to play in European affairs. Yeltsin's visit to Germany was a tremendous blow to Gorbachev's prestige and confirmation that the international community accepted the inevitability of Russia's emergence as the primary successor to the Soviet state.

Krasnaya zvezda, the Soviet Ministry of Defense daily, featured Yeltsin's visit to the Western Group of Forces (WGF). Yeltsin was leading while Gorbachev was fading. Yeltsin made firm statements that inspired some confidence. He repeated his basic position on the future structure of the post-Soviet military system. Each republic would have national guards but the main strategic assets and overall defense system would remain unified. Russia's national guards would be numerically small as well. This detail was important since many in the WGF were hoping to get positions in the Russian guards and to secure a decent career inside Russia. But Yeltsin was still working to preserve as much of the big Soviet defense system as possible. It was in Russia's national interests to do so since it surrounded Russia with a reliable shield and a significant defensive buffer zone, the other republics. "As President of Russia, I declare that Russia will not be the first to create its own armed forces and I call upon the other sovereign republics to do the same. I also support unitary nuclear forces including the Strategic Rocket Forces and the nuclear forces in the Navy and Air Force. They must unconditionally be under unitary command."[19]

On 25 November 1991, Gorbachev invited the heads of state to his Moscow country home at Novo-Ogaryovo for a final attempt to hammer out a basic treaty for a Union of Sovereign States. But the heads of state refused to give the Treaty their firm support. Gorbachev, Shaposhnikov, and Shevardnadze angrily stormed out of the meeting room. After a while Yeltsin and Shushkevich (Belarus) came after them and reported that the heads of state had agreed to a small step towards cooperation. They were willing to place the draft treaty before their respective parliaments but the latter would decide. Shaposhnikov finally understood that the civilians were unwilling to accept the political discipline required to preserve Soviet military assets: "I became more and more convinced that politics was a game and not always a clean one."[20]

On 1 December 1991, the Ukrainian electorate voted overwhelmingly (90 percent) for independence and chose Leonid Kravchuk to serve as its first democratically elected president. Gorbachev had underestimated Ukraine's drive for independence. When Union Minister of Defense Shaposhnikov raised the question, Gorbachev assured him that he could handle Ukraine. Gorbachev kept talking and acting as if the Union could be saved. Yeltsin evaluated the situation differently and believed that Ukraine's drive for independence had to be accommodated.[21] On 3 December 1991, Boris Yeltsin recognized Ukraine as an independent state. He said Russia and Ukraine would immediately build relationships appropriate to sovereign states based on the traditional friendship between the two countries and their respective and mutual international obligations—specifically, strategic arms limitations treaties, nuclear nonproliferation treaties, and human rights conventions.[22]

Soviet military personnel stationed in Ukraine, including draftees from outside Ukraine, were permitted to vote. The staff offices of the three Soviet military districts reported that about 60 percent of Soviet military personnel in the Kiev and Odessa military districts voted for Kravchuk. Soldiers in the Carpathian district also supported him but at a slightly higher rate. In the Sevastopol special naval district, 97 percent of the military voted and Kravchuk received 75 percent of their vote. His main opponent, Vyacheslav Chornovil, a Western Ukrainian, ran on a more radical, anti-Union, anti-Communist, independence platform. Chornovil was strongest in the Western regions where he received from 60 to 85 percent and weakest in the Russian districts where he got from 20–30 percent.[23]

The vote killed the Soviet Union and plans for unitary armed forces. At his first presidential press conference, Kravchuk explained that since 31 million voters had endorsed independence, the old Union was over. He reaffirmed Ukraine's intention to build independent armed forces but pledged to do so carefully and deliberately based upon agreements between Ukraine and the Soviet Ministry of Defense.[24] Since Yeltsin, not Gorbachev, was really the power behind the Soviet Ministry of Defense, it was necessary for Kravchuk to meet with Yeltsin. Gorbachev had already been marginalized.

Yeltsin and Kravchuk Dissolve the Soviet Union

On 5 December 1991, Yeltsin repeated the pledges he made during his November trip to Germany. He and the Russian Federation would take responsibility for defending the interests and paying the salaries of Soviet military personnel in Russia and abroad. He announced that military salaries would increase by 190 percent beginning January 1, 1992. He even used the phrase, "if there is no Union," in his public comments about the military's plight.[25] Then Yeltsin left Moscow for a closed-door summit with President Kravchuk of Ukraine which was hosted by Stanislav Shushkevich, the Belarussian head of state. Yeltsin had calmed the Soviet military in advance of his final blow against the Union and Gorbachev.

Shaposhnikov remained in Moscow but Grachev was with Yeltsin in Belarus. Gorbachev kept calling Shaposhnikov, "What are you hearing from Minsk (Belarus)?" At 10:00 P.M. Yeltsin called Shaposhnikov to fill him in *before talking with Gorbachev*. Yeltsin said that the three republics had formed a triple alliance (*troistvennyi soyuz*) and were inviting the other republics to join it. Russian historians call this set of agreements the Belovezhsky Accords[26]

Shaposhnikov asked Yeltsin questions and got information. He did not bargain with Yeltsin. He asked Yeltsin to read the key passages on military policy which he did. Nuclear forces would remain under strict central control. What about conventional armed forces? Yeltsin supported unified armed forces but that was not part of the CIS accords. Had Yeltsin talked with Nursultan Nazarbayev, president of Kazakhstan? Not yet, but they had discussed the general idea before. As soon as their conversation ended, Gorbachev was on the line. Shaposhnikov had words with his commander in chief who warned him, "Don't meddle. Its not your affair!" The next morning, Gorbachev called again. This time Shaposhnikov told him off. He and the country were tired of Gorbachev's indecisive leadership and needed action. Yeltsin provided that and the CIS was better than nothing.[27]

The fact that the three fraternal Slavic republics—Russia, Ukraine, and Belarus had met in secret and taken such important decisions alone bothered Shaposhnikov. He understood what Yeltsin was trying to accomplish. Yeltsin wanted to guarantee that the three Slavic republics would form a solid bond. This would unite about 70 percent of the population of the former Soviet Union into a major confederation. Yeltsin assumed that Kazakhstan would have to join them since 50 percent of its population was of Slavic ethnicity. This greater Slavic alliance would have controlled more than 75 percent of the former Soviet Union's resources. Would this precipitate a major rift between the Slavic republics and those of Islamic heritage? Such a rift had major security implications for Russia and all the former Soviet republics and Shaposhnikov wanted to prevent it.

Shaposhnikov called Nazarbayev and both expressed the same concern that rash actions could provoke "a wild, frightening" split along ethnic fault lines.[28] Shaposhnikov urged Nazarbayev and Yeltsin to discuss the situation immediately. The two spoke and agreed to hold an enlarged meeting for all the heads of state in Kazakhstan's capital, Alma Ata, on 21 December 1991. The Central Asian heads of state held their own meeting at Ashkhabad (Turkmenistan) on 13 December 1991 and announced that they would join the CIS at Alma Ata. But they also criticized the three Slavic republics for having taken action unilaterally in a manner that provoked negative ethno-national reactions. The Ashkhabad declarations endorsed firm, centralized control over strategic forces but did not call for unitary or even unified conventional forces.

Tensions were rising within the Soviet officer corps as a whole. The Belovezhsky accords made the Soviet military stateless. Were those agreements truly legal? At Belovezhsky, three heads of state—Yeltsin, Kravchuk, and Shushkevich stamped the word "former" on the Union state. The Russian Parliament acted quickly to give Yeltsin's bold move constitutional legitimacy. On 12 December 1991, it annulled the Union Treaty of 1922 and ratified the Belovezhsky accords by a vote of 188 for, 6 against and 7 abstentions.[29] Ukraine and Belarus did likewise.

Shaposhnikov followed Yeltsin's lead and allowed his legal commander in chief, Union president Gorbachev, to be sacked along with the Soviet state. Shaposhnikov kept the military cohesive as best he could during this awkward transition. He assembled the military district and service commanders in Moscow to discuss military reform. Both Gorbachev and Yeltsin invited themselves to the meeting and appeared in that order. Shaposhnikov remembers Gorbachev's talk as rambling and indecisive, one more confirmation that he should have retired voluntarily months ago, in August. Gorbachev expressed regret that he had not given enough attention to military affairs.[30] Gorbachev had lost the armed forces politically. Yeltsin had won them. Although Yeltsin could not promise that he could prevent any more defections from the unified forces concept, the military preferred him over Gorbachev. Russia was the key player and as *Krasnaya zvezda*'s editor Vyacheslav Lukashevich put it, "He who pays the piper calls the tunes." Yeltsin had the budget. Yeltsin promised the pay raises. Now it was up to Yeltsin to deliver.[31]

Although the three Slavic presidents had proclaimed that the Soviet Union had ceased to exist on 8 December 1991, Shaposhnikov continued to describe himself as the Soviet Union's Minister of Defense and to call the military, the Soviet Armed Forces. This posture helped preserve military cohesion between the Belovezhsky and Alma Ata meetings. Shaposhnikov's diplomacy extended to long meetings with foreign officials such as U.S. Secretary of State James Baker III who spent more than an hour with him on 16 December 1991. Baker came to Moscow to gather information and to support a smooth transition. Yeltsin asked for U.S. support for Russia's claims to the Soviet Union's international positions, embassies, seat in the U.N., etc. Baker communicated America's absolute support for the strictest central control over nuclear weapons but he refused to take a position on conventional forces. That was up to the sovereign states and he wished them well and urged them to avoid conflict.[32] After Russia, Baker visited Kazakhstan and Ukraine where he delivered the same basic message. Their future relations with the United States depended upon their position and actions on key questions related to nuclear weapons, economic reforms, civil rights, and democracy. The United States was not attempting to define their future relationships among themselves but it insisted upon strict implementation of international weapons agreements.[33]

Ukraine's March towards Military Sovereignty

After the Belovezhsky meetings, events in Kiev took a turn for the worse from Shaposhnikov's point of view. Ukraine's leadership realized that Ukraine could not be a viable sovereign state unless it built its own armed forces. Kiev's drive for security independence exacerbated tensions between Shaposhnikov and his chief of General Staff, Vladimir Lobov. The two had been competing ever since August. Lobov wanted a direct reporting line for himself to president Gorbachev and kept advocating his ideas even after Shaposhnikov and the military collegium had adopted different concepts as official policy. Now, Shaposhnikov forced Lobov to resign and replaced him with General Samsonov. Shaposhnikov had to stress leadership cohesion in the Ministry of Defense precisely because things were coming apart elsewhere. In Kiev, President Kravchuk and Minister of Defense Morozov evaluated Lobov's retirement as a positive move, the removal of a major stumbling block to a smooth partition of military assets.[34]

Kiev kept marching forward. Soviet military commanders became nervous and politically agitated. President Kravchuk called a special meeting with the top commanders of the Soviet military districts in Ukraine. He informed them that since the Soviet state no longer existed, he was their civilian commander in chief. He and Morozov exempted the strategic nuclear forces from this assertion of Ukrainian state, command authority over Soviet personnel and installations. Strategic forces in Belarus, Kazakhstan, Russia, and Ukraine would remain under central, unified control.[35] But what was that center? The CIS, a loose committee of those four states?

The situation put Shaposhnikov's diplomatic and political skills to the test. On the one hand, he supported Yeltsin over Gorbachev and was still backing him. On the other, Yeltsin had already made key concessions to Ukraine in military affairs. Shaposhnikov argued with Kravchuk but could not convince him to change his mind. On 13 December 1991, Shaposhnikov sent Col. General B. Pyankov and a delegation of generals from the General Staff to Kiev in order to encourage the Soviet commanders in Ukraine to adopt a positive, professional attitude towards developments there and to keep things under control. Kravchuk discussed military reforms directly with Shaposhnikov and the two reached a broad understanding about the process. Moscow expected Ukraine to give up all nuclear weapons and to build relatively small armed forces.[36]

The relationship between Russia and Ukraine had to be managed and it was better to cooperate and to hope that sovereign Ukraine and sovereign Russia would eventually sign a defense alliance than to alienate Ukraine by making threatening statements and encouraging military officers to resist Ukrainian authorities. Besides, Shaposhnikov had other problems on his hands. Soviet forces stationed in some parts of Moldova, Chechnya, Georgia, Armenia, and Azerbaijan found themselves in the midst of local armed conflicts. Shaposhnikov insisted that his forces remain neutral and had to make difficult decisions about how to preserve neutrality in zones where normal civilian authority had broken down. He calmed the military by explaining that his staff was preparing a draft defense alliance for the summit meeting scheduled for 21 December 1991. He ordered his commanders to prevent their officers and soldiers from being dragged into political conflicts. Their mission was to defend the external borders of the Soviet Union. They were not policemen or political armies. They defended the entire country against foreign threats.[37]

There would be no real surprises at Alma Ata. The two key military issues had been settled in advance. On 18 December 1991, during a visit to the Vatican, Yeltsin told the press that the Soviet Union's nuclear arsenal would be under his control but that each republic had the right to form its own conventional armed forces or to join a common defense system. He favored the latter but could not impose it.[38] On the summit's eve, Ukraine's parliament passed resolutions that reaffirmed Ukraine's independence and prohibited its representatives from ceding powers to the Commonwealth.[39]

The End of the Unitary Soviet Armed Forces

Yevgeny Shaposhnikov's flexible, responsible leadership and the Soviet military's cohesion and discipline permitted the civilian heads of state to settle the Soviet Union's estate without fear of major civil war. When they gathered in Alma Ata on 21 December 1991 to proclaim the end of the Soviet Union and the formation of the Commonwealth of Independent States, they were so confident in his abilities that they quickly agreed to appoint him supreme commander of the Unified Armed Forces of the Commonwealth of Independent States. However, in keeping with their well-established pattern of behavior, they refused to give detailed attention to military affairs and left the matter for future meetings after agreeing on several principles which did not please the military.

The heads of eleven newly independent states: Armenia (L. Ter-Petrosyan), Azerbaijan (A. Mutalibov), Belarus (S. Shushkevich), Kazakhstan (N. Nazarbayev), Kyrgyzstan (A. Akayev), Moldova (M. Snegur), Russia (B. Yeltsin), Tajikistan (R. Nabiev), Turkmenistan (S. Niyazov), Ukraine (L. Kravchuk), and Uzbekistan (I. Karimov) gathered in Alma Ata on 21 December 1991 to proclaim the end of the Union of Soviet Socialist Republics (USSR) and its replacement by a Commonwealth of Independent States (CIS). Georgia was not represented because its president Z. Gamsakhurdia was literally fighting for his power and his life against armed opposition forces who had him pinned down in his governmental office complex. Estonia, Latvia, and Lithuania did not attend because they were already free states and had no intention of joining.

Shaposhnikov hoped for a general military alliance to preserve the Soviet Union's most important defense assets. He lobbied for a five-year, military transition plan and a general prohibition against unilateral action by republics that might destabilize the military. He wanted the presidents to listen more carefully to the military point of view and to become better informed about the assets they were destroying. He got none of this. But instead of rejecting his ideas, the summit named him commander of the former Soviet forces and postponed further action on conventional forces until their next meeting in Minsk, nine days later. In Alma Ata, they focused on the nuclear question. The four nuclear states, Belarus, Kazakhstan, Russia, and Ukraine signed an eight-part agreement that placed the nuclear button under Yeltsin's control, reaffirmed preservation of a unitary military command system for strategic forces, named Shaposhnikov the military commander of the nuclear forces, and stated that Yeltsin could not use any nuclear weapons without first having the agreement of the other three powers. However, there were some differences over the nuclear question and the agreements required ratification by the respective parliaments.[40]

The presidents also approved Gorbachev's retirement plan but decided to leave him out of the CIS. They defined two coordinating bodies, a Council of CIS Heads of States of state and a Council of CIS Heads of Government. Both were supposed to meet on a monthly basis to resolve problems. Instead of naming someone—Gorbachev was the leading candidate, to chair the CIS Council of Heads of State, they decided that it would be better to have the position rotate among the presidents.

Gorbachev Passes the Nuclear Controls to Yeltsin

Gorbachev accepted the inevitable and prepared to resign and to close the office of the presidency of the Union of Soviet Socialist Republics on 25 December 1991. In modern times, the symbol of power is the nuclear kit not the orb and scepter. Shaposhnikov was tapped to conduct the nuclear kit from Gorbachev to Yeltsin. The transfer had legal/documentary and "hands-on" aspects. On 25 December 1991, shortly before Gorbachev's official address to the Soviet people and formal resignation, Yeltsin called Shaposhnikov and told him that he would prefer to stay away from the ceremony. He had already signed the papers. Would Shaposhnikov please call Gorbachev and inform him and make other suitable arrangements? Gorbachev understood and agreed that Shaposhnikov and his technical staff would convey the nuclear kit from the Kremlin to Yeltsin's residence. At 7:00 P.M. Gorbachev addressed the nation, bade farewell to his chief supporters, and then met with Shaposhnikov who took the nuclear kit to Yeltsin. He stayed with Yeltsin as technical experts taught him the special codes and routines. Towards midnight the two had a long chat.[41]

Conclusion

Who was responsible for breaking up the Soviet Union and splitting the unitary Soviet armed forces? Gorbachev? Yeltsin? Kravchuk? Were ambitious civilians more important in the process than the ambitious military officers who joined their teams? When Gorbachev abandoned Soviet dictatorship in favor of competitive elections, he doomed the unitary Soviet state and the unitary Soviet armed forces although this wasn't immediately understood by Soviet military and civilian leaders. The record shows that the civilians took the lead and the military followed and adjusted to their decisions. However, civil-military teamwork was an essential part of the larger process of state formation—the creation of sovereign, viable states based upon the fifteen Soviet republics. States do not achieve viability until they have effective systems for making and implementing decisions within their borders and can defend themselves.

The rise of an independent Russia undermined the Soviet state's viability. Boris Yeltsin's actions made Gorbachev a lame duck and deprived the Soviet state of the decision-making power and revenues it needed to sustain the Soviet defense system. It also shattered the legal foundations for coherent civilian command and control over the Soviet military machine. The August coup failed to block Yeltsin's steady attack upon the unitary Soviet state and it provoked Ukraine into speeding up its drive towards independence fortified by Ukrainian control over Ukrainian armed forces. The big Russia problem became the dominant political issue in the Soviet Union and will continue to be the dominant feature of post-Soviet regional political, economic, and military institutional development. The second most important issue is the relationship between Russia and Ukraine. The third is the relationship between Russia and Kazakhstan, a subject discussed more fully in the next two chapters.

Events moved rapidly and simultaneously on many levels. The Soviet military leadership responded by relying upon extralegal but effective standards of behavior rooted in Soviet political culture. Under Marshal Shaposhnikov's statesmanlike leadership they accepted Yeltsin, maintained cohesion during the transition from Union to Commonwealth, and helped avert civil wars. The Soviet military was used to a double standard. Under normal conditions it functioned within the law and the Soviet military codes. When special problems or emergencies arose it accepted extralegal direction from the country's political elite. Such dictatorship was supposed to work things out and effectiveness gave it legitimacy. The political culture accepted extralegal solutions as the only practical way to resolve difficult problems efficiently within the cumbersome Soviet bureaucratic system. Although Gorbachev wanted to increase legality and respect for law, he needed reasonably stable political structures in order to accomplish that objective. Instead, he faced instability, the unanticipated consequences of his reforms. The military abandoned Gorbachev, its legal commander in chief, because he was ineffective not because it disagreed with the basic thesis that the Soviet Union's economic and political system needed to be modernized generally along Western lines. The military followed Yeltsin because he appeared to be resolving the main problems of state and Russia controlled the main purse strings. Effectiveness bestowed legitimacy upon him. Yeltsin became bolder and more confident in his role as de facto commander in chief.

Political institutions had to adjust to the new political forces, namely demands for independence. As one of the most important attributes of state power, the military also had to adjust to the change. With backing from the world's nuclear states, the Russian state and the ethnic-Russian core of the former Soviet armed forces dominated the military reconstruction process and claimed the Soviet Union's rights and reponsibilities in world affairs. Although the Kremlin agreed to permit the other fourteen republics to form national armed forces if they so desired, it intended to establish a greater Russian security zone that covered their territories. Thus, Yeltsin could honestly say that he supported the retention of a common security system for the former Soviet Union while accepting national armed forces in each republic.

Although Yeltsin preferred bold moves, he acted more cautiously on the military systemic front than in some other areas. Instead of proclaiming the formation of independent Russian armed forces in fall 1991, he slowed the process down and regularly reassured the Soviet officers that they would not be abandoned. Nevertheless, it was clear that the military system would have to adapt to the Soviet Union's division into fifteen sovereign states and the emergence of a new, Russocentric regional system.

Successful adaptation required some degree of pattern maintenance to assure system viability and to keep changes under reasonable control. Too much resistance could have provoked armed confrontations so could a rapid, irresponsible division of personnel and weaponry. It is clear that Shaposhnikov understood the problem and rapidly developed into an excellent military statesman, one of the top half dozen leaders who managed the Soviet state's collapse. He is one of the unsung heroes of the anti-Communist revolution. Konstantin Morozov played a similar role in Ukraine and in relations between Russia and Ukraine. By December 1991, it was clear that the former Soviet republics would demand and get their own armed forces. It was also clear that there would be major differences in the domestic political systems of the republics which would make it difficult to establish relationships of trust among the republics. No solid, collective security system was likely under such conditions.

Notes

1. See Robert V. Barylski, "The Caucasus, Central Asia, and the Near-Abroad Syndrome," *Central Asia Monitor*, vol. 2, no. 5, pp. 31–37, and no. 6, pp. 21–28.

2. See Stepankov and Lisev, *Kremlevskii zagovor* (Moscow: Ogonok, 1992), pp. 112–15.
3. Testimony given on 22 November 1991. *Ibid.*, pp. 116–17.
4. See *Ibid.*, p. 115.
5. See *Krasnaya zvezda,* 21 August 1991.
6. See Lt. Colonel A. Polyakov, "Iz Kieva: Press-konferentsiya L. Kravchuka," *Krasnaya zvezda,* 28 August 1991.
7. Boris Yeltsin's address to the nation, Radio *Rossiya,* 29 August 1991. *Krasnaya zvezda,* 30 August 1991.
8. See Minister of Defense Shaposhnikov's interview for *Krasnaya zvezda*; *Ibid.*
9. See Shaposhnikov, *Vybor: Zapiski glavkomanduyushego* (Moscow: Nezavisimoe Izdatel'stvo, 1993), p. 70.
10. See S. Balykov, "Naznachen ministr oborony Ukrainy" (Ukraine's minister of defense named), *Krasnaya zvezda,* 5 September 1995.
11. See *Krasnaya zvezda,* 24 September 1991.
12. Interview with Chief of General Staff, Army General B. N. Lobov, *Krasnaya zvezda,* 7 September 1991.
13. Shaposhnikov interview, *Krasnaya zvezda,* 31 August 1991.
14. I discussed these issues with General Morozov on 8 May 1995 at his office at Harvard's Ukrainian Research Institute where he was dictating his memoirs and refining his ideas about the optimal grand design for Ukraine's armed forces.
15. Col. General Konstantin P. Morozov, "Voiska na Ukraine podchinyayutsya ministru oborony SSSR" (Armies in Ukraine are subordinated to the USSR ministry of defense), *Krasnaya zvezda,* 18 December 1991.
16. See Shaposhnikov, *Vybor,* pp. 109–12.
17. See Captain V. Urban, "Kakim budet voennyi byudjet 1992 goda?" (What kind of military budget for 1992?), *Krasnaya zvezda,* 3 December 1991.
18. *Ibid.*
19. Boris Yeltsin as cited by Col. V. Markushin and Lt. Col. V. Khabarov, "Prebyvanie B. N. Yel'tsina v ZGV" (Yeltsin's visit with the WGF), *Krasnaya zvezda,* 26 November 1991.
20. Shaposhnikov, *Vybor,* p. 121. *Krasnaya zvezda* reported that he had quite the meeting for understandable reasons. See Urban, "Kakim budet voennyi byudjet 1992 goda?"
21. See Shaposhnikov, *Vybor,* pp. 103–4.
22. G. Tallayev, "Iz Moskvy: B. Yel'tsin o priznaii nezavsimosti Ukrainy," *Krasnaya zvezda,* 4 December 1991.
23. Col. A. Polyakov, Captain V. Pasyakin, and Col. A. Ladin, "Kto segodnya prezident?" (Who is president today?), *Krasnaya zvezda,* 3 December 1991.
24. Col. A. Polyakov, "Iz Kieva: L. Kravchuk o Soyuznom dogovore" (Kiev: L. Kravchuk on the Union treaty), *Krasnaya zvezda,* 7 December 1995.
25. RIA, "Iz Moskvy: Rossiya beretsya soderzhat' voennosluzhashchikh" (Moscow: Russia will support military personnel), *Krasnaya zvezda,* 7 December 1991.
26. The adjective refers to the place they met in Belarus, a retreat in the Belovezhsky forest and game preserve near the Polish-Belarussian border.
27. See Shaposhnikov, *Vybor,* pp. 127–28.
28. *Ibid.*, p. 129.
29. See Capt. V. Ermolin, "Rossiiskii parlament skazal Yel'tsinu 'da'" (Russian parliament said 'yes' to Yeltsin), *Krasnaya zvezda,* 13 December 1991.
30. See Shaposhnikov, *Vybor.*, p. 137.

31. Vyacheslav Lukashevich, "Kak nas teper' nazyvat'—SSG, SNG, ili vse zhe SSSR?" (What are we called now—USS, UIS, or still the USSR?), *Krasnaya zvezda*, 12 December 1991.
32. TASS, "B. Yeltsin: vazhnye utochneniya" (B. Yeltsin: important clarifications);) and "Vstrecha v ministerstve oborony (Meeting in the ministry of defense), *Krasnaya zvezda*, 17 December 1991.
33. See *Krasnaya zvezda*, 19 and 20 December 1991.
34. See Col. A. Polyakov, "Iz Kieva: Byla sovetskoi a teper..." (Kiev: Used to be soviet, what now...), *Krasnaya zvezda*, 14 December 1991.
35. *Ibid.*
36. TASS, "L. Kravchuk o pozitsii Ukrainy" (L. Kravchuk on Ukraine's position), *Krasnaya zvezda*, 17 December 1991.
37. Lt. Col. O. Vladykin's report on Marshal Shaposhnikov's press conference on 13 December 1991, "Armiya vne politicheskikh igr" (The army is outside the political games), *Krasnaya zvezda*, 14 December 1991.
38. TASS, "Rossiya seichas ne khochet imet' sobstvennuyu armiyu" (Russia doesn't want its own amy now), *Krasnaya zvezda*, 19 December 1991.
39. "Zayavlenie Verkhnogo Soveta Ukrainy" (Decree from Ukraine's supreme soviet), *Krasnaya zvezda*, 21 December 1991.
40. The Alma Ata agreements were published in *Krasnaya zvezda*, 24 December 1991.
41. See Shaposhnikov, *Vybor*, pp. 137–38.

Part II

The Military and the New Russian State

7

Military Officers as a Political Force

During the Cold War analysts discovered that civil-military relations in the Soviet Union had some key points in common with standard, modern, Western practices. First, in both systems the military was expected to be loyal to the political system but to stay out of partisan politics. Second, the military was encouraged to concentrate upon developing professional expertise in the art of warfare but to defer to civilian decisions about war and peace, which weapons systems to develop, and other basic policy questions.

In Western practice, democratic civilian control meant that the military obeyed democratically accountable civilian leaders. It did not mean that the military had an inherent right to organize its professional life in a democratic or even semidemocratic manner or to discuss national political affairs freely in society at large. The military was expected to speak through second and third parties who mediated between civilian and military leadership groups. The most powerful civilian leader normally served as the supreme commander but that power was shared with legislative bodies and the judicial system in order to prevent presidents from using the military for personal and partisan political purposes. By a combination of tradition and law military participation in civil society and key policy debates especially during warfare was muted. Civilian experts on national defense were expected to predominate, not professional military officers.

In Gorbachev's Soviet model, democratic civilian control deviated from Western practice. Gorbachev initiated a series of changes that gave the military a voice in politics and permitted semidemocratic governance mechanisms to begin developing inside the armed services. These swelled into military demands for a strong, direct voice in politics. This chapter analyzes the rise of such military activism, efforts to tame it, and measures adopted to choke it off and to return to classical, semi-authoritarian patterns of civilian control. The top civilian and military leadership faced a period of testing during which some officers' groups began to take political initiatives which, if left unchecked, might have undermined military cohesion and civilian control. Later chapters discuss other aspects of civilian control such as the task of building checks and balances into the democratic control system to prevent presidents from abusing their power to command the armed forces.

The Military's Patterns of Political Participation

Instead of debating whether the Russian military are active or passive elements in political life, it is more productive to analyze the relationship between military activism and other, general political conditions. Since the armed forces are an essential part of any viable political system, they are always *political* in the broadest sense of the term. However, they aren't always active politically as individuals or as an institution.

When Tsar Nicholas II abdicated in 1917, he released the imperial officers from their oaths to serve him and he transferred their allegiance to the Provisional Government.[1] However, the Provisional Government was competing with popular councils or soviets which also claimed the authority to command the armed forces. Further, separatist armies were forming in various parts of the former Russian empire. It took a bloody civil war, 1917–21, and some 8,000,000 to 10,000,000 deaths to settle the postimperial political and military question. Leon Trotsky's Red Army rebuilt military cohesion and discipline, conquered most of the former tsarist empire, and established the Soviet Union. From 1922, the year the Union was proclaimed, until 1991, the year it was dissolved, the military was under civilian control and the civilian who served as commander in chief was the general secretary of the Communist Party of the Soviet Union. In 1985 officers knew that Mikhail Gorbachev had become their ultimate commander in chief when he was selected to serve as general secretary by the Party elite.

When Kravchuk, Shushkevich, and Yeltsin proclaimed the end of the Soviet Union on 8 December 1991, they created a potentially serious command and control problem. On 8 December 1991, three republics created the Commonwealth of Independent States (CIS) but, as the previous chapter explained, all three had different positions on the future of the armed forces and could not identify a legitimate civilian commander in chief or even a single state to which the Soviet military owed its allegiance. Ukraine insisted that the Commonwealth was not a state and refused to endorse any effort to give the CIS the power to make and enforce decisions inside Ukraine's borders. The Soviet armed forces had become temporarily stateless. They were in political limbo. The CIS presidents expected Marshal Yevgeny Shaposhnikov, the "former" Soviet minister of defense, to preserve military cohesion until they decided the Army's fate.

Political science predicts that a cohesive military is more likely to become involved in political life when civilian leadership becomes ineffective. If so, Shaposhnikov should have become a political leader during the transitional period when the old Soviet state was disappearing and the new, post-Soviet states were struggling to attain viability. Further, if and when the new states achieved viability, Shaposhnikov's political role should have decreased. Events in the former Soviet Union generally followed the pattern which political theory predicted. Theory also points to the importance of military ideology. When military leaders believe it is necessary and legitimate for the Army to become heavily involved in national decision making and in law enforcement, they are more likely to lead the armed forces into domestic political activities than when they consider such tasks entirely inappropriate for military professionals.[2]

Soviet revolutionary tradition legitimized military participation in political life. However, military participation had been highly ritualized and carefully controlled by civilians *except* at the beginning and the end of the Soviet state. In the beginning, when the tsarist state was collapsing, revolutionary soviets of soldiers and sailors proclaimed that military personnel had full political rights and they exercised them; but as the Bolshevik state achieved internal cohesion and viability, it reversed military democratization and denied the military any independent voice in politics. It wasn't until 1989–90 that military personnel started to become active politically again. Gorbachev's democratic reforms infused new power into the traditional Bolshevik idea that soldiers have full political rights. They ran for office, won competitive elections, and held political office. Majors, colonels, generals, and marshals enjoyed the same political rights and immunities as civilians in the Soviet Union's parliaments. As *individuals*, they were in politics because they were full citizens. However, the military as an *institution* was supposed to stay out of partisan politics and to follow orders from legitimate civilian authorities.

If there are only semilegitimate authorities or if several groups are competing for power, should the military stand back and await the outcome or take a position? In 1990 and 1991, the military took positions. In November 1990 at the confrontational meeting between Gorbachev and 1,100 military officers who held elective office, it demanded that Gorbachev demonstrate firm control over the levers of state power and it contributed to his shift to the political right. The next major demonstrations of military influence over political change came in August and December 1991. When Yazov agreed to join the state of emergency conspiracy, he committed the military to the dictatorship project's credibility. When he withdrew from the coup, he doomed it. When Shaposhnikov endorsed Boris Yeltsin over Mikhail Gorbachev in August and December 1991 and kept the military cohesive and "neutral," the military helped Yeltsin to achieve his immediate political objectives. The military's conduct enhanced Yeltsin's political authority but reduced Gorbachev's. The military abandoned its legitimate civilian commander in chief, Gorbachev, and transferred its primary allegiance to a rising civilian star, Yeltsin, who had popular legitimacy but only a dubious legal claim to command the Soviet armed forces. Yeltsin was simply the president of one, albeit the largest, of the fifteen Soviet republics and he had no right to command the Soviet armed forces which belonged to the Union of fifteen Soviet republics which was headed by Union president, Mikhail Gorbachev.

The military's role in bringing down Gorbachev and elevating Yeltsin bore at least a weak resemblance to what the military high command had done to Nicholas II in February-March 1917 when it pressed him to resign and rallied to the Provisional Government and its Minister of War Guchkov. We should also remember that the high command supported Khrushchev against Beria in 1953 and against the Malenkov group in summer 1957. However, in October 1964, it supported Brezhnev's political coup against Khrushchev. In October 1964 the military leadership abandoned Commander in Chief Khrushchev before he had relinquished his positions as head of party and head of state. In December 1991, it abandoned Gorbachev before he had resigned his position as the legal head of the Soviet state.

Byzantine, Corporate, and Anarchic Participation

There are three primary models for military participation in Russian political life: Byzantine, corporate, and anarchic. The Byzantine model fits military participation in Khrushchev's 1953 and 1957 insider political struggles for power at the top. Neither the general public nor the officer corps as a whole was involved or made aware of what was actually taking place. However, top military leaders joined the Khrushchev conspiracies against his civilian rivals. Similarly, when the political elite, including the military, had grown weary of Khrushchev's politics of disruption and his bullying leadership style, they combined in a Kremlin intrigue and forced him to retire. The same happened to Gorbachev and to the SEC in August 1991. Although that was a complex double coup, it was primarily an insiders operation supported by some public demonstrations in Moscow and St. Petersburg. Gorbachev was toppled and the Union was destroyed by a political oligarchy that obtained high-level military cooperation. The officers as a whole were not asked in advance. In the Byzantine model, the civilian conspirators initiated the conspiracies and then drew the top military leadership into them. There must have been some signaling and probing into military leadership reactions and intentions, a delicate affair when the top civilian leader is the target.

The corporate model fits more normal times during which the Ministry of Defense represents the military in the regular competition for budget. Unless the corporate leadership has the authority to commit the armed forces to implement its decisions, it cannot command respect at the political bargaining table. Therefore, in order to function well, the corporate model requires a cohesive military system with a strong chain of command. Democracy and corporate professional discipline are fundamentally incompatible in large bureaucratic organizations.

The anarchic model requires that the military system be democratized and it is incompatible with the corporate model. If military institutional life were democratized, the minister of defense and the high command would soon find themselves struggling to keep order within the armed forces. Such democratic anarchy started to develop as an outgrowth of military participation in competitive elections and the revival of officers assemblies.

Gorbachev's reforms were intended to increase pressure on the military leadership from below and from society at large. They produced a semidemocratized military corporate model and it began to create qualitative changes in the national defense system which posed a danger to Soviet political stability. The minister of defense began to lose the ability to speak for the military as a whole. Officers who held elective office had the right to criticize the minister of defense, to take legislative initiative, and to investigate military behavior. Various nationalist political movements began to challenge the military's right to draft youth into the Soviet armed forces. Civic organizations began to probe into military life, especially questions related to the high rate of noncombat deaths and conduct that violated basic military codes of conduct. Independent trade unions started to organize inside the armed forces.

Gorbachev's Perestroika and Officers Assemblies

Gorbachev's minister of defense, Dmitry Yazov instituted officers assemblies on 1 August 1989 as part of perestroika in the armed forces. These institutions were supposed to encourage officers to take an active role in improving military life and to promote "democratization of the armed forces." They conducted elections through secret ballot to form leading bodies and to send delegates to higher level assemblies. The first year's elections had normal, rather conservative results. Some 70 percent of the elected leaders were senior commanders or political officers while only 30 percent were junior officers.

Gorbachev and Yazov encouraged the officers to discuss political and economic reforms as well as military issues and made positive examples of assemblies that invited civilian political leaders to meetings with the professional soldiers.[3] Thus, the first generation of "democratic" assemblies were dominated by the people who normally commanded and controlled the units where they were formed. However, they had the potential to develop into political institutions through which the officers as a group could protest against the policies of their military and civilian leaders. And this is precisely what happened.

Yeltsin, Shaposhnikov, and the Officers Assemblies

Officers assemblies survived the Soviet state's collapse and gave disgruntled officers an official vehicle for organizing themselves to demand a hearing from senior civilian and military leaders. Officers began assembling to discuss the political situation. This was a natural reaction to the collapse of the Soviet state and the realization that Boris Yeltsin was not going to prevent the sovereign republics from breaking the Soviet defense system into pieces. The assemblies passed resolutions demanding an all-Union meeting.

CIS Supreme Commander Shaposhnikov was caught in a bind. If he ignored demands for a hearing coming from the officer corps, he might face a rebellion. If he gave into their demands and then lost control over the officer corps, he would be fired and civil-military tensions would sharply increase. In December 1991, he came under pressure to hold an All-Army Officers Assembly in Moscow. Shaposhnikov gave his approval for a session with about 1,000 officers "freely elected" by officers assemblies throughout the military system. The assembly was to have been a one-day affair, on 14 January 1992—the eve of the next CIS civilian leadership summit. The Ministry of Defense agreed to pay for travel and related expenses.[4] CIS civilian leaders could not but realize that the military was planning to use the officers assembly to apply pressure on them to preserve as much of the former Soviet defense system as possible. That was Shaposhnikov's personal and professional goal. But could he control the officers who increasingly saw him as Yeltsin's ally and one of the people responsible for destroying the Soviet state?

The Political Mood Prior to the All-Army Officers Assembly

In the Soviet days, the Communist Party's MPA would have controlled the elections to the officers assembly and guaranteed Shaposhnikov a governable meeting. However, Shaposhnikov and Yeltsin abolished the MPA in August 1991 and replaced it with a department of military educational and personnel affairs. The new department was still uncertain of its mission and authority. Should it control the officers from above or facilitate professional self-governance? Initially it seemed to lean towards the latter in keeping with Shaposhnikov's more democratic style of military leadership. Its deputy head, Col. Aleksandr Zyuskevich, described the upcoming All-Army Officers Assembly as a major political event: "The point is that the future of the army and the navy is neither to be decided in the quiet of private offices nor in the corridors of the highest ranking authorities. Problems will be placed on the agenda for discussion by the entire officer corps of the Armed Forces. This is also an impressive fact of the times."[5] The CIS heads of state were invited to attend the officers assembly.

What Zyuskevich said points towards the fundamental difference between the Byzantine and more democratic models for military participation in national political life. The Byzantine conspiratorial model is inherently elitist. The key political bargaining takes place within a narrow leadership circle. Officers resented the political facts that the Kremlin's leaders had imposed on them and the country. They wanted their views and their representatives to participate in policy making at the highest levels. Shaposhnikov also wanted a stronger military voice because he disagreed with the turn of events, the trend towards dividing the Soviet armed forces and defense system. He could not increase his influence and military corporate influence unless the civilians could be convinced that the Soviet military was solidly behind him. On the one hand, a well-organized All-Army Officers Assembly that supported his preferred position on the post-Soviet military system would be an asset. On the other, an assembly dominated by extremists would damage his credibility and effectiveness with Yeltsin and the other leaders. The democratic corporate model is inherently threatening to military cohesion and to civilian control over the armed forces, all the more so during times of political disunity.

Zyuskevich's interview appeared on page one of *Krasnaya zvezda,* to the right of a banner headline that summed up the Ministry's point of view: "SOLDIERS MUST SWEAR AN OATH TO THE PEOPLE, POLITICIANS TO COMMON SENSE."[6] The headline stood above a photograph of an armed soldier contemplating his military oath and was accompanied by an editorial by Vladimir Urban that concluded with a warning about repetitions of 1917 when various political commissars began dividing the military into "ours" and "theirs." The fact that the Union was coming apart and the post-Soviet states had not given the military clear answers about their present and future status was the main concern. However, officers were also worried about economic reforms and the strong, antimilitary and antidefense line the Yeltsin administration appeared to be taking with encouragement from the Western powers.

Yeltsin began 1992 with a pledge to implement deep economic reforms, Russia would finally take the path that other "civilized" states had taken. Prime Minister Yegor Gaidar would implement market reforms beginning with price liberalization. The civilianization of the Russian economy was part of the Yeltsin administration's economic reform plan. The military budget would be cut but the defense spending cuts would be aimed at bloated defense procurement budgets. Yeltsin promised to increase salaries and benefits to keep pace with the inflationary burst expected in 1992.[7] Further, some budget cutters expected to achieve defense savings by reducing the size of the armed forces. With fewer people on the military payroll, the Russian treasury might be able to maintain and even improve salaries and benefits without increasing total spending, at least in theory.

The Planned Assembly Swells to 5,000 Officers

Such news and events caused more and more officers to demand representation at the Moscow assembly. Shaposhnikov kept Yeltsin informed and conferred with him about the best way to handle the meeting. Yeltsin pledged to take part in the meeting and agreed that the officers deserved to be heard and to get answers directly from top civilian leaders. This was consistent with Yeltsin's populist political style. Yeltsin invited the officers to assemble within the Kremlin walls in the prestigious Palace of Congresses and issued the necessary orders to the Kremlin staff and guards.[8] The number of authorized representatives was increased from 1,000 to 5,000. The date was moved from 14 January to 17 January 1992. This gave more time to prepare and permitted the CIS heads of state to meet prior to the officers rather than immediately after the officers. The CIS summit was set for 16 January 1992. In the weeks before the Assembly, the Ministry of Defense published one strong editorial after another, numerous letters from disgruntled officers, and motions formally adopted by local and regional officers assemblies.

On 10 January 1992, the officers assemblies of the Moscow region sent delegates to an all-Moscow regional officers assembly which was to consider the main military issues facing the country. Because this body represented the former Soviet Union's most prestigious military institutions and elite armed forces, its views were politically significant. Its resolutions warned that the political games being played with the armed forces had become dangerous to civil peace, Commonwealth security, and to military personnel who were hostage to politics. They warned that the tragedy affecting the military could spread across the entire former Soviet Union. But instead of demanding the restoration of the Soviet Union and an end to the formation of national armed forces, the Moscow officers assembly endorsed the right of the new sovereign states to form their own armed forces. However, the officers endorsed linking the national armed forces into a common defense system and retaining unified armed forces for air defense and strategic nuclear deterrence. Therefore, their official declaration followed the line of reasoning which Marshal Shaposhnikov had using since August 1991. The Moscow assembly reminded all military personnel that they had sworn an oath to protect the people. Since no one had released them from those oaths, it was their duty to exercise restraint and to guarantee the calm environment the politicians needed to adopt new laws governing the armed forces and to complete basic reforms successfully. Military cohesion and self-discipline could prevent civil war. It was up to the officers to guarantee civil peace.[9]

The military had a serious political problem. The nationalists in the republics attacked the armed forces as "the last bastion of empire." The radical democrats speculated about the "military threat" to democratic reform and were eager to cut defense spending and to reduce the size of the armed forces. The fact that some 5,000 officers were about to gather and were virtually demanding that the CIS presidents appear before them only enhanced such concerns. Was it prudent to permit the military to gather in such an overtly political manner during a time of crisis?[10] Shaposhnikov supported the right of officers to meet and to express their professional views on matters of national concern. The soldiers had maintained good discipline so far and had not permitted themselves to be dragged into ethno-national and partisan political conflicts. Shaposhnikov's ideal of the Army was a strong force that continued to serve the higher interests of all the peoples of the former Soviet Union by refusing to yield to provocative attacks. Was that about to change?[11]

Shaposhnikov practiced a noblesse oblige philosophy in which the officer protects the higher national interests by maintaining stability and defending the country while the civilian politicos do their best to find solutions to basic problems. The Army was outside petty, partisan politics but it was the primary guarantor of the political process. This philosophy gave the officer a sense of political superiority over the politician and made the armed forces the superior guardian of national interests and security. Such ideas could nurture a climate favorable to praetorianism. Since Shaposhnikov and many officers were convinced that politicos were damaging the common defense, the military's corporate interests, and the personal interests of military personnel as a whole, civilian politicians had good reason to be concerned. Shaposhnikov understood those concerns and took them seriously: "I saw my main task at that time as preventing confrontation between the Army and the political leadership of the CIS states."[12] He believed the best way for the civilian leaders to avoid confrontation with the former Soviet armed forces was to adopt responsible, effective military policies, to communicate them to the military, and to implement them. Time was of the essence since the officers were demanding answers and putting pressure on Shaposhnikov. His leadership effectiveness was also on the line.

CIS Heads of State React to Military Pressure

The CIS heads of state met in Moscow on 16 January 1992. Shaposhnikov's staff had prepared a number of basic policy statements and agreements for their consideration, the set he believed had to be approved in order to keep things manageable. The CIS heads of state approved two sets of agreements covering key military issues and thereby gave Shaposhnikov some positive information to report to the officers assembly. But he could not report CIS unanimity since there was none. And, if the CIS heads of state refused to accept CIS political cohesion, how could they support a cohesive military system? Only nine of the former fifteen Soviet republics came to the CIS civilian summit and there were serious differences among the nine about the direction of military reform. The voting patterns confirmed that the civilian leaders would not agree to build a common defense system. Nevertheless, the heads of state did address some military concerns. The fact that the officers assembly was staring them in the face certainly made them pay attention to the armed forces.

The first set of agreements was designed to give military personnel hope that they would be treated fairly and professionally by the new states. This was the essential vote because the outcome affected every military family. Would they be treated like an alien army of occupation or given the full protection of the host state? Would they get to keep their apartments and/or receive fair compensation for them if they decided to relocate to another CIS state? Armenia, Azerbaijan, Belarus, Kazakhstan, Kirghizstan, Russia,

Tadjikistan, Ukraine, and Uzbekistan pledged to treat the military fairly and to place the armed forces under the protection of law. They further pledged to create the legal base for such guarantees rapidly.[13]

The second set of agreements addressed military oaths and command and control. The military demanded to know whom they now served. The CIS heads of state reaffirmed Marshal Shaposhnikov's authority and authorized him to decide when and where the new oaths of allegiance would be administered. However, these agreements and guidelines confirmed the fact that the CIS states were divided. Instead of one agreement on oaths, they had to pass two. Eight heads of state voted for the first; five heads of state for the second. The first was for military personnel serving in the CIS's joint forces. It was supported by representatives of the five republics that intended to form a defensive alliance: Armenia, Kazakhstan, Kirghizstan, Russia, and Tadjikistan. The second was for military personnel serving in the CIS strategic forces. It was adopted by Armenia, Azerbaijan, Belarus, Kazakhstan, Kyrgyzstan, Russia, Tajikistan, and Ukraine. Both oaths were identical in content. The soldiers swore to uphold the constitution and laws of their state and of the states where they serve and to obey their commanders.[14]

These agreements solved specific problems but they did not add up to a coherent legal foundation for the post-Soviet military. The CIS heads of state got what they wanted, an agreement that required the military personnel stationed on their territory to recognize that they had to obey the laws of the respective republics. Shaposhnikov got what he needed, an agreement that required the officers to obey their commanders. This reinforced military cohesion and discipline. In effect, this meant that he would have to resolve political problems that developed when the republics passed laws and/or issued decrees affecting the status of the military on their territory. This required an understanding between him and the heads of state that neither side would initiate any major policy changes without advanced consultation.

Shaposhnikov asked all the presidents to join him at the officers assembly. Which presidents were willing to face the 5,000 officers the next morning? Yeltsin and Kazakhstan's Nazarbayev argued that all heads of state should attend. Shaposhnikov supported that position. But Ukraine's Kravchuk disagreed. He proposed that Yeltsin be delegated to represent the CIS civilian leadership. Nazarbayev insisted upon attending and participating. Further, Uzbekistan's president, Islam Karimov, informed the meeting that he wanted to be represented there and was authorizing his representative to the CIS summit to perform that function in his absence. The CIS civilians resolved the issue by designating Yeltsin and Nazarbayev to serve as their official representatives. Uzbekistan's V. R. Niyazmatov also attended and spoke.[15] The military regarded Kravchuk as the wrecker, the CIS politician who destroyed the military's ability to form a powerful post-Soviet defense system built upon the strategic triangle of Russia, Ukraine, and Kazakhstan. The military regarded Nazarbayev much more positively even though he was a non-Russian of Turkic-Kazakh and Islamic heritage. Nazarbayev was popular with the military because he supported unified defense, a common defense space, and interethnic cooperation. The military regarded Yeltsin with ambivalence. Yeltsin had some political repair work to do with the soldiers because he had not delivered on his pledge to do his best to retain as much of the former Soviet military system as possible. and the demokraty in his entourage were slashing Russia's defense spending plans.

17 January 1992: A Turning Point

Marshal Shaposhnikov remembers the 5,000-delegate officers assembly as a political catharsis—the point at which tension between the officers and the civilian leadership peaked and then began to subside. On the whole, traditional military conservatism prevailed over military radicalism but not without first being put to the political test. If Shaposhnikov failed to maintain his authority and prestige in the face of 5,000 tense and concerned officers, the assembly could degenerate into the democratic-anarchic model of politics. Yeltsin's political enemies were already trying to recruit the military for their neosocialist, neo-authoritarian political movements which were more popularly known as Red-Browns and fascists.

Nazarbayev, Niyazmatov, Shaposhnikov, Stolyarov,[16] and Yeltsin took their places on the stage before some 5,000 or more officers plus reporters. Yeltsin's vice president, Col. General Aleksandr Rutskoi did not attend since he was recovering from an illness. The "administration's" first task was to impose order. Major General Stolyarov presided as the assembly debated the agenda. Stolyarov, a former political officer and defender of the White House in August 1991, was known for his ability to remain calm during acrimonious debates and to steer rowdy meetings in a positive direction. It was tense. For an hour people blew off steam and competed to dominate the meeting but Stolyarov nevertheless got an acceptable agenda. Some radicals demanded that the officers stage a "sit-in" in the Kremlin until all the CIS presidents show up. However, the agenda was set and Stolyarov called a thirty-minute break.

These details suggest that the "administration" had a responsible majority in the assembly but that there was a substantial radical minority that would attempt to push the 5,000 towards extreme positions which neither Shaposhnikov nor Yeltsin could accept. After the recess, the president who enjoyed the greatest popularity with the officers, Nursultan Nazarbayev, took the floor.

Nazarbayev's task was to convince the officers that the situation was under control and that the civilian leaders were behaving in a responsible, effective manner. The best way to do that was to describe what the CIS presidents had just done. He reported on the agreements the CIS presidents had made the previous day and described what would be done by their next session to settle key military questions, especially the status of military officers and their families. Nazarbayev's goal was to alleviate military anxiety and to appeal to their professional values. He said that he agreed with the officers: military questions were the most serious the CIS faced, deserved high priority, and more careful, responsible treatment. Nazarbayev's talk strengthened his military popularity and reputation. He advocated unitary armed forces to give the newly independent states the stability required to institute basic reforms successfully.[17]

Shaposhnikov followed Nazarbayev. The CIS supreme commander had to address the political issue: Did the military and this assembly constitute a threat to civilian rule? He noted that the press was warning that he and the military were out of control and threatening the legitimate civilian leadership. He denied such charges and repeated his basic pledge: "I will never permit our Armed Forces to be used against its people either to settle interethnic or political conflicts."[18] He reiterated his enormously reasonable assessment of what should be accomplished and called for a two-to-three-year transition period during which the post-Soviet defense system would be organized. He told the officers that he understood their reluctance to swear new oaths and stated that the new oaths would only be required of new recruits and conscripts. The military was the key to success or failure in the immensely difficult times the people faced. It was their duty to prevent conflict. Although some new states were creating tensions by forging ahead unilaterally with new policies that affected military interests, the military had to maintain discipline and cohesion. In the final analysis, each sovereign state had the right to decide whether it would have an independent army. The officers assembly should contribute to reform by identifying ways to preserve the security advantages offered by the old system under new political conditions.[19]

A brief rumpus occurred when delegates evicted Vitaly Urazhtsev, a Russian congressmen, military officer, and independent military trade union organizer. Otherwise, the discussions and speeches continued more or less normally. Black Sea Fleet Commander Admiral Kasatonov repeated Shaposhnikov's basic call for cohesion and discipline but did not fail to lambaste Ukraine for repeated destabilizing initiatives aimed at the Black Sea Fleet. As expected, he called for preserving the navy's unity to the maximum extent possible. Then General Patrikeyev and Colonel Butenko described the civil wars and tensions in the Caucasus. By preventing the former Soviet armed forces from being pulled into those civil wars, the officers were preventing a bad situation from degenerating into chaos. They argued for military restraint but firmness when faced with illegal attacks upon the troops and efforts to seize arms. Their description of the fighting in the Caucasus was a graphic warning to the rest of the country about what could happen.[20]

In keeping with the times, the Church had its say. The Orthodox clergy were represented by Metropolitan Kirill, the bishop of Kaliningrad and Smolensk. After the usual declaration that the Church was not entering politics, he gave a brilliant spiritual, political speech that received a standing ovation. He reported that the Church was disturbed to see the unitary army being divided. He reaffirmed the Church's decision to reclaim its traditional role in building military morale and values. He reminded the officers that the Church keeps them in its prayers because they take lives which are sacred to God and are called upon to give their own lives for the country. He recalled the major soldier saints, George and Alexander Nevsky, and asserted that the unitary military system was an integral part of the 1,000-year-old cultural heritage that bound the peoples together. Bishop Kirill spoke about balances of power, geopolitics, and how the multiplication of armies and states increased the potential for war. He reminded the officers that war or peace depended upon them, that they must examine themselves carefully because all people can generate emotions that cause war or peace.[21] (Bishop Kirill kept in touch with the military situation and reappeared during the September-October 1993 political crisis as one of the clergy working to mediate differences between Yeltsin and Parliament.)

Boris Yeltsin followed Metropolitan Kirill but no standing ovation was reported after Yeltsin's address. Yeltsin's performance had tarnished his charisma. He needed to rebuild his image as a competent, effective leader. He reminded the officers that the old Union had been destroyed in August 1991 and that the CIS was now their best chance to advance the common interest. He confirmed that strategic forces were under central control and that he and Marshal Shaposhnikov had the two nuclear buttons. He confirmed that conventional force issues had not been settled but promised to protect the interests of former Soviet military personnel and their dependents in those states which were not cooperating in the CIS process. He addressed the situation in the Baltic republics where ethnic nationalists were demanding an immediate Russian military withdrawal and making life difficult for military dependents and ethnic Russians especially in Latvia and Estonia. Yeltsin rejected charges that concern for Russians living in the former Soviet republics or near-abroad was a new form of Russian imperialism. Yeltsin insisted that it was his duty to guarantee that the Russian diaspora's human and social-welfare rights be respected. He argued that the CIS was making progress on military redevelopment and pledged to have definite, concrete results soon. He repeated Nazarbayev's basic report on the most recent CIS summit. He pledged to settle more military questions at the next summit scheduled for 14 February 1992. By giving a date specific, he reinforced the impression that he was in charge of events and getting things done effectively.

Yeltsin knew the officers were worried about bread and butter issues: housing, salaries, repatriation rights, military downsizing, and so on. He needed a positive way to present defense spending cuts and had found one. Yes, his administration had decided to change defense spending priorities. But, instead of spending more on R&D and procurement, the Yeltsin administration would put its resources primarily into personnel and related expenses such as adding 120,000 apartments in Russia for retiring and repatriating officers. Yeltsin described his new policy this way: "For the first time in the entire history of our army in Russia, a people-oriented military budget was adopted."[22] Some 60 percent of defense spending would be on personnel and 40 percent on military hardware. Yeltsin further pledged to index their salaries, pensions, and benefits and to make regular adjustments. (Later in the year, he revised his 60/40 plan to a 75/25 allocation between personnel and military hardware respectively.) He insisted that the officers and their dependents were his primary concern and reasoned that if they were saved from despair, national defense as a whole would survive. This was good politics since he owed his August 1991 victory to the military and did not want to lose its support. He was more concerned about the military officers than about reactions from managers in the military-industrial complex who faced huge cuts in government defense procurement orders.

Yeltsin promised to fire regional administrators if their midyear evaluations revealed that they had not supported the military properly especially on housing and relocation issues. He reported that the mayors of Moscow and St. Petersburg had pledged enough land for 70,000 officers to build private housing. He promised but only for the near term to give the Ministry of Defense a significant portion of hard currency earned through foreign military sales to support its personnel and housing budget. He authorized the military districts in Russia to sell surplus property in order to enhance spending on personnel.

Yeltsin assumed that the unitary Soviet military system could not be restored. However, he maintained that he was resisting that trend. "The Russian leadership's position on this question is definite and clear—Russia stood for and firmly stands for unified armed forces," he declared. But the specific adjectives Yeltsin used confirmed that the unitary (*yedinye*) armed forces would at best become the (*obyedinennye*) unified armed forces. Yeltsin explained, "Russia has shown great restraint. We did not pioneer the development of national armies. But if the majority of the republics start forming national armies, we will be compelled to do the same."[23]

Col. Viktor Alksnis, the most prominent leader of the Soyuz movement, followed Yeltsin to the podium. As usual, Alksnis was sharp tongued, bold, and incisive. In the past he had attacked Gorbachev's policies and correctly predicted that they would lead to the Union's destruction. Soyuz helped topple Gorbachev by undermining his legitimacy in the armed forces. Now he was firing at Yeltsin. He delivered a radical attack on the CIS process and Yeltsin's role in breaking up the Union. He accused Yeltsin of having destroyed the

Union through his own state coup (*gosudarstvennyi perevorot*). Alksnis mocked the CIS as an empty shell, a fiction without state power. He urged the officers assembly to organize, elect leaders, and demand a seat at the next CIS summit. He argued that by shedding its blood in various conflicts caused by political breakdown, the military had earned the right to direct representation.[24] Major General V. Vostorgin made a similar proposal. He proposed that all 5,000 officers reassemble on 14 February 1992 when the next CIS summit plans to meet. The officers could thereby confront the presidents with their direct representatives as they decide the military system's future.[25]

When the speeches ended, the time to vote on resolutions and to elect a permanent coordinating body for the officers assembly was at hand. As the discussions began on basic principles such as unitary or unified armed forces, the unitarians seized the initiative and forged ahead. This put Shaposhnikov in a difficult position. He had already gone down the other path along with Boris Yeltsin. He could not "fly in reverse." He rose to argue against demanding what was no longer possible even though he like his fellow officers really preferred the unitarian system. Just then, another speaker broke in on a microphone from the balcony and declared: "Gorbachev should be tried for neglecting the Armed Forces and for destroying the USSR; Shaposhnikov should be retired for having destroyed the Armed Forces."[26]

Shaposhnikov's nerves began to snap. He gathered up his papers and said, "If the officers want the supreme commander to retire, then I can do it immediately." He walked off stage. The hall grew silent. Then, someone shouted an invitation to come back. Shaposhnikov returned and made a powerful, brief speech. He hammered away at the realities and at what they had experienced as military professionals who had been dragged into civil wars and political games in Tbilisi, Baku, Vilnius, Riga, and Moscow. He repeated his pledge to prevent the army from being used against the people and to keep it out of partisan conflicts. If his fellow officers truly rejected those policies and really wanted to return to August 1991, then he could not be their leader. With that he left the stage a second time.

For the next twenty minutes his supporters held the podium and seized the momentum. His position won and they brought him back into a hall where the 5,000 gave him a standing ovation. Shaposhnikov would continue to lead the military through the difficult transition. He remembers this moment as the turning point after which the military as a whole cooperated with him and with the CIS presidents. The armed forces maintained good discipline and prevented civil war.[27] From a political point of view it was an extraordinary event. The officer corps of the former Soviet military had acted to confirm their support for Shaposhnikov and his policies. Did this mean that the officers expected to have the right to confirm the military system's top leadership in the future? Is a semidemocratic, military corporate model a viable way of structuring civil-military relations?

Military Democratization Again?

The officers assembly elected Col. Aleksandr Mochaikin to chair its coordinating council. The assembly passed one, long compromise motion which endorsed unitary armed forces but recognized that the peoples representatives, the parliaments will decide policy questions.[28] Was the military trying to institutionalize its political voice by building a permanent organization in Moscow known as the officers assembly? Apparently so. It scheduled its next All-Army Officers Assembly meeting for 17–18, June 1992. That meeting would give the civilian politicians six months to resolve basic military issues before facing the officers again. The assembly created a large Coordinating Council with 126 people. The Council immediately began developing its own, military positions on proposals that the CIS heads of state were expected to take up at their forthcoming meeting on 14 February 1992.[29] In early May 1992, its Presidium published its by-laws and defined itself as the "Armed Forces officer corps's *permanently* operating civic action organization It independently defines its forms and methods of work aimed at implementing the principles of democratization in military-service relationships and social justice in military units and on board ship. These principles require improving and strengthening unity of command on a democratic foundation in the Armed Forces."[30]

The Council invited new officers assemblies to form at all levels and elect representatives to a CIS-level organization. The principle of "democratic centralism" was to govern relationships between the various levels; that is to say, lower assemblies were to be bound by decisions taken by higher representative bodies of the officer corps. Commanders were to provide space for Assembly meetings and offices. The assemblies could collect dues and maintain accounts. They could discuss just about anything of importance to military service personnel and issue resolutions. They were to participate in the selection of commanders. Commanders were expected to give careful consideration to the resolutions and to implement them. If not, they were to ask the assembly to reconsider. If a disagreement persisted, the commander and the assembly were supposed to appeal to a higher assembly or commanding officer.[31]

Captain Mochaikin's organization attempted to operate as a political lobby on behalf of its members. When the CIS heads of state met, he sent them recommendations. For example, Mochaikin's group distributed materials to the Tashkent, May 1992, CIS summit which met to discuss and sign the first formal CIS Collective Security Treaty. He lobbied for the continued existence of CIS Unified Armed Forces, the foundation upon which his organization operated.[32]

Taming the Officers Assemblies

The officers assembly of 17 January 1992 made a negative impression on civilian leaders. It was a radical challenge to the standard models for civilian control over defense affairs and a threat to the military's traditional authoritarian operating principles, the chain of command. The idea that military officers had a right to an organized, independent voice in national political life was rejected by Soviet authoritarian tradition and by Western democratic tradition. The idea that the military as an institution should be operated in a semidemocratic manner was likewise rejected by democratic and authoritarian political systems. The officers assemblies developed when civilian leadership was confused and divided. They were choked off as soon as the Russian state crossed the Rubicon and nationalized the bulk of the former Soviet Armed Forces.

In May 1992 Boris Yeltsin promulgated the Russian Ministry of Defense and made Pavel Grachev post-Soviet Russia's first minister of defense. Grachev tamed the officers assemblies by issuing orders that redefined the parameters for their activities. He ruled that officers assemblies were appropriate only at lower levels and may not be permitted to develop into independent national political bodies. Grachev blocked the Mochaikin group's efforts to build a self-governing network of officers assemblies from the bottom to the top of the Russian military system. Grachev's Russian Ministry of Defense would not permit a repetition of Shaposhnikov's grand All-Army Officers Assembly that brought 5,000 officers to Moscow. Times had changed and Yeltsin and Grachev intended to restore a cohesive command and control system. Thereafter, it was the anti-Yeltsin ultranationalists and Unionists who organized their own officers assemblies and used them as overtly political bodies. However, Grachev neither paid for them nor permitted them to operate on Russian military facilities.

On 12 September 1992, Grachev promulgated new regulations on officers assemblies to replace those that Soviet Minister of Defense Yazov had issued back on 1 August 1989 when the Soviet Union still existed. Grachev's move was designed to reinforce the legal point that Mochaikin's officers assemblies were unauthorized civic organizations that had no right to operate in the Russian Armed Forces. Henceforth, the only officers assemblies permitted inside the military system had to follow Grachev's regulations. The new assemblies were to promote patriotism, honor, duty, and professionalism. There would be no more, officially sponsored, All-Army Officers Assemblies.

The official military historians developed an appropriate, imperial Russian foundation for these officers assemblies. Instead of political organizations, they were to be professional associations that supported military professionalism and which stayed out of partisan politics. Their roots were found in the Imperial Armed Forces, not the Bolshevik revolutionary tradition. They were traced back to the officers' clubs, restaurants, hostels, and associations which formed in the nineteenth century and which promoted collegiality and professionalism. Such professional associations had deep Russian roots and could be used to promote fraternity and patriotism.[33]

Grachev had difficulty reining in the officers assemblies especially in the Baltic republics where Russian military personnel were feeling stress and anxiety due to their precarious political and economic status. His main strategy was to prevent disgruntled officers from holding larger regional and national meetings. He was criticized by democrats and conservatives for such practices. Grachev refused to permit himself to be pilloried by officers assemblies or their representatives. The neo-Communists in *Pravda* criticized him for this because they believed that the assemblies could be used to give government policy a conservative, nationalist bias.[34] In the Russian Parliament, moderate reformers such as Sergei Stepashin thought Grachev had gone too far and urged him to relax his controls a bit.[35] More radical reformers such as Deputy Urazhtsev who had been evicted by the rather conservative-minded officers assembly of 17 January 1992, wanted Grachev to permit free trade unions to form in the armed forces, a position which the Minister of Defense rejected except for nonmilitary employees of his ministry.[36] Grachev refused to recognize or to give any official or even semi-official status to the so-called Coordinating Council of Officers Assemblies, the body that formed out of the 17 January meeting. He called it an attempt by the old guard to revive the political commissar system, the old MPA. Nevertheless, Grachev promised to permit officers to elect assemblies at the unit and perhaps the division levels but not higher. He was determined to prevent any repetition of the type of anarchy created by 5,000 member national meetings.[37]

Terekhov's Union of Officers

As the Ministry of Defense brought the officers assemblies operating inside the Armed Forces under tighter control, Stanislav Terekhov's Union of Officers became the vehicle for giving voice to radical discontent.[38] The Union of Officers was organized after the All-Army Officers Assembly of 17 January 1992. It used patriotic, strong Russia, even Unionist themes to attract former officers, veterans, Cossacks, and various and sundry military, police, and security personnel into a new national political force beyond the control of the Ministry of Defense and the president of Russia. It encouraged national opposition to Yeltsin and Grachev. Terekhov's Union of Officers was coordinating its activities with the other anti-Yeltsin groups. It was presenting itself as the military wing of the anti-Yeltsin opposition coalition.

Officers were unhappy with Yeltsin and Grachev. Terekhov hoped to turn this discontent into a national political force. At the time of the August coup, there were around 3,000,000 military personnel. The postcoup Russian government set is target at around 1,500,000 military personnel by the end of 1995. This meant that there would have to be a 50 percent reduction in the number of military officers. Such cuts naturally created tension in the officer corps. But that was just the beginning of the morale problem. The reductions took place at the same time that Russia was pulling its troops out of Germany, the Baltic, etc. and the unitary armed forces were being divided into national armies.[39] *Moscow News* reported that, "About two-thirds of the officers would like to have a military-based regime introduced in Russia. National-patriotic forces count on 70 percent support from among the officers."[40] Retired military and KGB generals who had supported the August 1991 coup, such as Col. General Albert Makashov and KGB General Aleksandr Sterlingov, were active in Terekhov's movement. So was former Soviet First Deputy Minister of Defense, Col. General Vladislav Achalov who had played a prominent role in the August coup and who would reemerge during the political confrontation between Yeltsin and Parliament in September-October 1993.

Terekhov's movement announced that it would hold an All-Russian Officers Assembly in Moscow on 21–22 February 1993. The dates were selected to lend support to Parliament in its struggle with President Yeltsin over the division of powers between the legislative and executive branches of government and over the main direction of economic reform. Terekhov's officers assembly met inside the Russian Parliament building, an act that sent a clear political message from Ruslan Khasbulatov, the leader of Parliament, to the Yeltsin administration. Terekhov was taking sides in the political battle that was brewing between Yeltsin and Parliament. Terekhov boasted that he had 30,000 active duty officers organized in underground cells. Terekhov's assembly rebuked Yeltsin and Grachev for incompetent leadership that was turning Great Russia into a third-rate power. The Red-Browns in his organization made their usual neo-Communist, nationalistic, anti-American, anti-Zionist charges against Yeltsin and the demokraty. They poked fun at Yeltsin's economic advisers ("Little boys in pink shorts") and ridiculed Minister of Defense Pavel ("Pashka") Grachev as Yeltsin's errand boy in the armed forces. The officers assembly passed a resolution demanding that Col. General (Ret.) Achalov's be made minister of defense in place of Grachev.[41] Simply put, Terekhov wanted to revisit the choices of August 1991 and to change the political outcome. He wanted a strong political regime and a statist strategy to rebuild Russian power rapidly.

An associated group, the Russian All-National Union met right after the officers assembly. It brought together a motley collection of nationalists and radicals including Viktor Anpilov whose Trudovaya Rossiya movement seemed to be advocating sedition. Vladimir Kryuchkov, Oleg Baklanov, Oleg Shenin, Anatoly Lukyanov, Army General (Ret.) Varennikov—some of the top leaders of the August coup attended and were treated to a hero's welcome. Generals Sterlingov and Terekhov made their familiar charges against Yeltsin, Grachev, and Gaidar. They claimed that the Yeltsin team had "betrayed" Russian national interests and had to be replaced.[42] They asked and got the Russian All-National Union to pass a resolution calling for Grachev's removal and Achalov's appointment as minister of defense. The rightists paraded through the streets in large demonstrations on Armed Forces Day.[43] They marched down Tversky Boulevard and held a large rally on Manege Square below the Kremlin walls. Even though some of their speakers called for the violent overthrow of the Yeltsin regime, no legal action was taken against them. Still, there were some fights, beatings, and window smashing at elegant Western shops.[44]

Grachev and Yeltsin Respond to the Challenge

Both Yeltsin and Grachev had to respond to the political attacks aimed at them by groups claiming to represent military officers, veterans, and other patriotic forces. Yeltsin gave a special interview in commemoration of Armed Forces Day during which he reminded the military of the severe repression and abuse the professional soldier had experienced under the Soviet regime. Yeltsin emphasized that only a democratic Russia could protect the military against a new round of political repression. He rebuked the nationalist extremists who promoted ethnic conflict and social discord in the name of patriotism. He admitted that his reform program was running into difficulty and making life harder for military personnel and he pledged to take corrective action. He reminded the armed forces of their duty to keep the peace: "The armed forces in no small way are the guarantee of stability in society."[45]

Grachev responded to specific charges hurled at him. Terekhov and Company claimed that he had dismissed 30,000 officers for political reasons. Grachev said that the actual number was three, just three cases of dismissal for overt violation of the rules that prohibit partisan political activity in the Russian armed forces. Yes, officers were being furloughed in large numbers but that was in conjunction with the normal cuts in military manpower which the government had mandated. Grachev argued that Terekhov's recent meeting and the street riot in Moscow demonstrated the danger inherent in efforts to politicize the military. The so-called officers assembly had been organized by and used by political parties for partisan political purposes and had little to do with military professional interests. Nevertheless, Grachev agreed with critics who believed that he needed to devote more attention to his own officers assemblies and he pledged to do so. He announced that he had ordered his top commanders to fan out across the country to talk with officers assemblies about the general situation and to explain what the Ministry of Defense was doing to promote their interests and national defense. He would personally meet with a Moscow regional officers assembly on 4 March 1993.[46]

Grachev met with his Moscow assembly and stated his policy: "The current leadership of the Armed Forces will not permit the Army to lean to the Left or to the Right. It will strictly fulfill the laws and the Constitution of Russia." He rebuked, Terekhov, Anpilov, and others for advocating the use of force to overthrow the government and to change policy. He ordered the military to stay within the law and to uphold the Constitution. In order to assuage military concern about the Yeltsin administration, he reported that the president would soon hold special meetings on military and defense issues and take action to improve the overall situation.[47] Grachev warned the commanders that political emissaries would be trying to enter military bases during the forthcoming extraordinary session of Congress. He instructed his commanders to prevent political activities on their bases and to keep the armed forces out of partisan politics. He reminded them that the military's primary energy should be focused on military reform and professional development. He expected the officers assemblies to focus on those activities.[48] In a related move, Grachev upgraded the positions of political/personnel officers from "commanders assistants for personnel work" to "deputy commanders." It was generally felt that the military had neglected political indoctrination since the downfall of the MPA and needed to begin rebuilding military morale and understanding of the officer's role in post-Soviet society.[49]

Conclusion

The two officers assemblies, Shaposhnikov's and Terekhov's demonstrated that the military had the potential to develop into an autonomous political force. The reforms which Grachev instituted after the Russian state nationalized the bulk of the Soviet armed forces halted much of the anarchy that had taken hold in military affairs. However, elements of the anarchic tradition persisted. So did public debate about military issues and military discussion of public affairs.

Shaposhnikov's January 1992 assembly demonstrated that officers were deeply concerned about their personal interests, military-institutional interests and the post-Soviet national interest. Although the session was emotional and tense, on the whole it represented the victory of political rationality over emotionalism. In the final analysis, the military reaffirmed its key values and stayed cohesive and obeyed its commanders and civilian leaders. It also got some of the attention it demanded from the civilian heads of states. Yeltsin responded to military criticism and decided to appease the officers at the expense of the military-industrial complex. Military political pressure influenced Yeltsin's decisions on the 1992 Russian national budget. He gutted the defense procurement order and spent those funds on military salaries, housing, and other benefits instead of new weapons and research and development.

Terekhov's February 1993 officers assembly demonstrated that anti-Yeltsin political forces were still courting the national defense constituency. The competition for military loyalty wasn't over and some radicals were prepared to take up arms against the Yeltsin administration. The fact that prominent August coup leaders such as Col. General (Ret.) Vladislav Achalov and KGB Chairman Vladimir Kryuchkov were encouraging Terekhov's movement was a warning to the Yeltsin administration that steps had to be taken to prevent the armed forces from being drawn into radical political movements.

Grachev and Yeltsin responded to this political challenge and took steps to assure military cohesion and political reliability. Grachev briefed his commanders and told them that they would be held personally accountable for an immediate improvement in military discipline and cohesion. He also accelerated the organization of officially sanctioned officers assemblies. He wisely began to fill the political space with Ministry of Defense professional activities. Yeltsin tried to appease the officers by pledging to take more effective action to solve their immediate problems; he also worked harder at demonstrating his foreign policy independence from the United States. Yeltsin had to repair his relationships with the armed forces before launching his final political offensive against the Khasbulatov Parliament. It was Grachev's task to firm up military cohesion and to prevent the armed forces from being drawn into political conflict. Military neutrality in this situation strengthened Yeltsin's position.

When Grachev and Yeltsin reminded the military about the Soviet past— the ordeal of trying to build a professional career under Soviet political conditions, they were appealing to the professional soldier's desire to join the rest of the "civilized" world. It was this hope that inspired many to support perestroika and to resist the SEC in August 1991. Rowdy political assemblies were incompatible with modern professionalism and threatened societal reform. The military establishment disliked incompetent, radical politicians and said as much in its official publications. Grachev did not ask the military to make a choice between Terekhov's radicals and the Yeltsin administration. He ordered them to focus on professional work such as improving combat readiness and building their post-Soviet organizational structures. His professional instincts were sound in that he rejected calls from the Left and the Right to permit officers to organize for political purposes.

Military political culture was in conflict with itself. On the one hand, some older radical ideas—part of the Bolshevik revolutionary heritage, took on new life when perestroika created officers assemblies, sanctioned political office-holding by military officers, and reaffirmed that the military was in politics in the grand sense of the term. On the other hand, the new military professionalism valued cohesion and rational deliberate problem solving by military experts and considered politics a necessary evil at best. Although the new professionals could long for improved professional status and freedom from irresponsible political interference, the state which they served lacked the stability and viability required to give them the type of semi-autonomous professional life they desired. On balance it appears that the Soviet military legacy of professionalism was generally well-suited to adapt to Western models. The civilian side of the political equation was the problem.

The Russian military could not enjoy Western-style professional benefits until Russia had an effective, stable, prosperous democratic state. Second, in order to reduce the military's vulnerability to capricious meddling and partisan interference in professional life, Russia needed effective checks and balances on executive power. Civilian control over the military had been democratized in as much as a democratically elected president controlled the armed forces. However, President Yeltsin treated the military as his fiefdom and the legislative branch had virtually no influence over key military appointments. Minister of Defense Grachev stayed close to Yeltsin politically and did not cooperate with Parliament's efforts to gain a foothold in military affairs.

But Grachev was not silent and his voice wasn't muted. He debated with his critics and made provocative statements to the press. He did not pull all military officers out of political life and officers continued to serve in the national legislature. Broadly speaking, the military continued to exercise political rights it received under Gorbachev although Grachev and Yeltsin worked hard to keep such activities from undermining military cohesion and reliability. Civil-military relations began to take on a distinctly Russian flavor. They were modern and Western in the sense that the military were under the control of elected civilian authorities; but the Russian military was more vocal, visible, and varied in its political participation than its Western counterparts.

Notes

1. See George Katkov, *Russia 1917: The February Revolution* (New York: Harper & Row, 1967), p. 352 for Tsar Nicholas II's message to the officer corps.
2. The connection between military indoctrination that made the soldier the defender of higher national values and military coups and/or military participation in authoritarian regimes has been observed and described in enough detail to identify a paradigm in which military participation in politics increases. See chapter 4, "The Praetorian Army and the Praetorian State" in Amos Perlmutter, *The Military and Politics in Modern Times* (New Haven, Conn.: Yale University Press, 1977). Soviet literature from the same period during which Perlmutter wrote his classic, identified similar domestic determinants but gave far more emphasis to external factors, particularly U.S.-sponsored military training which encouraged officers to stand guard against civilian political system breakdown. See A. F. Shul'govskii, *Armiya i politika v Latinskoi Amerike* (Moscow: Nauka, 1979).
3. See Lt. Colonel V. Chernobylov, "Ofitserskoye sobranie: god spustya" (The officers assembly: one year later), *Krasnaya zvezda*, 3 August 1990.
4. Col. V. Semenov's interview with Col. Aleksandr Zyuskevich, deputy chairman of the Committee for Personnel Work, "Ofitserskii korpus prosit slova" (The officer corps asks to be heard), *Krasnaya zvezda*, 9 January 1992.
5. *Ibid.*
6. "VOIN DOLZHEN PRISYAGAT' NARODU, A POLITIKI—ZDRAVOMU SMYUSLU," *Ibid.*
7. See Captain Oleg Odnokolenko, "Prezident Rossii B. Yel'tsin otmetil, shto sokrashchenie voennogo byudzheta ne dolzhno provoditsya za schet zhiznennykh nuzhd voennykh" (President of Russia B. Yeltsin said that military budget cuts must not be made at the expense of the vital interests of military personnel), *Krasnaya zvezda*, 17 January 1992.

8. See Shaposhnikov, *Vybor: Zapiski glavkomanduyushego* (Moscow: Nezavisimoe Izdatel'stvo, 1993), p. 142. Built under Khrushchev, the Kremlin "palace of congresses" was the site of former Communist Party meetings and other major, political conventions.

9. "Iz obrashcheniya ofitserskogo sobraniya Moskovskogo garnizona" (From the appeal of the officers assembly of the Moscow garrison), *Krasnaya zvezda*, 15 January 1992.

10. See Captain V. Chupakin's front page editorial in *Krasnaya zvezda's* edition for 17 January 1992, the day the officers assembly met in Moscow.

11. See *Ibid*'s large, political cartoon by Capt. V. Maryukha.

12. Shaposhnikov, *Vybor*, p. 139.

13. "Zayavlenie glav gosudarstv uchastnikov sodruzhestva nezavisimykh gosudarstv" (Declaration of the heads of state of the commonwealth of independent states), *Krasnaya zvezda*, 18 January 1992.

14. "Soglashenie o voennoi prisyage v silakh obshchego naznachenia" and "Soglasheniye o voennoi prisyage v strategicheskikh silakh," *Krasnaya zvezda*, 18 January 1992.

15. See Shaposhnikov, *Vybor*, p. 143.

16. Major General of Aviation, Nikolai Stolyarov headed the successor to the MPA, the so-called Committee for Work with Personnel. He was a political officer who supported Yeltsin at the White House in August 1991. A year earlier, he became a conciliator at the divisive First Congress of the Russian Communist Party. See Lt. Col. Tokarev's interview with Stolyarov, "Nadezhda na razum" (Hoping for reason), *Krasnaya zvezda*, 15 January 1992.

17. Reported by Col. V. Miranovich, "Vsearmeiskoe ofitserskoe sobranie: Armiya dolzhna byt' edinoi" (All-army officers assembly: the army must be unitary), *Krasnaya zvezda*, 18 January 1992.

18. Yevgeny Shaposhnikov, cited in *Ibid.*

19. Yevgeny Shaposhnikov as reported in *Ibid.*

20. See main report on the Assembly by Col. G. Miranovich, Lt. Col. O. Vladykin, Lt. Col. A. Dokuchayev, Lt. Col. V. Zyubin, Lt. Col. V. Rudenko, and Major A. Egorov, "Vsearmeiskoe ofitserskoe sobranie: strastnyi prizyv k blagorazumiyu politikov" (All-army officers assembly: passionate call for reason to politicians), *Krasnaya zvezda*, 21 January 1992.

21. Metropolitan Kirill, cited in *Ibid.*

22. Boris Yeltsin, cited in *Ibid.*

23. Boris Yeltsin, *Ibid.*

24. Col. Viktor Alksnis, *Ibid.*

25. Major General V. Vostorgin, *Ibid.*

26. Shaposhnikov's account, *Vybor*, p. 144.

27. *Ibid.*, pp. 145–47.

28. See "Obrashchenie k narodam, parlamentam, glavam pravitel'stv sodruzhestva nezavisimykh gosudarstv i lichnomu sostavu vooruzhennykh sil" (Appeal to the peoples, parliaments, heads of government of the commonwealth of independent states and the personnel of the armed forces), *Krasnaya zvezda*, 21 January 1992.

29. See Col. A Dokuchayev, "Ot otnosheniya k zashchitnikam Otechestva zavisit prochnost Sodruzhestva" (The Commonwealth's cohesion depends upon its relationship with the Fatherland's defenders), *Krasnaya zvezda*, 31 January 1992.

30. "Ustav Ofitserskogo sobraniya OVS SNG" (Rules of the officers assembly of the CIS UAF), *Krasnaya zvezda*, 7 May 1992.

31. See *Ibid.* The bylaws took one full page of newspaper space.

32. See Col. V Astafyev, Capt. V. Ermolin, "Tashkent gotovitsya k vstreche..." (Tashkent prepares for the meeting...), *Krasnaya zvezda*, 13 May 1992.
33. See Col. Mikhail Shevchenko, "Ofitserskie sobraniya v rossiiskoi armii" (Officers assemblies in the Russian army), *Krasnaya zvezda*, 20 February 1993.
34. See for example, Oleg Meshkov, "Moratorii na vyvod voisk iz Pribaltiki" (Moratorium on troop withdrawals from the Baltic), *Pravda*, 3 November 1992.
35. See Stepashin's speech of 5 December 1992 at the VIIth Congress, *Krasnaya zvezda*, 9 December 1992.
36. Reported by *Krasnaya zvezda*, 9 December 1992.
37. Grachev's press conference, reported by Col. Anatoly Dokuchayev, "Vooruzhennye Sily Rossii na storone Zakona i Konstitutsii" (Russia's armed forces on the side of the law and the constitution), *Krasnaya zvezda*, 18 December 1992.
38. See Sergei Popov, "Soyuz ofitserov prizyvaet provesti 'depolitizirovannoe' ofitserskoe sobranie: no bez politiki poka ne poluchayetsya" (Union of officers calls for a 'depoliticized' officers assembly: but can't be done without politics), *Krasnaya zvezda*, 14 January 1993.
39. Military "shock therapy" is discussed in chapter 16 below.
40. Major General Vladimir Dudnik, "What to expect from the army at the referendum," *Moscow News*, no. 7, 11 February 1993.
41. Reported by Alexander Zhilin, "Is the army in opposition?" *Moscow News*, no. 9, 25 February 1993.
42. Reported by Tatyana Mikhalskaya, "Patriots will make the Kremlin shudder," *Moscow News*, no. 9, 25 February 1993.
43. Reported in *Krasnaya zvezda*, 24 February 1993.
44. Reported by Andrei Kolesnikov, "calls for violent overthrow of the regime again permitted to go scot-free," *Moscow News*, no. 10, 5 March 1993.
45. See Vladimir Chupakhin's report on Yeltsin's Armed Forces Day interview, "Vooruzhennye sily—odin iz garantov stabil'nosti obshchestva" (Armed Forces—one of the guarantors of stability in society), *Krasnaya zvezda*, 23 February 1993.
46. Grachev's press conference, reported by Anatoly Dokuchayev, "Opasno, esli armiya raskoletsya i stanet po raznye storony barrikad" (Dangerous if the army splits and stands on opposite sides of the barricades), *Krasnaya zvezda*, 4 March 1993.
47. Col. Aleksandr Oliinik, Lt. Col. Sergei Popov, "Armii nuzhny ne politicheskie igry, a uglublenie reform," *Krasnaya zvezda*, 10 March 1993.
48. See *Ibid.*
49. See S. Ishchenko, "Net obyanannostei bez prav" (No obligation without rights), *Krasnaya zvezda*, 16 March 1993.

8

Dividing the Army Monolith Responsibly

This chapter analyzes one of the most important military-political events of the twentieth century—the Soviet military machine's reformation into the Russian armed forces and fourteen other national armies. A Soviet military professional—Marshal Yevgeny Shaposhnikov, deserves much of the credit for its success. He demonstrated that the Soviet military could produce statesmen as well as field commanders.

Boris Yeltsin was a political generalist with little knowledge of military affairs. Yeltsin needed high-level professional military support, people he could trust and entrust with extremely delicate assignments. Yeltsin respected Shaposhnikov's abilities and had confidence in his political judgment. However, there were policy differences between them. Yeltsin gave higher priority to the Russocentric model for post-Soviet defense while Shaposhnikov argued for greater investment in collective defense and CIS military cooperation. In the end, Shaposhnikov yielded graciously to Yeltsin's strategy and the rise of the Russian Ministry of Defense which rapidly eclipsed the institutions which Shaposhnikov had started building under the aegis of the Commonwealth of Independent States. By yielding to Yeltsin, Shaposhnikov reaffirmed civilian control over the armed forces in the post-Soviet state. By making a substantial contribution to early CIS defense affairs and related diplomacy, he confirmed that military professionals can participate in politics at the highest levels in a responsible manner.

The choice of roles was dictated partly by history and partly by the civilian leadership. Yeltsin used Shaposhnikov's skills well at a time when they were very much needed. Shaposhnikov was a diplomat and a military manager. He was also an internationalist who was uncomfortable with ethnic chauvinism and Russian state nationalism.

The Marshal Stays in Politics

As of 25 December 1991, the Union was dead but Yevgeny Shaposhnikov still hoped to convince the republics that unified strategic and conventional forces offered the best defense. His general's mind organized the case in a clear, logical, and didactic manner. He laid out a three to five year transition period for an ideal fusion of Commonwealth and national armed forces. But the civilian politicians wouldn't buy it. Shaposhnikov was so upset that he stormed out of the first CIS summit which was held on 30 December 1991. Boris Yeltsin chased after him, ordered him to calm down, convinced him to stay at his post, and gave him an immediate assignment. Yeltsin insisted that Shaposhnikov outline measures required to avert a deep military crisis during the next two months. The marshal hesitated and told the president to take direct command of the military himself. Shaposhnikov did not want to go down in history as the minister of defense who presided over the destruction of the unitary armed forces.[1] However, he was deeply concerned about civil war and decided to stay on for the good of the military and the peoples of the former Soviet Union.

Yeltsin's press conference recapped the summit's results. The CIS heads of state agreed to maintain strictly centralized nuclear forces but reaffirmed the right of each former Soviet republic to decide whether to have independent or collective conventional forces. Three states announced that they intended to build and command independent armed forces: Ukraine, Azerbaijan, and Moldova.[2] Only six of the fifteen Soviet republics supported the concept of CIS common defense: Russia, Armenia, Kazakhstan, Kyrgyzstan, Tajikistan, and Uzbekistan. Georgia wasn't attending CIS meetings due to armed conflict between its president and opposition forces; the three Baltic republics refused to join the CIS let alone any alliances; Turkmenistan preferred a bilateral arrangement with Russia over any collective security system; Azerbaijan, Belarus, Moldova, and Ukraine intended to build independent national armed forces although they were CIS members. The situation was extremely difficult to manage. Shaposhnikov had troops in fifteen former Soviet republics plus Germany, Cuba, and other former Soviet outposts. He reported to a committee of bickering civilian heads of state who expected him to keep order no matter what they did.

Whom do I Serve?

When they received their commissions, Soviet officers swore an oath to a specific government and country: "I will always be ready on orders from the Soviet government to defend my country—the Union of Soviet Socialist Republics..."[3] On 8 December 1991, the heads of three republics proclaimed that the Soviet government and the Soviet Union had ceased to exist as a legal entity. On 21 December 1991, eleven heads of state reaffirmed that claim. On 25 December 1991, the head of the Union government, Mikhail Gorbachev, reluctantly confirmed that political fact, closed his office, and transferred his powers over the Soviet nuclear arsenal to Boris Yeltsin. However, Gorbachev could not give Boris Yeltsin the legal power to command all the armed forces of the former Soviet Union because Yeltsin had already given his word to the other presidents that he supported their right to divide the conventional forces although he argued against that step. Therefore, the Soviet military was in limbo; it had no new head of state or single government to obey. As yet, there was no new oath of allegiance to the CIS.

There were 726,000 former Soviet military personnel in uniform in Ukraine on 3 January 1992 excluding the personnel of the Black Sea Fleet.[4] Ukraine decided that it had to move quickly to consolidate its national military sovereignty in spite of the fact that Yeltsin, Shaposhnikov, Nazarbayev and others were demanding time to think things through and the CIS summit appeared to have reached a consensus against unilateral actions that could spark conflict. During the very first week of 1992, on 3 January, President Kravchuk forced the issue and Minister of Defense Morozov started administering new oaths of allegiance to military personnel serving in Ukraine. He further insisted that all Soviet military assets on Ukraine's territory were the property of Ukraine and could not be moved without Ukraine's permission. This extended to the Black Sea Fleet ships and to Soviet Air Force planes normally based in Ukraine. The fact that some of these military assets were part of the CIS strategic weapons system made no difference. Everything belonged to Ukraine.

Shaposhnikov held a long press conference in which he appealed to the peoples, parliaments, and leaders of the sovereign states to reject the splitters and to retain a common defense system. However, there was contradictory information circulating about what he and Russia were planning to do. On the one hand, he hammered away at Ukraine's actions as if he expected to be able to reverse them. On the other, he pointed to NATO as a good model to follow and NATO was an alliance of sovereign states three of which were independent nuclear powers. He criticized Ukraine for administering new oaths but he suggested that the CIS armed forces could swear oaths of allegiance to their states and to uphold the laws and the constitution of the states in which they are stationed. He also reaffirmed his pledge that as long as he remained commander, the military would neither be used against the people nor for partisan political purposes.[5] The evidence suggests that Shaposhnikov and Yeltsin were wavering and finding it difficult to decide how to proceed.

The evidence from early 1992 suggests that Yeltsin and Shaposhnikov had difficulty making up their minds about the best way to control CIS military reform. They were of two minds. On the one hand, at the 30 December 1991 CIS Summit, Shaposhnikov urged Yeltsin to claim the entire military system and to declare himself its commander in chief. This would have given the military the type of clarity that officers understood and valued. The republics were prepared to accept Yeltsin's claim to the Soviet military forces stationed outside the former Soviet Union. But they could be expected to resist granting him powers over Soviet troops and facilities in their countries. This was not an easy problem to solve. Further, Yeltsin had repeatedly pledged not to be the first to split the unitary Soviet armed forces. Wouldn't it be better politics to let Ukraine and President Kravchuk take the blame? Soviet military-political rage could be deflected towards Kiev. The military might start dividing the CIS heads of state into "good" and "bad" presidents.

Yeltsin's Bold Initiative: Hasty Big Step Forward

Was Yeltsin preparing to follow Ukraine's example and to proclaim the establishment of the Armed Forces of the Russian Federation? It appeared that way on 5 January 1992 when he published an oath of allegiance to the Russian Federation along with instructions about how to administer it.[6] He sent the new oaths out to former Soviet troops stationed in the other fourteen republics. Kravchuk and Morozov crossed the "forbidden" line first when they began administering Ukrainian oaths on 3 January 1992. But when Yeltsin and Shaposhnikov followed through and published a new oath to Russia on 5 January 1992, they met with immediate resistance from two sources. First, Shaposhnikov was sharply criticized by military officers who warned that such an act by Russia would greatly aggravate military and political fragmentation. They demanded a hearing in Moscow and began electing representatives to the All-Army Officers Assembly which was discussed in the previous chapter. Second, Yeltsin was rebuked by CIS presidents who believed that he had grossly violated their national independence. They argued that the president of Russia had no right to issue orders to former Soviet troops stationed in their countries.

The Russian military oath of 5 January 1992 addressed foreign service and reflected Shaposhnikov's strong belief that the military must not be used for partisan political purposes. It was designed to serve the armed forces of a democratic Russia which had national and international duties to perform. It obliged military personnel to serve anywhere they were sent by the Government of Russia and to respect the laws of the state on whose territory they served. It also addressed Russian domestic politics and required that soldiers swear "Not to take up arms against my people and its legally elected organs of power."[7]

If former Soviet officers of Russian ethnicity who were stationed in Kazakhstan took the new Russian oath, such officers would immediately mark themselves as being troops in the service of a foreign power. If some officers in Ukraine took the oath to Russia while others took the oath to Ukraine, there would be two armies in Ukraine, one native and legitimate and the other foreign. The situation demanded a solution. The political life of the CIS and its Supreme Command had to be extended until things could be sorted out.

Kazakhstan's Support for Unified Armed Forces

In his effort to make the CIS into a substantial military alliance, Yevgeny Shaposhnikov had one important ally, Kazakhstan's president Nursultan Nazarbayev. In Kazakhstan where the population of some 17,500,000 was roughly evenly divided between citizens of Slavic European and Turkic Central Asian ethnicity, Yeltsin's preemptive strike had caused deep concern. Because roughly 50 percent of Kazakhstan's population was "Russian," Yeltsin apparently assumed that Kazakhstan was permanently "bolted" to Russia and did not have to be treated as carefully as Ukraine which was 80 percent Ukrainian. Further there were some 726,000 former Soviet military personnel in Ukraine and only about 200,000 in Kazakhstan. Ukraine had 10 percent of the former Soviet nuclear arsenal while Kazakhstan had only 6 percent. Although key Soviet nuclear and space facilities were located in Kazakhstan, those towns were Russian-speaking and the Kremlin tended to regard them as Russian possessions. The population of Kazakhstan's capital city, Almaty was 75 percent European by ethnicity.[8] In December 1991, about 95 percent of the military officers in the former Soviet forces stationed in Kazakhstan were ethnic Russians, Ukrainians, or Belarussians.[9]

Nazarbayev had to respond firmly and rapidly to prevent Yeltsin from seizing all former Soviet military assets in his country. He had to prevent Russian commanders from administering the new Yeltsin oaths of allegiance to the former Soviet troops in Kazakhstan and he had to work to keep the CIS alive as a military institution. Nazarbayev needed Shaposhnikov and the CIS military institutions far more than Ukraine's Kravchuk did. Kazakhstan's viability as an country was far more fragile than Ukraine's.[10]

Nazarbayev demanded that Yeltsin withdraw the orders and he called CIS Supreme Commander Shaposhnikov and insisted that the process be stopped.[11] He argued that it would be better to contend that the Soviet oath had been transferred to the CIS and its supreme commander than to force all officers to make an immediate choice between the republic where they were stationed, the republic where they intended to make their permanent homes, and the CIS. Nazarbayev met with the military commanders of the armed forces stationed in Kazakhstan and explained his position. He guaranteed that they and their families would receive equal treatment in Kazakhstan along with citizens of the republic. He was in no hurry to require nonresident Russians to decide between Kazakhstanian and Russian citizenship. He promised that he would not require them to take any new oaths of allegiance. He reaffirmed his support for a unified CIS military and economic system.[12] Nazarbayev emphasized CIS cooperation and the common heritage, a type of post-Soviet identity that could help bind the CIS states together. By taking the policy high road, Nazarbayev gained practical political advantages. By stressing inter-ethnic harmony and warning Yeltsin to be sensitive to ethnic issues, he prevented his country from being partitioned into a northern Russian zone and a southern Kazakh zone. By insisting upon collective governance of post-Soviet affairs through the CIS, he made it more difficult for Russia to dictate policy to Kazakhstan.

On 14 January 1992, Shaposhnikov flew to Kazakhstan for consultations with Nazarbayev. After their meeting, reporters asked him about the military oath issue but he had no clear answers. Shaposhnikov talked about three oaths. The soldier's first oath would be his people, the second would be to the Constitution of the state on whose territory he is serving, and the third would be to obey the orders of his commanders. This would permit a Russian to serve in Kazakhstan and a Kazakh to serve in Russia in the CIS armed forces. However, he also said that members of the CIS armed forces would probably take an oath to serve the Commonwealth rather than a specific country, "as long as we still have unitary forces." Shaposhnikov praised Nazarbayev's constructive approach to post-Soviet military affairs and reported that relations with Kazakhstan were far more positive and constructive than with Kiev. He looked forward to having Nazarbayev's support for responsible military reform at the forthcoming CIS summit and the officers assembly.[13] The two discussed possible models for the CIS ministry of defense and agreed that it should provide for a clear differentiation between civilian and military leadership areas in Commonwealth defense, a civilian in charge of civilian aspects and a military professional in charge of implementing military aspects of defense.

After his meeting with Nazarbayev, Shaposhnikov flew to Kyrgyzstan and Uzbekistan for direct discussions with presidents Akayev and Karimov respectively. Such travel had become routine for Shaposhnikov, an Air Force general who had become a statesman, who met with CIS heads of state, and who lobbied for certain policy positions. However, he did not see himself as a potential military dictator and he regarded his work as constructive and necessary given the extraordinary political situation in the former Soviet Union. This experience did not prevent him from advocating civilian leadership in military affairs.

Belarus Supports Choice

Kazakhstan was not alone in its resistance to Yeltsin's plans to push ahead with a military oath of allegiance to Russia. Little Belarus with a population of some 10,000,000 also reacted negatively. The news from Belarus confirmed that Yeltsin had actually ordered former Soviet troops in Belarus to swear an oath to Russia. It also reported that Shaposhnikov had signed the orders and that the process was supposed to have been completed from 10–12 January 1992. The Belarussian parliament reacted very negatively and condemned Yeltsin's hasty move.[14]

Instead of following Ukraine's example, President Shushkevich joined President Nazarbayev in insisting that Yeltsin adopt a more cautious, deliberate reform strategy. Belarussian pragmatists warned that little Belarus could not afford to pay for the military personnel and assets that were stationed within its borders. Further, it was not anxious to face citizenship problems for the 6,500 Russians and Ukrainians, 3,000 Uzbeks, and 1,000 Azeris serving in the Belarussian Military District. The Belarussian parliament adopted an appeal to all CIS states which called for a moratorium on further unilateral actions. Belarus insisted that the CIS meet and adopt basic ground rules to govern changes in military affairs.[15] Although, Belarus decided that it would eventually create its own armed forces because they were an indispensable attribute of national sovereignty, it insisted upon a careful, evolutionary strategy. Nevertheless, Belarus was reluctant to criticize Ukraine.

How the Oath Problem was Solved

The CIS heads of state met in Moscow on 16 January 1992. Shaposhnikov's staff had prepared a number of basic policy statements and agreements for their consideration, the set he believed had to be approved in order to keep things manageable. The CIS heads of state approved three key documents and thereby gave Shaposhnikov positive information to report to the Officers Assembly on 17 January 1992. However, only nine of the former fifteen Soviet republics attended the CIS Moscow summit and differences among the nine about the direction of military reform were confirmed by the voting.

The first agreement was designed to give military personnel hope that they would be treated fairly and professionally by the new states. This was the essential vote because the outcome affected every military family. Would they be treated like an alien army of occupation or given the full protection of the host state? Would they get to keep their apartments and/or receive fair compensation for them if they decided to relocate to another CIS state? All nine CIS states present endorsed the agreement: Armenia, Azerbaijan, Belarus, Kazakhstan, Kyrgyzstan, Russia, Tajikistan, Ukraine, and Uzbekistan.[16]

But whom did the military serve and what new oaths would the military be required to take? This key issue produced two agreements. *Both gave Marshal Shaposhnikov the power to decide when and where any new oaths would be administered.* The first was for military personnel serving in the CIS's all-purpose forces and it was supported by the representatives of the five republics that intended to form a defensive alliance: Armenia, Kazakhstan, Kyrgyzstan, Russia, and Tajikistan. The second was for military personnel serving in the CIS strategic forces and it was adopted by Armenia, Azerbaijan, Belarus, Kazakhstan, Kyrgyzstan, Russia, Tajikistan, and Ukraine. Both oaths were identical in content and followed the general pattern described by Shaposhnikov in his Alma Ata press conference on 14 January 1992.[17] The soldiers swore to uphold the constitution and laws of their state and of the states where they serve and to obey their commanders.[18]

The CIS summit was a tremendous victory for the republics because Russia gave up its claim to the former Soviet military personnel and to Soviet military installations in the other fourteen republics. The fact that many Soviet officers had been reluctant to swear a new oath to Russia, played into the hands of the republic nationalists. Instead of preserving a common defense space as they had hoped, they had discouraged Yeltsin from forming that space by taking all of them under his authority. Extremely expensive military sites such as the former Soviet space center went to the republic in which they were located. Thus Kazakhstan became a space power as well as a nuclear power. Over the coming years and months Nazarbayev would bargain with Russia about such facilities and require Russia to sign rental and lease agreements in order to continue using them.

Ukraine's Military Independence Strategy

Russia was still entangled in a matrix of partially resolved defense issues but Ukraine was pressing ahead and building its own armed forces. Although the first news from Ukraine focused on tension, the story soon changed. Ukraine's bold political offensive was paying off. Moscow discovered that Kiev was quickly winning supporters among the former Soviet military.

Officers had at least four reasons to cooperate with Kiev. First, they needed job security and there was no guarantee of military employment in Russia which had announced that it would be cutting its armed forces. Further since Russia had to repatriate Soviet military from abroad and the other republics, competition for positions would be keen. Second, if they really believed in internationalism and were culturally at home in Ukraine, their presence in the Ukrainian national army could be justified as forging personal links between Ukraine and the other republics. Third, Ukraine was more attractive than Russia because its security problems were far simpler than Russia's. The Russian state inherited an unsettled imperial legacy for which there were no simple solutions. Fourth, neither President Kravchuk nor Minister of Defense Morozov had given into nationalist demands to require the military to conduct its business in Ukrainian, a decision that made it possible for Russian-speaking military professionals to remain at work in Ukraine.

Some military officers in Ukraine criticized the hasty actions taken by Kravchuk and Morozov and endorsed the "no new oaths" strategy. Major General M. Bashkirov, commander of a strategic bomber group, quipped that he had more nuclear buttons than all the presidents together. He argued for delay until the status of all strategic forces had been settled. Black Sea Fleet Commander Admiral Kasatonov adopted a similar position.[19] Some officers who had refused to swear allegiance to Ukraine were repatriated "home" to Russia and the other republics. Some pilots flew valuable aircraft to Russia in defiance of Morozov's orders to keep all former Soviet military assets in Ukraine. Kiev had nationalized or at least laid a claim to everything in its territory.[20] Strategic forces began removing nuclear warheads and transporting them into Russia. Ukraine protested and insisted that the process be carefully supervised in order to guarantee that Ukraine received appropriate reimbursement for such valuable assets. Nuclear warheads were quickly becoming pawns on a political chessboard where Russia and Ukraine played but America paid the bills.[21] In early January 1992, there were 1,408 nuclear warheads on ICBM's and strategic bombers and 2,605 tactical nuclear warheads in Ukraine.[22]

During the first two weeks of the oath administration process, Ukraine's minister of defense, Morozov had gained the momentum and was winning the political war to nationalize former Soviet military assets. The trend towards acceptance of service in Ukraine won out. The officers who commanded the three former Soviet military districts in Ukraine—Kiev, Odessa, and Carpathian, were invited to official celebrations at which they were to make a public display of their allegiance to Ukraine. It was scheduled for 18 January 1992, the day after the grand officers assembly in Moscow. The results are telling.

In Kiev, 99.4 percent of the officer corps, those who commanded the Kievan military district, swore an oath to the people of Ukraine. Their commander, Col. General Viktor Chechevatov did not since he was still in Moscow due to flight cancellations caused by bad weather. His chief of staff, Lt. General V. Boriskin commented that the crisis period had passed in Ukraine. Minister of Defense Morozov, who was keen on giving each officer a definite status, arranged temporary contracts for those who intended to relocate to another republic in the near future. In Odessa, the numbers were lower due to the confusion about the Black Sea Fleet's future. However, 70 percent of the commissioned officers and 85 percent of the NCOs took the oath at the ceremonies. Virtually all the generals and military district commanders swore allegiance to Ukraine. The primary exception was Lt. General L. Kovalyev, chief of staff, who had been elected to the Russian parliament before being transferred to Ukraine and who intended to serve in Russia. In the Carpathian military district, 77 percent of all military personnel swore the oath including the district's chief of staff; however, the commander and deputy commander postponed their decisions.[23]

Morozov's Political Wisdom

Why did the Ukrainian strategy work so well? Morozov's policies were based upon sound political psychology and legality. Instead of backing Russian-speaking military professionals into a corner, Morozov gave them reasonable choices. He also defined their status legally which increased their sense of security. They could continue their careers in the Ukrainian national armed forces more or less normally and with reasonable expectations of tenure. Officers who intended to repatriate to Russia or some other republic could serve temporarily under a short-term contract. Retirees could stay and receive normal benefits and citizenship. Those who were hostile to Ukrainian military independence were not accepted into the Ukrainian officer corps.

Ukraine's strategy produced far less tension than that applied by the nationalist governments in the Baltic republics, especially Latvia and Estonia where anti-Russian nationalists had the upper hand and were insisting upon evicting the Russian military as rapidly as possible. In Latvia and Estonia, the Russian military, their dependents, and military retirees were holding meetings, organizing, and demanding that Boris Yeltsin take immediate action to defend their interests.

Morozov's strategy was similar to the one Yeltsin used during and after the August 1991 coup against his enemies in the military. Yeltsin did not back the officers who supported the coup into a corner, he let them join him. Only a handful of officers were jailed, those who were deemed unfit for leadership in the postcoup armed forces were retired on good pensions. Democrats complained that Yeltsin had been too lenient and had left too many hardliners in the armed forces. Ukrainian nationalists complained that Morozov had been too generous and that there were too many Muscovite Russians in Ukraine's armed forces.

Competition for good postings increased because Ukraine could not afford to maintain a 726,000 position army and there were some 150,000 additional military professionals of Ukrainian origin serving outside of Ukraine who wanted to return "home."[24] Although the Ukrainian Rada set the military's authorized size at 400,000, even that was too large given the economic problems besetting the country after the collapse of the Soviet common market and the disruption of economic relations. Morozov could not repatriate them all and give them positions without evicting the Russians and other non-Ukrainian military professionals who were serving in his army. Those who hoped to play the ethnic card in order to win the position and appointment game tended to support a nationalist group called the Union of Ukrainian Officers, a civic-action organization that emerged during the last years of Soviet power.[25] The nationalists argued that only those officers who gave positive and convincing answers to the question—"Are you prepared to fight Russia? should be retained in high military command positions. [26] But the political problem within the officer corps was more complex than competition between Russians and Ukrainians. Ukraine had to design its military system to suit Ukraine's defense doctrine and it had to begin moving a new generation of officers through the ranks. This meant that senior officers had to be retired to make room for the younger generation.

After three years of independence, Ukraine lost its attraction for Russian-speaking Ukrainian officers who had good positions in the Russian armed forces. In 1994 Russian sources reported that Ukrainian officers who were serving in the Russian military and who could make a claim for Ukrainian citizenship were opting for careers in Russia. Young officers graduating from Russian military academies with high demand specialties were the main exception to the rule. Kiev was recruiting them.[27]

Competitive Elections and Military Issues

The approaching 1994 presidential elections encouraged polarization and the incumbent, Leonid Kravchuk needed nationalist support to defeat his main opponent, Leonid Kuchma, a prominent defense industrialist who called for moderation in Russo-Ukrainian relations. As Kravchuk moved into the election campaign and began to encourage officers to support him, tensions increased. In October 1993, Morozov resigned as minister of defense. He was replaced by General Vitaly Radetsky. Thereafter tensions with Russia increased across the range of outstanding military issues. Two chronic problems generated the most strain: the Crimea and the strategic nuclear forces.

The incumbent president, Leonid Kravchuk tried to build a winning coalition by appealing to Ukrainian nationalists and moderates. His challenger, Leonid Kuchma's strategy called for building a bloc of moderates and voters sympathetic to policies that would improve relations with Russia. In this situation, Kuchma was vulnerable to pressure from the nationalists because their defection from his coalition would certainly cost him the election. Therefore, it made good political sense for Kuchma to stand up to the Russians in the Crimea and in matters pertaining to control over strategic forces personnel.

The familiar syndrome reasserted itself. Ukrainian nationalists provoked Russian nationalists. In March 1994, there were several minor skirmishes between Russians and Ukrainians in the Crimea. This was mainly posturing and bluffing and there were no fatalities.[28] Kravchuk and others were grandstanding at the expense of military calm in order to win nationalist support in the forthcoming election. Russian nationalists responded in kind by encouraging some Crimean politicians to distance themselves from Kiev and to press local autonomy to the maximum. During this same period Kiev revived demands that military personnel serving in the units that maintained the remaining strategic nuclear installations in Ukraine swear an oath to Ukraine. This was logical since Russia had taken the nuclear control functions from the CIS in June 1993. (See below.) Although Defense Minister Radetsky was uncomfortable with the politicization of sensitive military issues, he had to support Kravchuk and made political appearances with him. Given this close political association, he probably knew that a Kuchma victory would cost him his position.

Civilian or Military Professionals
as Ministers of Defense

Leonid Kuchma won the election by a small margin. The July 1994 election results confirmed that Western Ukraine tended to be more pro-independence and anti-Russian while the East was more interested in cooperation with Russia. Kuchma pledged to defend Ukraine's independence but to promote cooperation with Russia for the sake of economic revival. Tensions in Russo-Ukrainian military relations began to ease as soon as Kuchma took power. However, that was not the only policy change Kuchma made; he broke new ground by appointing a *civilian* minister of defense, Valery Shmarov, a person who knew finance and management well.

In addition to heading the Ministry of Defense, Shmarov was given the rank of vice premier in the Kuchma government. This enhanced his status and was a signal that defense issues would indeed be integrated into general national economic policy. With Shmarov's appointment Ukraine tried a Western pattern for the political governance of defense affairs. Kiev could claim that it was more European than Moscow.[29] Shmarov was responsible for overall policy leadership across a broad range of defense issues. He knew the military industrial complex well. More strictly military professional issues became the primary responsibility of his chief of General Staff, Army General Anatoly Lopata. Shmarov's main problem with the armed forces was the pressure to cut positions from the military payroll not his civilian background. Shmarov needed to trim the officer corps and to bring military planning into line with budgetary realities.[30] He managed to cut the military's size to 400,000 by May 1995.[31] Although any departure from tradition is difficult at first, the move from military to civilian leadership was appropriate even from a military professional point of view because the minister of defense in a democratic, competitive political environment is a political figure with partisan attachments not a nonpartisan, military professional.

The civilian appointment was to be the embodiment of the constitutional principle of civilian control over the military. It also was supposed to distance the military from partisan politics. Independent Ukraine's first two ministers of defense, Morozov and Radetsky, were military professionals but its third was a civilian, Shmarov. The CIS and independent Russia also began with military professionals as ministers of defense in the Russian ministry of war tradition. However, even Russia leaders considered idea of appointing civilians to the top position. Marshal Shaposhnikov broached the idea in August-September 1991 and in January 1992. He knew that circumstances had transformed him into a hybrid civil-military political figure. On a daily basis he had to address high political and narrow military issues. He was a general and a CIS politician and statesman. Although he managed those roles well, he and Nazarbayev recommended that the CIS and Russia place a civilian in the top defense position. However, Yeltsin rejected that advice and appointed Pavel Grachev.

In July 1996, Ukraine reverted to the greater Russian tradition and replaced its first civilian minister of defense with a military professional. The civilian defense administrator—Valery Shmarov, resigned and Lt. General Aleksandr Kuz'muk—a professional soldier, took his place. Analysts commented that military officers who had been raised in the Soviet military tradition found it more difficult to work well with a civilian than a military minister of defense. Shmarov pushed through military downsizing and imposed spending restraints which the military resented. The fact that he was a civilian made the process all the more tense.[32]

In the Russian tradition civilian control over the military is exercised through professional military leaders and the chief civilian executive deals directly with the chief military commander of the nation's armed forces. The former Soviet republics generally followed the Russian pattern. In July 1996 when President Yeltsin decided to replace Minister of Defense Grachev, he reaffirmed the tradition and appointed Colonel General Igor Rodionov to the top defense post. However, in December 1996, at Yeltsin's insistence, Rodionov exchanged his military uniform for a business suit and became a civilian. Rodionov was thereby transformed into post-Soviet Russia's first civilian minister of defense. Yeltsin explained the change as one befitting Russia's progress towards democracy but it was sparked by problems with military discontent with his administration (see chapter 17). But in May 1997 Yeltsin replaced Rodionov with a military professional. Col. General Igor Sergeyev. The military minister tradition dies hard.

Downgrading the CIS and Building Russia's Ministry of Defense

The political history of the CIS Unified Armed Forces and Strategic Command formed a U-shaped pattern. It had high short-range utility, only modest mid-range value, but a considerably higher long-range potential. Russia delayed forming its own Ministry of Defense and armed forces in order to give the CIS concept a chance to become established. The CIS was useful in the first few months of post-Soviet history and would be useful in the future. But, by mid-1992, Russian leaders decided that it had become an impediment to Russian state development. Instead of scrapping the CIS entirely, they retained it in a modest form more in keeping with political realities.

In December 1991 Yevgeny Shaposhnikov was responsible for some 3,000,000 military personnel, vast conventional forces at home and abroad, and the former Soviet nuclear arsenal. He presided over a huge staff and conducted military diplomacy with world heads of state. However, on 7 May 1992, Boris Yeltsin nationalized most of Shaposhnikov's operation and appointed Pavel Grachev to serve as Russia's first minister of defense. Two weeks later, Shaposhnikov was packing his things and moving out of the former Soviet Ministry of Defense. The CIS had been downgraded in importance. Shaposhnikov was only assigned a staff of some 250 people to open a stand-alone CIS headquarters on 41 Leningradsky Prospekt, the former home of the Warsaw Pact's Moscow offices.[33]

However, Shaposhnikov still retained the title supreme commander and was the official steward of the CIS nuclear kit. General Maksimov[34] and the nuclear football moved with him to No. 41 Leningradsky Prospekt because the CIS was still the legally authorized command center for the former Soviet strategic arsenal. Colonel General Samsonov also came along to serve as Shaposhnikov's chief of staff. Further, each member state was expected to send a deputy chief of staff, its permanent representative to the CIS. Lt. General Leonid Ivashov was named secretary to the Council of Ministers of Defense, a group that was expected to meet regularly, to prepare recommendations to the heads of state and to coordinate the implementation of CIS policy and agreements.

Reporters were skeptical about Shaposhnikov's future and asked him if his office had really been equipped with all the special communications links required to command the CIS strategic forces. Yes, there were direct lines to the presidents of the four nuclear powers: Belarus, Kazakhstan, Russia, and Ukraine, and to the former Soviet nuclear command center.[35] Further, Yeltsin's ukaz forming the Russian armed forces specifically stated that the strategic nuclear forces on the territory of Russia were under the CIS Supreme Command not the Russian minister of defense.[36] Shaposhnikov still waxed eloquently about plans for a Collective Security Council where the CIS states would develop security strategies and implementation programs. He still believed that the former Soviet republics needed their own version of NATO. He was an excellent planner and a fine statesman but the domestic forces at work in each of the fifteen republics prevented him from building a strong CIS alliance system. The idea was premature.

The free press insisted upon giving every shift in power a personal dimension. Yevgeny Shaposhnikov's career was hitched to the Commonwealth of Independent States. Pavel Grachev's was linked to the Russian Federation. Therefore, the media turned the institutional competition into personal political competition, Shaposhnikov vs. Grachev. Both officers were careful to deny such allegations and generally refrained from making ad hominem comments. However, there was some personal tension between them and it erupted during the war to prevent Chechnya's secession from the Russian Federation.[37]

Yeltsin, Shaposhnikov, and Grachev all understood the primary reason why they had to reverse the order of priority given to CIS multinational and Russian national defense system building. The CIS lacked *stateness* or *gosudarstvennost'*. It could not command effectively because its head was an unstable cluster of sovereign leaders who were free to reject any decision the CIS Council of Heads of State made. They were not required to implement what the CIS majority wanted. The CIS created uncertainty but Russia's national interests required crisp definitions of decision-making powers. The CIS armies had no state, no flag, no national anthem, and no oath of allegiance.[38] Only Russia could provide the leadership they needed and this had to be done through military alliances based upon a strong Russian military system.

The Russocentric defense system took shape as Russia negotiated bilateral and multilateral agreements with former Soviet republics. By fall 1995,

Minister of Defense Grachev reported that he had signed more than 200 such military agreements. He also had made arrangements for Russian military bases in Armenia, Georgia, Moldova, and Tajikistan. He continued to advocate a CIS military-political alliance.[39]

The Russian Ministry of Defense

Yeltsin told the stormy January 1992, All-Army Officers Assembly that Russia would take direct charge over its military affairs if the majority of CIS states refused to support unified armed forces. At the February and March 1992 CIS summits, the patterns became clear. Russia and four Central Asian states—Kazakhstan, Kyrgyzstan, Tajikistan, and Uzbekistan, plus Armenia were willing to build CIS Unified Armed Forces; that is to say, only six out of the former fifteen Soviet republics. Turkmenistan wanted a direct relationship with Russia and did not want to be encumbered by CIS defense complexities. Belarus was wavering on the issue. Ukraine was definitely out as were the three Baltic republics. Georgia and Azerbaijan insisted upon conditions which Moscow was reluctant to meet. This was not the type of political foundation on which a solid collective security system could be built. It was better for Russia to take charge directly and to build a Russocentric defense system primarily through bilateral relations with the republics in Russia's near-abroad.

In early April 1992 President Yeltsin gave the definitive signal that the Russian Ministry of Defense was coming soon. He named his blue ribbon commission to prepare the shift. Military historian, Col. General Dmitry Volkogonov chaired the group. His two first deputies were Pavel Grachev and Andrei Kokoshin, a civilian.[40] There was much public discussion about the merits of military versus civilian ministers of defense. Russian pre-revolutionary tradition favored the military ministry model. The Soviet experience was mixed but primarily military.[41] Shaposhnikov and Nazarbayev had been recommending a civilian-led ministry in which the civilian minister was the primary interface between the military professionals and the civilian political world. This fit the pattern that had become the norm in "civilized" Western democracies.

On 7 May 1992, Boris Yeltsin issued ukases that appointed himself commander in chief of the Russian Armed Forces and defined those forces. He also promoted Pavel Grachev to the rank of army general and named him first deputy minister of defense of the Russian Federation and acting minister of defense.[42] This raised speculation about Yeltsin's ultimate decision. Would he appoint a civilian to the top position or a military professional? On 18 May 1992, Yeltsin ended speculation about the top position and named Army General Grachev to serve as Russia's Minister of Defense.[43] Andrei Kokoshin, a civilian, became Grachev's first deputy minister of defense. Kokoshin concentrated on defense industry, research and development, conversion, and financial issues—the civilian side of the defense kitchen. Grachev focused on military professional affairs and on military diplomacy, solving military problems in the near-abroad of which there were many.

Although the defense ministry organizational chart showed Army General Grachev at the top, he did not have the professional background required to be able to coordinate all aspects of Russian defense planning, everything from financial planning to negotiating base agreements with Armenia, Georgia, and Moldova. He was an airborne forces commander not a general manager. The coordinating functions were in the Kremlin rather than in the Ministry of Defense. Over the coming years, this political fact permitted a gap to open between the army and the government especially over defense financing. Further, the bifurcation between Grachev and Kokoshin reflected another split and a competition between military personnel and the military-industrial complex for increasingly scarce funds. Yeltsin's model did not create a powerful, integrated ministry of defense. Policy integration was supposed to be handled through the Russian Security Council which included the most powerful ministers and which reported to Yeltsin.

Grachev was responsible for all the former Soviet military personnel and installations within the Russian federation except the strategic forces and all former Soviet forces abroad, roughly 2,900,000 military personnel of diverse ethnic heritage.[44] (See Table 8.1) He had to oversee the repatriation of Russian forces from Germany, Poland, Mongolia, and Cuba. He had to establish withdrawal agreements with Latvia, Lithuania, and Estonia. He had to deal with armies and groups of forces in Moldova and the Caucasus whose precise legal status was in dispute. Consequently, although Grachev was a paratrooper commander by training, he like Shaposhnikov, would soon find himself engaged in military diplomacy. Grachev's blunt, soldierly style ruffled civilian feathers but on the whole he managed to do what needed to be done.

Russia was trapped in its Eurasian heritage. There was no easy retreat from Soviet empire and even older problems rooted in tsarist multinational empire. A strong collective security system might have become a trap for Russia, a multinational body that prevented Russia from establishing its own security priorities and deciding where and when it needed to become involved in the rich array of near-abroad trouble spots. Thus, although President Yeltsin signed a Collective Security Treaty with Armenia, Kazakhstan, Kyrgyzstan, Tajikistan, and Uzbekistan on 15 May 1992, the Russian parliament did not ratify it until a year later. Further when it was signed, there was a mixed reaction. On the one hand, it was a step towards the type of common defense that Russian leaders had been advocating. On the other, it could be a trap forcing Russia to bear the full cost of all trouble created by states over which it had little control. Tajikistan was already sliding towards civil war. Armenia and Azerbaijan were fighting an undeclared war over borders. Russian troops in Moldova's

TABLE 8.1
Ethnic Composition: Armed Forces of the Russian Federation

Ethnicity	Officers	NCO's
Russians	79.7	73.1
Ukrainians	11.7	15.5
Belarussians	3.8	4.0%
Armenians	0.4	0.8%
Moldovans	0.2	0.5
Kazakhs	0.13	0.4
Azeris	0.15	0.3
Georgians	0.12	0.3
Uzbeks	0.08	0.1
Latvians	0.04	0.03
Tajiks	0.05	0.07
Kyrgyz	0.02	0.03

Source: Russian Federation's Ministry of Defense, Personnel Division. Published in Oleg Falichev, "Navestit' starushku mat'," *Krasnaya zvezda*, 3 June 1995.

Transdniestrian region were being pulled into local ethno-political struggles. There were two or three small wars in Georgia. And, the Chechens, under Dzhokhar Dudayev were refusing to recognize Moscow's authority over their region even though Chechnya was part of Russia.

Ending CIS Stewardship over Nuclear Weapons

In early 1992, Russia had about 80 percent, Ukraine 10 percent, Kazakhstan 6 percent, and Belarus 4 percent of the Soviet nuclear arsenal.[45] On 23 May 1992, Belarus, Kazakhstan, and Ukraine signed the Lisbon protocols to the nuclear nonproliferation treaty and reaffirmed their political pledges to become nonnuclear powers. The U.S. and Russia shared a national interest in encouraging Belarus, Kazakhstan, and Ukraine to shed their nuclear weapons in a speedy and secure manner. The United States provided financial and technical support to encourage Russia, Belarus, Kazakhstan, and Ukraine to move with deliberate speed on the strategic weapons removal and destruction front. The three "temporaries" tried to maximize that support by refusing to return nuclear weapons to Russia for destruction until they had been paid by the Americans in one way or another. Various aid packages and loan guarantees were arranged.

In July and August 1992, the dispute over the Black Sea Fleet's status demonstrated why Russian civilian leaders and the Russian Ministry of Defense could not permit their security interests to be handled by cumbersome CIS institutions. Although Shaposhnikov tried to mediate the dispute between Russia and Ukraine, he had no authority to make decisions and the two presidents, Boris Yeltsin and Leonid Kravchuk, preferred to settle matters face to face and between the Russian and Ukrainian ministries of defense. They decided to remove the Black Sea Fleet from Shaposhnikov's command even though it contained nuclear components and was supposed to be under Shaposhnikov. Yeltsin and Kravchuk agreed that the Black Sea Fleet belonged primarily to Russia and Ukraine and that they were jointly responsible for commanding and maintaining it. They informed the fleet that it now had two civilian commanders in chief, Boris Yeltsin and Leonid Kravchuk who jointly appointed the fleet commander.[46]

The Black Sea Fleet tensions were symptomatic of a deeper, chronic problem with the CIS defense system. Neither Russia nor the international community was fully comfortable with the idea that a nonstate, the CIS was responsible for the fate of the former Soviet nuclear arsenal. Russia was primarily responsible and the CIS structure only complicated matters. If the CIS nuclear command served any purpose, it was a prophylactic, political device. It helped to discourage nationalists in Belarus, Kazakhstan, and Ukraine from demanding stronger national control over nuclear arsenals. As long as the CIS supreme commander, not the Russian minister of defense, had the nuclear kit, it was a bit easier to restrain the nuclear nationalism. This gave Russia, the United States, and other powers directly interested in preventing nuclear proliferation time to bolt down nuclear nonproliferation and weapons transfer and destruction agreements with Belarus, Kazakhstan, and Ukraine.

Although possession of the nuclear kit enhanced Shaposhnikov's importance and put him in an elite category in the world power structure, he believed that Russia should become the sole nuclear power and he was uncomfortable with stateless nuclear weapons. The Kremlin decided to negotiate nuclear weapons management agreements directly with Belarus, Kazakhstan, and Ukraine. Belarus signed agreements in Moscow on 20 July 1992 that recognized Russia's responsibility for maintaining and managing the nuclear weapons on its territory.[47] Shaposhnikov endorsed such arrangements. It was Ukraine's reluctance to recognize Russian authority to command any troops on Ukrainian territory, including nuclear forces and military specialists, that prevented Russia from closing down the CIS nuclear shop on No. 41 Leningradsky Prospekt. Boris Yeltsin and the Russian Ministry of Defense warned that Kravchuk's attempts to play supreme commander over nuclear specialists in Ukraine posed a grave security risk. Russia insisted that it must have the unimpeded authority to take immediate, effective action without asking permission of Kiev.[48]

Shaposhnikov mediated this dispute and reached an agreement with Kravchuk that Shaposhnikov would call Kravchuk any time Grachev needed to send nuclear specialists. Further, Kravchuk recommended that Grachev name a commander to coordinate nuclear weapons support services in Belarus, Kazakhstan, and Ukraine and to agree to place such Russian officers under CIS Supreme Commander Shaposhnikov.[49] This infuriated the Kremlin and strengthened its determination to remove the CIS middleman from nuclear affairs. Such maneuvering also convinced the Kremlin that it could not afford to invest more time and energy in CIS institutional building at the expense of laying the foundations for a Russocentric defense system.

Russia decided to end the CIS nuclear role and did it without first holding a formal meeting of the CIS heads of state. The policy shift came in summer 1993 and was part of a larger pattern, a turning point in Russian politics. Boris Yeltsin decided to stop wavering back and forth on issues of fundamental importance to Russian *gosudarstvennost'*. He was drafting a new constitution for Russia and preparing himself psychologically and politically for a decisive showdown with Parliament over the distribution of power between the nation's executive and legislative branches of government. The political coalition that overthrew the August 1991 coup, the Union state, and President Gorbachev had pulled apart. Yeltsin neither trusted his vice president, Col. General Aleksandr Rutskoi, nor the Russian Security Council's secretary, Yury Skokov. Yeltsin made Skokov resign in May 1993 and he broke with Rutskoi in July 1993. Yeltsin announced that Vice President Rutskoi had no duties. On 1 September 1993, Yeltsin broke the news that Rutskoi had been charged with corruption and his office had been sealed.[50] By August 1993, there was open speculation about a possible coup against Yeltsin led by Rutskoi and Skokov.[51]

During this period Yeltsin reviewed the CIS idea and the competition between the CIS and the Russocentric, national defense strategies. Shaposhnikov was still arguing for the CIS model, a strong defense alliance. However, he knew that of the 100 or so military agreements that had been approved by the CIS, very few had been carried out properly. Given the rise of national self-consciousness in the republics and fears of Russian domination, even Shaposhnikov had to admit that near-term prospects for a cohesive CIS military system were low.[52] Since Yeltsin was preparing for a major political confrontation with his own Parliament and the CIS Supreme Command might have become a complicating factor during a confrontation, he decided to concentrate power in the Russian Ministry of Defense and Minister of Defense Grachev, a trusted political ally. Shaposhnikov, after all, had repeatedly pledged that he would never permit the armed forces to be used for partisan political purposes. He was perhaps a bit too independent to be left in an important command position during a major political crisis in which force could not be ruled out as an option.

In June 1993 the Russian Security Council, chaired by Boris Yeltsin, decided to implement the Russocentric model and to end the CIS's role in nuclear weapons command and control. Russia also decided to abolish the office of

the CIS supreme commander, Shaposhnikov's job. The media had been specu-
lating about a rivalry between Grachev and Shaposhnikov. Yeltsin convinced
Shaposhnikov to resign his CIS supreme commander position and to take
Yury Skokov's former position as secretary of the Russian Security Council.
The new role had prestige and gave Shaposhnikov an opportunity to influence defense policy. On 12 June 1993, Shaposhnikov's new appointment was
announced to the public and the nuclear kit moved out of No. 41 Leningradsky
Prospekt and back to the Russian Ministry of Defense. *Moscow News* re-
ported it this way:

> Immediately after the appointment of Yevgeny Shaposhnikov as Secretary of the
> Security Council of the Russian Federation, he got a call from Defense Minister
> Pavel Grachev who tactfully demanded that the cherished suitcase be handed over
> to him. On the same day a group of armed people, arriving at the Marshal's office,
> "expropriated" the nuclear button, henceforth the bosses of the "retribution
> weapon" are Boris Yeltsin and Pavel Grachev.[53]

The paper claimed to have received copies of Grachev's report to the Security
Council which included a strong recommendation that Russia takeover the
CIS's nuclear responsibilities and that Russia block efforts to create major,
joint armed forces (JAF) under CIS command. He also argued against transferring more Russian military personnel to CIS peacekeeping institutions.[54]

For all practical purposes, the dual ministry period ended on 12 June 1993.
Grachev's point of view won out because it fit Eurasian realities better than
Shaposhnikov's. Both understood the situation well. Grachev was moving
with Boris Yeltsin and the Russian state. Shaposhnikov was still trying to
advance the CIS ideal and he continued to do that until Boris Yeltsin essentially recalled him from his CIS assignment. In any event, the CIS operation
at No. 41 Leningradsky Prospekt had been under Russian military management and dependent upon Russian state funding. Shaposhnikov and his top
deputies were ethnic Russians and Russian Federation citizens. The CIS Supreme Command existed as long it was useful to Russia. When Shaposhnikov
moved to the Russian Security Council, he took his personal staff along.

However, the Secretary of the Council of CIS Defense Ministers, Lt. General Leonid Ivashev, criticized the Russian government for taking matters
into its own hands without first holding the two meetings required by CIS
agreements. The process should have started with a regular meeting of the
Council of CIS Defense Ministers which should have approved a motion to
recommend personnel and position changes to the Council of CIS Heads of
State. However, before either meeting took place, Russia abolished the CIS
Supreme Command, transferred Shaposhnikov to the Russian Security Council, and took possession of the CIS nuclear kit. The Kremlin showed disrespect for CIS agreements and procedures. The pattern was more in keeping
with Soviet than democratic tradition.[55]

The CIS ministers of defense met in Moscow two weeks after the fact on 23–24 August 1993. Shaposhnikov did not attend. Belarus, Russia, Tajikistan, and Uzbekistan were represented by their respective ministers of defense. Armenia and Kazakhstan sent their chiefs of staff. Kyrgyzstan sent the chair of its parliament's defense and security committee. Azerbaijan and Georgia sent observers since they were not CIS Collective Defense Treaty members. Ukraine just sent a representative from its Moscow embassy because Kiev insisted upon military independence. This diversity confirmed Grachev's main criticism of the CIS; its motley, cumbersome, unreliable nature prevented it from serving as a reliable collective security system. Grachev opened the meeting by stating that although Russia was definitely interested in establishing joint armed forces with any interested country, Russia regretfully concluded that in its present condition the CIS had neither the legal, the economic, nor the political wherewithal to support joint armed forces effectively Therefore, in the near future, he argued that CIS should concentrate on military assistance and cooperation. In the future as the member states developed stronger military capabilities, the CIS would become a more effective collective security alliance. Consequently, for the present, it was no longer appropriate to have a CIS supreme commander and the position should be abolished. Grachev put the matter to a vote and it passed unanimously. Next came the question of appointing someone to lead the new program. Grachev nominated Col. General Viktor Samsonov to serve as the general secretary of the coordinating staff for CIS military cooperation and set the CIS Moscow staff at 250 personnel. These motions also passed unanimously.[56]

Conclusion: Shaposhnikov's Military-Political Legacy

Although Yevgeny Shaposhnikov argued and tried to convince civilians to do otherwise, they divided the Soviet defense system. Nevertheless, he will go down in history as the last Soviet military leader in the best sense of the term and the person who helped divide the Union and its armed forces peacefully. He kept his word and did not use the armed forces against the people and he discouraged civilian politicians from using the armed forces for partisan purposes.

He was a Eurasian statesman not an ethnic Russian nationalist who was insensitive to the values and feelings of non-Russian peoples. Although the Soviet system strove to inculcate such qualities in its military and civilian leaders, it often fell short of the mark though certainly not always. Soviet political indoctrination and Soviet life had given Shaposhnikov a multinational perspective, one shared with many officers who took their oath to the entire Soviet Union seriously. Such crosscutting politically relevant affiliations gave the Soviet Union a complex political sociology.[57] The main ethnic parts were visible, generally viable but incapable of complete separation from one another. Further, there were numerous smaller divisions within the various republics which also mitigated against a simple, crisp separation into fifteen independent nation states.

The fact that the first ministers of defense of Ukraine and Kazakhstan were sensitive to ethnic dimensions of military reform helped to calm the military and contributed to peace. This chapter discussed Konstantin Morozov's work in Ukraine. The third part of the strategic triangle—Kazakhstan, began building its national armed forces under the leadership of a World War II veteran of Turkic-Kazakh ethnicity, General Sagadat Nurmagambetov who enjoyed wide respect in the Soviet armed forces. His civilian leader, Nursultan Nazarbayev was Shaposhnikov's most steadfast supporter among the CIS heads of state.

It is easy to confuse the old Soviet ideal with neoimperialism and Russian chauvinism. Internationalism can be grafted to imperialism just as national self-determination can fuse with extreme nationalism. Shaposhnikov consistently condemned all extreme nationalists and refused to accept their claim to be patriotic forces. Shaposhnikov was keenly aware of the power political leaders had to reduce or increase ethnic tensions. He worked hard to prevent violence and ordered the soldiers under his command to refuse to take sides. He believed that the CIS needed and could build strong peacemaking forces. Most CIS civilian leaders shared at least some of these transnational values but they were restrained by domestic political considerations from acting positively upon them.

Although the once mighty Soviet military machine had been divided and was suffering from falling budgets, political instability, and other difficulties, the military profession made some progress. Shaposhnikov helped to liberate the Soviet military professional from the Communist yoke, the political commissars and the Olympian clique of Party bosses. He prevented the military from breaking into warring factions and had prevented the Yugoslavianization of the Soviet Union. He set good precedents for military leadership in civil society by leading from principle in a pragmatic and open manner. He practiced the art of compromise. He often emphasized these points and returned to them in his memoires.[58] He demonstrated that soldiers could be responsible citizens, engage in a dialogue with society about security issues without imposing their views, and provide a stabilizing force during periods of stress without reverting to dictatorship.

There is a final point to make about changes in the military under Shaposhnikov. The official daily of the Soviet Ministry of Defense, *Krasnaya zvezda*, developed into a much better source of news and views. The positive trends that began during the last years of perestroika continued under Shaposhnikov and were not curtailed under Grachev. The paper became the best available overall source of information about the armed forces. Although it did not permit the military's sharpest critics equal time or give them more than brief mention, it reflected the general military point of view on events.

One of its main themes became that of the patriotic military professional who serves, carries out orders, and makes the best of the mess created by civilian politicos. Impatience with such politics was very much in evidence but duty required perseverance. Such themes fit Shaposhnikov's philosophy well.

Political historians work at analyzing and sorting information into neatly structured patterns and generally tidy up the record as they explain what happened. Our explanation of why the unitary, extraterritorial Soviet military system divided into fifteen national armies is based upon what might be called the ethno-political imperative: Each people living within a contiguous space will naturally seek to insure its survival by forming political institutions and armed forces. This seems to be a fundamental sociobiological imperative. But what if survival requires cooperation, alliances, and even unification of peoples? Will they reverse the process? Shaposhnikov argued that they should unite into a common defense system. However, there was no common external enemy to provoke that natural reaction and the main player in the regional system, Russia, decided that the CIS defense system could not be strong unless Russia first built its own powerful military machine.

After April-May 1992 when Pavel Grachev became post-Soviet Russia's first minister of defense, he became Russia's most prominent military leader. The other generals who got on the Yeltsin bandwagon in August 1991 were also active politically. Army General (Ret.) Konstantin Kobets served as one of Grachev's deputy ministers and used his contacts with Parliament, the government, and the executive branch to help solve various administrative and financial problems for the military. Grachev and Yeltsin placed Col. General Boris Gromov in charge of the military's relations with the near-abroad, tasks such as relocating and repatriating troops from the Baltic republics to Russia. Gromov was well-suited for such diplomatic military work and had some of Shaposhnikov's diplomatic ability. Gromov ran those operations and completed the withdrawals quite smoothly. Later, in winter 1994–95, Gromov broke with the Yeltsin administration over the Chechen war and was reassigned to the Ministry of Foreign Affairs, an appropriate and sensitive decision on Yeltsin's part.

Lt. General Aleksandr Lebed remained an outsider as did Col. General Aleksandr Rutskoi even though the latter was Yeltsin's vice president. Lebed became commander of the 14th Army, a Russian force in ethnically divided Moldova. Shaposhnikov, Grachev, Gromov, and Rutskoi were all promoted by Yeltsin but Lebed was not. This maverick soldier continued to hold the rank of lieutenant general until he quit the military. Yet, he had served Russia's interests by keeping the Slavic enclaves in Moldova under reasonable control. In mid-1992 when civil war broke out between the Slavic Transdniestrian region and Romanian-speaking Moldovans. Lebed helped stopped the carnage and became something of a local caudillo. But instead of keeping politically quiet and cooperating with orders from Moscow, he often criticized

Kremlin political antics. Like Gromov, he condemned Yeltsin's handling of the Chechen secession problem. Lebed held on in Transdniestria until summer 1995 when he finally resigned from the service and made national politics his full-time job.

Shaposhnikov, Grachev, Gromov, Lebed, and Rutskoi— some of the generals who helped bring down the August coup, stayed in politics and helped shape Russia's political future. They could not have played such roles without Boris Yeltsin's support and tolerance. He was a novel president and they were novel generals. The relationship between the president and the generals grew out of the Soviet system's habitual commingling of civilian and military elites. That system's liberalization created the novel situation in which neither side of the civil-military equation really understood how to behave. On the whole Shaposhnikov's precedents were positive for political liberalization and military professionalism. The same will not be said about all generals who entered political life as subsequent chapters will show.

Notes

1. See Shaposhnikov, *Vybor: Zapiski glavkomanduyushchego* (Moscow: Nezavisimoe Izdatel'stvo, 1993), pp. 140–41.
2. See *Krasnaya zvezda*, 31 December 1991.
3. Cited by Yury M. Voronin in *Svitsom po Rossii* (Machine-gunning Russia) (Moscow: Paleya, 1995), p. 171. Voronin was the Russian Parliament's chief budgetary expert and Speaker Khasbulatov's first deputy. He cited the oath to make the point that the officers had broken it by allowing Yeltsin et al. to destroy the State and the Government they had sworn to protect.
4. Source: Minister of Defense Valery Shmarov, *Krasnaya zvezda*'s 50th Anniversary of Victory in Europe, 4 May 1995.
5. See Captain V. Chupakhin's long report on Shaposhnikov's press conference, "'Ya obrashchayus' k narodam, parlamentam, rukovoditelyam suverennykh gosudarstv" (I appeal to the peoples, parliaments, and leaders of the sovereign states), *Krasnaya zvezda*, 7 January 1992.
6. Boris Yeltsin, "Ukaz Prezidenta Rossiiskoi Federatsii o tekste voennoi prisyagi Rossiiskoi Federatsii" (Ukaz of the President of the Russian Federation: text of the military oath of the Russian Federation), *Krasnaya zvezda*, 9 January 1992.
7. *Ibid.* The oath bound officers to obey their commanders and orders placed on them in a lawful manner. This introduced the problem of how an officer is to know the difference between an order that was awful and one that wasn't.
8. See Mikhail Guboglo (Deputy Director of the Institute of Ethnography and Anthropology, USSR Academy of Sciences), "Demography and Language in the Capitals of the Union Republics," *Journal of Soviet Nationalities*, Winter 1990–91, vol. 1., no. 4, p. 7.
9. Source: Kazakhstan's Minister of Defense, Col. General Sagadat Nurmagambetov. See "Soglasie, ravenstvo, i vzaimodeistvie (Accord, equality, and joint action)," *Armiya*, no. 16, August 1992, pp. 20–23.
10. See Robert V. Barylski, "Kazakhstan: Military Dimensions of State Formation over Central Asia's Civilizational Fault Lines," in Constantine in Constantine P. Danopoulos and Daniel G. Zirker, eds., *Civil-Military Relations in Soviet and Yugoslav Successor States* (Boulder, Colo. Westview; 1995).

11. See Anatoly Ladin's report from Alma Ata in "Tak li nado reformirovat' vooruzhennye sily?" (Is this the way to reform the armed forces?), *Krasnaya zvezda*, 10 January 1992.
12. See Col. Anatoly Ladin, Lt. Col. V. Rakhmankulov, "N. Nazarbayev: Prodolzhat' sluzhit' Rodine. Ona u nas etc" (Continue to serve the motherland. We have one), *Krasnaya zvezda*, 14 January 1992.
13. Col. A. Ladin, "Marshal aviatsii E. Shaposhnikov: Vstrecha s Nazarbayevym vselyaet nadezhdy" (Meeting with Nazarbayev sparks hope) *Krasnaya zvezda*, 15 January 1992.
14. See Col. P. Chernenko, "Parliament Belarusi: Voennye voprosy reshat' bez toroplivosti" (Belarus Parliament: Solve military questions without haste) *Krasnaya zvezda*, 11 January 1992.
15. See Col. P. Chernenko, "Belarus: I svoye ministerstvo i svoya prisyaga" (Belarus: Its own ministry and oath), *Krasnaya zvezda*, 14 January 1992.
16. "Zayavlenie glav gosudarstv uchastnikov sodruzhestva nezavisimykh gosudarstv" (Declaration of the heads of state of the commonwealth of independent states), *Krasnaya zvezda*, 18 January 1992.
17. See Anatoly Ladin, "Marshal aviatsii E. Shaposhnikov."
18. "Soglashenie o voennoi prisyage v silakh obshchego naznacheniya" and "Soglasheniye o voennoi prisyage v strategicheskikh silakh," *Krasnaya zvezda*, 18 January 1992.
19. See Col. V. Kaushanskii, Col. A. Polyakov, "Komanduyushchie vystupili protiv ukrainskoi prisyage" (Commanders came out against taking Ukrainian oath), *Krasnaya zvezda*, 11 January 1992.
20. See Vladimir Urban, *Ibid.* 9 January 1992.
21. Kazakhstan and Belarus also used the nuclear issue to gain American financial assistance. See Barylski "Khazakhstan." The Bush and Clinton administrations were actively involved in resolving the nuclear issues between Russia and the three temporary nuclear powers.
22. See Lt. Col. D. Antolyev "S territorii Ukrainy nachalsya vyvod yadernogo oruzhiya" (Removal of nuclear arms from Ukraine has started), *Krasnaya zvezda*, 14 January 1992.
23. Col. V. Bogdanovskii, Col. V. Kaushanskii, and Col. N. Mulyar, "Vybor sdelan, prisyaga prinyata na ocheredi— Vseukrainskoe soveshchanie ofitserov" (Choice made, oath taken, next in line the Ukraine-wide officers conference), *Krasnaya zvezda*, 21 January 1992.
24. See Vladimir Kushanskii's interview with Ukraine's minister of military conversion, Viktor Antonov, "Khochet li Ukraina stat' bezyadernym gosudarstvom?" (Does Ukraine want to be a non-nuclear state?), *Krasnaya zvezda*, 8 November 1992.
25. See p. 170, Taras Kuzio, "Ukrainian Civil-Military Relations and the Military Impact of the Ukrainian Economic Crisis," in Bruce Parrot, ed., *State Building and Military Power in Russia and the New States of Eurasia* (Armonk, N.Y.: M. E. Sharpe, 1995).
26. See Anatoly Polyakov's interview with Kuchma's chief of presidential staff, Dmitry Tabachnik, "Dmitry Tabachnik: Nikomu ne udastsya vbit' klin mezhdu nashimi narodami, nashimi armiyami" (No one will succeed in driving a wedge between our peoples, our armies), *Krasnaya zvezda*, 15 September 1994.
27. See Vladimir Maryukha, "Bylo vremya—i tseny snizhalis' pri novoi sovetskoi vlasti," *Krasnaya zvezda*, 27 September 1994.
28. See Oleg Odnokolenko, "My ne dolzhny stat' zalozhnikami momenta" (We must not become hostages of the moment), *Krasnaya zvezda*, 13 April 1994.

29. The Western powers were encouraging the former Soviet republics and satellites to move in this direction.
30. See Anatoly Polyakov, "Ukrainskaya armiya s trudom prinimayet grazhdanskoye litso v roli ministra oborony" (The Ukrainian army is receiving a civilian in the role of defense minister with difficulty), *Krasnaya zvezda*, 6 December 1994.
31. Source: Minister of Defense Valery Shmarov, *Krasnaya zvezda*, 4 May 1995.
32. See Grigory Nesmyanovich, "Ministr oborony Ukrainy ushel v otstavku" (Ukraine's minister of defense departs...), and, "Chetvertyi ministr" (The fourth minister), *Krasnaya zvezda*, 11 July and 31 October 1996.
33. See Elena Agapova's interview with Yevgeny Shaposhnikov, "Pozitsiyu OVS otstaivayu ne iz lichnykh interesov" (I'm not defending the UAF for personal interests), *Krasnaya zvezda*, 29 May 1992.
34. Maksimov served under Shaposhnikov as commander of the former Soviet nuclear forces.
35. See Col. O. Falichev, "Leningradskii prospekt , 41," *Krasnaya zvezda*, 30 May 1992.
36. B. Yeltsin, "Ukaz Prezidenta Rossiiskoi Federatsii: O sozdanii Vooruzhennykh Sil Rossiiskoi Federatsii" (Ukaz of the President of the Russian Federation: On the formation of the Armed Forces of the Russian Federation), *Krasnaya zvezda*, 9 May 1992.
37. See chapter 18 below.
38. See Boris Yeltsin's comments, "Boris Yeltsin schitayet shto situatsiya v armii sevodnya spokoinee chem kogda by to ni bylo" (Boris Yeltsin considers the situation in the army today calmer than it had been), *Krasnaya zvezda*, 28 May 1992.
39. See Gennady Miranovich's report on Minister of Defense Grachev's press conference of 15 November 1995, *Krasnaya zvezda*, 17 November 1995.
40. See *Krasnaya zvezda*, 14 April 1992.
41. See chapter 6 above.
42. *Krasnaya zvezda*, 9 May 1992.
43. *Ibid.*, 20 May 1992.
44. In November 1995, Grachev told the press that he started with 2,822,000 positions in May 1992, cut 1,122,000 positions from May 1992 to November 1995 and had a total of 1,700,000 military personnel under him as of early November 1995. See Gennady Miranovich's account of Grachev's major press conference of 15 November 1995, *Krasnaya zvezda*, 17 November 1995.
45. See Col. Anatoly Dokuchayev, "Po probleme yadernogo naslediya SSSR ne dolzhno byt' negovorennostei" (On the nuclear legacy problem there should be no disagreements), *Krasnaya zvezda*, 14 October 1992.
46. Their fourteen-point agreement was published in *Krasnaya zvezda*, 8 August 1992.
47. Reported in *Krasnaya zvezda*, 22 July 1992.
48. See "Pravitel'stvo Rossii sdelalo zayavlenie po voprosu razmeshcheniya na territorii Ukrainy yadernogo oruzhiya" (The government of Russia issued a declaration on nuclear weapons located on the territory of Ukraine), *Krasnaya zvezda*, 6 April 1993.
49. See Viktor Litovkin, "Marshal Shaposhnikov nedovolen dogovorom o kollektivnoi bezopasnosti" (Marshal Shaposhnikov is not pleased with the CIS collective security treaty), *Izvestiya*, 29 May 1993.
50. In order to make things appear "fair," Yeltsin also suspended a supporter, Vladimir Shumeiko. See *Krasnaya zvezda*, 2 September 1993.

51. See Vladimir Orlov, "How Rutskoi will save the country," *Moscow News*, no. 35, 27 August 1993; and Andrei Zhukov, "Vice-President has to defend himself," *Ibid*. Rutskoi claimed to have solid evidence of major corruption in Yeltsin's entourage.
52. See Col. Gennady's Miranovich's interview with Shaposhnikov, "Evgeny Shaposhnikov: Ya budu prodolzhat' sluzhit' i Sodruzhestvu" (Yevgeny Shaposhnikov: I will continue to serve, the commonwealth as well), *Krasnaya zvezda*, 17 June 1993.
53. "Grachev: the new 'master' of Russian nuclear weapons," *Moscow News*, no. 30, 23 July 1993, p. 30.
54. See "Commander in chief—Minister: dispute is not over?"
55. See Nikolai Poroskov, "Dolzhnost' glavkommanduyushchego OVS SNG ne mozhet schitat'sya uprazdnennoi" (The CIS JAF supreme command cannot be considered abolished)," *Krasnaya zvezda*, 6 July 1993.
56. Col. Gennady Miranovich, "SNG: Voennoe sotrudnichestvo—na real'nuyu osnovu" (CIS military cooperation on a realistic foundation), *Krasnaya zvezda*, 25 August, 1993.
57. The phrase and the concept are from Seymour Martin Lipset's classic, *Political Man: The Social Bases of Politics* (New York: Anchor Books, 1963), p. 77. Lipset's political sociology is relevant to the study of contemporary post-Soviet politics. See especially, chapter 3, "Social Conflict, Legitimacy, and Democracy" in *Ibid*.
58. See Shaposhnikov, *Vybor.*

9

Presidential or Parliamentary Armed Forces?

Democratic political systems distribute power among various institutions in a never-ending search for the right balance between political effectiveness and political pluralism. During post-Soviet reconstruction, the president and Parliament competed to determine whether Russia would become a parliamentary or a presidential republic. The inherited political culture, at least in military circles, seemed to encourage the presidency as did the crisis atmosphere caused by the breakdown of normal political and economic arrangements. But, the inherited, Soviet-era Constitution favored the legislative branch over the executive branch and competition between Parliament and the president over power and policy became the dominant feature of Russian political life in 1992 and 1993.

Simple logic suggests that there were three positions the military could take in the struggle between Parliament and the presidency: pro-parliament, neutral, or pro-president. Military political culture favored the executive branch and positive neutrality and mitigated against organized military political intervention against the President on behalf of Parliament However, there is also a fourth logical possibility, military factionalism. In theory, a significant military faction might have broken away from the Ministry of Defense and thrown its support to Parliament either during political negotiations or during armed confrontation. Although such behavior ran against deeply held, military corporate values which emphasized military cohesion, Parliament tried to exploit military discontent in order to win the military's neutrality if not its active support against the Yeltsin administration. By summer 1993, Parliament had taken on some of the trappings of a government in opposition. It had become far more than the national legislature, it had become the focal point for opposition to the Yeltsin administration which went beyond normal legislative opposition to strong-willed presidents.

Ruslan Khasbulatov—the speaker of Parliament, became the central civilian leader in the competition with Yeltsin's presidential administration. A number of former military and security officers climbed on Khasbulatov's political bandwagon. This commingling of civilian and military opponents converted the Parliament building into a proto-government. The Parliament center and the Kremlin both claimed the right to lead Russia.

Parliament was armed; it had its own security forces directed by former Soviet First Deputy Minister of Defense Vladislav Achalov—one of the leaders in the August 1991 coup. It also became the last political redoubt for Colonel General Aleksandr Rutskoi, Yeltsin's politically estranged vice president. And, as the previous chapter noted, Parliament's leadership core become associated with extremists in the national-patriotic constituency. The coalition that formed around Parliament argued that Yeltsin had mismanaged post-Soviet reconstruction and damaged Russian national interests. This constituency was promoting Achalov to replace Grachev as minister of defense and trying to organize opposition to Grachev and Yeltsin inside the Russian armed forces through Stanislav Terekhov's officers movement.[1] They condemned Yeltsin for destroying the Soviet Union and the economic, military, and social security the Union state had given its citizens.[2]

Prior to the August 1991 coup, Achalov had been a member of Parliament. (Lt. General Aleksandr Lebed was his informal campaign manager in the 1990 elections to Russia's Parliament.) Although he was arrested by Russian federal authorities for his role in the August coup, he was not held for long and the case disintegrated along with the Soviet Union. By spring 1993, Achalov was working in Parliament for Khasbulatov on relations with the military and on the development of paramilitary guards to defend Parliament against a possible presidential coup. However, Parliament was neither isolated from pro-Yeltsin military nor from the top leadership in the Ministry of Defense. When the political showdown came in September-October 1993, all the key players knew one another and were able to maintain communication throughout the crisis. Parliament lost to Yeltsin because the Ministry of Defense backed the president. Although there were many reasons why the top military leadership supported Yeltsin over Khasbulatov and Rutskoi, political loyalty to Yeltsin was an important factor. Yeltsin had appointed the top military leadership and retained the power to remove it. He was the sole commander in chief. Parliament had failed to prevent him from making the military into a presidential fiefdom.

Presidential or Parliamentary Control

In 1992, as Yeltsin prepared to establish the Russian Ministry of Defense, Parliament prepared a comprehensive Law on Defense designed to make the Russian legislature an effective check on Presidential power in military affairs. Parliament insisted that it have veto power over key military personnel decisions. It refused to pass legislation that granted the President the power to appoint and remove the commanders at will. However, Yeltsin ignored Parliament and his presidential team controlled all key military appointments and shaped a new military administration that was beholden to him. He argued that his power was legitimate since he was the supreme commander and the democratically elected president of Russia.

Parliament and the President were supposed to cooperate and to share ideas about important legislation. Consequently, key bills in draft form were sent from Parliament to the presidential staff for comment and suggested revisions. As drafted by Parliament, the Law on Defense granted the president the power to nominate the minister of defense, the chief of General Staff, the deputy ministers of defense, and the service and territorial commanders; *however, they were to be appointed only with the consent of Parliament.* Yeltsin bristled at this and tried to get it changed. His staff deleted "with the consent of Parliament" from the draft bill and sent it back to Parliament. However, Parliament refused to grant him the sole power to appoint the top military leaders.[3]

Yeltsin dismissed charges that he was creating a presidential dictatorship in Russia and argued that it was in the national interest to effect military personnel changes efficiently and rapidly. In the end, Yeltsin compromised with Parliament. He agreed to support and sign legislation that gave Parliament the power to confirm or deny appointments in exchange for Parliament's acceptance of all the military appointments he had already made. This was a step in the right direction. It would have given the military and the country some protection against the abuse of power by Russia's presidents. In the Russian context it was easier to establish civilian control than to institutionalize it in a manner that encouraged responsible civilian control which supported military professionalism and nonpartisanship.

The final bill which President Boris Yeltsin signed into law on 24 September 1992 requires Russia's presidents to obtain parliament's consent for all top military appointments. Parliament had won its point in law but not in practice.[4] The principle was sound: in a democratic Russia, the military must not be permitted to become the personal armed force of the presidents. However, there is reason to believe that Yeltsin never really accepted that fundamental principle of democratic civilian control. Yeltsin signed the bill not because he agreed with all its provisions but because he had already shaped the military high command to his liking and it would have been unwise to prolong the period during which the military had to operate without a post-Soviet basic law on defense. Further, he insisted and Parliament agreed that the section of the law that gave Parliament veto power over top military appointments be held in abeyance until the then current Constitution had been amended. Parliament issued a special decree that permitted Yeltsin to continue making the key military appointments during the interim. But the decree also required the Ministry of Defense to furnish more information to Parliament about military reform plans and to implement military downsizing.[5] The president, the Parliament, and the Ministry of Defense were engaged in *politics,* the competition to determine which branches and departments of government would determine basic policy directions, allocations of power, and distributions of funds.

Yeltsin signed the Law on Defense but subsequent actions demonstrate that he never intended to grant Parliament any major voice over military appointments and defense affairs. Yeltsin's game plan was to get a new Constitution that legitimized presidential power to dominate appointments and to control the military high command. The new Constitution which was adopted in a referendum in December 1993 grants the President the power to appoint and remove the top military leaders without Parliament's consent.[6] This makes the military high command an extension of the president's executive staff. Presidential power to appoint and remove the military high command gives the Ministry of Defense and the top military leadership a keen interest in presidential elections and partisan politics. On the one hand, Yeltsin created a situation in which it will be difficult for the military to be politically neutral during elections. On the other hand, the Law on Defense completely prohibited partisan political activity in the armed forces and made it illegal to use military assets, facilities, or personnel for partisan political purposes.[7]

Neither the Law on Defense nor Yeltsin's new Constitution rescinded the political rights which military personnel gained under Gorbachev. They continued to run for office and to serve when elected. The Ministry of Defense and other branches of government such as the Central Electoral Commission issued special regulations and policy statements to define how military personnel exercise their political rights without violating the prohibition against partisan political activity in the armed forces. Minister of Defense Grachev was uncomfortable with such political activity even though it was legal. He repeatedly referred to the new Law on Defense in order to justify his efforts to keep the military from being drawn into partisan political competition. Grachev himself held no elective offices and argued that military officers should decide between politics/public administration and the military profession instead of trying to combine the two.[8]

As the Law on Defense was being drafted, Parliament considered proposals to break with Russian imperial and Soviet tradition and to redefine the Ministry of Defense into a primarily civilian institution. The final bill which Yeltsin signed into law opened the door to change by stating that the positions of the minister of defense, the deputy ministers of defense, and other executives officers in the armed forces of the Russian Federation "could be filled by civilians."[9] But it did not require civilians to hold the leadership and policy coordinating positions in the Ministry. Thus, the door was open for Yeltsin and future presidents to begin moving civilians into leadership positions in the Ministry of Defense but they were not required to do so.

The new laws differentiated between civilian and military professional employees in the Ministry of Defense. The civilians could organize trade unions and negotiate with the Ministry but the solders could not. This was a victory for the Ministry of Defense over the radical democratizers such as Vitaly Urazhtsev, leader of Shield (*Shchit*) who argued that military civil rights should include the right to collective bargaining. The Ministry warned that Shield, independent officers unions, and similar groups would undermine military cohesion and thereby damage the Ministry's ability to keep the military under reliable and effective control. Parliament agreed and limited collective bargaining to civilian employees. Thus, Parliament supported Grachev's efforts to reinforce the cohesive military chain of command. Although it endorsed democratic civilian and rejected military system democratization, it tried to prevent the Ministry of Defense from operating as a closed system. But the Ministry was unwilling to share much information about its operations with Parliament.

Armed Forces Personnel in Politics

Russian law permitted armed forces officers to serve as peoples' deputies and to hold leading positions in government simultaneously. This weakened Parliament's ability to serve as an effective check on the executive branch. For example, Sergei Stepashin, Yeltsin's deputy minister of Russian security, was also an elected congressman and in 1993 he chaired the legislature's main Committee on Defense and Security Affairs. In 1993, Yeltsin promoted Stepashin to lt. general and in 1994 he became the head of the Russian Security Service, the main successor to the KGB. Stepashin's career began in the MVD where he was trained for responsible positions as a political officer. He joined the Yeltsin faction in the Russian Parliament before the collapse of the Soviet Union and was one of the insiders who organized Yeltsin's support during the August 1991 coup.

In October 1992, the Ministry of Defense's officer's journal *Armiya* reported on the status of forty-four military personnel who had been elected to the Russian Congress in March 1990. Forty percent were senior command officers and some 33 percent were former military political officers. In October 1992, three chaired Parliamentary committees: Lt. Colonel A. Korovnikov chaired the committee on veterans and invalids; Lt. Colonel A. Tsarev chaired a subcommittee on defense and security; and Lt. Colonel S. Yushenkov chaired the subcommittee on the mass media and information. In addition to the forty-four officers serving as peoples deputies, another 300 military officers were assigned by the Ministry of Defense to various parliamentary committees and offices, governmental departments, and the presidential staff and committee system.[10] Two of the forty-four peoples' deputies were also serving as President Yeltsin's special administrative representatives in Chelyabinsk and Krasnodar respectively. Another two served as heads of city administrations in Ryazan and Borisogleb.

When the forty-four military deputies ran for office, most faced from three to nine opponents. Three won in two-candidate races. The largest field of candidates was fifteen. The mid-point was six. Deputy Minister of Defense Achalov, Army General Kobets, Col. General Volkogonov, and Col. General Rutskoi constitute an interesting cluster in the data. They all defeated a field of nine candidates.[11] In October 1992, thirty-seven of the forty-four officers still remained on the military's personnel lists and only seven had been furloughed.

Thus, there were extensive military-civilian contacts which linked Parliament, the Ministry of Defense, and the presidency. Vice President Rutskoi was a member of Congress as well as a colonel general and Yeltsin's vice president. General Kobets was a member of Congress and Yeltsin's "insider" in the top echelon of the Ministry of Defense. Col. General (Ret.) Achalov was a member of Congress, a leader in the nationalist opposition, and a special adviser to Ruslan Khasbulatov, speaker of Parliament.

Rising Tensions between President and Parliament

Yeltsin refused to cede patriotism and national defense to the radical opposition. He reaffirmed his commitment to modern, professional armed forces and reminded the military of the repression it had suffered under the former system. The new Russia was building a new professional army and ridding itself of negative habits such as blind obedience and crude treatment of military personnel. He warned the military against those who would attempt to play the army card in domestic political power games. He called for a new Russian nationalism that reflected the Russian state's multiethnic traditions and denounced "those compatriots who permit themselves haughty scornful behavior towards other peoples, their history, culture, traditions, and way of life."[12]

Yeltsin's stand was positive and progressive; his opponents were extreme and uncivil. When Varennikov, Pavlov, Tizyakov, and Baklanov led a big march down Tversky Boulevard towards the Kremlin, part of their group turned violent. Fancy new shop window fronts were broken and "foreigners" were attacked including a Czech press photographer and a Russian citizen of Jewish ethnicity. Some speakers called for armed rebellion on 17 April 1991, but Moscow authorities claimed they lacked sufficient evidence to bring charges or to arrest them.[13] Minister of Defense Grachev warned his officers against dividing and taking up positions on the opposite sides of the political barricades.[14]

Yeltsin met with the Russian high command to discuss military reform, the broad outlines of a new national military doctrine, and the general international and domestic situation. Top commanders then attended an expanded meeting of the Russian Federation Security Council.[15] The Ministry of Defense's daily paper, *Krasnaya zvezda* editorialized that the nation had reached a decision point. The choice that had to be made was deeply constitutional, a matter of revising the balance of power between the legislative and executive branches. Effective national leadership and a strong state required a strong presidency.[16] Khasbulatov and Parliament responded to the Yeltsin administration's strong state themes by accusing the Kremlin of plotting to impose presidential dictatorship on the country.

Minister of Defense Grachev saw a major political confrontation brewing between the president and Parliament. On 5 March 1993, he organized his own Officers Assembly for the commanders of the units in the greater Moscow region. He stated flatly, "The current leadership of the Armed Forces will not permit the army to lean to the left or to the right; it will strictly fulfill the laws and the Constitution of Russia." He denounced the radicals who were trying to exploit military discontent and to convince officers to take up arms. He reminded the commanders that it was their duty to keep the military out of political battles and to prevent bloodshed and civil war. He warned that radicals would send emissaries to military installations and attempt to pull the military into politics. Grachev instructed the commanders to keep the military cohesive and busy with intensive military professional activities during the upcoming political confrontation. Grachev also touched upon military problems, the sources of military discontent and tried to give the officers the impression that the Ministry of Defense, the Parliament, and the president were making some progress though not nearly enough. Grachev also dispatched personal military representatives to meet with his commanders in the regions.[17]

On 9 March 1993, Grachev appeared before the citizen-soldiers, the military officers serving in the Russian Congress, to discuss the political situation and what the legislature could do to improve national defense and military life. They covered a broad range of issues ranging from military housing to national military doctrine. In addition to promoting military professional interests, Grachev urged the deputies to make it perfectly clear to all concerned that the Ministry of Defense would neither permit the armed forces to split along partisan political lines nor be dragged into the impending political confrontations.[18]

Ruslan Khasbulatov issued an appeal to the nation to defend the Constitution against attempts by Boris Yeltsin to impose presidential dictatorship: "Bitter experience has led the deputy corps to conclude that Russia must reject extraordinary measures and extraordinary powers. Society can develop normally only when all state leaders and institutions of power, political parties, and movements, every citizen follow the Constitution without deviation. Khasbulatov's view was that Yeltsin's administration had not been effective because of it refused to cooperate with Parliament and tried to impose unpopular and unwarranted policies on the country.[19]

The military's main problem was the Russian political economy's deplorable condition. Yeltsin's problem and that of the demokraty was political accountability for that situation. The military wanted an effective government and a solid economy which generated a steady stream of revenues and new technologies, the resources needed to give post-Soviet Russia a first-class military system. Instead, it faced an unstable political system and a declining economy. The democratic system of institutional checks and balances seemed to have degenerated into political paralysis. Radical nationalists were appealing to the military to drive the Yeltsin administration out of office. The president demanded that the military reject those appeals and support state strengthening under his leadership. He reminded them that radical solutions imposed by political extremists would create a politically charged dictatorship in which modern military professionalism could not flourish. They also knew that Yeltsin had the power to appoint and dismiss them, a fact that gave each top commander an incentive to support the president.

Yeltsin's First Attempt to Impose Presidential Rule

On 20 March 1993 Yeltsin launched a preemptive political strike against Parliament while Khasbulatov was in Kazakhstan conferring with its president, Nursultan Nazarbayev. Yeltsin addressed the nation and declared that he felt compelled to take bold action to solve the constitutional impasse that was crippling the government. He would govern through special presidential rule while the nation prepared for a referendum on the division of powers and his stewardship. His speech made direct reference to the armed forces: "As Supreme Commander I issued orders to the Minister of Defense not to permit the armed forces to be used for political purposes. I reaffirm that in the future concern for the Armed Forces and military personnel will be one of the most important tasks of the Russian state."[20] But instead of general support, Yeltsin faced a torrent of protest from major *civilian* constitutional officers. Federal Prosecutor Valery Stepankov and Vice President Rutskoi took to the air waves and denounced Yeltsin's imminent imposition of presidential rule as an unconstitutional and destabilizing act. The head of the Federal Constitutional Court, Valery Zorkin made similar statements and called the plan "an attempted state coup."[21]

What was the military's official position at the height of the crisis? On the day when the full Congress assembled, *Krasnaya zvezda* published the following message from the minister of defense and the Collegium of the Ministry of Defense to the armed forces. It was Constitutionally correct. Instead of siding with either the President or Parliament, it called for strict neutrality, calm, and discipline:

> Soldiers of the Russian army! The Collegium of the Ministry of defense appeals to you in connection with the complex political situation in the country. To achieve their own goals various political forces have started a struggle for influence in the army which today remains one of the guarantors of stability in Russia. Efforts to split the army, to divide the officer corps, to draw it into political struggle, to provoke the military into using force have not stopped. All this could have the most serious consequences right up to the collapse of statehood, territorial integrity of Russia, and the most frightening—bloodshed.
>
> Under these conditions the army acts and will continue to act in keeping with the Constitution and the law of the Russian Federation. The leadership of the Armed Forces considers it impermissible to drag the army into political struggle.

Commanders at all levels therefore must strengthen their efforts at explaining the legislation regulating the activity of the Armed Forces, and above all the *law on defense* which prohibits all political agitation in the Armed Forces including the establishment of any social or other organizations pursuing political aims.

All military personnel must take all necessary measures to preserve military discipline and order in the units and on board ship, the required level of military readiness and fleet strength, reliable control of the armies.

The Collegium expresses confidence that the personnel of the Armed Forces of Russia will remain loyal to their military duty, show restraint, calm and organizational discipline, and will do all to preserve peace and civil accord in society.

The same issue's front-page headline read: "The Army Must Have Reliable Immunity to Political Stress." [22]

The National Referendum: 25 April 1993

In the face of widespread opposition, Yeltsin backed down and never formally issued the decree which he had already read over national television on 20 March 1993. But he insisted on keeping his political offensive going. Instead of imposing a temporary presidential dictatorship, he settled for a more democratic device which Justice Zorkin advised was within his constitutional powers, a national referendum. However, Yeltsin wanted to do more than measure public opinion. He wanted to use the referendum to win popular approval for a new Constitution.[23] Parliament refused to agree to allow him to circumvent its constitutional authority by employing the referendum device. The existing Constitution gave Parliament the power to make constitutional revisions Yeltsin notwithstanding. Parliament refused to endorse a referendum on a new Constitution. Nonetheless, the two sides compromised. They agreed to hold a referendum that asked the voters these four questions:

1. Do you have confidence in the President of the Russian Federation, B. N. Yeltsin?
2. Do you approve the social-economic policies followed by the President of the Russian Federation and the government of the Russian Federation since 1992?
3. Do you consider it necessary to hold early elections for the Russian Federation President?
4. Do you consider it necessary to hold early elections for the peoples deputies of the Russian Federation?[24]

They set the referendum for 25 April 1993; and they agreed to form a special commission to work efficiently on constitutional revisions. Yeltsin believed that the referendum would strengthen his hand in the negotiations with Parliament about constitutional changes. However, in retrospect, it is clear that he had agreed to a set of questions which did not address the key constitutional issues directly.

The military establishment reacted in a thoughtful editorial written by *Krasnaya zvezda's* parliamentary correspondent, Captain Vladimir Ermolin. He recommended that citizens who want to strengthen Russia and to give the new political system a chance to achieve viability should vote *yes* on the first two questions and *no* on the second two. Endorsing the president and his program would strengthen the executive branch and encourage the legislative branch to be more cooperative. However, holding new elections for either the president or the parliament was a bad idea because new elections would disrupt post-Soviet reconstruction. The tables were already piled high with partially and nearly completed bills. It was in the national interest to complete that work not to disrupt it. Responsible citizens should vote accordingly.[25]

Parliament's Defense and Security Committee issued a statement confirming that the Russian military had the right to vote in the national referendum of 25 April 1993. It reminded officers and Ministry of Defense officials that Russian legislation conferred full citizenship upon the military including the right to run for office. However, the Law on Defense prohibited partisan political activity within armed forces institutions. Parliament's declaration stated: "To all Russian fighters: make your decisions independently on the questions of the referendum according to your conscience and sense of duty." It instructed commanders to prevent any agitation, speeches, or other activity that might prevent military personnel from exercising their free will. It gave the same admonition to President Yeltsin and all political leaders.[26] Parliament was warning the president to refrain from any actions aimed at intimidating members of the armed forces into voting one way or the other.

Parliament encouraged the military to leave its bases and military institutions and to vote with civilians in regular civilian voting places. This was a definite break with Soviet practice. Lt. General (Ret.) Yevgeny Popov worked with the Central Electoral Commission to facilitate military voting. He reported that 95 percent of military personnel voted, even those stationed abroad received their ballots in time. By contrast, only 62 percent of the general population voted. About 33 percent voted of armed forces personnel voted at civilian polling places. Popov commented that it was an important trend that should be expanded, a new practice designed to protect military civil rights.[27]

The Yeltsin administration beat the drums for a vote against Parliament. It wanted new parliamentary elections. Western funds and advertising experts helped to craft slick ads that chanted "yes-yes-no-yes" mantras on the Russian mass media. But on 25 April 1993 the public voted as *Krasnaya zvezda's* Vladimir Ermolin had recommended not because his paper was terribly influential with the public at large but because the ideas he expressed were a better reflection of public opinion than the Kremlin point of view. The Russian people gave Yeltsin and his policies a vote of confidence but rejected his calls for early presidential and parliamentary elections.[28] There were significant regional differences in the vote. On the one hand, voters in St. Petersburg endorsed all four points and thereby called for both Yeltsin and Parliament to step down. On the other, Muscovites voted to retain Yeltsin but not the current parliament.

Military Impatience with Civilian Political Irresponsibility

The Ministry of Defense's editorial writers were relieved that the country had avoided another governmental crisis; however, they warned the civilian politicos that the people were tired of politics and wanted responsible, effective leadership: "We hope the main conclusion drawn from the referendum will be that it was not a vote of confidence but the last grant of credit of the people's patience with governmental institutions of power and their leaders."[29] Yeltsin's leadership style was part of the problem; so was Khasbulatov's. The military longed for stable, effective government.

Yeltsin's inner team, the Presidential Council gathered to evaluate the election in the great Catherine Hall of the Kremlin. Their plan was to proclaim victory. The press was invited to hear the results but was excluded from the meeting itself. Grigory Satarov, a Presidential Council member who developed and managed systematic public opinion polling and data analysis for the Yeltsin administration, interpreted the results as a significant victory. Yeltsin's senior military-political adviser, Colonel General Dmitry Volkogonov claimed that the overwhelming majority of the military personnel and military dependents, some 8,000,000 voters supported their commander in chief.[30] However, he did not elaborate or disclose any details about military voting.

The vote as initially reported by the Central Electoral Commission showed that Boris Yeltsin was more popular than his policies. About 58 percent gave him a vote of confidence but only 53 percent approved his policy line. Some 33 percent called for new presidential elections. A higher percentage of the voters, 42 percent, called for new parliamentary elections. It was a modest victory for the president but hardly a resounding vote for the radical proposals he had made on 20 March 1993.[31] Nevertheless, Yeltsin vowed to press ahead with plans for a new Constitution. But that effort kept running into the same problem. The existing Constitution gave Parliament the power to revise and adopt the nation's basic law, not the president. Khasbulatov declared that there had been neither winners nor losers in the referendum. Parliament was unwilling to cede national political leadership to the president.

Yeltsin's In-House Opposition: Vice President Rutskoi

Yeltsin had sworn an oath to uphold the Constitution. If he overthrew the Constitution, he could be impeached and replaced by his vice president, Col. General Aleksandr Rutskoi. During a political crisis, Parliament might declare Rutskoi the acting president of Russia. Since Rutskoi's political views were closer to the parliamentary majority than the Yeltsin administration, Yeltsin had a serious political rival inside his political camp. Further, Rutskoi was an Afghan war veteran and had supporters in the so-called national patriotic movement.

Col. General Aleksandr Rutskoi, Hero of the Soviet Union, was staking out the Center-Right in the Russian political spectrum. This was natural given his political psychology. Rutskoi came from a military family. He served in Afghanistan and was shot down twice, once by Stinger missiles which the U.S. supplied to the mujaheddin. As deputy commander of the Soviet air forces in Afghanistan, he served under Boris Gromov. Earlier in his career he had attended the General Staff's Academy with Pavel Grachev. Although the Soviet government made him a Hero of the Soviet Union, his military superiors decided not to promote him from colonel to general after the war even though Grachev and Gromov were so honored. Rutskoi was considered a maverick.

Rutskoi decided to run for political office in the first competitive elections for Gorbachev's Soviet Congress in May 1989. But he was defeated in a Moscow district where the elite demokraty (Yevtushenko, Korotich, etc.) sharply criticized his Communist views. However, he next tried his luck in his native town, Kursk, where he was elected to the Russian Republic's Congress. He ran as a reform Communist, a person who believed the country needed a thorough reform led by firm, effective leaders. He considered perestroika and the demokraty incompetent and therefore dangerous to Russia's national interests. He deeply resented the way the Soviet leadership treated the soldiers sent to Afghanistan and resented incompetent political leaders who made mistakes and left the soldiers to take the blame. For example, in January 1991, when Gorbachev failed to control his Unionist show of force in Vilnius and young soldiers were ordered into battle against civilians, Rutskoi joined Yeltsin in condemning Gorbachev's actions. Rutskoi argued that a firm, law-governed state, could prevent such abuses of power in the future. He saw no contradiction between the rule of law and Communist Party membership. He warned that unless the leaders were made subject to the law, "who could guarantee that tomorrow we won't see tanks on the Moscow River embankment by the White House."[32]

In March-April 1991 when Gorbachev tried to unseat Yeltsin from his leadership position in the Russian republic's Congress and to block Yeltsin's effort to amend the Russian Republic's constitution to establish a popularly elected president and vice president, Rutskoi formed a political alliance with Yeltsin against Gorbachev. Gorbachev blundered by imposing a ban on political demonstrations in Moscow and surrounding the Russian Congress with security troops ostensibly to protect the deputies from intimidation when they voted on Yeltsin and the constitutional amendment. But the deputies were enraged and they turned their wrath against Gorbachev. When the critical vote came, Gorbachev tried but failed to hold the Communist majority together. Rutskoi led that Communist defection and announced that he had formed a new political movement, Communists for Democracy. This was sufficient to save Yeltsin and to get the popularly elected presidency through the Congress.[33] Those votes changed Russian history.

When it came time for Yeltsin to choose a running mate, he selected Rutskoi on 18 May 1991, the last day possible. Rutskoi knew what the political game had to be. Yeltsin needed a military patriot to draw votes away from rivals in the center (Vadim Bakatin, Nikolai Ryzhkov) and on the right (Col. General Albert Makashov, Vladimir Zhirinovsky, and Aman Tuleyev). However, Ryzhkov had the same idea and he linked up with another Afghan war hero, Rutskoi's former commander, Col. General Boris Gromov. The military knew its 4,000,000 votes were being courted and discussed it openly in the Ministry of Defense daily, *Krasnaya zvezda*.[34] Yeltsin went after the military vote and began his campaign with a patriotic appearance at the Northern Fleet. The strategy worked well for the Yeltsin-Rutskoi and Ryzhkov-Gromov tickets. Yeltsin came in first; Ryzhkov second; and the others trailed far behind. The Yeltsin-Rutskoi ticket captured 57.3 percent of the popular vote in the first round at the June elections. The Ryzhkov-Gromov ticket received 16.8 percent. Only 3.74 percent voted for the Col. General Makashov.[35] (General Makashov's radical Russian nationalist, authoritarian rhetoric found little popular support.)

After the June elections, events moved rapidly towards the collapse of the Gorbachev regime and the August coup. Rutskoi maintained close relationships with some Unionists such as former KGB General Aleksandr Sterlingov, a relationship that sheds light on some of the more complex political alliances that took shape during the August coup when the democrats and the statists joined forces to topple Gorbachev. Sterlingov flew to Foros on the "rescue mission" which Rutskoi led and which returned Gorbachev to Moscow but not to power. In January 1992, Rutskoi had hoped to attend the All-Army Officers Assembly but illness kept him away. Sterlingov did attend and he organized a group of officers into a new political lobby called "Officers for Russia's Renaissance (Offitsery za vozrozhdenie Rossii). Five of the eight officers who founded that organization were members of Vice President Rutskoi's staff, including Sterlingov. At the end of January 1992, Rutskoi stated that he would be prepared to head the government if offered the position of prime minister. He then began publishing his views in a series of articles, interviews, and speeches.[36]

Elected vice presidents are a potential political problem for their presidents in any political system. Rutskoi's political orientation was more conservative and statist than Yeltsin's and he rapidly became an outsider within the Yeltsin administration. He scorned the group led by Yegor Gaidar. He called them "little boys in pink shorts" because these pro-Western reformers lacked substantive administrative or military experience. They mistrusted him as an unstable, ambitious figure with populist, authoritarian leanings. By the end of December 1992, Rutskoi had joined the opposition to Gaidar and the Westernizers but he continued to cling to his office. Rutskoi contended that he had been directly elected by the people and was as much their representative as Yeltsin. Rutskoi should have resigned but didn't. As a military professional who had achieved the rank of Colonel General, Rutskoi certainly knew that he was damaging cohesion within the executive branch by hanging on. Yeltsin had an avowed political rival in the Kremlin but there was no provision for removing the vice president unless some serious crime had been committed.

Yeltsin assigned Rutskoi two difficult portfolios, agricultural reform and the war against crime and corruption. On 15 April 1993 Yeltsin withdrew the agricultural portfolio. The next day Rutskoi held a press conference, displayed suitcases filled with documents, and suggested that his investigation into crime and corruption was pointing to some very high places. Yeltsin reacted angrily and he ordered the Kremlin guards to cut Rutskoi's security team down to the bare minimum, three people.[37] By this time, the president's Kremlin Guards and Parliament's special security forces had stopped cooperating. The former were excluded from Parliament and the latter were prevented from entering the Kremlin.[38] Earlier in the year, Khasbulatov put Col. General (Ret.) Achalov in charge of Parliament's guards. Since Achalov had been one of the August coup's more avid supporters and the commander of the Soviet military's elite paratroopers, his paramilitary role in the Khasbulatov-Rutskoi camp was a definite concern to the president.

Parliament decided to give Rutskoi's situation official public attention and it scheduled a special hearing on corruption for 29 April 1993. Yeltsin angrily and clumsily withdrew Rutskoi's anticrime portfolio the day before on the 28th.[39] Finally, on 7 May 1993, President Yeltsin announced that Vice President Aleksandr Rutskoi had no assigned duties whatsoever. Since the existing Constitution gave the president the power to define the vice president's duties, Yeltsin was within his rights.

On 1 September 1993, President Yeltsin locked Vice President Rutskoi out of his Kremlin offices and offered a two-part explanation. First, Rutskoi was under investigation for alleged corruption. Second, he has no duties since it is up to the president to define them and Yeltsin had given him none. In order to appear evenhanded in the war against corruption in high places, Yeltsin also suspended Vice Premier Vladimir Shumeiko, a Yeltsin supporter and Kremlin insider.[40] The real political aim was to discredit Rutskoi and to isolate him physically as Yeltsin prepared for his putsch against Parliament. Since Rutskoi had allied himself with Khasbulatov, he had to be shut out of the Kremlin. Given his negative experience with Vice President Rutskoi, Boris Yeltsin decided that it would be best to eliminate the office of the vice-presidency from the Russian political system. However, he could not do so without changing the Constitution. This strengthened his determination to change the Parliament and the Constitution and he decided to do so even if he had to resort to extreme measures.

Conclusion

Rather than recommend either presidential or parliamentary domination over military affairs, the best democratic experience supports constitutional governance, a law-governed process that protects society and the armed forces from capricious abuses of power. However, effective constitutional governance presupposes a high degree of societal agreement about the proper aims of government and regular elections which place politicians in office who reflect that consensus. It also requires political habits and a political culture that work inexorably towards compromise and centrist positions. The best democratic practice also distributes power among several institutions and levels of government. When the parts cooperate and make compromises in a timely manner, the distribution produces healthy checks and balances and the political system is effective. When the parts fail to cooperate, the political system's policy making and implementation functions operate poorly.

Competition between the president and Parliament impaired military operations in four ways. First, it led to delays in legal, regulatory, and overall policy clarification which encouraged drift in the military reform process. Second, it produced confusing and contradictory signals about how civilian control over military affairs would be exercised. Third, it contributed to the national economic recession and the sharp drop in federal revenue collection which disrupted military financing, added to general military discontent, and pushed the military into nontraditional income generating activities. Fourth, the competition for power increased tension within the military because opposition leaders such as Achalov and Rutskoi were deliberately trying to attract military support.

Yeltsin refused to allow Parliament to serve as an effective check on presidential control over military personnel actions. He appointed and dismissed the leading officials in the Ministry of Defense and the top military commanders without the advice and consent of Parliament. Strictly speaking this was democratic civilian control since Boris Yeltsin was a democratically elected president. But it deviated from more sophisticated forms of democratic control which are designed to discourage excessive concentrations of power in the hands of the executive branch of government.

The official military press grew impatient with civilian political inefficiency. The Ministry of Defense tried to shield military personnel from partisan politics but it remained officially loyal to the President who was the supreme commander. This created a situation in which Yeltsin could be assured of the military's positive neutrality. Parliament's political tactics helped to drive the Ministry of Defense towards the presidential camp. By embracing radical groups such as Stanislav Terekhov's anti-Grachev union of officers, promoting Vladislav Achalov as an alternative to Pavel Grachev as minister of defense, and working with Yeltsin's renegade vice president, the Parliament compromised itself in the eyes of progressive military circles and in Russian society. The military leadership distanced itself from such Red-Brown extremists but it did not embrace either the demokraty or the shock-therapy economic reformers because those groups demanded rapid military downsizing and demilitarization of the national budget.

Authoritative military analysts writing in *Krasnaya zvezda* understood the progressive concepts of democratic civilian control and military professionalism and of dynamic competitive markets. They frequently contrasted and compared the Russian situation to those ideals and provided readers with specific comparisons based upon information drawn from Western sources. Their assessment was that the Western model remained highly attractive though less readily attainable than believed in the euphoria of August 1991. The ability to see beyond the confines of traditional political culture and to imagine a better future is one of the most intriguing human abilities and one not well understood by political science. Instead of demanding an immediate return to Soviet dictatorship and high defense spending, the Russian military continued to support political and economic reconstruction. Yeltsin's remarks to the military leadership and rank and file always appealed to such progressive ideals and promised that the awaited economic upturn would surely take place.

Notes

1. See Alexander Zhilin, "Is the army in opposition?" *Moscow News*, 25 February 1993.
2. See Tatyana Mikhalskaya, "Patriots will make the Kremlin shudder," *Moscow News*, 25 February 1993.
3. See Major A. Krokhmalyuk's interview with Lt. Colonel Aleksei Tsarev, who chaired Parliament's subcommittee on defense and security affairs during this period, in *Armiya*, no. 16, 1992, pp. 13–15.
4. See Article V. Powers of the President of the Russian Federation in Defense (in Russian); *Zakon Rossiiskoi Federatsii—Ob Oborone, No. 3531-1*. The text is in *Armiya*, no. 20, 1992, pp. 3–10.
5. See Supreme Soviet of the Russian Federation Decree No. 3532-1, 24 September 1992, "On the manner in which the Russian Federation Law on Defense will be implemented" (in Russian), *Armiya*, no. 20, 1992, p. 10.
6. See Article IV. New Constitution's text, in *Krasnaya zvezda*, 10 November 1993.
7. See Article XVIII, Law on Defense, *Armiya*, no. 20, 1992.
8. See changed his position in summer 1995 and encouraged trusted officers to stand for election to the Duma. See below.
9. See Article XIV.
10. See "Kto oni segodnya—deputaty-voennosluzhashchie?" (Who are they today, our military service deputies?), *Armiya*, no. 20, 1992, pp. 43–48.
11. See *Ibid*. I drew the information of each race from the deputy biographical material provided in *Armiya*.

12. See Vladimir Chupakhin, "Vooruzhennye sily—odin is garantov stabil'nosti obshchestva," *Krasnaya zvezda,* 23 February 1993, for Yeltsin's speech on Russia's defenders of the fatherland holiday.
13. See Andrei Kolesnikov, "Calls for the violent overthrow of the regime again permitted to go scot-free," *Moscow News,* 5 March 1993.
14. *Krasnaya zvezda* report, 2 March 1993.
15. See Anatoly Dokuchayev, Vasily Fatigarov, "Boris Yeltsin provel zasedanie Soveta bezopasnosti," *Krasnaya zvezda,* 4 March 1993; and Vladimir Ermolin, "Shto my zhdem ot vneocherednogo Syezda? Tol'ko ukrepleniya grazhdanskogo soglasiya (What do we expect from the extraordinary Congress? Only the strengthening of civil accord)," *Ibid.,* 10 March 1993.
16. See Vladimir Urban's editorial in *Krasnaya zvezda,* 4 March 1993.
17. See Col. Aleksandr Oliinik and Lt. Col. Sergei Popov, "Armii nuzhny ne politicheskie igry, a uglublenie reform," *Krasnaya zvezda,* 10 March 1993.
18. See A. Stasovskii, "Vstrecha ministra oborony RTF s narodnymi deputatami Rossiiskoi Federatsii," *Krasnaya zvezda,* 10 March 1993.
19. For Khasbulatov's appeal see, "Obrashchenie k grazhdanam Rossiiskoi Federatsii," *Krasnaya zvezda,* 16 March 1993. Although Grachev was supporting Yeltsin, he did not prevent the official military press from reporting the content of the opposition's views. Yeltsin's competition with the opposition was in the military's interests because it forced Yeltsin to improve support to the armed forces.
20. Boris Yeltsin cited in *Krasnaya zvezda,* 23 March 1993.
21. See Radio Free Europe/Radio Liberty News Briefs, 22–26 March 1993.
22. See *Krasnaya zvezda,* 26 March 1993 (author's translation).
23. See Boris Yeltsin, "O deyatel'nosti ispolnitel'nykh organov do preodeleniya krizisa vlasti," *Krasnaya zvezda,* 24 March 1993.
24. See *Krasnaya zvezda,* 31 March 1993.
25. See Vladimir Ermolin, "Vy za sil'nuyu i stabil'nuyu Rossiyu? Da. Net. Nenuzhnoe zacherknut" (Are you for a strong and stable Russia? Yes. No. Strike out what's not needed), *Krasnaya zvezda,* 31 March 1993.
26. See "Obrashchenie komiteta verkhovnogo soveta RF po voprosam oborony i bezopasnosti ob uchastii voennosluzhashchikh v vserossiiskom referendume 5 aprelya 1993 goda," *Krasnaya zvezda* 10 April 1993.
27. See Vladimir Urban and Vladimir Ermolin, "Na referendume narod svoyu pozitsiiu vyrazil. Teper' delo za politikami," *Krasnaya zvezda,* 27 April 1993.
28. See *Ibid.*
29. See *Ibid.*
30. Oleg Odnokolenko, "posle referenduma, prezidentskii sovet podvel itogy i opredelil strategiiu," *Krasnaya zvezda,* 30 April 1993.
31. See Vladimir Ermolin, "Referendum, kotoryi nikogo ne otpravil v otstavku" (A referendum that sent no one into retirement), *Krasnaya zvezda,* 28 April 1993.
32. Cited by Krotov in *Ibid.,* p. 24.
33. See *Ibid.*
34. See Vyacheslav Lukashevich, "Rossiiskie pretendenty: reverans pered armiei" (Russian pretenders: reverence before the army?), *Krasnaya zvezda,* 1 June 1991.
35. The electoral commission reported that 79, 498, 240 people voted out of an electorate of 106, 484, 518 or 74.66 percent. The results were: Yeltsin (57.30 percent), Ryzhkov (16.85 percent), Zhirinovsky (7.81 percent), Tuleyev (6.81 percent), Makashov, (3.74 percent), Bakatin (3.42 percent). See *Krasnaya zvezda,* 20 June 1991.

36. See N. Krotov, "Aleksandr Rutskoi: Politicheskii Portrait," pp. 22–40, in D. A. Mayorov, ed., *Neizvestnyi Rutskoi: politicheskii portret* (The unknown Rutskoi: a political portrait) (Moscow: "Obozrevatel'," 1994).
37. See O. Dias, "Moya fizinomiya ne ponravilas, no ya ostalsya" (They didn't like my physique but I stayed on), pp. 20–21, in D. A. Mayorov, ed., *Neizvestnyi Rutskoi.*
38. See *Ibid.*
39. See Vladimir Ermolin, "Borby s prestupnost'yu vozglavil lichno Prezident," *Krasnaya zvezda*, 30 April 1993.
40. ITAR-TASS. "Prezident RF prinyal reshenie ob otstranenii ot dolzhnosti Aleksandra Rutskogo i Vladimira Shumeiko." *Krasnaya zvezda,* 2 September 1993.

10

The Armed Forces and Yeltsin's Presidential Putsch

Early in the morning of 4 October 1993, Minister of Defense Grachev's tanks fired on Parliament. That event marks the end of the first stage in post-Soviet political reconstruction. Boris Yeltsin used the military to dissolve Parliament and to impose a temporary presidential dictatorship on Russia. He ruled by decree from September through December 1993. Although hundreds of decrees flew out of the Kremlin into Russian political space, there were no major improvements in national political cohesion or state viability. If anything, his actions damaged respect for constitutional law and the cardinal rule of democratic political culture, a willingness to compromise. Furthermore, the general economic recession deepened.

The president resorted to armed force to convert the Russian political system from a parliamentary to a presidential republic. Instead of siding with Parliament and defending the existing Russian Constitution, the military sided with the president and delivered him a victory in Moscow. Key parliamentary and opposition leaders were taken prisoner in this political war and locked up to prevent them from campaigning in the new competitive elections which Yeltsin promised the people. Yeltsin argued that Russian national interest was a higher value than respect for the existing constitution. But, if there is a higher national interest which stands above the existing constitution, perhaps some day the military will appeal to it in order to remove an incompetent president or to overthrow a president and a parliament which the military leadership believed had severely compromised national security. The idea that a higher national interest justifies law breaking is a serious problem for democratic development. It displaces more sophisticated ideas about institutional political culture that are absolutely essential to effective democratic government. How should presidents behave within the executive branch? Towards the judiciary? Towards the legislative branch? How should members of parliament behave towards one another? Towards the executive branch? How should the military behave in a democratic system of checks and balances? How will it behave when the institutions and leaders that make up the national political context are misbehaving?

245

Military Opinion Makers on the Political Cultural Problem

On 4 August 1993, I spent a morning and lunch discussing these issues with four people who shaped military opinion at the Ministry of Defense daily, *Krasnaya zvezda:* Vyacheslav Lukashevich, Oleg Odnokolenko, Manki Ponomarev, and Vladimir Zhitarenko. They were all deeply concerned about the way civilian political instability, individual competition, and inter-institutional rivalries were affecting state viability and the military's ability to function well.

Lukashevich, as the senior editor, wrote a weekly column during the months when the Gorbachev regime was breaking down. He wrote candidly about the jockeying for power on the eve of the August coup. He pointed out that Gorbachev had in effect abandoned his cabinet (Pavlov, Kryuchkov, Yazov, et al.) in order to win Yeltsin's agreement to sign a new Union Treaty. This political "tip" made subsequent political surprises understandable. During the coup itself, *Krasnaya zvezda* printed reports on resistance to the coup and on foreign reactions in addition to the SEC's official statements. After the coup the paper continued to develop into a very decent source of news and views although certainly not a wide-open publication. It remained the Ministry of Defense's daily but was far more than an in-house propaganda outlet. From December 1992 through March and April 1993, after every political confrontation between Yeltsin and Parliament, it expressed regret that the nation's civilian political institutions were in disarray and urged civilian leaders to pull together in order to make the government work effectively. In August 1993, Lukashevich and his staff were very concerned about the rising political tension between the president and Parliament.

Odnokolenko's trademark became the incisive critique of politics—it reflected the way younger professionals felt as their country's leaders mismanaged national affairs. When Gorbachev's policies were upsetting the national defense system, he wrote about Khrushchev's bullying and misguided intervention in military affairs. Later when it became possible to write more directly about current politics, Odnokolenko tended to push his commentaries to the edge of what was permissible. In person, he was realistic about the general mess on the political landscape and deeply concerned about it. Odnokolenko and his colleagues understood the situation, were unhappy about it, but saw no easy solutions on the horizon. Their complaints were also laments. They were not calls to restore the old order but they were a call for effective order.

Ponomarev's editorials covered Russian foreign policy, particularly relations with the West, NATO, and the United States. He wrote from a realist perspective and this meant confronting the unavoidable signs that Russia was in decline as a world power. In the West, he was seen as a nationalist who could not rid himself of old ways of viewing the world. But as a realist, he insisted upon asking the unpleasant questions about Russia's inability to command respect and to defend its interests in the near-abroad. The Russian state had major problems defining its defense perimeter. The United States and other powers had a definite policy towards Russia's near-abroad which encouraged the former Soviet republics to expand relations with the greater international community rather than to focus primarily on rebuilding economic and defense ties with Moscow. Ponomarev saw this and explained its implications for Russian efforts to build a near-abroad system.

Zhitarenko wrote about soldiers who served in hot spots. He saw them as people trying to do their professional best under difficult political, physical, and psychological conditions. When we talked, he had just returned from the border between Tadjikistan and Afghanistan where Russian servicemen were being targeted by extremists who used hit-and-run tactics. He insisted upon showing how difficult it was to serve there, so far away from home in a generally hostile environment and with less than adequate material and political support from home. Zhitarenko focused on the human, personal sides of the Russian soldiers who risked their lives to keep the near-abroad from degenerating into civil war. He wanted the public and the politicians to remember the soldiers and to give them proper support and understanding. He and his colleagues were internationalists in the Soviet sense of the term and were troubled by ethnic conflict and its impact upon military morale. A little over a year after we talked, Vladimir Zhitarenko was shot dead by a sniper in Chechnya just after midnight on New Year's Day 1995. He was killed while walking out to a group of soldiers who were defending a Russian post. He had been writing about them to remind policymakers and general readers that real people were fighting and dying in Chechnya. He wanted to wish them a better New Year.

The consensus of opinion at *Krasnaya zvezda* in August 1993 was that post-Soviet political reconstruction wasn't going well. Something needed to be done to make the political system more effective. There was no simple cause and there would be no simple cure. Political leaders and institutions did not have a clear sense of their personal professional and institutional responsibilities. The signals had already been given that the president would make a move and that the military might have to be used; but the idea of using soldiers for domestic political purposes was an unwelcome development.[1]

The president's civilian political advisers were working on the new Constitution, draft decrees, and issues related to his anticipated confrontation with Parliament. Georgy Satarov—a world-class political scientist, understood the overall situation as well as anyone person could from theoretical perspectives and from his pioneering work building political information systems to monitor Russian political change. He was also deeply concerned and aware that it would be impossible to achieve a crisp ideal outcome. But it was possible to improve the political system's effectiveness. The federal institutions upon which the Russian state's overall viability depended were immobilized at the top. That impasse had to be broken. It would be best to reach a progressive compromise with Parliament but a combination of personal, institutional, and policy rivalries made that unlikely. The progressive intelligentsia had its patriotic duty and needed to provide appropriate professional guidance and reliable information about political trends.[2]

Preparing the Military for Temporary Presidential Rule

In June 1993 Minister of Defense Grachev assembled the military high command to evaluate military reform and military preparedness. President Boris Yeltsin addressed the group on a wide range of issues. It was a good speech, quite candid with regard to major tasks and problems. The Russian armed forces were achieving organizational viability within their new contours. The tremendous change from the unitary armed forces of the Soviet Union to some fifteen different national armies took place under extremely difficult conditions. All things considered, it had been handled rather successfully. Russia's military officers helped prevent civil war and were a tremendous factor in domestic political stability. Yeltsin thanked the officers for their continued support and renewed the Yeltsin bargain to continue working cooperatively with the military on reorganization and reform.

Yeltsin talked about the opposition and its efforts to drive a wedge between him and the military. Yeltsin told the officers that he expected the military to reject the political opposition and to support his policies. He demanded what I have called positive neutrality from them because he and his policies had been endorsed by the people more than once, most recently in the referendum of 25 April 1993. Yeltsin explained, "Our principled position was and remains the following: the armed forces must be outside the parties, outside political struggle. But this does not in any way mean some sort of opposition to government policy. Quite the opposite, our mutual direct obligation is to follow the course the people selected." On the one hand, he agreed that the military should not be used to settle political scores at home; on the other, he refused to exclude domestic military roles from the military mission. Yeltsin concluded: "Today's army is more than the guarantor of the country's security. It is called upon to be the guarantor of stability, the guarantor of economic and political reform in Russia."[3]

After spending May, June, July, and August attempting to find a way to replace the existing Soviet-era Constitution which created a parliamentary republic with a new constitution designed for a presidential republic, Yeltsin decided to prepare for a showdown with Parliament and the motley coalition of opposition forces that had gathered around Khasbulatov and Rutskoi. On the second anniversary of the August 1991 coup, Yeltsin held a press conference at which he announced his two-stage plan for resolving the national political crisis. Yeltsin said that during August he would complete his plans and during September he would implement them through decisive actions perhaps continuing into October. He left no doubt about his goals. He wanted a new post-Soviet Constitution and a new post-Soviet legislature.[4] This required new elections and a national referendum.

Yeltsin's Final Preparations for the Putsch

On 1 September 1993 Yeltsin announced Rutskoi's suspension, locked him out of the Kremlin, and spent the day shoring up relations with the armed forces. Yeltsin promised the troops that such presidential days with the military would become a regular monthly affair, a new demonstration of his personal interest in the country's armed forces. He visited the Taman and Kantemirsky divisions in the Moscow military district, precisely the forces that had been trained to defend the capital. He posed with troops and made a great show of being an understanding but strong commander.[5] Yeltsin made two such outings before launching his political attack on Parliament. In his second political biography, *The Struggle for Russia,* Yeltsin admits that he was actively working on plans to suspend Parliament but he disingenuously claims that the military visits were not connected to his preparations for the putsch.[6] However, Khasbulatov and Rutskoi followed Yeltsin's moves and their own insider military sources reported that Yeltsin had asked the soldiers revealing questions such as: "How long would it take your division to come to full combat readiness and to take up positions in the center of Moscow?" [7] Rutskoi's sources said that Yeltsin reminded all the military units he met that he was their supreme commander and that all his orders had to be obeyed.

On the weekend of 12 September 1993, Yeltsin went over putsch plans with Minister of Defense Grachev, MVD Chief Yerin, Acting Minister of Internal Security Golushko, and Foreign Minister Kozyrev. They decided that the MVD's crack Dzerzhinsky Brigade would be used to seize Parliament on Sunday 19 September 1993 while Parliament was in recess. Shortly after this planning session, Yeltsin scheduled his second presidential day with the armed forces. This time he visited the MVD's Dzerzhinsky Brigade which was stationed outside Moscow. The MVD's Dzerzhinsky units were supposed to be combat ready and prepared to move immediately to carry out any special assignment in the capital district.[8] The national media pictured Yeltsin in the Dzerzhinsky Brigade's cap and cape and also carried the news that Prime Minister Viktor Chernomyrdin had just signed decrees granting the armed forces 180 percent salary increases retroactive to 1 September 1993.[9] The Dzerzhinsky forces were trained for domestic conflict and were part of the MVD's network of internal armies not part of the Ministry of Defense. This visit fit Yeltsin's strategy and agreement with Grachev that MVD forces not the military would be used if armed force became necessary during the struggle with Parliament. The military was supposed to defend the Russian state against foreign enemies; the MVD was supposed to handle domestic conflict situations.

Khasbulatov and Rutskoi issued a public warning that an anticonstitutional, presidential putsch was near at hand; they delivered a stinging condemnation of Yeltsin's economic and political record; and they called upon all CIS states to send representatives to a Eurasian parliament to discuss their common security and economic interests.[10] When they argued that a threat to Russia's emerging parliament was a threat to all CIS parliaments, they had a point. Presidential rule in Russia would appeal to would-be presidential dictators in the former Soviet republics. Khasbulatov and Rutskoi also beefed up Parliament's paramilitary defense forces in anticipation of Yeltsin's next moves. They were deliberately raising the stakes just as they had done in August 1991 when they stood together with Yeltsin against the SEC. They were raising the price Yeltsin would have to pay to defeat them.

But Yeltsin decided to push ahead. He feared that another retreat would destroy his credibility and effectiveness. His three power ministers knew that he wanted nothing but plans guaranteed to bring Khasbulatov and Rutskoi down. Yeltsin ordered more MVD troops into the city but masked that move as part of his anti-crime and corruption program. He insisted that the MVD and the federal security forces, not the military, be given primary responsibility for law and order during his putsch and expected ministers Yerin and Golushko to confirm their ability to meet that challenge. Minister of Defense Grachev's task was to keep the Russian military cohesive and insulated from the political fray. According the final plan, no additional Russian military forces were to be brought into Moscow and none were to join the cordon that would be tied around the Parliament center.

Yeltsin told Yerin and Golushko that he wanted no bloodshed. This was understandable from a personal political and psychological point of view. But did it make sense from a pragmatic, operational point of view? Was Yeltsin giving the MVD's internal armies an impossible assignment? General Mikhail Barsukov, Yeltsin's presidential security chief spoke up and warned that the plan was flawed. Parliament was armed. It had volatile supporters. The police would have to use or threaten to use lethal force in order to be effective. If they were under strict orders to not to shoot, Parliament's supporters would find out and break through their lines. But Yeltsin refused to think this through. He wanted action. Yeltsin rebuked Barsukov for his "mutiny" and told him to take a vacation.[11] Thus, Yeltsin put the MVD in a no-win situation. However, instead of supporting Barsukov's point, the other power ministers kept their silence at that critical juncture in Russian political history. The flawed plan went forward because Yeltsin had intimidated them. The incident is an excellent example of how small group psychology operates to the detriment of good planning. Leaders sometimes intimidate their subordinates and do not get the best possible professional advice from them.

Grachev's immediate goal was to keep the military out of the unavoidable confrontation between the president and Parliament. The MVD had sufficient personnel and equipment to handle the tasks and should have been able to cope. And there were additional special security forces and commandos that the President could call upon. Although Grachev understood that he might have to get involved, his main message to the military commanders was that the MVD rather than the Ministry of Defense had been handed the volatile, political hot potato.

On 20 September 1993, the day before Yeltsin was to suspend Parliament, Grachev convened a special meeting of the military collegium. The commanders needed this face-to-face meeting and advanced warning to prepare themselves psychologically and politically for a sharp rise in national political tensions and to block efforts by Khasbulatov, Rutskoi, Achalov, and Terekhov to separate the military from Yeltsin. The opposition was interested in that meeting and it left two interesting accounts gleaned from insiders. Rutskoi's version describes Grachev as firm but cautious. He told the commanders to prevent the military from being pulled into the political struggle. They were to remain loyal to the president and to be prepared, if all else failed, to support military action to enforce the president's ukaz. Grachev emphasized that MVD forces, not the military, had been given the primary responsibility. The military was there as an emergency backup if things began to get out of control.[12]

Yury Voronin's story is more dramatic. He claims that Boris Yeltsin placed a call to Grachev during his meeting with the military commanders. According to Voronin, Yeltsin told Grachev in no uncertain terms that the military commanders had to be made to understand that they needed to be prepared to take action if ordered to do so. They were not to leave the meeting feeling complacent that everything had been left to the MVD. Grachev supposedly tried to respond that "the Army is outside of politics." But Yeltsin persisted and this jolted Grachev who had to leave the meeting briefly to take a pill. He returned to explain the situation in all its stark reality.[13] By this time, Yeltsin had apparently realized that Barsukov had been right all along. Barsukov knew some of the key security professionals working at Parliament since some used to work for him in the Kremlin. It turned into a three-ministry operation. The Ministry of Defense, the MVD, and the FSS (former KGB) all had roles to play and none was permitted to stand outside as a neutral observer.

Military Efforts to Avoid Armed Confrontation

High-ranking military officers tried to convince Khasbulatov and Rutskoi to accept political defeat peacefully for the good of the country and their personal safety. The fact that they knew one another made this easier. Extensive contacts between the military and Parliament facilitated communication but may have convinced Parliament that its colleagues in the armed forces would never agree to attack them with lethal weapons.

Rutskoi wrote that contacts began on the day before the presidential putsch. After Grachev's 20 September 1993 closed meeting with the military collegium, General of the Army, Konstantin Kobets paid a confidential visit to Parliament where he tried to convince Khasbulatov of the seriousness of the situation. He encouraged him to give in to the president's demands. In the event that Parliament cooperated, Kobets pledged to use his influence to assist the leadership and to continue working for democratic reform.[14] He warned them that the administration would use force if necessary. After Kobets had gone, Khasbulatov immediately called Minister of Defense Grachev and tried to get him to agree to come over to Parliament for a face-to-face discussion about the general situation. Grachev declined and offered a variety of excuses. However, he agreed to send Chief of General Staff, Colonel General Nikolai Kolesnikov to Parliament. Kolesnikov verified what Kobets had said and gave Khasbulatov the same advice. Kolesnikov repeated that the military hoped to stay out of the situation but only "time will tell."[15]

Rutskoi's account is reasonable. Voronin confirms it in the main and adds that he and Kobets agreed to keep a confidential channel of communication open for the duration of the crisis.[16] It was better to convince Parliament that the military was standing by the president than to allow it to think that there could be a chance that the military would either stand aside or help tip the scales towards Parliament. If so, it is likely that Yeltsin approved of this confidential exchange of information. It would be absurd to believe that he wanted to send the tanks against the Parliament which met in the very White House that had become the icon of Yeltsin's own victory over the SEC in August 1991. The military high command was engaging in high level politics by signaling to Khasbulatov and urging him to avoid putting them in a position where they would have to use force against him. Khasbulatov had to be convinced that they were psychologically and physically prepared to obey Yeltsin's orders if and when they were issued.

Ukaz No. 1400

On Tuesday, 21 September 1993 at 8:00 p.m. Yeltsin's prerecorded speech was broadcast to the nation. Presidential Ukaz No. 1400 was officially promulgated. It opened with key ideas designed to appeal to the military and national patriotism: "A political situation threatening the country's state and societal security has developed in the Russian Federation."[17] He argued that Parliament repeatedly and deliberately prevented the president from implementing reforms which the people had endorsed in the referendum of 25 April 1993. Political paralysis had set in and had to be cured. The Constitution requires that the president take action to defend national security. Therefore,

Parliament was suspended, new legislative elections would be held along with a referendum on a new Constitution. Yeltsin explained that the old system had created an impossible political tangle. He said "the security of Russia and its peoples is a higher value than the formal observation of contradictory norms established by the legislative branch of power." He ordered the three power ministries—defense, internal affairs, and security, to give him daily reports and authorized them "to take all measures necessary to guarantee state and public security."[18] Yeltsin suspended the Constitutional Court lest it declare him in violation of his oath of office. He did the same to Rutskoi, suspending his position as vice president in order to prevent him from using it to proclaim himself acting president of Russia. Yeltsin also suspended some newspapers and deprived Parliament of direct access to national television and radio.

Parliament tried to defend itself against Yeltsin's presidential putsch by using tactics that Yeltsin had used against the SEC in August 1991. At midnight Parliament voted that Yeltsin had flagrantly broken his sacred oath to uphold the Constitution of the Russian Federation and named Aleksandr Rutskoi acting president. It likewise "removed" the three power ministers—Grachev, Yerin, and Golushko from office since they were now serving an anti-constitutional dictator. It named Col. General (Ret.) Achalov acting minister of defense. Achalov and Rutskoi immediately issued urgent orders to the military commanders of the Russian armed forces to report to them. Valery Zorkin, chief judge of the Constitutional Court advised Parliament in writing that the majority of the Court's members considered Yeltsin's act unconstitutional.[19] And Parliament's supporters began erecting barricades just as Yeltsin's had done in August 1991.

Not all deputies supported Khasbulatov's move to replace Yeltsin and Grachev with Rutskoi and Achalov. Col. Aleksei Tsarev, chairman of the subcommittee on defense and security affairs, spoke against it. He warned against efforts to resubordinate the military, police, and security forces of Russia to acting ministers named by Parliament. He argued that such moves push the political confrontation to the brink of armed confrontation. He and fellow military officers argued that the military would not take action against Parliament unless it was provoked. Khasbulatov, Rutskoi, and Achalov dismissed their arguments and forged ahead. Minister of Defense Grachev ordered all military deputies to leave Parliament immediately and to report to their commanders at once. Tsarev reported to his unit in the Strategic Rocket Forces. Therefore, after the first day of the crisis, no military deputies who were loyal to the Ministry of Defense and President Yeltsin remained in Parliament.[20]

Instead of backing the peoples deputies into a corner, Yeltsin offered them all material and professional incentives. All who supported him were given title to a Moscow flat, a pension, and a promise of employment in public administration. At least 100 deputies took him up on the offer. But some 500–

600 continued to meet as an extraordinary, emergency Congress in defiance of the President.[21]

In August 1991, Yeltsin had made himself temporary commander in chief over all Soviet armed forces in Russia and issued special decrees that assured officers that he would protect them for disobeying orders from the SEC. In September 1993, Rutskoi and Achalov used the same tactics. They issued decrees which explained that Yeltsin had violated the Constitution: "Citizens of Russia! The President has taken extreme, previously planned actions to overthrow the constitutional order and to topple democracy. A state coup has taken place in Russia..." They released Ministry of Defense, MVD, and FSS personnel from the illegal orders that Yeltsin had imposed. They warned officers that anyone who carried out the regime's illegal orders would be prosecuted. They urged the armed forces to prevent civil war.[22]

It was imperative that Grachev and the high command demonstrate their loyalty to President Yeltsin and publicly repudiate Parliament's appointment of Rutskoi as acting president of Russia. Therefore, Grachev assembled his deputy ministers and key service commanders for a press conference on 22 September 1993. Grachev appeared before the cameras with his military commanders and denounced Parliament's demand that the armed forces report to new leaders. He told reporters that he had taken measures to keep the military united and out of the political struggle. He said that Parliament had sent at least forty packets of its orders to commanders in the Moscow region. Therefore, Grachev had been compelled to issue special orders that prohibited commanders from implementing any orders except his written orders. Although he did could not categorically rule out the option of using some military power to restore order, he insisted that police and internal security services would take primary responsibility for controlling events. Grachev summarized: "The army must be left in peace, outside of politics. It guarantees Russia's security and will not meddle in questions of internal security up to the point where political passions cross into general confrontation. If the blood of innocent people is spilled, the army will have its say."[23] According to this logic, if Parliament's supporters caused bloodshed, then Grachev could order military units to intervene in the political crisis.

On Wednesday 23 September 1993, Boris Yeltsin sent a special message to the armed forces: "Dear Soldiers of the Russian Armed Forces! My Sons! I appeal to you at a critical moment for Russian statehood and our Fatherland." He covered the familiar ground about the erosion of state viability and the need for decisive measures to end the protracted national crisis. He described the difficulties the army and the nation faced because of national political paralysis. He urged the soldiers to stay united and focused on their professional tasks and to reject pseudo-patriots who would drag them into political adventures: "Remember that the prevention of national collapse and civil war and the prospects for the revival of a great Russia depend upon your firm, responsible position."[24]

Discrediting the Union of Officers: The Terekhov Incident

According to some reports on 23 September 1993 in the late afternoon, Viktor Anpilov, head of Trudovaya Moskva, harangued the crowd that had gathered outside Parliament. He allegedly urged armed radicals, "those who are really men," to attack CIS military headquarters at No. 41 Leningradsky Prospekt. Anpilov yelled that the orders had been given by Stanislav Terekhov, head of the Union of Officers. This evoked shouts accusing Anpilov of being an agent planted by the Kremlin. Fights broke out and had to be stopped by Parliament's security guards. The fact that these details were printed in *Krasnaya zvezda* suggests that reporters were likewise suspicious of Anpilov's motives.[25]

Another story attributed to government sources reported that at 8:50 P.M. a car full of militants arrived, killed militia guard Valery Sviridenko, and wounded a civilian living next door, Vera Malysheva. The government media picked up the theme that Moscow was threatened with bloodshed and anarchy because armed extremists were taking up positions in the city.[26] The next morning Grachev and Kobets accused retired, opposition generals Achalov, Makashov, and Rutskoi of complicity in the death of innocent people. They said that it was deeply disturbing that Rutskoi had taken such action after the army had promised not to take Parliament by force. Grachev said that this was proof that Parliament was distributing arms and inciting violence. He argued that the threat to civil peace justified bringing additional troops into the city and he ordered more elite armed forces to take up positions in Moscow. Grachev described the incident as an attack on the military by Parliament's supporters, part of an effort to drag the military into the political confrontation.[27] It is interesting that the generals apparently said nothing about Terekhov. A separate news brief stated that some unnamed witnesses claimed that they had seen Stanislav Terekhov among the attackers that night and therefore he had been arrested by the military procurator in Moscow. This all smacked of old-style KGB manipulation and disinformation.

Khasbulatov convened the Tenth Extraordinary Congress at 10:00 P.M. on 23 September 1993. It ran into the predawn hours. At 5:00 A.M. on 24 September 1993, Congress adopted a resolution that called for simultaneous new presidential and parliamentary elections.[28] This compromise with Yeltsin was designed to defuse the crisis. However, instead of focusing on Parliament's so-called "double-zero" option, the Yeltsin administration behaved as if Moscow were threatened by anarchy and emphasized the stories about armed extremists in the city.

Rutskoi disclaimed the attack on CIS headquarters and called the incident a deliberate provocation launched by Parliament's enemies to give Yeltsin an excuse to use military power to get his way. Rutskoi demanded that the authorities produce Terekhov and permit the media to speak with him. Three members of Terekhov's Union of Officers—Col. General Albert Makashov, Lt. General M. Titov, and Lt. Col. E. Chernobrivko held a press conference and denounced the Yeltsin administration for arresting Terekhov and accusing him a launching a patently absurd attack on CIS military headquarters. They saw it as a political attack aimed at the Union of Officers and a warning to all officers who supported Parliament's cause.[29] The opposition claims that Terekhov was arrested, taken to the militia where Sviridenko had worked, and left to be beaten by militia men who had been told that he had just killed their colleague. He was then handled by military rather than civilian authorities and confined to Butyrka prison by a military procurator. The entire case was dropped after the crisis in Moscow had passed.[30]

The opposition further charges that deliberate, excessive cruelty was shown towards members of the Union of Officers when Grachev's forces attacked Parliament on the morning of 4 October 1993. Six members of Terekhov's movement were shot dead during the assault.[31] When Grachev's tanks opened fire, they aimed their guns directly at the twelfth and thirteenth floors of Parliament because that is where Grachev's opponent, Col. General Achalov had established his headquarters.[32]

The Patriarch Mediates: "Thou Shalt Not Kill."

The Church invited Parliament and the president to send representatives to talks at the Danilovsky Monastery in Moscow, the location of Patriarch Aleksy II of Moscow and All Russia's city offices. Bishop Kirill, who addressed the January 1992 Officers Assembly, became an important go-between. The Holy Synod met and warned that it would anathematize those responsible for any bloodshed.[33]

Yeltsin was in an extremely uncomfortable personal psychological and political position. If he compromised once again, the national political crisis would continue though in a milder form. If he moved decisively against an armed Parliament, he would be responsible for bloodshed. Not only would his reputation suffer but it would be a deep personal blow given that building's symbolic importance to Yeltsin and the democratic movement. It was a lose/lose situation. General Barsukov had been correct. The militia and security forces were not coping well. Parliament was assembling a ragtag army of nationalist extremists from various parts of the country.

The Terekhov incident had raised many disturbing questions about covert operations. Terekhov had been arrested but the person who had been seen urging the crowds to take arms against the government, Viktor Anpilov, was still free. He reappeared on Tuesday 28 September 1993 and organized the mobs that attacked police lines. A militia man, a father of five was killed. Yet, Anpilov was not arrested for provoking that incident either. Was Yeltsin's order that the militia shed no blood crippling its effectiveness or was all this staged? As the crisis dragged on, the pressure on Yeltsin mounted and his democratic image became increasingly tarnished. He issued special orders that any officer who does not support the laws of the Russian Federation including presidential Ukaz No. 1400 will be immediately removed from the armed forces. Further, all commanders were to be held personally account-able for their units and for the disposition of all weapons within them.[34] The pressure worked. Only some forty to fifty active-duty personnel rallied to Parliament.[35] Some 2,000,000 did not. Thus, Yeltsin appeared to have won that battle for control over the military. However, the political struggle's out-come was uncertain.

The Ministry of Defense daily, *Krasnaya zvezda*, reported favorably on the negotiations to settle the crisis. Military cohesion guaranteed the stable environment in which the political leaders could find a peaceful way out of the crisis. Yeltsin's orders to remain cohesive and stable were understood as a positive contribution to the settlement process. The paper rebuked Parlia-ment for continuing to arm itself and for urging volunteers from all over Rus-sia to assemble in Moscow to defend the Constitution.[36]

Parliament called upon all elected political bodies to defend their rights against the Kremlin's efforts to impose presidential dictatorship on the country. Parlia-ment urged representatives of regional legislatures to assemble in Moscow. Representatives from fifty-four of Russia's eighty-eight main political units or *subyekty* arrived in Moscow. They met in the Constitutional Court building and insisted that the political confrontation be settled peacefully through compro-mise. The patriarch joined the "civilian" politicians for that session.[37]

As various regional governments took positions for or against the presi-dent or Parliament, the political crisis in Moscow began to threaten national political integrity. Both sides were courting the regions. The military press commented negatively on this development and cited the lessons of Russian history. Whenever feudal princes divided the country into warring domains, Russia fell victim to attacks from outside. Why repeat this mistake at the end of the twentieth century? The Russian Federation is neither the totalitarian Soviet Union nor the imperial prison house of nationalities. It deserves pro-tection. "As to the military, its interest in a united Russia is definite.... We must diffuse the situation as fast as possible and exclusively through peaceful means.... Compromise is as vital as breadth."[38]

Will the Military Continue to Obey Orders?

Time was working against Yeltsin. Public violence was working against Rutskoi. The Yeltsin administration claimed that there was a serious danger of anarchy and insurrection in Moscow and that Parliament had become the general headquarters for Red-Brown revolution. Parliament denied those charges and offered to open itself for inspection. Civic leaders pressed for compromises such as the "double-zero" plan. Rutskoi sent the patriarch a written pledge that Parliament would not fire its weapons first. Further, Parliament insisted that an impartial commission of military experts be formed and sent into Parliament to investigate charges that its self-defense forces represented a generalized threat to Moscow and the country. On Saturday, 2 October 1993, at 4:20 in the afternoon, negotiators at the Danilovsky monastery agreed upon a list of six high-ranking military officers whose task was to take a full inventory of Parliament's weapons and paramilitaries. The idea was to demilitarize the situation and to end the dangerous military stand-off before major violence erupted.[39]

Foreign journalists and diplomats kept probing for answers from the military. What was the army going to do about the political crisis? Would it intervene to settle it or not? Aleksandr Gol'ts published a frank editorial on the subject in 2 October 1993 issue of *Krasnaya zvezda*, the issue printed and distributed to the military on the weekend when the crisis peaked. After noting the great interest from journalists and diplomats in the political position of Russia's armed forces, he said: "The situation where the military is outside of politics is axiomatic in societies that have firmly absorbed democratic values. But for Russia this is still a theorem."[40] He reminded readers that the military still deeply resents the way it was used and abused in Tbilisi, Baku, Vilnius, and Moscow (August 1991). None of those attempts to use the military to resolve political problems was successful. Further, the military developed a deep resentment towards such political games and this helps explain why the armed forces are maintaining their restraint and cohesion in the face of various efforts to pull them into the current political crisis.

But would the military obey orders to end Parliament's defiance of the president's orders? Gol'ts made it absolutely clear that the military did not want to face such orders and that Yeltsin's prestige and authority would be damaged if he issued them. The military served the country not one political faction or another: "If one politico or another hopes to have authority among the armed forces, he must contend with this deeply rooted, military self-awareness as sons of the *Fatherland* not just supporters of this or that political line." "This week the military has demonstrated by its calm and restraint greater sense than the politicos. Therefore, in this instance, society could draw a lesson from the military."[41] But what about the answer to the tough question? Would the military obey orders? "There can be no greater danger for an army than the violation of this principle, 'one set of orders.'"[42] I think the answer was clear and honest. In the final analysis, the military would have to obey orders to intervene. However, by issuing such orders, the President would severely damage his moral capital and authority with the military.

The Sunday Violence

As the country headed into the weekend, there was reason to believe that the crisis had peaked. Patriarch Aleksy's efforts had yielded good results. On

Sunday morning 3 October 1993 Yeltsin left for his country home after several hours of work in his Kremlin office. Things seemed relatively calm in the city. He stopped to chat briefly with troops and then drove off. But early that afternoon the opposition fielded huge demonstrations that swept the militia aside. Although there were thousands of militia, security, and military forces in central Moscow, the mob "liberated" Parliament and broke the blockade. The three power ministries either failed miserably or collaborated in scheme to entrap Khasbulatov, Rutskoi, Makashov, Achalov, et al.

Voronin was still negotiating at the Danilovsky monastery when his bosses at the White House lost their heads. All the political work done to deprive Yeltsin of his main objective evaporated. Khasbulatov and Rutskoi blundered miserably. They started by clearing MVD troops out of neighboring buildings. The operation was so successful that they became overconfident and called for one group to march on the Kremlin to throw out the usurpers and another on the national radio and television center, Ostankino. Rutskoi began lining up men, building armed formations for an immediate attack before the window of opportunity closed.[43] Barsukov called Yeltsin on his private line to tell him what was really happening in Moscow.[44] Yeltsin had to take formal action at some point to rescind his original orders against the use of violence and to take decisive action against the insurrection. Meanwhile, Parliament's mini-revolution moved forward. Their convoy moved through Moscow unimpeded and by 7:00 P.M. was massing outside Ostankino station, some 100 armed attackers and up to 4,000 unarmed demonstrators. At 7:30 P.M. Col. Gen. (Ret.) Makashov ordered Parliament's forces to attack! At 8:00 P.M. the main channels went off the air, an event that heightened the sense of national political emergency. Units of the Dzerzhinsky division moved into place to begin the retaking of Ostankino but did so only slowly.

Observers accused Boris Yeltsin of incompetent leadership that led to bloodshed that might have been avoided. They raised questions about his actions on the afternoon and evening of Sunday 3 October suggesting that he was neither in control of himself nor the situation. Yeltsin attempted to shift responsibility to Pavel Grachev and claimed that his generals were distraught and psychologically immobilized: "I was trying to bring my combat generals out of their state of stress and paralysis. I saw that the army, despite all the assurances of the defense minister, for some reason, was not able to come quickly to Moscow's defense and fight the rebels."[45] But Yeltsin's reconstruction of the events leaves too many questions unanswered.

Yeltsin's team had given Khasbulatov and Rutskoi the leeway, the political rope to hang themselves and they took it. The political game had been played on covert and overt levels by both sides. But it was Rutskoi who made the greatest mistake and who initiated the last rounds of violence precisely when he was winning the political conflict at the conference table in the

Danilovsky monastery. He failed a critical test of leadership. He was more a bullheaded fighter than a statesman.

National Armed Forces or Yeltsin's Political Army?

Yeltsin collapsed under the psychological burden. The strain had been too great for him. As commander in chief and president of Russia, it was Yeltsin's duty to lead the state through the crisis by choosing and legitimizing the main strategy and by giving the power ministries their orders. His first strategy had failed. He had been ineffective as chief national strategist and he placed his legitimacy at risk by violating the Constitution and by rejecting compromises that prominent civic leaders had brokered. The second strategy was working but it was costly. People had been killed and law enforcement professionals were not doing their jobs properly. It all smelled of cynical political manipulation. Yeltsin's credibility had been permanently damaged. When the crisis peaked, Yeltsin was in no condition to lead in public or in private. The first leader to appear on national television to announce that the administration was taking control of the situation was Prime Minister Chernomyrdin not Boris Yeltsin. Further, Chernomyrdin chaired the crisis management committee for Yeltsin on the night of October 3–4, 1993 when Grachev and the key players met to discuss options and actions. The session started without Yeltsin. When Yeltsin arrived, he sat to one side and did not take a position at the head of the table.[46]

Yeltsin recalls that "the generals' expressions were grim, and many had lowered their heads. They obviously understood the awkwardness of the situation: the lawful government hung by a thread but the army couldn't defend it—some soldiers were picking potatoes and others didn't feel like fighting."[47] But this interpretation is ridiculously self-serving and insulting to the Russian armed forces. The generals were stressed because they knew that their commander in chief had deliberately created and then mismanaged a political crisis that he would now order them to end by using lethal fire power against their fellow citizens. The Tbilisi syndrome had raised its head again.

It was 3:00 a.m. when Chernomyrdin's session with the military collegium completed hearing a plan for the military's taking of Parliament by force. Army tanks were to strike directly to demonstrate the utter hopelessness of the Parliament's position. Chernomyrdin, not Yeltsin, called the question. The plan was adopted. Yeltsin then told Grachev that he had his orders. At this point Grachev made a difficult but correct decision. He asked President Yeltsin for formal written orders, a step that angered Yeltsin who seemed to have misunderstood or to have pretended to misunderstand the situation. But Yeltsin agreed to send written orders and then left for the Kremlin.[48]

In Tbilisi, Baku, and Vilnius the armed forces killed civilians without the benefit of written orders. After the Tbilisi incident the military was supposed to implement such operations only upon receipt of written, legitimate orders from the appropriate commanders. The military's brush with civil war in August 1991 reinforced its fear of being manipulated into no-win situations. After the August coup, Minister of Defense Shaposhnikov pledged that the military would never be used against the people during his watch and issued policy directives that required all orders to use lethal force in domestic operations be put in writing. Therefore, when his successor, Pavel Grachev insisted that President Yeltsin provide written orders, he was defending the interests of the armed forces and setting an important precedent that contributed to the institutionalization of responsible civilian control over the armed forces. Boris Yeltsin had to take responsibility for his decision, the orders to use rifles and tanks against the defenders of Parliament.

But a larger problem remained. Although the military had written orders from its civilian commander in chief, Boris Yeltsin, the soldiers were still being used for blatantly partisan political purposes. The military's isolation from domestic political conflicts requires sufficient domestic political stability which depends upon the actions of civilian and military leaders. Pavel Grachev was Yeltsin's appointee and he behaved as part of the political leadership core by working closely with Yeltsin on the overall plan for the presidential putsch against Parliament. Boris Yeltsin rejected the idea of armed forces neutrality and made that point clear in his visits to the Taman and Dzerzhinsky divisions before he issued presidential Ukaz No. 1400. That attitude was clear as Yeltsin rebuilt the Soviet and the Russian military high command. They were his commanders since his policies were the best for Russia and he had been chosen by the people to implement them. Yeltsin made the top military appointments without consulting with Parliament and intended to keep that power for himself. The new Yeltsin Constitution that the voters would approve by a small margin on 12 December 1993 concentrated those powers directly in the hands of the president. The high command became the president's to appoint and dismiss. [49] Further, on 2 November 1993 through presidential Ukaz No. 1833, Boris Yeltsin promulgated a new military doctrine that legitimized the domestic use of all the armed forces to counter threats to state security and public order.[50]

Yeltsin's Military Assault on Parliament

Col. Vladimir N. Taranenko, a member of Rutskoi's personal security guard, reported that Grachev's deputy Minister of Defense, Mironov, called Rutskoi at Parliament before dawn and warned him that a showdown was inevitable and urged him to evacuate the building.[51] Yuri Voronin, Parliament's deputy speaker, confirms that Parliament was informed about the orders Yeltsin had given.[52] This suggests that Grachev and his commanders still hoped to be able to avoid an ugly confrontation with Parliament and the inevitable political and psychological fallout. But Rutskoi refused to surrender and convinced himself that the president was bluffing, trying to frighten him into giving up. According to Taranenko, Rutskoi kept insisting that his armed supporters exercise extreme caution and refrain from firing upon Grachev's troops. Parliament would not fire the first shot. But it was too late for Rutskoi to play this card. He had incited violence and was deeply implicated in the Sunday bloodshed.

The cannonade began at 6:30 A.M. as Grachev's tanks aimed directly into Col. General Achalov's headquarters on the twelfth and thirteenth floors of Parliament. Voronin called the Ministry of Defense and reached Col. General Dmitry Volkogonov, the respected military historian and Yeltsin's military adviser. Voronin poured out a mixture of questions and anti-Yeltsin invective. But, it was useless to try to convince the military leadership to disobey. Volkogonov confirmed that Commander in Chief Boris Yeltsin had issued formal, written orders to the military and his orders would be obeyed as required by law. Law and order would be restored in Moscow. The insurrection would be crushed. Parliament should surrender peacefully.[53] Volkogonov was helping coordinate military and political aspects of the operation.

Yet, the standoff dragged on. Grachev's forces, one small unit at a time, moved into the White House. The military was systematically building up its forces inside, around, and above the White House. but it wasn't the military's job to arrest political leaders. In post-Soviet Russia as in the Soviet Union, that job belonged to special security units who were taking their orders from the Kremlin. In this case, it was several, Alfa commandos who entered the building and worked their way to the leadership. They put down their guns on the marble floor and asked to be taken to Khasbulatov and Rutskoi. They had been instructed to tell them that they could leave the building and live or face the consequences of the final assault which had already been ordered and prepared. Alfa had orders to guarantee their personal safety as they exited the building. Khasbulatov and Rutskoi feared for their lives given the highly charged atmosphere and what they had done on Sunday. They accepted the Kremlin's offer and prepared to surrender. They made ceremonial speeches and the remaining defenders signed a special memorial book to record their presence in Parliament on that historic day. Voronin also called constitutional court justice, Valery Zorkin and urged him to get legal personnel into Parliament as soon as possible in order to take possession of important documents and evidence and to witnesses the surrender. Parliament's materials included records of military communications and lists of officers who had given the orders to attack. Parliament's deposed leaders intended to press charges against Yeltsin and the military at some later date.[54]

The Alfa commandos told Rutskoi and Khasbulatov that they were going to be taken to the Moscow subway and released; but they were taken to Lefortovo prison. A second bus with important political prisoners such as

Generals Achalov and Makashov was similarly handled. Otherwise, the scene was bizarrely anarchic and Voronin ended up running through the streets and taking shelter in a perfect stranger's apartment.[55] The official government report states that there were 878 casualties. A total of 145 people were killed by both sides on 3–4 October. About 100 died in and around Parliament and forty at Ostankino. There were 121 civilians killed. The MVD lost eighteen personnel, the Ministry of Defense, six. Sixty-two MVD and forty-two military personnel were hospitalized.[56] By the end of the day, the rebellion had been defeated militarily and politically.

But the operation's technical messiness suggested that there had been some command and control problems which remained hidden from the public until after the crisis. According to Major General (Ret.) Yury I. Drozdov, the elite commando units hesitated and resisted when Grachev first ordered them to take Parliament and to arrest elected deputies on October 4, 1993. Although they finally carried out his orders, after the putsch, Yeltsin decided that they had to be transferred from the military to the MVD. However, the elite commando officers regarded the shift as a major demotion professionally. They considered the military more important and prestigious than the police (MVD). Further, they were unhappy with the Yeltsin administration's behavior. As a result, more than 1,000 highly qualified professionals left the armed forces in disgust and found immediate employment in private security organizations.[57] This loss of highly trained talent would damage the Yeltsin administration's ability to respond to terrorist incidents in 1995 and 1996.

From Arrest to Amnesty

The Russian state charged Rutskoi with the crime of calling for the violent overthrow of the constitutional order. But he claimed that it was actually "units of the toiling masses" who rose to defend the Constitution, the courts, and their rights and freedoms which had been trampled under foot by Yeltsin. He objected to efforts to paint him as a "Communo-fascist" and pledged to keep fighting for the Soviet peoples against those who destroyed the Motherland.[58] When interrogators accused him, he repeatedly accused "Mr. Yeltsin—and his clique who under the collective pseudonym 'President of the Russian Federation' carried out a state, anti-constitutional coup." He lashed out at the West for supporting and encouraging Yeltsin to take preventative action to block the growing national, popular movement against the country's destruction. Yeltsin had usurped power and destroyed an institution that represented the people's will. [59] It was Communists of the Yeltsin type who turned a powerful state into the CIS (Commonwealth of the Impoverished and the Starving).[60] The real *fuhrer* is the one in the Kremlin who sends tanks against Parliament and muzzles dissent.[61] The greatest crime against the State was the Belovezhsky conspiracy in December 1991. And this was followed by a pattern of threats and deeds that violated the constitutional order: December 1992, March 1993...September 1993.[62]

Day after day, Rutskoi and his lawyers read into the legal record every step taken by Yeltsin to intimidate Parliament, to bend the law, to undermine the opposition, to intimidate the military by making political visits to special forces units, by promising pay increases on the eve of the September crisis, by building a personal army of some 18,000 in the presidential guards, and by manipulating and reorganizing command structures for the Alfa and Vympel special commandos.[63]

In February 1994, Parliament's direct successor, the Duma which was elected in December 1993, voted to amnesty all who had been arrested in connection with the August 1991 coup and the events of September-October 1993. This "double-zero" gesture was designed to permit political wounds to heal. It was the prelude to a Yeltsin administration effort to build a national political consensus around a grand *soglasie* or national political accord. All soglasie signatories were morally bound to play the political game within the constitution and laws of Russia. Rutskoi refused to sign and continued to argue that Boris Yeltsin had done major damage to post-Soviet political reconstruction by flagrantly violating the Constitution and imposing a temporary dictatorship on the country.

Conclusion

President Yeltsin's actions in September-October 1993 damaged prospects for democratic development in four ways. First, by appealing to a higher national interest greater than the rule of law and the constitutional process, Boris Yeltsin set a dangerous precedent. He put into the post-Soviet political record precisely the type of thinking needed to justify military juntas and presidential dictatorships. Second, by refusing to agree with Parliament to implement a compromise based on a "double-zero" option, he reinforced authoritarian values and increased the presidency's isolation from society. Nongovernmental organizations such as the Church were working responsibly towards solutions which he rejected. Third, he damaged the credibility and professional morale of MVD and law enforcement organizations in Moscow by intimidating their leaders into supporting bad policy decisions and by imposing no-win conditions on policy implementation. Fourth, he deliberately pushed the military into the domestic political struggle instead of allowing it to remain neutral.

Colonel General (Ret.) Aleksandr Rutskoi's behavior was also damaging to democratic development. Rutskoi set two negative precedents for military officers with political ambition. Vice President Rutskoi was disloyal to his president and irresponsible in his use of military skills. He should have resigned as soon as it became clear that he could not support the Yeltsin program. When Rutskoi lost his head and began an armed insurrection along with allies such as

Col. General (Ret.) Albert Makashov on 3 October 1993, he became a threat to Russia's political integrity and security. This damaged the military's image and confirmed that there was some danger to civil society from some soldiers.

Parliament's actions were also damaging to the development of democratic political culture. By associating itself with the extreme opposition to the Yeltsin administration and with groups that were actively promoting opposition within the armed forces, Khasbulatov and Rutskoi showed little understanding of democratic political culture and left a poor legacy for the future. They made the legislative branch into a quasi-government complete with its own little army. By summer 1992—a year before the showdown, all entrances were guarded by special security forces toting automatic weapons, hardly the type of environment one would associate with an open democratic institution.

Thus, the opposition bears much of the blame for the situation, particularly the anarchic violence. Nevertheless, neither Yeltsin nor the three power ministers satisfactorily explained why they permitted that violence to develop and failed to arrest known extremists such as Viktor Anpilov even after he openly incited armed attacks on state institutions. The facts point towards efforts to manipulate the affair into a crisis situation. The only other explanation is gross incompetence which is even less flattering to Yeltsin and the power ministers.

The Ministry of Defense's record is mixed. Grachev should have supported General Barsukov's effort to prevent Yeltsin from making the flawed decisions which led to armed confrontation. Nevertheless, once the cards had been dealt, Grachev's staff worked hard to convince Parliament to give in without fighting. From 20 September through 4 October 1993 the military leadership communicated with Parliament and consistently advised it that the armed forces would support the president. When the final showdown came and Yeltsin gave Grachev verbal orders to send tanks against Parliament, Grachev keenly understood that his reputation and military legality were at stake. By insisting that President Yeltsin give him formal written orders, Grachev won a small victory for the military. By putting those orders in writing, Boris Yeltsin moved civil-military relations in right direction and accepted personal responsibility for them.

In theory, Grachev might have refused to use force and resigned on the night of October 3–4, 1993. However, after Rutskoi's huge blunder and the violence on Sunday 3 October 1993, it became much harder to resist the president. By demanding written orders and obeying them, Grachev did the best he could with a very bad situation. To Grachev's credit most of the leading actors in the drama on Parliament's side survived the assault and were taken into custody safely. Grachev picked Achalov's office suites in Parliament as the primary target for the tank gunners and members of the Union of Officers were killed during the assault. On the one hand this appears vindictive; one the other, it made military-political sense to hit Parliament's armed forces rather than its civilians. Things could have been much worse. Grachev showed raw political courage if not professional sophistication by taking personal command of the assault. But this did not solve one of the most important dilemmas in civil-military relations.

How can a minister of defense decide between legal and illegal orders from a president? How can officers decide between two sets of orders, one set from Grachev and another from Achalov? There are no easy answers to such questions. The military supported the President for three main reasons. First, Boris Yeltsin appointed the high command and he threatened to remove any commander or officer who hesitated to implement his orders. Second, Parliament had associated itself with political extremists who were trying to split the armed forces. Military professional values such as military cohesion and the military's general duty to guarantee national security favored the president over Parliament in this confrontation once the anarchy began. Third, prior to launching Ukaz No. 1400, Yeltsin established personal contact with the military units that were most likely to be used. Such personal attention helped assure the officers that they would not be abandoned and left to bear the blame for the killing. He also gave the military a pay raise and promised to address their concerns more systematically. This was good "politics."

It can be argued that the Russian military were under democratic civilian control and that civil society was emerging in Russia. But it was still only embryonic democratic control and civil society had insufficient influence over the political elite. Yeltsin was a democratically elected president but not democratically orientated in his personal leadership style. He refused to come to terms with Parliament's insistence that he moderate his reforms and be more cautious. He had a Communist-like aversion to compromise. Although he regarded himself as the real father of Russian democracy, he refused to listen to society when prominent citizens including religious and secular leaders lobbied to avert the showdown with Parliament. He should have accepted their compromise plan. That step would have nurtured an environment favorable to responsible civic activism. Instead Yeltsin engaged in conspiratorial manipulations which gave rise to semi-anarchy in Moscow before calling in the troops and blasting the Parliament center into submission. This was at best an example of primitive democratic civilian control of the military.

It is easy to explain the entire affair as the result of deficiencies in Russian political culture, particularly civilian democratic political culture. But thoughtful military leaders understood the issues involved quite well. Civilians had to learn more new roles than the soldiers. The military could remain basically hierarchical and authoritarian within its own sphere because that is the way militaries are expected to be even in democratic societies. Under Grachev's leadership the military reaffirmed traditional discipline and tried to undo the damage caused by experiments with military democratization without reverting to the type of authoritarian excesses that undermine modern professionalism. The high quality of much of the reporting and analysis found in *Krasnaya zvezda* reflected that general striving. It also revealed concern that the country as a whole was coping poorly with economic and political reconstruction. The military wanted to live in a Russia where the general political situation permitted the armed forces to stay out of partisan politics and to focus on national defense.

Notes

1. Author's interviews at *Krasnaya zvezda*, 4 August 1993.
2. Author's conversations with Georgy Satarov, July 1993.
3. Captains V. Chupakhin and A. Dokuchayev, "Armiya vystoyala v ispitaniyakh i sposobna razvernut' polnomashtabnuyu reformu," *Krasnaya zvezda*, 11 June 1993.
4. See Aleksander Pel'ts, "Nameren navodit' poryadok v Rossii po vsem napravleniyam," *Krasnaya zvezda*, 20 August 1993.
5. See Oleg Falichev and Aleksandr Oliinik, " Narod vy krepkii i deistvitelno mozhete vypolnit' liubuyu zadachu" and "Prezident RF prinyal reshenie ob otstranenii ot dolzhnosti Aleksandra Rutskogo i Vladimira Shumeiko," *Krasnaya zvezda*, 2 September 1993.
6. Boris Yeltsin, *The Struggle for Russia* (New York: Times Books/Random House), p. 243.
7. Aleksandr Rutskoi, "Podgotovka" (The preparations), *Nezvisimaya gazeta*, 27 January 1994 in D. A. Mayorov, ed., *Neizvestnyi Rutskoi:politicheskii portret* (The Unknown Rutskoi: a political portrait), (Moscow: "Obozrevatel'," 1994), p. 95. Mayorov's volume is a collection of writings by and about Rutskoi.
8. See ITAR-TASS, "Sevodnya-ocherednoi 'voennoi den' ' Prezidenta," *Krasnaya zvezda*, 16 September 1993; and Vladimir Maryukha "Krapovyeberety vruchayut ne kazhdomu. Boris Yeltsin posetil diviziyu vnutrennykh voisk MVD RF," *Krasnaya zvezda*, 18 September 1993.
9. See Yury Gladkevich, "Nakonets, i voennym oklady povysheny. Vot tol'ko vse li ikh poluchat vovremya?" *Krasnaya zvezda*, 16 September 1993.
10. See Vladimir Ermolin, "Na parlamentskoi tribune—Khasbulatov, Rutskoi i Lobov," *Krasnaya zvezda*, 18 September 1993.
11. Yeltsin, *Struggle*, pp. 253–54.
12. See Aleksandr Rutskoi, "Podgotovka" (The preparations)," *Nezvisimaya gazeta*, p. 95.
13. See Yury Voronin, *Svitsom po Rossii* (Moscow: Paleya, 1995), p. 183. Voronin was second to Khasbulatov in the Parliamentary leadership.
14. See Rutskoi, "Podgotovka."
15. See *Ibid.*
16. See Voronin, *Svitsom po Rossii*, pp. 183–87.
17. President Boris Yeltsin, "Ukaz Prezidenta Rossiiskoi Federatsii, 'O poetapnoi konstitutsionnoi reforme v Rossiiskoi Federatsii' (Ukaz of the President of the Russian Federation: On step sequential constitutional reform in the Russian Federation); Krasnaya Zuezda, 23 September 1993.
18. *Ibid.*
19. V. D. Zorkin and Yu. Rudkin, "Zaklyuchenie Konstitutsionnogo Suda Rossiiskoi Federatsii (Opinion of the constitutional court of the Russian Federation);" 21 September 1993; Yury Voronin, *Svitsom po Rossii*, pp. 80–81.

20. See Anatoly Stasovskii, "Aleksei Tsarev: Novomu parlamentu ot voennykh problem ne uiti" (The new parliament will not be able to get away from military problems), *Krasnaya zvezda*, 9 November 1993.

21. See Voronin, *Svitsom po Rossii*, pp. 50–55.

22. Appeal from the Presidium of the Supreme Soviet of the Russian Federation (in Russian), 21 September 1993. Documents in Yury Voronin, *Svitsom po Rossii*, pp. 82–83.

23. See Vladimir Maryukha, "General Armii Pavel Grachev: U armii zadacha odna—zashchita otechestva," *Krasnaya zvezda*, 23 September 1993.

24. Boris Yeltsin, "Obrashchenie Prezidenta Rossiiskoi Federatsii—Glavnokomanduyushchego Vooruzhennymi Silami Rossii," *Krasnaya zvezda*, 24 September 1993.

25. See Vladimir Ermolin, "A tem vremenem v Belom Dome," *Krasnaya zvezda*, 25 September 1993.

26. "From the Council of Ministers of the Government of the Russian Federation" (in Russian), *Krasnaya zvezda*, 25 September 1993.

27. See Aleksandr Pel'ts, Sergei Pyatakov, "Kommentarii rukovodstva Ministerstva oborony RF," *Krasnaya zvezda*, 25 September 1993, and "Moskva: khronika sobytii." in *Ibid.*

28. See Vladimir Ermolin, "A tem vremenem..."

29. See Yury Voronin, *Svitsom po Rossii*, pp.165–67.

30. *Ibid.*, pp. 167–68.

31. *Ibid.*, p. 216.

32. *Ibid.*, p. 197.

33. See "Declaration of the Holy Synod of the Russian Orthodox Church" of 1 October 1993, in *Ibid.*, pp. 153–56.

34. "Ukaz Prezidenta predpisyvayet ofitseram derzhat'sya ot politiki podal'she," *Krasnaya zvezda*, 30 September 1993.

35. See Aleksandr Pel'ts. "Armiya byla vynuzhdena deistvovat' reshitel'no," *Krasnaya zvezda*, 8 October 1993.

36. See Oleg Odnokolenko, "Blagorazumie predpolagayet postoyannyi poisk mirnogo vykhoda iz krizisa" (Good sense demands a steady search for a peaceful way out of the crisis), *Krasnaya zvezda*, 1 October 1993.

37. See *Ibid.*

38. Vladimir Gavrilenko, "Tsentr-regiony: smozhem li uberech' nash obshchii dom ot bezumiia razvala? (Center-region: can we save our common home from senseless destruction?)," *Krasnaya zvezda*, 2 October 1993.

39. The agreement's text, the commission's mission, and its membership are in Yury Voronin, *Svitsom po Rossii*, pp. 159–60.

40. Aleksandr Gol'ts, "armiya ostayetsya garantom grazhdanskogo mira. Mozhet byt', edinstvenno nadezhnym" (The army remains the guarantor of civil peace. Perhaps the only reliable one)," *Krasnaya zvezda*, 2 October 1993.

41. *Ibid.*

42. *Ibid.*

43. Voronin, *Svitsom po Rossii*, pp. 171–72.

44. Yeltsin, *Struggle*, p. 271.

45. *Ibid.*, p. 276–77.

46. *Ibid.*

47. *Ibid.*

48. *Ibid.* pp. 278–79.

49. The 1993 Constitution, Chapter IV, Article 83, as printed in *Krasnaya zvezda*, 10 November 1993.

50. For new Military Doctrine's Russian text see *Krasnaya zvezda,* 19 November 1993.
51. See Vladimir N. Taranenko, "Ryadom s Rutskoi (Along Side Rutskoi)," p. 18 in D. A. Mayorov, ed., *Neizvestnyi Rutskoi: politicheskii portret* (The Unknown Rutskoi: A political portrait) (Moscow: Obozrevatel, 1994).
52. See Yury Voronin, *Svitsom po Rossii,* p. 195.
53. See *Ibid.,* p. 196.
54. *Ibid.,* p. 202.
55. *Ibid.*
56. Valery Yakov, "Number of Casualties During Events of Oct. 3–4 in Moscow Has Been Established" (in Russian), *Izvestiya,* 25 December 1993 (*CDSP,* vol. XLV. no. 52, 1993), pp. 20–21.
57. Vladimir Berezko, "Yury Drozdov, 'Nash *Vympel*—ne perekhodyashchii'," *Krasnaya zvezda,* 30 September 1995.
58. Aleksandr Rutskoi, Official Declaration; 8 October 1993, at Lefortovo prison. Voronin, *Svitsom po Rossii,* pp. 42–43.
59. Aleksandr Rutskoi, Interrogation Stenographic Record, 21 October 1993. *Ibid.* p. 45–50.
60. *Ibid.,* 22 October 1993, p. 52.
61. *Ibid.,* p. 53.
62. *Ibid.,* pp. 54–55.
63. Ibid., pp. 56–57.

11

The Military's Politics after the Crisis
of September-October 1993

President Yeltsin promised the nation a new, more viable Russian state under a strong executive branch but he failed to deliver. On the surface, he appeared strong. He sat in the same Kremlin offices and was pampered like the Communist general secretaries of old. He assembled a large presidential staff and housed it in the former Central Committee of the Communist Party's office building. He was the direct successor to the general secretaries and his presidential staff was a reformed version of the old Central Committee. The Russian Ministry of Defense, as the continuation of the Soviet Ministry of Defense, expected the president to solve its problems and to make the key decisions just as Communist general secretaries had done in the past.

The presidential staff cranked out decrees to fix every major problem and Yeltsin signed them and sent them into the vast Russian political space where they were swallowed up in a new web of regional political bosses. Why? Because Russia had no effective public administration system. The Communist Party used to guarantee the integrity of public administration. In 1991 when Yeltsin smashed the Party's organizations, he destroyed the federal system's administrative integrity. The former Communists and other regional elites responded by reorganizing into local and regional political-economic machines and fended for themselves. In 1991 when Yeltsin choked the Soviet state by refusing to transfer normal taxes and revenues to the Soviet treasury, he set an example for the regions to follow. Now the regions and the big industrial groupings were doing the same to him. Since semicapitalist states must run on money instead of orders from dictators and without money Yeltsin's quick fix programs could not go very far, as federal revenues declined so did his real power. Further, as revenues decreased, the battle for the budget intensified and the military found itself competing with teachers, pensioners, and the national police for increasingly scarce funds. Yeltsin tried to ease tension by printing more and more money. This produced inflation which undermined sound financial planning in every state agency and in the new market economy as a whole.

This chapter analyzes the military's efforts to understand and to respond to the changing political, social, and economic environment in Russia. It examines the Ministry of Defense's relationships with the presidency, the Duma, and society. It demonstrates that the military was part and parcel of the general political process and a well-identified competitor in the political game. The Ministry of Defense received much less than it wanted and often fell into acrimonious debate with the demokraty without winning much sympathy from the proto-Communists. Nevertheless, new forms of civil-military relations were developing in Russia. On the whole these changes were part of the larger process nurturing a more open society and competitive political system. The military was participating in the public debate about the future of national defense.

Yeltsin's Post-Putsch Relationship with the Military

The military seemed eager to put the October crisis behind it and to get on with the work of military reconstruction. Although, it did not conceal its disappointment with the manner in which the president and Parliament had mismanaged national political affairs, it hoped for a new, stronger presidency to restore Russian state viability. But the public as represented by the free press wanted answers and Grachev felt that he had to defend the military and tried to do so without alienating his political superior, Boris Yeltsin.

Although Yeltsin ordered the attack on Parliament, it was Grachev and the military who carried it out. The political images were of Russian tanks waging political warfare in central Moscow not of Boris Yeltsin giving the orders. The press kept turning to Grachev for answers because Boris Yeltsin failed to provide the type of national political leadership expected of a democratically elected president. Grachev complained that he was tired of politics and wanted to take the military back to normal professional work and to keep it there. He said that he would not get involved in the post-putsch debates about the legitimacy of Yeltsin's actions. The country needed to move ahead.[1]

Yeltsin finally pulled himself together and addressed the nation on the evening of 6 October 1993, two days after the bloody showdown in Moscow. Yeltsin defended the use of force and said that it was one of the main lessons gained from the crisis: "The main lesson in this is that democracy must be reliably defended. The state must use force when threats arise...without that there is no democracy." He accused Khasbulatov and Rutskoi of deliberate conspiracy: "Their goal was the establishment in Russia of a bloody Communo-fascist dictatorship. Now it is all clear that this was being prepared for months." The White House—which had been the symbol of democracy in Russia "had become a citadel of terrorism with a huge supply of arms and ammunition, a symbol of broken promises and deception."[2] He pledged to hold new, democratic, competitive elections. However, he intended to prevent "those that participated in the conspiracy" from participating. He intended to restore the judicial branch but not the current Constitutional Court because it had violated the principle of judicial neutrality and independence by siding with Parliament on controversial issues. He intended to press his policy of renewing government and holding new elections to legislatures into the rest of the country. Post-Communist political reconstruction required more than changes in the national Parliament.[3]

Instead of simply mouthing the Kremlin political line, the Ministry of Defense added its own point of view which held civilian leaders accountable for the mess: "On that tragic Monday, the army was forced to engage in what is not its business. Forced because those who were obligated to cope failed to do so. It was necessary to save people, to save the city, and, in the final analysis, to save the very state from the real threat of bloody chaos." The military was upset that some members of Yeltsin staff were shifting blame to the armed forces by accusing the commanders of waiting too long before coming to the support of Yeltsin. "The idea that the Army is outside politics was not dreamed up by Grachev. It is the law which the Armed Forces of all civilized states live by."[4]

Russia was politically divided and would remain a strained political system. Therefore, the military had to emphasize military cohesion and obedience to orders. Otherwise, civil war and national political disintegration would surely follow. Officers who disagreed with Yeltsin's policies and with the manner in which he handled the political confrontation with Parliament were nonetheless expected to behave in a manner that preserved armed forces unity: "In these situations it is extremely important to remember one thing: unity of command is the pivot that holds the Army structure together. One Fatherland, one oath, one set of orders—any retreat from this leads to schism in the military ranks."[5] Cohesion and unity of command could not be improved unless the prestige of the professional officers, particularly the commanders were raised. The Ministry of Defense had to repair and rebuild military cohesion. "Is it really normal that during the last few years, the very figure of the commander has receded into the background?" "The Army is the Army and unlimited democratization cannot be permitted."[6]

Presidential Control and Expanded Domestic Military Roles

Boris Yeltsin also drew military-political lessons from the events of September–October 1993 and decided to strengthen his constitutional and legal authority to appoint and remove commanders and to order the military to fight in domestic political conflicts as a tool of state power. On 2 November 1993, he issued Ukaz No. 1833 which promulgated a new Military Doctrine for Russia, a major policy document written, revised, debated, and approved by his Security Council. Although the full text is secret and cannot be released, the Yeltsin administration published excerpts and summaries.

The November 1993 Military Doctrine cited domestic threats to Russian state security and legitimized using the military and other armed forces to remove such threats. For example, if nationalist, separatist, or other organizations that aim to destabilize the domestic situation or to violate its territorial integrity threaten to use force, the Military Doctrine authorizes the state to use the full range of armed forces, including the military, to protect the national interest.[7] The choice of which forces to use in what order is left to the President. In other words, there is nothing that would require Russia's presidents to make the MVD rather than the Ministry of Defense the primary instrument for keeping the domestic peace.

Next, Yeltsin published the draft of his new Constitution which gave him and future presidents the power to appoint and dismiss the high command of the armed forces of the Russian Federation without the advice and consent of the Duma.[8] Neither the Duma nor the Federal Council is given any check on the president's power to appoint and remove the top military officers. Yeltsin was willing to consult on positions of lesser importance such as the appointment of ambassadors but not on the military. The Constitution gave him similar powers over all of Russia's military, police, and security forces. The importance of this concentration of power in the hands of the executive branch should not be underestimated. It violates democratic practice and is suitable to authoritarian regimes.

Grachev Signals a Major Shift: No Politicking

The revolutions of 1917 gave active-duty officers, soldiers and sailors the right to get into politics. Lenin and Stalin preserved the outward forms of military participation but systematically blocked the military from any independent political activity. Gorbachev's reforms produced a qualitatively different situation in which military political activity expanded. It survived the collapse of the Soviet Union and became one of Russian democracy's distinctive features; however, Minister of Defense Grachev did not approve of such practices. Therefore, he actively discouraged military officers from running for office in the Duma elections of December 1993.

The Russian legislature that Yeltsin abrogated on 21 September 1993 had been elected in 1990 only a few short months after the Soviet legislature amended the Soviet Constitution to break the Communist Party's monopoly on political power. At that time, the Ministry of Defense took the position that the best way to prevent the officer corps from dividing into rival political factions was to keep the officers inside one political organization, the Communist Party. Therefore, officers who expected to be promoted had to toe the line and stay with the Communist Party. And the forty-four military officers who were elected to the Russian Parliament in 1990 were members of the military branch of the Communist Party at the time of election. Ministry of Defense policy changed in August 1991 when Yeltsin and Shaposhnikov made

Gorbachev abolish the Communist Party's branches in the armed forces. Thereafter, officers were encouraged to be nonpartisan or *partyless*. The justification for this shift was clear. Since the military defended the entire country, including all the parties and factions that uphold the Constitution, it should be nonpartisan.

After the experience of trying to hold the military together through the political crisis of 1993, Minister of Defense Grachev decided that it was in the best interests of the armed forces to discourage officers from becoming heavily involved in political life. He regarded politics and public administration as a distinct profession, a type of service that required full attention. He also knew that political engagement would inevitably damage military cohesion since the officer corps was not united behind one political movement.

Grachev set the tone for the military. Officers could not afford to ignore his warning that those who want to build successful military careers should not attempt to combine them with politics. In the old days, Communist Party membership was absolutely necessary to career success. Now, partisan political activity was frowned upon. Grachev could not officially order his officers to give up their constitutional right to run for office but his personnel officers could make recommendations to that effect. Grachev's chief military personnel officer, Lt. General Konstantin Bogdanov said, "In this context, we recommend that military service personnel refrain from offering their candidacy in the coming elections." People who want politics to be their field of work were encouraged to resign from the armed forces. As Bogdanov explained, "There is a profession called defending the Motherland. And the right place for people in military uniforms is performing military functions in their military units."[9] This message had the desired affect. With few exceptions prominent, *active* military professionals who might have been elected did not run for the Duma in the December 1993 elections. Yet, Grachev did not intend to ignore the Duma which had the power to write laws and to set the national budget. His plan was to provide expert advice and information to Duma deputies and committees and he created a department of parliamentary relations for that purpose.[10]

However, it would be several months before a new parliament or Duma would be in session. Meanwhile, political power was concentrated in the executive branch of government which poured forth hundreds of decrees. Therefore, the Ministry of Defense and Russia's defense industrialists focused their aspirations on Boris Yeltsin and tried to get as much done as possible during this brief period of presidential dictatorship.

The Elusive National Defense Constituency

Although Grachev actively discouraged military officers from running for office, the Ministry of Defense had reason to believe that political competition would be good for the defense constituency. As candidates and parties competed for votes, the political significance of the national defense constituency became widely understood. Who could deny that the Russian State's security was threatened by economic decline and national political disunity?

In theory, there was an enormous national defense constituency buried in the Russian body politic. In practice, the Ministry of Defense competed with defense-industrialists for increasingly scarce funds. During the immediate post-Soviet reconstruction period, the defense community—military personnel, dependents, and MIC employees and their families, did not consolidate into a cohesive national political force. The Ministry of Defense gave highest priority to direct and indirect support for military personnel, relocation, and investment in the new infrastructure required to operate the post-Soviet military system. There simply was not enough money to meet immediate operational needs and to maintain previous levels of defense orders for new equipment. Yevgeny Shaposhnikov faced that dilemma in winter 1991–1992. He resolved it in favor of current operational expenses. Investment in new weaponry would have to be postponed. Pavel Grachev continued in that vein.

The Defense Spending Problem before the Putsch

The main problem was financial system breakdown rather than the struggle between advocates of Western "shock therapy" and a Russian version of Deng Xiaopingism. Political instability in 1991 undermined the state budgets for 1992. The Union's fragmentation upset the normal budgetary process and state agencies such as the armed forces had to muddle through. Initially, the republics were supposed to share the costs of defense spending. Russia pledged to cover 61 percent of the defense bill, Ukraine 17 percent, and the other republics were to cover the remaining 31 percent.[11] But this deal fell apart as the Union fragmented. During 1992 the Yeltsin administration was making policy on the run. Yeltsin could not stop the political and financial clocks in order to assess the real situation and to lay out a comprehensive strategy for bringing revenue and expenditures under reliable control. State agencies and departments were in a financial and regulatory limbo. Sources of funding and rules and regulations governing the generation and expenditure of funds were murky at best.

The Yeltsin administration's 1992 budget cut defense procurement spending by 67 percent compared to the last Soviet-era defense budget. Yegor Gaidar is normally considered the Kremlin driving force behind this "shock therapy" which the Yeltsin administration imposed on the military-industrial complex. The 1992 budget was marketed as proof that democratic Russia had broken with the bloated defense budgets of the Soviet period. The full truth is certainly more complex. To some extent, the Kremlin was making a virtue out of necessity. Income was falling because the Soviet Union's fragmentation disrupted economic relations and caused a depression. Market oriented "shock therapy" may have contributed to the problem but the main cause was the fragmentation of the Soviet common market. Further, instead of honestly working for open markets, Communist bureaucrats were privatizing public assets. This went on in the military-industrial complex as well as in traditional civilian-orientated enterprises.[12]

When the economy collapses in a democracy, the incumbent president's popularity falls unless a scapegoat can be found. In Yeltsin's case, Yegor Gaidar became the scapegoat in fall 1992. Arkady Vol'sky's leagues of industrialists and entrepreneurs demanded that the government put experienced managers and industrialists in charge of policy making rather than academics like Gaidar. They insisted that the 67 percent cut had been far too drastic and pressed Yeltsin to increase the defense procurement order for 1993.

In October 1992 Yeltsin yielded and asked Gaidar to make a conciliatory speech to industrialists and to build bridges to the military. Gaidar announced a 10 percent increase in the defense budget for 1993 and assured the defense constituency that the Yeltsin administration would not destroy Russian defense capability.[13] Gaidar supported national defense but was concerned about signs that statist ideology might revive, a way of thinking that justified State domination of the political economy instead of a society in which individuals and corporations determined the general direction of change. He believed that the military understood that it had also been a victim of Soviet statist ideology and that modern military professionalism was incompatible with the old style of political dictatorship. However, he also knew that groups interested in restoring military power and prestige, defense spending, and defense employment security were deliberately distorting his views. Congress was looking for people to hold accountable for the nation's economic problems, was determined to remove Gaidar and the "little boys in pink shorts," and wanted to replace them with solid managers who had demonstrated their ability to handle large-scale enterprises during the Soviet era. In the end, Yeltsin agreed to make gas industry executive, Viktor Chernomyrdin his prime minister in exchange for pledges of improved cooperation from the full Congress and its smaller standing body, the Parliament.

The Ministry of Defense was pleased to see Gaidar go. It hoped that Chernomyrdin would support the defense constituency and move more steadily and cautiously along the nation's economic fronts. But few changes were made. Chernomyrdin had to face the consequences of economic recession and declining revenues just like Gaidar. Further, the more liberal reformers in and near the Yeltsin camp, believed that the Ministry of Defense was dragging its feet on reform and trying to save a bloated military system. The demokraty wanted to keep Grachev on a starvation diet until he shed the military fat.

The demokraty had some military deputies in their camp. In Parliament's defense committee, Colonel Vladimir Lopatin, candidly pointed out that the military was using Russia's domestic instability and security problems along the southern borders of the former Soviet Union to retard military reform and downsizing. For example with a uniformed force of about 1,800,000 personnel in mid-1993, the Russian army had 2,218 generals while the U.S. military had only 1,008 generals for its 1,800,000 soldiers. The total number of officers was 690,000 or more than twice as high as the international standard. Further military pay had improved relative to other civil servants and had reached 1.4 to 1.5 times corresponding civilian positions. The military continued to enjoy great professional autonomy: "The old principle that the military decide military questions still dominates in practice." The minister of defense was a military professional and the Ministry did not report its actual sources of income and expenditures with the relevant committees of Parliament. How much was the army costing Russia? "No one can answer that question today. Those who could compute it have no interest in doing so. And those who would like to know lack the means of finding out." Lopatin concluded that military reform would not take place until the president as commander in chief had a strong civilian-led branch of government to administer the armed forces, a strong legislative branch to set and monitor the overall budget and military policy, and a strong judicial system to handle law enforcement and prosecution of violations.[14]

Russia desperately needed a long-term defense redevelopment plan, one which addressed Ministry of Defense and military-industrial complex requirements. Grachev top civilian employee, Deputy Minister of Defense Andrei Kokoshin, was supposed to handle those dimensions of military development while Grachev dealt with the commanders, the hot spots, and the near-abroad. Kokoshin and others worked hard on planning. The Yeltsin administration created special policy planning and interdepartmental coordination groups under the Security Council, in the Ministry of Defense, and under the prime minister. However, it was extremely difficult to make solid plans because inflation, political instability, and privatization had disrupted normal financial accounting systems, revenue flows, and contractual relationships. The new committees and departments lacked the power to do what the Soviet system was capable of doing through the Five-Year Plan, the State Planning Agency (Gosplan), and special defense planning and control departments. Further, when there were problems under the old system, the general secretary settled them and issued the appropriate orders.

Yeltsin's One Hundred Days: A New Pro-Defense Image?

The combination of national economic crisis and political instability made it extremely difficult to make much headway in national defense affairs. For this reason, the defense constituency rallied to Yeltsin's putsch and saw it as a window of opportunity. During the one hundred days of temporary presidential dictatorship from 21 September 1993 to the Duma's first session in January 1994, Yeltsin could make decisions efficiently.

On the surface, the one hundred days was a temporary reversion to Soviet-style politics. Yeltsin behaved more like a general secretary than a democratic president. He made the key decisions about new rules and distributions of national assets without the checks and balances provided by either an effective legislature or judiciary. However, the one hundred days lacked the political clout of the old Soviet system for two reasons. First, he could not force the country's political and economic institutions to implement his decrees. The old Party machine and discipline had given way to pluralism and numerous de facto checks and balances between and within different levels of government. Second, the he lacked the financial power to fund his decisions because the economy was in decline and the post-Soviet revenue estimation and collection system was working poorly.

Nevertheless, the chief interest groups involved in national defense tired to make the most out of the one hundred days. Deputy Minister of Defense, Andrei Kokoshin prepared a 200 enterprise plan which identified the essential core of Russia's military-industrial complex (MIC). It called for putting a floor on defense spending that guaranteed the 200 enterprises, on average, state orders at some 25–30 percent of their 1988 levels. Kokoshin and the 200 industries and research and development organizations represented by the plan argued that they could save the best, the most vital parts of Russian defense industry.[15] The Russian MIC intended to resume and expand foreign arms and technology sales to supplement its income. The MIC's future health would stand on three legs: guaranteed government orders, foreign arms sales, and more civilian products sales. Yeltsin agreed with Kokoshin's general idea. On 6 November 1993, he issued presidential Ukaz No. 1850, "On the Stabilization of the Economic Situation in the Enterprises and Organizations of Defense Industry and Measures to Guarantee the State Defense Orders."[16] The seven-point decree called for a comprehensive attack on the problem by government and industry. Yeltsin understood the importance of stable financial guarantees to defense industries; however, he could not guarantee that his treasury would have the resources required or keep inflation from ravaging the cost estimates. Yet, the MIC was happy to be receiving higher priority.

Yeltsin spent two days working with MIC leaders and visiting the troops in mid-November 1993. They met at Tula—the historic center of Russian arms production and the home base for elite paratroopers. Tula was an appropriate site to demonstrate a serious presidential commitment to rebuilding *Russian* national defense. High level officials from the Ministry of Defense, military commanders, Security Council members, and others conferred about the new MIC 2000 Plan and Russia's new Military Doctrine. Yeltsin said he was committed to steady financing for defense industry and defense conversion, support for foreign arms and technology sales, and a firm defense development plan. He also praised the military units he visited and noted the humanitarian missions they performed in near-abroad hot spots. This was a reminder that the Russian military had the capacity to move rapidly into the near-abroad if Russia's interests or the Russian-speaking population were threatened.[17] After the Tula meetings, Yeltsin convened his Security Council and it approved the establishment of a new state committee on defense industry chaired by Viktor Glukhikh.

The Russian double-headed eagle was rising and Russian state power was being restored—that what Yeltsin intended to convey to Russia and the world by giving higher priority to military power and defense industry. On 30 November 1993, he signed the decrees which made the imperial double-headed eagle the official emblem of post-Soviet, democratic Russia. Yeltsin's eagle was golden rather than the imperial black that had flown over Russia from Peter the Great to Nicholas II. Yeltsin's emblem retained the imperial orb and scepter and the crest of St., George, the emblem of the Princes of Moscow, a reminder that Moscow is the center and heart of the Russian Federation.[18]

The December 1993 Elections: Duma and Constitution

The military was hopeful that democratic competition would be good for defense. The Russian public had never had a chance to vote on key national defense issues because the radical changes in defense policy had been made by presidential fiat first by Gorbachev and later by Yeltsin. Boris Yeltsin tried to change his image from blundering reformer to Russian patriot and state builder. He knew there was a large protest vote brewing in Russia, a growing demand for effective leadership. He was deliberately distancing himself from his own record and the people associated with it such as Yegor Gaidar. As Russia headed into the December 1993 elections and referendum on the new Constitution, the President wanted to ride the popular demand for change rather than be swept away by it.

Virtually all political parties were courting the various defense constituencies. They were all for a strong Russia. Why? Because the defense constituencies would be as large as 20 percent of the general electorate of some 105,000,000 million people, even larger if veterans are included. There were still at least 2,300,000 military personnel on the Ministry of Defense payroll. They and their families were all worried about defense cuts. The size of the MVD was similar. Defense industrial employees were triple the number of armed forces personnel. Because the national defense constituency numbered at least some 20,000,000 adults, no major political party or candidate dared to call for additional defense cuts in the 1993 election campaign. As a result, the military and the national defense lobby expected to improve their relative position in the 1994 federal budget. However, the centrist and more democratic and Western-oriented parties were reluctant to beat the patriotic and national defense drums.

Krasnaya zvezda's analysts poured over the party lists and found only four out of thirty that had no military officers on them. The most "militarized" party was Vladimir Zhirinovsky's Liberal Democratic Party which had nine military candidates on its Duma list. Even the RDDR, a democratic coalition assembled by Anatoly Sobchak and Gavril Popov, had six. However, no members of Defense Minister Grachev's high command were running as candidates. Most of the so-called military candidates were outside the military leadership circle. This was a major change from the Soviet practice in which the high command expected to be elected to the highest legislative bodies as a mark of high status in society. *Krasnaya zvezda* endorsed no political parties or movements but offered them space to state their main views.

However, on 7–8 December 1993, Minister of Defense Grachev assembled the top commanders and key Ministry of Defense administrative officers for a Ministry of Defense collegium devoted to the political situation. The collegium issued an official opinion on the referendum and urged a positive vote for the new Constitution because the country needed it to complete political and economic reform successfully.[19] Yeltsin addressed the nation on 9 December 1993 and focused on the Constitution. He argued that experience had shown that without a stronger presidency Russia will not be able to solve its political and economic problems. The new Constitution was designed to give Russia the type of executive power it needed and it was vital that the people vote for it. He endorsed no political parties but urged people to vote for candidates who would work hard for Russia.[20]

Krasnaya zvezda's headline editorial in its last edition published before the election urged the military to vote for the Constitution and to vote responsibly. It warned military voters against being taken in by populist candidates. It expressed regret that the parties and candidates had not focused much on military issues during the campaign and those that did usually limited their comments to generalities. Therefore, it invited the main parties to submit material to *Krasnaya zvezda*. The paper urged military voters to think hard about the promises being made, the potential for new waves of destabilizing change, and the quality and experience of the people standing for election. Such advice was clearly aimed at Zhirinovsky et al.[21]

The major parties were interviewed by *Krasnaya zvezda* for the preelection issue.[22] All expressed support for a strong Russia and a strong military and called for reexamination of the national budget's allocations. Some were more cautious than others but all wanted to be pro-defense. Vladimir Zhirinovsky's LDPR attacked the Yeltsin administration's record. Zhirinovsky's bombastic criticism of the Russia's decline and his pledge to restore Russian power was an extreme manifestation of a more general political phenomenon. Even Yegor Gaidar pledged that if elected his Russia's Choice party would reevaluate defense spending. However, he insisted that Russia's national interests would be best served by a common security system with the West.

When Russia voted on 12 December 1993, there were no prominent military leaders elected to and seated in the new Duma. The best known military candidates were former Soviet Minister of Defense, Marshal Yevgeny Shaposhnikov and military historian, Col. General Dmitry Volkogonov. Shaposhnikov ran on the RDDR ticket. Volkogonov ran on Russia's Choice's. The RDDR failed to get enough votes to surmount the 5 percent barrier in the party-list competition and therefore got no seats. The RDDR's poor showing, only 4 percent of the vote, demonstrated that prominent urban democrats such as mayor Sobchak of St. Petersburg and former mayor of Moscow, Gavril Popov did not have a national constituency. Admiral (Ret.) Vladimir Chernavin's Civic Union party got less than 2 percent. Col. General (Ret.) Grigory Yashkin's Dignity and Charity movement received less than 1 percent. Merely placing military candidates on the party's list wasn't enough to attract voters. Russia's Choice received 15.5 percent and Col. General Volkogonov won a seat in the Duma; however, poor health prevented him from playing an active role in politics.

The big winner was Vladimir Zhirinovsky and his LDPR which received 23 percent of the popular vote while Yegor Gaidar's Russia's Choice received only 15 percent. The Communists came in third with about 12 percent. The Agrarians, a rural party with Communist roots, won about 8 percent.[23] The LDPR, Communists, and Agrarians received about 44 percent of the popular vote. Russia's Choice and other democratic and centrist parties captured about 35 percent. The remainder went to movements that occupied the political space between those two extremes. Thus, the new Duma which met on 11 January 1994 had a moderate to conservative bias. It was neither an endorsement of Yeltsin's policies nor a call the restoration of Soviet dictatorship. It reflected the state of national political confusion and popular discontent with the economic depression. The military vote went primarily to the protest movements. Some analysts claim that Vladimir Zhirinovsky's LDPR captured about 70 percent of the total military vote. Yeltsin said it was only 33 percent.[24] The Ministry of Defense issued a statement criticizing claims that the military voted in the main for Zhirinovsky. Its public relations officers insisted that the results used to support the claim were based on a very small sample—just 1 percent of the total military vote, polling places at military bases. In order to preserve the confidentiality of the military vote, the Ministry of Defense and the federal electoral commission arranged to have military personnel vote at civilian voting places near military institutions. Further, the Ministry protested that attempts to probe into the military vote were a threat to the secret ballot, a fundamental democratic principal.[25]

Krasnaya zvezda's report on the Murmansk region, which has a heavy military population, confirmed that Zhirinovsky's party was far more popular with military personnel than Gaidar's Russia's Choice. Foreign Minister Kozyrev ran in Murmansk for one of the single-manadate seats. He won as an individual but his party, Russia's Choice was clobbered by Zhirinovsky's LDPR on the party ballot. He evaluated the results correctly and said the people were protesting against the general economic situation, they were demanding action.[26] But the Murmansk report was the exception that proved the rule. Clearly, the Ministry of Defense did not want the military press to discuss the military's right-wing protest vote. The main evidence is the absence of any in-depth writing on the election results in *Krasnaya zvezda*. However, there were several rather frank editorials which affirmed the protest vote's validity.

It was a military protest against the general situation and a demand for change. "The Army voted for itself and for state interests not for petty, narrow, corporate interests. It voted for a strong, united, and patriotically oriented Russia. It voted so that future politicians would not pull it into their games. It voted to be respected and properly supported. It voted for an opportunity for new entrants to serve with dignity and for its veterans to live in dignity."[27] When Yeltsin held a press conference to discuss the election results and offered to work with all groups willing to solve problems constructively, *Krasnaya zvezda* approved.[28] Democracy was working to put the national leadership in touch with popular sentiment. Yeltsin's administration had been governing in the old way, in the imperial-authoritarian tradition. The fact that the president had accepted criticism instead of trying to destroy the opposition was a positive development. In this sense, reform was working.[29]

Krasnaya zvezda's evaluation was accurate rather than a revival of Soviet ideology.[30] Western-oriented elitists had ignored popular sentiment to the point where Westernization itself was threatened by extremists who were riding the wave of discontent into the Duma. The military protested more strongly than the general population because its corporate interests had been severely damaged by the changes that took place under Yeltsin. The president had not given the military steady attention and his recent attentiveness had blatant political motives. He had used the military to settle domestic political conflicts and he had sent the military into near-abroad hot spots without backing the soldiers with moral and material support.

The military blamed Yegor Gaidar, the leading figure of Russia's Choice—the "little boy in pink shorts," for inflicting huge cuts on the military-industrial complex and unleashing inflation which ravaged woefully inadequate budgets. The soldiers would not vote for him. Yeltsin should not have permitted Gaidar to head the democratic ticket and should have worked harder to build a democratic coalition. Instead of leading, Yeltsin tended to play the political referee while others battled things out. Although Yeltsin took note of these mistakes, he was unable to change his basic leadership style.

Yeltsin did better on the Constitutional referendum. The neo-authoritarians such as Zhirinovsky endorsed it as a fine basic law for a future Zhirinovsky presidency. The official results claimed that the Yeltsin Constitution was endorsed by about 60 percent of those who voted but some doubted that more than 50 percent of the pool of registered voters had actually voted for the Constitution, a requirement to make the referendum valid. Doubts were never removed because the Yeltsin administration refused to make enough voting records available to satisfy its critics.[31] The Ministry of Defense reported that 74 percent of the military who voted, endorsed the new Constitution.[32]

Reasons for Military Anxiety and Protest

Minister of Defense Grachev and the Russian military had more or less successfully muddled through the most difficult phase of post-Soviet military reconstruction. At the end of December 1993, Grachev reported on the vast scale of change. Here are some of the key numbers.

The military stood at 4,250,000 funded positions when Gorbachev began the cutting in December 1988. That cut lowered the number of authorized military personnel to 3,750,000.[33] When Grachev formed the Russian Ministry of Defense in May 1992, he had some 2,900,000 positions. From mid-1992 to the end of 1993, the Ministry of Defense cut about 500,000 positions, a drop from 2,800,000 to 2,300,000 military personnel. Grachev wanted to halt the cutting and hoped that the Duma would support him by rejecting the old Parliament's military manpower target of 1,500,000. The armed forces continued to experience problems with draft resistance but received little support from civilian politicians on this front. Grachev reported that the military's actual level of staffing was 40 percent below planned targets for positions to be filled by draftees. Further, the military budget was too lean to permit the Ministry of Defense to close this gap by hiring people to serve under contract.[34]

During 1993, the Ministry of Defense repatriated some 640,000 military personnel from Germany, Eastern Europe, and the near-abroad. Russian forces completed their withdrawal from Czechoslovakia, Hungary, Poland, Mongolia, Lithuania, and Cuba. This massive removal and relocation of people and materiel required an extraordinary effort but it was accomplished in a very short period of time. Neither housing nor military base infrastructure could be built fast enough in Russia. Grachev still had some 120,000 homeless officers, officers and families without decent housing or support facilities. Further, inflation was ravaging the defense budget.[35]

The military demonstrated its corporate vitality by completing the withdrawals and changes without losing either its fundamental cohesion or fighting ability, according to Pavel Grachev. Further, he asserted that the military had saved the country from civil war and helped bring the September-October 1993 political crises to an end. Consequently, he hoped the new Duma would understand the army's importance to societal stability and national defense and reevaluate the military budget.[36] Grachev expressed concern about politically motivated attempts to isolate the military vote for special analysis. He insisted that the data were not available because the military mainly voted at civilian polling places.[37]

Military Personnel in the Duma

In spite of Minister Grachev's admonition against mixing military and political careers, eleven military officers were elected to the Duma. Their election demonstrated that military officers could run and could be elected. Because the eleven were from various districts spread across Russia, were not involved in partisan politics, and held no powerful military posts, it was highly unlikely that they would develop into influential leaders in the Duma. The eleven did not constitute an important faction in the 450-member Duma.

Nine were elected from single-mandate districts and only two won seats based on party voting. Only one claimed to be a member of a political party while ten were partyless. Captain Yevgeny Logunov won a seat on the Zhirinovsky ticket. Logunov was a student at the main military political academy in Moscow. Col. Aleksandr Zaitsev, a member of the Russian infantry's central staff, won a seat on the Communist list but claimed to have no party affiliation. The nine deputies who represented districts claimed no party affiliation and none held important positions in the national military leadership. Since the Duma political game would revolve around party factions, the partyless military deputies were condemned to the political sidelines. One member of the military cohort, Major General Nikolai Stolyarov, was reasonably well-known since his involvement in the August 1991 coup as a Yeltsin supporter. Stolyarov was elected from a Moscow district. However, his career had moved into consulting, business, and teaching—appropriate for a former military political officer; and he was not part of the national military leadership.[38]

The New Duma's "Anti-Military" Line

By voting for the LDPR, the Communists and other nationalists and populists, the soldiers thought that the Duma would naturally be sympathetic to national defense; but they were disappointed. Although various and sundry neo-Communists and nominal national patriots had a near majority in the Duma that was elected in December 1993, they seemed immune to military calls for financial relief. The Duma kept to the old Parliament's general line and set defense spending at 5 percent of GDP or no more than 20 percent of the total federal budget for 1994 and insisted that the Ministry of Defense accept a target of 1 percent of Russia's total population or 1,500,000 as the military's ideal size. Demilitarization of the economy remained a key goal in post-Soviet reconstruction plans. These targets were less the problem than the country's overall economic and political performance. The economy continued to slide towards an elusive post-Soviet bottom and the polity continued to weaken because laws and regulations were not enforced evenly and swiftly throughout the country.

It took two years before the Yeltsin administration's budgetary cuts, the falling economy, and raging inflation took their full toll on the military and the military-industrial complex. Thus, although Gaidar cut defense procurement orders sharply in 1992, the full impact of those cuts did not really hit until 1994. Neither the military nor the defense industrialists had really understood what was coming when Russia emerged as a sovereign state in December 1991 and began post-Soviet reconstruction. Two years later in late 1994, defense industrialists lamented that they had missed a key turning point. They should have been active in late 1991 and early 1992. Although there was much talk about the threat from the Soviet defense lobby, there was no effective lobby and no constructive plan of action. Attempts were made to begin building an effective defense lobby in mid-1994. But it was difficult for the military and the industrialists to cooperate because the Ministry of Defense's highest priorities were current personnel and operating expenses.

The military wanted the public to understand its situation, to support a revision in national spending priorities, and to enforce the draft laws. The Ministry of Defense asserted itself through a campaign to influence public opinion and Duma votes. Grachev's chief budgetary officer, Col. General Vasily Vorobyev supplied the basic data to support the contention that real defense spending had fallen by 66 percent since Soviet days.[39] The Ministry used comparisons with America to make its points. From 1990 to 1993, the American per capita GNP had grown from $24,252 to $24,303. In Russia it plummeted from $3,152 to $1,134 during the same period. In 1990, the Americans spent $1,339 on national defense for every American citizen and $1,151 in 1993. Thus, although American defense spending was also declining, American political leaders had moved cautiously and responsibly compared to their Russian counterparts. Russia's defense per capita spending had collapsed from $239 to $57, and was less than one-twentieth of the American level.[40] When Col. General Vorobyev translated Russia's 1994 military budget into dollars at the official exchange rate prevailing in October 1994, it amounted to a mere $6 billion compared to $297.2 billion for the U.S.[41]

How can we make sense out of these figures given the vast differences between the Soviet and the American political economies? Since the Soviet Union was not part of the world market and domestic prices and valuations were politically determined, it is very difficult to make cost comparisons. Nevertheless, I use a very rough rule and multiply Soviet-era figures by ten based upon personal experience with Soviet salary and price levels in general. When that is done, we find that the defense burden that the average Soviet citizen carried was at least twice as large as that borne by their American counterparts. This conclusion also fits the Russian sense of things, that the Soviet military burden was excessive and had to be trimmed to the 5 percent figure set by the Duma. However, by 1993–94, the economic situation was so bad that the 5 percent figure resulted in a military budget that was far too low to sustain the existing military system.

As inflation raged, it became more and more difficult to keep accounts and to make meaningful year-to-year comparisons. Further, in an effort to slow inflation, the Ministry of Finance began to delay transfers from the treasury to the Ministry of Defense and other federal agencies. As a result, the Ministry could not make its payroll or pay its normal operating expenses on time. The gap between 1994 Duma authorized spending and the amount of money the Ministry of Finance actually sent the Ministry of Defense for fiscal 1994 had grown to 6,892,000 trillion rubles by 24 October 1994.[42] In effect, underfunding had cut the military budget by some 15 to 20 percent even before taking 1994's inflation (280 percent) into account. In order to give meaning to these numbers, the Ministry of Defense released data that suggested the once mighty Soviet military machine had almost come to a standstill. For example, as of October 1994, some 85 nuclear submarines were docked because the navy could not afford to operate them.[43]

Thus, one year after the military had saved the Yeltsin regime and restored order in Moscow, the Ministry of Defense felt betrayed by the president and the Duma. In fall 1993, Yeltsin had pledged to improve military funding and to design and adopt a midterm plan designed to prevent the best military-industrial enterprises and research and development programs from collapsing. In a piece on the first anniversary of the October 1993 events, *Krasnaya zvezda* cited a letter from a thirty-six-year-old Lt. Colonel, Andrei Startsev. He wrote, "We don't want to get into politics. We have so many unresolved problems of our own. But it seems that it is easier for politicians to get their way by using us and our arms. That is how it was in the USSR and how it has already been in Russia."[44] Boris Soldatenko, the journalist who reported on military opinion, concluded: "The Armed Forces are the guarantor of stability in our society. It certainly isn't healthy that this guarantor now resembles a hungry bum."[45]

The campaign had an impact. President Yeltsin addressed military concerns in a press conference on the anniversary of the October 1993 putsch. He spoke of Russia as a great power and said that he highly values the leadership of the Ministry of Defense.[46] Yeltsin convened a special interagency working group to address the military's most pressing financial needs. Grachev reported on his must urgent problems and the commission instructed the Ministry of Finance to release more funding for current military expenses and accumulated operating expense debts.[47] The Ministry of Defense wasn't the only state agency to suffer from tight funding; neither was it the only to benefit from some loosening of the purse strings. The problem was that the Kremlin treasury lacked the cash to meet the Duma approved budget. It had to print money to meet its obligations and the ruble crashed to 4,200 to the dollar on 12 October 1994. Shortly thereafter, Prime Minister Chernomyrdin reported that for fiscal 1994, total government spending would be about 215 trillion rubles or some 72 trillion more than the 145 trillion he expected to collect in taxes and other revenues.[48]

The income shortfall meant that the military would have to postpone plans to increase the percentage of professional contract service soldiers and would have to continue to rely primarily on the military draft for the immediate future. Although it was not a popular move, Boris Yeltsin began to roll back some of the liberal deferment practices that pushed Russia's effective draft yields down to some 20 percent. The president decreed that civilian educational institutions must accelerate academic work and graduate students with certain military deferments by 25 December 1994. The Ministry of Defense was particularly short of educated draftees and intended to draft the new graduates immediately.[49] In 1993 approximately 70,000 draftees evaded the draft but criminal charges were only brought against 1,531 individuals—another sign that the civilian authorities no longer felt obliged to give the military full legal support. Now, after years of sloppy and irregular enforcement of draft laws under Gorbachev and Yeltsin, the Ministry of Defense hoped matters would change. Grachev told Yeltsin that on average military units were under staffed by some 40 percent. Yeltsin decided to take action and set the fall 1994 draft quota at 251,600 youth.[50] He was also willing to increase the length of obligatory service for those already in the armed forces by six months. The Duma refused to apply such changes retroactively but it agreed to return to the standard two years of service for the next call-up.

Soldiers Enrich Yourselves!

One of post-Soviet reconstruction's strategies might be called "branch self-reliance." Instead of depending upon the federal government for financing and orders, the vast state agency system was supposed to find creative ways to finance at least part of its annual operating budget. Thus, defense industrialists were supposed to convert to civilian production, to earn more through foreign sales, and to complete mergers and spin-offs. In order to break their state agency mentality and habits, the Yeltsin administration slashed defense procurement orders by 50 percent in the 1992 budget.

The Kremlin also encouraged the Ministry of Defense to find ways to generate income. This invariably led to confusion about what was and was not authorized. What was a criminal act several months ago had just become official policy. The full gamut of opportunists, from honest entrepreneurs to outright crooks, had already been circling over choice military bases and storage depots. Now they could move in for the feast and consider it their patriotic duty to convert surplus property into funds which the military could use to build new facilities and housing. Russia was liquidating Soviet military bases in Germany, Hungary, Poland, Latvia, Lithuania, and Estonia. Every base had some assets that someone wanted. There were large amounts of surplus tanks, other military hardware, oil, gasoline, and kerosene.

Officers and soldiers saw civilians scrambling to enrich themselves as state property was transferred to individual and corporate ownership. The Ministry of Defense knew that federal funding was either frozen or based on unsound, inflated rubles, that inflation was raging, and that military personnel needed immediate support. It was also under pressure to liquidate certain foreign assets as rapidly as possible in order to meet troop repatriation and foreign base closing deadlines—all of which had been imposed on the military by civilian political leaders. The Yeltsin administration put the military into a corrupting political and financial environment. It was hard on military discipline and military morale.

Political Tensions Peak: Dmitry Kholodov's Murder

The Ministry of Defense was agitating for more support. It began working closely with the League of Defense Industrialists. The national defense coalition began taking shape. The Ministry of Defense's daily paper *Krasnaya zvezda* began publishing regular reports on the military industrial complex. The demokraty were concerned lest this military political offensive reverse national spending priorities. Popular newspapers such as *Komsomolskaya pravda* published provocative, investigative reports on allegations of corruption and featherbedding in the armed forces. Warnings from the Ministry of Defense that military personnel might rebel were not appreciated by the civilian leadership. Grachev seemed to be threatening society and he became a frequent target of editorials published in the liberal press. Reporters hinted that the Kremlin had become concerned about civilian control over the armed forces and that Yeltsin was considering either removing Grachev or trimming his wings.

The public controversy reached a feverish pitch in mid-October when Dima Kholodov, an investigative reporter with *Moskovsky komsomlets* was murdered. Kholodov had been investigating corruption in high military circles when a confidential source offered to get him a suitcase filled with incriminating documents. He picked it up and brought it to *Moskovsky komsomlets*. The suitcase was a booby trap.[51] It contained a bomb device which killed Kholodov. Dima Kholodov's murder was immediately understood as a terroristic act aimed at Russia's free press, a warning from the new criminal elements that reporters would be killed if they went too far.

Kholodov's murder unleashed a torrent of anti-Grachev commentary. Kholodov had been investigating the Western Group of Forces and its last commander, Col. General Matvei Burlakov. Grachev had recently made Burlakov a deputy minister of defense even though allegations involving very large sums had been circulating for months. Therefore, the demokraty linked Grachev to Burlakov and by implication to Kholodov's death. Minister of Defense Grachev fought back and filed charges against a reporter who had been particularly vicious. Grachev insisted that he had civil rights just like everybody else and had to defend his honor and that of the military: "I am a veteran and a military man and have often been under fire and am not afraid to defend myself.... In keeping with the laws of Russia, I am asking the Procurator General to begin action for anti-defamation." (A year later the courts ruled in favor of Grachev but no punishment was imposed on the reporter.) Grachev saw the killing as a major attack on the military, one that had to be fought. He would not permit things to be settled quietly at his personal expense. He insisted upon exercising the rights that democratic Russia guaranteed, namely, the presumption of innocence. He likened the public campaign against him to practices used in the totalitarian past to purge people.[52] Boris Yeltsin issued a brief, firm statement that said he did not think Grachev was involved and called Grachev a solid statesman (*krupnyi gosudarstvennyi deyatel'*).[53]

Although Grachev bristled with anger at the way the press as a whole was treating the affair, his own newspaper, *Krasnaya zvezda*, immediately condemned the murder and said all the right things. Captain Oleg Odnokolenko wrote: "The act of terror at *Moskovsky komsomlets* was not just an effort to silence the *fourth estate*, it was an attack against all of society, a crime of society-wide proportion. There can be no other conclusion."[54] The Ministry of Defense posted a $20,000 reward to go to the organization that is responsible for finding the killer.[55] Odnokolenko warned that there will be no one left willing to tell the truth unless the killer is found and punished.

Moscow News said that newspapers had been asking the MVD and the Federal Counter-Intelligence Service to investigate threats being made against journalists who were writing about corruption in high places, not just in military commercial activity but in the government in general. Its editorial on the memorial service for Kholodov warned that crime was killing freedom of conscience, freedom of entrepreneurship, and freedom of speech.[56] Sergei Yushenkov, chairman of the Duma's defense and security affairs committee, promised to investigate allegations of corruption in the Western Group of Forces.[57] Yegor Gaidar and the leadership council of Russia's Choice called for the immediate resignation and replacement of the top leadership in the Ministry of Defense. Others pointed the finger at civilian Commander in Chief Boris Yeltsin who supported General Burlakov's transfer from Germany to a high position in Moscow. Stories began to circulate alleging that Yeltsin had deliberately squelched major, intelligence service reports about military corruption.[58] Parts of the key report written by Yury Boldyrev, Russian Federation chief state inspector, were leaked to the press. Boldyrev risked and lost his position for pressing the matter and causing embarrassment to the administration.[59] Boldyrev was also a senator or member of the Federal Council. The fact that the Yeltsin administration denied his request to share the report with the Duma and the Federal Council damaged the Ministry of Defense's credibility in the legislature. It added to the popular suspicion that a group of generals was living like Russia's new capitalists and getting rich while most officers and draftees faced severe hardship. This reinforced resistance to Grachev's efforts to get the Duma to increase defense spending. General Lebed added to Grachev's difficulties by declaring: "Burlakov is a common thief who is wanted by all prosecutors in Russia," and threatened to prevent his airplane from landing if he dared to attempt to conduct a scheduled inspection of the 14th Army in Transdniestria.[60]

The pressure on Grachev and the Ministry to release more information about military corruption intensified and continued until late November when the war for the control of Chechnya erupted into the headlines. Two weeks after Kholodov's death, President Yeltsin suspended Col. General Burlakov who later went into retirement.[61] The Duma debated what if anything it should do to get to the bottom of the allegations. The Duma leadership opted for a combination of public and closed hearings. Grachev was asked to address a public session which turned out to be rather supportive of the military.[62] The Duma decided to conduct closed hearings into military corruption and Col. General Burlakov to testified. Burlakov's main defense was that he followed orders issued by the Ministry of Defense's Central Department of Trade (Glavnoye upravlenie torgovli). Yes, he was the commanding officer over the Russian forces in Germany but he neither negotiated nor evaluated the contracts the Ministry granted for supplies, the disposal of property, etc. He further reported that the major commercial decisions were made by civilian departments not the military.[63] The press took his comments seriously. As a result, the search for guilty parties and profiteers could not be confined to the military.

The Military and the Battle for the 1995 Budget

Minister of Defense Pavel Grachev had become a political leader in his own right. His blunt military style did not sit comfortably with the demokraty as a whole but he fought to save his position, his honor, and refused to keep silent about the true state of national defense. Defense was stuck with its 5 percent and the Government and the Duma built their budgets around such percentages. The military could not jump its share to 10 percent without knocking another interest group's allocation down. Nevertheless, Minister of Defense Grachev tried and submitted a request for a 90 trillion ruble 1995 defense budget instead of the 40.6 trillion he had been given in 1994. This went over like a lead balloon and Prime Minister Chernomyrdin recommended a 45 trillion ruble defense budget to the Duma.[64]

Yeltsin addressed the military leadership's annual enlarged meeting of the military collegium on 14 November 1994. Grachev opened the meeting and declared to the president that the armed forces were combat ready and capable of defending Russian security. However, instead of giving full blown political support to Grachev, Yeltsin distanced himself somewhat and tried to bring Grachev down a notch or two by announcing that he would speak directly to the commanders as necessary. Yeltsin told the commanders that he wished to meet with them personally and had instructed the Minister of Defense to authorize such meetings. Was this a sign that Yeltsin was unhappy with Grachev or a clever way to appear to be punishing Grachev while actually protecting from ambitious rivals?[65]

Whenever the commander in chief begins to circumvent his minister of defense, he damages his minister of defense's authority. Grachev's chief of staff, Col. General Mikhail Kolesnikov delivered the main report on military reform and the status of the armed forces of the Russian Federation, not Grachev. Yeltsin offered no hope on the military budget except that he pledged to require the Ministry of Finance to deliver funds in the amounts authorized by the Duma and in a timely manner. Yeltsin also spoke about the need to improve cooperation between the military, the Russian border forces, the MVD, and security forces. Yeltsin praised the military and said they were indeed becoming the armed forces of which Great Russia could be proud.[66]

The Ministry of Defense continued its public information campaign against the current and proposed budgets. If Great Russia needed strong armed forces it would have to find a way to pay for them. The core of Russia's continental defense, the Russian Infantry was understaffed by 100,000 soldiers and non-commissioned officers. No large scale training exercises had been held since 1992. During 1994, the infantry received only 9 percent of the funding it needed to hold training exercises. The Russian Air Force had to cut training flights by 44 percent from 1993 to 1994. Aircraft are not being properly maintained due to insufficient funding for maintenance and repair. The Strategic Rocket Forces could not hold talented young officers, some 2,500 were furloughed on their own initiative in 1994 alone.[67]

Less than two weeks after Yeltsin's speech to the military collegium, an incident in Grozny revealed that the Yeltsin administration had been running covert operations to unseat Djokhar Dudayev's secessionist regime. On 26 November 1994, Dudayev captured Russian military personnel who had just pushed their way into the center of Grozny disguised as a pro-Moscow Chechen force. This added to Grachev's political woes. Although the President had made the decisions to use covert operations against Dudayev and the military personnel who engaged in them were under special contract to federal secret services, the military's image suffered. The Army had been used again for a ill-conceived, domestic political operation. The list had now expanded to Tbilisi, Baku, Vilnius, Moscow, and Grozny.

Conclusion

Yeltsin's one hundred days and the surge of nationalism seen in the 1993 Duma elections gave the impression that the tide had turned in favor of the national defense lobby. However, things developed quite differently as the Zhirinovskyites and Communists adopted the same formula-driven approach to defense spending that Yegor Gaidar had imposed. Grachev criticized and cajoled but the formula-driven approach held firm. The total number of authorized military positions was to be no greater than 1,500,000 or 1 percent of Russia's population. Defense spending was capped at about 20 percent of the total federal budget and no more than 5 percent of total GDP. The Ministry of Defense was competing for a diminishing supply of real funds. It continued to be unpopular with the democratic and pro-Western camp and had to keep its distance from Yeltsin's political enemies in the nationalist camp. Therefore, it could not build a strong, pro-defense lobby in the Duma.

For civilian control over defense affairs to work well, a president must lead rather than referee. The president must draw the lines for his commanders and for his ministers. However, in post-Soviet Russia, Yeltsin behaved more like a political referee than a powerful president while the Duma, the Ministry of Finance, and the Ministry of Defense argued about military budgets, reform, and investigated allegations of military corruption. Yeltsin tolerated dissonance and self-assertive behavior. Yeltsin's personal leadership style encouraged the Ministry of Defense to play the political game.

Grachev was inclined to end military politicking because it threatened military cohesion. Stray officers and soldiers had to be collected and placed in their administrative pens in the chain of command. Military personnel had to be assembled and mobilized for military reform and reconstruction. However, Grachev could not stay out of politics for four main reasons. First, the civilians would not leave the military alone to do its professional work. Second, the federal budget could not provide the military with the financial support it needed. Third, the military would not permit its leader, Defense Minister Grachev, to ignore its complaints and to sit back while other interest groups hacked away at the defense budget. Fourth, the civilian commander in chief, Boris Yeltsin refereed instead of leading during many a political game.

The military overestimated the presidency's ability to solve defense problems, underestimated the importance of working openly and constructively with the Duma, and failed to convince society at large to make the sacrifices required to avert radical military downsizing and/or a sharp drop in overall combat readiness. No effective military-industrial complex lobby took hold in post-Soviet Russia during Yeltsin's first term. The military was on the political defensive in a declining economy. It faced a political consensus that demanded military downsizing and a rather bleak field of potential political allies.

Notes

1. See Aleksandr Pel'ts, "Press-konferentsiya ministra oborony Rossii" (Russian minister of defense's press conference), *Krasnaya zvezda*, 6 October 1993.
2. Boris Yeltsin, "Obrashchenie Prezidenta Rossiiskoi Federatsii," *Krasnaya zvezda*, 7 October 1993.
3. *Ibid.*
4. Vladimir Leonidov, "Okazhetsya, Rossiyu spasla Akhedzhakova" (It seems that Akhedzhakova saved Russia), *Krasnaya zvezda*, 7 October 1993.
5. Unsigned, front page headline story and editorial, "Posle razyazki: nuzhny spokoistvie, vyderzhka, bditel'nost' i splochennost'" (After the denouement: calm, self-control, vigilance, and unity are needed), *Krasnaya zvezda*, 6 October 1993.
6. Unsigned, lead story and editorial, "Chem storozhe vertical' edinonachaliia tem prochnee i nadezhnee sama armiya" (The stricter the vertical in the unity of command, the more cohesive and reliable the army), *Krasnaya zvezda*, 16 October 1993.
7. See "Osnovnye polozheniia voennoi doktriny Rossiiskoi Federatsii" (Basic provisions of the military doctrine of the Russian Federation), *Krasnaya zvezda*, 19 November 1993.
8. See Article IV. President of the Russian Federation in the new Constitution; *Krasnaya zvezda*, 10 November 1993.
9. Lt. General Konstantin Bogdanov, interviewed by Lt. Col. Aleksandr Andreyev and Capt. Leonid Mrochko, "Armiya i vybory: kak budem golosovat'?" (The army and the elections: how will we vote?), *Krasnaya zvezda*, 6 November 1993.
10. See Anatoly Stasovskii, "Aleksei Tsarev: Novomu parlamentu ot voennykh problem ne uiti" (The new parliament will not be able to get away from military problems), *Krasnaya zvezda*, 9 November 1993.
11. Captain Vladimir Urban, "Kakim budet voennyi budjet 1992 goda" (What will the 1992 military budget be like?), *Krasnaya zvezda*, 3 December 1991.
12. See Yegor Gaidar, *Gosudarstvo i evolyutsiya* (State and evolution) (Moscow: Evrazia, 1995).
13. See Vladimir Urban's positive interview with Gaidar, "Prestizh voennoi professii budet vosstanovlen" (The military profession's prestige will be restored), *Krasnaya zvezda*, 9 October 1992.
14. Vladimir Lopatin, "Armiya dlya gosudarstva, a ne gosudarstva dlya armii," *Izvestiya*, 26 May 1993.
15. See Valentin Rudenko, "Oboronke nuzhny opredelennost' i vzveshennye, produmannye reformy" (Defense needs definition and carefully weighed, thoughtful reforms), *Krasnaya zvezda*, 27 October 1993.
16. The text of *Ukaz No. 1850* was published in *Krasnaya zvezda*, 20 November 1993.
17. See Aleksandr Pel'ts and Anatoly Stasovksii, "Tul'skiye desantniki pokazyvayut, chto armiya sposobna zashchitit' rossiyan" (Tula paratroopers demonstrate that the army is capable of defending Russians), *Krasnaya zvezda*, 18 November 1993.
18. "Simvolika: Gosudarstvennogo gerba Rossiiskoi Federatsii" (The symbolism of the state seal of the Russian federation), *Krasnaya zvezda*, 3 December 1993.
19. "Rukovodstvo Vooruzhennykh Sil Rossii—za prinyatie Konstitutsii RF" (Armed forces leadership for adoption of RF constitution), *Krasnaya zvezda*, 10 December 1993.

20. Boris Yeltsin, National Address, "Nam nuzhna Konstitutsiya, esli my khotim sokhranit' mir v Rossii" (We need a Constitution if we are to keep peace in Russia), *Krasnaya zvezda*, 11 December 1993.
21. Unsigned, "Nuzhen parlament, gde preobladalo by konstruktivnoe otnoshenie k armii" (Needed, a parliament wit a constructive relationship to the army), *Krasnaya zvezda*, 10 December 1993.
22. See *Krasnaya zvezda*, 10 December 1993.
23. See Richard Sakwa, "The Russian Elections of December 1993," *Europe Asia Studies*, vol. 47, no. 2, 1995, p. 213.
24. See *Ibid.* Sakwa judiciously warns that the data on the military vote are controversial.
25. Ministry of Defense, "Armiya i vybory" (The army and elections), *Krasnaya zvezda*, 17 December 1993.
26. See Vladimir Urban, "Vstrecha A Kozyreva s Zhurnalistami" (A. Kozyrev's meeting with journalists), *Krasnaya zvezda*, 18 December 1993.
27. Yury Velichenko, "Ne nado klyast' Rossiyu" (Don't curse Russia), *Krasnaya zvezda*, 22 December 1993.
28. Vladimir Ermolin, "Dialog mezhdu vlastyu i narodom nuzhno nalazhivat' kak mozhno skoree" (Dialogue between the people and the authorities must start as soon as possible), *Krasnaya zvezda*, 24 December 1993.
29. Aleksandr Gol'ts, "Ponyat' svoi sobstvennyi narod" (To understand your own people), *Krasnaya zvezda*, 25 December 1993.
30. For a different point of view, see Thomas M. Nichols, "'An Electoral Mutiny?' Zhirinovsky and the Russian Armed Forces," *Armed Forces & Society*, vol. 21, no. 3, 1995, pp. 327–47. Nichols argues that the military retained more Soviet ideals and tended to yearn for a strong, authoritarian state—a reformed version of the former Soviet Union.
31. See Richard Sakwa, "The Russian Elections."
32. *Krasnaya zvezda*, 14 December 1993.
33. Oleg Falichev, "Lyudi v pogonakh" (People in uniform), *Krasnaya zvezda*, 2 August 1994.
34. Grachev's press conference of 29 December 1993, reported by Aleksandr Pel'ts, "Uroki na zavtra" (Lessons for tomorrow), *Krasnaya zvezda*, 31 December 1993.
35. *Ibid.*
36. *Ibid.*
37. Aleksandr Pel'ts, "Armiya sdelala glavnoye: ne dopustila grazhdanskoi voiny" (The army accomplished the most important: it prevented civil war), *Krasnaya zvezda*, 30 December 1993.
38. Deputy biographies are in *Armiya*, No. 5, 1994; p. 2.
39. Interviewed by Lt. Col. Ivan Ivanyuk, "Den'gi na oboronu strany..." (Money for the country's defense...), *Krasnaya zvezda*, 1 October 1994.
40. Oleg Vladykin, "Trudnye vremena zakonchatsya" (Hard times ending), *Krasnaya zvezda*, 19 November 1994.
41. Ivan Ivanyuk, "Den'gi na oboronu strany."
42. See Ivan Ivanyuk, "Voennyi budjet na 1995 god: pri vvedenii zhestkikh mer ekonomiki nado uchityvat' predel prochnosti" (The 1995 military budget: economic soundness must be considered when implementing tough measures), *Krasnaya zvezda*, 4 November 1994.
43. See Ivan Ivanyuk, "Den'gi na oboronu strany."
44. Cited by Boris Soldatenko in "Tak khochetsya spokoino zhit' , spokoino delat' svoye delo" (We really want to live peacefully and to do our job peacefully), *Krasnaya zvezda*, 1 October 1994.

45. *Ibid.*
46. Yeltsin's press conference of 4 October 1994, reported by Vladimir Ermolin, *Krasnaya zvezda*, 5 October 1994.
47. Ivan Ivanyuk, "Pravitel'stvo obespokyeno khodom podgotovki armii k zime" (The government is worried about army preparations for winter), *Krasnaya zvezda*, 8 October 1994.
48. See Vladimir Ermolin, "I voennosluzhashchie za nizkoyu inflatsiyu v 1995 godu. No ne za shchet razvala armii" (The military also want low inflation in 1995 but not at the cost of the army's collapse), *Krasnaya zvezda*, 28 October 1994.
49. Oleg Falichev, "Prizyv-93 byl samym trudnym. Chto nam ozhidat' osen'yu 94-go?" (The 1993 call-up was the worst. What can we expect in fall 1994?), *Krasnaya zvezda*, 8 October 1994.
50. See *Ibid.*
51. Sergei Bychkov, "In War of Words Russia Gains a Martyr," *Moscow News*, no. 42, October 21–27, 1994.
52. Minister of Defense, Army General Pavel Grachev, "Zayavlenie ministra oborony Rossiiskoi Federatsii" (Declaration by the minister of defense of the russian federation), *Krasnaya zvezda*, 22 October 1994.
53. Boris Yeltsin, "Ne nado lit' potoki gryazi na armiyu i eye rukovodstvo" (Shouldn't pour filth on the army and its leadership), *Krasnaya zvezda*, 22 October 1994.
54. Oleg Odnokolenko, "Eto uzhe ne prosto Rossiiskoe ubistvo" (Not just another Russian killing), *Krasnaya zvezda*, 20 October 1994.
55. See E. Galumov, the fund's president, in *Krasnaya zvezda*, 21 October 1994.
56. "We Will Not Retreat From Threats: Dmitry Kholodov's death is a terrorist act against freedom of speech in Russia," *Moscow News*, no. 42, October 21–27, 1994.
57. "Coming Hearings on Corruption," *Moscow News*, no. 42, October 21–27, 1994.
58. "Who's Behind Kholodov's Assassination?" *Moscow News*, October 28–November 3, 1994.
59. See Aleksandr Minkin, "The Rich Generals of a Poor Army," *Moskovsky komsomolets*, 28 October 1994. *CDSP* translation, vol. XLVI, no. 45, 1994, pp. 9–12.
60. Alexander Zhilin, "Conflict Erupts in Russia's Armed Forces," *Moscow News*, November 4–10, 1994.
61. Yeltsin retired Burlakov in February 1995. See *Krasnaya zvezda*, 10 February 1995.
62. Natalya Gevorkyan, "Defense Duma Passes a Duma Test," *Moscow News*, no. 47, November 25–December 1, 1994.
63. Reported by Oleg Odnokolenko, "Tak stoilo li podnimat' antiarmeiskii shum?" (Was the anti-army ruckus worth it?), *Krasnaya zvezda*, 26 November 1994.
64. Vladimir Ermolin, "I voennosluzhashchie za nizkoyu inflyatsiyu v 1995 godu" (Military also for low inflation in 1995), *Krasnaya zvezda*, 28 October 1995.
65. Some liberal reporters believed Yeltsin was protecting Grachev rather than preparing to remove him. See Alexander Zhilin, "Military Soap Opera Continues," *Moscow News*, no. 46, November 18–24, 1994.
66. See Anatoly Dokuchayev, "Oblik Vooruzhennykh Sil stanovitsya vse bolee dostoinym Velikoi Rossii" (The armed forces' make-up will become more worthy of great russia), *Krasnaya zvezda*, 15 November 1994.
67. Oleg Vladykin, "Urovnem podgotovki armii opredelyaetsya moshch' gosudarstva. Vse li ponimayut eto?" (The level of military preparedness defines the state's power. Do all understand this?), *Krasnaya zvezda*, 18 November 1994.

Part III

Testing the Russian State's Viability

12

The Chechen War and
Civil-Military Relations

The war between the Russian federal government and General Dzhokhar
Dudayev's rebel Chechen regime was the first major military confrontation
on Russian soil since World War II. It became a formative event in post-
Soviet, Russian political development. The Chechen war tested and shaped
relationships between the military, civilian political institutions, and society
at large.

Careful analysis of the war provides evidence about democratic development in Russia and the military's role in the transition from Soviet dictatorship
to a democratic state, one with a government which is accountable to society
and which observes constitutional norms. It also yields insights into the relationship between war and state formation. This chapter examines how the Yeltsin
administration made and implemented the decision to resort to war, how it and
the military responded to public criticism of the war; and, how the war affected
civilian control and leadership over the Russian armed forces.

Contradictory trends pulled at the Russian military system. On the one
hand, society demanded military downsizing and kept squeezing military
budgets, a phenomenon intensified by severe economic recession. The end of
the Cold War and the emergence of new military technologies made Russia's
big, heavy military divisions obsolete. On the other hand, while heavy missiles and tanks were being destroyed, the military was handed a new expanded
mandate in domestic political-military conflict inside Russia, in former Yugoslavia, and in several former Soviet republics. This required highly mobile
and politically sophisticated armed forces. Given its experience with revolution and national liberation struggles, one might have expected the Russian
state to wage combined military and political warfare with great sophistication especially within the former Soviet Union. The Chechen rebels drew
upon this legacy and were surprisingly successful. The federal forces did not.
Their strategy and tactics were mismanaged from the Kremlin.

From the outset Russia's top military professionals realized that their civilian leaders were imposing bad policies on them and on the nation. However,
they were caught in the classical dilemmas faced by military professionals ev-

erywhere under such circumstances. Obedience to civilian authorities who make bad policy decisions has costs which society as a whole pays to preserve the principle of civilian control. Americans paid that price in Vietnam and Russians paid it in Afghanistan and Chechnya. Russian society and the Russian military criticized the Chechen war from the outset but resistance was passive and did not reach the level of civil disobedience and insubordination required to stop Yeltsin. It was the presidency that eluded general societal control not the military. This is a complex and extremely rich case study which should disabuse readers of simplistic notions about civil-military relations in Russia and about the assumed popularity of the Russian imperial tradition.

War as Domestic Politics

In December 1994, the Russian military was handed a new function, waging war against fellow Russian citizens. President Yeltsin and Minister of Defense Grachev launched an offensive by some 24,000 soldiers against the secessionist regime in the Chechen statelet nestled in the foothills of Russia's North Caucasian region. The Chechen campaign was part of President Yeltsin's larger Russian state-building strategy. The September-October 1993 putsch, the December 1993 Constitution, and the Chechen war were linked. They were part of Yeltsin's overall effort to restore integrity and efficiency to the Russian political system. Yeltsin used brute force against parliament in October 1993 instead of accepting mediation and compromise. He also showed little respect for existing constitutional processes. Yeltsin displayed a similar leadership style as he dealt with the Chechen rebellion. However, it would be unfair to blame Yeltsin alone for the resort to force. In both cases the opposition must share a considerable part of the responsibility. Parliament's top leaders armed themselves and called for insurrection. Chechnya's rebel regime threw down the gauntlet by declaring independence and preparing to defend it with arms.

The Chechen rebellion was but the most extreme manifestation of a more general political malaise, a tendency by regional and local governments to exploit political "wiggle room" to the maximum. This looseness developed naturally when local political machines realized that the state's administrative enforcement mechanisms had withered away along with the unitary Communist Party dictatorship. Russia had destroyed the unitary dictatorship but had not yet become an integrated, law-governed state. Yeltsin argued that force was required to achieve political viability.

The Yeltsin administration described the Chechen secessionists as a criminal gang that had taken on the attributes of statehood. However, as Charles Tilly has argued, there are similarities between *states* and organized crime.[1] All states offer protection (defense, police, law enforcement) in exchange for money (taxes and fees). Further, war has been a normal part of state formation throughout history, a way to define borders and to establish hegemony within borders. It was difficult to define the difference between criminality and legality because so much of what used to be illegal had just become legal with the collapse of the Soviet state and the successor states were still struggling to achieve internal political viability. Yeltsin based his claim to political supremacy in Chechnya on his 1993 Constitution, the basic law which Russia adopted through a national referendum. However, Russia's Chechen region boycotted that referendum because it had already declared and ratified Chechen independence from Russia through its own elections in open defiance of the federal government in Moscow. Which was the higher value? The Russian state's political integrity and its Constitution or the Chechen people's right to self-determination? Two regimes claimed the same territory and both were armed and willing to fight.

War and the Formation of Sovereign States

The Chechen independence movement had organized and armed itself under the leadership of a military professional, Dzhokhar Dudayev, a former major general in the Soviet Air Force, who certainly remembered the Leninist admonition that all Soviet officers had been taught: "No revolution is worthy of the name unless it is capable of defending itself." Dudayev gave his statelet credibility by building self-defense forces. He was not unique in this regard. His was one of three major secessionist movements in the greater Caucasian region. All three had armed themselves to fight the governments which they opposed. Further, all began with arms and officers from the former Soviet armed forces though not all their arms and personnel were products of the Soviet military system.

The Armenian nationalists in Nagorno-Karabakh led the way by creating an armed force to support their secessionist struggle against Azerbaijan.[2] Next, Abkhazian separatists armed themselves against the Georgian government. Chechen volunteers under Shamil Basayev fought in Abkhazia and they later emerged as the core of the Chechen secessionist regime's special commando forces. Moscow treated each secessionist movement differently. Moscow aided and abetted the Armenians and the Abkhazians but tried to overthrow the Chechens. Moscow appeared to be using wars of secession to undermine state viability in Georgia and Azerbaijan because strong, viable states under nationalist leaders would have ruptured the Russian state's traditional hold on the Caucasus and the oil-rich Caspian region.[3] But the instability that Moscow tolerated in Georgia and Azerbaijan violated the key principle upon which political stability depends, the political integrity of existing states. It created a regional environment favorable to rebellion and one in which the flow of arms became increasingly difficult to control.

The Russian state had two primary reasons for attempting to defeat Chechnya's drive for independent statehood. First, the government in Moscow felt compelled to defend Russian state integrity. Second, it was attempting to build a sphere of influence which in effect meant imposing limitations on the state sovereignty of Armenia, Azerbaijan, and Georgia. The use and manipulation of armed conflict served both political goals and illustrated the reason why the Russian military argues that armed forces are inherently political.

The Mountain Caudillo: Dzhokhar Dudayev

Dzhokhar Dudayev was the first former Soviet general to lead an armed rebellion against his government. Dudayev established his regime in Chechnya during the August 1991 coup. He based his claim to legitimacy on the right to self-determination. Dudayev proclaimed that Chechnya was a sovereign and independent state. This was at least the third Chechen rebellion against Muscovite rule. During the nineteenth century imperial Russia fought and won a forty-year war against the Chechens, conquered the region and held it captive against its will. When the tsarist state collapsed in 1917, the Chechens rebelled again but were reconquered by the Red Army. In 1944 Stalin tried to eradicate the Chechen problem by deporting the Chechens, the Ingush, and other "rebel" peoples to Central Asia. However, in 1957, Khrushchev permitted them to return and to rebuild a statelet within the Russian republic in their traditional homeland. Dzhokhar Dudayev was born in 1944 just before the deportations. He spent his childhood in Kazakhstan and returned to Chechnya with his family under Khrushchev's dispensation.[4] Dzhokhar Dudayev entered the military and enjoyed a successful career in the Soviet Air Force. He commanded a division of heavy bombers that was stationed in the Baltic republics until the Baltic independence movements became powerful enough to cause Moscow to withdraw its nuclear bombers in mid-1990. At that time, Dudayev resigned from the military and devoted himself to politics. He liked to describe himself as a mere foot soldier in the Chechen national movement.[5]

The Chechen-Ingush republic included two related peoples, the Chechen and the Ingush plus a significant ethnic-Russian population, some 450,000 living mainly in the urban centers and parts of the lowlands. Under the Soviet dictatorship, the Soviet military, MVD, and KGB were present in the Chechen-Ingush republic and kept the pro-Moscow, Communist regime in power. During 1990 these key state agencies began to suffer from internal operational confusion partly caused by Yeltsin's rivalry with Gorbachev and the rise of Russian as opposed to Soviet political power. When Yeltsin rebelled against Gorbachev, Dudayev demanded independence from Yeltsin. In June 1990 the Russian Congress passed a declaration of Russian state sovereignty over the USSR. In November 1990, the Chechen-Ingush statelet's legislative body did the same to the Russian state of which it was a part.[6] This raised questions about the Russian state's ability to hold together if and when it freed itself from the Soviet Union. In August 1991 when Yeltsin defeated the State of Emergency Committee and simultaneously crippled Gorbachev's Soviet institutions, Dudayev organized his own revolutionary coup inside the Chechen-Ingush republic, ousted the pro-Moscow bosses and legislature, proclaimed independence, and announced that elections would be held to confirm independence and to form a new government. These actions produced a cohort of anti-Dudayev, pro-Moscow Chechens—politicians whom Dudayev ousted, sometimes at gunpoint. Some worked with Moscow against Dudayev.

The First Confrontation: A Standoff

In October 1991, President Boris Yeltsin and the Russian Parliament agreed that Dudayev's drive for independence had to be blocked. However, they could not come up with a satisfactory policy to achieve that objective. Yeltsin dispatched Vice President Rutskoi to Grozny, the rebel statelet's capital, with orders to have Dudayev and the rebel leadership arrested. But Dudayev's Chechen nationalist movement had already armed itself and Yeltsin was confronted with a difficult choice between armed conflict and a temporary political defeat. Instead of fighting and getting embroiled in a civil war, Yeltsin backed off and recalled the Rutskoi mission.

The manner in which Yeltsin handled the problem convinced Dudayev that he had a real chance to win independence. Moscow seemed confused and ineffective. Yelstin had given Dudayev three days to disarm. Yeltsin had warned that "all necessary measures" would be taken to restore the constitutional order. But that decree wasn't even published in Grozny until the day it expired, 22 October 1991. Yeltsin also named Akhmet Arsanov, an ethnic Chechen, to serve as his official representative and plenipotentiary in the Chechen-Ingush region.[7] But Arsanov could not dislodge Dudayev merely by sending letters and making phone calls. Dudayev's regime was armed and was in control of some territory. Since it made and enforced decisions over a territory and had armed forces, it had become a proto-state, if not a state in fact. Although Yeltsin was the president of Russia, the Soviet military was still under Gorbachev and Yeltsin had only limited authority to command some National Guard units.

Until May 1992 when Yeltsin created his own armed forces, his ability to use military power to overthrow the Dudayev regime was in doubt. Thus, in fall 1991, during the critical beginning months of Dudayev's rebellion, the Soviet Union still existed and the military were under Marshal Yevgeny Shaposhnikov whose legal civilian commander was USSR President Gorbachev *not* Russian President Yeltsin. Then, from late December 1991 to May 1992, the military and Shaposhnikov officially reported to a committee of CIS heads of state. This command structure was too cumbersome and could not serve Russian state interests effectively. Dudayev understood this and took advantage of the institutional and political confusion in Moscow. It gave him time to build his own defenses.

Yeltsin could issue decrees but he lacked the military and police power to back them up. For example, Yeltsin forbade Dudayev to hold elections in fall 1991 but Dudayev refused to be intimidated and posted Chechen national guards at some voting places and near some Soviet military and police facilities. Soviet forces stayed on base and voting took place in electoral districts that were under Chechen rebel control. Dudayev's independence movement won the truncated elections of 27 October 1991. Nevertheless, the fact that not all of Chechnya had voted permitted Yeltsin to argue that Dudayev did not have a valid mandate from the Chechen people. Russia's federal Parliament declared the truncated elections to be invalid. Further, Moscow's secret services encouraged opposition groups to advertise themselves as the true representatives of the Chechen people. On 7 November 1991, Yeltsin issued a formal ukaz which imposed a state of emergency on Chechnya, a form of temporary dictatorship. However, Yeltsin and the Russian Parliament decided that this could not be enforced without warfare and Yeltsin concurred when the Parliament did not ratify it.[8]

Although Dudayev's rebellion had important implications for Russian statehood, in fall 1991 the stakes at risk in the Chechen problem seemed quite small compared to the main political game to determine the future of Gorbachev and the Union state. While Yeltsin focused attention on his competition with Gorbachev and the Union, Dudayev quietly reinforced his statelet. Although his government wasn't recognized, it was becoming more effective and it controlled Grozny, the main industrial city and administrative capital of Chechnya. Its representatives nurtured contacts with the Chechen diaspora in Turkey, Jordan, and other states.

In spring 1992, Dudayev obtained enough arms and military supplies to build a small army and to arm a larger militia. Since Russia, Ukraine, and the other republics had nationalized Soviet military assets on their territories, Dudayev claimed the same rights for his statelet. Further, his paramilitary forces kept the Russian military under constant pressure. When faced with a choice between compromise and armed confrontation, Yeltsin accepted compromises which later plagued him. Russian federal troops withdrew from Chechnya under duress and Russian federal authorities gave in to Dudayev's demands. The Russian military agreed to leave him about 50 percent of its military assets. However, Dudayev ended up with some 80 percent of the materiel, an abundant supply of hand weapons and a small army of forty-five tanks and fifty-five armored personnel carriers.[9] Although Yeltsin, Grachev, and Shaposhnikov were involved in those 1992 decisions, three years later when Dudayev used those weapons against Yeltsin's federal armies, no one was willing to take either the credit or the blame for them.

During 1992 and 1993, the Yeltsin administration tried to whittle Dudayev down to size and to undermine him through covert operations. Dudayev's span of control never extended across all of Chechen-Ingushetia. It was mainly confined to the ethnic Chechen portion of the statelet. Moscow encouraged the Ingush to demand separation from the Chechens and they did so. In early 1993 the federal government formalized the division and appointed a military officer, General Ruslan Aushev, to govern the new Ingush republic. This political move by federal authorities was popular with the Ingush since Aushev was an ethnic Ingush and an Afghan war hero. In March 1993, elections were held and General Aushev became president of the Ingush statelet.[10] Now there were two generals in power at the head of two statelets that controlled a small but strategically important border region of the Russian Federation. One general was loyal to Moscow; the other continued to demand independence. Aushev encouraged Dudayev to strike a compromise deal with Moscow but Dudayev refused. However, Aushev opposed the militants in the Yeltsin administration who wanted to use military power to overthrow Dudayev. Aushev warned that it would be impossible to conduct a simple, effective war. Instead of a quick and dirty corrective military coup, an attack on Dudayev could produce a long, difficult civil war.

From a strictly military point of view, Dudayev's statelet did not constitute a major security threat to Russia. However, the Kremlin worried about his rebellion's impact on Russia's domestic political integrity and upon its ability to prevent Turkey and its Western allies from pulling the Caucasus and the greater Caspian region out of Russia's sphere of influence. Nevertheless, Aushev and other moderates favored patience because they considered the potential for communal violence and civil war—precipitated by federal military action, to be more immediate dangers. Yeltsin tried to use covert operations and indirect methods to dislodge Dudayev. However, those methods failed for two reasons. First, Dudayev turned out to be the more skillful player. Second, the new Russian security services were less effective than the former Soviet security services because the Yeltsin administration's democratic reformers had deliberately weakened them after the August 1991 coup and the fall of the Soviet Union.

By 1994 Yeltsin became convinced that he had to overthrow the rebels because Dudayev's continued resistance was undermining Moscow's credibility in the international game for control over the future oil flows from the greater Caspian region. It was imperative that Moscow demonstrate its ability to defend the pipeline route from Azerbaijan to Novorossiisk which passed through Chechnya. Russian diplomats considered Dudayev to be a de facto ally of Turkey and those groups working to pull the Caucasus out of the Russian sphere of influence. For this reason, his rebellion had become intolerable to Moscow's strategic thinkers. It was reasonable for Yeltsin to expect to be able to topple him and to demand that the appropriate federal agencies develop an effective plan. It would have been extremely difficult for the three Russian power ministers to tell their president that they could not handle the Chechen statelet and still retain their jobs.

Grozny: Yeltsin's Bay of Pigs

By summer 1994, the Chechen statelet's population had been halved to about 1,000,000 for two reasons: the split with Ingushetia and political flight. From 1991 to 1994, about 250,000 Russian-speakers fled Chechnya for more stable areas of Russia. The Chechen proto-state was on the brink of civil war because the Russian state's federal security services had armed three to five opposition movements. Chechen nationalists, bandits, and real estate speculators made life difficult for ethnic Russians in areas under their control.[11] Those citizens had a legitimate claim on federal assistance but the Kremlin seemed more interested in toppling Dudayev than is supporting refugees.

It was relatively easy for federal agencies to nurture rival opposition groups since the Chechens have traditionally organized themselves into competing clans and Dudayev had made political enemies. Further, Chechnya's oil wells, refineries, and pipelines promised the victors high incomes. Even the politically disgraced speaker of the former Russian Parliament, Ruslan Khasbulatov took up residence in Chechnya, his home republic, and suggested that he might someday head a new Chechen government of national reconciliation.[12] But Dudayev continued to denounce the Kremlin and its local allies. He refused to join any Moscow-sponsored political roundtable. Therefore, the Yeltsin administration concluded that a show of force would be required to persuade Dudayev to cooperate. In September 1994, as the Yeltsin administration was completing plans and preparations for an armed attack against Dudayev, former Soviet defense minister, Yevgeny Shaposhnikov warned Yeltsin against using war to achieve his political goals and urged him to meet directly with Dudayev. However, Yeltsin rejected Shaposhnikov's advice.[13]

On 26 November 1994, a column of twenty-six Russian tanks and some seventy-five Russian military personnel disguised as Chechen rebels pushed its way into Grozny and waited for Chechen opposition forces to stage a general uprising and to proclaim the end of the Dudayev regime. But there was no general rebellion. The tanks and troops waited for several hours until Dudayev's forces moved in and took them prisoner. Dudayev found Russian officers among them including servicemen from the elite Taman and Kantemirov divisions which are normally stationed outside Moscow. Russia's free press soon arrived on the scene, began questioning the captives, and publishing the sensational news. This incident became an enormous political humiliation and defeat for the Yeltsin administration.

At first, the Yeltsin administration decided to stick to its official, obviously false, description of the events. However, because Russia had a free press, the truth came out. At first, the Ministry of Defense supported the Kremlin line with a deceptive explanation. None of its "regular" armed forces was involved; the fighting was done by politicos and hirelings. From a legal, technical point of view, the Ministry's statement was true. Professional soldiers, on leave from the Ministry of Defense and under contract to federal state security agencies participated in the operation, not "regular" soldiers. Ten days later, the Ministry published a frank description of the covert operation including the high salaries (400 to 500 percent higher than normal levels) that were promised to participants[14] This material appeared in the military press after it had come out in the civilian media.

Dudayev threatened to deal harshly with the captives unless the Yeltsin administration admitted that they were Russian military personnel and stopped claiming that they were an authentic, Chechen opposition movement. He warned Russian mothers and families that the Yeltsin administration was preparing to send even more of their children into war, an ugly civil war in which there would be many casualties. He reminded them of Kremlin mistreatment of Russian draftees during the Afghanistan war. He urged them to block Yeltsin and to force Yeltsin to deal responsibly at the highest level with his government.[15] Dudayev wanted direct, high-level negotiations with the Kremlin.[16]

Yeltsin rebuffed Dudayev and continued to describe Chechnya as a part of Russia where civil war had broken out among contenders for power. The Kremlin refused to deal solely with Dudayev because such negotiations would have amounted to de facto recognition of his claim to be a legitimate head of state. Yeltsin kept making the case required to justify a major military-political intervention. Yeltsin insisted that criminal gangs and irresponsible local politicians had created a lawless situation that deprived Russian citizens of basic civil liberties and endangered Russia's vital interests.[17] On 29 November 1994, Yeltsin ordered all sides to disarm within forty-eight hours. If not, he threatened to impose an emergency regime and to use "all means at the disposal of the State" to restore constitutional order in Chechnya.[18] On 1 December 1994, aircraft bombed parts of Grozny. The Kremlin did not claim responsibility for the bombing. Instead it insisted that a civil war was raging and that armed forces controlled by a so-called Chechen Provisional Council had actually conquered part of Grozny's suburbs.[19] The pro-Moscow, Provisional Council offered to stop fighting and to turn in its weapons if Dudayev did the same.[20] Dudayev rejected Yeltsin's ultimatum and insisted that Yeltsin treat him as a legitimate head of an independent state.

The Autonomous Presidency and the Duma

The Duma erupted into debate and charged Yeltsin with violating the spirit if not the letter of the Constitution. However, it failed to serve as an effective check on presidential power. Russia's Constitution and federal laws obliged the president to take timely action to defend the constitutional order and to end crisis situations that endanger civilian life. Further, Russian military doctrine authorized the use of military power in domestic crises that threatened vital national interests. Secession certainly fit that class of events and it was Yeltsin's duty to end it. Finally, Yeltsin was supreme commander over all the armed forces—military, national police, special security forces, border forces, etc., and had the power to dismiss or promote any officer without the Duma's approval.

Yeltsin played his legal cards in a crafty manner that relegated the Duma to the political side lines. Yeltsin could have issued a presidential ukaz to impose a State of Emergency on Chechnya; but he decided not to because the Russian Constitution requires post facto legislative ratification of official states of emergency. That constitutional provision was designed to make the legislature an effective check on presidents. However, Yeltsin simply dictated federal policy on Chechnya without declaring a formal state of emergency. As a result, the federal government moved towards civil war without legislative approval of its war policies. Instead of the Duma, Yeltsin used the Russian Security Council, a body he appointed, to legitimize his policies. Again, this illustrates the extent to which the Russian presidency was able to operate autonomously within Russian society against the wishes of its elected representatives in the Duma. But this did not prevent Duma deputies from attempting to bring influence to bear on the crisis.

On 1 December 1994, a Duma delegation arrived in Grozny to investigate, to seek peaceful solutions to the conflict, and to win freedom for the captives. The political atmosphere was tense because aircraft had just bombed key airfields and installations in and near the city. Col. Sergei Yushenkov, chairman of the Duma's defense and security committee, led the mission which also included Vladimir Lysenko, Ella Panfilova, and Anatoly Shabad.[21] On the first day of their two-day visit, they interviewed the captives and passed the information they obtained to the press. On the second day, they talked directly with Dudayev. He released two prisoners who returned to Moscow with the Duma deputies. Deputy Lysenko warned that it was going to be difficult to settle the conflict because Yeltsin and Dudayev were unlikely to compromise. He complained that the Yeltsin administration was refusing to seek the Duma's advice and consent. The Duma had very little power over the president. Yushenkov, Lysenko, et al. concluded that Russia needed a constitutional amendment to make the Security Council accountable to the Duma.[22]

President Yeltsin and Minister of Defense Grachev damaged their political relationships with the Sergei Yushenkov and the Duma's defense and security committee by leaving them out of the policy loop. The Duma wanted to avoid civil war and its speaker, Ivan Rybkin, tried to move federal policy towards all-round assistance to Chechnya, a set of positive incentives to remain in Russia. The Ministry of Defense seemed to endorse Rybkin's call for positive engagement and steady, determined work to find an acceptable compromise that kept Chechnya within the Russian Federation.[23] This fit the pattern seen in previous conflict situations. The military urged civilian leaders to resolve their differences responsibly and peacefully. Bitter experience had taught the military that society tends to blame the armed forces for the killing even though it is civilian leaders who order the military into action. In early January 1995, to strengthen national political unity behind the war policy, Boris Yeltsin made Ivan Rybkin and Vladimir Shumeiko voting members of the Security Council by virtue of their positions as speakers of the State Duma and of the Federal Council respectively.[24]

Although the Duma failed to prevent military escalation, it legitimized dissent. The free press covered the Duma debates and speeches. The Duma legitimized and institutionalized political debate and gave the war's critics and Yeltsin's rivals a legitimate way to organize their dissent. When Yeltsin added Rybkin and Shumeiko to the Security Council, he made a constructive effort to improve consultation with the legislative branch of government. On the one hand, this was a positive development because it placed the armed forces and security service chiefs at the same national security table with the two leaders of parliament and thereby facilitated communication between the executive and legislative branches of government. On the other, it may have weakened the legislative branch's role as an independent critic of presidential policy.

Yeltsin's War Strategy: Rational but Too Complex

The national interest case for defeating Dudayev was easy to make; the military-political planning required greater subtlety. The justification litany was simple to recite. His rebellion had been tolerated for too long. Russia's political integrity was at stake so was its ability to hold the Caucasus and the Caspian in its near-abroad security zone. Some politicians in Tatarstan and other parts of Russia were eager to follow Dudayev's example. But what about the reliability of intelligence estimates about the strength of Dudayev's self-defense forces and of popular support for a war of independence? These had just been proven wrong and had resulted in the grand blunder of 26 November 1994. Yeltsin might have fired his top security officers, made them responsible for the fiasco, and used their mistakes as an excuse to open talks with Dudayev. Instead, he retained them and demanded a victory plan from them even though they had just given him a humiliating defeat. His Security Council designed an excessively complex, all-forces strategy that prevented the military from using its coercive power efficiently and created command and control problems..

Yeltsin's decision to escalate fit the pattern seen during his political conflict with Parliament in 1993. After making several threats and backing down, he decided to crush his opponents and to ignore societal calls for compromise. Once he had decided to crush Parliament, he demanded that the three power ministries provide winning plans not excuses. But he also imposed politically motivated restrictions on what the armed forces could do. In the 1993 crisis he initially ordered the armed forces to avoid bloodshed in Moscow. This approach failed and Yeltsin ended up using tanks against Parliament. He used military power to win a political victory instead of accepting a brokered compromise. The confrontation between Yeltsin and Dudayev was falling into the same tragic pattern.

In the October 1993 crisis Grachev ended up taking the public lead and initially bore the brunt of public anger and criticism as his tanks fired on Parliament. In December 1994 Grachev found himself in a similar predicament at the head of a far more serious military-political operation. Yeltsin gave him the overall command of the war against Dudayev. What did he advise Yeltsin? Some have accused him of encouraging the President to believe in an easy military victory, a Russian version of Operation Desert Storm. Grachev's story is quite different. He pointed out that Russia had the firepower, more than enough, to destroy Dudayev and Grozny easily. But he warned that such destruction was not what the president had in mind. If the president wanted to defeat Dudayev without destroying Chechnya in the process, then a more sophisticated approach had to be designed, one that suited the president's political objectives. However, Grachev cautioned that the more limitations the war's political managers placed on the types of weapons and operations the military could use, the longer the war would be.[25] Grachev warned that the defense budget had been so low that the military had not been able to train properly for the last two years. He repeated the military's standard litany of complaints about poor funding, an inadequate military draft system, and problems with equipment and supplies. But he was unable to get Yeltsin or the Security Council to give him either the time or the financial support the military needed to prepare properly for a new escalation in Chechnya.[26]

Yeltsin probably lost patience with Grachev's litany of complaints. On the one side, Grachev had some 1,900,000 military personnel and the MVD under Yerin had another 350,000 or so professionals in its internal armies. Further, Russia was spending trillions of rubles on defense. On the other side, according to Russian intelligence estimates, Dudayev's statelet had some 11,000 to 12,000 professional fighters plus a large home guard. Grachev could not effectively argue that he did not have enough resources to crush Dudayev without opening himself up to severe criticism for the mismanagement of national defense. So he came up with a general plan for the Security Council, a strategy that seemed logical. If Dudayev forced a fight, the Ministry of Defense military would use its superior air and land power to take out Dudayev's tanks, planes, heavy artillery, and larger fighting units. As soon as the heavy fighting was over, the MVD would move into place and take charge of security in the villages, towns, and cities. Federal security units would handle special intelligence operations. Federal border troops would isolate Chechnya. The foreign ministry would handle the war's external diplomatic requirements. The appropriate departments of government would mobilize for economic reconstruction, move rapidly, and demonstrate to Chechnya's population that the federal government was working on their behalf by restoring normal economic and social life.

The Russian Security Council named Pavel Grachev to head the team effort. The elite group included Nikolai Yegorov, Yeltsin's plenipotentiary representative in the Chechen Republic, Viktor Yerin head of Russia's MVD, Col. General Anatoly Kulikov commander of the MVD's internal armies, Col. General Andrei Nikolayev commander of Russia's Border Forces, Sergei Stepashin head of the Russia's security service or FSS, Boris Pastukhov a deputy minister of foreign affairs, plus representatives from federal disaster relief organizations. Grachev established Chechen operations headquarters in Mozdok, a major Russian military base near Chechnya.[27]

On the organizational charts, the plan was rational. There was one operational commander, Minister of Defense Grachev. He was given the command authority to coordinate MVD, Border Forces, and the FSS personnel assigned to the Chechen operations. He had additional diplomatic support from the Ministry of Foreign Affairs. But there were three flaws. First, the president and the Security Council retained overall "civilian" managerial authority over Grachev. Second, they used this power to impose constraints upon him and insisted that his troops not open fire first, a politically motivated order that gave the rebels tremendous advantages. Third, they refused to speak directly with Dudayev.

The press zeroed in on Grachev. The war's critics accused him pushing war to enhance the military's political clout in Russia. Grachev was on the political and the military front-lines while Yeltsin and others watched from relative safety behind the Kremlin walls. Grachev opened Chechen conflict resolution talks at Mozdok during the first week of December. However, only the pro-Moscow groups in the so-called Provisional Council showed up. Dudayev refused to send authoritative representatives to Grachev's Chechen roundtable. Grachev said that he was ready to meet in groups or separately with Dudayev but there were two preconditions which Dudayev could not accept. First, Dudayev would have to recognize that Chechnya was under the Russian Constitution and an integral part of the Russian Federation. Second, he would have to begin disarming immediately.[28]

The Security Council's political and military strategies were flawed. The Security Council's terms required Dudayev to surrender in advance just to get a seat at the negotiating table. This was hardly a constructive beginning. Grachev appears to have been given too little wiggle room to make any serious headway with Dudayev. Further, the Security Council's war strategy only made sense if Dudayev agreed to engage federal troops away from urban centers, towns, and villages. But Dudayev refused to limit his defense to open field warfare and he used Chechnya's towns and cities for cover. Heavy concrete buildings including administrative centers and civilian housing became his fortresses. He prepared for urban and rural guerrilla warfare—a strategy that would force Yeltsin to destroy Chechnya's cities and towns.

Grachev's Diplomacy and Dudayev's Appeal for Talks

Grachev tried one last time to break the deadlock and arranged a personal meeting with Dudayev on 6 December 1994. The two former Soviet generals met behind closed doors for over an hour. They seemed to have made progress. After the meeting Dudayev announced that all Russian military prisoners would be released to federal authorities. Grachev told the press that he had only discussed military affairs with Dudayev. He said that he was pleased with the talks and hoped to meet Dudayev again. The two generals had spoken with no strings attached and had demonstrated that former Soviet officers might be able to resolve problems efficiently. *Krasnaya zvezda* presented this news under the headline title: "There is No Conflict between Russia and Chechnya: Just a Battle for Power." Dudayev's chief of staff, another former Soviet officer, Aslan Maskhadov took charge of the prisoner exchange. The captives were handed over to Russian authorities on 8 December 1994. Grachev flew their relatives in for the ceremony. Dudayev sent word to Yeltsin that he wanted a direct, face to face meeting. Various political leaders urged Yeltsin to take that step towards peace but he refused to do so. But President Yeltsin continued to insist upon prior conditions that amounted to surrender in advance.[29]

Civil Society and the Semi-Autocratic Presidency

There were signs that civil society was attempting to form in post-Soviet Russia and competing with the still vibrant autocratic tradition. Society had access to competing points of views from domestic and international sources. Various political parties and movements were taking positions. The legislative branch of government was showing vitality and getting involved. However, the Kremlin—the semi-autonomous presidency of Boris Yeltsin refused to engage in a serious dialogue about policy with its critics. The Duma's security and defense committee, former Soviet President Gorbachev, Minister of Defense Grachev, and others were trying to bring Dudayev and Yeltsin together. But Yeltsin rejected their efforts and did as he pleased. On 8 December 1994 the Duma held a closed-door session on the Chechen crisis with representatives of the Yeltsin administration. The Duma called for a peaceful resolution of the crisis.[30] Mikhail Gorbachev offered to mediate.[31]

Instead of negotiating, Yeltsin rejected mediation. Yeltsin convened the Security Council on 7 December 1994 and heard reports on the latest developments from the Caucasus. When the meeting ended, Yeltsin issued a presidential ukaz naming Nikolai Yegorov, an ethnic Russian, to lead the Chechen crisis team and promoted him to the rank of vice premier of Russia. In other words, the civilian Yegorov replaced Grachev as the overall coordinator of the Kremlin's Chechen policy.

Grachev's Demotion and Military Dissent

The Kremlin demoted Grachev from overall coordinator of Chechnya policy to its military operations coordinator. This lesser role was more appropriate for the minister of defense. However, it would have been even wiser for Grachev to appoint a military subordinate to serve as general for the highly unpopular Chechen operation. Grachev might have distanced himself from direct responsibility for war's conduct. But Grachev's initial attempts to do so failed and that strategy did not fit Grachev's leadership style. Grachev's first choice for the onerous assignment, General Vorobyev, refused the command and resigned from the armed forces. Grachev decided to take charge himself and to take the political lumps. He had done that on 4 October 1993 instead of assigning a deputy to command the attack on Parliament. This seems foolhardy and immature, scarcely the most prudent course to take. However, Grachev was willing to take responsibility for success or failure instead of hiding behind others. This earned him support and sympathy in military circles even though the military did not like the Chechen war.

In April 1995, a responsible national survey found that 70-80 percent of Russia's adult citizens did not believe that Chechnya should be forced to remain a part of Russia against its will. They also blamed the war more on Russian politicians who blundered early and permitted Dudayev to build his regime (38 percent), President Yeltsin (31 percent), and Dudayev (19 percent). The public's willingness to let the Chechen's decide their future status did not resolve Russia's state integrity problem. Only 7 percent said that the army and the power ministries were the main cause.[32] Public opinion opposed the war but did not see the Russian military as the engine that generated the war. The public image of the military was close to the Ministry of Defense's point of view—the soldier was carrying out orders as required by the Constitution even though the soldier was critical of the civilians for their mismanaged domestic politics which led to war.

Grachev took risks and carried out flawed missions instead of resigning or putting other officers on the firing line. But now events were moving towards civil war, precisely what he and other officers had hoped to prevent. Even worse, the Kremlin politicos severely damaged the Ministry of Defense's ability to mobilize and train forces properly for the coming war. Yeltsin and the Security Council moved hastily: Yeltsin's covert operation was defeated on 26 November 1994. Yeltsin promulgated the presidential ukaz that authorized the use of armed force to restore the constitutional order on 9 December 1994. Yeltsin set the offensive's starting date for 11 December 1994. Units that had never fought together had to be rushed to Mozdok from various parts of the country, from various federal agencies, and from different units within those agencies. Grachev selected an experienced military commander, Col. General Edvard Vorobyev, to assess and to help organize the mobilization. But Vorobyev refused the appointment, put his career on the line, and tendered his resignation: "My personal fate is not so important at this point; it is necessary to save Russia and get out of the situation that has developed in the country, in Chechnya, and in the Armed Forces."[33]

Should Grachev have also threatened to resign unless his civilian commander in chief, Boris Yeltsin gave him more time to prepare the military properly for the Chechen offensive? Or unless Yeltsin agreed to lift restrictions he imposed on the military conduct of the war? Vorobyev argued that Grachev should have demanded more time and risked his position to obtain it. According to this line of reasoning, the military was not ready to fight the war and it was Grachev's professional duty as a professional military officer and a responsible leader to impress that fact upon Yeltsin.[34]

After less than a week of fighting it became clear that the first war plan was flawed. It tried to minimize fighting while encircling key towns, especially the capital Grozny. It underestimated Dudayev's determination and ability to organize military and political resistance. Therefore, Yeltsin faced another decision point and had another opportunity to fire officials and to open negotiations with Dudayev. Instead, he kept the three key power ministers in office and decided to escalate rapidly. On 26 December 1994, he gave Grachev only five days to prepare for a more decisive military drive to take Grozny and Dudayev's presidential palace. Troops were drawn from all across Russia in order to double the fighting force to over 40,000.

The Generals Who Took a Stand

Once Yeltsin had given his orders, defense minister Grachev had to implement them. Grachev had to pull the military leadership team together and to secure its active support. Disagreements within the military high command made Grachev's work more difficult and could not be ignored. Three deputy ministers who did not support the Chechen operation had to move aside: Col. General Boris Gromov, Col. General Valery Mironov, and Col. General Georgy Kondratyev. The purge was handled gracefully and presented as a decision to reduce the size of the top leadership group, a natural part of the ongoing military reform process. Although the three generals conducted themselves with good discipline and did not engage in barefisted politics, they criticized the Chechen policy after their removal from top leadership positions.[35] Gromov complained that the Yeltsin administration, including Grachev, had made the key decisions for war without convening the top leadership council of the Ministry of Defense. Gromov disagreed with their methods *not* with the goal of restoring order in Russia. He revealed that his dissent began when Yeltsin forced the military to fire upon parliament in October 1993. Gromov explained, "I would like to stress that I am not against establishing order in Chechnya and in the country as a whole, but I am against methods which are incompatible with the concept of *constitutional order* and *democracy*."[36]

A more vocal critic, Lt. General Aleksandr Lebed managed to hold on to his position at the head of the Russian group of forces based in Moldova's Transdniestrian region until summer 1995. In early January 1995 Lebed accused Yeltsin and Grachev of gross incompetence and mocked them bitterly for sending soldiers to their deaths and provoking Chechens into fierce resistance. He published blatantly insubordinate material under his own signature: "The whole world has come to know the main Russian military secret: the reforms of the armed forces under the leadership of *the best defense minister of all times and peoples* has ended up with their complete collapse. It is terrible and bitter to understand. Russia no longer has an army—what it has is only military formations of boy-soldiers which are hardly capable of achieving anything."[37] Lebed called the Yeltsin administration's explanations of the Chechen population's views "a pack of lies" and said that the federal armed forces, by using "barbaric" firepower against the towns and cities, had so enraged the Chechen people that the conflict had become a "people's war."[38] On 14 June 1995, President Yeltsin signed the orders relieving Lebed of his Moldovan command. Lebed resigned from the military to devote himself to politics.

Lebed's insubordinate behavior started before the Chechen war in summer 1992. It had gone on for three years. Why had Yeltsin and Grachev tolerated him? In February 1995 Lebed suggested an explanation. Neither Yeltsin nor Grachev felt secure enough to remove him because they did not have the generals under reliable control: "The defense minister is not the Defense Ministry. I have excellent relations with generals and officers in the central apparat who are really concerned over the future of the armed forces and are worried by the fact that the current pseudo-reforms drive the army into a dead end. They are generals Semyonov, Vorobyev, Gromov, Mironov, the flower of our army elite who are, unfortunately barred from active duty now."[39]

Human Rights and Soldiers' Rights

Boris Yeltsin's own presidential commission on human rights became the focal point for some of the sharpest criticism of federal decision to use war to settle the political dispute about Chechnya's future status. Sergei A. Kovalyev, the commission's chairman, took up residence in Grozny and demanded that the Kremlin stop making war on its own people and pushing its military professionals into combat against fellow citizens of Russia. He reasoned that the Kremlin had the most power and therefore the most responsibility for ending the civil war while it was still relatively easy to do so. As a long time dissident, former Gulag inmate, and close associate of the icon of Soviet dissent— the late Andrei Sakharov, Kovalyev hit hard and emotionally instead of offering, statesmanlike evaluations of the situation.

Kovalyev and others who condemned the war on humanitarian and human rights grounds described Yeltsin's policy as fundamentally criminal and warned that civilian and military leaders who gave the orders to use lethal force, especially against mixed targets where civilians were killed, might be brought to justice after the war. Yeltsin formed a new, temporary, human rights commission and charged it with responsibility for monitoring and reporting on human rights issues related to the "process of restoring the constitutional order on the territory of the Chechen republic. He named MVD Col. Valentin Kovalyev, a deputy in the Duma, to serve as its chairman. Now there were two human rights commissions and two chairmen operating simultaneously, both were Duma deputies, and both had same family name, Kovalyev. One was "evenhanded" and the other was deeply disturbed about Yeltsin's policies and refusal to meet Dudayev.[40]

In this war, at least at the beginning, the soldiers killed were named and described in normal, human terms. The military press asserted its own right to "human rights" and refused to play the role of the heartless, professional killer. *Krasnaya zvezda* regularly printed personal profiles in a series called "Soldiers Don't Pick War." The free press—particularly *Komsomolskaya pravda* picked up where the military press left off and criticized the military establishment for not supporting its soldiers properly and for not printing full lists of those killed. In October-November 1996, Grachev's successor Igor Rodionov discussed military openness with *Komsomolskaya pravda* and gave the paper a full list of Russian military casualties. Defense Minister Rodionov reaffirmed the post-Communist commitment to treat every death as a tragedy and to honor the fallen. He then published the full list of soldiers killed since from November 1994 through November 1996.[41]

The Ministry of Defense's reporter who pioneered this humanistic type of military journalism in the post-Soviet era, Col. Vladimir Zhitarenko, was shot dead by a Chechen sniper, the first victim of the war in 1995. Zhitarenko had gone to the front lines to describe Russian soldiers doing their duty under extreme psychological and physical conditions. He left the safety of the command post to go out to wish troops he had been interviewing a better New Year. He went out without his helmet since it was a holiday. A sniper picked him off just before he reached the men. His memorial service in Moscow was a large event which underlined his view of the war and of the Russian soldier who had to fight it. He had covered the "hot spots" and risked his life to present the military professional as a citizen performing the most difficult work society required.[42]

But the New Year's offensive began as ordered. Fighting was heavy and federal and rebel forces suffered the greatest losses of the war during the first days of January. Moscow wanted to break Dudayev's resistance and morale. Bombing became more extensive as did the protests from the antiwar and human rights groups. Yeltsin ordered a bombing halt on 5 January 1995, a political step resented by the federal forces. Reports suggested that the bombing had continued in violation of Yeltsin's orders. Yeltsin chastized Grachev during a public broadcast of the opening minutes of a special Security Council session but did not remove him. Yeltsin tried to get the rebels to accept a cease-fire but they refused his conditions and the war resumed. Yeltsin repeatedly interfered with the war effort for political reasons; he still hoped that Dudayev would see reason and accept a compromise rather than permit the war to destroy Chechnya's capital and urban infrastructure. But Dudayev made Yeltsin and the people pay that price.

The immediate commanding officer of the unit that finally took Dudayev's presidential palace in Grozny, Lt. General Lev Rokhlin commented, "In any war the most fundamental right, the right to life is denied you. That is the way it is and why the decisions are taken by the politicos. I fought and did my duty and brought my corps back to Volgograd and I am the first to bow before the families of the fallen."[43]

As the war ground on, one incident in April 1995, the federal offensive against the town of Samashki, caused the greatest furor. Antiwar activists such as Sergei Kovalyev charged federal troops with atrocities against civilians, including the murder of women and children. Stanislav Govorukhin, also a Duma deputy, conducted his own investigation and concluded that Kovalyev and the human rights activists had greatly exaggerated what happened there. But professional military officers did not conceal the fact that the federal armed forces included some units that had serious disciplinary problems.[44] By this point in the war Kovalyev and Govorukhin had fallen into a pattern, each tending to take the opposite position. The human rights activists kept the pressure up and insisted that any soldiers on either side guilty of wanton killing should be held criminally accountable. The Duma was inclined to grant a general amnesty after the war to encourage reconciliation.[45] International human rights groups generally rallied to Kovalyev and honored him for his work.[46]

The war generated human tragedy but it was also a test of post-Soviet, Russian society's capacity to tolerate debate and dissent during a time of crisis. Neither the Yeltsin administration nor the armed forces relished the constant barrage of criticism; yet, Yeltsin permitted it and even protected it. Lt. General Rokhlin was right to view the war as a tragedy in which the basic right to life was being taken away from soldiers and civilians alike. Kovalyev was right to struggle against the war and military officers were justifiably concerned about the antiwar movement's negative influence on combat discipline and morale. Under the Soviet dictatorship things would have been far neater. The state would have defended its political integrity more vigorously and crushed the first signs of Chechen national rebellion. The Soviet repressive machine would never have permitted nationalists to arm themselves. Gorbachev's reforms weakened the repressive machinery enough to allow armed rebellion to develop. Yeltsin's attack on the remnants of one-party and KGB rule virtually guaranteed that they would develop in some parts of Russia. The Chechen war made democracy's inherent messiness all the more apparent. Unfortunately, civic culture had not matured to the point where it could prevent politicians such as Dudayev and Yeltsin from precipitating a civil war.

Although the military press tended to complain about Kovalyev and the antiwar movement, the military also benefited from post-Soviet Russia's radically expanded freedom of speech and human rights movements. During the Afghan war, the dead and wounded were treated shabbily and denied public honors. During the Chechen war the military demanded better treatment and benefits for its combat veterans. Further, society pressed the military to improve medical care and general support to those at the front lines and to the wounded. The Ministry of Defense made a genuine effort to put relatives in touch with soldiers recovering from wounds and even learned to direct parental concern in constructive directions. However, the army's internal problems, funding shortages, declining morale, and staffing problems created an overall situation in which it failed to achieve its goals of treating its personnel in keeping with the standards set by the advanced, "civilized" states.

Lt. General Lev Rokhlin: Stoic Patriot

The symbol of Russian military and political humiliation was Dudayev's presidential palace in central Grozny. It continued to hold out against Russian attacks and became the site of fierce urban warfare during which corpses were mutilated and left for dogs to eat, part of the psychological war against the federal troops. The war had turned ugly and threatened to run out of control.

On 19 January 1995, the federal troops finally took possession of Dudayev's presidential administrative center in downtown Grozny. The federal Russian flag now flew over a miserable urban landscape reminiscent of World War II. Lt. General Lev Rokhlin, who commanded the forces that delivered this highly symbolic victory to Yeltsin, refused to play the traditional hero role in this war. Rokhlin did his duty and fought hard right with his men but he refused all awards and medals. Rokhlin's military column of some 500 vehicles moved across twenty kilometers of Chechen roads in order to reach Grozny and the battle for the presidential palace. The Afghan war veteran negotiated with Chechen civilians before his forces moved into their towns and was able to prevent some fighting. But in Grozny he faced severe urban warfare in streets too narrow for his tanks to operate effectively. Dudayev's fighters hit his vehicles with grenades and mortar fire at close range from the relative safety of the massive foundations of large urban buildings.[47] As Rokhlin moved closed to victory. Grachev lashed out against the limitations the civilians had imposed upon him: "I could have ended this war faster and with fewer casualties and less damage but I am being interfered with and am not allowed to fight in a manner that I know would have been more successful."[48] Vladimir Maryukha described the solders grinding their way towards the presidential palace in religious terms. It was Golgotha and they were forced to bear someone's else's cross.[49] In January 1995, the federal armed forces in Chechnya circulated a protest statement which was adopted at various meetings on 24 January and published in *Krasnaya zvezda* four days later. The soldiers' document was addressed to President Yeltsin, Prime Minister Chernomyrdin, Federal Council Speaker Shumeiko, Federal Duma Speaker Rybkin, Defense Minister Grachev, and Chief of General Staff Kolesnikov.[50] The protest's content was consistent with Rokhlin's realistic and bitter view of the war and the civilian leadership's response to it.

Lt. General Rokhlin became a national hero, a symbol of the soldier doing his patriotic duty under the most difficult circumstances. Instead of celebrating and playing the conquering hero, he refused to give the war false glamour and insisted on describing it realistically. He found it impossible to accept Yeltsin's Hero of Russia medal given his deep feelings about the war as a national tragedy. Political parties courted him and he agreed to run for a seat in the Duma at the December 1995 elections. Rokhlin associated himself with the statist party, Russia Our Home, and appeared on its official party list. But he ran for a single-mandate district seat and won on his own. The new Duma selected him to chair its Defense and Security Committee.

The Budyennovsk Incident: Terrorism and Society

Terrorism against innocent civilians—the type seen in various parts of the world, took root inside the Russian Federation as a result of the Chechen war. Neither the Russian armed forces nor Russian society had prepared for such developments. The Budyennovsk incident demonstrated the link between armed violence and politics. The rebels achieved a minor political victory by resorting to extremism. This planted a negative precedent in post-Communist Russian politics. Even though the Russian government—led by Prime Minister Viktor Chernomyrdin nobly tried to rise above the standard dilemmas all governments face in such situations, the extremists demonstrated that Russian society was vulnerable and that terrorism could be effective.

By early summer 1995, federal armed forces had reoccupied most of Chechnya and Dudayev's rebels had been driven into the underground and the mountains in the southern part of the region. The Yeltsin administration expected to start rebuilding the region's political, economic, and social institutions on its own terms. However, Dudayev and the rebels refused to concede defeat and executed a bold terrorist attack inside Russia in order to shatter the Yeltsin administration's confidence. Paradoxically, the Budyennovsk incident also confirmed that the Russian state's social and political institutions were viable though they did not operate neatly and efficiently. The Yeltsin administration recovered its equilibrium and actually agreed to some compromises with the rebels and the Duma.

On 14 June 1995, a Chechen commando led by Shamil Basayev seized a hospital complex in the town of Budyennovsk and held nearly 2,000 people hostage. However, President Yeltsin flew to a G-7 meeting in Halifax instead of remaining in Moscow to manage the crisis personally. But the incident damaged his claim to represent a great power in world affairs. It confirmed that his administration had not yet demonstrated effective control over a strategically significant part of its territory. Budyennovsk was 100 kilometers from Chechen-held territory and well within the North Caucasian Military District, the district with the largest number of Russian military personnel. Why hadn't Russian military and security forces prevented the attack?

The terrorists demanded an immediate end to the war, federal troop withdrawal from Chechnya, and direct talks between presidents Yeltsin and Dudayev. Moscow rejected the demands and ordered federal forces to attack on 17 June 1995 at 12:10 A.M. Ninety-five people were killed and another 142 were wounded in the hostage taking the fighting that ensued. The assault by federal commandos stalled because Basayev used the hostages as human shields and the Yeltsin administration decided against a massacre. Chernomyrdin was handed the task of negotiating with Basayev. Chernomyrdin conducted part of his negotiations live on Russian national television. Chernomyrdin struck a deal that gave Basayev and his fighters safe passage back into rebel-held territory in exchange for the hostages. Federal and Chechen rebel leaders also agreed to resume settlement talks in Grozny. On 19 June 1995, the terrorists returned to rebel lines under federal protection.[51]

Yeltsin Makes Compromises with War Critics

Terrorism had won a tactical victory. Dudayev had been threatening to take the war deep into federal territory, even to Moscow. Yeltsin warned the public against overreacting. He said that the rebels were deliberately trying to provoke the federal forces into a cycle of interethnic violence. He insisted that a clear distinction be made between the radical terrorists and the Chechen people as a whole.[52] Chernomyrdin argued that his decision to grant safe passage and to start talks under the OSCE's aegis in Grozny was not too high a price to pay to save the lives of the innocent civilians who had been taken hostage by the fanatics. He lashed out against Zhirinovsky and other politicians who called for a hard line and punitive action.[53] Chernomyrdin later commented: "The Russian state, almost for the first time in its history, I repeat, almost for the first time, put the life of its citizens above any political expediency."[54]

The Duma became the primary vehicle through which public exercised its democratic right to hold the government accountable for the mismanagement of national security institutions. According to the Russian Constitution, the Duma could register its protest in the form of a no-confidence vote in the Chernomyrdin cabinet. However, it takes two such votes to force a government to resign and after the second vote, the president has the option of dissolving the Duma and holding new elections or forming a new government. On 21 June 1995, the Duma voted solidly for a motion of no-confidence, 241–72. Following this vote, negotiations began between Duma leaders, Yeltsin, and Chernomyrdin over the future of the three power ministers, Grachev, Stepashin, and Yerin.[55] Instead of rejecting the Duma's call for changes at the top, Yeltsin decided to agree with their assessment that action had to be taken. He moved in two ways. First, he used his powers to increase security in the capital region and in the North Caucasus. Second, he used the Security Council, which included the speakers of the Duma and the Federal Council, to conduct an overall evaluation of the national security situation.

While the president and the Duma were attempting to reach a compromise on the power ministries, Shamil Basayev made new threats and boasted that he had special units ready to launch attacks in the capital. Because of such threats, Yeltsin needed to reassure Muscovites that the capital was safe so he ordered Grachev to provide 4,000 paratroopers and Yerin to assign 7,000 MVD troops to begin patrolling the capital immediately. He also pressed Stepashin to make security surveillance more effective. Military personnel complained that they were not being used properly—they were trained for warfare not for guarding markets, city bridges, and checking cars and trucks for weapons. They were paratroopers, not policemen. However, their commander, Col. General Yevgeny Podkolzin pledged to carry out the national security assignment with distinction.[56]

Yeltsin sent his Security Council secretary, Oleg Lobov, to Budyennovsk to determine how and why Russia's security services had performed so poorly. Yeltsin also scheduled a special session of the Security Council to evaluate the Budyennovsk incident and to take appropriate actions. The investigation did not single out the military for blame since domestic peace-keeping is the primary responsibility of the MVD and the federal security service. What had happened to the strong military, MVD and KGB commando units that democratic Russia had inherited from the Soviet dictatorship? The Yeltsin administration had reduced and weakened such units because democratic reformers viewed them as a serious threat to civil liberty. Now, that Russia needed more effective national security services, it would have to rebuild them.

The military used to have a Vympel unit that was trained to take heavily fortified urban targets. In February 1994 Yeltsin decided to transfer it from the Ministry of Defense to the MVD, a move that most Vympel officers regarded as a mistake and a major demotion. The military considered the MVD to be an inferior service. Therefore, 400 out of Vympel's 430 officers quit the unit. The KGB's best commando forces, the Alfa units had been reduced in size and kept in the Moscow region. They were highly trained—an expensive, elite unit considered too valuable to use in the Chechen conflict.[57]

Yeltsin consulted with Duma leaders about changes in the power ministries and settled upon retaining defense minister Grachev and replacing MVD chief Yerin and federal security boss Stepashin. He also removed Nikolai Yegorov who had been his plenipotentiary in Chechnya.[58] Once these changes had been agreed upon informally, Yeltsin convened the Security Council on 29 June 1995 to announce them as formal decisions. Yeltsin explained: "Russia and the entire world saw a demonstration of the low level of ability of our special forces to carry out assignments given to them." Consequently, new leadership was required. He also announced that a new, special antiterrorism center would be created and based upon units drawn from the three power ministries. But instead of escalating the war in Chechnya, Yeltsin endorsed the Grozny peace talks as the best way to end the conflict.[59] The political crisis blew over and the struggle for power between federal forces and the independence movement in Chechnya entered a new phase.

Professional Soldiers or Draftees?

The Ministry of Defense decided to increase the number of contract soldiers and to decrease the percentage of draftees serving in Chechnya. By April 1996, the number of contract professionals was 50 percent of the total military contingent in Chechnya. The Ministry of Defense expected to increase its weight to 100 percent over the coming year assuming that the main fighting was over and total number of personnel serving in Chechnya could be reduced.

This was not an isolated policy decision. It was the logical end result of democratization of Soviet society and of military efforts to follow America's lead and to build an all-volunteer army. The first trend developed in 1988–89 when Gorbachev's reforms gave the public the ability to protest against the government's policy of sending draftees to serve in Soviet hot spots such as the Caucasus. In 1990–1991, the fifteen republics placed restrictions on how and where their draftees could serve in the unitary Soviet armed forces. The Ministry of Defense resented such restrictions upon military service but adapted to them. The general rule had already become that only volunteers could be sent to serve in hot spots when the Soviet Union collapsed and the Soviet military was divided into republican armed forces.

The second trend—the transition from heavy reliance upon the military draft to an all-volunteer military, also began under Gorbachev as the armed forces and society learned more about the variety of military manpower systems in the advanced industrial states and began debating reform. Conservatives on the issue warned that contract servers were mercenaries not citizen-soldiers and that it would be better for society to retain the principle of universal military service. Progressives argued differently. Instead of focusing upon citizenship and the citizen-soldier issues, they concentrated upon military professionalism and compared the way military professionals were treated in the Soviet Union with their American counterparts. They argued that modern warfare required longer training and a heavier investment in each soldier—a real military career as opposed to a quick two years as a draftee. Military officers found the all-volunteer model attractive because it had positive implications for their own conditions of service.

Popular resistance to using draftees to serve as military pawns in ethnic-conflict zones and the general push for an all-volunteer army merged. The Duma supported the public and the Ministry of Defense decided to convert its main forces in Tadjikistan—a chronic "hot spot," into a completely all-volunteer or contract service operation.[60] In April 1996, all Russian military personnel in the main Russian contingent in Tajikistan—the 201st motorized division, were under contract and considered volunteers. Further, all Russian military personnel serving in former Yugoslavia were contract professionals. And, as noted 50 percent of those serving in Chechnya were volunteers but the Ministry planned to raise that to 100 percent.[61] According to Colonel General Vyacheslav Zherebtsov, chief of manpower mobilization, there were 270,000 personnel serving under contract out of a total Russian military force of some 1,600,000 in April 1996.[62] The defense ministry's long range plan was to increase the professional contract service or *profi* contingent to 50 percent of 1,500,000 by the year 2000, a target that could not be met due to insufficient funding.[63]

The Chechen war probably increased popular support for the all-volunteer army concept just as the public displeasure with the Vietnam war had done in the United States. The idea that all citizens were expected to spend some time directly contributing to national defense weakened in Russia and America. Modernization theory's emphasis upon increasing specialization and differentiation of function in society supports the trend.

The Uneasy Truce: Losing Slowly

The talks produced mixed results. Dudayev's representatives agreed to a military cease-fire but rejected Moscow's main demand that Chechnya must remain part of Russia. In order to get the cease-fire, a key rebel negotiator, Commander Aslan Maskhadov, accepted federal demands that illegal armed forces be disarmed and that the process begin immediately. He argued that political matters could not be settled until later and only if truly free elections were held. Shamil Basayev's brother was part of the negotiating team and he commented that free elections would have to permit the rebels to run independence candidates including Dudayev. Skeptics warned against accepting a cease-fire under these conditions. They expected Dudayev to use the peace to rebuild the rebel underground and to infiltrate areas under federal control.[64] Rebels showed Russian military reporters that they were still present in Grozny and the other cities that were supposedly under federal control.[65] To appease critics and to demonstrate his intention to keep Chechnya within the Russian state, Yeltsin issued an ukaz ordering the Russian military to establish permanent military bases in Chechnya. But he forgot to inform his negotiating team in advance. The Chechens threatened to end the talks and the Russian team temporarily degenerated into a bickering lot. But the cease-fire continued.[66]

The military began to complain that although they had virtually won the war, the civilians were losing the peace. Instead of pressing the military advantage, the Yeltsin administration focused on talks but avoided the most difficult political questions including bringing Shamil Basayev to justice for the terrorist attack at Budyennovsk. Major General Vladimir Burlakov commented: "We for some reason are giving in and forgetting about the losses that our armies suffered in Chechnya and our peaceful civilians in Budyennovsk." He found much in common between Dudayev's tactics and those the *mujaheddin* used successfully against the Soviet forces in Afghanistan.[67]

Nevertheless, Yeltsin pressed to extend and deepen the cease-fire. Contacts between federal forces and rebel fighters increased. Because the heavy fighting ceased, the Russian military took second place to the MVD. Yeltsin promoted commander of federal forces in Chechnya, MVD Col. General Anatoly Kulikov to Yerin's former position at the head of the entire MVD. Moscow wanted to believe that Dudayev had been defeated militarily and that the MVD could handle the task of restoring law and order in Chechnya. Duma deputy and military historian, Col. General Dmitry Volkogonov explained that in some cases no solution is a solution, that is, the Korean Armistice. In Korea the two sides stopped fighting but never agreed to a permanent settlement. He suggested that the same could happen in Chechnya, a way to buy time until the political situation matured to the point where a compromise settlement became possible.[68] Dudayev approved the military cease-fire but refused to abandon his ultimate goal, independence for Chechnya. He called his state the Republic of Ichkeria and issued his opinions as if he were the head of a sovereign nation. Volkogonov's prediction seemed to be coming true, Military press editorialists wondered why it had been necessary to fight and die for such an outcome?[69]

President Yeltsin confirmed that the war was over and offered his condolences to the families of those who died: "I bow my head in memory for those who gave their lives defending the fundamental values without which no state could survive. I express my deepest sympathy to the families, relatives, and to those near and dear to the Russian soldiers, officers, and peaceful civilians who died." Yeltsin agreed to begin withdrawing federal troops if and to the extent that the rebels disarmed illegal military formations. He

agreed to a relatively small permanent federal military presence in the republic, one MVD brigade and one military brigade. He accepted international monitoring by the OSCE. He announced that the Chechen side had
agreed to condemn terrorism and to assist in the search for those responsible for the terrorist acts at Budyennovsk.[70] He also spoke about his views
about the future. He insisted that the Chechens participate in the next regular elections to the Duma and the Federal Council. He pledged to rebuild
and revive Chechnya as part of Russian Federation. However, Dudayev had
never agreed to those points and Yeltsin was overselling the deal.

Instead of taking action to require rebels to disarm, the new commander of
federal armed forces in Chechnya, Lt. General Anatoly Romanov entered into
talks. In some places, rebels began transforming themselves into "legals" by
taking up positions and keeping order in areas that the federals did not control. Federal armed forces knew of such cases but as a rule did not force the
issue. They were supposed to keep the peace and engage in confidence-build-
ing measures with the locals. Local commanders were making unofficial deals
with one another to avoid conflict. This permitted the rebels to strengthen
their positions. They apparently counted upon becoming official, "legal"
members of the Chechen military and police forces in the near future. The
rebels neither disarmed nor accepted federal claims that they were "illegal
armed formations." Dudayev instructed them to consider themselves the legitimate armed forces of the Republic of Ichkeria. Chechen flags of independence and portraits of Dudayev began to appear.[71] Military analysts warned
that Dudayev was rebuilding his forces and winning a quiet victory. General
Kulikov warned that military force would have to be used if the Chechens
refused to disarm voluntarily.

The Yeltsin administration was not prepared to resume the warfare and the
Dudayev regime was not prepared to give the federal authorities peace. His
fighters began a series of mainly small scale attacks, just enough to keep the
pressure on Yeltsin and to intimidate the federal forces. Dudayev's message
was clear. No federal position was safe. Security council secretary Oleg Lobov
reported that the rebels had only turned in some 600 out of the 70,000 weapons that his intelligence sources said they had.[72] Yeltsin made Lobov "plenipotentiary for normalization." Moscow began pulling military forces out of
Chechnya without first disarming the rebels. On 20 September 1995, the rebels
made an attempt on Lobov's life. Although he escaped unharmed, the message was clear. Dudayev could strike at anyone.

Yeltsin's Political Calendar and the War

Regularly scheduled democratic elections are supposed to make political
leaders—even headstrong presidents like Boris Yeltsin, pay attention to public opinion. The calendar was working in Russian society's favor. Yeltsin knew

the war was unpopular and that he was supposed to face presidential elections in June 1996. Therefore, as 1995 came to a close, he kept pressing for a face-saving settlement in Chechnya. The rebels took advantage of his political calendar and used cease-fires to infiltrate and entrench themselves at the expense of the federal forces. The military described what was happening and predicted the eventual outcome, a political and military defeat. The soldiers had little reason to fight hard or enthusiastically in this situation. It became absolutely clear that they were in a no-win situation dictated by Kremlin political calculations.

Russia's military intelligence reported that Dudayev had appointed his own military commanders in every district of Chechnya. In the first half of September 1995, there were 408 attacks on federal forces and twenty-six federal troops were killed.[73] Dudayev blamed federal commander Lt. General Romanov for the increased tension. Yeltsin's special representative at the ongoing talks at Grozny, Arkady Vol'sky said disarmament was going normally. Romanov argued to the contrary. Defense Minister Grachev supported commander Romanov's assessment and said most of the so-called weapons that had been turned in were hunting rifles that belonged to elderly villagers. Dudayev had lost the main war but he retained the ability to mount small hit and run operations and was planning to do so indefinitely.[74] In October 1995, Chechen terrorist bombs severely wounded Lt. General Anatoly Romanov. In November, terrorists wounded Doku Zavgayev, the head of the federal reconstruction government for Chechnya. The rebels targeted Zavgayev because he was leading the pro-Moscow, Chechen reconstruction program.

President Yeltsin insisted that the residents of Chechnya hold elections on 17 December 1995 for regional leaders and deputies to the federal Duma. Dudayev threatened to disrupt the elections and launched small attacks, the most serious being on the town of Gudermes which resulted in several hundred casualties. However, federal authorities held elections and Doku Zavgayev was proclaimed the winner. This completed a long cycle that began when Dudayev ousted Zavgayev in September 1991. An ethnic Chechen in the Russian armed forces, Col. Ibrahim Suleimanov, ran for the Duma and was elected. Yeltsin proclaimed that the elections, although imperfect, marked Chechnya's restoration to the constitutional system. Dudayev vowed to continue his resistance.

Dudayev retained the ability to strike at federal positions and continued to fight into spring 1996. In January 1996, his special commandos staged another hostage-taking like the earlier Budyennovsk incident. This time they struck in Daghestan just to the East of Chechnya. That incident ended inconclusively though the fighting was heavier. Their next major attacks came in March 1996 and included fighting in and around Grozny. This compelled Yeltsin to thrown federal troops at Dudayev's bunkers in former Soviet ICBM silos around the town of Bamut. Yeltsin kept hinting that he would announce a dramatic policy shift to end the war but Dudayev kept federal military and political forces off balance. Dudayev held out for independence but was willing to give Russia security guarantees and to join the CIS. However, he insisted that Russian troops withdraw. Yeltsin kept backing Zavgayev.

After one year of armed struggle to defeat Dudayev's rebellion militarily, the Ministry of Defense reported that the total number federal military personnel killed was 1,928. The number of soldiers wounded in combat was placed at 5,487.[75] Civilian deaths were generally estimated at some ten times the number of federal combat losses, a number that confirmed that Dudayev had deliberately fought the war in a manner that put civilians at risk. Towns and villages were his cover.

Constitutional Court Considers the War's Legality

The Russian Constitution grants the president the power to impose a state of emergency on a region but requires him to notify the upper house or Federal Council and to obtain its approval in order to keep it in effect. Antiwar and anti-Yeltsin politicians raised this question in the Duma but could not get the Constitutional Court to agree to address the war's legality until the main fighting appeared to have ended in summer 1995.

In July 1995, the Russian Constitutional Court agreed to rule on the Chechen war's legality. Vice premier Sergei Shakhrai presented the Yeltsin administration's case. Yelena Mizulina (Federal Council) and Anatoly Lukyanov (Duma) argued for the opposition. The plaintiffs asked the Court to rule against the presidency in order to make the legislative branch of government an effective check on presidential dictatorship. They insisted that the Russian Constitution clearly intended to prevent presidents from using troops and waging war inside the Russian Federation without legislative approval. They pointed out that Yeltsin had in fact imposed a de facto state of emergency on Chechnya without following the procedures outlined in the Constitution for imposing a legitimate state of emergency. Shakhrai and the administration cited Russian laws and parts of the Constitution that empower and require the president to defend law and order and recited the familiar litany of Dudayev's violations of federal law.[76]

Because the case had enormous implications for the Chechen rebels and the federal forces, the talks in Grozny went into recess to await the Court's ruling. On 1 August 1995, the Court ruled that the use of armed force in Chechnya was legal and constitutional and that President Yeltsin had acted in keeping with his authority and responsibility.[77] There were dissenting opinions in the Court's report which was read to reporters and which took forty-five minutes to read. The Court argued that the fact that the war itself was constitutionally legitimate did not absolve those who did the fighting from legal responsibility for their actions. This was a bow towards the human rights activists who were deeply concerned about civilian casualties which were estimated at some 40,000. However, by refusing to rule against the Yeltsin administration, the Court averted a major national political crisis but it also set a dangerous precedent. The first president of post-Soviet Russia had fought a civil war without obtaining proper authorization from the Russian legislature. The Yeltsin administration continued to manage the Chechen affair as an executive branch operation.

The armed forces could never completely resolve the problem of what to do about potentially illegal orders from civilian and military commanders. After the August 1991 coup, Soviet Defense Minister Shaposhnikov wrestled with the problem and concluded that the military had to obey orders; otherwise, the military system could not operate. Therefore, he insisted upon written orders from civilian leaders, a step that made the civilians more accountable than the commanders. Grachev continued this policy by demanding that Yeltsin give him written orders to use the military on 4 October 1993. This practice was expanded for the federal campaign to restore federal power in Chechnya. President Yeltsin, the Security Council, and the Chernomyrdin government backed federal actions with official, published decrees. The president repeatedly reassured the armed forces that they were acting legally. But all this "legitimacy" came from just one branch of government, the executive branch and the post-Soviet, presidency until the Court took action and ruled that it was constitutional.

Conclusion

In democratic theory the state's governmental institutions are presumed to be tools which serve the people, a complex network of institutions created and maintained by the people for certain purposes. State institutions, including the professional armed forces, consist of public servants who serve the people and who are ultimately accountable to them. In post-Soviet Russia the uniformed soldier was both a sovereign citizen—one of the people, and an armed public servant skilled in the use of coercion to achieve political ends. When they were on duty and on military facilities, Russian law required soldiers to obey legitimate orders and prohibited them from engaging in partisan political activity. However, when they were off duty and off base, Russian soldiers had the right to criticize public policy—including war policy and to run for office. Nevertheless, in any political system, is difficult for soldiers to present themselves as loyal public servants and military team players if they are actively protesting government policies during their off-duty hours. In practice, the military is expected to obey civilian leaders and to stay out of partisan politics.

Russia's political problem was more societal control over the presidency than civilian control over the military. The Chechen war was launched by the executive branch of government without approval or endorsement from the legislative branch. The military and the Duma complained about insufficient consultation. The president of Russia, Boris Yeltsin made the key decisions with his Security Council, a dozen or so officials whom he had appointed and who depended upon his goodwill to stay in office. Had the president consulted with the Duma leadership and sought Duma endorsement, he would have been pushed towards negotiations with Dudayev. Had the president consulted more fully with the military leadership, he would have at least delayed the start of hostilities. Such delays would have reinforced the antiwar mood in the Duma and given Dudayev and antiwar politicians time to place more political and military obstacles in Yeltsin's path.

There is little evidence to support the idea that the Russian military wanted a war to improve its influence and status. From the outset, the military criticized the war and resented the civilian politicians who imposed war on an army that was neither psychologically nor professionally ready for it. The military accepted civilian control but resented civilian control by inept political leaders. Prominent and respected military professionals who dissented were removed from central leadership positions in the Ministry of Defense—a necessary and appropriate measure to reinforce civilian control and military cohesion. They paid a high price for professional honesty in a very difficult situation. The military system obeyed its civilian commander in chief and went to war but it never invested its best efforts in that conflict..

The decision to go to war was unpopular but not unpopular enough to cause either the Duma or the military to challenge President Yeltsin directly, to put him on the political spot by taking actions to force the issue. For example, the Duma might have tried to impeach the president. However, the impeachment process requires agreement between the Duma, the Federal Council, and the Constitutional Court. Further, it would have added danger and confusion to the situation in Chechnya and weakened military cohesion and viability.

The war's military critics, such as generals Gromov, Lebed, Mironov, and Vorobyev, pointed out that the Ministry of Defense collegium had not been asked to debate and vote on the war. Did they mean to argue that the collegium or top two dozen or so military leaders should have veto power over presidential decisions regarding war and peace? No, but they did imply that fuller consultation between military and civilian leaders would help prevent bad policy decisions. They were trying to initiate a discussion about how to make civilian control work more effectively. Under what conditions does civilian control produce better decisions? Worse decisions? On the one hand, it is difficult to argue with the notion that fuller discussion should produce better decisions. On the other, the principle of civilian supremacy requires that the military accept decisions that run counter to what military professionals believe is appropriate. But neither military nor civilian leaders benefit from situations where military professional advice is ignored or the military is bullied into ill-conceived operations by civilian leaders. Institutional arrangements can encourage consultation but will not guarantee that the political process will produce the best decision in every instance.

Yeltsin tried to repair relations with the military and the Duma. He made institutional changes to give the legislative branch a voice in key policy decisions by appointing the speakers of the Duma and the Federal Council full voting members of his Security Council. This thoughtful institutional change deserves praise. Yeltsin also began to consider ways to change the military's reporting relationship to the presidency and there was talk about naming a civilian minister of defense while retaining a military chairman for the General Staff. But that decision was postponed. Grachev remained loyal to Yeltsin and helped to keep the military cohesive and obedient to its civilian commander in chief. Grachev's work was as much political as military as he responded to antimilitary attacks from the antiwar movement, kept the war effort going, tried to enhance the military's share of the federal budget, represented Russia in international and near-abroad military affairs, and struggled to make headway on military reform. He was attempting to do too much and needed to rely upon stronger subordinates.

There is a fundamental contradiction between glasnost' or the open discussion of policy issues by military officers and the requirements of military cohesion. However, neither President Yeltsin nor Minister of Defense Grachev tried to prevent the military from thinking out loud and in print about its problems within reason. All democracies have formal and informal limitations upon policy discussion and debate within governmental agencies, particularly security agencies. In the Russian military, the first post-Soviet norms were quite liberal, a radical change from Soviet practice.

It was the first war the military had to fight without comprehensive political support from the Russian government, the mass media, and societal institutions. It was a war that the military itself criticized. It was the first time in modern Russian history since the Bolshevik revolution that an antiwar movement enjoyed the protection of the law. Officers and their civilian commanders in chief knew how to behave under dictatorship and were just learning how to behave in civil society. Mild treatment of dissent and opposition within the military was a definite break with Soviet political culture. New mores and expectations were beginning to emerge. Things had changed from the Soviet system which required the military to praise the national civilian leaders even when they made huge policy blunders and committed major crimes against military professionals and civilians alike. The post-Soviet military was developing an independent point of view which must have made some civilians uneasy.

Notes

1. See Charles Tilly, "War Making and State Making as Organized Crime," in Peter Evans, Dietrich Rueschemeyer, and Theda Skocpol, eds., *Bring the State*

Back In (Cambridge: Cambridge University Press, 1985).

2. In July 1990, Gorbachev ordered the Armenian irregulars to disarm but they refused. Gorbachev compromised and allowed them to become "regulars" under Levon Ter-Petrosyan's non-Communist, nationalist, Armenian government. This compromise ended the Soviet regime's monopoly on armed force and was a sign that the unitary Soviet state was breaking up.

3. See Robert V. Barylski, "Russia, the West, and the Caspian Energy Hub," *The Middle East Journal*, vol. 49, no. 2, 1995, pp. 217–32.

4. See pp. 192–93 in N. N. Novychkov et al., *Rossiiskiye Vooruzhennye Sily v Chechenskom Konflikte: Analiz, Itogi, Vyvody* (The Russian armed forces in the Chechen conflict: analysis, conclusions, and lessons), (Paris & Moscow: Holveg-Infoglob, 1995).

5. See *Ibid.*

6. See *Ibid.* p. 6.

7. See Sh. Aushev, "Iz Groznogo: O situatsii v Checheno-Ingushetii" (Grozny: Situation in Chechen-Ingushetia), *Krasnaya zvezda*, 23 October 1991.

8. See N. N. Novichkov et. al., *Rossiiskiye Vooruzhennye Sily*, p. 7.

9. See "Official Statement by the Ministry of Defense of the Russian Federation" (in Russian), *Krasnaya zvezda*, 18 January 1995. See pp. 13–17 in N. N. Novichkov et al., *Rossiiskiye Vooruzhennye Sily*.

10. See Vladimir Gavrilenko, "Kazhdyi politik dolzhen byt' gosudarstvennikom" (Every politician needs to be a statesman), *Krasnaya zvezda*, 24 February 1993.

11. See Dmitry Balburov, "Chechen opposition leaders make strange bedfellows," *Moscow News*, no. 36, September 9–15, 1994.

12. Elke Wendisch, "Does Chechen Crisis Mark Khasbulatov's Last Encore?" *Moscow News*, no. 40, October 7–13, 1994.

13. See p. 13, N. N. Novichkov et al. *Rossiiskiye Vooruzhennye Sily.*

14. Vladimir Ermolin, "Dvoe rossiiskikh voennosluzhashchikh uzhe spaseny" (Two Russian military servicemen already rescued), *Krasnaya zvezda*, 6 December 1995.

15. Alexei Venediktov, "Dzhokhar Dudayev: 'This is Intervention, Pure and Simple...,'" *Moscow News*, no. 48, December 2–8, 1994; and Vladimir Ermolin, "Dvoe rossiskikh voennosluzhhashchikh."

16. See Aleksandr Pel'ts, "Chechen Knot: Presidents Actions Fully Constitutional" (in Russian), *Krasnaya zvezda*, 2 December 1994.

17. Yeltsin used a word for "Russians" which means all the peoples of Russia (*Rossiyane*) not just ethnic-Russians (*Russikye*). English translations fail to convey the proper meaning of most of his speeches because the English language has only one word for *Rossiyane* and *Russkiye—Russians*. The former really means "inhabitants of Russia." The latter refers only to the ethnic Russians.

18. Boris Yeltsin, "President's address to participants in the armed conflict in the Chechen Republic" (in Russian), *Krasnaya zvezda*, 30 November 1994.

19. *Krasnaya zvezda*, 30 November 1994.

20. Aleksandr Pel'ts, "Chechen knot."

21. These surnames suggest that the committee was of Jewish, Russian, and Ukrainian heritage. It wanted to promote civil liberties, human rights, and inter-ethnic accord.

22. Vladimir Lysenko, "Chechen Trap for the Democrats," *Moscow News*, no. 49, December 9–15, 1994.

23. See. for example, comments by lead editorialist Aleksandr Gol'ts, "Nad propast'yu vrazhdy" (At the edge of the abyss of hatred), *Krasnaya zvezda*, 3 December 1994.

24. There were twelve members in addition to President Yeltsin. Yeltsin had the power to appoint of dismiss members by presidential *ukaz*. The council consisted primarily of the heads of the foreign, military, security, police, border defense, and intelligence services. See Ilya Bulavinov, "Changes in the Makeup of the Security Council," *Kommersant-Daily*, 11 January 1995; *CDSP*, vol. 57, no. 3, 1995, p. 19.

25. Minister of Grachev's press conference at Mozdok on 11 January 1995 as reported in *Krasnaya zvezda*, 12 January 1995.

26. See pp. 18–19 in N. N. Novichkov et al., *Rossiiskiye Vooruzhennye Sily*.

27. Aleksandr Pel'ts, "Zona konflikta: voiska gotovy deistvovat' reshitel'no" (Conflict zone: armies ready for decisive action), *Krasnaya zvezda*, 7 December 1994.

28. "V poslednii chas" (The latest...), *Krasnaya zvezda*, 7 December 1994.

29. "Konflikta mezhdu Chechnei i Rossiei ne suchchestvuyet. Est' lish' bor'ba za vlast'" (It is really a battle for power. There is no conflict between Russia and Chechnya), *Krasnaya zvezda*, 9 December 1994.

30. Petr Karapetyan and Vladimir Ermolin, "Na zasedaniyakh palat Federal'nogo sobraniya" (At the Federal Assembly), *Krasnaya zvezda*, 9 December 1994.

31. Aleksandr Pel'ts, "Chechnya: obstanovka ostayetsya slozhnoi" (Chechnya: situation remains complex), *Krasnaya zvezda*, 10 December 1994.

32. Rozalina Ryvkina and Yury Simagin, "Expert Opinion: The Status of Chechnya: The Population vs. The Authorities' Position," *Sevodnya*, 18 July 1995. *CDSP*, vol. 47, no. 30, 1995, pp. 13–15.

33. Cited by Pavel Felgengauer, "Protest: General Vorobyev On The Reasons For His Resignation," *Sevodnya*, 24 December 1994. *CDSP*, vol. 46, no. 51, 1994, pp. 7–8.

34. See pp. 60 and 178–80 in N. N. Novichkov et al., *Rossiiskiye Vooruzhennye Sily*.

35. V. G., "In Brief: Col. Gen. Kondratyev Is Confident He's in the Right," *Nezavisimaya gazeta*, 21 January 1995. *CDSP*, vol. 47, no. 3, 1995, p. 25.

36. Col. General Boris Gromov, cited by Aleksandr Zhilin in "Chechnya Plans Kept From Deputy Defense Minister," *Moscow News*, no. 2, 13–19 January 1995.

37. Lt. General Aleksandr Lebed, "Regiments of Bob-Soldiers Suffer A Defeat," *Moscow News*, no. 1, 6–12 January 1995.

38. *Ibid.*

39. Lt. General Lebed as cited by Aleksandr Zhilin in "General Lebed Has Passed the Test," *Moscow News*, no. 5, 3–9 February 1995.

40. "Chechnya: khronika sobitii" (Chechnya: chronicle of events), *Krasnaya zvezda*, 31 December 1994.

41. See Yury Gavrilov, "Poslednii dolg pavshim" (Final duty to the fallen), *Krasnaya zvezda*, 10 November 1996. See chapter 6 below.

42. See *Krasnaya zvezda*, 5 & 6 January 1995.

43. Interviewed by Anatoly Borovkov, "General-lietenant Lev Rokhlin: 'Ya svoi dolg vypolnil chestno" (I fulfilled my duty honorably), *Krasnaya zvezda*, 9 June 1995.

44. It should be remembered that the federal armed forces consisted of various military and MVD units. The MVD's OMON units had earned a bad reputation in 1990–1991 and were involved in the Samashki incident.

45. See Ivan Rodin, "Parliament: Stanislav Govorukhin vs. Sergei Kovalyev," *Nezavisimaya gazetas*, 20 April 1995. *CDSP*, vol. 47, no. 16, 1995, pp. 5–7.

46. Dmitry Pogorzhelsky, "Award: Sergei Kovalyev is First Winner of International Human Rights Prize," *Sevodnya*, 19 September 1995.

47. Vladimir Maryukha, "Soldat voinu ne vybirayet" (The soldier doesn't pick war), *Krasnaya zvezda* 13 Janaury 1995.

48. Pavel Grachev, Press conference at Mozdok on 11 January 1995; *Krasnaya zvezda*, 12 January 1995.

49. Vladimir Maryukha, "Soldat voinu ne vybirayet" (The soldier doesn't pick war), *Krasnaya zvezda*, 12 January 1995.

50. "Obrashchenie voinov chastei i podrazdelenii rossiiskikh voisk, nakhodyash-chikhsya v Chechenskoi respublike" (Appeal from the fighters of the units and detashments of the Russian armies stationed in the Chechen republic), adopted on 24 January 1995 and published in *Krasnaya zvezda,* 28 January 1995.

51. Vitaly Strugovets, Anatoly Stasovskii, "Khronika tragedii v budyennovske" (Chronicle of the tragedy at Budyennovsk), *Krasnaya zvezda*, 20 June 1995.

52. See "President Boris Yeltsin's Appeal to the Russian People" (in Russian), *Krasnaya zvbezda*, 20 June 1995.

53. See Oleg Odnokolenko, "Net nichego tsennee zhizhni..." (There is nothing more valuable than life...), *Krasnaya zvezda,* 20 June 1995.

54. Cited by Steven Erlanger, "Yeltsin Shakes Up Top Cabinet Posts To Quell Criticism," *New York Times,* 1 July 1995.

55. Yevgeny Yuryev, "Plenary Meeting of the State Duma: The Government's Defeat Does Not Mean A Victory For The Duma," *Kommersant-Daily,* 22 June 1995. *CDSP,* vol. 47, no. 25, 1995, pp. 14–15.

56. Konstantin Petrov, "Voiska v Moskve—mera vynbuzhdennaya..." (Armies in Moscow—a necessary measure...), *Krasnaya zvezda,* 24 June 1995.

57. See p. 67 in N. N. Novichkov et al., *Rossiiskiye Vooruzhennye Sily.* Based on Russian press accounts, *Moskovskii komsomolets,* 5 January 1995.

58. In August 1995 Yeltsin announced that the former head of the Kremlin guards, Mikhail I. Barsukov, had replaced Stepashin at the head of the Federal Security Service.

59. Boris Yeltsin's televized remarks at the Security Council meeting of 30 June 1995, *Krasnaya zvezda,* 30 June 1995.

60. However, there were indications that when asked to volunteer for service in the 201st motorized infantry in Tajikistan, officers believed that their military careers would be quickly terminated unless they accepted.

61. See Oleg Falichev, "Prizyv-96: kto vstanet pod boevye znamena" (The 1996 call-up: who will stand under military banners), *Krasnaya zvezda,* 11 April 1996.

62. See *Ibid.*

63. See Oleg Falichev, "Voennaya reforma kak zerkalo rossiiskoi ekonomiki" (Military reform-a reflection of the russian economy), *Krasnaya zvezda,* 10 April 1996.

64. Petr Karapetyan, "Peregovory v Groznom podoshli k reshayushchemu rubezhu" (Negotiations in Grozny have reached a decisive point), *Krasnaya zvezda*, 4 July 1995.

65. Col. Aleksandr Andryushkov, "Skhron v Groznom" (Hideout in Grozny), *Krasnaya zvezda,* 30 June 1995.

66. Petr Karapetyan, "Peregovory v Groznom..." (The talks in Grozny...), *Krasnaya zvezda,* 5 July 1995.

67. Col. Aleksandr Andryushkov and Col. Sergei Pryganov, "U Dudayevskikh boevikov" (With Dudayev's fighters), *Krasnaya zvezda,* 7 July 1995.

68. Dmitry Volkogonov, "...A budushchee uzhe nachato" (But the future is already here...), *Krasnaya zvezda,* 18 July 1995.

69. Oleg Odnokolenko, "Chechenskaya voina zakonchilas?..." (Is the Chechen war over?...), *Krasnaya zvezda,* 3 August 1995.

70. Boris Yeltsin, "Real'naya vozhmozhnost' ustanovleniya mira v Chechne, a znachit, i v Rossii" (A realistic chance to establish peace in Chechnya means in Russia as well), *Krasnaya zvezda,* 5 August 1995.

71. Anatoly Mikhailov, "V poslednyi chas" (The latest), *Krasnaya zvezda,* 11 August 1995.
72. Vladimir Ermolin, "Sredi razvalin Chechni..." (In a ruined Chechnya...), *Krasnaya zvezda,* 1 September 1995.
73. Vladimir Gavrilenko, Anatly Stasovskii, "Chechnya: na Olega Lobova soversheno pokushenie" (Chechnya: Attempt made on Oleg Lobov), *Krasnaya zvezda*, 21 September 1995.
74. Pavel Grachev, Press conference of 25 September 1995; *Krasnaya zvezda,* 27 September 1995.
75. Ministry of Defense Information Service, "They Fulfilled Their Military Duty To The End" (in Russian), *Krasnaya zvezda*, 10 Decembver 1995.
76. See Aleksei Kirpichnikov's reports in *Sevodnya*, 18 & 19 July 1995. *CDSP*, vol. 47, no. 29, pp. 10–11.
77. Aleksandr Pel'ts, "Konstitutsionnyi sud priznal: prezident deistvoval v rankakh Konstitutsii Rossii" (Constitutional court ruled the president acted within the bounds of the constitution of the Russian federation), *Krasnaya zvezda*, 2 August 1995.

13

The Military's 1995 Political Offensive

Russian military officers returned to the political front in 1995. An ideologically diverse group of active and retired military professionals crossed the dividing line between the military occupations and full-time, civilian political work. Although the military candidates assembled under different political banners, they shared a common goal—the election of enough pro-defense officers to tip the Duma's political balance towards stronger defense policies, higher military spending, and overall state strengthening. The Ministry of Defense fielded some 120 non-partisan military candidates. But there were others who ran on party lists. Some were notorious military figures who several years earlier had tried to overthrow President Yeltsin and Defense Minister Grachev. Others were democratically oriented critics of the administration's policies. If elected, military discontent from the left, right, and center would have a constitutionally protected voice.

This chapter begins with Grachev's decision to encourage officers to run for Duma seats, describes his 120 nonpartisan candidates, and examines Russian military views about military participation in politics. It then briefly discusses the most prominent officers who ran on partisan and opposition tickets, analyzes the election's results, and evaluates the new "militarized" Duma defense committee which was chaired by Lt. General Lev Rokhlin. The chapter concludes with remarks about what this episode in Russia's civil-military relations contributes to our general understanding of the military's role in political life.

Civilian Control: Personalities and Political Culture

During 1994 and 1995, Minister of Defense Pavel Grachev and Duma defense committee chairman Sergei Yushenkov became political enemies. To some extent this was both a clash of personalities and a confrontation between old and new political culture. Neither the imperial nor the Soviet political heritage had prepared the Ministry of Defense and the president for the new politics. The Ministry of Defense was not used to cooperating with democratically empowered civilians and lower-ranking officers who, as elected peoples deputies, claimed the right to penetrate its hallowed domain, to gain a full understanding of its budgets and policies, and to begin reshaping them. It was difficult for Army General Grachev to accept the fact that elections had made Colonel Sergei Yushenkov, a former military professor of Marxist-Leninist philosophy, one of his primary civilian controllers.

Yushenkov tried to make the Duma's defense committee an effective vehicle for civilian control over the military. Yushenkov was familiar with how legislative oversight worked in the industrial democracies. He attended Western seminars on civil-military relations and visited with American and European legislators. He also knew that neither Russia's Ministry of Defense nor Russia's president was inclined to give the Duma committee a powerful voice in defense affairs. This inevitably led to tension between him and Grachev and between him and the presidential administration which treated the armed forces as its exclusive political space. This was understandable since the executive branch of government had directly controlled the military throughout Russian history. It had been that way under the imperial tsars and the Communist general secretaries and was continuing under Russia's first democratically elected president, Boris Yeltsin. Even Duma deputies friendly to the military complained that Grachev never provided the Duma with enough information.[1]

In 1994 when the Russian press was debating military corruption and the murder of Dmitry Kholodov, Yushenkov argued that military reform would fail unless Russia established stronger civilian control over the military and appointed a civilian minister of defense. When the Yeltsin administration went to war in Chechnya, Yushenkov criticized the war policy, Grachev's management of its military aspects, and Yeltsin's failure to seek the Duma's consent before making war. After nearly a month of such criticism, Grachev lashed out. He denounced Yushenkov, questioned his motives, and came close to calling him a traitor. At a 20 January 1995 press conference at the Mozdok military base, Grachev bitterly criticized Yushenkov, antiwar Duma deputies such as Sergei Kovalyev, and the press:

> And this peacemaker, Deputy Kovalyev! But no place has been left to put another stigma on him! He is an enemy of Russia, a traitor to Russia!...This Yushenkov, this skunk, for whom no other epithet can be found, reviles the very army which gave an education and rank to him. Regrettably, in keeping with a resolution, he is still a colonel in the Russian army. And he, this skunk, is defending those scoundrels who want to ruin the country. I don't understand this.[2]

It wasn't just the criticism that bothered Grachev, he was furious that Kovalyev, Yushenkov, and others were able to build enough political pressure in Moscow to get Yeltsin to offer truces and cease-fires to Dudayev, halts in the fighting which disrupted and confused Grachev's war plans. He regarded such civilian control as negative and misguided interference in military combat operations, incompetent meddling that would cost the Russian armed forces lives, prolong the fighting, and undermine the Russian position in Chechnya.[3]

Instead of giving Grachev his full support, Yeltsin decided to reaffirm *civilian* presidential authority to command the armed forces. In mid-January 1995, Yeltsin made two related moves which appeared promising but which in fact solved nothing. First, Yeltsin decided that it would be best to place some distance between the Chechen war and Grachev. Yeltsin transferred overall responsibility for the federal armed forces in Chechnya from the Ministry of Defense to the Ministry of Internal Affairs (MVD). Second, he started reevaluating the Ministry of Defense's reporting relationship to the office of the presidency.

Yeltsin Wrestles with Command and Control Problems

Since the Ministry of Defense's primary mission is defense against *external* enemies and the Ministry of Internal Affairs' primary task is defense against *internal* enemies and the Chechen war was an internal rebellion rather than a foreign war, it was appropriate to put the Minister of Internal Affairs in charge of the combined federal forces operating in Chechnya. On paper and in Yeltsin's Security Council, the shift appeared logical. But in practice the MVD lacked the organizational talent, military experience, and political clout to coordinate and lead the war effort well. MVD chief Sergei Stepashin had been an MVD political officer and a politician not a manager. Even though he lacked high level administrative experience, Yeltsin made him the leader of the country's internal police and armed forces. Stepashin had neither major combat command experience nor real political clout. Further, although Stepashin and the MVD were supposed to coordinate all armed forces operations in Chechnya, the Ministry of Defense continued to regard the MVD as a lower level, junior military organization. And it was. Therefore, Yeltsin could not rely upon Stepashin alone and wanted direct links to the military.

Yeltsin opened a direct reporting line to Chief of the General Staff Mikhail Kolesnikov, Grachev's immediate subordinate.[4] Now there were two top military leaders reporting to the president—the minister of defense and the chief of the General Staff. This was a warning to Grachev that he might be sidelined. The command line was supposed to run straight from Yeltsin to Kolesnikov and on to the field commanders fighting in Chechnya. This strengthened Yeltsin's wartime role as commander in chief of the Russian Armed Forces. Grachev retained overall responsibility for military reform, relations with the near-abroad, and general management of military affairs. These changes seemed to be pointing towards a future reform, Grachev's probable replacement by a civilian defense minister. However, instead of following through and pressing this dual-ledership model on the Ministry of Defense, Yeltsin quietly backed out of it and Grachev remained the paramount leader in military affairs. Yeltsin announced the dual-leadership reform on 11 January 1995 but only three days later it was being described as just a policy option, one model among several being considered.[5] Grachev's media liaison, Elena Agapova, suggested that no major changes in the Ministry's structure could be considered until the national economic and political situation had stabilized. Other military commentators denounced the plan as Yushenkov's effort to split the Army from Grachev.[6]

Military Needs Its Own Lobby in the Duma

The military's general discontent with the Chechen war, the defense budget, and national politicians needed a constructive outlet. In early 1995, the Ministry of Defense's daily *Krasnaya zvezda* began promoting the idea that the armed forces and its natural allies in the military industrial complex had to learn to play the political game. They had to get directly involved in elections by supporting some candidates and denying support to others.

Aleksander Piskunov—deputy chairman of the Duma's defense committee, an expert on the defense budget, and a friend of the military, reminded military leaders that politics often counted more than substance when the federal budget was being carved up. Piskunov explained that the agricultural lobby, the new commercial groups, the oil and gas industry, and the bankers had their own lobbies. Each jealously guarded its share of the budgetary pie and refused to surrender any part of it to the military. Although business people, bankers, oil, and gas industry people understood that Russia needed strong national defense, their own sectorial interests came first. Piskunov concluded: "This raises the question of the Army's participation in parliamentary elections. The Army needs its own representatives in the deputy ranks."[7]

Ministry of Defense editorial writers repeated that theme: "The Army needs its own people in parliament just like the agrarians and Gazprom, the banks, and the others."[8] The paper promised to tell its readers how various deputies and Duma factions voted on key bills and urged them to use such information, rather than political campaign promises, to judge the candidates during the next Duma elections in December 1995. Aleksander Gol'ts, a prominent military editorial writer, held up America as a model for Russia. Gol'ts explained that America's national defense lobby was so popular in the United States Congress that the Pentagon received more than it asked for in 1995! Given the size of Russia's military and Russia's military-industrial complex, he concluded that Russia could have a defense lobby as strong as America's and argued that defense interests should unite to build one.[9] However, he also warned military personnel against giving their votes to extremist political parties and urged them to support responsible candidates. Gol'ts was advocating that the military advance its interests by learning to play the new political game well. This was quite different from radical nationalists who called for major structural changes in the new democratic order.[10]

The Defense Ministry's Policy Shift

In April 1992 when Yevgeny Shaposhnikov reviewed the country's experience with military personnel holding elective office, he told the Russian Parliament that the practice was of little benefit to the country or its Armed Forces. He noted that most "civilized countries" prohibit it. However, when Parliament wrote its first set of post-Soviet laws on defense, it reaffirmed the military's right to run for office, to be elected, and to serve. Nevertheless, Pavel Grachev, post-Soviet Russia's first minister of defense, disagreed with Parliament and, like Shaposhnikov before him, warned officers against trying to mix military and political careers. Grachev set the tone for the military as a whole and discouraged officers from running in the 1993 Duma elections. His warnings had the anticipated chilling affect on would-be candidates among active-duty personnel.

Grachev somewhat naively expected the Duma which was elected in December 1993 to be pro-defense even without experienced combat generals and military administrators among its ranks because all major parties and candidates had called for a strong Russia during the electoral campaign. But he was wrong and the new "anti-Yeltsin" Duma did not challenge the Yeltsin administration's basic defense spending guidelines. The Duma kept the defense budget at roughly 5 percent of GDP and 20 percent of the total federal budget even as GDP fell and inflation raged. The Duma rejected Grachev's calls for an upward revision in the 1,500,000 position target for Russian military personnel and forced Grachev to cut hundreds of thousands of positions a year. (He was some 400,000 positions above the 1,500,000 target.) Further, the Duma refused to revise the military conscription system and to enforce draft laws properly. The Duma set defense procurement orders and research and development contracting so low that Russia was in danger of losing its ability to produce new weapons and falling behind in the global competition for military modernization. Russian society was still reacting against Soviet militarism—the excessive defense burdens that the Soviet state had imposed on the people. National defense was caught between popular resentment and declining federal revenues. The people's representatives in the Duma were not going to cut social services, education, and subsidies to agriculture in order to increase defense spending.

Therefore, the top military leadership reassessed its position and decided that the military needed its own voice in the Duma. Grachev told Soviet reporters that he discussed the policy change with the Ministry of Defense Collegium and that the military leadership approved it.[11] Since Grachev reported to President Boris Yeltsin who had the power to appoint and remove all top military administrators and military commanders, it is reasonable to assume that Yeltsin either approved Grachev's new policy or, at a minimum, found it tolerable. Because the anti-Yeltsin opposition was actively courting military officers and urging well-known military dissidents to stand for election, the

Yeltsin administration probably decided that it would be prudent to have some of its "own" military in the Duma, officers who could be counted upon to serve as a stabilizing force.

The Ministry of Defense wanted candidates who supported strong defense but who rejected political radicalism. Lt. General Sergei Zdornikov, the Ministry's chief of military political education, expressed it this way: "Military personnel are convinced that Russia must not permit another *revolutionary upheaval,* a radical change in national policy directed by ambitious leaders asking us to believe one more time in some *beautiful future*...Russia needs stability...and the revival of a great and powerful State.... That is who we will vote for and not for those fly by night birds who are mainly interested in comfortable nests for themselves."[12]

Personal, institutional, and national political interests were at stake in the elections. The Ministry needed Duma deputies who shared its views of the proper role of the army and not all civilian and military candidates fit that profile. Some anti-Grachev, retired military officers were running for office. If such dissident officers were elected and took control of the Duma committees responsible for defense, police, and security affairs, Grachev and others could find their positions and policies in jeopardy. Since the Duma writes the laws and sets the national budget, the entire military establishment had a stake in the elections. So did the country as a whole since the state's ability to provide for the national defense would be affected by the quality and efficiency of the Duma's legislative work and of the Duma's political relationships with the president, the government, and the Ministry of Defense.

The Ministry of Defense's Nonpartisan Candidates

There are 450 seats in the Russian Duma. Half are elected from single-mandate electoral districts and half are elected through party-list voting. When candidates run for one of the 225 single-mandate seats, they have the option of running either as partisan or nonpartisan candidates.

Grachev knew that the Ministry of Defense was supposed to be nonpartisan and he wanted normal, stable military professionals to win Duma seats. How could he encourage active-duty military officers to run and still successfully ward off accusations that he had violated federal legal prohibitions against partisan politicking inside the armed forces? He solved the problem by getting active-duty officers to run as nonpartisan candidates for the single-mandate seats. The nominations were made, the signatures were gathered, and the "vetted" military candidates were entered in the political race. The officers ran as independents rather than as members of electoral blocks or parties. The total number of such "vetted" candidates was roughly 120 which was divided into some forty generals and admirals and some eighty middle-level officers.[13]

As soon as they had registered and been accepted as candidates by the Central Electoral Commission, Grachev put them on temporary leave from military work but they continued to receive their military salaries in keeping with Russian law. The also had access to free media time and to some campaign expense money from public funds. Grachev adopted a correct public position towards these candidates and avoided blatantly using military resources to promote them although all received some coverage in the official military press. *Krasnaya zvezda* published a list of 119 military candidates on 15 December 1995, only two days before Duma election day. However, during the month prior to the list's publication, the paper carried feature stories on about a dozen such candidates but those stories did not say that they were running for office.

Krasnaya zvezda's candidate list gave each military candidate's name, rank, position, and electoral district. Although this isn't a great deal of information, when sorted by rank it yields some interesting data. Grachev wanted mature military personnel to run for office and he got a professionally mature set of candidates, one dominated by full colonels, generals, and admirals. It included: five admirals, thirty-six generals, sixty-seven colonels, four majors, six captains, one sergeant.

At first glance it appeared that Grachev was going to conquer the Duma by mobilizing the full voting power of the entire military industrial complex behind the 120 candidates. One of Grachev's rivals, then recently "retired" Lt. General Aleksander Lebed claimed that Grachev had told commanders that he would factor politics into their annual professional evaluations because he and the military needed pro-defense deputies in the next Duma. Lebed said that Grachev wanted at least fifty elected and had circulated a list of their names.[14]

A Military Coup via the Ballot?

A large military bloc would have been a power within the Duma. What were the 120 candidates' political aims? Were they entering politics to support the president or to promote military corporate interests? Were they inspired more by patriotism, military professional interests, or personal ambition?

One of Grachev's listed candidates, Rear Admiral Valery Aleksin spoke about the elections as a functional substitute for a military coup. He began by sounding the patriotic alarms: "Russia is heading for catastrophe." Aleksin argued that it was time for the 40,000,000 people whose fates were linked to national defense to act through the ballot box. He saw the electoral process as a peaceful alternative to a violent coup: "The most progressive, clear-headed, and responsible elements in the Russian officer corps, those with a high level of organizational ability and administrative experience, have to enter the new Duma in order to use legislation to guarantee the bloodless correction of the reform for the sake of society and the state and to save Russia."[15]

Aleksin knew that his remarks were upsetting some civilian political analysts. But he pointed out that most of the so-called demokraty were former Communists themselves. He characterized them—not without some justification, as a group of former teachers of Marxism-Leninism, academic researchers, graduate students, actors, directors, and evening school instructors who declared themselves "democrats" and took power. From his vantage point, because they lacked major political and administrative experience, they were not qualified to lead Russia. Their ill-conceived reforms had brought Russia to the brink of collapse. Therefore, Russia needed new leadership. Aleksin insisted that the Russian military was precisely the reservoir of patriotic, selfless, leadership talent that the nation required.[16] Although it sounded as if Aleksin was advocating a legal, "corrective" military coup, he and Grachev really wanted something more modest, a purge of the Duma's defense and security committees. They were after Yushenkov. There was also some truth behind Admiral Aleksin's charges that political officers rather than experienced commanders and administrators had used politics to take control over national defense affairs in the legislature.

Colonel Sergei Yushenkov, the chairman of the outgoing Duma's defense committee, was precisely one of those political instructors that Admiral Aleksin had criticized. When Yushenkov first ran for national office, he was teaching philosophy at the Lenin Military Political Academy in Moscow. Through politics professor Yushenkov won the power to shape military laws and budgets and to badger the Ministry of Defense and the minister of defense. Yushenkov's deputy chairman, Colonel Aleksandr Piskunov, the Duma's expert on military budgets, was running the computer operations at the Plesetsk space center when he ran for national office.[17] Elections, not a long apprenticeship inside the Ministry of Defense's financial management organization, made him the Duma's top expert on the military budget. Similarly, Sergei Stepashin, the chairman of the defense committee in the parliament that Yeltsin toppled in October 1993, was a political officer in the MVD when he ran for office. By standing for election and winning, Stepashin leaped into the highest levels of policy making in national security affairs. Then by joining Yeltsin's faction and working with him during the August 1991 coup, Stepashin earned Yeltsin's confidence and respect and this led Yeltsin to make him chief of the MVD. Thus, politics got Stepashin to the very top leadership position in his profession. By the same token, it was politics that gave Grachev the top position in the Ministry of Defense, Grachev's close association with Boris Yeltsin before, during, and after the August 1991 coup.

When the press first learned that Grachev was placing a political army of some 120 military candidates into the December 1995 Duma elections, there was a predictable flurry of articles that criticized the Ministry for getting into politics.[18] Yushenkov knew that he was Grachev's main target and he reacted angrily. Yushenkov warned that Grachev was trying to fill the Duma with obedient people "who, without thinking, will vote to increase the terms of service, the size of the Army and military spending, without any explanation as to where the money will go." He further suggested that "Grachev would have done better to keep his mouth shut, then everyone would at least have been able to pretend they hadn't noticed that the Defense Ministry is headed by an incompetent man who is out of touch with Russia's interests and thinks only about himself and his close associates."[19]

Should Military Professionals be Full-Time Legislators?

However, prospects for a Duma dominated by Grachev's 120 candidates were rather bleak for four reasons. First, the fact that a candidate wore a military uniform and had a military career was not enough to attract favorable public attention. Second, Russian law prohibited the Ministry of Defense from using its resources aggressively to promote its 120 candidates and their opponents watched this very carefully. Third, the 120 were running as independents without the backing of any major political movement such as the Communists and the Liberal Democrats. Further, the major parties had their own military candidates on their tickets and they represented diverse political points of view rather than a single military line. Fourth, given the diversity of party and nonparty military candidates, it was difficult to convince readers that the group would coalesce into a cohesive "military" threat.

Although *Krasnaya zvezda* gave some of the 120 military candidates special feature stories, it also printed a thoughtful interview with Aleksei Tsarev who contended that military expertise was insufficient preparation for success at politics in the legislature. Tsarev used his career as an example. Tsarev started his political career as a political officer, a commander's assistant for military education with the rank of lt. colonel.[20] He served briefly as a mayor before getting into national politics where he chaired a security affairs sub-committee under Sergei Stepashin in the Russian parliament (1990–1993).[21] Tsarev admitted that most deputies, including himself, neither knew how to run the legislative process efficiently nor had the technical expertise required to write good laws. Further, by the time he and his colleagues had learned their new political jobs and had started to produce better legislation, Yeltsin disbanded their Parliament. Then came the new elections and most of the team that had been writing defense and security legislation was replaced by a new set of legislators who had to learn the process from scratch. Now, just as they began functioning smoothly, another round of elections was about to turn out them out of office.[22]

Tsarev's story contained important lessons for the Russian military. There is no easy transition from being an effective officer to being an effective legislator. It is not the same profession. Merely getting officers elected to the Duma will not guarantee that they will be effective at writing law or at making the political deals required to move their legislative agenda forward. Further, it takes time to adjust to the new roles, to learn how to operate politically, and to master the intricacies of writing law.

If we apply Tsarev's insights to the list of 120 military candidates that the Ministry of Defense was promoting, we find a rather motley group, one not well prepared for legislative work. On the whole they were neither well known nor particularly well informed about the military's overall needs. There was only one highly visible military commander among them, Colonel General Yevgeny N. Podkolzin, commander of Russia's elite paratrooper forces. He ran in the 149th electoral district in Ryazan, a city with a large military constituency. Most of the other generals on the list were heads of military conscription boards, political commissars, political officers, or heads of military institutes or departments within them. The list included twenty-one military commissars. Although the position title sounds impressive, military commissars are the administrative heads of the military conscription organizations for cities and regions—hardly popular figures during an unpopular war. It made no political sense to put this group into the electoral process unless Grachev really could not get stronger candidates to agree to run.

There were also fourteen political officers or commander's assistants for educational work running as candidates on Grachev's list. Back in 1990, a cohort of political officers was elected and became to core of the military reform group in the Russian parliament. However, Tsarev's point was valid. Experience as a political officer was better training for public speaking and campaigning than for writing laws and making the political system work effectively. Further, after August 1991, political officers or educational specialists fell to the bottom of the military profession. Their numbers had been slashed and their status had been downgraded by the military itself which had long resented Communist political military educational and control officers in its midst.

Another sixteen military candidates were either faculty or administrators in the military educational system. There were about fifty candidates who were either departmental chiefs (*nachalniki*) or deputy department heads from a wide range of military administrative offices or commanders of small to middle-sized military units in one service or another. Such middle-level military professionals did not have high level administrative experience and were not prepared to grasp the entire defense budget in its full complexity. The presence of a large number of military commissars, political officers, military academics, and middle level administrators on Grachev's lists could not but undermine prospects for success. There must have been something more to this than mere political naiveté. One possible explanation was that the military leadership did not want to get on either the pro-regime or pro-Grachev political bandwagon. It was safer to act through the secret ballot than to stick one's neck out politically.

The Military and the Pro-Regime Party

Under the Soviet system, the military was required to align itself with the ruling Communist party. However, under the post-Soviet, Yeltsin "system," the secret ballot and the practice of having military personnel vote at civilian polling places enhanced the average soldier's ability to make a free choice. Opinion surveys prior to the election suggested that most military personnel would vote for opposition parties such as the reformed Communists and the neofascist, nationalist Liberal Democratic Party of Russia.

The Soviet dictatorship controlled professional rewards and punishments and trained the officers to toe the regime line. Soviet elections were rituals through which the military demonstrated its political loyalty by supporting the regime slates. That practice started breaking down under Gorbachev and Yeltsin ended it when he abolished special Communist Party and all partisan organizations inside the military system. But instead of building a national political party of his own to replace the Communist Party, Yeltsin tried to manage without one. And when his regime's supporters finally got around to realizing that they needed a strong national political party in order to be effective in the 1993 Duma elections, it was too late. Further, Yeltsin never gave their efforts his full personal support. Instead, he presented himself as a national patriot who stood above partisan politics. Meanwhile the Communists began to rebuild and to appeal to popular discontent with the Yeltsin administration's record.

For the 1995 Duma elections, the regime's supporters faced a major challenge. Prime Minister Viktor Chernomyrdin became the figurehead for the pro-regime political party called Russia Our Home (Nash Dom Rossiya). The party's message was that Russian national interests required that the Russian government persevere and carry its reform program to completion. Its chief rivals, the Communist Party of the Russian Federation (CPRF) and the Liberal Democratic Party of Russia (LDPR) argued that the regime had failed and that the Russian people should use their votes to protest against the regime's policies. Instead of standing firmly with Chernomyrdin and campaigning vigorously, Yeltsin distanced himself from Russia Our Home. It wasn't just a matter of Yeltsin's poor health (major heart problems) because Yeltsin could have used taped messages, etc. It was more a matter of political judgment and attitude. He simply did not give high priority to party building. However, this did not mean that leading members of the Yeltsin administration could belong to opposition movements or remain strictly neutral. Thus, defense minister Grachev was expected to give at least mild public support to Russia Our Home which was a signal to top officers that they and their families ought to do the same. Grachev told reporters that he was supporting President Yeltsin and Russia Our Home.

But, Russia Our Home's leaders were unhappy with the military's decision to run independent, military candidates. Sergei Belyaev, Russia Our

Home's chief organizer, expressed concern about the military vote and the military's strategy. Belyaev pointed out that instead of aligning itself with the Yeltsin administration, the military had distanced itself. Grachev had used the non-partisan lists to avoid being forced to get on the Russia Our Home bandwagon. Grachev's 120 "nonpartisan" candidates were a warning from the military to the Yeltsin administration that the military was seeking political autonomy and leaning towards the opposition.

> It would seem that if the president of the country and the minister of defense have defined their positive attitude toward Our Home, the military must support them. In reality, however, even the representatives of the higher command personnel have been divided among different blocs. Moreover, many seek to get a seat in the Duma to stand up solely for the army's interests there. The lobbying by the military for their own interests to the detriment of the interests of the whole nation is an extremely dangerous phenomenon.[23]

Belyaev predicted that the military would mainly vote for the Communists (CPRF), the moderate nationalists of the Congress of Russian Communities (CRC), and the administration (ROH). He also expected a significant vote for Zhirinovsky's LDPR.[24]

Why? Because military officers were unhappy with Yeltsin's record. This was confirmed by information obtained from the Ministry of Defense's internal sociological research staff. Based upon polling data from 1990–1995, the Ministry knew that there had only been a small improvement in positive sentiment since the low point in 1992 when 12 percent were satisfied while 88 percent of military officers were dissatisfied with material conditions. Sentiment improved somewhat from 1992 to 1993, when 29 percent said they were satisfied. Then it began to slide as the economic depression and inflation took their toll. On the eve of the 1995 Duma elections, only 21 percent of the officers told military sociologists they were satisfied which meant that 79 percent were discontented.[25]

If the Yeltsin-Chernomyrdin administration had adopted a more pragmatic political attitude towards the defense constituency in 1993 and 1994, it would not have found itself facing a potentially serious defense constituency voter "rebellion" in 1995. The warning signs were patently clear ever since the 1993 Duma elections but the Kremlin and the Duma persisted in ignoring complaints from the armed forces and the defense industrialists. The military saw itself politically isolated and abused. It had become the scapegoat that carried away the accumulated public resentment towards the Brezhnev administration's heavy defense spending and its foreign policy misadventures such as Afghanistan. Gorbachev's perestroika had an antimilitary, antidefense orientation. Yeltsin's policies for post-Soviet reconstruction continued in that vein. Although his spending priorities favored military personnel somewhat more than defense procurement, he could not deliver on his promises. The military was unhappy with its professional condition and with the situation in the country as a whole.

Lt. General Lev Rokhlin: Russia Our Home's General

The regime's party knew that an antiregime protest vote was looming and that the national defense constituency would be part of it. Therefore, Sergei Belyaev tried to improve Russia Our Home's appeal to military voters. Yeltsin and Chernomyrdin cooperated by promising to pay military back salaries and government debts to the military-industrial complex. However, they refused to promise any large increases in defense spending.[26] Belyaev needed more than that and hoped to get popular generals onto the Russia Our Home ticket. He therefore courted Lt. General Lev Rokhlin—the soldier who fought to victory in central Grozny for the federal government in January 1995 but who later rejected military honors for that "victory." Rokhlin was the very embodiment of the military's anger and disappointment with Chechnya and of its stoic ability to maintain discipline and loyalty to the State and Russia. Russia Our Home hoped that the military would follow Rokhlin's example and stick it out for the long haul by voting for pro-regime candidates.

Rokhlin allowed Russia Our Home to place his name near the top of its party list. This meant that if the party won more than 5 percent of the popular vote, Rokhlin would be given one of the 225 party-list seats in the next Duma. Thereafter, he would have an opportunity to work for a strong Russia and a strong national defense as a national political leader. But Rokhlin told reporters that he was not cut out for politics and he warned that he would not take his seat if elected.[27] I don't think that Rokhlin was being disingenuous. He knew that the federal government wasn't functioning well but as a military professional, he tended to see partisan politics as one of the main sources of Russia's difficulties and he could not see himself in the Duma as a Duma politico, a military version of either Zhirinovsky or Gaidar. Politicking wasn't like soldiering. It did not fit the military professional's view of how life's problems should be solved. Generals tend to think that the best form of administration is a highly rational bureaucratic system in which experts solve problems and subordinates obey their decisions. In that vein, Rokhlin argued that "honest, well-organized and uncorrupted people from our ranks" will be capable of getting the country moving.[28]

Other Military Candidates

With the exception of Rokhlin, the best known military candidates ran for office under opposition banners; that is to say, they were not on Russia Our Home's party list. There were about a dozen such retired notables arrayed along the political spectrum. At one end there were progressives such as Col.

General Edvard Vorobyev who had resigned in protest over Yeltsin's handling of the Chechen war. At the other end there were semi-authoritarian ethnic-Russian nationalists such as Col. General Vladislav Achalov. Further, there were at least three generals running for the Duma who were regularly mentioned as future presidential candidates: Gromov. Lebed, and Rutskoi. Therefore, the Duma elections became a test of their ability to attract the Russian electorate.

Lt. General (Ret.) Aleksandr Lebed joined a political organization called the Congress of Russian Communities (CRC), a party that supported a strong Russia and protection of Russian interests in the near-abroad.[29] Although Lebed helped defeat the August 1991 coup, he never gained Yeltsin's confidence and was "exiled" to Moldova where he mixed military and political work as the controversial commander of Russian 14th Army in Moldova where the Russian-speaking Transdniestrian enclave had tried to achieve political autonomy. Although many credited Lebed for having stopped a major civil war between Slavic Transdniestrians and the Romanian-speaking majority in Moldova, he used his command and his Transdniestrian base as a political fortress from which he frequently criticized Yeltsin and Grachev. They tolerated his maverick behavior for three years until they reorganized and downgraded his command. Lebed resigned from the military in July 1995 rather than accept a lesser posting.

Thus, in fall 1995 Lt. General (Ret.) Lebed was at liberty to operate as a full-time politician even though he continued to describe himself as a patriot and an officer. He claimed that politics was an extension of his military-patriotic duty to defend the nation's security. He presented himself as a statesman, patriot, and soldier—anything but a politico.

In order to give himself two chances to be elected, Lebed ran for an individual seat in the Tula region and on the CRC party list—a practice allowed under Russia's electoral system.[30] Lebed did not disguise his presidential ambitions. Prior to the Duma elections, Lebed was often mentioned as a Yeltsin rival and a figure who could unite the national defense lobby. However, during the Duma electoral campaign, he neither established a clear image of himself nor offered the voters a definite reform program. At times he worked with military statists such as Col. General Igor Rodionov, commandant of the General Staff's military academy, to promote a political movement within the armed forces under the guise of conferences to discuss professional improvement and change. Rodionov invited top officers and military attaches representing foreign governments to the first conference of the Honor and Homeland movement in October 1995. The Lebed-Rodionov conference's success provoked an immediate response from Grachev and the Yeltsin administration. They quickly organized their own national conference on military reform in order to prevent Lebed and Rodionov from seizing the initiative.[31] Lebed's candidacy, his links with Rodionov, and the conference were signs that confirmed that there was some political activity within the military, political activity which neither Yeltsin nor Grachev could control. Further, Yury Skokov, who headed the Russian Security Council until his political break with Yeltsin, was also working with Lebed in the CRC. Skokov's ties to the military industrial congress were expected to benefit the CRC but Lebed and Skokov could not work together effectively.

Gennady Zyuganov's Communist Party of the Russian Federation (CPRF) did a better job at courting the national defense vote than either Russia Our Home or the CRC. The Communists had the most effective national political organization and the largest number of supporters in fall 1995. Zyuganov asked voters to throw the dilettantes out of office and to replace them with experienced political and managerial professionals such as Anatoly Lukyanov, the speaker of the last Soviet parliament, Pyotr Romanov a prominent industrialist, and "war horses" such as Col. Generals (Ret.) Albert Makashov and Valentin Varennikov. The CPRF presented itself as the responsible opposition, a better choice for voters than the radical extremists clustered around Vladimir Zhirinovsky's LDPR and smaller radical groups. However, Makashov's presence on the CPRF ticket was a warning that there were elements in the CPRF coalition who, if given a chance, would probably support a new state of emergency regime, one under CPRF leadership.

Makashov had been one of Gorbachev's most vocal critics when perestroika's unanticipated consequences began to undermine the USSR. Makashov helped organize military support for development of a Russian Communist Party in 1990–91 in opposition to Gorbachev's group which controlled the Communist Party of the Soviet Union. Yet, Gorbachev did not deprive him of his command at the head of the important Volga-Urals military district. Makashov supported the state of emergency coup against Gorbachev in August 1991. After the coup, Makashov was forced into retirement by Shaposhnikov, Gorbachev, and Yeltsin when they purged the top military leadership. Yet, Makashov refused to stay out of politics and became a radical, para-military opponent of the Yeltsin administration. Makashov led pro-Parliament fighters in an assault on the Ostankino radio and television center on the night of 3–4 October 1993. For that political violence, he was arrested and held in prison until the amnesty of February 1994.

Col. General (Ret.) Valentin Varennikov, another prominent actor in the August 1991 coup, also got on the CPRF bandwagon. During the August 1991 coup Varennikov was deputy minister of defense and commander of Soviet land forces. He was part of the elite delegation of military and civilian coup leaders sent to confront Gorbachev at Foros. After "telling" Gorbachev to line up behind the coup, Varennikov flew to Kiev to bully Ukraine's president, Leonid Kravchuk into accepting the new order. During the coup Varennikov demanded that the wobbly coup leaders act decisively. After the coup, he was retired as part of the post-coup purge of the military leadership.

In 1995, Varennikov was using democratic elections to continue his fight for a strong State and for the reintegration of most former Soviet republics into an effective economic and defense organization.

The CPRF also lined up Lt. General (Ret.) Mikhail Surkov, the last head of the Soviet Communist Party's special branch inside the Soviet armed forces. Surkov claimed that the coup's leaders had left him out of the August coup's planning; however, in the weeks immediately before the August coup, he issued special appeals to Communist officers in the military, called for vigilance and unity, and supported the military's criticism of Gorbachev's "weak" leadership. By training and career Surkov was a military political professional whereas Makashov and Varennikov were soldiers and military commanders. Surkov served on the Politburo of the Soviet Communist Party from April to August 1991. At that time, he advocated economic and political reform under a strong regime and resisted efforts to free Soviet military officers from the political discipline imposed by mandatory membership in the Communist Party. He argued that Gorbachev's reform program could only be implemented by a well-disciplined political party. However, in spring 1991, Surkov opposed using the Soviet military for coercive domestic political operations.[32] After the August coup, Surkov said, "I've been at the Central Committee for a year and at the Supreme Soviet for two—that's enough, I'm sick and tired of big-time politics."[33] But in December 1995, he was back in politics.

On the one hand, the Communists correctly argued that the Russian electoral system rewarded big coalitions and punished splinter movements. Therefore, it made sense for the opposition to unite under the CPRF banner. This appealed to the older generation in the military opposition. On the other hand, the Party had neither a clear program nor an organizational system that could forge a stable consensus within its ranks. Thus, the more diverse elements it gathered under its banner, the more difficulty it had running an effective campaign. The Party wanted to present itself as a constructive alternative to Yeltsin but its radicals condemned Ivan Rybkin who had served constructively as speaker in the previous Duma. They claimed that he had made too many compromises with the Yeltsin administration. He had been too constructive. The rift between Rybkin and Zyuganov resulted in a split and Rybkin organized his own small electoral block.

More generals who played important roles in the political events of 1991 and 1993 were on other tickets. Col. General (Ret.) Vladislav Achalov and KGB General (Ret.) Aleksandr Sterlingov created their own political movement, the Union of Patriots to field its own candidates in the 1995 Duma elections. The CPRF was too moderate for them and too cosmopolitan. The Achalov-Sterlingov Union was an ethnic nationalist movement with a strong anti-Western orientation. Sterlingov continued to charge that the West had engineered the Soviet Union's collapse. He and Achalov demanded that all Union candidates demonstrate that they are authentic ethnic Russians.[34]

(Achalov had served as commander in chief of the Soviet elite paratroopers before becoming Yazov's first deputy minister of defense. In that capacity he coordinated military preparations for the coup.) The Union of Patriots condemned Zyuganov's Communist Party as the successors to the non-Russian, cosmopolitans who for some seventy years brought ruin to the country. Their murky ideology combined ethnic-Russian nationalism and authoritarianism with calls for national repentance and reconciliation. Sterlingov's former boss, Vladimir Kryuchkov who headed the KGB during the August coup and Viktor Anpilov who repeatedly incited violence in September-October 1993, ran on another party's ticket, that of the radical "true" Communists who accused the mainline CPRF of abandoning authentic Communist positions. Stanislav Terekhov, the chairman of the radical nationalist Union of Russian Officers ran for a Moscow district as a member of the National Republican Party of Russia—another neo-fascist movement. On the other hand, former KGB General Oleg Kalugin—one of the "old" KGB's most prominent liberal critics, was also running for office but on the ticket of a small party called For an Honest Russia.

Former vice president of Russia, Col. General (Ret.) Aleksandr Rutskoi refused to cooperate with the Communists, the ethnic-nationalists, the pro-Yeltsin statists, and the Zhirinovskyites. Rutskoi organized his own statist party called Derzhava or Power in the sense of "state power." Although he had presidential ambitions, Rutskoi continued to be a maverick and to have difficulty building any stable political coalition.[35] After being elected vice president in June 1991, Rutskoi became alienated from his president, Boris Yeltsin, and sided with Parliament. Rutskoi was arrested for inciting armed insurrection on 3–4 October 1993 and released under the February 1994 amnesty.

Several deputy ministers of defense who had broken with Grachev over the Chechen War also ran for Duma seats. Col. General (Ret.) Edvard Vorobyev ran as an independent and Col. General Boris Gromov organized and registered his own political movement, My Fatherland[36] although Duma speaker Ivan Rybkin had tried to bring him into the Ivan Rybkin bloc.[37] Gromov was still on active duty but he was working in the Ministry of Foreign Affairs on Russia's international military relations, especially the near-abroad portfolio.

Duma speaker Ivan Rybkin supported the military's effort to get more officers and supporters into Parliament. He argued that the military and the Duma needed to be better informed about military needs and the national budget's ability to provide for them. He was generalizing upon his own political experience. Just as he had learned to make constructive compromises, he expected any newly elected citizen soldiers to strive to do the same once they had taken their seats in the Duma and seen the bigger national picture. The Army needed to learn to work the political ropes. Other groups had been better at the political process and the military was late coming to the game. Duma speaker Rybkin concluded that the electoral process was the right vehicle: "I am not frightened by the Army's preelection activity. It would be much worse if the military used arms to press its demands as happened in 1917." [38]

The 1995 Duma Elections: An Overview

Russia's 1995 Duma elections were highly competitive and the political spectrum was decidedly fragmented. Grachev's 120 nonpartisan candidates faced stiff competition. For the 225 single-mandate seats, there were some 2,600 candidates competing or an average of about ten candidates per seat.[39] The maverick and independent soldiers who refused to join any of the larger parties also faced stiff competition. Russia's election laws set a 5 percent barrier which parties must cross to get into the distribution of party-list seats. All groups which receive 5 percent of the popular vote or more share the 225 seats proportionally. Groups which fall below the 5 percent line receive no seats whatsoever.

The electoral system was designed to discourage small political parties. By dividing themselves among dozens of parties and/or running as independents, the candidates were not behaving rationally.[40] Such irrational behavior was widespread and there is no reason to believe that military candidates were any smarter politically than their civilian counterparts in this regard. It would take more experience with the system for basic political-technical knowledge to become widespread in Russia.

The Russian Federation's basic Law on Defense bans all partisan political activity from Russian military institutions and prohibits military personnel from using Ministry of Defense assets, institutions, and personal to support or to oppose any candidates or parties. Strictly speaking, Grachev could not use military institutional assets of any kind to support particular candidates. But he was also prevented from blocking military access to political information. The Central Electoral Commission (CEC) ruled that it was appropriate to permit would-be candidates to inform military personnel about their intentions and to collect signatures for their nomination petitions. CEC Chairman, Nikolai T. Ryabov, issued various interpretations of the laws and rules to the Ministry of Defense.[41]

Grachev set up a small department under Col. Vladimir Vlasov to provide organizational and technical support for the electoral process in the Army. The Ministry decreed that the military commanders at all levels were accountable for the proper implementation of Russia's electoral laws in the institutions and bases they administered.[42] On the one hand, military district, base, and unit commanders were instructed to be strictly neutral and to prevent any partisan political activity inside military facilities. On the other, they were supposed to facilitate the exercise of military political rights.[43] Grachev was adamant about where partisan meetings, candidates nights, and the actual voting were to take place—off base and outside military institutions.

Politicians knew the law but tried to get around it. Vlasov complained: "They try just about everything to get into the military bases and into the garrisons in order to agitate and to advertise their programs and platforms.... There is practically no region where the parties have not tried to get representatives into the military units."[44] Since there were some four dozen parties and electoral blocks and thousands of nonpartisan candidates who wanted military signatures for their petitions, the commanders had their hands full.

The Ministry insisted that military voting be done with civilians at civilian voting polling places because Grachev wanted to make it very difficult for political analysts to identify the military vote as a separate item for public political discussion. After the 1993 elections, analysts noticed that the military voted overwhelmingly for the Communists and the Liberal Democrats. This information was a political embarrassment to Grachev. However, it was also proof that Yeltsin and Grachev did not control the military vote. Things had changed from Soviet days when soldiers had to vote for the regime's candidates. Under the Soviet system, group votes were sometimes turned in by commanders. Further, officers were permitted to cast several votes as a matter of convenience to free members of their families and units from actually having to vote. Soviet officials demanded virtually 100 percent participation and some 98–100 percent of the vote was supposed to be for the regime's slate. All such Soviet political habits were supposed to be changed. People had to vote in person, in secret, and at civilian voting places.[45] The ballots caste by military voters abroad were sent back to Russia and mixed into the election reports for civilian polling places. For example, ballots from Russian military units stationed in Georgia, Armenia, and Azerbaijan were to be sent some 400 miles away to a Russian city for tabulation.[46] Such procedures protected the secrecy of the military vote, enhanced the military's ability to vote without fear of reprisal, and helped protect Grachev and the commanders from political backlash.

Although it was clear to all political observers that the pro-Yeltsin forces were going to suffer a major set back at the elections, President Yeltsin rejected suggestions that the Duma elections should be postponed. He sent word from the hospital where he was recovering from an October heart attack that he believed it was extremely important to hold the elections as provided by the law. He was categorically against postponement and criticized efforts being made to raise doubts about their legality.[47]

A recovering but still weak Yeltsin addressed the Russian people on 15 December 1995 and urged them to vote and to caste their votes for parties, individuals, and groups that were dedicated to reform. He delivered a similar message in December 1993, one that set him above the political fray as president of all the Russians. He directed his message to the different generations. To the older citizens who were more inclined to support the CPRF and the LDPR, he spoke about the terrible suffering the country had experienced under previous regimes and urged them to persist and to persevere until the current reforms bore fruit. To the younger generation, he provided encouragement and urged them to vote to strengthen the reform process and to reject the radical politicians. He complained that his fellow citizens had been judging him "harshly, at times mercilessly" and asked them to be as hard on themselves and to think very carefully before casting a vote for an extremist. Though, he avoided naming any party, the message was clear.[48]

The Ministry of Defense followed the Yeltsin line in its editorials but added mild endorsements for responsible military candidates. It urged voters to reject extremists and reminded them that there were responsible military candidates in the field and concluded that their participation had on the whole raised the quality of the political debate. It suggested that the public had stopped fearing the military and expected the officer corps to generate at least some leaders capable of helping Russia to solve its problems: "Today you can hear the thought from authoritative political scientists and sociologists that namely from military circles a new constellation of sober-thinking, responsible, political actors could arise." Since democratic countries such as the United States had elected top officers to the highest political office, it would be "normal and natural" for the same to happen in democratic Russia.[49]

On election day, the military voted in large numbers. Defense Ministry sources reported that over 90 percent of military personnel voted and the voting process was handled in a well-organized, correct manner.[50] Military participation was far higher than the 64 percent participation rate for the general population, a fact that politicians would certainly notice. Civilian reporters tried to isolate the military vote for special analysis but had difficulty since military and civilians voted together. However, there are voting districts with large military populations and where defense industries were the dominant employers. In those areas, according to spotty reports in *Krasnaya zvezda*, the voters followed the national trend and voted primarily for opposition parties. The CPRF and the LDPR received the largest number of votes in the military areas. There were clusters of votes for the pro-Union, Communist die-hards from military personnel in the Caucasian republics.[51]

The national results on the party-list voting were as follows: 22.3 percent voted for the CPRF, 11.2 percent for the LDPR, 10.1 percent for ROH, and 6.9 percent for Yabloko (Yavlinsky's democratic reformist group). No other party received more than 5 percent of the vote. Therefore, all the 225 party-list seats went to just four parties: 99 to the CPRF, 50 to the LDPR, 45 to ROH, and 31 to Yabloko. In the 225 single-mandate districts the voters generally rejected the LDPR which won only one such seat! The CPRF won 58, ROH won 10, and Yabloko won 14 seats. The remaining single-mandate seats went to a combination of nonpartisan and party-identified candidates. The initial, combined tally of party list and single-mandate seats gave the Communists about one third of the Duma's 450 deputies. The four main parties were the: CPRF (157 deputies), ROH (55), LDPR (51), and Yabloko (45).[52] When the Duma assembled in January 1996, there were some 120 delegates who did not belong to any of the four main parties. Some joined together to form independent factions but the CPRF, ROH, and Yabloko party faction leaders dominated the Duma committee assignment process. The CPRF was the dominant party within that group and one of its leaders, Gennady Seleznyev became the Duma's speaker.

Only ninety deputies were veterans of the 1993 Duma. This meant that 80 percent were "freshmen."[53] Although the Duma elected in December 1993 served just two years, the new Constitution stipulated four-year terms for the Duma deputies elected in December 1995. However, they were not guaranteed a four-year term because the Russian Constitutions empowered the President to dissolve the Duma and to call new elections if an impasse developed between the executive and legislative branches of government.

Military Candidates: Winners and Losers

Most of Grachev's military candidates lost. Only two of the 119 officers who ran as single-member district candidates were elected: Colonel Ibrahim A. Suleimanov who represented Chechnya and Colonel Yevgeny Zelenov who represented a Novgorod district. Suleimanov was the military commissar for Grozny. (Since Grozny was in ruins and under military occupation, that election cannot be considered normal.) Zelenov was a deputy unit commander in the air force. The remaining 117 "vetted" officers lost. In the overwhelming majority of cases, they were defeated by civilians.

Six lost to other military candidates. In four of the six cases, the victors were well-known national figures: Colonel General Boris Gromov, Colonel Sergei Yushenkov, Colonel General (Ret.) Edvard Vorobyev, and veteran cosmonaut German Titov. The fifth winner was Colonel Yevgeny Loginov, an outspoken supporter of Zhirinovsky's LDPR and a former instructor in the military's national political academy. The sixth, Major General Nikolai M. Bezborodov defeated a regional military commissar. All six winners belonged to the opposition, that is to say, they were opposed to the Yeltsin administration's national defense policies and/or handling of the Chechen war. But they did not constitute a united opposition. Grachev's most prominent military candidate and commander, Col. General Mikhail Podkolzin, ran in Ryazan's 149th district. Although Ryazan had a large defense industry, the voters elected Leonid M. Kanayev, a civilian industrial manager who ran under the CPRF banner.

The Communists did well. Col. General Varennikov, Col. General Makashov, and Lt. General Surkov, were elected to the Duma and thereby gained special rights and immunities. This strengthened their ability to organize retired and active duty officers into a more effective political lobby and opposition movement. Cosmonaut Titov, also a CPRF member, was expected to cooperate with them. The generation of military leaders that was defeated in August 1991 regrouped under the CPRF's banner and under the protection of the 1993 Constitution and won a protected voice in national political life.

But the radical nationalists and Union restorationists—Achalov, Anpilov, Kryuchkov, Sterlingov, and Terekhov were all soundly defeated.[54] So was the perennial maverick, former Vice President Aleksandr Rutskoi. Political structures and public opinion worked against them The electoral system was designed to reward politicians who joined broad coalitions and to punish those who insisted upon creating their own splinter movements. And it worked precisely that way. Small parties did poorly. But the main reason the extremists lost was that the public rejected their ideas.

In some cases, a popular individual survived involvement with a weak party. Lt. General (Ret.) Aleksandr Lebed was elected to represent Tula, a region that has been part of Russia's military-industrial complex for more than three hundred years. He got some 40 percent of the popular vote in his district; however, the political party he had linked up with, the Congress of Russian Communities did poorly. It received only 4.29 percent of the popular vote in the party-list balloting. For all practical purposes, the CRC had no influence in the Duma and Lebed would have to cooperate with other parties and politicians in order to have a voice in Duma affairs. But since he presented himself as an honest, independent, and uncompromising political leader, he did not fit in and he received no major committee appointments.

Some independent military reformers were elected in the Duma. The group included Vladimir Lopatin who had started pressing for military downsizing, contract service, alternative service for conscientious objectors, and for stricter enforcement of the military code in Gorbachev's legislature, and Nikolai Stolyarov, a moderate reformer who helped Gorbachev to restrain Makashov's hardliners politically at the Russian Communist Party's congress in summer 1990 and who supported Yeltsin during the August 1991 coup. However, because Lopatin and Stolyarov were elected as independents in single-mandate districts and were not part of the "big four" parties in the Duma, they could not expect to be given any important Duma committee assignments.

Russia Our Home—the party that supported the Yeltsin administration got two military candidates into the Duma, Lev Rokhlin, the "hero" of the battle of Grozny, and Sergei Petrenko, head of the Russian Afghan war veterans organization. Lt. General Rokhlin quickly emerged as the Ministry of Defense's preferred candidate to take command of the military and defense lobby or, more accurately, to pull the diverse factions together to form an effective national defense lobby. Rokhlin had absolutely no experience in legislative politics. He was a soldier's soldier whom the media had made into a national political figure, a military officer who upheld his oath to obey legal orders and simultaneously criticized the entire bloody mess. He agreed to run because the country needed a sober-minded, battle-scarred general on the administration's ticket. Still, he threatened to refuse to be seated if elected.

The New Defense Committee

But Yeltsin and Grachev needed Rokhlin to save them, the military, and Russian security from a major political crisis. They could not permit the new Duma to place its national defense committee in the hands of the Communist war horses—Makashov, Surkov, and Varennikov. Neither could they accept either Gromov or Vorobyev at its head since they had broken with Grachev and Yeltsin over the Chechen war. Yet, these two former deputy ministers of defense were far better prepared for political and legislative leadership than Rokhlin. In theory, General Lebed was also available but he had two strikes against him. First, he was a maverick whose political views were still changing. Second, he was not a member of one the Duma's four main political parties. What about former Duma defense committee chairman Sergei Yushenkov? He was too liberal and too independent for the Communists and too unpopular with the Ministry of Defense's leadership. The most he could hope for was a general position on the committee.

The CPRF, Russia Our Home, the LDPR, and Yabloko faction leaders negotiated and bargained over the Duma committee chairmanships. Their negotiations produced a defense committee with a balanced, diversified membership. Although Lt. General Rokhlin was a member of the Russia Our Home faction which had only one-third as many deputies as the CPRF, the four main parties agreed to make him chairman.

Lt. General Lev Rokhlin presided over a committee with 23 members, himself included. The party breakdown was as follows: LDPR 7, CPRF 5 , Agrarians 1, ROH 4, Yabloko 1, small parties and independents, 5. Although the LDPR had the largest single party group on the committee—including LDPR chief Vladimir Zhirinovsky, the committee had a moderate majority.[55] Chairman Rokhlin had four deputy chairman: Aleksei Arbatov (Yabloko), Major General Nikolai Bezborodov (Narodovlastiye), Colonel (Ret.) Mikhail Musatov, and Lt. General (Ret.) Mikhail Surkov (CPRF).[56] The rest of the committee included: Vladimir Zhirinovsky (LDPR), Mikhail Glushenko (LDPR), Colonel Yevgeny Loginov (LDPR), Stanislav Magomedov (LDPR), Yegor Solomatin (LDPR), Col. General (Ret.) Albert Makashov (CPRF), Aleksandr Mikhailov (CPRF), Svetlana Savitskaya (CPRF), Vladimir Volkov (CPRF), Anatoly Yaroshenko (Agrarian), Aleksandr Martynov (ROH), Col. Ibrahim Suleimanov (ROH), Roman Popkovich (ROH), Lt. General (Ret.) Aleksandr Lebed (independent), Col. (Ret.) Sergei Yushenkov (independent), Col. General (Ret.) Edvard Vorobyev (independent), Colonel Yevgeny Zelenov (Russkiye regiony).[57]

There was no room on the defense committee for early reformers Vladimir Lopatin and Nikolai Stolyarov, Cosmonaut German Titov, Col. General Boris

Gromov, or Col. General (Ret.) Valentin Varennikov. However, Varennikov was given chairmanship of the Duma's committee on veteran affairs a position from which he could organize support for the CPRF among military retirees and veterans. Gromov, Lopatin, and Stolyarov were in limbo so to speak because of their non-partisan status which in effect excluded them from powerful committee positions.

Rokhlin's Leadership Ideal—No Politics!

Lt. General Lev Rokhlin brought military-professional values to parliament. His first task was to instruct his deputy chairmen, general committee membership and staff to put aside partisan politics and to get down to work. Their main duty was to the country and their main goal was the improvement of national defense. Therefore, Rokhlin stressed military professional values such as patriotism, technical competence, and teamwork.[58]

Instead of treating his four deputy chairmen as representatives of four different political orientations, he described them as three experienced military professionals and one responsible civilian who had served in the previous Duma and therefore had useful knowledge of the parliamentary process. Rokhlin argued that their sense of patriotism and professional commitment to teamwork and cohesion would permit the committee to work efficiently and productively. Rokhlin formed nine subcommittees and assigned his deputy chairmen areas of primarily responsibility. He conducted a broad assessment of existing and pending legislation governing national defense and began to establish priorities with the seventeen-member technical and support staff group which he inherited from the previous Duma. He praised this team for its substantive knowledge of national defense affairs and his solid experience in the armed forces, the Ministry of Defense, and various governmental agencies. Instead of lashing out at the previous Duma for the gaps it failed to fill, he described the work that had to be done in a matter of fact manner. He was demonstrating the very spirit of nonpartisan, professionalism that he wanted his entire committee to follow.[59]

Rokhlin extended teamwork beyond the Duma and immediately created special working groups charged with completing revisions to legislation. One such committee brought together members of his committee, the presidential administration, several governmental agencies, and the upper-house or federal council. Their task was to reach agreement with the executive branch over issues that prevented the president from signing an important defense law which had been passed by the previous Duma. Rokhlin opened lines of communication to the chairmen of other key Duma committees and to various departments of government. He clearly understood that they were the other "generals" in the Duma and that he needed productive working relationships with them in order to advance the national defense agenda. Rokhlin also consulted with the Ministry of Foreign Affairs and placed items on his work list that were dictated to Russia by the Council of Europe, conditions that Russia had to meet in order to join the Council of Europe.[60]

When running for office, Rokhlin pledged to keep the military, military dependents, and veterans high on his personal agenda and he took a personal interest in revising the basic law on the Status of Armed Forces Personnel. His comments demonstrated a clear understanding of the need to increase both rights and responsibilities in order to raise military professional standards and the military profession's prestige in society. He instructed his committee to prepare legislation that would finally establish a centralized military police force armed with tougher codes of military justice.

But politics without partisanship is as unlikely as war without fighting. Politics is the process which sets the main rules and divides the budget and there will inevitably be competition and shifting alliances in politics. There were even hints of politics in some of Rokhlin's carefully written description of his committee's membership structure and agenda. He warned that the Duma would prepare a bill about national security that would require certain state officials and political leaders to think more carefully before entering into strategic arms and other security agreements that were potentially damaging to national interests. He also complained about salary and benefits differences that had emerged between the different armed services over recent years. In particular, he complained that the soldiers serving under the Ministry of Defense were not receiving the new higher benefits package that had been granted to soldiers serving in the Russian Border Forces. It is also noteworthy that he mentioned a dozen officials at various levels of government who were working productively with his committee. The list included First Deputy Minister of Defense Andrei Kokoshin and Chief of the General Staff, Col. General Kolesnikov, but not Minster of Defense Pavel Grachev.[61]

In a democracy national defense policy cannot be legislated, funded, and implemented without partisan politics. Groups compete for resources and for their points of view on defense affairs. Therefore, in the final analysis, Rokhlin had to compete, to negotiate and to make compromises. There was no other way to be effective. The fact that three of his four deputy chairmen and eleven of the twenty-three members of his committee had military backgrounds could not guarantee that they would work cohesively for his agenda. His fellow citizen soldiers had different political orientations which would certainly produce different ideas about national defense policy and spending.

Conclusion

The 1995 Duma elections showed that active-duty and recently retired military professionals continued to be involved in Russian politics. Instead of leaving the political domain to civilians, soldiers had a legitimate role in national political life. The Duma elections allowed them to test their political abilities, to gain political experience, and to call national attention to themselves.

The Ministry of Defense's political offensive failed, perhaps intentionally. Grachev's 120 "vetted" candidates did poorly and were probably a diversionary operation organized with Yeltsin's approval in order to draw votes and attention away from the main opposition's attack which was led by senior retired military officers such as generals Makashov, Surkov, and Varennikov who were working through Zyuganov's Communist Party. The fact that the 120 were for the most part defeated by civilians suggests that the public did not regard them as its legitimate representatives. By contrast, the Communist Party did quite well and drew many votes from the disaffected military and defense sector constituencies. However, he alleged defense constituency was at best a very loose coalition without a political party really dedicated to solving its problems. The national political consensus still looked upon defense spending unfavorably and the Chechen war had made military service generally unpopular.

Lt. General (Ret.) Aleksandr Lebed won a single-mandate seat from a relatively safe district but his national political organization, the CRC failed to make the 5 percent needed to get a portion of the party-list seats, and the other parties and factions in the Duma did not promote his political interests when the new Duma formed its internal leadership structure. He was still a political outsider. Instead of Lebed, the politicians moved Lt. General Lev Rokhlin into the chairmanship of the Duma defense committee. Thus, the military had won the key committee chairmanship. Chairman Rokhlin espoused a constructive mission and denied any presidential or ministerial ambitions. Rokhlin insisted that he did not like politics. Therefore, he was no immediate political threat to either Yeltsin or Grachev in national defense affairs. Yeltsin coopted Rokhlin into the national defense effort by giving him a seat on the Security Council, a reasonable and constructive effort to improve cooperation between the executive and legislative branches in defense matters. Rokhlin also gave Yeltsin direct input from the field commanders who were unhappy with the overall defense situation and the Chechen war.

The Duma election confirmed that there were dozens of military officers in national politics, individuals with diverse points of view on national policy. However, no charismatic, intelligent political leader had yet emerged from that group to mount a powerful national campaign. But the fact that dozens of military officers were actively engaged in politics suggested that the military would remain part of Russian political life for some time to come and it probably increased the likelihood that one or several would break into the ranks of the national political elite. The military were participating in various political movements along with civilians instead of assembling into an isolated, anticivilian political force. Nevertheless, the military did not favor the demokraty and military participation in politics enhanced the forces that were demanding that the political and economic reform process be disciplined and sanitized. Yeltsin and Grachev were not popular. Soldiers voted against the administration's candidates and exercised their political rights with more freedom than had ever been possible in Russian history. That was progress but it also was a warning to the Yeltsin administration that it had lost support in a very important part of the national power structure.

In Russian politics, democratic constitutional control over the military did not require military-professional exclusion from national political life. Civil-military relations were inclusive. The fact that Lt. General Lev Rokhlin moved from the battlefront in Grozny to the chairmanship of the Duma defense committee in less than a year's time illustrates that point. Military professionals like professionals from any other field could participate directly in national political life. Their presence improved the flow of accurate information between the armed forces and the political elite and helped to keep the military integrated into the national political process. Instead of withdrawing and becoming a hostile political force, the military was engaged and engaged in a pluralistic manner. Such engagement challenged both soldiers and civilians to understand national defense issues as part of the full spectrum of problems Russia faced.

Notes

1. See for example, Deputy Mariya Dobrovolskaya's comments in Vitaly Strugovets, "V parlamente malo lyudei, boleyushchikh za armiyu" (Few in parliament are hurting for the army), and Deputy Aleksandr Piskunov in *Krasnaya zvezda*, 14 September and 10 November 1995.
2. Press Conference, Pavel Grachev, Mozdok, January 20, 1995, "General Grachev: 'We Won't Stop,'" *Moscow News*, no. 4, January 27-February 2, 1995.
3. See *Ibid.*
4. Reported by *Golos Rossii*'s World Service, 11 January 1995 and the ITN World News.
5. INTERFAKS, "Strukturnye izmeneniya v Minoborony RF-ne povod dlya sensatsii" (Structural changes in the ministry of defense, no excuse for sensationalism), *Krasnaya zvezda*, 17 January 1995.
6. See Vadim Markushin, "Rossiiskaya armiya vypolnila postavlennuyu zadachu" (Russian army fulfilled its assigned mission), *Krasnaya zvezda*, 26 January 1995.
7. Vladimir Ermolin, "Budet li uchteny uroki chechenskoi tragedii?" (Will the lessons of the Chechen tragedy be studied?), *Krasnaya zvezda*, 25 January 1995.
8. Vladimir Ermolin, "Kto i kak golosuyet v Gosdume" (Who votes how in the State Duma), *Krasnaya zvezda*, 3 March 1995.
9. Aleksandr Gol'ts, "A est' li u nas VKP?" (Do we have a MIC?), *Krasnaya zvezda*, 4 March 1995.
10. Anatoly Stasovskii, "Predvybornyi tuman nad nami proplyvayet" (The pre-election fog is about to descend upon us), *Krasnaya zvezda*, 30 May 1995.
11. See Anatoly Veslo, "Fighting Men: Pavel Grachev Decides to Upgrade the Duma with his own Subordinates," *Sevodnya*, 26 September 1993. *CDSP*, vol. XLVII, no. 39 (1995), page 4.

12. Lt. General Sergei Zdornikov, interviewed by Vasily Semenov, "Kakaya zhe ideologiya nuzhna segodnya Rossiiskoi armii" (What kind of ideology does the russian army need today), *Krasnaya zvezda*, 8 September 1995.
13. See Aleksandr Pel'ts, "Na vashe reshenie—16,600 variantov" (For you to decide—16,000 choices), *Krasnaya zvezda*, 15 November 1995.
14. Aleksander Lebed's interview by Sergei Yastrebov, "Generals Storming the Duma," *Moscow News*, no. 33–35, September 15–21, 1995.
15. Rear Admiral Valery Aleksin, Chief Navigator of the Russian Naval Forces, "Deputy v pogonakh ili za chem voennye idut v politiku" (Deputies in uniform or why the military are entering politics), *Krasnaya zvezda*, 7 December 1995.
16. See *Ibid.* Aleksin used America as an example for Russia because every president since World War II, with the exception of Bill Clinton, had served in the armed forces and had presented that service as a positive qualification. Such presidents understood defense affairs and promoted American democracy, economic development, and military power.
17. See "Kto oni segodnya—deputaty voennosluzhashchie?" (The military deputies—who are they today?), *Armiya*, no. 20, October 1992, pp. 46, 48.
18. See Anatoly Veslo, "Fighting Men: Pavel Grachev Decides to Upgrade the Duma With His Own Subordinates," *Sevodnya*, 26 September 1995; *CDSP*, vol. XLVII., no. 39, 1995, p. 4.
19. Cited by Pyotr Zhuravlyov, "Officers: Sergei Yushenkov—The Ministry of Defense Wants To Be A Political Party," *Sevodnya*, 28 September 1995; *CDSP*, vol. XLVII., no. 39, 1995, p. 4.
20. See *Ibid.*
21. Neither Stepashin nor Tsarev became deputies in the Duma elected in December 1993. However, Stepashin became Yeltsin's Minister of Internal Affairs and Tsarev joined Duma speaker Ivan Rybkin's staff as an advisor on armed forces affairs.
22. Aleksei Tsarev, interviewed by Vladimir Ermolin, "Sochustvuyut armii mnogie. Reshit' eye problemy v Gosdume smogut tol'ko professionaly" (Many sympathize with the army. Only professionals can solve its problems in the state duma), *Krasnaya zvezda*, 8 December 1995.
23. Cited by Vadim Akchurin, "Don't Rule Out the Danger of Another Nationalization," *Moscow News*, no. 47, 1995.
24. *Ibid.*
25. See "Will the Army Become Hazardous to Society?" *Moscow News*, no. 47, December 1–7, 1995.
26. See Viktor Chernomyrdin's special interview for the military, "My nauchilis' ne tol'ko vyzhivat'" (We learned to do more than just survive), *Krasnaya Zvezda*, 14 December 1995.
27. Konstantin Krasnopolsky, "Party Life in Russia: General Rokhlin: I Have No Use For A Seat In The Duma," *Kommersant-Daily*, 20 September 1995; *CDSP*, vol. XLVII, no. 39, 1995, pp. 3–4.
28. *Ibid.*
29. However, Lebed refused to endorse ethnic-Russian nationalism and reminded listeners that he intended to defend the interests of all the citizens of Russia: ethnic Russians, Jews, Bashkirs, Chechens, etc. See Aleksandr Lebed as interviewed by Sergei Yastrebov, "Generals Storming the Duma," *Moscow News*, no. 33–35, September 15–21, 1995.
30. Lebed commanded the Tula paratrooper division from 1988–1991.
31. Vadim Yegorov, "The Army" CRC Establishes 'Honor and Homeland' Move-

ment," *Nezavisimaya gazeta*, 17 October 1995; *CDSP*, vol. XLVII, no. 41, 1995, pp. 3–4.

32. See Surkov's comments in *Krasnaya zvezda*, 11 April 1991 and 7 August 1991.

33. Lt. General Mikhail Surkov as cited in "The Army: Communist committee shut," *Moscow News*, no. 39, 29 September-6 October 1991.

34. Viktor Khamrayev, "Scope: Union of Patriots Proposes to Save Russia By Restoring A *Russian* Government," *Sevodnya*, 9 September 1995; *CDSP*, vol. XLVII, no. 38, 1995, pp. 6–7.

35. Valery Musin, "Parting: Aleksandr Rutskoi Will Strike 'Slanderers' of 'Great Power' From His Slate," *Sevodnya*, 2 September 1995; *CDSP*, vol. XLVII, no. 38, 1995, p. 6.

36. See *Krasnaya zvezda's* list of parties and blocs, 15 November 1995.

37. Pyotr Zhuravlyov, "Left Center: Ivan Rybkin Doesn't Intend to 'Force Himself On Anyone," *Sevodnya*, 8 September 1995; *CDSP*, vol. XLVII, no. 38, 1995, p. 1. By creating his own bloc, Ivan Rybkin weakened the *Agrarian* party on whose ticket he had been elected in 1993.

38. Ivan Rybkin as cited by Vladimir Ermolin in "Duma dolzhna obespechit' dostoinoe financirovanie armii" (Duma must guarantee the army appropriate financing), *Krasnaya zvezda*, 10 November 1995.

39. Aleksandr Pel'ts, "Na vashe reshenie—16,6000 variantov" (For your decision, 16,600 variations), *Krasnaya zvezda*, 15 November 1995.

40. See pp.198 ff. in Steven White, Richard Rose, and Ian McAllister, *How Russia Votes* (Chatham, N.J.: Chatham House Publishers, 1996).

41. See Nikolai T. Ryabov's interview by Vladimir Ermolin, "Izbiratel'noe pravo voennosluzhashchego zashchishcheno Konstitutsiei RF" (RF constitution protects military service personnel electoral rights), *Krasnaya zvezda*, 31 August 1995.

42. See Colonel Vladimir Vlasov's long interview by Anatoly Stasovskii, "Armiya i vybory" (The army and the elections), *Krasnaya zvezda*, 2 September 1995.

43. See Major Yury Krotov's description of how this worked in the Volga-Urals military district (not without controversy), "Komandiry postupayut po zakonu" (Commanders acting according to the law), *Krasnaya zvezda*, 10 November 1995.

44. Vlasov, "Armiya i vybory."

45. Staff, "17 Dekabrya—vybory deputatov v Gosudarstvennuyu Dumu" (17 December—elections for deputies to the state duma), and Aleksandr Pel'ts, "Golosovat' nado umeyuchi…" (Need to vote knowingly…), *Krasnaya zvezda*, 16 December 1995.

46. Vitaly Denisov, "Trudno golosovat' na rasstoyanii" (Hard to vote from far away), *Krasnaya zvezda*, 23 November 1995.

47. *Ibid.*

48. Boris Yeltsin, "Obrashchenie Prezidenta RF k grazhdanam Rossii 15 dekabrya 1995 goda," *Krasnaya zvezda*, 16 December 1995.

49. The Editors, "17 Dekabrya—vybory deputatov v Gosudarstvennuyu Dumu" (17 December—elections for deputies to the state Duma), *Krasnaya zvezda*, 16 December 1995.

50. Aleksandr Pel'ts, "Vybory v Gosdumu: aktivnost' izbiratelei prevozhoshla vse ozhidaniya" (Duma elections participation surpassed all expectations), *Krasnaya zvezda*, 19 December 1995.

51. Petr Karapetyan, Anatoly Stasovskii, "Vybory v gosdumu" (Duma elections), *Krasnaya zvezda*, 19 December 1995.

52. See Karapetyan in *Ibid.*, 17 January 1996.

53. There were forty-six female deputies, or just over 10 percent of the new Duma. Two-thirds of the Duma deputies were fifty or older,
54. Terekhov received only 2.9 percent of the vote. He was defeated by Irina Khakamada a member of the non-partisan, Common Cause (*Obshchee delo*). Sterlingov did better with 8.9 percent but was defeated by Ivan Rybkin. Achalov, head of the All-Russian Officers Assembly, got only 3.09 percent of the vote in his Tatarstan district. See Sergei Polivanov, "Fascists' Dismal Poll Failure," *Moscow News*, no. 10, 14–20 March 1996.
55. See Vladimir Ermolin, "Komitety Gosdumy sforimoravany" (State Duma committees formed), *Krasnaya zvezda*, 1 February 1996.
56. See Vladimir Ermolin in *Ibid.*, 26 January 1996.
57. See Vladimir Ermolin, "Komitety Gosdumy sforimorivany."
58. Lt. General Lev Rokhlin as interviewed by Vladimir Ermolin, "Glavnoye—znat' armiyu. A parliamentskii opyt pridyet" (The main thing is to know the army. Parliamentary experience will come), *Krasnaya zvezda*, 2 February 1996.
59. Lt. General Lev Rokhlin, "Voennym nuzhny deistvennye zakony" (Military needs effective laws), *Krasnaya zvezda*, 16 March 1996.
60. *Ibid.*
61. *Ibid.*

14

The 1996 Presidential Campaign

At the year began, Yeltsin's popularity ratings were in the single digits and it was widely believed that he was too ill to campaign vigorously and to keep his Kremlin elite under reliable control. However, as the months passed, the Yeltsin campaign team did remarkably well. By the May holidays Yeltsin was pulling ahead of his Communist opponent, Gennady Zyuganov; but neither expected to win enough votes to be elected in the first round on 16 June 1996.

The campaign had two phases based upon Russia's two-stage election system. During the first phase some ten candidates competed knowing that under Russia's election rules if none received more than 50 percent in the first round on 16 June 1996, only the top two vote getters would be permitted to run in the second vote some two weeks later. This chapter examines the first phase which ran from 15 February to 15 June 1996. It analyzes the electoral campaign's influence on civil-military relations and argues that the Yeltsin administration left a mixed legacy. Some of its campaign actions set good precedents for democratic institutional development. Others did not. On the whole, the 1996 election experience probably made the military more political than it wanted or needed to be. The next chapter examines the actual voting, Yeltsin's alliance with Lebed, and the dramatic changes it precipitated in national military and security leadership.

Winning a competitive election is a learning process. Players who cling to unpopular positions and to political allies who are out of favor can damage their chances of winning. Yeltsin learned faster and adapted his behavior more quickly than his rivals. He modified his positions on military and security issues and changed his allies in order to enhance his prospects for winning the popular vote. But his campaign's national defense component did not begin well. It improved as election day drew nearer and Yeltsin became more candid and more energetic in pursuit of the national defense constituency. But, there was no easy, responsible way to convert military discontent and concern about Russia's decline into pro-Yeltsin sentiment.

The Campaign Begins: Mixed Signals on National Defense

On 15 February 1996, Boris Yeltsin formally announced that he was running for a second term and introduced his main campaign theme. Yeltsin said, "On June 16th we will be choosing not only a President but also what our life is going to be like in the near future; we will be deciding the fate of Russia."[1] Yeltsin urged Russians to focus on the future and to keep their impatience with current hardships from confusing their judgments about long-term goals. He wanted the 1996 election to reaffirm the national commitment to liberal economic and political reform. He argued that people were better off than in the Communist past in spite of all the unanticipated difficulties the reform process had brought.

Reporters asked Yeltsin about national defense, the Chechen war, and military reform. His answers gave the national defense constituency little to cheer about. Yeltsin said he favored strong defense, had a comprehensive plan to end the Chechen war, and was completing one for military reform. But he blamed the Ministry of Defense for shortcomings in military reform and charged that the Ministry had been unable to reform itself and had kept raising new concerns and asking for more funding. For these reasons, he created an independent commission on military reform whose recommendations would go to the Security Council which would maintain strict control over the military reform process in the future.[2] Yeltsin was equivocating in a manner that placed the top military leadership in political limbo and could not have pleased the armed forces. If reform had been mismanaged, why hadn't Yeltsin replaced Defense Minister Grachev? Was Yeltsin cunningly waiting until the right moment in the presidential election game to play his military cards? Why hadn't Yeltsin offered Russians a more balanced assessment of the military, one more sensitive to military views? Why hadn't he praised the military for having remained cohesive, manageable, and loyal through an extremely difficult four-year period? Yeltsin seemed to be sticking to a rather negative line on national defense at a time when he should have been seeking political support in the national defense constituency.

Yeltsin's *Poslanie* or State of the Federation Message

On 23 February 1996 Yeltsin delivered his State of the Federation message (*poslanie*) to the Federal Assembly.[3] The document bears the telltale marks of the democratic intelligentsia on Yeltsin's team. It is more about the sweep of Russian history than political meat and potatoes—precisely the type of political analysis that Gorbachev valued and which Yeltsin used to criticize. It fit the Soviet political tradition which demanded that grand social theory legitimize state policy. The new social theory is the universal theory of modernization developed by Western social scientists. It argues that competitive political and economic systems adapt far more rapidly to political, technological, and economic challenges than bureaucratic command systems and produce better politics and a higher standard of living than dictatorship.

Yeltsin reviewed twentieth-century political history with that in mind. He condemned the destruction of "civil society" by radical utopians—the Bolsheviks. He described the totalitarian model's mobilization regime including the police state and repressions. He discussed its reform under Khrushchev and the structural dilemma the reformers faced. (The political elite knew that decentralization was required to infuse dynamism into the stagnating economy but it feared losing control and therefore delayed reform.) He confirmed Gorbachev's claim that the income earned from foreign sales of Soviet oil and gas had saved the Brezhnev economy from collapse.

Yeltsin then painted a mixed picture of Gorbachev's perestroika. He praised glasnost' and democratization but criticized its half way measures in economic and political reform. He cited "secret" reports to Moscow from regional leaders warning Gorbachev that they could not meet basic targets for meat and milk. Yeltsin charged that Gorbachev started deficit spending and inflation but admitted that he had also given Russians a dose of inflation. What was the difference? "In 1991, the shelves were empty and now they are full."[4] In 1991 the Soviet Union suffered a negative balance of trade but by 1995 it had turned positive and the Russian State Bank had the equivalent of some 12 billion dollars in hard currency on reserve. Yeltsin took the credit for leading Russia through the most difficult years and argued that Russia had built the foundation for an authentic market economy and political democracy. He admitted that mistakes had been made and major problems remained including crime, corruption, abuses of power, and the secessionist war. Yeltsin asked the citizens to give him a second term to complete the job started in 1991.

There was nothing "Eurasian" or fundamentally anti-Western about his Poslanie. In fact, Yelstin was coaching his people to believe that they had what it takes to persevere and to make their final breakthrough into progressive forms of politics and economics. He wanted them to reflect upon the past and to reject the proto-Communists and the proto-patriots who were promising them quick solutions and a better life under some type of semi-authoritarian regime. Yeltsin lashed out against those who argued that Russian political culture had no democratic tradition and no capacity to sustain a democratic society. He called upon the people to become citizens and to take responsibility for their future: "Today I call upon all the citizens of Russia to start living as if this were your own home!"[5]

Yeltsin on Military Spending and the Military "System"

Yeltsin's ideas on defense spending fit perestroika and post-perestroika views that the Soviet regime—from Stalin to Brezhnev, had spent excessively on its military-industrial complex. Yeltsin granted that Stalin had made Russia into a mighty industrial and military power but criticized the enormous cost in human lives and values. Yeltsin reminded Russians that Brezhnev's drive for military parity with the West had deprived the Soviet people of any chance of reaching a high standard of living: "The attempt to maintain military parity with the *capitalist world*, to help the countries of the *socialist camp* and all *progressive forces*, sucked the last juices from the economy and destroyed the consumer sector."[6] Yeltsin noted that during the 1970s and 1980s the Western economies adjusted to rising energy costs, pressed for more efficient production methods, and began building the new computer-driven economies. "In Russia," Yeltsin explained, "the effect was quite different and petro-dollars went to satisfy administrative ambitions, dubious *projects of the century*, and foreign policy and military adventures."[7] Russia ended up producing more and more guns and less butter.

Yeltsin was sensitive to charges that he had damaged Russian economic and security interests by destroying the Soviet Union. Yeltsin blamed Gorbachev and insisted that he was salvaging what he could: "By declaring Russia to be sovereign, we prevented Russia from being used as a military staging ground for armed struggle against the other republics and we opened the way for efforts to retain the Union on an entirely different foundation."[8] In other words, by refusing to make Russia the military core of a Unionist dictatorship, Yeltsin made it possible for Russia to develop democratically and for the republics to achieve formal independence. However, he could not permit Russia itself to disintegrate and this is why he went to war in Chechnya but only after several years of unsuccessful attempts to settle the affair peacefully.

If Russia's soldiers expected to hear their supreme commander praising them for their bravery and the sacrifices they had made in Chechnya, they were disappointed. Instead of cheering them on, Yeltsin admonished them to target bandits and rebel fighters, not the Chechen people who are all Russian citizens: "All of us, especially our military personnel, must be absolutely clear that the force of state coercion was and is aimed at the bandits who possess an enormous quantity of arms. Federal forces assist the Chechen Republic's legal authorities to lay the foundations for a normal, secure life for its inhabitants."[9] Instead of dwelling on the tragedy and of helping to heal the wounds by expressing condolences to all who died because politics failed to keep the peace, he just repeated the Kremlin line about Dudayev's bandits having been all but defeated. But he did state that he was prepared to make compromises to achieve a settlement and to start settlement talks "but not with bandits" and not behind the backs of the Chechen authorities.

Yeltsin made two points that conveyed a negative attitude towards the military leadership. First, he said that the military's personnel system did not always reward true professional competence: "One of the most important goals of military reform is the creation of a flexible and just system of military service that promotes those who really carry the burdens of military service and dedicate themselves to the service of their Fatherland."[10] Second, he confirmed that civilian control had to be enhanced and suggested that this would improve the public's attitude towards Russia's soldiers: "The second special aspect of military reform in a democratizing society is the strengthening of state and civilian control over Armed Forces operations. This has to be done according to modern standards and has to take Russian specifics into account. This will increase the people's love and confidence in the defenders of the Fatherland."[11]

Propagating the Yeltsin Point of View in the Military

The president's message did little to repair the military's deep sense of alienation and it had forgotten to recite the standard patriotic litany that begins with Aleksandr Nevsky and ends with the sacrifices being made for Russia in Chechnya. Nevertheless, in early March 1996, *Krasnaya zvezda* reported that Defense Minister Grachev had ordered General Sergei Zornikov's Main Administration for Educational Work to launch a comprehensive informational campaign focused on President Yeltsin's State of the Federation message. This decision resembled a Communist-era political education campaign. Yeltsin was making the military study his new "party line." All officers would be required to spend four to six hours discussing Yeltsin's thesis. The military academies were instructed to insert it into the curriculum immediately. Further, military dependents and civilian leaders were to be invited to public lectures about Russia's past, present, and future. Regional heads of civilian administration were expected to attend. Military editors and producers were told to support the campaign by giving Yeltsin's message priority attention in their publications and broadcasts. This was a blatant abuse of executive political power. Yeltsin was using his position as supreme commander to promote his political campaign in the armed forces.[12]

Grachev and Zornikov faced a difficult political task. They were supposed to replace the military's negative attitude towards the Yeltsin administration's defense cuts, erratic defense financing, and inept handling of the Chechen conflict with a positive one. Yeltsin's message was a poor vehicle for doing that since most officers would certainly recognize it as a partisan political document. In the December 1995 Duma elections the military—like most of the Russian electorate had supported opposition parties rather than the motley collection of demokraty grouped around the Yeltsin regime. Turning the military voters around would not be easy. Yeltsin could force Grachev to make the official military press toe the political line and he could even make officers parrot it; however, he could not control how they would actually vote without violating fundamental democratic principles such as the secret ballot which the military supported and took steps to reinforce after the 1993 and 1995 Duma elections.

Military Discontent and Activism: The Money Problem

Yeltsin's Poslanie boasted that the Kremlin treasury had built up reserves and was running a positive balance of trade. But the military knew that the Yeltsin administration had collected far less in taxes than required to fund the 1995 and the 1996 federal budgets. The situation produced a certain degree of social and political tension. Draftees were struggling through the Chechen winter, fighting, and dying for Russia while the new bourgeoisie was salting away millions and enjoying the prosperous life and the government did not have the funds to pay basic military salaries and benefits on time. Soldiers were supposed to be patient, to endure, and to persevere. But instead of immediately endorsing Yeltsin's positions, the armed forces continued to lobby for increased spending and were bold enough to suggest where the money could be found.

On 9 February 1996, Army General Anatoly Kulikov—Grachev's counterpart at the head of Russia's domestic armed forces and police or MVD, presented his own plan to a federal cabinet meeting and then held a press conference about it. Kulikov insisted that national defense and security could be funded properly, identified the sources, and laid out a comprehensive plan for collecting the revenues. Kulikov called for higher rates of taxation on Russian corporations, the nationalization of the most important banks, the restoration of state monopolies in oil and gas, and an end to all unnecessary spending including pork-barrel items such as a 50 billion ruble allocation for a Russian samovar festival.[13] General Kulikov's proposals were more radical and daring than the Communist Party's. Kulikov argued that renationalization of key industries and enterprises was in the national interest . The Communists were more circumspect.[14] Kulikov was responding to his constituency—police and internal troops who had not been paid and who had been organizing strikes in some regions.[15]

On 15 February 1996, the same day that Yeltsin announced his presidential candidacy, Defense Minister Grachev spoke to a national meeting of fellow Afghan war veterans. Grachev charged that "politicians had betrayed the lives of an entire generation" by throwing youth into the Afghan adventure. Further, the peace they dreamed of when they withdrew from Afghanistan was never achieved. Russian soldiers were still fighting in hot spots from Chechnya to Tajikistan. Grachev said that the military was losing patience and could spin out of control: "In the very near future an irreversible process could start." In his blunt, soldierly manner, Grachev warned, "Don't keep testing the military's patience and pushing it to the breaking point."[16]

Thus the ministers of defense and internal affairs had both warned Yeltsin that the troops were restless and did not buy the explanation that the government could not support national defense. Their point of view was that the current federal government lacked the will to take the actions required to support defense and to rein in the new bourgeoisie. *Krasnaya zvezda's* lead editorialist Aleksandr Gol'ts put it this way.

> There is a Russian capitalist problem here. They don't seem to understand that they have to pay and to pay for social peace and this means paying their taxes and paying wages properly. The only lessons they have learned from history is that they have to prepare for their flight abroad in advance and to get their resources and funds out. So millions are fleeing the country now.[17]

Gol'ts was troubled by the existence of widespread corruption and a potential conflict between national security interests and private interests in the natural resource industries and in the military-industrial complex. He wanted Yeltsin to attack corruption and to make the new economy work by honest and fair rules. He called for a law-governed market and a fair tax system.

The national defense lobby also wanted Yeltsin to impose a general plan on the industrial reorganization process, one that would give priority to the preservation and development of national defense industry and technology. In early 1996, there was a sharp policy debate in Kremlin leadership circles. Some top administrators in the military-industrial complex (MIC) also supported MVD General Kulikov's point of view that natural resources exports and key defense industries are natural state monopolies and should be treated as such.[18] The head of the Yeltsin administration's interdepartmental agency for national defense industry (Goskomoboronprom), Viktor Glukhikh came out against privatization of key industries: "We are totally against the privatization of those firms upon which national security most fully depends."[19] He insisted that the government address the needs of the seventy Russian cities where defense industries are the dominant employers: "They have to be given work."[20] He pointed out that Russian defense had to scramble for foreign sales to stay afloat financially because "foreign sales are now two to three times as large as Russian defense purchasing." In 1995 the MIC deliveries to the Russian military were only 6 percent of 1991 levels. Such numbers were not good for Yeltsin's political campaign. Further, Glukhikh did not campaign for pro-Yeltsin candidates during the December 1995 Duma elections and most candidates nominated by the military-industrial complex were leftists.[21] Yeltsin fired Glukhikh and replaced him with Zinovy Pak

Defense Spending and Presidential Election Politics

The political process had set the level of national defense spending and that could not be changed significantly unless the balance of political forces shifted towards a pro-defense majority or the economy improved dramatically. Neither was likely to happen quickly. In spite of all that the military and the MIC had done to lobby for higher defense spending from 1992–1996, neither the president, nor the government, nor the opposition-dominated Duma had been willing to increase military spending at the expense of other, more popular constituencies. The national political consensus supported lower defense spending and smaller armed forces.

In theory, Yeltsin's Communist opponents led by Gennady Zyuganov had a good chance to win the general military protest vote. However, their own Duma voting record, from 1993 to 1996, reflected the national consensus and kept military spending down. Zyuganov's Communists had too many constituencies to satisfy and could not cut pensions, agricultural supports, and subsidies to civilian industry in order to increase defense spending. The same held true for Zhirinovsky's Liberal Democrats. The Russian military was reasonably well informed about the national political and financial situation although it was not happy with it.

Aleksei Arbatov, deputy chairman of the Duma's defense committee and the Yabloko party's leading military expert, argued that Russia had to cut its military personnel to less than the 1.5 million figure set by Yeltsin and the Duma for two reasons. First, Russia had no major external enemies and did not need large standing armies. Second, since the Kremlin treasury could not properly support a 1.5 million position army, it made sense to cut total manpower by another three to five hundred thousand positions. Otherwise, Russia could not afford to create, highly trained, well-equipped, mobile armed forces. World experience demonstrated that smaller, more effective armies required higher per capita investment in personnel and defense technology. Russia had to make a choice between quantity and quality. Arbatov published his thesis in the independent Russian national daily, *Nezavisimaya gazeta*.[22] But the Ministry of Defense continued to insist that Russia needed no less than 1.7 million soldiers.

The General Staff provided additional information that reinforced the impression that current reform plans were impractical. Even downsizing had turned out to be more expensive than anticipated. From 1992–1996, Russia slashed 1.1 million positions from the Ministry of Defense payroll but the severance pay and benefits packages granted to furloughed officers cost the country about as much as it would have taken to keep them on active duty.[23] Similarly, the idea of replacing the military draft with professionals under contract was beyond the military's means. General Staff experts argued that Russia could not afford that option even though it had strong public support and was appealing to the military. Grachev reaffirmed that he would prefer a completely professional military but warned that "such a force would be so costly that the entire country would have to work to support it. Russia simply cannot afford such expenditures."[24] The General Staff's chief of operations planning, Col. General Barynkin, had all but abandoned the goal of making 50 percent of the Russian military professional by the year 2000 because, as a military professional, he judged it to be impractical.

Ending Conscription

Practical or not, Yeltsin knew that military conscription was unpopular, that he was running for reelection, and that he had the power to issue decrees changing the military system. Why not use that power to improve his popularity? Precisely one month before the elections, he issued two decrees designed to win votes. Ukaz No. 722 ordered the Ministry of Defense to plan to end military conscription by the year 2000. Ukaz No. 723 ordered the armed forces to stop sending draftees to hot spots unless soldiers volunteered for such service. Thus, by virtue of the powers vested in him by the 1993 Constitution, Yeltsin unilaterally changed the anxiety-producing situation faced by Russia's eighteen year olds and their families. Senior military leaders had to endorse those moves and to treat them as responsible, welcomed policy changes.

Yeltsin endorsed smaller, better-trained, all-professional armed forces even though he did not have the financial wherewithal to support them. The political opposition complained and pointed out that Yeltsin was reading the public opinion polls and making policy accordingly. However, the main idea had long been popular with the military for two reasons. First, the military hoped that an all-professional military system would permit it to recruit and hire higher quality personnel. Second, the reform fit the trends seen in the advanced industrial states upon which military progressives hoped to model the new Russian army. However, there was good reason to be skeptical since it would take higher salaries and benefits to attract better qualified personnel and there was nothing to indicate that the government was either willing or able to increase military salaries in the near term.

Yeltsin was playing politics with military reform issues and bringing policy closer to what the general public wanted even though the Kremlin treasury could not afford it. He also demonstrated concern for the military's difficult financial situation but delayed some to avoid precipitating a surge in inflation before the presidential elections. He demanded that the Russian government pay the military its back pay and benefits in the first quarter of 1996. Then, on 12 June 1996, a mere four days before the elections he decreed that salaries and benefits be increased for all members of the armed forces.[25]

Lebed—"I am a Russian officer with a conscience."[26]

There was one military officer among the leading presidential candidates, Lt. General (Ret.) Aleksandr Lebed and not even he believed that defense spending could be increased significantly in the short run. However, he did believe that funds could be spent more efficiently and that the military system needed thorough reform. He ran on a vague progressive and nationalist reform platform which charged that Russia's political leadership needed a thorough purging to get rid of corruption and criminality. He was the people's warrior determined to make certain that the people get their fair share of the benefits the new society promised to bring. But he insisted that there be no return to lawlessness and Communist dictatorship. He argued that he represented the majority of Russian voters who wanted a democratic Russia and saw their hopes being dashed by incompetent and corrupt politicians.

Lebed presented himself as the honest, patriotic Russian officer who had entered politics to put an end to irresponsible politicking and to start rebuilding the Russian state. He was an ethno-nationalist who defined Russia as a triangle formed by the Church, the Army, and the People. He warned that tsars, general secretaries, and presidents come and go but the people remain and he saw himself as the personification of the best in the people, the Russian officer.[27] He had little patience for social theory but favored common sense and pragmatism. Yet he understood the case for democracy and market competition and insisted that these new ideas were superior to the corrupt personal Communism of the past and to post-Communist corruption. Yet all this nationalist, patriotic populism at least recognized the problem of numbers and accountability and Lebed argued that Russia would have to rebuild slowly and steadily. Although Lebed was competing with the Yeltsin campaign for some of the same voters, he was also competing with the Communists and drawing protest voters away from them.

Back in summer 1992 when Lebed was trying to control the military and political situation in Transdniestria and operating like a military governor, the Yeltsin administration had difficulty restraining him. Grachev ordered Lebed to stay out of politics but Lebed defied him in writing. Lebed published the relevant official military correspondence in 1995. His defiant response reveals a personal conviction that leadership should be above politics and that real officers are bound by higher moral obligations to lead. Grachev charged that Lebed had become another military man meddling in politics. Lebed gave this response: "I categorically deny those accusations and declare to you that I will continue to speak as a Russian officer who has a conscience."[28] He defended himself and insisted that he, a *responsible* Russian officer, had taken bold action to end the civil war, communal violence, and grabbing for wealth and power. Yes, he refused to obey orders to enter into constructive discussions with Mircea Snegur, Moldova's head of state, because Snegur, according to Lebed, had blood on his hands. Lebed sent his declaration to Boris Yeltisn and to the heads of state and the parliaments of all fifteen former Soviet republics. It ends with a cryptic warning to the "comrade politicos" (*tovarishchi politiki*) that the People are the highest authority.[29] Grachev persisted, reaffirmed the orders to work with Snegur, and warned Lebed that the Kremlin was taking his resistance very seriously. But Lebed still refused to work with Snegur and denied charges that he was betraying the confidence that President Yeltsin had placed in him. Lebed's official response ended with these words: "I am a Russian army general and have no intention of betraying her."[30] Lebed believed that officers had a higher duty than service to specific politicians.

Yeltsin and Grachev finally stripped Lebed of his command and forced him to retire with presidential Ukaz No. 591 of 14 June 1995. Nevertheless, it was an honorable discharge and Lebed retained the right to wear the uniform of a lt. general of the Russian Army. He published the discharge papers in his political autobiography and attached the following defiant comments to Grachev: "A TEMPORARY FINISH?!"[31]

The Yeltsin Administration's Dialogue with the Military

Political incumbency has advantages and disadvantages. On the one hand, Yeltsin had a mixed record and could not escape blame for it. On the other hand, he could use his office to try to influence the military constituency. There would be ten or eleven officially registered presidential candidates but only one, Boris Yeltsin, had direct access to the military elite and military press. Russian federal law prohibits partisan political activity inside the armed forces but neither the Duma nor the Russian courts were powerful enough to challenge him on this. Yeltsin's team used presidential access to promote his candidacy. On 5 April 1996, Georgy Satarov, Yeltsin's chief political adviser, addressed senior military leaders. On 12 April 1996, Nikolai Yegorov, Yeltsin's chief of presidential administrative staff, appeared before them. On 23 May 1996, Yeltsin sent a special policy letter to the armed forces which Grachev ordered all officers to study and to discuss with their subordinates. On 29 May 1996, Yeltsin spoke directly to a major assembly of senior military leaders. And, two days later he signed a new Law on Defense which reinforced his direct control over all key armed forces operations.

The Yeltsin's administration's messages to the military changed between February and June 1996. Yeltsin's first major public commentary—the Poslanie or State of the Federation message, was quite negative and could not have pleased the armed forces establishment. Satarov's presentation concentrated on modernization theory and reminded officers why the military wanted and needed a dynamic political economy. Yegorov tapped nationalist sentiment and read like chapter from Aleksandr Lebed's political biography. Yeltsin's political rivals charged that he was engaging in blatant political opportunism and coopting the opposition's program but competitive elections are supposed to produce such behavior. Political opportunism is a form of democratic accountability.

Georgy Satarov's Meeting with Military Leaders

Defense Minister Grachev invited Yeltsin's chief political advisor, Georgy Satarov, to explain the national political situation and the president's political strategy to the senior officers at an expanded meeting of the military collegium.[32] Satarov found the situation somewhat ironical but not without political import. Although he was a democratic intellectual and a political scientist of international caliber, fate handed him a traditional Soviet political role. He was to explain the Yeltsin party line to the top military officers whom Grachev had already ordered to study Yeltsin's Poslanie. Satarov thanked the military for the invitation and said that he would focus on two subjects—the Poslanie's central ideas and the most important political event of 1996, the presidential elections.[33] Satarov was also observing his audience and gauging the senior military leadership's political mood.

Satarov said there were no specific models for Russia to follow but there were general laws of nature governing complex systems including societies and countries. These demonstrate that adaptation (adaptivnost') is the key to survival and progress. The most successful organisms, societies, and governments constantly adapt to changing circumstances. The Soviet model—like most forms of centralized dictatorship, was adequate for short-term goal attainment but could not support long-term adaptation. It fell behind. Satarov reminded the officers that they had supported perestroika precisely because they knew that the Soviet military-industrial complex was lagging behind: "I think that many of you know that one of the fundamental reasons why perestroika was started was the colossal technological gap and the Army's and the MIC's dissatisfaction with the system's inability to support their development."[34]

Although the senior officers certainly understood the main point, Satarov still had to defend Yeltsin's record—the choices the Yeltsin administration made and why other models such as China under Deng Xiaoping or Chile under Pinochet were rejected. Didn't Russia need an authoritarian regime for a given transitional period? Hadn't the Yeltsin administration overthrown the Parliament in 1993? Satarov argued that the Russian people rejected dictatorship when they voted for Yeltsin in 1991 and that Yeltsin was doing his best to establish effective government without dictatorship. Satarov insisted that there is no foreign model that Russia could use to guarantee a smooth transition from Soviet dictatorship to democracy and a market economy. He admitted that Russia had paid a price for change but argued that the political economy was starting to operate according to new rules, those closer to the laws of nature, and was beginning to produce better political and economic results. It would be a tragedy and a disaster to thrown all that away in favor of some new variation on the old dictatorship, he concluded.

Satarov presented the case for Yeltsin as social science, common sense, and the struggle for freedom. He urged military officers to exercise responsible leadership by explaining the past, the present, and the future to their subordinates and colleagues. He described Yeltsin as a the leader with the right values and ideas for Russia. He also explained Yeltsin's overall campaign strategy and named the people responsible for managing the campaign organization. He reported that public opinion data—one of Satarov's areas of professional expertise—showed the president just behind Zyuganov but he noted that the trend favored Yeltsin. The campaign team was convinced that Yeltsin would win the election because the numbers improved as soon as he began campaigning actively and demonstrated that he had the energy to lead effectively. Public opinion surveys showed that Russians were more concerned about his political will and health than about specific steps taken to improve popularity such as progress made on the back-pay problem.[35]

The military did not ask Satarov any questions about modernization theory. Their concerns were more practical. Did their supreme commander really know what was happening inside the military? How would he react if the Chechen rebels took advantage of the cease-fires and the partial federal withdrawals that Yeltsin had just announced? Satarov reassured them that Yeltsin knew what was going on and relied upon multiple channels of information. Satarov said: "To be frank, the President does not know every division's situation perfectly. That would be unrealistic and impossible. But Boris Nikolayevich receives information on the situation in the army from more than the Ministry of Defense. I emphasize, the president's working principle is multiple sources of information."[36] On Chechnya, Satarov confirmed that Yeltsin would authorize adequate military responses to any attack by rebel forces on federal troops.

Nikolai Yegorov's Meeting with Military Leaders

A week after Satarov's talk, Grachev assembled the officers for Yeltsin's chief of presidential administration, Nikolai Yegorov. Yegorov insisted that the Yeltsin team really understood the military's situation and was sympathetic to it. His speech was historical, analytical, and deeply political. He used history to explain why the military should reject Yeltsin's three rivals: the Communists, the radical democrats, and the Zhirinovsky nationalists. He described Yeltsin as the best representative of a fourth electorate, the majority of Russians who wanted honest reform. Yegorov reminded officers that it was the Communists who destroyed Russia's military cohesion and viability as a deliberate act of political sabotage designed to destroy the tsarist state and the democratic Provisional Government. He also criticized radical democrats and liberals who failed to understand the importance of state-building and defense spending after Russia's defeat by Japan in 1905. Yegorov's lessons of history included many of the same points that Aleksandr Lebed had been making.[37]

Yegorov added much that Yeltsin should have been saying to the military to win their support. He referred to the enormous tasks the military accomplished when it repatriated some 1,200,000 military personal and more than 45,000 pieces of military hardware, withdrew nuclear weapons from Belarus, Kazakhstan, and Ukraine, cut its overall size by some 900,000 positions, fought an unpopular civil war in Chechnya without inadequate funding or societal support, and laid the foundation for a new regional, territorial defense system. Yegorov agreed with military critics who claimed that Gorbachev's diplomatic concessions and the defense cuts made by radical democratic reformers in 1992 had damaged Russian security interests and that they had imposed those changes without due regard for military professional opinion. They had cut defense spending too deeply and had nurtured an antimilitary climate in Russian society. The world system was taking advantage of Russia's weaknesses and moving into Russia's traditional sphere of interest. Yegorov claimed that Boris Yeltsin had taken steps to correct prior mistakes in foreign and domestic policy. Yeltsin is described as having saved Russia from internal collapse and civil war and having installed the foundation for a powerful, democratic, and prosperous country. Yegorov concluded: "It is above all to the credit of the President of the Russian Federation that we broke that negative trend and adopted a realistic, truly statist ideology and policy for military development."[38] Yegorov insisted that there was a new positive, cooperative relationship between the Yeltsin administration and the military: "We entered into a new state in the relationship between the highest government leadership and the senior group in the Armed Forces, a stage of close cooperation on military development questions and army combat readiness and real measures to improve the living conditions of those who dedicate themselves to the defense of the Fatherland."[39]

Yeltsin's Military Letter and Meeting with Senior Leaders

On 23 May 1996, Boris Yeltsin published a letter addressed to all military personnel. It combined ideas and cited some of the same facts used by Satarov and Yegorov. It was far more positive on national defense than his State of the Federation Message and far less negative on the Communists and his nationalist opponents than Yegorov's report. Yeltsin was trying to position himself to receive voters from the nationalist opposition, people who were planning to vote for Lebed and Zyuganov. Yeltsin listed eight main points that will guide his military policy and made concern for military personnel his highest priority. This time he did not criticize the military for dragging its feet on reform; instead, he acknowledged that it, like the rest of Russian society, had made progress under very difficult conditions. He confirmed that he supported a smaller, more mobile, better equipped and trained, all-professional military. He touched briefly on the main elements of military system reconstruction. Defense Minister Grachev ordered all officers and soldiers to study the letter and explained that officers were to describe it as proof that the national leadership understood their problems and was taking action to remedy them.[40]

Yet, on balance the letter was bland, lacked candor, and probably evoked a negative response. Further, there were rumors circulating that Yeltsin was planning some dramatic shifts in military leadership, part of an alleged last-minute attempt to make himself more popular. Yeltsin decided that he needed to speak directly to the national military leadership. Grachev set the date and invited senior military administrators, commanders, educators, and related civilian experts and governmental leaders. The audience was looking for important political signals. Yeltsin's talk sent three.[41]

First, Yeltsin signaled that he really understood the military's deep sense of frustration and really valued the sacrifices it had made for Russia. He thanked the military for shedding its blood to defend Russia's political integrity and security. He admitted that he and civilian politicians in Moscow and Chechnya shared some of the blame for the mistakes that caused the war, kept it going, and brought so much destruction. He noted that inconsistent policy leadership and interagency coordination problems had sometimes left the army to fend for itself in contradictory situations. He added that inexperience with such conflicts on Russian territory had also contributed to the war's costs and mistakes. The war revealed weaknesses in the armed forces system that had to be corrected. Nevertheless, Yeltsin concluded, the military accomplished its mission and prevented the secessionists from beginning a process that would have destabilized all of South Russia.

Second, he signaled that he would stick to his basic line on military reform. Yeltsin admitted that the administration had underestimated the costs of military reform and the amount that could be saved by reducing total authorized positions by some 1,000,000 positions. Yeltsin said that the armed forces showed over 100 divisions on paper but in fact most were understaffed and some were not fit for combat. He supported more cuts and organizational streamlining in order to produce fewer but better trained and equipped divisions. He noted that some military experts were skeptical about the state's ability to replace draftees with paid professionals but said that they would find the means once they had been ordered to do so. He also briefly discussed the new Ministry of Defense Industry and the need for close coordination with the Ministry of Defense.[42]

Third, he signaled that he was generally pleased with the military and was even planning to increase its importance by restraining some of the other armed forces that had grown at its expense. Yeltsin denied rumors that he was about to make sensational changes in military leadership in order to improve his electoral prospects. He insisted that he was primarily interested in stable, constructive reform. He came to win their support not to frighten them. Yeltsin said, "On the whole I am satisfied with the work of the Minister of Defense's leadership group and the Ministry of Defense." He went on to say that "not everything is well with the reconstruction of the military and the other armies of the Russian Federation" but he focused on high costs not personalities.[43] Yet, listeners should have noticed that he did not praise Minister of Defense Grachev by name.

Armed Forces Checks and Balances

Yeltsin confirmed what many had believed. The total number of personnel under arms in Russia had not decreased since 1992 even though the military had cut some 1,000,000 positions! Other militarized forces grew rapidly while Russia's regular military had been cut. Although it was Yeltsin who originally approved that redirection of national resources, now he was complaining that it was wasteful and poorly administered. He instructed the military's General Staff to design new administrative models for bringing all Russian armed forces under a coordinated national security plan.[44] This was a significant political step that appealed to the military which resented the fact that the Federal Security Service, the MVD, and other militarized forces that had grown at their expense. When the lists of Ministry of Defense personnel, the MVD's internal armies, and the Border Forces are combined, the total number of professional armed forces at Yeltsin's command crosses the 3,000,000 line even without counting the special Kremlin security guards. All the federal armed forces were competing for the same shrinking pool of draftees. In spring 1995, for example, 210,000 were drafted but only 129,000 went to the military while 80,000 went into the other armed forces.[45]

Why had Yeltsin favored the MVD, the Border Troops, and the special security forces over the mainline military? From 1992 to 1996, Yeltsin had increased those armed services at the military's expense because his experts believed that the main threats Russia faced were domestic and in the border regions. But that wasn't the only reason. Military organizational analysts knew that there were political reasons for this practice. For example, Col. General Gennady Borzhenkov candidly stated that the civilian leadership kept the armed forces divided in order to create a system of checks and balances.[46]

Yeltsin did not invent the system of checks and balances. The model came from the Soviet period and was developed under Stalin. Soviet leaders had deliberately kept the country's armed forces divided into different services and ministries under different commanders as a way of holding them under reliable control. They used one armed force against another at various turning points in history. For example, Stalin used the security services against the military; Khrushchev reversed the pattern and used the military against the KGB in 1953; and, Yeltsin used the military against Parliament's armed security service in October 1993. Was Yeltsin now preparing to use the military as a balance against special security forces? Was he only interested in saving money or was he trying to save his political power from a perceived threat? The answer is both.

Yeltsin's staff discussed the organizational problem with Lt. General Lev Rokhlin whose Duma defense committee passed a new Law on Defense in late April 1996. Yeltsin signed it on 31 May 1996, two days after his appearance before the military. Rokhlin said that the other armed forces complained vigorously and charged that the military was trying to take them over.[47] But

Yeltsin did not want to push things that far. He opted for a middle position that created an armed forces planning and coordinating group within the General Staff. It gave Yeltsin a new institutional device for keeping tabs on the nonmilitary, armed forces but avoided creating one, extremely powerful Russian military machine that could threaten civilian political supremacy. When the General Staff established the new coordinating and planning division, each armed force was supposed to retain its own autonomous, militarized chain of command.[48] This move enhanced Chief of Staff Mikhail Kolesnikov's political importance to Boris Yeltsin and gave Yeltsin a new source of information about his domestic armed forces, domestic security forces, border forces, railroad troops, customs service, leadership security guards, and other special forces.

Yeltsin's Uses the Advantages of Incumbency

When they run for reelection Russia's presidents enjoy political advantages rooted in the powers associated with the office they hold. Yeltsin's campaign organization used those advantages to promote their candidate's interests and they did so without reverting to Soviet-style intimidation and coercion. Thus, on the whole, they set a modestly positive precedent for the future as they tried to coopt parts of the Communist and national-patriotic opposition's platform and to win over as many of their voters as possible. Nevertheless, there is reason to criticize some of his campaign's political activity with the military's senior leadership and the officer corps. The democratic process is supposed to encourage presidential candidates to move towards the middle of the political spectrum and that is what Yeltsin was doing in the Russian context. The two strongest opposition movements, the Communists led by Gennady Zyuganov and the reform patriots led by Lt. General (Ret.) Aleksandr Lebed found Yeltsin courting their "natural" constituencies.

Every senior officer knew that the 1993 Constitution gave the President the power to appoint and remove any officer and that the new Law on Defense enhanced presidential powers. Therefore, every senior officer's career depended upon the outcome of the presidential elections. By ordering the officer corps to study and hold meetings on the presidential Poslanie, staging meetings with Yeltsin administration insiders, sending letters to the military, and directly addressing the military leadership, Yeltsin was abusing the powers of the office of the presidency and practicing the art of political intimidation. But he was doing so with restraint. Defense Minister Grachev cooperated in this type of moderate partisan political activity and signaled that officers were expected to give their supreme commander their political support. However, neither Supreme Commander Yeltsin nor Defense Minister Grachev asked the senior officers meetings they held in Moscow to pass political resolutions supporting Yeltsin's candidacy.

The official military press became blatantly pro-Yeltsin in April 1996 and continued cranking out pro-Yeltsin news day after day on page one right up to the voting on 16 June 1996. The official organ of the Ministry of Defense, *Krasnaya zvezda*, followed Yeltsin's campaign and maintained an almost complete news blackout on his nine opponents. However, this was not a full scale regression into Soviet-style political control, not even at *Krasnaya zvezda* which continued to carry high quality reports on many important issues but not on the campaign. Its editorials were quite intelligent though they were all pro-Yeltsin. For example, Aleksandr Pel'ts's editorial of 20 April 1996 described the relationship between the campaign tours and changes in Yeltsin's positions on various issues. The campaign brought the president into direct contact with popular sentiment and he was changing his views to reflect the electorate's concerns about basic economic and social issues. The country wanted a broad coalition, honest discussion of past and recent policy mistakes, and steady work to correct them. If the broad coalition strategy meant that democratic reformers had to learn to be comfortable with some Communist symbols, more nationalist self-assertion, and military parades, so be it. Thus, when the president ordered the Red Flag of Victory (*Znamya pobedy*) to be restored to a place of in honor of those who gave their lives to defeat Hitler while serving under it, Gol'ts supported the decision. The main thing was to pull the nation together in order to continue the work of national reconstruction. The flag decision signaled that Yeltsin was running as the president of all the people. He would not concede the older generation and veterans to the Communists.[49]

Yeltsin's campaign organization created a special section for veterans affairs. Yeltsin addressed the leaders of all major veterans organizations at a special Kremlin reception. Next his campaign created a special presidential veterans advisory council which held national and regional meetings and reported to Yeltsin who responded positively by taking steps to repair the country's political-historical fabric and to improve veterans benefits and services.[50] On the other hand, the Communist opposition was also courting the veterans with Col. General (Ret.) Varennikov leading the effort through the Duma committee on veterans affairs which he headed. However, the Duma was less powerful and there was less prestige associated with it. By dealing directly with the veterans organizations, bringing them into his campaign, restoring the Red flag, and increasing veterans benefits, Yeltsin was outsmarting his Communist rivals and coopting their program.

What about defense industry and defense workers? The campaign targeted them as well. Yeltsin visited major defense industrial centers, criticized the government's handling of defense orders and payments, and pledged to take immediate action to improve the situation. He revived a theme that was popular with defense industrialists but generally ignored during his first term—Russia's industrial modernization should be based upon the military-industrial complex. He praised defense workers for enduring the personal sacrifices necessary to save national defense industry and announced that he was implementing a defense plan through the year 2005. "The worst is behind us" was his theme. Defense Minister Grachev reinforced these campaign themes.[51]

Managers wanted more than words. On 8 May 1996, Yeltsin used his powers of decree to transform Goskomoboronprom into a regular, free-standing ministry and named Zinovy Pak to serve as Russia's minister of defense industry.[52] Two weeks later a national MIC convention that represented labor and management from more than 500 defense industrial enterprises and research institutions assembled in Moscow to discuss national policy. Yeltsin addressed the meeting and pledged to improve financial and administrative support; however, other speakers reaffirmed that national defense planning and spending were still in poor condition even though the Yeltsin administration had been promising to take effective action for years.[53]

What about Cossacks and other nationalistic, ethno-Russian political forces? Was there room in the Kremlin for them? In order to court that constituency, Yeltsin went to the Cossack heartland in the North Caucasus and addressed huge public rallies. At Krasnodar, the Yeltsin campaign team brought forth *atamans* or Cossack headmen representing some 300,000 Cossacks. While the crowd shouted its approval, Yeltsin pledged to create a Supreme Administration for Cossack Armies that would report directly to the president and signed the necessary ukazes in their presence at the biggest rally. He then went on to Budyennovsk, the site of the hostage incident of summer 1995 and pledged to end the Chechen conflict successfully. He declared that Russia would never abandon its southern outposts and that only Russian power could guarantee all the peoples of the Caucasus civil peace and order.[54]

While Yeltsin was trying to rally the military, the veterans, and the national defense constituency behind his candidacy, his main opponent, Gennady Zyuganov, was working to encourage the armed forces to support the Communist political offensive. In early April, *Moscow News* obtained what it believed was a confidential forty-page report dated 26 March 1996 from an unidentified source in the Defense Ministry's Main Education Department on how the senior officers were leaning politically. However, two days later, the paper learned that the report had been prepared for the Communist Party on "confidential orders" from Gennady Zyuganov and was not a Defense Ministry document.[55] Nevertheless, even that was news and the paper printed a summary of the report's main conclusions which included results from an alleged military opinion poll showing Zyuganov gaining in popularity among military personnel with 14.1 percent in August 1995 and 21.5 percent in January 1996 compared to Yeltsin's 6.2 and 4.2 percent respectively. The idea was to show Yeltsin dropping and to give the impression that it would be a serious mistake for any officer to climb aboard his sinking ship.

The Communist report claimed that the senior officers for the most part could not be considered solidly in Yeltsin's camp and grouped them into five different political categories. It placed Defense Minister Grachev in the set of "unpredictable" generals who were ready to support any victor who could protect their careers and positions. Yeltsin's main supporters were clustered about First Deputy Defense Minister Andrei Kokoshin and Army General Konstantin Kobets—a Yeltsin ally since the last years of the Gorbachev regime. Chief of the General Staff, Army General Mikhail Kolesnikov and key senior military administrators near him were classified as political neutrals who were playing a waiting game. The group willing to criticize Grachev and Yeltsin's reforms openly consisted of Gromov, Kondratyev, Lebed, Mironov, and Vorobyev; but they were not in senior positions and some were recently retired. The report found little support among senior military leaders for vocal members of the opposition such as retired generals Lobov and Varennikov but found some for Achalov. It further claimed that if Yeltsin tried to avoid an electoral defeat in June 1996 by fomenting disturbances in the country and artificially creating a situation in which he could declare a state of emergency, then part of the military would side with the Communists. The report's most serious claim was that pro-Yeltsin generals had manipulated military voting and tampered with ballots in a manner that increased Russia Our Home's final results and amounted to 70 percent of that party's votes in December 1995's Duma elections.[56]

The press treated Zyuganov's report as news that there were political divisions within the senior command and that Yeltsin and Zyuganov were competing for military loyalty. The Ministry of Defense felt compelled to deny those reports and issued a political statement in the name of its top leadership council, the Collegium of the Ministry of Defense. It rejected allegations that the nation's top military professionals were divided over key political issues. It stated that the alleged surveys were fabrications designed "to disorient society and army and naval personnel on the eve of the presidential elections, in order to create the impression that there is a secret opposition inside the military leadership. "The collegium considers the spread of all manner of fabrications about the army for political purposes to be intolerable and declares that the Ministry of Defense leadership is united on all questions of military development and completely supports the reform program underway and the preservation of stability in the country."[57]

The episode demonstrated that the Russian political framework—the Constitutional provisions that put the senior military leadership squarely under the president's control, made it extremely difficult for the military to build and to hold to a neutral position even though, as I have argued, they would have preferred to be nonpartisan. In other words, the constitutional structure encourages the military to get on the reelection political bandwagon since they owe their jobs to the sitting president. This is especially true when the incumbent has a strong chance of winning. This system damages military professionalism and military cohesion.

Communists are Irresponsible, Incompetent, and Dangerous

On 15 March 1996, the Communists and their allies in the Duma passed a resolution condemning the *Belovyezhskiye Accords*, the December 1991 deal between Yeltsin, Kravchuk, and Shushkevich that dissolved the Soviet Union. They claimed that it was an illegal act which contradicted the March 1991 referendum in which the majority across the USSR endorsed a reformed Union of Sovereign States. The Duma resolution's purpose was to remind voters that Yeltsin had killed the Union as part of his drive to defeat Union president Gorbachev and that Yeltsin was responsible for the damage that act had done to the general economy. However, the Communist gambit backfired and the Yeltsin camp immediately took advantage of the blunder. They accused the Communists of political irresponsibility—gross ineptitude that could only damage relations between the former Soviet republics and which if pushed to its logical conclusion might provoke armed conflict between the republics and civil war. Zyuganov had delivered a political gift to Yeltsin.

The campaign to elect Yeltsin charged that Zyuganov was at best a Trojan horse—a means by which the real Communist hardliners intended to take power and to repudiate the democratic revolution. In mid-April, *Moscow News* reporters were claiming that Zyuganov had already picked his future cabinet and intended to make Col. General (Ret.) Albert Makashov his minister of defense and to give control over the media to Viktor Anpilov. Further, the future Communist minister of agriculture was to be Starodubtsev—who served in the SEC's three-day government in August 1991.[58] Zyuganov soon realized that extremists inside his political coalition had become his main liability and he tried to convince industrialists and other Russian elites that he would never give power to radicals such as Col. General (Ret.) Albert Makashov and Viktor Anpilov.[59] In September-October 1993, the two helped push the Khasbulatov-Rutskoi camp into rash actions that gave Yeltsin the excuses needed to throw the military against them. In spring 1996, their radical statements damaged the Zyuganov campaign which needed to present itself as a responsible alternative to the Yeltsin administration. They played into Yeltsin's hands by giving his campaign political ammunition against the Communists.

Nevertheless, the competitive electoral system was nudging Zyuganov towards the center of the political spectrum and he and Yeltsin found themselves competing for the same group of swing voters. In order to convince voters of his political moderation and desire to build a broad coalition, Zyuganov announced that if elected he would reserve about 20 percent of the presidential nomenklatura for people now in the Yeltsin camp and non-

Communist parties now represented in the Duma. However, the Yeltsin nomenklatura used its influence over the state media to crank out anti-Communist specials and kept the Yeltsin campaign's "Communist threat" theme before the public.

The Chechen War and the Elections

The electoral campaign had three impacts on civil-military relations. First, since the war was unpopular, the president tried harder to end it and this led to more intensive fighting and peacemaking. Although that mixture seems inherently contradictory, that strategy made better political and military sense than the one followed from November 1994 to April 1996. Second, Yeltsin imposed changes in military conscription and military service assignment patterns in order to make himself more popular with the voters. Third, he tried to confront his own role in the conflict more candidly and to identify systemic problems that contributed to the war policy's shortcomings. The role of the prodigal president who had learned his lessons and could now lead better had some appeal but it prevented him from using political scapegoats effectively.

The rebels had used every cease-fire to regroup and to gather strength for the next round in fighting—the military warned Yeltsin that any new cease-fire would be the same. The military argued that a political settlement could only be achieved after Dudayev's forces had been defeated militarily. Yet, Yeltsin proclaimed another cease-fire for 1 April 1996 and even offered to meet with Dudayev without first requiring him to abandon his drive for independence. Reporters compared Yeltsin's struggle with Chechen rebels to Israel's with Palestinians. After years of refusing to meet with the PLO and Yasir Arafat, Israel changed its policy and made progress towards a settlement. Terrorism had achieved for the Palestinian cause what normal warfare could not achieve given Israel's military superiority. Wouldn't meeting with Dudayev confirm that point? Yeltsin agreed but predicted that Dudayev would moderate his position and accept a treaty that gave Chechnya the maximum autonomy permissible short of independence.[60]

Weren't the Russian elections working in Dudayev's favor? Why should Dudayev give up his independence goal and settle now? Yeltsin did not have a good answer. Instead, he claimed that Dudayev would try to keep the war going in order to enhance the Communist Party's prospects since the world community would be more likely to support a rebellion against a Communist regime than against democratic Russia and the chaos that would follow a Communist victory in Russia would benefit his rebellion.[61]

What about the military problem? How would Yeltsin prevent Dudayev from taking advantage of the current cease-fire? Yeltsin had no answer. Instead he stressed that federal troops would immediately begin limited withdrawals because more and more of Chechnya had come under reliable control.[62] Thereafter, every town and hamlet that signed a *soglasie* or reconciliation agreement that pledged to prevent rebels from operating within its administrative borders was listed as a zone under federal control. By mid-April 1996, the Yeltsin administration claimed that some two thirds of Chechnya or 203 cities and towns had signed such agreements.[63] Federal troops were not supposed to take military action unless fired upon but they did set up check points and tried to monitor and to prevent rebel forces from moving about the country.

Two weeks after Yeltsin's new cease-fire, rebel forces attacked a federal military convoy and killed fifty-three federal troops and wounded another fifty-two. The incident took place in the Shatoi region whose authorities had signed the reconciliation agreement. It supported the military's contention that rebels were abusing the cease-fire and would not accept peace until they had suffered a more complete military defeat. The attack sparked a new round of political debate on the war just as the Russian central electoral commission announced the full list of presidential candidates and Yeltsin was touring the North Caucasus.

The Duma erupted and demanded immediate hearings. Antiwar deputies attacked Defense Minister Grachev and accused him of deliberately sabotaging the president's policies. The media had a field day with the hearings but Grachev persisted and demonstrated why from a military operational point of view the cease-fire was a bad policy. Duma defense committee chairman, Lt. General Lev Rokhlin wanted the military's professional assessment rather than a partisan attack on the armed forces. Defense Minister Grachev provided full details on the Shatoi convoy incident which illustrated how bad political policy and sloppy military discipline contributed to the slaughter. Federal troops had left themselves open to attack. (Later, Grachev sacked the officers in charge of the operation.) Grachev told the Duma, "Nothing good will come out of a situation in which the army is suspended between war and peace, *neither war nor peace*."[64]

Duma Deputy Kharitonov asked Grachev how many federal troops had been killed since the president's cease-fire went into effect? The answer was 122 of which 102 were soldiers in the regular military and twenty were in either the MVD and the local militia. He went on to express his understanding and support for the Russian soldier who continued to uphold the state and to obey orders.[65] Kharitonov tried to turn the debate into a search for solutions rather than a search for scapegoats.

Grachev lost his temper as various deputies demanded his resignation. When Deputy Shchekochikhin told him to step down, Grachev said, "Well, first I am the Minister of Defense not the Minister of Health or Culture. Therefore, my duty is to carryout orders and to fight. How I fight is another matter. That probably does not solely depend upon the will of the Minister of Defense. Yes, I deeply regret the deaths. But I also deeply regret the fact that I was prevented from defeating the remaining rebel bands." He went on to remind the deputies that it was the civilian politicians who had created the mess in the country and the war, not the soldiers." Grachev continued blasting away: "If you peoples deputies believe that all the disorder happening in the country and in part in the army and those losses that the federal forces suffer depend just on the Minister of Defense personally, then, under those circumstances, I am ready to resign now."[66]

But Grachev then argued that the rebels were primarily to blame for the war. Grachev reminded the deputies that, on Yeltsin's instructions, he had met with Dudayev, the Chechen rebel leader, for three hours at the beginning of the war. Dudayev allegedly told Grachev that he could not agree to a settlement since his entourage would never permit it. He further argued that even now the Chechen rebel side is disunited and cannot make authoritative decisions at the current talks. Grachev advocated a talk and fighting strategy that would force the rebels to submit.[67]

Next Deputy Galina Vasilyevna Starovoitova accused Grachev of insubordination and warned that there was a "creeping military coup underway in the country." Grachev countered with three points. First, some military officers had indeed used insubordination to build their political reputations but he had always been loyal to the supreme commander. Second, the armed forces were under reliable control and capable of fighting successfully. Third, he said, "Galina Vasilyevna, you need to listen very attentively. I did not say that I am in opposition to the peace plan. I said that as a result of this peace plan, in my view, the enemy was able to organize himself, to dig in, and to prepare for large scale future actions. This is what he showed us on 16 April 1996."[68]

Military Offensives, Dudayev's Death, and a New Cease-Fire

Grachev survived the latest round of calls for his resignation and it appears that Yeltsin decided to take his advice. The federal side stepped up military pressure on rebel strongholds in remote southern regions of Chechnya, especially the Bamut rebel center which was housed in a former Soviet strategic missile complex. Further, on the night of 21–22 April 1996, Dudayev was killed by federal missiles, but Yeltsin never took credit for the ultimate political act, the assassination of the leader of the opposition. For years the federal side either lacked the capability or had deliberately restrained itself from using sophisticated technology to locate and attack Dudayev by tracking his communications signals. Yet, on that night, Dudayev was killed while trying to place a call allegedly related to the peace process. Dudayev was standing in an open field holding a special telephone which used international satellite links when he was killed. His funeral took place shortly thereafter without any air attacks.[69]

On 2 May 1996, Yeltsin renewed his offer to meet with Chechen rebel leaders, even in Chechnya if necessary. Yeltsin envoys tried to get direct talks going. Meanwhile federal troops launched a major attack with troops, artillery tanks and air power and destroyed the rebel command center on or about 24 May 1996. Three days later, on 27 May 1996, Zelimkhan Yanderbiyev, Dudayev's successor, was flown to Moscow under special protection guaranteed by Boris Yeltsin for talks in the Kremlin. Yeltsin announced that there would be a new cease-fire and that work would begin immediately on a treaty between Chechnya and the federal republic. He put Premier Chernomyrdin in charge of taking the next steps and another meeting with rebels was held on 28 May 1996 after which they returned to Chechnya. By using its military power more aggressively, the federal side had pushed the rebels to the conference table. Yeltsin tried to exploit this breakthrough politically and all but declared victory in the war to preserve Russia's political integrity. He flew to the war's military headquarters at Mozdok to thank the troops and to explain his policy and then went on to make several appearances inside Chechnya. The troops were concerned lest this the latest cease-fire follow the familiar pattern in which rebels simply regroup for more fighting. Yeltsin and Grachev told soldiers that things would be different this time since the key rebel strongholds had been destroyed and the federal side would not permit them to abuse the cease-fire.[70] Yeltsin reassured the troops, thanked them, and admitted that he had made errors that had kept the war going too long. " I do not deny my own guilt in that," the president said. He repeated the basic legal case for the war. "You functioned on a legal foundation by carrying out the orders of the Supreme Commander and the Minister of Defense. You are under the protection of the Constitution and the President." He distributed medals and awards to soldiers and explained that the time had indeed come to move from the military draft to a completely professional army.[71]

Conclusion

What had the Chechen war politics of April and May illustrated about the state of civil-military relations in post-Soviet Russia? Three main points need to be made. First, there was a healthy public dialogue on the war and the military participated in it. Defense Minister Grachev spoke candidly and tried to shape national policy. He could not have done so without the passive approval of his supreme commander, Boris Yeltsin, who permitted members of his cabinet to express personal views on policy issues. Second, the military learned to carry out national policy even when it did not fully agree with it. And, it learned to function with national and international media watching and commenting upon its actions. Third, the need to win votes motivated the president to work harder at ending the war successfully. This led to heavier fighting and to greater concessions and risks such as direct negotiations with the rebel leaders. It also led to popular but unfunded promises such as the pledge to end the military draft.

The campaign reaffirmed and therefore reinforced the practice of treating the military and the national defense community as political constituencies that need to be courted. By giving increased attention to military salary, benefits, and housing problems, Yeltsin was doing what politicians normally do when running for election, promising what the voters wanted within reason. But the Yeltsin campaign went beyond normal, democratic courtship and abused presidential power by imposing self-serving, partisan political activity on the officer corps. Although some such behavior is to be expected, it is extremely important for the development of the democratic political process that incumbents be prevented from using state assets, institutions, and public employees for partisan political purposes. Sitting presidents should not be permitted either to order or to persuade military officers to study their political tracts or to teach them to the troops as part of normal military institutional life. They should not be allowed to impose partisan editorial policies on official military publications. They should not be able to subject senior military officers to partisan political lectures by senior presidential aides. Yeltsin did those things and set a poor precedent for the future.

He went too far in promoting his political platform inside the armed forces but he did not go far enough in training his "power" ministers to support his policies consistently in their dialogue with the public. It damaged the president's authority as supreme commander when power ministers advocated their own policy ideas to the media. Such behavior created the impression that the Yeltsin did not control the top generals which implied that the armed forces were not under reliable constitutional control. On the one hand, Grachev, carried out Yeltsin's orders in Chechnya and regularly declared that the Russian military were cohesive and combat ready. On the other, he openly criticized Chechen war political strategies from a military point of view and warned that the armed forces had lost patience with civilian leaders and were close to running out of control. On the one hand, MVD chief Kulikov worked within the federal budget and concentrated on internal law and order issues; on the other, he criticized federal revenue collection and allocation policies and advocated major changes in governmental regulation of banks, energy, and other "natural" monopolies. Special political security force chief Korzhakov's behavior was even more controversial as will be shown.

The idea that the Fatherland will not be restored until military officers present themselves to the people, win their support, and take high office moved from the realm of theory into practice. Lt. General (Ret.) Lebed's entry into the presidential campaign reinforced the idea that patriotic Russian soldiers can and should displace irresponsible and incompetent civilian politicos. Winning votes was more important than military professionalism in determining who would have the strongest influence over national defense policy.

The combination of competitive elections and civil liberties had changed Russian political life and the way Russia fights wars. Society at large watched, participated, reacted, and influenced policy. The military participated in that political dialogue. Such affairs of state were no longer the exclusive purview of a small elite. Nevertheless, there was no easy solution to the Chechen affair or to the general problem of reconstructing Russia's military capabilities to meet post-Soviet challenges more effectively.

Notes

1. Boris Yeltsin cited by Tatyana Malkina, "Candidate: Boris Yeltsin: Starting with Good Intentions," *Sevodnya*, 16 February 1996; *CDSP*, vol. XLVIII, no. 7, 1996, p. 1.
2. Leonid Posdeev, "Boris Yel'tsin ofitsial'no obyavil reshenie o tom, shto on budet ballatirovat'sya v Prezidenty Rossii na vtoroi srok" (Boris Yeltsin officially declared his decision to run for the presidency of Russia for a second term), *Krasnaya zvezda*, 16 February 1996.
3. The Federal Assembly is Russia's two-house legislative branch of government. The lower house is the State Duma. The upper house is the Federal Council.
4. My translation from the official *State of the Federation* text: Boris Yeltsin, "Poslanie Prezidenta Rossiiskoi Federatsii Federal'nomu Sobraniyu—Rossiya za kotoruyu my v otvete, 23 February 1996," *Krasnaya zvezda*, 11 March 1996, pp. 3–5. Hereafter: Boris Yeltsin, Poslanie. In addition to the official text which Yeltsin supplied, there is a translation of the speech which he delivered, a shorter and less formal version of the official written text. See *CDSP*, XLVIII, no. 8, 1996 for an English translation of the shorter speech. My citations are from the official *State of the Federation* text.
5. Boris Yeltsin, *Poslanie*.
6. *Ibid.*
7. *Ibid.*
8. *Ibid.*
9. *Ibid.*
10. *Ibid.*
11. *Ibid.*
12. Reported by Lt. Colonel Sergei Popov, "Rossiya, kotoruyu my zashchishchaem. Blizhaishei temoi obshchestvenno gosudarstvennoi podgotovki voennosluzhayushchikh stanet izuchene Poslaniya Prezidenta RF" (The Russia we defend. Study of the RF president's message to be immediate topic for military personnel education in civics), *Krasnaya zvezda*, 6 March 1996.
13. See "Details: What Is General Kulikov Proposing?" *Argumenty i fakty*, no. 7, 1996. *CDSP*, XLVIII, no. 7, 1996, pp. 8–9.
14. See Mikhail Berger, "A Gesture of Despair or Military-Economic Intelligence?," *Izvestiya*, 14 February 1996. *CDSP*, XLVIII, no. 7, 1996, p. 9.
15. See Mark Morozov, "Expert Opinion On A Plan: The Police Know Where The Money Is," *Obshchaya gazeta*, no. 6, 15–21 February 1996. *CDSP*, XLVIII, no. 7, 1996, p.9.
16. Pavel Grachev, cited by Oleg Vladykin, "Ne zbyt' tekh ognennykh dorog" (Do not forget those burning roads), *Krasnaya zvezda*, 17 February 1996.
17. Aleksandr Gol'ts, "Prezidentskii marafon: Dengi reshat vse" (Presidential marathon: money determines all), *Krasnaya zvezda*, 17 February 1996.
18. Comment by Vitaly Vitebsky, *Goskomoboronprom's* chief statistician; "Statistika: VPK v 1995" (Statistics: the MIC in 1995), *Krasnaya zvezda*, 17 January 1996.
19. Viktor Glukhikh, Chairman of *Goskomoboronprom* interviewed by Valentin Rudenko, "Rubikon, nazyvayemyi tabilizatsiei…" *Krasnaya zvezda*, 13 January 1996.

20. *Ibid.*
21. See Viktor Litovkin, "Military-Industrial Complex Entrusted to Master of Dual Technologies," *Izvestiya*, 25 January 1996. *CDSP*, XLVIII, no. 4, p. 17.
22. Reported by Oleg Falichev, "Voennaya reforma kak zerkalo rossiiskoi ekonomiki" (Military reform, a reflection of the Russian economy), *Krasnaya zvezda*, 10 April 1996. Arbatov was a member of Gregory Yavlinsky's *Yabloko* faction.
23. Falichev, *Ibid.*
24. Pavel Grachev cited by Falichev in *Ibid.*
25. On 12 June 1996, issued Ukaz no 861, "O dopolnitel'nykh merakh po sotsial'noi zashchite…" and Ukaz no 863, "O pravakh i lgotakh voennosluzhaschikh," Texts in *Krasnaya zvezda*, 14 June 1996.
26. Aleksandr Lebed's political autobiography, *Za derzhavu obidno* (Ashamed for the State) (Moscow: Moskovskaya pravda, 1995), p. 453.
27. *Ibid.*, pp. 422–49.
28. Lt. General Aleksandr Lebed, "Declaration by the Commander of the 14th combined guard forces of the Russian Army" (in Russian), 4 July, 1994, Tiraspol; p. 450, *Ibid.*
29. *Ibid.*, p. 454.
30. Aleksandr Lebed to Pavel Grachev, 5 July 1992, page 455, *Ibid.*
31. *Ibid.*, p. 463.
32. See Vitaly Strugovets, "Neobkhodima konsolidatsiya vsekh sil vo blago Rossii: Vstrecha v Ministerstve oborony s pomoshchnikom prezidenta" (Consolidation needed for Russia's sake: meeting at the ministry of defense with president's assistant), *Krasnaya zvezda*, 6 April 1996.
33. See Georgy Satarov, "Politicheskoe trebovanie vremeni—konsolidatsiya" (Consolidation—today's political demand), *Krasnaya zvezda*, 10 April 1996.
34. *Ibid.*
35. *Ibid.*
36. *Ibid.*
37. See pp. 422–49 in Lebed, *Za derzhavu obidno*.
38. Nikolai D. Yegorov, Chief of Presidential Administration, "Velikoi Rossii nuzhna sil'naya armiya" (Great Russia needs a powerful army), *Krasnaya zvezda*, 20 April 1996.
39. *Ibid.*
40. The letter and the editorial on how it should be studied are in *Krasnaya zvezda*, 25 May 1996.
41. See Boris Yeltsin, "Prezident Rossii Boris Yeltsin, "Ya primu vse mery dlya vsestoronnei podderzhki armii i flota" (I will take all measures to provide all-round support to the army and navy), *Krasnaya zvezda*, 31 May 1996.
42. *Ibid.*
43. *Ibid.*
44. *Ibid.*
45. Oleg Vladykin's interview with Maj. General Valery Astanin, Chief of Mobilization for the Ministry of Defense, *Krasnaya zvezda*, 22 July 1995.
46. Col. General Gennady Borzhenkov, "Voennaya reforma" (Military reform), *Krasnaya zvezda*, 30 June 1995.
47. See Captain Vladimir Urban's discussion of the new Law on Defense, "Zakon RF *Ob oborone* podpisan prezidentom i vstupayet v silu" (RF defense law signed by president and taking force), *Krasnaya zvezda*, 5 June 1996.
48. Reported by Oleg Vladikin, "Voiska vsekh silovykh vedomstv Rossii nachinayut uchitsya vzaimodeistviyu" (The armies of all the power ministries (departments) are beginning to learn to cooperate), *Krasnaya zvezda*, 1 June 1996.

49. See Aleksandr Pel'ts, "Vremya otritsat' otritsane" (Time to reject rejectionism), *Krasnaya zvezda*, 20 April 1996.
50. See Yury Gladkevich, "Znat' problemy i nuzhdy tekh, kto sluzhil Otechestvu..." (To know the problems and needs of those who served the Fatherland...), *Krasnaya zvezda*, 6 April 1996.
51. See Vitaly Strugovets, "Voenno-promyshlennyi kompleks—osnova tekhnologicheskoi modernizatsii promyshlennosti" (The military-industrial complex—the foundation for industry's technological modernization), *Krasnaya zvezda*, 13 April 1996; and Aleksandr Pel'ts, "Vremya raskachki proshlo" (The time of major shake-ups has passed), *Krasnaya zvezda*, 19 April 1996.
52. See Valentin Rudenko, "Zinovy Pak: 'Oboronka nachinayet zhit' tsivilizovannoi zhizn'yu" (Zinovy Pak: Defense begins living a civilized life), *Krasnaya zvezda*, 18 May 1996.
53. See Valentin Rudenko, Prezident Rossii obeschaet 'oboronke' podderzhku" (Russia's president pledges support to defense), *Krasnaya zvezda*, 30 May 1996.
54. Reported by Anatoly Borovkov, "Kazaki otvetili: *Lyubo*" (Cossacks responded *hurrah*), *Krasnaya zvezda*, 18 April 1996; and Sergei Knyaz'kov, "Severnyi Kavkaz—forpost Rossii" (North Caucasus: Russia's forward position), *Krasnaya zvezda*, 19 April 1996.
55. See Aleksander Zhilin, "Generals Divided Over June Election: The Balance of Power at the Defense Ministry and the General Staff in the Run-up to the Presidential Elections in June 1996," *Moscow News*, no. 14, 11–14 April, 1996.
56. See *Ibid.*
57. "Zayavlenie Kollegii Ministerstva oborony RF" (RF ministry of defense collegium declaration), *Krasnaya zvezda*, 10 April 1996.
58. See Sergei Roy, "ghostly Cabinet," *Moscow News*, no. 14, 11–17 April 1996.
59. See Maksim Sokolov, "Zyuganov has Made What the All-Russian Communist Party (Bolsheviks) Used to Call A 'Hostile Attack,'" *Kommersant-Daily*, 16 May 1996, *CDSP*, vol. XVIII, no. 20, 1996, p. 15.
60. Boris Yeltsin's press conference of 31 March 1996 as reported by *Golos Rossii*, Russia's international radio service, on the same date. Author's notes.
61. *Ibid.*
62. "Chechnya: 203 naselennykh punkta vstupayut za mir" (Chechnya: 203 settled areas go for peace), *Krasnaya zvezda*, 18 April 1996 (no author).
63. The full transcript of Grachev's remarks to the Duma hearings on 19 April into the incident of 16 April was printed in *Krasnaya zvezda* on 23 April 1996. *Neither war nor peace* refers to the disastrous Bolshevik policy towards the Germans in 1917–1918, a form of self-righteous capitulation.
64. *Ibid.*
65. *Ibid.*
66. *Ibid.*
67. *Ibid.*
68. *Krasnaya zvezda* cited ITAR-TASS reports and did not provided any inside military information on this event. See editions of 25 and 26 April 1996.
69. Reported by Anatoly Stasovskii, "Na peregovorakh v Moskve dostignut progress. Boris Yeltsin pribyl v Chechne s mirom" (Progress at Moscow talks. Boris Yeltsin visits Chechnya with peace), *Krasnaya zvezda*, 29 May 1996.
70. Anatoly Stasovskii, "Federal'nye voiska v Chechne vypolnili svoi dolg. Oni zashchitili tselostnost' Rossiiskogo gosudarstva" (Federal armies in Chechnya fulfilled their duty. They defended the integrity of the Russian state), *Krasnaya zvezda*, 30 May 1996.

15

President Yeltsin and General Lebed

Russian electoral politics were a mixture of authoritarian populism, democratic opportunism, political marketing, and Soviet-style intrigue. Yeltsin learned the new competitive electoral skills and used them better than his opponents and the overall outcome reaffirmed that a competitive electoral system was taking root in Russia. But he also demonstrated that the politics of oligarchy remained very much alive and that key members of the armed forces participated in them. Yeltsin's political dealing with Lt. General (Ret.) Aleksandr Lebed, one of his electoral opponents, illustrates how democratic opportunism and Kremlin rivalries were interwoven. This chapter explains why Yeltsin made Lebed his chief national security adviser and called him his heir apparent and why this event precipitated major personnel changes at the highest levels in the country's military and security leadership. Those events confirmed that Russia's armed forces—particularly the top leaders of military and security institutions, were very much involved in national politics and could not afford to ignore them. The political system made them vulnerable to high-level political wheeling and dealing instead of insulating them from it.

Yeltsin's Campaign Needs vs. Administrative Cohesion

Aleksandr Lebed's decision to run for the presidency turned out to be a fortunate development for the Yeltsin campaign but a very unsettling one for the Yeltsin administration's national security team. The Yeltsin campaign needed a political ally who could convince voters that the next Yeltsin administration would tackle internal problems such as corruption, criminality, and drift on key national defense and security reconstruction issues. The general was the only person on the list of presidential candidates who could do that and draw opposition voters away from the Communists and the radical nationalists. By 1996, the other prominent non-Communist radical nationalist, Vladimir Zhirinovsky, had thoroughly discredited himself with the Russian public and could not poll more than 5–6 percent of the vote. In effect, Lebed had conquered some of the political space that Zhirinovsky used to dominate.

As the election drew nearer and Yeltsin campaign pollsters and strategists gained a relatively accurate picture of the electorate's mood, they knew that the president would have to deal with the general in order to secure a solid margin of victory in the second round. These discussions precipitated some nervous behavior inside the Yeltsin security team since it was understood that the general would demand major changes in national security leadership.

The Yeltsin campaign used modern political science techniques to discover what Russian voters wanted region by region, constituency by constituency. Georgy Satarov and other political scientists led the expert analytical group which developed the political information and advised Yeltsin and his supporters about where to go, what to say, and what policy actions to take. Such applied political science gave the Yeltsin campaign advantages over its rivals. It drew upon international experience and employed some American experts as well. By May 1996 the news Satarov's pollsters had for Yeltsin was good but it also created political problems for Yeltsin inside the Kremlin. The good news was that Yeltsin was ahead of his main rival, Gennady Zyuganov but did not have nearly enough support to win the election on the first round which required more than 50 percent of the popular vote. Yeltsin had to prevent the opposition from congealing into a broad anti-Yeltsin coalition. Total popular support for the three leading opposition figures—Zyuganov, Zhirinovsky, and Lebed, added up to more than 50 percent. The three knew that they needed to join forces in order to defeat Yeltsin.

In that situation, the Yeltsin campaign had two logical choices. First, it could try to postpone the elections in order to give Yeltsin more time to build his political coalition to the point where he could take the election with more than 50 percent of the popular vote. Second, it could go ahead with the election and do its best to make certain that Yeltsin and Zyuganov would win the most votes in the first round and that Yeltsin would defeat Zyuganov by a slim margin in the second round. Yeltsin's primary goal was to prevent Zyuganov from building the triple alliance that could topple him. There was a political price to pay. Yeltsin had to make deals with political outsiders such as General Lebed who wanted some of the most important positions in the Yeltsin administration. Which Kremlin insiders and top leaders would be sacrificed to appease Lebed? There was also deep concern about President Yeltsin's health, his ability to complete the campaign and to convince voters that he was physically and psychologically fit.

The fact that Aleksander Lebed was emerging as the commander of a block of swing votes, the holder of political space that Yeltsin and Zyuganov both wanted to occupy—had tremendous implications for Yeltsin administration insiders who held the most important positions in national defense and security affairs. Lebed regarded the campaign as a process in which he gathered a popular mandate to give Russia an honest and effective progressive government and to restore Russian state power and prestige. At a minimum this required new leadership in military, security, and police affairs. Since Lebed believed he had the popular mandate and the legitimacy to make these changes, if Yeltsin wanted him to join the second Yeltsin administration, Yeltsin would have to empower him to make the changes that the "people" were demanding. Lebed saw himself as the agent of the people and the defender of Russian national interests against a corrupted political oligarchy. However, he did not want to be Zyuganov's general. Lebed's Russian nationalism and personal disgust for the crude manner in which Communist regimes had treated Soviet military professionals kept him from joining Zyuganov's "national-patriotic front."

The corruption, criminality, and incompetence issues had been on the agenda for years and little had been done to face them. Rutskoi and Yeltsin had split over such problems. Now a new crusading military officer was forcing them onto the political agenda and demanding to know why they had not been addressed by the officials responsible for national security and law and order. Since Yeltsin also knew that it was in his personal interest and in Russia's national interest to attack corruption and to let others take most of the blame for the Chechen mess, a political house-cleaning had appeal. It would give Yeltsin a chance to win the election and to go down in history as the man who gave Russia honest reform after listening to the people and making tough decisions. To make that happen he would have to purge part of his own administration. People who stood to lose their prestigious positions and their wealth and power were understandably nervous.

Competitive Politics and Leadership Renewal

After the strong Communist surge in the December 1995 Duma elections, Yeltsin shifted his leadership core modestly in an effort to appeal to voters who demanded a more assertive foreign policy, a more socialist reform program, proof positive that the president was fighting crime and corruption in high places, and immediate progress towards a settlement in Chechnya. In January 1996 Yeltsin replaced foreign minister Andrei Kozyrev with Yevgeny Primakov, Vice Premier Anatoly Chubais with Vladimir Kadannikov, and Chief of Presidential Administration Sergei Filatov with Nikolai Yegorov. However, the three power ministers—Barsukov (federal security), Grachev (defense), Korzhakov (elite political security), and Kulikov (MVD), retained their positions.

Grachev survived through the fourth anniversary of his appointment as Russia's first, post-Soviet minister of defense. He had taken the military through enormously difficult times; yet, he continued to be unpopular with the liberal media which tended to focus on what he had not done as opposed to what he had accomplished in spite of the national economic and political mess. In May 1996 when Grachev completed four years of service as defense minister, there were neither major honors from President Yeltsin nor celebrations in recognition of his contributions. He was just a presidential ukaz away from the political attic where figures like Gorbachev and Shaposhnikov already resided. Competitive politics, like the competitive economy, keep grinding forward and bringing new figures to the fore. Generals in senior military leadership positions are fair game and are affected by that competition because they are members of the national political leadership and are on the presidential nomenklatura or list of appointees. Getting promoted beyond a certain point puts a military officer into that part of national political space where military professional and civilian political criteria fuse.

General Korzhakov's "Threat" to Democracy

On 5 May 1996, General Aleksandr Korzhakov, chief of Russia's federal security services, stated that the presidential elections should be postponed because the Russian people had not had enough time to reach "mature conclusions" about the candidates and issues. At Russia's celebrations honoring the military who served in the war against fascism, Korzhakov told reporters, "Many influential people in Russia consider it desirable to postpone the election, myself among them, since we need stability." He claimed that there was strong public support for postponement and the security services knew this to be fact. Why? Because the elections would polarize society and lead to conflict no matter whether Yeltsin or Zyuganov won. He insisted that postponement was in the national interest.[1]

Yet, the Yeltsin campaign had been reporting steady gains and it was predicting that in the first round of voting on 16 June 1996, Yeltsin would receive more votes than Zyuganov, enough to prevent a Zyuganov victory though not enough to avoid a second round runoff. Korzhakov's public statements caused the campaign team serious embarrassment. Campaign chief, Sergei Filatov had to denounce them. Filatov warned that such thinking could lead to a return to the old politics of dictatorship. Yeltsin told reporters that he ordered Korzhakov not to poke his nose into politics and not to make any more such statements.

Korzhakov had been Yeltsin's loyal security guard and confidant through thick and thin. Lebed had characterized him as an opportunist who drank his way to the top and said the same about Defense Minister Grachev.[2] Korzhakov had been Yeltsin's human shield and personal body guard during the August coup and thereafter as required. Yeltsin's decision to sacrifice him if necessary in order to save his own power could not have been easy to make. Nevertheless, Yeltsin insisted that the elections be held on time and said that he had "faith in the wisdom of Russia's voters."[3] (The Communists denounced Korzhakov and demanded that the elections be held as scheduled; they needed democracy and the Constitution to protect their political rights.)

New Class Fears of Radical Populism

Korzhakov wasn't alone in seeking a way to reduce the risks inherent in the election. Russia's new wealthy class realized that radical populism threatened its power and position in Russian society. A new financial elite had grown up along with the Yeltsin administration and was intricately involved with it. The new elite did not have similar ties to the three main opposition movements which represented the majority of Russian popular sentiment. It was vulnerable to a Russian counterreformation with strong socialist overtones.

A week before Korzhakov's call for postponement, a group of thirteen prominent business leaders headed by Boris Berezovsky published an appeal that attacked the competitive electoral process because it was encouraging each faction to take extreme positions instead of combining forces for the good of the country. Instead of letting the elections decide who will govern, they proposed that all major political leaders meet to negotiate power-sharing pacts, a series of binding compromises. Their appeal insisted, "Russian politicians must be induced to make very substantial mutual concessions and to conclude strategic political accords and to codify them in legal form. There is simply no other way out."[4] They wanted a business merger instead of an election. They considered the democratic process a threat to Russian reconstruction along Western lines.

But did they have a real plan to block the election? One that would be supported by the armed forces? The armed forces were part of the problem, part of the threat to the new financial elite because the Ministry of Defense and the MVD had taken public stands critical of the new class's stewardship over national finances. The business elite was supposed to provide the State with economic prosperity and to insure an adequate flow of revenues into the Kremlin treasury. Instead, the economy was down by some 50 percent in overall industrial output since 1990 and the armed services were suffering from inadequate and irregular support. For years the official military press had complained about the poor quality of political and economic leadership. The most prominent retired generals in politics were in the opposition parties not in the pro-business group. This was not an environment in which the economic elite could expect the armed forces to save it from a populist rebellion.

Presidential candidate Lebed was playing it both ways. He demanded honest management of national economic affairs not a return to the socialist political economy. But his zealous attacks on corruption made the financial elite uneasy. Defense Minister Grachev also certainly knew that his days were numbered and must have shared mixed feelings with trusted colleagues though, to his credit, he did not make a public spectacle of them. Competitive politics aren't necessarily fair or always the best way to improve the professional quality of national leadership in the short run. The power ministers knew that Lebed was energetic, able, and experienced in some aspects of military and political affairs; but they also knew why he had been kept at a distance since August 1991 and must have been deeply concerned about this maverick's arrival at the Kremlin walls because of his inflated sense of historic mission and personal legitimacy.

Yeltsin and Zyuganov knew the political game as well as anyone and were both trying to improve their chances for victory by meeting with political rivals. The election system had been designed to encourage coalition building. If no candidate won more than 50 percent in the first round, a second election had to be held in which only the top two vote getters could run. Yeltsin said that he was ready to talk and began negotiating. The problem was the high price that "third force" politicians such as General Lebed and economist Grigory Yavlinsky were demanding for cooperation. By the time Korzhakov spoke out against the elections, he must have known that Lebed and Yavlinsky were both demanding major changes in the Yeltsin cabinet. His own position was at risk.

Maneuvering Correctly in Order to Win

Yeltsin explored coalition-building opportunities in a rational manner. Yeltsin met with General Lebed first, just before the May holidays at which Korzhakov called for postponing the elections. Rumors circulated that Yeltsin had offered Lebed a top position in his administration, including defense minister, in exchange for his support. Lebed did not reveal the details of his talks with Yeltsin but he decided to stay in the running instead of withdrawing in favor of Yeltsin.[5] Grigory Yavlinsky also met with Yeltsin but he was too bold and published a list of five demands, an unwise political move unless he never intended to join the Yeltsin administration.[6] Yavlinsky's list included military reform, a signal that he supported those who wanted to replace many senior military and security force leaders.

Some candidates moved towards Yeltsin on their own initiative. General Boris Gromov entered the political picture by rallying to Yeltsin. Gromov had been sidelined into military-diplomatic work after criticizing the Chechen war. He had been thought of as a viable presidential candidate in his own right. However, his campaign had gone nowhere and he decided to caste his lot with Yeltsin and recommended that all who had been supporting a "third force" choice do the same in order to prevent a Communist victory.[7] Thus, General Gromov was back in politics and offering his services to the Yeltsin administration and the nation. But since Gromov had no strong political movement of his own or block of votes to put on the bargaining table, he was not as important to Yeltsin as Lebed.

Yeltsin's Election Eve Military Promotions

Yeltsin took steps to improve military support for his candidacy just three days before the first round of voting. He promoted all five senior military commanders from the rank of colonel general to army general; but there were no honors or promotions for Pavel Grachev who had served Yeltsin loyally since the August coup in 1991. The commanders Yeltsin promoted were in charge of the troops, five branches of the Russia's armed forces. The official military press published the news on election eve. It was a signal that Grachev's future was in limbo. Yeltsin was reassuring and rewarding the commanders as he prepared for some politically necessitated shifts in Ministry of Defense and national security leadership. Grachev was out of the country and engaged in military diplomatic work with NATO and the Western European Union (WEU) during these days. He was advancing the administration's diplomatic agenda by urging greater military and security cooperation between Russia and NATO and between Russia and the WEU as a constructive alternative to NATO expansion at Russia's expense. If Grachev were sidelined, Supreme Commander Yeltsin and Chief of General Staff Kolesnikov could lead the military through the five newly promoted commanders: Petr S. Deinekin (air force), Feliks N. Gromov (navy), Viktor A. Prudnikov (air defenses), Vladimir M. Semyenov (land forces), and Igor D. Sergeyev (strategic rocket forces).[8]

After making these promotions, Yeltsin hit the campaign trail and worked at cultivating Lebed and the Lebed constituency. Reporters kept pressing Yeltsin for hard information about the political dealing. On 14 June 1996 he told them that he could already see the type of person that Russia needed to lead her in the year 2000. "Was that Lebed," they asked? At first he said it was too soon to be that specific. But when prodded later, Yeltsin answered, "You are thinking correctly."[9]

The First Round of Voting: June 16 1996

When Russian voters went to the polls on 16 June 1996, they could chose among ten candidates and none of the above. The voting was conducted fairly even though the Yeltsin administration had used its prerogatives in order to skew national radio and television campaign coverage towards an anti-Communist vote and the liberal media did likewise. Just under 70 percent of the electorate participated and the results were as follows:

35 percent—Boris Yeltsin
32 percent—Gennady Zyuganov
15 percent—Aleksandr Lebed
7 percent—Grigory Yavlinsky
6 percent—Vladimir Zhirinovsky
1 percent—Svyatoslav Fyodorov
0.5 percent—Mikhail Gorbachev
0.4 percent—Martin Shakkum
0.2 percent—Yury Vlasov
0.2 percent—Vladimir Brintsalov[10]

There are two ways of evaluating the vote. On the one hand, 65 percent of those voting had cast their ballots against Yeltsin, a clear warning that the public was unhappy with his record. On the other, the deep opposition, was smaller, about 52 percent if Zyuganov, Lebed, and Zhirinovsky votes are combined. Yeltsin had to make alliances in order to secure more than 50 percent in the next round. Since the moderates and democratic reformers who did not vote for him in the first round would either join him or abstain rather than support the Communists, he did not have to give them his primary attention. Further, all of them put together (Yavlinsky, Fyodorov, and Gorbachev) only added up to seven or eight percent, not enough to put Yeltsin over the top. Yeltsin needed most of Lebed's 15 percent or just under 11,000,000 citizens.[11] Further, if he could forge an alliance with Lebed, he might also pull some of the protest voters away from Zyuganov and Zhirinovsky. A deal with Lebed seemed imperative. The campaign needed it but parts of the administration loathed it.

The Yeltsin-Lebed Alliance

Yeltsin received Lebed on 18 June 1996 and struck a political deal that made Lebed Russia's national security czar. The deal was legitimized and formalized in a two-minute Kremlin ceremony carried by the Russian media. Yeltsin signed previously drafted ukazes that appointed Lebed to two powerful posts: presidential national security adviser and secretary of the Security Council. At the same time, the Kremlin announced that Grachev had submitted his resignation and that Yeltsin had accepted it. Yeltsin appointed Army General Mikhail Kolesnikov—the chief of the General Staff of the Russian armed forces, to serve as acting minister of defense.[12] Therefore, by using his presidential powers Yeltsin swiftly changed the top national security and defense leadership. The orders were signed and the system responded with some resistance that was quickly punished.

Lebed was elated and began to make statements that raised alarms. He endorsed Yeltsin over the Communists but reaffirmed his political autonomy as a special force with a mission from the people: "Eleven million people believed that I can create order and guarantee security. I am an officer and I am obliged to carry out those orders."[13] On domestic political conflict, his remarks were a warning to politicians and a pledge to the people: "The people of Russia must not suffer from the political wrecks politicians make...I am a soldier who has had enough fighting to hate war and will do all I can to make certain there is none on Russian soil."[14] But wasn't Lebed now playing politics himself by giving up his role as part of the opposition? Lebed bristled at that question and declared that he was sick of all the political incompetents who made a profession out of being in the opposition But would he actually campaign for Yeltsin? On this point, Lebed quipped that he wasn't an entertainer and he planned to get down to national security work immediately. Would his voters actually follow him into the alliance? Lebed predicted that about 20 percent would reject the decision but that the majority would vote for the new Russia, his euphemism for Yeltsin.[15]

Instead of pausing and trying to bridge the rift between Lebed and members of his administration before the second round of voting on 3 July 1996, Yeltsin explained that had forged an alliance with Lebed which required changes in his administration's political orientation. Yeltsin said that it was the unification of two programs not a short-lived alliance of convenience. Yeltsin said the vote for Lebed was a legitimate mandate for changes in national policy. He agreed with the voters who called for new approaches to military reform and to the fight against crime and corruption.[16]

The Military-Political Fallout

The Yeltsin campaign needed Lebed and it sacrificed key parts of the Yeltsin administration to win him over. This dealing precipitated events that led to the removal of some ten generals plus several key civilian members of the Yeltsin administration over the next several days On the night of 18–19 June members of Korzhakov's security team detained two leading members of the Yeltsin campaign team. Anatoly Chubais charged that Korzhakov and Barsukov were trying to scuttle the elections. On 20 June 1996, Yeltsin sacked his two highest-ranking national security generals—Korzhakov and Barsukov, and Oleg Soskovets—a deputy prime minister with close ties to conservatives in the military-industrial complex. Lebed pledged to use the full power of the Russian state to guarantee that the elections take place, to investigate the incident, and to present his findings to the president.[17] Defense Minister Grachev was also dismissed quietly. When the press asked Lebed about Grachev's fate, he gave a professionally restrained answer, "That step was necessary and came out of the situation that developed."[18]

Yeltsin gave a surprisingly candid explanation to the press. It was aimed at Korzhakov, Barsukov, and Soskovets, not Grachev. He said that the controversial trio had been causing him considerable embarrassment. He indicated that he had enough of the accusations that Korzhakov had been the real power behind the presidency and that Yeltsin took orders from him: "It is necessary to change cadres to bring in fresh people. I'm always getting criticized for Barsukov, Korzhakov, and Soskovets. Is the President supposed to work for them?" Yeltsin made the final judgment that damned them: "The power structures had to be replaced because they had starting taking on too much and giving too little." The world press carried these remarks as did the Russian military press though there was no explanation of Grachev's dismissal other than a perfunctory statement that it had been necessary in connection with Lebed's appointment as Yeltsin's national security adviser and secretary of the Russian Security Council.[19]

Some of Defense Minister Grachev's military colleagues allegedly began to organize some type of effort to get President Yeltsin to reconsider Grachev's dismissal. This led to more sackings and to talk that some generals had tried to use military pressure on Yeltsin. The *New York Times* reported that "Mr. Lebed said today that he had already foiled an attempt by a small group of military commanders to reverse Mr. Yeltsin's dismissal of General Grachev. The plot, Mr. Lebed explained, involved putting troops in the Moscow area on a high state of alert. "I believe the men who engaged in this will have to present their resignations.[20]

Yeltsin Invests Lebed: "I serve the Fatherland"

On 20 June 1996, there was no discussion and no dissent when Yeltsin used the rump Security Council to invest Lebed with formal authority. Yeltsin used the Security Council the way former general secretaries had used the Politburo. Yeltsin opened the meeting by saying there was a proposal on the floor to appoint Aleksandr Lebed national security adviser and secretary of the Security Council. With cameras rolling, Yeltsin said, "I don't think there is any need to discuss his combat record. There is a motion to confirm...unanimously. Congratulations. To battle!" Instead of thanking the president or pledging to serve him and the Constitution, Lebed answered, "I serve the Fatherland."

Yeltsin chaired the Security Council meeting and demonstrated that he was in charge, not Lebed. Yeltsin said that Lebed would be personally responsible for the following aspects of national security: strengthening society's security, the security of persons, and political stability in Russia. Yeltsin then issued orders to improve support to the military and to demonstrate that he intended to increase military discipline. He took note of the fact that military bases and facilities faced energy and fuel problems. He asked Prime Minister Viktor Chernomyrdin and Lebed to get together to draft the necessary ukazes for him to sign. Next, Yeltsin demanded tough measures to punish those who had misused military property and defense funds, some 250 billion rubles worth. He instructed acting Defense Minister Kolesnikov to take action and to report directly to him on actions taken.

After these public acts, the press left and the meeting went on behind closed doors. Later the press asked Lebed about the rest of the meeting and he said that in part corruption and crime was discussed. Asked about his views on Security Council reform, the said that his main concern was to strengthen professionalism.[21] This was a reassuring display of normalcy and restraint. It was supposed to convey the impression that the president was strong, in charge, and directing policy and that Lebed was his key assistant not his handler.

Lebed's Disturbing Behavior

Such displays of strong leadership were part of the Yeltsin reelection campaign. They came between the first and second rounds in the presidential election process. The campaign wanted the public to believe that Yeltsin was physically healthy and politically vigorous—fully capable of completing the job he had started in 1991. The image that Yeltsin was correcting mistakes made during his first term was part of the campaign strategy. In order to improve the executive branch's operations, Yeltsin announced that he would create a special commission to reevaluate the presidential nomenklatura.

On 25 June 1996, Yeltsin promulgated the Presidential Cadre Policy Council and named Lebed to head it. Yeltsin empowered the Cadre Policy Council to review credentials and to recommend appropriate action to Yeltsin as he filled positions in the civilian and armed services. Chairman Lebed was to be assisted by Yury Krapivin, the new leader of the special presidential security guards service. (Krapivin was Korzhakov's successor.)[22] This appointment gave Lebed enormous power over the executive branch and the armed forces. He was now sitting in the Kremlin and helping to determine who would rise, who would move, who would stay the same, and who would fall from power. This is how Stalin built his power base under an ailing Lenin. Stalin took charge of filling positions and thereby built a political machine that served his personal power interests. This was an ironic turn of fate since Lebed used to brood over the way he had been treated by Communist Party Central Committee cadre professionals when they examined his political reliability before approving him for military promotions.[23]

This was the second time that Lebed had been involved in a major committee on political and professional evaluations. His first such appointment was in September 1991, after the August coup. He sat on the commission which evaluated the military's political commissars and decided who stayed, went, or was transferred. He was fired from the committee before its third meeting. Further, instead of getting a plush position in Moscow after the August coup, he was sent to Moldova. His opinion of what was happening in Moscow at that time was not flattering: "Majors became Colonels, Lt. Colonels became Generals, and naked adventurists and passersby with democratic images stormed the still warm places at the feeding table and pushed onto the seats of power."[24] Such experiences deepened Lebed's conviction that politics is the problem and that honest professionals who are true patriots should govern without politics. Of course, this was terribly naive and mildly self-serving but it was what Lebed claimed to believe. He insisted that his personnel work would be informed by professional standards rather than politics.

The main problem wasn't politics or Lebed's military background. The problem was Lebed's personal psychology and leadership style. Lebed found it impossible to observe the rules of civilized, professional behavior that make it easier to conduct the work of governance. Lebed had disobeyed Yeltsin and Grachev while serving in Moldova and boasted about it. Such behavior had kept him out of more responsible leadership positions for five years. It was politics that gave him a second chance, a major opportunity to demonstrate that he had the personal discipline required to carry national political power and responsibly. But the old personality problems were still there and he began to boast that he intended to get Yeltsin to change his mind about key issues including the very nature of the postelection administration. Lebed argued that the new administration should give cabinet positions to all leading presidential candidates including Zyuganov, Zhirinovsky, and Yavlinsky.[25]

Lebed said that Russian society was divided into three camps and that this could develop into a two-camp split just as had happened in Vietnam, Korea, and Germany. He also told the press that he intended to ask Yeltsin to give him command over Russia's special security forces, the units that control national communication systems and carry out extraordinary military and security tasks.[26] His comments on Vietnam, Korea, and Germany made little sense. His request to take charge of the country's elite security forces was a warning that he was trying to grab too much power.

There were other signs that Lebed lacked the political maturity required to lead a modern great power's national security system. On 28 June 1996 as he addressed a meeting of ethno-Russian nationalists, the second conference of the Union of Patriotic and National Organizations, he pledged to build a rich and strong Russia, a normal theme. Some nationalists complained that he had abandoned his political struggle to build a new third force in Russian politics. He said it was time to unify Russia and that keeping the country divided into three camps was damaging to Russian national interests.[27] During the question and answer period he admonished one questioner for "talking like a Jew," a remark that quickly spread across the national and international media.[28] The Soviet military had given all its officers basic instructions to avoid ethnic slurs and to encourage interethnic cooperation and harmony and to many it was a matter of professional duty and honor to avoid such behavior. Yet, Lebed flouted those norms and still moved into the center of power. This was another warning signal to key members of Yeltsin's staff, people of diverse ethnic and religious heritage, who were trying to build an enlightened, democratic Russia. He later sincerely apologized for those comments and that incident did little additional damage his reputation. His huge appetite for power and lack of political manners not ethno-nationalism were his main problems. He was creating too many enemies too rapidly to survive as a democratic leader.

The very same day that Lebed took charge of the presidential cadre's commission another seven military professionals were relieved of their positions by presidential ukaz. This brought the figure to ten when Grachev, Barsukov, and Korzhakov are included. The list included, among others, Colonel General Barynkin, who as chief of operations development and planning had been critical of Yeltsin's handling of the military draft question, Colonel General Zdornikov, who as chief of personnel development and civics education had failed to convince the officer corps that Yeltsin had been an outstanding president. [29] Nevertheless, Yeltsin kept Lebed from taking charge of the Ministry of Defense and it was General Kolesnikov who assembled and led the first meeting of the Military Collegium or assembly of senior commanders and administrative personnel on 28 June 1996.[30]

Round Two: The Elections of 3 July 1996

The presidential electoral system was designed to nudge both candidates towards the political center and that is precisely what happened between the first and second rounds of voting. Yeltsin and Zyuganov found themselves competing for the same centrist voters. Yeltsin was more successful than Zyuganov and took the second round with Lebed's assistance.

Zyuganov tried to increase his support by pledging to form a coalition government of *natsional'noye soglasie* if elected. He proposed a Communist-led coalition that would be one-third Communist, one-third Duma deputies, and one-third government officials. Zyuganov also tried to capitalize upon Yeltsin's poor health and the instability in the Kremlin by presenting himself as a responsible alternative, a new leader who could mend the divisions in Russian society. But no major non-Communist leaders accepted Zyuganov's invitation. Prime Minister Chernomyrdin, Moscow mayor Luzhkov, and fourth-place presidential candidate Yavlinsky publicly rejected Zyuganov's offer.

Yeltsin took what was good in Zyuganov's idea and began to use it to his advantage. If Zyuganov could try to lure voters from Yeltsin's camp, Yeltsin could do the same to the Communists. Yeltsin therefore opened the door to cooperation with reform-minded Communists such as Ivan Rybkin whom Yeltsin invited to join a new national advisory council just before the elections. Yeltsin also invited non-Communist, democratic reformers to endorse him and some did.

Further, Yeltsin used his quasi-dictatorial powers to change election day from a Sunday to a Wednesday and to declare it a nonworking, special holiday. He did this because his political scientists advised him that it would improve his chances. They reasoned that the original date, 30 June 1996, favored the Communists since it was a summer weekend and many typical, urban Yeltsin supporters would prefer to take a holiday at their summer cottages than to stay in town to vote. It was thought that the Communist opposition had better organization and could achieve a high level of participation even on a summer weekend. The Central Election Commission complied with Yeltsin's orders even though they violated the basic laws on elections which state that the second round should be two weeks after the first.

Voting took place without any major problems and Yeltsin won more or less as predicted. Yeltsin received about 55 percent of the vote, Zyuganov took 40 percent, and the remaining 5 percent opted for "none of the above." Exit polling data suggested that about two thirds of Lebed's voters supported

Yeltsin this time while one third defected to the Communists, a political fact that damaged Lebed's political capital a little.[31] It had been a long, hard campaign. Yeltsin had fought his way back from very low popularity ratings of 8–10 percent in January. But the battles had inflicted damage on his health and on his administration's internal cohesion.

Rebuilding the Administration: Containing Lebed

Now that Boris Yeltsin had achieved his primary objective and won the presidential elections, he had to recover his political equilibrium and rebuild the executive branch of government. The alliance with Lebed had become terribly disruptive and had taken a toll on Yeltsin's psychological and physical health. Yeltsin's drinking problems, weak heart, and tendency to swing between optimistic manic and depressive behavior were well known and had contributed to the instability surrounding his political life ever since he had come to Moscow to join the Gorbachev administration in December 1985. Nevertheless he had always bounced back and recovered. Even though he was in danger of death from heart ailments, Yeltsin was not too ill to respond to dangerous political infighting within his administration before undergoing heart surgery.

Who would dominate postelection, administrative restructuring? Yeltsin? Chernomyrdin? Lebed? Yeltsin decided to demonstrate that he was in charge and that he would control the administrative restructuring. Yeltsin announced that Viktor Chernomyrdin would continue to serve as his prime minister and Chernomyrdin, not Lebed, would form the list and propose the new cabinet to Yeltsin. Further, since the Constitution empowers the prime minister to take over the presidency if the president dies or becomes incapacitated, by naming Chernomyrdin to serve as prime minister, Yeltsin was making Chernomyrdin his immediate constitutional successor not Lebed. If a president dies, the basic law requires that the acting president hold new presidential elections within three months.

Once Yeltsin had been reelected, politics began to work against Lebed who was no longer as important to Yeltsin. Lebed alienated some of the best professionals in the Yeltsin administration. Lebed grabbed for too much power too fast and had to be contained. Back in 1991 Lebed had been scornful of the coup plotters. He quipped that not even a third-rate Latin American general would have messed up such a chance to take power.[32] But how well would Lebed manage the Kremlin political game in 1996? Lebed either had to learn to get along with the professionals at the top or get out of the way. Anatoly Chubais—a close Yeltsin associate and former minister of "privatization," took the lead in criticizing the general much as he had criticized the generals Korzhakov and Barsukov when they invaded the political space reserved for civilians and began to challenge the basic power balances and political domains within the Yeltsin administration.[33] Yeltsin appointed Chubais to serve as chief of the presidential administration. This appointment created a balance in the Kremlin between two young, ambitious politicians—Chubais and Lebed. It also made good policy sense in that Chubais could promote economic reform while Lebed concentrated upon improving national security.

But Yeltsin did not want to give Lebed too much authority in national security affairs either. He therefore filled the vacancy created by Grachev's departure with Col. General Igor Rodionov, a respected, senior military officer who had shown political and military courage and an ability to accept unpleasant political decisions gracefully.[34] Although Lebed supported Rodionov's appointment and admired Rodionov, he was very much Lebed's professional senior. Under Rodionov's leadership the Ministry of Defense would not permit itself to be subjected to immature reorganizations and purges inspired by inexperienced and overly ambitious mavericks. Yeltsin completed Lebed's political encirclement and tried to solve a long-standing problem by creating a new Defense Council, under a civilian—Yury Baturin, to coordinate and report on the implementation of national defense policy.

Yeltsin presented Rodionov to the country's senior military leaders and announced the formation of the Defense Council on 18 July 1996 at a special meeting held outside Moscow at Barvikha where Yeltsin was resting and recovering from the strains of the campaign. This completed the process of rebuilding Russia's national defense leadership team, a major political operation that began when Yeltsin made his political approaches to Lebed in early May 1996, moved through a turbulent stage around 18 June 1996 when Grachev, Korzhakov, and Barsukov their jobs, and ended with the appointment of Igor Rodionov as Minister of Defense and the formation of a new Defense Council under Yury Baturin. The Defense Council suited Yeltsin's need for political checks and balances in the Kremlin and for an institution that could give national defense affairs the type of high-level, professional coordination it deserved. The idea had been recently floated by senior military political analysts such as Army General Makhmut Gareyev and published for discussion by the Gorbachev Fund.[35]

Thus, it only took two weeks for Yeltsin to clip Lebed's wings. Yeltsin bought Lebed's support by making him the presidential national security adviser and secretary of the National Security Council. He also announced that Lebed would be the gatekeeper for presidential appointments. By appointing Col. General Rodionov minister of defense, Yeltsin gave Lebed a highly intelligent and formidable leader to compete with. Rodionov was a statesman. Lebed was not. By creating a Defense Council and placing it under Yury Baturin—a civilian politician with strong ties to the military-industrial complex, Yeltsin gave himself an institutional alternative to the Security Council, a place to send virtually any security or defense matter that he did not want Lebed to handle. By reaffirming his support for Viktor Chernomyrdin as prime minister, and making Anatoly Chubais head of the presidential administration (some 1,200 authorized positions), Yeltsin left little political space for Lebed to conquer. In fact, Lebed had to start defending the turf that the Security Council used to occupy.

Conclusion

There are two ways of evaluating what happened in the first six months of 1996. The first explanation will be pleasing to the glass half-full approach to democratization. The second will appeal to the glass half-empty school. The optimistic and pessimistic assessments are accurate descriptions of the same glass. Both agree that the glass is half-empty but they disagree on the assumed direction of change. There is general agreement that Russia had neither completely consolidated its democratic political system nor its market economy; but which direction was it heading? Would Russia move from democratic take-off to democratic consolidation or would it repudiate political and economic markets? It is too soon to answer that question with certainly although there are grounds for optimism.

Optimists will emphasize the fact that Yeltsin stood for reelection and that some ten candidates competed openly. In this explanation Yeltsin's marriage of convenience with General Lebed was a positive, necessary though venal development. Democratic political institutions are supposed to encourage headstrong politicians to pay attention to public opinion and to change their policies accordingly. Yeltsin was doing precisely that and demonstrating that democratic accountability and political opportunism are two sides of the same coin. Yeltsin admitted that his administration had made mistakes and he invited Lebed to join his second administration in order to correct them. Russia had a political market and Western political marketing techniques helped Yeltsin to sell himself and to win more than 50 percent of the votes.

Pessimists will remember that General Korzhakov and Boris Berezovsky, representing the national security and financial elites respectively had argued in public that the elections should be postponed. They were ready to repudiate political markets when the markets appeared to have turned against them. They were not prepared to accept defeat by a Communist-led coalition even in a reasonably fair competitive process. Further, they were uncomfortable with Yeltsin's embrace of Lebed who had declared political warfare on the corrupted elite and who looked more like a populist threat to stability than their natural ally. The entrenched power elite did not intend to permit Lebed to set himself up as Yeltsin's successor and would dispose of him as soon as it became politically expedient to so. They would handle Lebed the way they had handled Col. General Rutskoi, the last ambitious military officer to dare to challenge them.

Lebed in 1996 was what Rutskoi had been in 1991, an expeditious way to get more votes. The two officers had similar personalities and neither could really be trusted to serve the President loyally. In June 1991 when Yeltsin first ran for the Russian presidency, he selected an Afghan war hero, Aleksandr Rutskoi, to be his vice presidential running mate. That decision demonstrated that the competitive electoral system was influencing the Yeltsin team's political behavior. The need to get 51 percent of the popular vote led to ticket balancing and coalition building tactics. The Yeltsin team wanted to improve its appeal to the national defense and conservative constituencies. Rutskoi agreed to run as Yeltsin's vice president and the Yeltsin-Rutskoi ticket won. But this alliance dissolved rather quickly; Rutskoi sided with Parliament against the Kremlin; and launched an all-out political war on Yeltsin which ended in defeat. In June 1996 for Russia's second presidential elections, Yeltsin had to face ticket-balancing problems once again but the same solution wasn't available since, after his negative experience with Rutskoi, he abolished the office of the vice presidency in 1993. Yeltsin's campaign team achieved a similar result by forging a political deal with General Lebed and appointing him to powerful Kremlin security posts. Since Lebed held only appointive offices, President Yeltsin could remove him at any time simply by signing the appropriate ukaz.

About eleven generals lost their positions at the top of the ministry of defense and national security system in the immediate aftermath of Lebed's negotiated entry into the Kremlin inner-circle. There are three main political structural reasons why this happened.

First, Russia's two-round, presidential election system promotes closed-door, elite bargaining. Changes in ministerial and cabinet-level appointments can be negotiated before or just after the first round. General Lebed demonstrated that it was worthwhile to enter the presidential race just to build a significant block of voters to take to the bargaining table. This phenomenon has more to do with the electoral system and the Russian Constitution than with Lebed's military background.

The second cause of the political purge of high-level military and security officials is the excessive concentration of power over all armed forces appointments in the hands of the President. If the Russian Constitution had given the Duma the power to reject or confirm such appointments, the nation's top armed forces professionals would have been better protected against political capriciousness. The Russian Constitution leaves them too vulnerable to politics. It makes their positions part of the political spoils system.

The third factor contributing to the purge, is the absence of strong national political parties in Russia. Russian politics turn more on personalities and intrigues than on small shifts between reasonably stable coalitions that are typical of stable democratic systems. With the passage of time, the Russian defense constituency should find its place in the political party system as politicians learn to court its votes.

Leadership style certainly influenced the manner in which the Yeltsin-Lebed alliance came together. Both leaders had a tendency to make rash decisions and to believe that bold offensives were better than slow moving statesmanship, the politics of compromise, and coalition-building. Lebed's personal psychology and societal discontent combined to give him the drive and the support required to move into national politics and to draw some of the protest vote away from the Communists. Lebed had campaigned on a "democracy with order" theme that attacked the disorder and the breakdown in law and order that the Yeltsin administration had brought the country. Lebed's ideas were the core of authoritarian populist ideology: the Fatherland needs order, democracy is disorderly, politics are venal, and only an uncompromising leader can provide the right balance between dictatorship and anarchy—such ideas are the standard elements in the authoritarian populist world view. Lebed was the Russian manifestation of this phenomenon which develops in societies where political institutions are not able to make and implement policy decisions effectively and elite interests are threatened by rising popular radicalism.

The elections of 1996 were a modest victory for democracy but they were also a warning that the Russian political system had not yet consolidated its competitive political or economic institutions. Military professionals were not protected against high-level partisan deal making. This was the new Russian politics—an eclectic combination of authoritarian elite bargaining and political marketing. *Krasnaya zvezda's* final editorial on the elections was politically sophisticated, mature, and nonpartisan. It reminded readers that it was their right to vote their conscience, mentioned Yeltsin and Zyuganov, but endorsed neither. It argued that healthy political systems have constructive oppositions and that Russia had already had its fill of monarchs and unitary political leadership. It said that Russia's goal should be to learn to hold elections and to transfer power peacefully as a normal societal function much like construction work or farming.[36] Russia held elections but since Yeltsin won, the critically important test of democracy—the peaceful and smooth transfer of power by the defeated to the winners, had not been run. Even so, the military experienced major changes in top leadership as a result of political deal making and was reminded that it was still in politics.

Notes

1. Reported by Tatyana Malikin, "Personal: Aleksandr Korzhakov Believes the Presidential Election Should be Postponed," *Sevodnya,* 6 May 1996. *CDSP,* vol. xlvii, no. 18, 1996, p. 1.
2. See Lebed, *Za derzhavu obidno* (Moscow: Moskovskaia pravda, 1995) pp. 379–80.
3. Reported by Stephen Kiselyov, "Instant Analysis: A Warning Shot to the Head," *Izvestiya,* 7 May 1996. *CDSP,* vol. XLVIII, no. 18, 1996, pp. 1–3.
4. B. A. Berezovsky et al., "Get Out Of The Impasse!" *Kommersant-Daily,* 27 April 1996. *CDSP,* vol. XLVIII, no. 17, 1996, p. 1.
5. Reported by Marina Shakina, "Consultations: Yeltsin Continues to Meet with Rivals," *CDSP,* vol. XLVIII, no. 18, 1996, p. 5.

6. Stepan Kiselyov, "Primary Source: Grigory Yavlinsky Met with the President on May 5 and Gave Him a Letter:" *Izvestiya*, 7 May 1996. *CDSP,* vol. XLVIII, no. 18, 1996, p. 6.
7. Anatoly Veslo, "Boris Gromov Becomes A Yeltsin Campaign Aide," *Sevodnya*, 14 May 1996. *CDSP*, vol. XLVIII, no. 19, 1996. pp. 12–13.
8. Announcements in *Krasnaya zvezda*, 15 June 1996.
9. See the military press's explanation of the deal, "Vstrecha Prezidenta Rossii Borisa Yeltsina s Aleksandrom Lebedem" (Yeltsin's meeting with Lebed), *Krasnaya zvezda*, 19 June 1996.
10. Results from the Central Electoral Commission as reported by Aleksandr Pel'ts, "Podvedenie itogov pervogo tura prezidentskikh vyborov prodolzhaetsya," *Krasnaya zvezda*, 19 June 1996. I rounded the figures.
11. The numbers of voters who voted for each candidate are reported in Aleksandr Pel'ts, "Okonchatel'nye itogi pervogo tura golosovaniya podvedeny" (Final results...); *Krasnaya zvezda*, 22 June 1996. The numbers: 123.065 for Vladimir Bryntsalov, 151,282 for Yury Vlasov, 277,068 for Martin Shakkum, 386,069 for Mikhail Gorbachev, 699,158 for Svyatoslav Fyodorov, 4,311,479 for Vladimir Zhirinovsky, 5,550,752 for Grigory Yavlinsky, 10,974,736 for Aleksandr Lebed, 24,211,686 for Gennady Zyuganov, and 26,665,495 for Boris Yeltsin.
12. ITAR-TASS, "Vstrecha Prezidenta Rossii Borisa Yeltsina s Aleksandrom Lebedem," *Krasnaya zvezda*, 19 June 1996.
13. *Ibid.*
14. Lebed cited by Aleksandr Pel'ts, "Press konferentsiya sekretarya Soveta bezopasnosti-pomoshchnika Prezidenta RF po natsional'noi bezopasnosti Aleksandra Lebedya," *Krasnaya zvezda*, 20 June 1996.
15. See Pelts on Lebed, *Ibid.*
16. ITAR-TASS, "Vstrecha Prezidenta Rossii Borisa Yeltsina s Aleksandrom Lebedem," *Krasnaya zvezda*, 19 June 1996.
17. Lebed cited by Pel'ts, *Ibid.*
18. *Ibid.*
19. See "Prezident prinyal reshenie po kadram" (President made personnel decisions), *Krasnaya zvezda*, 21 June 1996.
20. Michael R. Gordon, "Yeltsin Chooses A Defeated Rival for Security Post," *New York Times*, 19 June 1996.
21. ITAR-TASS, "Prezident prinyal reshenie po kadram," KZ 21. June 1996.
22. Presidential Press Service, "Kadrovye izmenenie" (Cadre changes), *Krasnaya zvezda*, 27 June 1996.
23. See Lebed, *Za derzhavu obidno*, pp. 215–17.
24. *Ibid.*, pp. 415–18.
25. *Golos Rossii* world service, 30 June 1996.
26. Boris Soldatenko, "Idti vpered, kak by trudno ni bylo" (Forward no matter how hard), *Krasnaya zvezda*, 29 June 1996.
27. Boris Soldatenko, "Aleksandr Lebed vybral kurs na bogatuyu i sil'nuyu Rossiyu" (Lebed sets course for a rich and powerful Russia), *Krasnaya zvezda*, 28 June 1996.
28. Reported by Alessandra Stanley, "For Yeltsin's New Kremlin Team, Chickens Come Home to Roost," *New York Times,* 28 June 1996.
29. Presidential Press Service, "Kadrovye izmeneniya" (Cadre changes); *Krasnaya zvezda*, 27 June 1996. The word *izmeneniya* has the same root as the Russian words for treachery and betrayal. An anti-Yeltsin barb?
30. "Zasedanie Kollegii Ministerstva oborony RF," *Krasnaya zvezda*, 29 June 1996.

31. Based upon an exit poll done by Mitofsky Intl. and CESSO Ltd. and reported by the *New York Times*, 4 July 1996, "How Russians Voted in the Runoff."

32. Lebed, *Zaderzhavu obidno*, p. 408. He said, "Pri takoi rasklade lyuboi srednei ruki yuzhnoamerikanskii general svoego shansa ne ustupil."

33. See Michael Gordon, "Russian Vote Sets Off Battle, This Time in Yeltsin's Camp," *New York Times*, 6 July 1996.

34. See chapter 3 for a discussion of Rodionov in politics, 1989–1990.

35. See Army General Makhmut Gareyev, "O kontseptsii rossiiskoi oboronnoi politiki" (Russia's defense policy concept), *Svobodnaya mysl'*; no. 7, 1996, pp. 50–59. The Gorbachev Fund publishes *Svobodnaya mysl'* in Moscow.

36. See Oleg Andreyev, "Delat' vybor—nashe pravo," *Krasnaya zvezda*, 2 July 1996.

16

Military Politics in Yeltsin's Presidential State

As the Russian state emerged from the Soviet Union, it tried to rebuild itself without crippling the four key governmental functions necessary to sustain state viability: political leadership, basic economic activity, domestic law enforcement, and external defense. Boris Yeltsin's state reconstruction strategy had to be a blend of institutional continuity and adaptation rather than radical change. It also had to take into account the struggle for political survival. His 1993 Constitution defined a powerful Russian presidency by adapting the Communist institution of the office of the general secretary to a society with emerging political and economic markets. It created a *presidential state* by concentrating political authority in the office of the presidency at the expense of the legislative and judicial branches of government. The president's authority over national defense and security affairs was enormous but this did not prevent individuals and institutions from competing for power and resources.

This chapter analyzes military politics in the presidential state. It is based upon a review of news from the Russian Ministry of Defense for the first six months of Yeltsin's second term, June through December 1996. As I analyzed the news for information about defense-related institutions, leaders, issues, and statistics, it became clear that certain institutions, individuals, and issues were linked in post-Soviet defense governance patterns and that some key institutions were performing functions similar to those which sustained the Soviet defense system. Such analysis also identified gaps, areas in which the post-Soviet defense governance system was not performing as well as its Communist authoritarian predecessor. It also identified progressive changes, system adaptation to the requirements of a more open, pluralistic, and law-governed society.

The Russian political system's inability to break with the tradition of strong executive leadership is the most striking element of continuity between Soviet and post-Soviet politics. Ironically, the more powers Boris Yeltsin claimed the more poorly the political economy performed in general and in the defense sector in particular. Defense system politics revolved around the office of the presidency and Yeltsin's efforts to build institutions capable of coordinating defense and security affairs, to place loyal, competent individuals at the head of such institutions, and to keep them cooperating in the national interest. But Russia's disappointing economic performance and the money problems it created were the predominant national concern not the presidency's formal powers. From 1991 through August 1996, defense production dropped by 85 percent while the overall economy's industrial output dropped by some 50 percent.[1] By 1996, the federal budget was only able to finance about 35 percent of the Ministry of Defense's continuing operating costs.[2] Financial difficulties plagued the Ministry of Defense and made it impossible to maintain normal professional military activities and combat readiness.

Russia had a strong presidency and reasonably strong ministries capable of managing various aspects of defense. The main weakness in the architecture of power was in the middle space between the president and the ministers. The system lacked stable coordinating and planning bodies. Ministers and departments were competing for increasingly scarce funds and trying to deal directly with the president and the prime minister. Solutions were found to one crisis after another but all the main players knew that Russia's state viability required more than ad hoc governance.

From General Secretary to President

From 1985 to 1995 control over the military moved from the general secretary of the Communist Party of the Soviet Union to the president of Russia. It can be argued that this shift placed the military under democratic, law-governed control because the president is democratically elected and the federal Law on Defense was passed by a democratically elected legislature, the Duma. However, the Constitution and the Law on Defense concentrated so much control over all key national defense policy and decision making in the hands of the president that it violated elementary principles of democratic control such as institutional checks and balances. When the Duma passed the law on 24 April 1996, it abdicated its democratic responsibility to serve as a check and balance on presidential power.[3] The Duma's hands had already been tied by the Yeltsin Constitution which had been written by the presidency for the presidency.

Like the Constitution, the Law on Defense gives the president some twenty powers and reserves only two for the Duma. The Duma passes the federal budget and writes the laws. Its powers are defined in just three lines of text in a law that takes one and a half pages of newspaper space. The Duma has no role whatsoever in the review of military appointments, the definition of national defense policy, or the use of military force at home or abroad. The president sets national defense policy, determines the organizational structure of the various forces, sets the numbers of authorized positions in each force, appoints the commanding officers, controls their movement inside the country, and decides when and where to use military power without consultation with the democratically elected Duma which is the most representative body in the Russian state.

In addition to the Duma, the Russian federal legislature has a smaller upper house or Federal Council made up of two representatives from each of the eighty-nine *subyekty* or political-administrative units that comprise the Russian Federation. Each unit sends its governor and the speaker of its assembly to represent it on the Federal Council. At first glance it appears that the Law on Defense intended to use the Federal Council as a check and balance on the powers of the presidency. However, closer examination reveals that the law did not close the gaps that Yeltsin exploited to wage war in Chechnya. The Federal Council has the power to approve or rescind presidential states of emergency. But in the Chechen war Yeltsin never declared a state of emergency. The Federal Council has the power to confirm or deny the president's right to use federal forces for nonauthorized purposes. But since the same law gives the president the power to define the authorized purposes, the Federal Council has little control over the use of armed force in Russia. Further, the president approves federal Military Doctrine which defines the domestic and foreign threats to national security and the types of forces that can be used to meet them. By granting power over Military Doctrine exclusively to the president, the constitution closed the Duma and the Federal Council out of the most important strategic debates. By contrast, the law and the constitution are specific on the use of Russian armed forces outside of Russia. This requires Federal Council approval.

It is conceivable that the Russian federal legislature will eventually convert its constitutional power to define the defense budget into substantive control over national security affairs. However, at present, it is weak and too young an institution to serve as an effective check on the president, the prime minister, and the three power ministries. In practice, the ministers at the head of the various armed forces determine how the funds which the Duma appropriated are actually spent and they have access to additional funds beyond the Duma appropriations. The prime minister and the government make tremendously important decisions about foreign arms sales, disposition of property, and the rescheduling and cancelling debts independently of the Duma. For example, they can require state-owned energy companies to supply the armed forces at reduced prices and to postpone collections. Such actions can increase or decrease the funds available to the armed forces by trillions of rubles. Thus, in November 1996, Defense Council Secretary Yury Baturin announced that the Ministry of Defense was being given an additional three trillion rubles to spend. When pressed for information about the sources of those rubles, Baturin explained that it was debt rescheduling.[4] When Defense Minister Grachev passed the leadership baton to Rodionov he left enormous unpaid debts, at least 30 percent of the military's annual operating budget.[5] Further, the defense industries were in similar financial condition and owed their suppliers some 55 trillion as of August 1996 according to Vitaly Vitebsky a leading economist at the Ministry of Defense Industry.[6] In this political-economic environment, the minister of defense's most important political relationships were with the president and the prime minister, not the Duma. The national financial crisis magnified their importance. However, Rodionov also used the media to gain attention. His press conference on the military's financial crisis attracted some 300 reporters. Two days later he met with Yeltsin who pledged immediate relief and instructed Prime Minister Chernomyrdin to make it happen.[7]

The Duma passes military funding bills that are quite global. The power ministries—especially the Ministry of Defense, do not share detailed information about expenditures with the legislature. The Duma has neither the staff nor the accumulated expertise required to challenge the President and the power ministers. As a political body the Duma came into existence in 1993 or 1990 at best. Further, it experienced tremendous turnover in the 1995 elections. In 1996, Lt. General Lev Rokhlin's Duma defense and security affairs committee had a full-time staff of just fifteen professionals plus several secretaries.[8] This little Duma army could not keep up with the three power ministries which employed some 3,000,000 personnel plus the millions more in the defense-industrial complex. If the power ministries and the military industrial complex actually provided Rokhlin with detailed reports, he and his small staff would have been buried in paper.

President Yeltsin's Weakness: Institutional Development

Yeltsin had the formal legal authority to lead defense and security affairs with little interference from the legislature, but he had difficulty institutionalizing that leadership under post-Soviet conditions. He lacked an overall architecture for presidential management of defense and security affairs. The Soviet system used to run on five-year plans which included huge defense components. The Soviet bureaucracy implemented the plans. Basic defense policy and resource allocation issues were made by the general secretary in consultation with a handful of top military and military-industrial managers and then implemented by the Soviet bureaucracy. The Soviet state had a strong capacity for strategic planning and coordination of armed forces development. Yeltsin's Russian state did not. It engaged in crisis management instead of strategic planning and coordination.

Yelstin had many levers of power but no power system. He needed an overall architecture of power. As of December 1996, President Yeltsin had the following major institutional resources and offices to assist him in the fulfillment of his constitutional duties in defense and security affairs:

Presidential Security Adviser;
Security Council of the Russian Federation;

Defense Council of the Russian Federation;
Armed Forces Appointments Commission;
Ministry of Defense and General Staff of the Ministry of Defense; CIS military cooperation and peacekeeping bodies;
Border Forces of the Russian Federation;
Ministry of Internal Affairs (MVD);
Federal Domestic Security Service (FSB);
Foreign Intelligence Service;
Presidential Guards/*Okhrana*;
Federal Communications Service (FAPSI);
Civil Defense/Emergency Services;
Railroad Troops;
Prime Minister of the Russian Federation;
Ministry of Defense Industry and related commissions;
Special Commission on Financing the Armed Forces;
Various Presidential Commissions on Cossacks, Veterans, etc.
Presidential Administration (formerly the CC CPSU).

In the Communist system the general secretary's work was supported by a large professional staff in the Central Committee of the Communist Party of the Soviet Union. Boris Yeltsin continued that practice. The post-Soviet edition of the Central Committee was called the Presidential Administration and it was housed in the former Central Committee building commonly referred to as Staraya Ploshchad. The Presidential Administration prepares reports on all major policy areas and monitors policy implementation. It also dispenses political rewards and punishments to increase compliance with presidential policy. People approach it with problems and seek favors there. But the Presidential Administration was too broad and amorphous to provide effective national defense and security coordination and could not fill the gaps created by the collapse of the Soviet Five-Year planning and control system.

Yeltsin understood that his personal interests and Russian national interests would be better served if the twenty-odd, defense-related institutions and departments were arranged into a clear hierarchy with a definite chain of command and put to work under long-range strategic plans. During the presidential campaign, Yeltsin's opponents hammered away at his chaotic management of national affairs. Yeltsin acknowledged the problem and pledged to correct it. In June 1996 he gave Lt. General (Ret.) Aleksandr Lebed overall responsibility for pulling things together and appointed him presidential national security adviser and secretary of the security council. Lebed eagerly accepted the assignment even though skeptics pointed out that he lacked the right training, experience, leadership habits, and political connections required to be successful. To his credit, Lebed promoted Col. General Igor Rodionov's candidacy—a much better strategic thinker than himself, to replace crisis manager Pavel Grachev at the head of the Ministry of Defense.

Firing the Ambitious Lebed

But instead of ending the period of crisis management, Lebed deliberately sparked controversy and provoked conflicts. Yeltsin responded to this "Lebed" problem by making more personnel and institutional changes. Although these were somewhat unsettling in the short run, they had the potential to develop into a better system for coordinating defense and security affairs under civilian leadership in the longer run.

Lebed was neither an institution builder not a team player. He had not been cured of the personal behavioral patterns that kept him out of the Kremlin leadership from August 1991 through June 1996. In late July 1996, a little over a month after Lebed took over the Security Council, Yeltsin created a rival institution called the Defense Council, gave it broad responsibility for defense and security planning, and named a civilian political ally—Yury Baturin, to head it. (Baturin had been Yeltsin's National Security Adviser until 18 June 1996 when he gave that post to Lebed!) Lebed was understandably disappointed when he learned that he was to be just one of fifteen members of that important body. Further, Yeltsin's Defense Council enabling decree authorized Baturin to hire some fifty-five professionals and to take another twenty-five experts from the armed forces to form the Defense Council's core. However, instead of changing his style and accepting his lowered status, Lebed staged another bold political offensive. When Chechen rebels launched a highly effective series of attacks on federal troops in Grozny, Lebed saw a chance to seize the initiative.

Chechen rebels timed the new fighting to embarrass Boris Yeltsin and it did. While the ailing Yeltsin was taking his presidential oath of office in the Kremlin's Palace of Congresses, feisty Chechen rebels were swarming over federal positions in Grozny and hundreds were being killed in the worst fighting of the entire war. Lebed rushed into the leadership vacuum and Yeltsin assigned him the task of ending the fighting. Lebed negotiated a power-sharing agreement with Aslan Maskhadov, a former Soviet officer like himself. The peace agreement made Lebed very popular at home and with most of the military. Lebed admitted that the rebels had won a major victory but he condemned the war and the politicians who had imposed it on all the citizens of Russia including the Chechens. Instead of making an unambiguous statement on the controversial settlement, Yeltsin left Lebed dangling for days. When Yeltsin finally endorsed it, he also instructed Lebed to stop taking stands on controversial issues without first clearing them with him.[9] But Lebed kept feuding with MVD chief, Army General Anatoly Kulikov and accused him and the MVD of having botched both the Chechen war and the overall war against crime in Russia. Kulikov struck back and charged that Lebed had capitulated to the Chechen rebels and sold Russia's territorial integrity and military honor down the river in the pursuit of personal political glory. (Lebed's cease-fire accords included an agreement that federal troops would withdraw from Chechnya and that Chechens could vote on national independence from Russia in 2001. He had won peace and gained time but the Chechen independence issue had not been settled.) Initially Yeltsin, Chernomyrdin, and Rodionov supported Lebed and tried to restrain his ambitious exuberance. But they turned against him in late September when he began making provocative statements that sounded as if he were promoting himself as Yeltsin's replacement and calling for a state of emergency.

Lebed called a press conference to share his evaluation of his first 100 days in office. He said that the armed forces were on the verge of mutiny and that national security was threatened by new nuclear accidents and other disasters. He called for better planning and leadership and was harsh on the Yeltsin's administration's leadership confusion. Lebed declared: "For the last 100 days I haven't been able to determine how decisions are made in this country."[10] He demanded immediate action to prevent disaster. But he failed to cooperate closely with Rodionov who was working to prepare the military for additional staffing cuts and reorganizations, including reductions in Lebed's former service—the elite paratroopers. Instead of supporting Rodionov on those cuts, Lebed was present at officers meetings in the Tula region where they were harshly criticized. Lebed also took Yeltsin's former chief of security, General Aleksandr Korzhakov to Tula for some political work aimed at getting Korzhakov elected to the Duma, a step that would have given him political immunity against Yeltsin. General Kulikov charged Lebed with plotting a coup and trying to create his own personal army.

On 17 October 1996 President Yeltsin fired Lebed for breaking ranks and provoking tension. Yeltsin pointed out that Lebed was prematurely and excessively interested in making himself president instead of working as a loyal member of the Kremlin administration. Yeltsin specifically noted that Lebed had been dealing with his recently disgraced former chief of Kremlin security, Korzhakov. In Tula, according to Yeltsin, Lebed was presenting Korzhakov as his political ally and likely successor at the head of Russian national security as soon as Lebed became president.[11] Yeltsin tried to strip General Korzhakov of his military rank for conduct unbecoming of an officer and gross violations of military etiquette. But Korzhakov promised to fight Yeltsin in the courts and threatened to reveal secret information about high-level corruption in the Yeltsin administration.

Although Rodionov had been linked to Lebed, he survived another seven months until Yeltsin fired him in May 1997. Rodionov tried to keep Lebed's quick fall from power and tried to keep defense affairs on a steady course.

This was difficult because Yeltsin had been making hasty personnel decisions that affected national defense When Yeltsin fired Lebed just before entering the hospital for heart surgery, he replaced him with a civilian, Ivan Rybkin, at the head of the Security Council. Agrarian Communist and former Duma speaker Rybkin was even less well-prepared than Lebed for major security coordination leadership. Yeltsin also floated the idea of creating a special Presidential Military Inspectorate to give him an independent source of information on how well the power ministries were fulfilling their duties and responsibilities. These moves suggest that Yeltsin was trying to strengthen his grip on the military; they also made good managerial sense.

The Presidential Military Inspectorate, the Security Adviser, the Security Council and the Defense Council could develop into powerful policymaking and control institutions. On paper those organizations formed an impressive architecture for a national defense and security affairs system. But they needed a constructive builder to turn the idea into reality. During his first term, Boris Yeltsin did not demonstrate such qualities. During the first six months of his second term, he continued to lead erratically.

Ministers of Defense and Defense Management

The Ministers of Defense were acutely aware of the national leadership problem which first arose under Gorbachev. Marshal Dmitry Yazov joined the conspiracy to impose a state of emergency on the Soviet Union because he and other top military leaders disapproved of the breakdown in strategic planning and control. His successor, Marshal Yevgeny Shaposhnikov fought a losing battle against the same deficit in political leadership vision. Yeltsin repeatedly pledged to put a "full-stop" to national leadership drift but he neither imposed strategic planning discipline on himself nor on his administration. Shaposhnikov kept insisting that Russia adopt a long-term defense reform strategy. Yeltsin agreed and appointed Shaposhnikov to head Russia's Security Council. But Yeltsin neither gave Shaposhnikov nor the Security Council the steady support needed to develop into Russia's primary national security planning institution. Shaposhnikov quit and ended up running Aeroflot after a stint trying to bring order to Russian foreign arms sales.

Defense Minister Grachev was the only top minister in the Yeltsin administration to have survived from spring 1992 through the first round in the presidential elections of 1996. Although there were frequent calls for Grachev's resignation from the liberal media, he persevered and stood his ground. Grachev coped with every crisis and kept the military cohesive, manageable and under civilian leadership. The Ministry had tremendous reserves of institutional resilience and carried on in the best Russian stoic tradition. There were times when Grachev told the press that the civilians were the root cause of his problems including the decision to wage war in Chechnya and the poor manner in which it was handled. But on the whole, he kept the military responsive to Yeltsin's orders. Since Yeltsin was erratic, military planners and administrators had to shift gears frequently and to grin and bear it. The Yeltsin leadership style was ill-suited to the habits of mind and professional discipline valued by top military professionals. By serving Yeltsin loyally, Grachev inevitably made himself unpopular with strategic thinkers and managers.

At the beginning of Yeltsin's second term, Defense Minister Igor Rodionov and Chief of General Staff Viktor Samsonov replaced Pavel Grachev and Mikhail Kolesnikov in the Ministry of Defense's leading positions. Rodionov's appointment was praised by Russian demokraty, moderates, Red-Browns, and Communist warhorses such as Army General (Ret.) Varennikov. Rodionov had spent the previous six years as commandant of the General Staff's military leadership training academy and was acutely aware of the deficiencies in national strategic planning and administration. When Yeltsin invested Rodionov, he invited top military leaders to assemble at the sanitarium where he was preparing for heart surgery. Addressing Rodionov, Yeltsin said, "Mister Minister, your top priority is to establish elementary order in the Army." But Yeltsin also signaled that he had heard and agreed with critics who demanded better strategic planning and management just as Rodionov had been advocating. When Yeltsin appointed Rodionov, he also announced the formation of the new national Defense Council.[12] Yeltsin instructed Rodionov and the top military leadership to enhance the General Staff's planning and strategic leadership functions and to give increased attention to military cooperation with the CIS.

Yeltsin demanded various strategic plans for Russian military and armed forces development thorough the year 2001 from the General Staff, the Defense Council, the Security Council, the Ministry of Defense Industry, etc. and habitually gave them only a couple of months to prepare them. The Rodionov-Samsonov military leadership team had the right intentions but political and economic circumstances were unfavorable to strategic management. Col. General Samsonov lamented, "I say quite openly that the General Staff cannot keep up with the continually changing tasks set by the politicians."[13] He also complained that the "professional and intellectual potential of the General Staff has declined over the last four years."[14]

The military suffered from two main problems. The first was the lack of stable, strategic leadership from the Kremlin. The second was economic—inadequate financing, irregular financing, and instability in ruble values and prices. Rather than point the finger at Supreme Commander Yeltsin, Defense Minister Grachev used to claim that the Duma and the Ministry of Finance were responsible for inadequate financing. The idea that the military could solve its chronic financing problems by getting more pro-defense deputies elected was naive. Defense Minister Rodionov also engaged in political advocacy designed to put pressure on the Duma and the Ministry of Finance;

however, he understood that the general economic situation was the greatest threat to Russian state security.

Defense Minister Rodionov insisted that the military leadership be better informed about the overall strategic picture. In early November 1996 he held a major national workshop where national leaders and experts lectured his commanders, answered questions, and debated points with them.[15] Rodionov also visited every military district and discussed the national situation and its implications for the armed forces with military and civilian leaders. He also did some touring with Prime Minister Viktor Chernomyrdin who candidly told officers that the only way to increase the budget substantially prior to an economic recovery would be to print rubles and that was unacceptable since it would rekindle hyper-inflation and undermine the country's financial viability. He admitted that the government had not collected taxes aggressively enough and announced that measures recently adopted to improve receipts were producing some positive results. He noted that foreign military sales were helpful but warned that Russia would never be able to collect the some $160 billion still owed from Soviet military aid programs. The sick economy remained the fundamental problem. Chernomyrdin told defense industry employees that their low pay was directly related to the state's inability to support high defense orders and its refusal to thrown them out of work by closing superfluous plants. The state could only afford to keep them on the payroll by paying wages lower than those being earned in the regular private sector.[16]

The Rodionov style was a mixture of Soviet revolutionary populism, high-level strategic thinking, and statesmanship. Although Rodionov understood the national economic situation, as the military's leader he was expected to lobby strongly for every additional ruble the military could get. However, he also agreed that the military would have to make additional cuts which would require basic organizational reconstruction. He lived comparatively frugally and permitted himself to suffer from late payment of salaries and benefits along with the rest of the officer corps. He abandoned Defense Minister Grachev's Mercedes and rode in Russian-made leadership vehicles. He advocated frank, responsible talk from his subordinates and rebuked the commanders for dressing up their reports in order to disguise the real decline in Russian military capabilities and combat readiness.

Cutting positions would not make him popular but he accepted that task. He agreed that number of authorized military positions would have to be reduced from over 1,500,000 to some 1,000,000 to 1,200,000 as soon as possible. Additional cuts would have to be made in the Ministry's civilian employment which stood at some 600,000 personnel. Yeltsin accepted Rodionov's argument that the military had to receive higher priority in defense and security spending and that nonmilitary armed forces would have to be cut by at least 15 percent in 1997. In early October, Yeltsin ordered Prime Minister Chernomyrdin to form a special commission on armed forces financing and to resolve back bay problems for the second time in 1996. Chernomyrdin admitted that declining state revenues had led to underfinancing once again and that back pay problems throughout the federal services was worse than it had been before the presidential elections.

Proposals to Reform the Ministry of Defense

Four ideas for changing the organizational/institutional structures for the supervision of national defense emerged during the Gorbachev era. One focused upon civilian control and the civilianization of the Ministry of Defense. The second involved the manner in which the minister of defense and the chief of General Staff reported to the president. The third addressed the problem of finding the right balance between unification of all the country's armed forces into one powerful ministry and their division into three to five separate ministries. The fourth centered on ways to coordinate defense industrial and military affairs.

The first reform proposal—that Russia should demonstrate civilian control over the military by appointing a civilian minister of defense, surfaced under Gorbachev. However, the military argued that it was preferable to keep a military officer at the top of the Ministry of Defense during the transition period from authoritarian to democratic socialism. The same logic prevailed in fall 1991 during the transition from unitary to national armed forces, and from empire to commonwealth. In spring 1992 when Yeltsin converted the Soviet Ministry of Defense into the Russian Ministry of Defense, he decided to work within Soviet and Russian tradition but he also made a small gesture towards the civilian reformers. Yeltsin appointed General Pavel Grachev—a military professional, to serve as Russia's first, post-Soviet minister of defense and Dr. Andrei Kokoshin—a civilian expert on defense affairs, to serve as first deputy minister of defense. The idea of replacing Pavel Grachev with a civilian Minister of Defense came up repeatedly and was delayed until the transition period could be proclaimed ended.

Yeltsin could have appointed a civilian Defense Minister in 1992 and given military professionals a less visible public, political role. That change would have brought Russian practice in line with the general European model. Yeltsin's decision to delay that shift was a wise one since Grachev was able to speak bluntly, soldier-to-soldier, with military officers during a tense period of rapid change that required frank and sometimes very difficult leadership interactions. Rodionov continued in that tradition. Placing a civilian at the top of the Defense Ministry would have increased military alienation from the Yeltsin administration.

The second reform proposal emerged after the August 1991 coup. In fall 1991, in light of Defense Minister Yazov's conspiracy against Gorbachev, Chief of Staff Marshal Lobov argued that civilian presidents needed two control lines into the Ministry of Defense in order to make it more difficult for military leaders to conspire against them. Lobov suggested that the president divide defense functions between the minister of defense and the chief of General Staff and make each report to him separately. This structural proposal had positive and negative features. On the one hand, it would give the president two sources of information about military operations and opinion. On the other hand, it would promote rivalry between the minister of defense and his chief operational officer, the chief of General Staff; and this would damage military cohesion.

Initially, president Yeltsin agreed with senior military leaders who urged him to reject Lobov's proposal because it violated the principle of military cohesion at a time when the military faced tremendous organizational strains. Later, however, when Yeltsin became concerned about his ability to control military behavior during the Chechen war, he announced that the chief of staff would report directly to him. However, instead of making that shift formal and splitting the military at the top, Yeltsin kept things the same on paper but began inviting Chief of General Staff Kolesnikov to deliver reports and to participate in policy development. Nevertheless, Yeltsin, Grachev, and Kolesnikov did not let this shift develop into a serious political problem and Grachev continued to be treated as the overall leader of military affairs. This, informal, two-headed system served Yeltsin well when he parted with Grachev in June 1996 and he appointed Kolesnikov to serve as acting defense minister. However, as a general principle it is not a good idea to structure military administration in a manner that promotes rivalry and suspicion between the minister of defense and the chief of General Staff.

The third reform proposal was driven more by cost considerations than by political necessity. The practice of dividing the armed forces into separate services under separate ministries came from the Soviet era. The general secretaries liked this system because it lowered the risk of an armed forces putsch against them. President Yeltsin continued the practice for the same reasons even though the military criticized it because it resulted in costly duplication. Yeltsin agreed that an effort should be made to reduce waste but he refused to unify all the armed forces under the Defense Ministry. In addition to political control issues, there were solid professional reasons for creating different organizational structures for specialized coercive functions. Thus, for example, the Russian state regarded the military as the state institution primarily dedicated to defense against external enemies and it expected the MVD troops to carry the main burdens of domestic peacekeeping. Different missions required different professional training and political indoctrination. This structural/functional logic is of universal applicability and all developed countries maintain differentiated armed forces.

The fourth institutional/organizational reform proposal was related to the third. What is the best way to coordinate defense industrial and military affairs? Russian leaders tried to avoid creating an enormous national defense institution that would be too powerful to control. Therefore, they normally kept national defense industrial affairs—control over the vast defense industrial complex, separate from the Ministry of Defense. The defense-industrial portfolio was normally given to civilians and to several departments. Brezhnev took personal responsibility for the coordination of national defense affairs and relied upon a small group of key, experienced Soviet administrators and experts for advice. They permitted defense spending to consume too large a percentage of the Soviet economy but they did imposed a general plan on national defense development. Planning and coordination weakened under Gorbachev who simply did not know defense affairs as well as his predecessors. Things did not improve during Yeltsin's first term.

Duma—The Legislative Branch and Defense Politics

The legislative branch of government made some progress even though it faced an uphill battle against the strong presidency and Defense Ministry tradition. The nation's senior military leaders refused to admit the elected deputies into their policy making circles. They preferred working with the executive branch in spite of its faults. Nevertheless, the Russian military had to learn to pay attention to the Duma because it formed the federal budget, wrote the nation's laws, held hearings and inquiries into national policy, and had the power to disrupt the smooth operations of government by calling for votes of no confidence. Although the President could slow down or speed up spending and had a tremendous impact upon who got what resources in what order, the basic budget had to come from the Duma. Successive Dumas reaffirmed this power but they also confirmed that there was a national consensus against high military spending, a consensus that ran all across the political spectrum from the demokraty to the Communists. The military watched as the Communists, Agrarians, and the Zhirinovskyites—the parties that had criticized Yeltsin for weakening the Russian state, insisted that they could not increase defense spending because the federal treasury lacked the funds. Besides, they had other commitments and other constituencies.

The practice of having some military officers in the Duma as full deputies with all the normal rights and privileges of deputies creates awkward situations for the senior leadership in the Ministry of Defense. The normal chain of command and principle of military cohesion is strained when some military officers have special political powers. The minister of defense is a public servant responsible to the people through the elected president *primarily* and to the elected Duma *secondarily*. The minister of defense can be questioned, even impolitely and unfairly, by lower-ranking military officers who have been elected to the Duma. Such questioning by citizen-soldiers tends to confuse the Ministry's policy development operations. There are two political problems here.

First, the classical problem all political systems face—the tension between professional experts and politicians. In theory, having the opposing points of view debated in public view is better than having them settled in private. In practice, some institutional arrangements are better than others for striking a balance between the competing values of military cohesion and professionalism on the one hand and political and civil rights for all military officers on the other.

Second, special problems develop when a military officer is elected to the Duma and becomes the head of its committee on national defense affairs. Col. Sergei Yushenkov led the first post-Soviet Duma's defense committee. Yushenkov became Defense Minister Grachev's rival. Yushenkov tried to lead defense reform, to assert the Duma's right to more information about how the Ministry spent its funds, and, through the Duma to give the public more influence and more knowledge about defense affairs. Yushenkov's successor, Lt. General Lev Rokhlin saw himself as the avowed representative of the soldiers in uniform, particularly those carrying the heaviest burdens and risking their lives in Chechnya, Tajikistan, and the other post-Soviet "hot spots." Rokhlin announced that he would try to prevent normal politics from damaging national defense. He intended to forge positive working relationships with all the branches of government, the key Duma committees and factions, and individual leaders required to advance the national defense agenda.

Rokhlin hoped to be effective without being in politics. Initially he decreased the level of inter-personal and inter-institutional tension by avoiding inflammatory language. However, he could not avoid the essence of politics which involves bargaining and deal making as well as drafting legislation and building budgets with the assistance of expert staff and representatives from the various governmental agencies and departments. As a soldier's soldier, Rokhlin pledged to protect the interests of those in uniform who bear the greatest burdens of national defense and to the fighting. This meant that there would be tension between Rokhlin and senior military professionals who were part of the chauffeured limousine and expensive-living elite, including Defense Minister Grachev. Rokhlin was a military populist and was predisposed to support Lebed's call for a serious campaign against corruption in civilian and military leadership circles. Both complained that federal laws, regulations, and military codes had not been properly enforced. They supported Grachev's resignation and praised Rodionov's appointment as his successor. This created better opportunities for constructive work between the Duma, the Defense Ministry, and the Security Council.

Ministers of Defense Yazov, Shaposhnikov, and Grachev were uncomfortable when soldiers mixed political and military careers. On the whole, the senior military leadership understood that in an ideally developed political system military officers neither ran for political office nor served in elective office without first resigning from the military. They also believed that Russia had not yet become a normal political democracy and that some abnormal military political activity might be necessary for the duration of the transition. But how long is a transition and what is the difference between a transition and a formative period in a political system's development? Some political habits that are excused as temporarily necessary could turn out to be quite durable.

Grachev discouraged officers from running for Duma seats in the December 1993 elections but then changed his mind in December 1995. He argued that the military needed its *own* lobby in the Duma, a set of legislators dedicated to rebuilding the Russian economy, the Russian state, and the Russian military. Grachev's vetted candidates failed to get elected; however, other soldiers and retired officers were elected on partisan lists. Grachev and other soldiers who disliked politics underestimated the role and importance of political parties—the organizations needed to mobilize the resources required to win office, to promote special interests in the national political institutions, and to hold accountable when they fail to deliver. It is difficult to be effective politically while remaining nonpartisan. As long as there are competitive elections, at least some politicians will be attracted to the national defense constituency and the military vote. It was the democratic process that gave the unhappy military voter the opportunity to protest against the Yeltsin administration by voting for opposition parties in the two Duma elections and which propelled Aleksandr Lebed into Yeltsin's entourage.

Military-Industrial Complex

Although the Soviet regime devoted enormous resources to defense spending, the Soviet military-industrial complex (MIC) did not know how to defend its interests either when the Soviet political system began to crumble or during the critical formative months and years when the post-Soviet, Russian state reset national spending priorities. The senior military officers, the leading industrialists, the workers organizations, and the politicians had no political machine to mobilize them to protect their interests. This is only partly explained by the collapse of the Communist Party.

The Yeltsin administration had to chose between money for military personnel and money for new weapons development, production, and purchasing. Marshal Shaposhnikov opted for money for soldiers as did Minister of Defense Grachev. Further, federal budget cutting, opportunities to make personal fortunes by privatizing parts of the national defense industrial sector, and potentially lucrative foreign arms and technology sales added to the goals confusion within the MIC. Yeltsin's planners decided that the defense sector should account for no more than about 5 percent of Russia's gross domestic product. For comparison, the figure was about 20 percent during the 1980s.[17]

Nevertheless, strategic thinkers understood that Russia needed a military-industrial complex, a national defense redevelopment strategy, and political institutions to set priorities and to implement them. Further, politicians could not afford to ignore the national defense constituency even though they knew that they could not satisfy its needs in the near term. The Yeltsin administration starting building such institutions: the Security Council, Rosvooruzhenie, and Goskomoboronprom. Prior to the Duma elections of 1993 and 1995 and the presidential elections of 1996, leading politicians pledged to bring order and stability to defense reconstruction and offered various general plans. In May 1996, Yeltsin decreed the formation of the Ministry of Defense Industry, a logical response to the national defense leadership and administration problem. In July 1996 Yeltsin authorized an increase in that Ministry's professional staff from 1,196 to 1,500 positions.[18] This step confirmed the importance of defense to Russian state viability.

Yeltsin also reaffirmed the old Soviet practice of keeping defense military and defense industrial affairs separate. Instead of having one grand, unified department to handle military and defense affairs, Russia would have two, separate institutions—a Ministry of Defense and a Ministry of Defense Industry. The Ministry of Defense would operate as a *military* ministry and concentrate on professional soldiering. The Ministry of Defense Industry would concentrate on weapons planning, development, production, and sales. The president would coordinate the work of the two ministries through special committees within his presidential administration, the Security Council, and the Defense Council. In theory, this structure enhanced the president's ability to exercise leadership authority and was a reasonable division of responsibility in national defense affairs. The soldiers handled soldiering and the defense-industrialists handled weapons production. The Defense Council was to established the strategic plans for weapons development.

The Mass Media

One of Gorbachev's most important contributions to Russia's political development was his decision to promote glasnost' or the ability to express dissenting opinions and to debate policy issues in the Soviet Union. Yeltsin deepened those reforms and civil liberties and the open media gained strength. Although Gorbachev and Yeltsin complained about what they considered irresponsible political reporting and used presidential influence to persuade state-owned and controlled national radio and television and official government publications to support their political lines, an independent media emerged from 1985 through 1996.

This development was important to soldiers who for the first time began to hear national defense policy questions debated in public and began to receive better information about the political history of the armed forces. By 1990–1991, they had access to diverse points of view, a broad spectrum ranging from the unofficial soldiers union—Shchit (Shield) to the right-wing nationalist organizations. Further, Russia's most popular independent, national papers developed a group of military analysts and regularly printed informative and provocative material. In this environment the Defense Ministry had to learn to defend its interests in the court of public opinion. The independent press made it necessary to respond to charges that draftees were still being abused, that the sale of surplus property and the awarding of contracts had bred major corruption, and that the war in Chechnya had been mismanaged.

Defense Minister Grachev faced the press in person and regularly. He even became involved in civil suits against reporters who accused him of criminal involvement in corruption and in the alleged cover-up of the murder of Dmitry Kholodov, the reporter killed by a bomb placed in a suitcase that was supposed to contain documents pertaining to military corruption. Although Grachev won several civil suits, he did not pacify his media critics. Grachev probably could have increased his popularity by sending the press military scapegoats from time to time but he preferred to keep his problems in-house, a political decision that rivals such as Aleksandr Lebed quite naturally exploited. By protecting his team, Grachev gave the appearance of supporting a systematic cover-up.

Yet, under Grachev, the official military press improved. Trends that began under Yazov strengthened. *Krasnaya zvezda* covered the Chechen war from a military-realist point of view, an enormous change from Soviet coverage of the war in Afghanistan. Reporters developed a post-Soviet, realist style which described soldiers as Russian citizens performing their professional tasks under extremely difficult physical and psychological conditions. Colonel Vladimir Zhitarenko's work is an excellent example of the genre. (He was killed by a sniper in Chechnya on 1 January 1995.) *Krasnaya zvezda* editorials consistently argued that Russia should strive to become more like the advanced industrial democracies in its civil-military relations and expressed deep regret every time the military was ordered to take action to settle or to attempt to settle a domestic political conflict that civilians had failed to resolve peacefully. Although some have criticized this independent-minded commentary, I would argue that it was constructive and progressive. Under the Soviet regime, the paper would have been forced to praise the government's action. Under Grachev it expressed a more objective, professional military perspective.

Nevertheless, *Krasnaya zvezda* reflected the Defense Ministry's general policy lines and did not permit its pages to be used by its critics. From time to time it engaged in self-serving attacks on the government and the Ministry of Finance for holding up military salaries and benefits. The paper seemed to be steering military anger towards the minister of finance instead of towards the President who bore the ultimate responsibility for the salary payment strategy which was designed to restrain inflation. Presidential policy could be criticized indirectly but no open editorial attacks on the supreme commander were allowed.

The paper took sides in the Duma and presidential elections. The partisan trend increased from the 1993 to the 1995 Duma elections. And, for the first round in the presidential elections, *Krasnaya zvezda* promoted the Yeltsin agenda quite shamelessly. However, it continued to report the news from Chechnya in a far less optimistic tone than the presidential campaign would have liked. And, after the paper saw Yeltsin dump Grachev in order to win Lebed's support, it moved closer to neutrality on the presidential elections and reminded the military that the country needed a constructive opposition and urged them to vote as they pleased. The paper reflected the military's impatience with civilian politicos as a whole and it occasionally gave space to officers who believed that Russian military personnel could provide effective national leadership as Eisenhower had done for America, de Gaulle for France, and Pinochet for Chile. But such naive comments appeared infrequently and the main editorial line reflected a more mature sense of concern about the political system's apparent inability to tackle basic reform tasks systematically.

Although it was unhappy with its treatment in the civilian mass media, the military leadership understood that it had to learn to use the press more effectively and to nurture a new generation of public relations professionals to serve the interests of national defense. Grachev established the precedent that Russia's Defense Ministers were prepared to appear before the press and to debate issues with journalists and the media. Senior military leaders were expected to be able to handle the press well. Defense Minister Rodionov granted interviews to papers that had regularly goaded his predecessor and tried to increase military openness. He also expanded and reorganized the Defense Ministry's press service. The press responded positively to his more dignified, diplomatic manner and his military frankness.[19]

Role Expansion? Competition? Coordination?

Yeltsin used the military as a domestic political tool and contributed to the militarization of political competition when he sent the tanks against Parliament and made war against the Chechen secessionists. But he did not invent the use of military force in domestic politics. He learned the importance of armed force in domestic politics by observing the events in Tbilisi, Baku, and Vilnius by dealing with Gorbachev's use of armed forces to intimidate the Russian Congress in March 1991, by analyzing the activities of the elite paratroopers in the Moscow region in September 1990 and summer 1991, and by responding to Defense Minister Yazov's betrayal of Gorbachev and the SEC's clumsy attempts to use military intimidation to impose its temporary dictatorship. Yeltsin could not have taken power and remained in power without having learned to use the military as a domestic political tool and this primarily meant building an effective relationship with the elite paratroopers and other special forces. Both Grachev and Lebed came out of that branch of the Russian military which conducted military-political interventions at home and abroad and which expected to continue to be needed in the future.[20]

There was no doubt about the existence of special political and personal bonds between President Boris Yeltsin and General Pavel Grachev, a coupling that was severely strained by the Chechen war and Yeltsin's electoral campaign needs. Similarly, another source of power within the Kremlin developed around the person responsible for high-level protection and security services, General Aleksandr Korzhakov. Although Grachev and Korzhakov were both Yeltsin's close personal associates and people who had rendered him vitally important services, he removed them in order to consolidate a new political alliance with General Aleksandr Lebed. When the Yeltsin-Lebed alliance collapsed, Lebed and Korzhakov drew together against their new common enemy—Boris Yeltsin. The fact that Lebed and Korzhakov were politicking together in Tula with the elite paratroopers sent Yeltsin into a rage. He certainly remembered that he had been to Tula before every major confrontation with Gorbachev and before and after his political showdown with Parliament.

Soldiers were in politics and civilian politicians were cultivating soldiers because the political system was failing to cope with basic governance problems well enough to support national security and defense institutions properly. The military was less interested in using armed force at home than in using political influence to insure a steady flow of financial support and resources into national defense. By 1996, the military leadership clearly understood that the armed forces needed a healthy economy more than soldiers elected to the Duma and placed on the Duma defense committee. However, military officers had not been educated to analyze and evaluate competing economic policies and were frustrated spectators rather than intelligent participants in the main reform debates.

Further, proud soldiers did not want to serve as domestic police. However, the Yeltsin administration increased the size of the various armed forces that perform domestic security and border protection and customs functions while it cut the size of the military. By spring 1996, they outnumbered the military and military analysts complained. Army General Makhmut Gareyev estimated their strength at about 2,000,000 compared with the approximately 1,500,000 in the regular or strategic military forces under the Ministry of Defense.[21] Some Russian analysts estimated that there were another 1,000,000 private guards at work protecting enterprises and institutions, a reflection of the state's failure to provide basic security for the emerging commercial and business classes.[22] General Lebed rode that wave of popular insecurity into the Kremlin. It moved representatives of the armed forces and the departments responsible for them into more prominent public leadership roles during the first half of the 1990s.[23]

Defense Minister Rodionov was a strategic thinker who understood the extent to which the Yeltsin administration had improvised instead of imposing a planned national defense reconstruction strategy on the country. He argued that the military could not undertake military reform successfully unless and until the country adopted a national defense reconstruction plan which embraced, industry, the police, and so on.[24] This position confirmed the military's support for comprehensive efforts to restore state viability. If civilian politicians and a democratic regime cannot provide that, then the military will probably gravitate to the opposition. Will it take over and try to govern the country on its own? The traditional Russian pattern is military participation but not the substitution of a military regime for civilian political administration. The military's record from 1985–1995 was rather progressive although its attitude towards the demokraty became quite negative. The Yeltsin administration bears much of the responsibility for that problem since it did not set the right tone for civil-military relations as a whole.

Over the coming years, the level of military involvement in politics will depend upon how well the civilian political leadership manages economic and social reform. There will be less military involvement in politics if the economy improves and social tensions decrease. There will be more military involvement in political life if the economy continues to deteriorate, the government is unable to fund national defense properly, and the civilian leaders fail to settle the Chechen and other political conflicts. Under those circumstances the military will find itself courted by the new financial and economic elite and the populist opposition forces. When discussing Yeltsin's offer of appointment, Rodionov warned the president that unless military salaries and benefits were improved, he could lose control over the armed forces.[25] He openly admitted that Russia's ability to defend itself was still falling and that military discontent was still rising.

Conclusion

The 1993 Constitution and the 1996 Law on Defense created a presidential state in which the executive branch dominated national defense policy with no effective checks and balances from either the Duma or the Federal Council. The presidential state is an adaptation of the Soviet state which centered dictatorial powers over the armed forces in the office of the General Secretary.

Ministers of defense had to give their main attention to cultivating productive political relations with the executive branch of government. Since the power to make authoritative decisions was centered in the presidency, the minister of defense had to stay close to the president and the presidential administration. The military's next most important political contacts were with the prime minister and various departments of government, especially the Ministry of Finance which controlled the flow of money from the federal treasury to the armed forces and the Ministry of Defense Industry. After the president and the prime minister came the Security and Defense Councils which set and coordinated Russian security and defense policies. The Duma was less important except when writing legislation that directly affected the military and when defining the annual budget. In the long run, the latter function could become the hook the Duma needs to become an effective check on the president's power over military affairs. Duma hearings also give society an opportunity to inquire into the workings of government and to ask probing questions. This power could also become more important over time.

The president directly supervises all the power ministries—defense, domestic police, border troops, and security forces. These practices originated in the Soviet dictatorship but the Soviet dictatorship managed them better because it had strong coordination and control mechanisms rooted in the five-year plans and the single-party dictatorship.

Without strong policy coordinating institutions, President Yeltsin was overwhelmed by political demands competing for his time and energy and could not focus his political attention long enough on any area to be very effective. This encouraged the power ministries to attempt to resolve problems on their own and to compete with one another other for resources. Yeltsin was advised to create strong policy development and coordination institutions. Instead, he kept trying to juggle some twenty-odd, defense-related institutions. The Lebed affair precipitated a number of institutional and personnel changes that had the potential to develop into a good architecture of power for presidential control and coordination of national defense affairs. The Security Council and the Defense Council could develop into such strategic planning and policy coordinating institutions. However, that could not happen unless Boris Yeltsin changed his political leadership style and started operating as a builder of stable institutions in national defense affairs.

Russia's first democratically elected president was a strong political gamesman but a weak administrator. He had enormous formal powers but did not wield them effectively. He was also lenient and tolerant of dissent—a trait that future presidents might not share. In the hands of a different leader, the Russian constitution could serve as the legal foundation for a powerful, semi-authoritarian state.

Notes

1. See Vitaly Vitebsky, "VPK v pervom polugodii" (MIC half-year report), *Krasnaya zvezda*, 26 October 1996. Vitebsky is a Ministry of Defense Industry economist. He publishes a quarterly report defense industry performance.
2. See Oleg Odnokolenko's interview with Aleksandr Piskunov, a member of the governmental team arranging emergency financing for the armed services, "Financy, byudzhet i reforma" (Finances, the budget, and reform), *Krasnaya zvezda*, 19 November 1996.

3. The Law on Defense is printed in *Krasnaya zvezda*, 5 June 1996. Yeltsin signed it into law on 31 March 1996.

4. See Aleksandr Pel'ts, "Sovet oborony: prioritety na budushchee" (Defense council's future priorities), *Krasnaya zvezda*, 22 November 1996.

5. Source Defense Minister Rodionov, reported by Vladimir Chupakhin, Sergei Knyaz'kov, Anatoly Stasovskii; "Nado zdelat' vse vozmozhnoe, shtoby armiya bystree vyshla iz kriziza" (Need to do everything possible to get the army through the crisis), *Krasnaya zvezda*, 2 October 1996.

6. Vitaly Vitebsky, "VPK v pervom polugodii (MIC at half-year), *Krasnaya zvezda*, 3 August 1996.

7. See *Krasnaya zvezda*, 2 and 4 October 1996.

8. See Lt. General Lev Rokhlin, chairman of the State Duma's Defense Committee's optimistic description of his small committee, "Voennym nuzhny deistvennye zakony," *Krasnaya zvezda*, 16 March 1996.

9. Presidential Press Service, *Krasnaya zvezda*, 22 August 1996.

10. Lebed as cited by Vasily Fatigarov, "100 dnei Aleksandra Lebedya," *Krasnaya zvezda*, 28 September 1996.

11. The world press carried Yeltsin's statement, so did the Ministry of Defense's daily, *Krasnaya zvezda*, 19 October 1996.

12. "Prezident Boris Yeltsin predstavil vyshemu rukovodstvu Vooruzhennykh Sil novogo ministra oborony RF general-polkovnik Igorya Rodionova" (Yeltsin presented the new defense minister to top armed forces leadership), *Krasnaya zvezda*, 19 July 1996.

13. Chief of General Staff Viktor Samsonov, interviewed by Alexander Zhilin, "General Staff Can't Keep Up With the Politicians," *Moscow News*, 31 October-6 November 1996.

14. *Ibid.*

15. See *Krasnaya zvezda*, 5, 6, 12, and 13 November 1996.

16. See the report on Chernomyrdin and Rodionov's visit to the Northern Fleet by Vladimir Gundarov, "Skvoz' prizmu reform" (Through the reform prism), *Krasnaya zvezda*, 26 November 1996.

17. See Nikolai Shmelyev, "Pyat' let reform—pyat' let kriziza" (Five years of reform. Five years of crisis), *Svobodnaya mysl'*, no. 7, 1996, p. 64; and V. V. Andreyevskii and Col. V. N. Tkachev, "K voprosu opredeleniya chislennosti Vooruzhennykh Sil Rossii" (The Question of defining the size of Russia's armed forces), *Voennaya mysl'*, no. 2, March-April, 1995, pp. 25. ff.

18. Reported in *Krasnaya zvezda*, 25 July 1996.

19. See "Sozdana press-sluzhba MO RF" (MoD press service formed), *Krasnaya zvezda*, 26 November 1996. Liberal military correspondents such as Alexander Zhilin at *Moscow News* welcomed these developments and were inclined to reinterpret their earlier negative attitude towards Rodionov's 1989 criticisms of relations between civilian politicians and the military.

20. *Ibid.*

21. Army General Makhmut Gareyev, president of the Academy of Military Sciences, "O kontseptsii rossiiskoi oboronnoi politiki" (Russia's defense policy concept), *Svobodnaya mysl'*, no. 7, 1996, pp. 50–59.

22. See Lt. General (Ret.) Vladimir Serebryannikov, "Voennoe nasilie v politicheskikh konfliktakh" (Military coercion in political conflicts), *Ibid.*, no. 6, 1996, p. 29–35.

23. See Airborne Forces Commander, Col. General E. N. Podkolzin, "Primenenie vozdushnykh desantov v lokal'nykh voinakh i vooruzhennykh konfliktakh"

(Using paratroopers in local wars and armed conflicts), *Voennaya mysl'*, no. 4, July-August 1996, pp. 15 ff.

24. See Rodionov's interview by Col. Oleg Vladykin, "Ministr oborony RF general-polkovnik Igor Rodionov" (The RF's Minister of Defense: Col. General Igor Rodionov), *Krasnaya zvezda*, 1 August 1996.

25. See Igor Rodionov's interview by Col. Oleg Falichev, "Vernem lyudam v pogonakh dostoinstvo i uvazhenie" (We will return honor and respect to the people in uniform), *Krasnaya zvezda*, 7 August 1996.

17

The Theory and Practice of Democratic Constitutional Control

This chapter reviews the Russian political and military leadership's response to a decade of change. It identifies positive and negative experience with military participation in national political life and discusses why Boris Yeltsin continued to have difficulty laying solid foundations for balanced, democratic control. It argues that Western insights become more relevant to Russian politics as new competitive political and market forces transform Russian society but it pinpoints a weakness in mainstream Western discourse on civil-military relations.

Western theory's central concept—civilian control, is too vague and needs specific institutional and ideological anchoring. How should civilian control be structured in order to encourage responsible leadership in defense affairs? If *civilian control* really means a refined system of constitutional checks and balances within a democratic political system, then Yeltsin's ukaz-governed state falls short of the mark. Although the Yeltsin administration was dominated by civilian politicians and therefore exercised *civilian* control over the military, it was a hybrid system, a mixture of authoritarian and democratic theory and practice.

The Historic Legacy: Authoritarian Theory and Practice

The Russian armed forces have been under various forms of authoritarian civilian control for hundreds of years. In the Russo-Soviet political context, civilian leaders were not civilians in the Western liberal sense of the term. They were a class apart from the general citizenry, something more than leading citizens. The tsars and the highest noble ranks did not think of themselves as civilians. The latter were commoners—tradesman, peasants, and the like. Soldiers were also commoners unless they advanced into the officer ranks. Nobles did not serve as common soldiers and when commoners became commissioned officers, they were simultaneously admitted to the noble orders. The nobility's control over society was the Russian imperial system's funda-

mental operating rule. The tsar's absolute control over the nobility and imperial state machinery including the military was the core of that system.

The idea that commoners were citizens with equal rights and that the state's
political leaders were accountable to the citizens was just starting to take root
in the Russian empire when the Bolshevik revolution aborted the process. It
should be remembered that Russia's first Constitution was granted to Russia
by the tsar in 1905 under duress and that it defined various classes of citizens
with different degrees of political power.

The two-stage Russian revolution of 1917 was partly a mutiny in the armed
forces, partly a general social revolution, and partly a failed corrective coup by
the military and civilian elite. The February-March revolution abolished citizenship distinctions based upon socioeconomic class and made all citizens equal.
The October-November revolution reimposed distinctions based upon socioeconomic class and made the workers and peasants—the so-called proletar-
ians, the citizenry. The Socialist Revolutionary and Bolshevik parties put imperial
officers under popular control by the mass of military personnel and they took
representatives from the armed masses into their revolutionary councils or soviets which became the foundation for the Soviet Union. Initially, the Reds
promoted two main principles—democratization of military life and full military participation in popular self-government. Later, they made one-party rule
the Soviet political system's basic operating principle. When soldiers advanced
into higher command positions, they were brought into the Communist Party, a
step that confirmed their enhanced leadership rank.

Party control was the main issue not civilian control and the great Bolshevik leaders such as Leon Trotsky and Joseph Stalin moved back and forth
between military and other state-building activities. So did Khrushchev and
Brezhnev. They deliberately prevented the military profession from evolving
into a closed, elite institution set apart from the Party and society. However,
they were respectful and suspicious of military power and created special
KGB units to provide personal security services to top military commanders,
a move that institutionalized surveillance and control. The general secretary
was the "general of generals" and could remove the top leadership in any
profession including the armed forces.

Thus, the noble-led state gave way to the Party-led state. The Party's absolute control over society became the Soviet political system's main operating
principle. The general secretary's absolute control over the armed forces flowed
from it. One type of authoritarianism replaced another.

The imperial state's ascriptive elitism was replaced by the Soviet state's
instrumental elitism. The imperial elite was composed primarily of people
born into wealth and power though not exclusively. The Soviet elite was composed of people who advanced through the Communist Party and their professions. Party membership was reserved for the managerial elite in all fields
including the armed forces. In Soviet theory the elite served the people, was

professionally competent, and was derived from the people. In practice, it was self-selecting and no open competitive elections were permitted. It refused to hold itself accountable to the people and it also tended to restrain debate within the professions.

Western Experience and Russian Practice

Gorbachev and Yeltsin argued that political competition would produce better societal leadership and that economic competition would create a more dynamic and productive economy. The military accepted that basic thesis and supported the main thrust of Gorbachev's reforms. In order to explain the new system, Western terms were introduced into Russo-Soviet political thinking but this does not mean that Western thinking has replaced Russo-Soviet thinking or that the terms have the same meaning in Western and Russo-Soviet political culture. Thus, the analyst who would understand the military's place in the post-Soviet political system must engage in the rectification of terms.

The Russian translation of the Western term, civil control, is *grazhdanskii kontrol*. As in English language, the adjective *grazhdanskii* has three related definitions: civil, civilian, and citizen. The term *civil control* is therefore too vague to be truly useful in the development of democratic theory and practice. We need to become more specific. Civilian control certainly doesn't meet the test because civilian control can be democratic, authoritarian, or totalitarian. *Civil control* is better but still too vague. *Civic control* would be preferable because it denotes general societal control which, after all, is the aim of democratic political movements.

The Soviet dictatorship's basic operating principle was Party control or *partiinyi kontrol*. It was clear and specific. The Communist Party controlled defense affairs and it did not subject itself to civic accountability until the Gorbachev reforms of 1988–1989 introduced competitive elections. His goal was constitutional control or *konstitutsionnyi kontrol* within a law-governed state or *zakonnoe gosudarstvo*. During Gorbachev's perestroika, Russian thinkers introduced those terms into the national political debate. They also borrowed another Western term, *civil society*, which they translated as *grazhdanskoe obshchestvo,* to describe the growth of pluralism and institutional self-governance that developed as the Party relinquished its vanguard role and society began to organize itself under democratically derived laws.

Russian political theory and practice deviated from Anglo-American concepts which were shaped by the battle for parliamentary control over the monarchy and over the armed forces in England. Standing armies were considered a threat to republican government; therefore, citizen militias were the armed force of preference in the early American republic and the United States Constitution specifically empowered the citizenry to form them. As a result, American thinking tended to be more interested in civilian control over standing armed forces and in congressional checks on presidential power than in how the professional soldiers exercise their rights of citizenship and bring their professional expertise into national policy debates. American political culture influences American political science which generally assumes that democratic theory and practice ought to place some restrictions on political participation by military professionals. Latin American political experience has reinforced this general American point of view because authoritarian military regimes impeded democratic development in a number of American states. The competition between civilian and military elites reaffirmed the general American democratic commitment to civilian control.

In Russian constitutional law and thought, the armed forces are part of civil society and armed forces personnel are considered full citizens. Russian political history celebrates the revolutionary soldier's contribution to the revolution against the imperial state. The soldiers are not set apart from civil society. They are included in the overall governance process which defines and implements national defense and security policy. All Soviet constitutions gave soldiers and sailors full political citizenship rights including the ability to hold elective office. Yeltsin's 1993 Constitution reaffirmed the such rights but forbade partisan political activity within the armed forces.

Yeltsin tolerated a high level of military participation in policy debates. He also worked directly with uniformed officers who headed his power ministries. These face-to-face political activities included confidential planning for the use of armed force to achieve domestic political objectives. He brought the armed forces into inappropriate domestic political activity and illustrated the danger of giving presidents too much control. That experience suggests that military professionals are coopted by civilian elites and used for domestic political purposes.

From the American vantage point, Russia made a mistake when it granted the president the right to appoint and dismiss military commanders without confirmation by the Duma and when it continued the Soviet revolutionary practice of including armed forces personnel in the political process. Although American views were shaped by Anglo-American history, they may not be ethno-culturally bound. Those who design constitutions to support democratic republics, even presidential republics, need to consider how the distribution of power over the armed forces affects political behavior and how the presence of military officers inside the competing branches of government influences the forms of competition.

Russia's constitution made it relatively easy for inappropriate coercive political behavior to develop out of natural political competition between the executive branch and the legislature and between the federal government and the regions. For example, soldiers in the last Soviet parliament contributed to the militarization of the political conflict between president and Parliament. And, President Yeltsin's direct power over all the armed forces made it easy for him to plot against Parliament with the three power ministers and he did. Soldiers in the Chechen nationalist movement—Dzhokhar Dudayev and Aslan Maskhadov, rapidly converted the Chechen nationalist assembly into an armed rebellion. Yeltsin's direct control over federal armed forces permitted him to go to war against the Chechens without seeking prior approval from the Duma.

One bad practice supports and encourages another. Having colonels and generals in the Duma makes it all the more necessary to unify and centralize control over the armed forces in order to prevent policy battles between the Duma and the presidency or within the Duma from penetrating into the armed forces. Too much power in the hands of the presidency tempts ambitious presidents to use armed force to win their domestic political battles. Therefore, the design solution to this problem would have to address the presidency, the Duma, and the military's political rights. The president, the Duma, and the army would have to give up something.

The president would have to give up exclusive control over military appointments and transfer some of that power to the Duma. To permit the Duma to serve as an effective check on presidential abuses of power, the armed forces need to give up their right to serve in the Duma. Otherwise, there will be conflicts of interest and presidential suspicion that the Duma is a politically protected space where members of the opposition and military deputies are conspiring against the presidency. Two examples of such problems have been noted. First, anti-Yeltsin military officers in the Russian Parliament, 1990–1993, did indeed conspire against the presidency. Second, Lt. General Lev Rokhlin's chairmanship of the Duma defense committee was a conflict of interest which compromised the Duma's ability to serve as an independent political monitor over military affairs.

But would the national interest gain from a better system of checks and balances? In societies where there is a strong political consensus and the executive and legislative branches cooperate, the answer is positive. In divided societies where there are major divisions between the executive branch and the legislature and the legislature is divided, the answer is far less clear. In such cases, checks and balances can result in system *immobilisme* and a general weakening of the state's ability to respond effectively to domestic and foreign security threats. Yeltsin used such arguments to defend his 1993 Constitution and the presidential state it created.

Military Glasnost'

The main goal behind Gorbachev's glasnost' or openness reforms was to give Soviet society the ability to generate the positive benefits enjoyed by open societies. Society gains when it receives accurate information and solid professional advice from the armed forces about national security issues and when military and civilian experts engage in a substantive dialogue about national security issues. The military benefits from political knowledge about the balance of interests in the country and how public opinion is moving on issues related to national defense. It can also benefit from increased public support assuming that society values national security and a strong military and will respond in a timely manner to security threats. But too much openness can damage military cohesion and manageability and lead to a confusion of military and civilian roles and functions in society. Russia has experienced both the benefits and drawbacks of military citizenship and openness.

Gorbachev proclaimed glasnost' to Russian society as a whole. This was essential to modernization's institutionalization of change which requires the right to debate ideas freely. The fact that armed forces personnel joined the national debate was somewhat disconcerting but it was a normal development in the Soviet context. Military professionals were present in the Soviet legislatures which Gorbachev transformed into forums for debate and lawmaking. Military professionals were tired of being bossed by politicians and wanted to have their say. They had ideas to propose and interests to defend as much as fellow citizens working in other professions. If the emerging bankers and business tycoons could be involved in the formation of national economic policy, military professionals should have similar rights and opportunities to be involved in national security policy formation.

The military may not have liked the general direction post-Soviet politics was taking but it could not but recognize the fact that demilitarization of the economy and big cuts in standing armies were supported by society as a whole. The process that Gorbachev initiated not only continued under Yeltsin but it deepened. When Gorbachev took power in 1985, the Soviet military had some 4,200,000 authorized positions plus civilian employees. A decade later the Russian Defense Ministry had recognized and accepted the inevitability of drawing the numbers down but was trying to hold the line somewhere between 1,500,000 and 1,700,000 positions. A year later in fall 1996, Defense Minister Rodionov had accepted the inevitability of more cuts and a new base of 1,000,000 to 1,200,000 authorized military positions and some 500,000 civilian employees. He realized that even those numbers could not be properly supported and maintained by Russia's weak economy. Although the military quite naturally complained and competed to get every ruble it could from other federal agencies, it realized that its main problems were the public's resistance to high military spending and the country's economic decline.

The Ministry of Defense has had mixed feelings about military participation in political activity. On the one hand, it has tried to use the military's political rights to advance its departmental agenda, to win funding increases, to amend draft laws, to influence policy development, and so on. On the other hand, it recognized that partisan political activity is a definite threat to military cohesion and to the chain of command's integrity. Military discontent peaked in winter 1991–1992 but it was channeled through the Officers Assemblies which demanded and received a hearing from Boris Yeltsin and Defense Minister Shaposhnikov. That experience confirmed the right to be heard but it also defined the line that once crossed leads to a general breakdown in military discipline and constitutional control.

On balance, official Ministry opinion favored depoliticization in a viable state capable of supporting the armed forces properly. Thus, its support for depoliticization was conditional and based upon an assumed division of labor between political-governance professionals and military professionals within the Russian state. As long as the political professionals provide overall effective leadership, the military should be content to stay out of politics. Similarly, as long as military professionals manage internal military affairs competently, they should experience little direct political intervention in their military professional activities. In post-Soviet Russia, there were weaknesses in national political leadership and in internal military governance which encouraged contestation in both directions. Civilians probed into military affairs and the military complained bitterly about civilian mismanagement of national affairs. The public debate became so acrimonious that Defense Minister Grachev ended up taking journalists to court and won several suits for libel.

It would be hard to imagine a military professional serving as secretary of defense of the United States of America let alone a top general in acrimonious debates and law suits with the press. American political culture conditioned its military to remain silent even when civilian leaders waged war incompetently as in Vietnam during the Kennedy, Johnson, and Nixon administrations. The situation was quite different in post-Soviet Russia when the Yeltsin administration waged war incompetently in Chechnya. The official military press criticized the war's strategy and tactics from beginning to end but the military still obeyed Yeltsin's orders. Lt. General Lev Rokhlin, the commander who conquered Grozny for Yeltsin, was one of the war's most pragmatic critics. Rokhlin ran for office and within a year was heading the Duma's defense committee. It would be difficult to imagine an American military commander such as General William Westmoreland running for a seat in the United States Congress during the Vietnam War on an antiwar platform, winning, and being given leadership over the most important defense committee.

The Russian military had access to society and society had unprecedented access to the military even at war. The Russian military was also exposed to direct societal pressures typical of civil wars. Mothers' organizations rapidly developed and sent representatives into the combat zones where they both besieged military officers with pleas to release their sons from service and helped to organize humanitarian assistance to the soldiers and the wounded. Even Lt. General Rokhlin admitted to having released several soldiers from the battle of Grozny when their mothers came to him with desperate pleas. Reporters and civil and human rights organizations also penetrated the war zones and the Russian public found itself receiving special reports from all sides. The Russian state lost control over the war story immediately and never regained it. Russian society saw itself at war without any embellishments.

Mixing Military and Political Leadership Functions

Civil war and instability led to a breakdown in the simplistic explanation about what war is and isn't and to a fusion of military and political functions. Was Lt. General (Ret.) Aleksandr Lebed a civilian politician or a military leader when he negotiated the Chechen settlement with Chechen chief of General Staff, Aslan Maskhadov? Was Maskhadov a civilian or a military leader when he simultaneously served as chief of General Staff and acting prime minister? Chronic, unstable conditions produce leaders that combine political and military functions. The Russian state's North Caucasian districts were ripe for government by local *caudillos* either in alliance with or in opposition to the federal government. Chechnya's immediate neighbor, Ingushetia also had a col. general in the Russian Armed Forces serving as its elected president, Ruslan Aushev.

Lebed's July-August 1996 cease-fire agreements with the Chechen rebels granted the rebels the right to control the armed forces inside the Chechen republic but refused to recognize Chechen independence from Russia. This legitimized the Chechen anomaly or gap in the Russian federal military system. Federal forces withdrew from Chechnya and Chechen forces which totally rejected President Boris Yeltsin's right to serve as their supreme commander assumed responsibility for maintaining law and order. Chechen rebels regarded federal troops as a threat to self-determination and liberty and refused to agree to permit them to be stationed in the Chechen lands. Would other parts of the Russian Federation make similar demands? Federal states can and do grant federation units some powers to form and command their own armed forces in addition to supporting federal armed forces. American experience confirms that principle. American governors command state troopers and national guards. However, the president becomes the commander in chief over the national guards in times of war or major national emergency. This follows the general rule that the central political authority in any state must be able to control the use of armed force within its borders. The Chechens refused to accept this principle. Lebed granted the Chechens control over armed force within Chechnya but not Chechen power to control air space and international borders. These were reserved to Moscow—the federal government.

The Military and the Rising Economic Elite

During the Soviet period, Marxist-Leninist analysis of civil-military relations insisted that armed forces are created and maintained by particular socioeconomic classes in order to defend their class interests. Thus, the military serves the socioeconomic elite and defends its wealth and power against the masses except in truly democratic socialist societies where they are essentially armed citizens. For this reason, Soviet analysts used to argue that when Western political scientists supported civilian control they really meant control by society's wealthy elite. Since Soviet thinking always assumed that the Soviet Union was in the process of becoming a classless society, it started with the premise that "the Army and the people are one." Therefore, the idea of blocking the peoples soldiers from participating in societal governance was considered wrong and condemned as typical of bourgeois elite regimes. If post-Soviet Russia is in the process of becoming a class society with an emerging financial and commercial elite, will official Russian thinking about civil-military relations change to reflect the new socioeconomic realities? Who will command the armed forces? The general citizenry or the new elite?

Russia did not have a legacy of competition between civilian politicians and military officers for control over the levers of power in society. In Gorbachev's Soviet Union, top military officers were still part of the national elite but the nature of the national elite was beginning to change. By the mid-1990s in Yeltsin's, post-Soviet Russia, the military was far less certain about its social status and regularly complained about its relative decline. New financial elites were emerging and the comparatively impoverished military was not part of that class. Those top level officers who imitated the new elite's habits were derided as illustrated by the case of Defense Minister Grachev's Mercedes and a host of related tales about posh military dachas in the Moscow suburbs.[1] The Russian military wasn't closely associated with the new financial elite and tended to see it as antidefense in its domestic policies and insufficiently patriotic in its general economic orientation. Aleksandr Lebed reflected such populist and nationalist sentiments.

Tension between the rising elite and the populists developed during the 1996 presidential campaign. Post-Communist tycoon, Boris Berezovsky called for postponing the elections when he and other business leaders feared that Yeltsin might be defeated. Military populists played to the public's distrust of the new entrepreneurs who were financing Yeltsin's campaign and who were getting richer while the average Russian was getting poorer or at least less secure. Lt. General Aleksandr Lebed called for a thorough campaign against corruption in high places. However, Lebed quickly fell from power; and after his fall, Yeltsin appointed tycoon Berezovsky to the Russian Security Council, a step that reaffirmed Yeltsin's close links to the rising business elite.

Yeltsin decided that the Security Council needed to promote teamwork between the moderate socialists, the armed forces, and the rising tycoons. He therefore made a democratic socialist, Ivan Rybkin, Security Council secretary and gave him two assistants for armed forces and economic affairs respectively: Col. General Leonid Mayorov and Boris Berezovsky. This was a pragmatic response to a strategic political problem. Yeltsin wanted the new tycoons, the socialist populists, and the armed forces to find common political ground, a general strategy for rebuilding the Russian economy rapidly enough to prevent social and military breakdown.

The populist tradition isn't necessarily deeply democratic or even liberal. It can associate itself with both authoritarian and democratic political methods. Lebed's claim that the people demand a take-charge regime because the Fatherland is in danger and the run-of-the-mill politicos are corrupt and incompetent is the foundation for authoritarian populism. When Yeltsin took Lebed into his administration, he said that it was a merger of two political programs not just a temporary political alliance of convenience. Yeltsin thereby validated some aspects of the authoritarian populist criticism of his first administration's record.

The military's overall behavior was predicted by modernization theory. Russian military professionals supported the grand reform project and wanted a law-governed society where military professionals could hope for better standards of living and honorable careers. Since 1985 the Soviet military elite supported progressive national political change even though it was deeply critical of the way civilian politicians handled their responsibilities. Such impatience runs through the comments and actions of the four successive ministers of defense—Generals Yazov, Shaposhnikov, Grachev, and Rodionov who led the military from 1987 to 1996. It was the main complaint from the military opposition to Gorbachev that formed around the Soyuz faction in the Soviet Congress. It was deeply embedded in vice president, Col. General (Ret.) Rutskoi's thinking when he broke with Yeltsin and rallied to Parliament in 1993. It was Lt. General Lev Rokhlin's main reason for rejecting military honors for his service in Chechnya and deciding to run for a seat in the Duma in December 1995. It was the foundation for presidential candidate Lt. General (Ret.) Aleksandr Lebed's criticisms of the first Yeltsin administration and the basis for Lebed's reformist agenda as Security Council Secretary in Yeltsin's second administration. And it was one of Defense Minister Pavel Grachev's main complaints and deeply embedded in his successor, Col. General Rodionov's outlook ever since the Tbilisi events of April 1989.

Political Cleavage Patterns that Limited Military Influence

The military, the other armed forces, and defense industry still represent a potential political force of some 15 percent or more of the electorate.[2] Although the military was highly critical of how civilians had managed national reform, it neither joined forces with a particular party nor attempted to imposed a regime of technocratic colonels and generals on Russia. The military's overall relationship with society and Russia's leading political parties was complex. Within that complexity there were definite patterns, three political cleavages which discouraged the military from realizing its full political potential either within a major political coalition or as an autonomous political force. Because the military could not cooperate effectively with the main political parties, the other armed forces, or the Russian defense industry, no cohesive national defense lobby formed during the first Yeltsin administration, 1991–1996.

The first political cleavage was between the Soviet military and society as a whole. The military was both the beneficiary and victim of democratization. Although the military moved with Russian society when it supported political and economic reform, neither the Yeltsin administration nor society at large supported the military's position on defense spending. Individual military leaders were powerless against this wave of antidefense spending sentiment. The national political consensus demanded sharp cuts. The general economic depression prevented the Kremlin from supporting the armed forces adequately and made the battle for resources more intense. The Chechen conflict pitted military draft boards against Russia's draft-age youth and their families and widened the gap between the armed forces and society. Better-educated, better-placed youth received deferments while lower-class workers and farmers were drafted. Politicians paid more attention to their influential civilian constituencies than to the war's needs and the military's requirements. Instead of healing the cleavages between civilian opinion makers and the military, the Chechen war made them worse. It also created tensions within the military. Field commanders such as Lt. General Lev Rokhlin resented the fact that soldiers fighting in Chechnya had become third-class members of the Russian military system. The senior military elite lived comparatively well in Moscow, some service branches such as the Strategic Rocket Forces received priority funding, and the boys fighting in Chechnya got what was left over.

The second set of cleavages operated between the military and the Russian state's other armed forces. These cross-cutting cleavages decreased the likelihood that all the armed forces could coalesce around a particular political leader or demand. Yeltsin exploited this diversity by building up the MVD, the Border Forces, and special security forces at the military's expense; and, he also made several politically loaded references to the need for a new personnel system that rewarded professional competence. This appealed to middle and lower level officers who were eager for promotion and who resented the military elite's affluent living. By taking the military populist Aleksandr Lebed into his administration and permitting him to begin a campaign against corruption and incompetence in leading military circles, Yeltsin was playing politics with the military as much as supporting reform. When Yeltsin removed Grachev in order to satisfy Lebed's demands, he confirmed that senior military positions were on the political bargaining table. Such actions enhanced factional competition within the senior officer corps for the top leadership positions. When Yeltsin introduced Grachev's successor, Col. General Rodionov, to the military high command, he told senior officers that Rodionov would fight corruption in the armed forces and address the promotional criteria and methods problem. On the one hand, such steps were necessary to strengthen the military as an institution. On the other, they benefited Yeltsin by keeping the military involved in internal military affairs instead of joining Lebed for a general political attack on corruption and incompetence in civilian and military spheres.

The third cleavage developed between the military and the defense industrial establishment. When faced with a choice between money to fund military salaries and benefits and the defense procurement order, the military supported its own immediate personnel and operational requirements. When Yegor Gaidar was prime minister, the Yeltsin administration slashed spending on new arms development and production in order to be able to pay some of the bills for repatriating 1,200,000 military personnel and dependents to Russia. The defense order spending cuts remained in place after Yeltsin replaced Gaidar with Viktor Chernomyrdin in December 1992. In late 1992 and 1993 when Yeltsin wanted support from the national defense constituency, he pledged to improve national defense spending but he could not keep those promises. Therefore, the military and the defense industrialists continued to compete for the same pool of inadequate funds. Innovative measures did not help much. When civilian politicians and enterprising officers tried to enhance the federal defense budget by promoting foreign arms sales and all manner of creative selling and trading in surplus and abandoned military property, the wheeling and dealing bred corruption and rule bending and breaking which damaged the military's public image and produced internal strains within the military organism.

The political divisions between the military and society over military spending prevented the Communist-led opposition from uniting with the military-industrial complex. The antidefense spending consensus prevented society from dividing along one deep political fault line with demokraty on one side and all the armed forces, the national defense constituency, and the Communist-led opposition on the other. The military had no solid political home of its own. It leaned towards the opposition but the opposition was not prepared to support the higher defense spending that the military wanted. However, there are two main reasons why the military will eventually find political support. First, since political parties need votes to achieve power and the armed forces and the defense industrial sector represent a definite constituency, sooner or later the politicians will find their way to these voters and make the deals required to win their support. Second, the Russian state will need armed forces and a military-industrial complex and will have to address those fundamental issues.

Military Leaders as Political Leaders

Each major political change since 1985 sheared off part of the military organism, gave some officers a chance for rapid promotion, and sent others out into the national political pool where they joined various movements and parties. Because senior military leadership positions were dependent upon civilian politics, officers could not afford to be indifferent towards them. This had positive and negative implications for democratic development. On the one hand, it reaffirmed civilian control and accelerated military leadership renewal and adaptation to changing national circumstances. On the other hand, it made it more difficult for senior military professionals to justify nonpartisanship and to turn a deaf ear to political activists who urged them to get more deeply involved in the competition for power.

From 1985 to 1989, the velocity of change in individual careers, military institutions, and national defense policy began rising. It accelerated rapidly from 1990 to 1993 and then began to decline. The war in Afghanistan, the transfer of power from the Brezhnev to the Gorbachev generation, perestroika's anticipated modest changes and its unanticipated radical changes, the state's use of military force in domestic political conflict, the transfer of power from Gorbachev to Boris Yeltsin, the breakup of the Soviet Union, Yeltsin's 1993 putsch and subsequent parliamentary elections, post-Soviet economic decline, the Kremlin's military suppression of the Chechen rebellion, the parliamentary elections of 1995, and the political posturing for the presidential elections of 1996—these events all had military dimensions that affected every officer's career interests, the military's institutional interests, and national strategic interests. All officers, soldiers, defense contractors, defense workers and their dependents were part of the grand political process that destroyed the unitary, multinational Soviet state and its one-party political system.

Some ambitious officers such as Pavel Grachev made the right political moves at the right times and were rewarded with rapid political and professional advancement. Lt. General Grachev developed a relationship of trust with Yeltsin and supported him during the August coup and the subsequent collapse of the Soviet Union. Yeltsin promoted Grachev to the rank of army general and made him Russia's minister of defense. Others, such as Soviet Minister of Defense Dmitry Yazov, destroyed their military careers by making the wrong political choices. Even more tragic was the fate of Soviet Marshal Sergei Akhromeyev who also joined the coup and committed suicide when it collapsed. Some officers rode the political roller coaster. Aleksandr Rutskoi is a good example of the military political phoenix. By siding with Boris Yeltsin in spring 1991, Col. Rutskoi became Russia's first democratically elected vice president. For helping Boris Yeltsin through the August 1991 coup, Colonel Rutskoi won a military promotion and became Col. General Rutskoi. However, when he broke with President Yeltsin, sided with Parliament, and tried to make himself president, Yeltsin defeated him with Grachev's help and Rutskoi was arrested and imprisoned in October 1993. Yet, by mid-1994, he had been amnestied was promoting himself as a potential presidential candidate in the 1996 elections. Although his presidential race did not get off the ground, he managed to get himself elected governor of Kursk, a position that also gave him a seat on the Federal Council.

Lt. General Aleksandr Lebed also played a key role in Yeltsin's victory in August 1991; however, he quickly fell off the Yeltsin bandwagon and became a political maverick. This hurt him in the short run but after five years in the opposition, he ran a credible presidential campaign and won 15 percent of the popular vote which he traded in for positions that he hoped would make him the dominant player in Russian defense and security affairs and Yeltsin's successor.

Although Kremlin politics were hard on military leaders, they offered the greatest opportunities to serve. Yazov, Shaposhnikov, and Grachev never achieved the type of military reform the military desired but all three made positive contributions to Russian political change. Of the three, Yazov's record is the most controversial. Yazov kept the military cohesive through the first policy shifts that led to the collapse of the Soviet system even though he saw the collapse coming and hoped to prevent it. From August 1990 to August 1991, Yazov supported the hard-line on the Union and urged Gorbachev to take stronger action to enforce the military draft and to disarm illegal, nationalist paramilitary organizations. Those efforts failed and the Soviet state began to lose its monopoly on the use of organized armed force and its political integrity. In August 1991 Yazov joined the putsch in a vain attempt to save the Soviet state and the unitary military system. The effort to impose an emergency dictatorship with or without president Gorbachev set a dangerous precedent, damaged military cohesion, and threatened state viability. To his credit, Yazov pulled the military out of the coup and condemned it to failure before the political situation degenerated into widespread violence.

Shaposhnikov also faced a difficult situation and had to serve two presidents simultaneously. He moved with Yeltsin against Gorbachev and when Yeltsin formally dissolved the Soviet Union. Shaposhnikov's moderation and diplomacy helped to prevent civil war. His record is more positive than Yazov's but it shows how difficult it is to lead the military during times of civilian political instability. By supporting Yeltsin, he deprived Gorbachev of state power and took sides in the most important political struggle of the day. Yeltsin and Shaposhnikov were improvising rather than following well-established constitutional procedures.

Marshal Shaposhnikov understood the dilemmas that the military faced and articulated them well. He was the type of military statesman that the former Soviet Union needed in order to prevent military-political excesses during the transition from Union to national armed forces. He tried to preserve more of the Union's unitary defense system than was politically possible. It made sense for Yeltsin to replace Shaposhnikov with a new leader to implement policies which Shaposhnikov did not fully support. Yeltsin preferred Grachev to Shaposhnikov and Shaposhnikov handled the power transfer gracefully. Russia lost a military statesman when Shaposhnikov moved out of Kremlin policymaking circles. He had many of the leadership qualities that would have enhanced the prospects for a better relationship between the military and the demokraty and other key constituencies in Russia and the former Soviet republics. Shaposhnikov set the precedents that made the defense minister a national political figure and an international statesman.

Grachev continued playing those roles though without Shaposhnikov's grace and civility as he tackled the enormously difficult tasks of Russian military system reconstruction from 1992 to 1996. Instead of keeping a low public profile and concentrating on military professional affairs, Grachev became a prominent and controversial figure in Russian politics. Grachev fought the military's political battles with the media and the Duma because Yeltsin chose not to do so and gave him wide latitude. Grachev also negotiated international defense agreements instead of leaving most of that work to the Ministry of Foreign Affairs. He repatriated some 1,200,000 military and civilian employees to Russia, perhaps the largest and fastest peacetime redeployment of military power in history. He also laid the foundations for a comprehensive Russian defense system that included new defense agreements with former Soviet republics and other powers. Grachev's dedication to Yeltsin, to military cohesion, and to speaking his mind on the Chechen war and other domestic and foreign policy issues was on the whole positive for Russia's democratic development. He was the only minister of defense of a major world power who spoke his mind so often and so openly. This permitted the military to vent its frustration and probably helped keep Russia stable. However, the fact that Russia was deviating from the advanced industrial democracies in this regard was a warning that the practice was unwarranted. The Russian president should have taken the public lead more openly and more often.

Grachev had to implement decisions of dubious constitutional validity—the October 1993 attack on Parliament and the Chechen war. Yeltsin cited national interest and the president's highest obligation to national security when he suspended key provisions in the Russian constitution and closed Parliament. Grachev wanted no part in the actual fighting but Yeltsin insisted. When Grachev required Yeltsin to take formal legal responsibility for those actions and asked for written orders, Grachev took a positive step in the development of civil-military relations. It was better to attack Parliament with formal written orders than without them and to express deep concern about the breakdown in civilized political behavior instead of proclaiming that the entire affair had great merit. To his credit, Grachev criticized the militarization of political competition even though he carried out Yeltsin's orders.

In June 1996 when Yeltsin struck the political deal with Lebed, a step that made it politically impossible for Grachev to continue as minister of defense, Grachev stepped down. Some of Grachev's associates were accused of conspiring to get the president to reconsider and they also lost their positions. Grachev entered the Kremlin as Yeltsin's political ally and he left the Kremlin when that alliance was no longer useful to Yeltsin. His rise to national leadership, his controversial service, and his departure demonstrated that Russia's senior military positions were still part of the political spoils.

The Transition from Political Games to Institution Building?

Grachev's departure created a military-leadership void which Yeltsin filled with Col. General Igor Rodionov, a respected senior figure who could help Yeltsin to keep Lebed, the overly ambitious junior in line and provide intelligent, mature leadership in national defense affairs. But good politics at the Kremlin level has to be more than individual competition. It has to address national interests and institutional development. The great Kremlin politicians will manage to do all three simultaneously and seize upon ideas that have that threefold quality. To institutionalize the new balance of power in the Kremlin while addressing legitimate national security needs Yeltsin seized upon the idea of creating a Russian Defense Council, a fourth body in addition to Aleksandr Lebed's Security Council, Igor Rodionov's Ministry of Defense, and Zinovy Pak's Ministry of Defense Industry. The president and the four key defense institutions made a formidable organizational set.

President
Security Council
Defense Council
Ministry of Defense
Ministry of Defense Industry

The organizational theory behind the four-element set made managerial sense since it was based upon a rational division of labor and it enhanced the president's ability to coordinate national security and defense affairs. But it required a gifted and able president to lay the foundations for the system by selecting and supporting the new administrators and expert teams. It also required a president who was willing to risk what general secretaries had not been willing to do, the centralization of strategic planning and administration for all the federal armed forces in a small set of powerful institutions. Yeltsin authorized the General Staff to study the matter of uniting some aspects of managing the MVD's domestic armed forces, the Border Forces and other federal troops. On the one hand, the idea was attractive because it promised substantial savings. On the other hand, it would have violated the basic rule all general secretaries had followed. They kept the armed forces divided in order to prevent them from becoming a threat to their power. In December 1996, the Duma passed and sent a resolution to the still recuperating Yeltsin which urged him to define each institution's charter more fully, to determine which department would have responsibility for which aspects of military reform, and establish plans governing defense redevelopment through the year 2005.[3] The Duma deputy pressing the issue was Lt. General Lev Rokhlin who argued that Russian national security interests were being damaged by the absence of steady presidential leadership. The Duma was prodding the president to fulfill his constitutional obligations properly not trying to weaken his office.

The Universal Model and Russian Experience

Military political activity operates on three levels—individual, institutional, and systemic. Individual officers compete for prestige and position but their competition is influenced by military values, military institutional habits, Russia's formal political structures and informal ways of building politically significant networks. Further, changes taking place in the larger political system and society as a whole push and pull at military institutions and individual officers. Some officers try to shape history by deliberately working to encourage some changes and to discourage others.

At times leaders were carried by larger systemic changes in directions they otherwise would not have taken. The larger system can overpower the individual leader. Being armed with modernization theory did not prevent Gorbachev from losing control after his reforms released political forces that Soviet dictatorship had long suppressed. By focusing on his competition with Gorbachev and accepting the breakdown of the unitary Soviet state, Yeltsin rode the new political forces and defeated Gorbachev even though Yeltsin had little interest in grand theory. In the end the Army moved with Yeltsin but not without regretting the loss of the Soviet Union and its mighty defense system and not without developing an independent perspective on political events. Although the military had broad access to the political process and to the media, it did not have broad public support for high levels of defense spending and it lacked powerful, influential political allies. It had become an alienated political constituency in search of an appropriate ally capable of rebuilding the national economy and of restoring defense system viability.

The rise and fall of military leaders and the institutional shifts which followed the 1996 presidential elections support this book's main thesis: the military is in politics, always has been, and always will be as long as the Russian state maintains armed forces. The military profession cannot escape politics for two reasons. First, it is an attribute of state power. Challenges to the Russian state's territorial and political integrity increased after 1991. The president fought Parliament over the basic division of powers and Chechen rebels fought the federal government for independence. Second, it competes for state funding. Competition for funding increased after 1991. Democratization brought more groups into the competition and economic recession reduced the amount of money available. The Russian military started to produce a new type of politically sophisticated senior officer, one willing to engage with the press, the presidency, the prime minister, the Security Council, the Defense Council, the Ministry of Defense Industry, and the Duma. Individual officers and the military as an institution were learning new ways to advance their interests.

A new type of political activist, the military politician emerged in post-Soviet Russia. Military politicians challenged one another for predominance and they also challenged civilian politicians including the very president of Russia, Boris Yeltsin. The first to challenge Yeltsin was his own vice president, Col. General Aleksandr Rutskoi. Although Yeltsin won that competition and the brief armed conflict with Parliament in October 1993, Rutskoi remained alive politically and was elected governor of the Kursk province in July 1996. The second challenge came from Lt. General (Ret.) Aleksandr Lebed who, like Rutskoi before him, entered Yeltsin's political camp and then tried to build an independent power base. Yeltsin's negative experience with Rutskoi and related skirmishes with General Aleksandr Korzhakov convinced him to reevaluate the practice of bringing military professionals into top federal leadership positions.

The Russian system for managing military affairs differed from Western practice in four important ways. First, the 1993 Constitution created a presidential state and concentrated too much power over Russian military personnel and policy in the hands of one person, the president. Second it gave the Duma too little power over military affairs. Third, it permitted the *military* to become directly involved in national political life. Fourth, it placed military professionals rather than civilians at the head of the Defense Ministry.

Yeltsin Zig Zags on the Military Ministry Tradition

In December 1996, after reviewing his experience with military politicians and the overall defense governance system, Boris Yeltsin decided that it was time to break with the dominant Russian tradition and to redefine the Ministers of Defense as federal-level political leaders. He therefore declared that the minister of defense should have civilian rather than military status. However, this did not mean that Yeltsin was displeased with Army General Igor Rodionov's record as minister of defense or that he doubted his ability to lead the strategic thinking and management that Russia needed to rebuild its defense system. Yeltsin retained Rodionov as his minister of defense and praised his abilities.

Yeltsin argued that he was changing the Defense Ministry from a military ministry into something broader and more important. Prime Minister Viktor Chernomyrdin supported that evaluation and noted that the defense minister had to function as one of the nation's top political leaders and had to work with every major department of government. This was a thoroughly political role, one that would be enhanced and facilitated by civilian status. Chernomyrdin added that he was confident that Rodionov would lay the foundations for this new type of Defense Ministry and set excellent precedents for the future.[4] Yeltsin pointed out that this shift brought Russian practice into alignment with that of the world's democratic states.[5]

Thus, as 1996 ended and Yeltsin noted the fifth anniversary of the breakup of the Soviet Union and Russia's emergence as an independent state, the key departments which managed military affairs were under civilian administrators. The Security Council was headed by Ivan Rybkin a democratic socialist political generalist. The Defense Council was headed by Yury Baturin, a political generalist familiar with defense industrial affairs. The Ministry of Defense Industry was under Zinovy Pak, a civilian expert on defense industrial affairs. The Ministry of Defense was headed by Igor Rodionov, a military professional whom Yeltsin made into a civilian as a sign of his promotion into the ranks of top national leadership. Now Rodionov was expected to represent the national interest rather than military departmental interests. Yeltsin had imported the Western principle of civilian control which includes at least a mildly negative attitude towards direct military participation in high-level politics.

Yeltsin's decision to convert a quintessential military professional into a civilian statesman was a smart political move as well as a positive contribution to Russian political development. A close working relationship between a strong president, prime minister, and defense minister would enhance Russia's prospects for recovering from economic and political decline during Yeltsin's second term. It could create a powerful troika that could move Russia either towards democratic consolidation or authoritarian interludes. However, the model failed and within five months Russia had a new military minister of defense (see chapter 19).

Although the troika model was potentially very powerful, it could not achieve its potential as a political power machine unless the president gave it his steady attention for the remainder of his second term. But as Yeltsin's political adviser, Georgy Satarov told the military leadership in April 1996, the president insisted upon keeping several independent channels of information and authority operating simultaneously.[6] Such habits encouraged pluralism and bureaucratic competition instead of authoritative command and control. Russia's deepening economic depression made the battle for rubles all the more intensive and Rodionov refused to accept the Yeltsin administration's public line that the president was funding national defense properly. This led to his downfall and the first failure of the civilian defense minister model. In May 1997 Yeltsin removed Rodionov and replaced him with Col. General Igor Sergeyev, another consummate military professional. Six months later in November 1997, Yeltsin reinforced Russia's military ministerial tradition by promoting Sergeyev to the rank of Marshal of the Russian Federation. (See pp. 478 ff. below.)

Conclusion

In the final analysis the Russian state will be neither democratic nor viable, neither stable nor secure unless it solves its economic and military problems. Building the right institutions to structure the political process would help and there is evidence that institutions do shape behavior over time. The interplay between the president, the Duma, the Defense Ministry, and the press began to resemble aspects of the common democratic experience. However, the Russian state had not achieved viability by the end of 1997. Its overall economic performance was weak and the state was not collecting enough revenue to support basic functions properly including national defense.

The ideal system is balanced, democratic control by the chief executive with checks on that power from the legislative and judicial branches of government. Such democratic governance produces a military leadership system where the officer serves a legitimate civilian commander in chief within an effective constitutional structure which keeps that chief accountable to the people and which grows a modern, relatively prosperous economy. The tsarist Russian and Soviet Russian states maintained civilian control over the armed forces but were political dictatorships. Neither system rested upon a civil society. Democratic Russia's challenge is to maintain civilian control while making the state accountable to the people and effective at providing for the national defense.

In June and July 1996, Russia held its first, post-Soviet, competitive presidential elections, a major event in post-Soviet political reconstruction. But since Boris Yeltsin was reelected and Viktor Chernomyrdin remained prime minister, the elections did not really test the political system's ability to require one political elite to cede power and privilege to a democratically elected opposition. Further, the Yeltsin administration had not yet passed the economic test. The economy was still in decline in winter 1996–97. A tight political alliance between the president, the prime minister, and the defense minister could be used to stabilize Russia during troubled times. That thought certainly entered Yeltsin's mind as he read the negative news from the economic front and faced more strikes and demands for effective action as the new year began.

Notes

1. See for example, Denis Baranets, "Demob Power Chords," *Moscow News*, no. 27, July 11–17, 1996.
2. There were 108,000,000 eligible voters and 71,200,000 voted in the July 1996 presidential elections. The 3,500,000 armed forces personnel and the roughly 3,000,000 people directly employed in defense industry (Viktor Glukhikh, *Krasnaya zvezda*, 13 January 1996) add up to 6,500,000. If that number is doubled to include dependents, then it is about 15 percent of the enrolled electorate.
3. See Vladimir Ermolin, "Duma ozabochena sostayniem armii," *Krasnaya zvezda*, 5 December 1996.
4. ITAR-TASS, "Prezident vysoko otsenivayet deyatel'nost' ministra oborony," *Krasnaya zvezda*, 15 December 1996.
5. See *Ibid.*
6. See chapter 14, above.

18

Serving Under the Imperial Eagle

This chapter offers a brief discussion of an enormous subject, the post-Soviet military's political and ethno-civilizational orientation. Although the topic represents a slight detour from our main line of inquiry, it is vital to any understanding of the general atmosphere in which the military professional functions. The evidence reaffirms the eclectic quality of post-Soviet society and politics, an ironic, post-modern blending of Russian imperial, red Soviet, and progressive democratic ideas and symbols. It gives the soldier a renewed sense of historic mission but offers little guidance for democratic state building.

Russian Heritage Revivalism

Yeltsin is a classic example of a political hybrid, neither fully democratic nor fully authoritarian. His personal political style—a firm belief that he must take the political offensive in order to survive and to advance the political and economic reform agenda, fits inherited Soviet authoritarian political culture. The fact that Yeltsin used the tsarist term—ukaz, for his fiats and issued them on official presidential paper emblazoned with the imperial double-headed eagle speaks for itself. He adopted the tsarist heraldry and terms on his own authority without formal authorization from the Duma. He likewise imposed imperial military heraldry on the Russian military without Duma approval. In May 1994 Boris Yeltsin decreed that henceforth the Russian presidency will have its own special flag consisting of the double-headed eagle emblazoned in gold on the Russian tricolor. Further, the president's full name and date of inauguration is affixed to the standard in silver. The "original" was kept in the president's working office in his Moscow residency. Copies were to be flown over his Moscow residency and to accompany him as he traveled.[1] (See figure 1.)

Yeltsin also imposed his personal preference for imperial symbolism on the armed forces and replaced the red star and hammer and sickle with several forms of the double-headed eagle. At first the military began using the same late imperial, double-headed eagle, used by the president himself. However, on 27 January 1997, Yeltsin issued presidential Ukaz No. 46 which in

FIGURE 1
The Flag of the President of Russia

effect imposed an older form of the double-headed eagle, one dating from the time of Peter the Great on the Russian military.[2] (See figure 2.)

Continuity—the military's historical role as the backbone of the Russian state for over 1,000 years, became the new general line in military education. This filled the gap left by the collapse of Soviet military-political history. Why hadn't the Yeltsin administration picked up where Gorbachev had left off? Gorbachev had stressed the military's role in defending perestroika. He argued that the armed forces had to provide the international and domestic stability required to implement deep reform. Shouldn't the Yeltsin administration have taught the military to defend constitutionalism, democratic values, and due process? The principled answer is clear and affirmative. But the practical answer was muddled and qualified. Yeltsin himself rejected strict constitutionalism and due process and ordered tanks to fire on Parliament. He became an imperial president and made the military the bulwark of an imperial presidency. His choice of imperial symbolism over the simple tricolor of the democratic revolution of 1990–1991 betrayed his ideology of power which posited a higher constitution called Russian state interest. In this world view,

FIGURE 2
The Russian Federal Military Emblem

the army, the president, and the state are one. In the Soviet system, the army, the general secretary, and the state were one though it constantly trumpeted that the army and the people were one. In a law-governed state, the nation is formed through a common commitment to constitutionalism and due process and the professional soldier is protected by the constitution and subject to it. The main binding force is a personal and professional commitment to a political process inspired by democratic political values.

What should the Russian military be taught about its duty during political crises such as Gorbachev's fall from power, Yeltsin's rise, and the Soviet Union's dissolution? There are no simple rules to apply when the state you have sworn to serve is breaking down and its leaders are competing for power. But values do come into play and military leaders determined to avoid civil war, dictatorship, and ethnic conflict can and do make a difference as they maintain cohesion and civil peace during periods of change. As a practical matter, the military understood that by obeying its commander in chief, it helped to preserve domestic peace and tranquillity during times of political crisis.

New Military Holidays and Old Eurasian Rivalries

Military battles are central to the history of the rise, fall, and reconstruction of successive Russian states. The Russian soldier both builds and guarantees the survival of the Russian state. Russian national interests require a strong military and the dedicated soldier is the state's bulwark. State viability and military system viability are organically linked. Such ideas form the core of Russian military-patriotic ideology. They argue that there can be no strong Russian state without a strong military system. They also link the state, the army, and the church and make post-Soviet Russia a state of Orthodox Christian heritage. In practice this meant that the Russian Orthodox Church had access to the military and was present at major events to invoke divine blessings upon Russia's multiethnic and mainly agnostic armed forces. Although the Yeltsin administration condemned regressive, traditional ethno-Russian nationalism's anti-Western, anti-Islamic, and anti-Jewish prejudices, its decision to revive traditional history tended to revive some of the old prejudices. The lessons of history assigned ethno-religious minorities to the defeated enemy role in the drama.

On 10 February 1995, the State Duma passed legislation defining an official set of military holidays.[3] What is the list's ethno-civilizational significance? When the list is sorted according to the enemy's national origin, the results are instructive. The Germans (seven entries) take first place on the list of Russia's historic enemies but the Turks and Tartars come in second (four entries). If year after year Russian military political officers teach this list, the Germans and the Turks will emerge as the most important and relatively permanent rivals of the Great Russians in the competition for spheres of influence in Western and Southwestern Eurasia.[4]

Although the Muscovite state fought German states head on twice in the twentieth century, it regarded Turkey with suspicion and assumed that Turkey would emerge as a natural ally of Russia's rivals in the West. Why? Because the struggle between Slav and Turk for control over the Black Sea, the Volga River Valley, the Transcaucasus, and the Caspian Sea is the bedrock of Russian state history. Russian—that is Eastern Slavic, Orthodox Christian civilization and settlement, expanded at the expense of Turkic and allied Islamic peoples from 1380 until 1917. The Soviet state became the direct successor of imperial Russia. For this reason, the anti-Soviet, national independence movements in the Islamic heritage regions of the former Soviet Union have taken on anti-Russian dimensions.

By January 1992 the Russian public had become familiar with a pan-Turkic and pan-Islamic scenario in which Turkey—with United States encouragement, hoped to move into the political vacuum left by the collapse of the Soviet Union in the Caucasus and Central Asia. Moscow's main evening news reports explained Turkey's plans to redraw the geopolitical map by pulling the flow of oil and wealth from Azerbaijan, Kazakhstan, and Turkmenistan through Turkey into world markets. Moscow and Ankara were competing for control over oil pipeline routes and the oil transit fee revenue. The idea that Russia and Turkey are permanent rivals was taken up by military historians and military strategic thinkers who saw Russian influence weakening in the

Black Sea and the Caucasus. Therefore, Russia decided to increase its military presence in the North Caucasian Military District (NCMD) which covers the land bridge between the Black and Caspian seas. Moscow transferred military assets from former East Germany and the Baltic States to the NCMD. This new defensive strategy reaffirmed Moscow's view that Turkey had replaced Germany as its primary rival. While serving as Yeltsin's national security adviser, Lt. General (Ret.) Aleksandr Lebed pointed out that Turkey maintained a standing army of 600,000 and a large navy and air force.[5] Turkey was becoming proportionately more powerful in the greater Black Sea region and Russia was declining.[6] Russia's weakening combined with China's strengthening, Western support for Turkey, and NATO's expansion into Eastern Europe cannot but raise alarms about the Russian state's ability to defend Russian territorial integrity let alone Russian spheres of influence.[7]

Moscow is also concerned about the two pockets of compact Islamic-heritage settlement inside the Russian Federation—-Tatarstan and to a lesser extent Bashkortostan on the Middle Volga, and Chechnya and the Islamic-heritage statelets in the North Caucasus along the border between Georgia and Russia and Azerbaijan and Russia. The Tatars and the Bashkirs belong to the Turkic-speaking group of peoples and have shown an interest in expanded, free relations with Turkey and other Islamic countries since the collapse of the Soviet Union.

The Russian state is concerned about political and economic stability in Kazakhstan and Central Asia. Ethnic Russians and other peoples of European heritage have been leaving Central Asia since 1990. This confirms the main trend—the line between Russian-dominated and native Turkic and Islamic heritage-dominated politics is migrating northward. Kazakhstan is the most sensitive area since some 8,000,000 Russians live in Kazakhstan just south of the Russian border and are the majority ethnic group in a large band of territory. Since 1991, Kazakhstan's native Kazakhs have been steadily nationalizing the top political positions in the country including those that control the military and police forces.[8] The same general process has taken place in all the newly independent states of Islamic heritage. Thus, ethnic Russians are indeed being displaced by new elites of Islamic heritage and mainly of Turkic ethnicity.

But the most unstable region in Central Asia is Tajikistan where the battle for power turned violent as the Soviet state collapsed. No simple description of that complex struggle for power between ethnic groups and clans is possible. Nevertheless, Moscow is convinced that it must be contained and has done so with the assistance of Uzbekistan, Kyrgyzstan, and China. Russian military personnel guard Tajikistan's border with Afghanistan and maintain armed forces inside Tajikistan. Several dozen Russians are killed there annually. However, the military teaches those border-keeping forces that they are protecting Russian national interests by preventing Islamic political extremists from launching a series of destabilizing military-political conflicts that would threaten Russia itself. Thus, the Russian state sends its soldiers to fight on the Tajik-Afghan border so that they will not have to fight in Russian cities such as Astrakhan.[9]

A Special Eurasian Orientation?

Could a common anti-Western orientation unite Russian Orthodoxy and Russian Islam? Although there can be no doubt that the Russian state's expansion into the Crimea, the middle and lower Volga, and the Caucasus involved major conflicts between Slavic Christians and Turkic (and other) Muslims and large population shifts which changed the demographic balance of those regions, Islam survived and has now won for itself the right to redevelop in the regions of traditional Islamic settlement and in Moscow and other major Russian cities. Mosques are being rebuilt and Muslims are insisting that there be an Islamic presence at major Russian patriotic sites associated with the Great Patriotic War such as Poklonnaya Hill outside Moscow. Democratic Russia cannot preserve its territorial integrity unless it permits its peoples of Islamic heritage to rebuild Islamic cultural and religious institutions.

Between January 1991 and January 1993, the number of officially registered Islamic religious communities on the territory of the Russian Federation increased from 870 to over 4,000 and continued to grow. Such data convinced Russian students of Islam in Russia such as R. G. Landa that post-Soviet Russia will be multiconfessional and a unique country where strong Islamic communities operate within a large mainly Christian heritage country.[10] Landa reports that Russians are learning to live with Islam and to differentiate between different peoples of Islamic heritage, countries, and political movements instead of viewing all as part of a unified, general Islamic threat.

The Chechen war opened old wounds by renewing the battle between Russian Christians and peoples of Islamic heritage for control over the strategic passes linking Russia with Georgia, Armenia, and Azerbaijan. But it also tested the Russian military's ability to view the war as something other than a war between Muslims and Christians. The official military press was careful to avoid fanning those flames. Yeltsin likewise described the conflict in general political terms—defending Russian state integrity against secessionists. But the ethno-civilizational issue was there and the Chechens used it to win support in the greater Islamic world.

Is Russia Primarily an Orthodox Christian-Heritage State?

Military holidays that celebrate victories over Catholic and Protestant armies will contribute to the Russian soldier's sense of difference if not alienation from mainstream Western Christendom. Russia has been on the outside and continues to be regarded as distinct and threatening by its immediate neighbors in the West. Estonia, Latvia, Lithuania, Ukraine, and Moldova present themselves as bona fide candidates for membership in the European family of states and raise doubts about *Eurasian* Russia. Four Russian military holidays reinforces this view. Russia is shown as having to fight its way into Europe with European powers resisting and attacking.[11]

A new Minin and Pozharsky holiday was created as a post-Soviet, Russian patriotic substitute for the Great October Socialist Revolution holiday, traditionally celebrated on 7 November. It is presented as a warning that Russia will fall to foreign conquest if its regional military-political chieftains fail to unite under Moscow. It has a populist twist since Russia's national rising against the Polish occupation in 1612 is presented as a people's war of liberation inspired by lower nobles and commoners nto grand princes and boyars. It also has an anti-Western and anti-Catholic flavor which favors traditional Great Russian ideas of a unique Orthodox Russian civilization.

The Russian military is supposed to see itself as the direct successor to Alexander Nevsky, Dmitry Donskoi, Generals Kutuzov and Suvorov, and Marshal Zhukov. New memorials to Marshal Zhukov were erected in time for the fiftieth anniversary of the Soviet Union's victory in the Great Patriotic War. "The Banner of St. George the Victorious stretches through them all," from St. Alexander Nevsky's victory over the Teutonic Knights to the Battle of Stalingrad—that was how Yury Rubtsov, a *Krasnaya zvezda* editorialist explained historical continuity.[12]

For the grand celebrations of the fiftieth anniversary of the allied victory in Europe over Nazi Germany, the Yeltsin administration promoted a new, expanded cult of Marshal Georgy Zhukov—a solid ethnic-Russian war hero and left Stalin lurking in the shadows instead of confronting the problems of Stalin's poor civilian leadership of national defense affairs head on.

Gaps in Twentieth-Century Military History

The new list of military holidays retained a spurious event, Stalin's Armed Forces Day. Anyone who has tried to determine exactly when Lenin and Trotsky created the Red Army of Workers and Peasants has run into this problem. Soviet historians wanted to hide the fact that their revolutionary tactics gutted the imperial army's cohesion and dealt a major blow to the Russian war effort. Stalin also wanted to obscure Lev Trotsky's decisive leadership of the Bolshevik military effort from the October 1917 coup through the 1921 victory in the Civil War. Therefore, Stalin needed a date, an event that could be celebrated as a national armed forces holiday and presented as a moment when people pulled together to defend the new Socialist Fatherland. Stalin's military-political historians and propagandists seized upon a rather unimportant battle against German forces in February 1918 and made that Soviet Armed Forces Day.

Early twentieth-century Russian military history is really dominated by two Soviet leaders of non-Russian ethnic heritage. Trotsky—the real founder of the Red Army was of Jewish ethnic heritage. Stalin—the despot who built the modern Soviet state and led the Soviet Union to victory over Nazi Germany, was of Georgian ethnic heritage. Yet, both were thoroughly Russian and thoroughly Soviet. There is no simple way to sort this out and it is particularly difficult to do so in English which lacks the proper vocabulary to convey the nuances of ethnicity which developed in the Russian empire.[13] Focusing on Zhukov finessed the Stalin issue for the fiftieth anniversary of Nazi Germany's defeat, but democratic Russia needs new political histories that show why certain political structures are superior to others. Post-Soviet Russia also needs a sense of citizenship that is linked to democratic values rather than ethnicity and it would be helpful to teach the military its true history, one showing that a person's ethnicity counts less than a person's principles and professionalism and which explains and illustrates why it is unwise to place too much power in the hands of the executive branch of government.

Russian military historians still choke on the fact that the Red Army was built by an internationalist named Lev Davidovich Trotsky (Bronstein) who was of Jewish ethnicity and who was even popular in his political lifetime. In 1992, the late great, Soviet military historian, General Dmitry Volkogonov published a two-volume, post-Soviet political biography of Trotsky. It began the process of restoring historical truth; however, the official military press still generally ignored Trotsky and the internationalist question.[14] In keeping with Yeltsin's Russian heritage revivalism, the Ministry of Defense did some of what Trotsky himself tried to do. It began to rehabilitate parts of the imperial officer corps and to show how military professionals dealt with problems of military professionalism under the tsars and during the revolutionary period. Trotsky nationalized a substantial part of the imperial Russian state's military talent and took the remnants of the imperial General Staff from Petrograd to Moscow. Although Trotsky prosecuted the Civil War with Bolshevik ruthlessness, he recognized that talented military professionals from the imperial officer corps could become Soviet patriots and openly defended such officers and their ideas against Stalinist-led, politically inspired purges. Stalin ousted Trotsky from his position as commissar of war and moved against his protégés in winter 1924–25. Stalin then systematically distorted early Soviet military history. To this date, Trotsky's record has not been properly reconstructed and taught. His Jewish ethnic heritage is certainly part of the reason.

The Russian Jewish community's dynamism—a controversial part of Soviet history, did not end in 1991 with the death of the Soviet state.[15] Russians of Jewish heritage—political leaders such as Foreign Minister Yevgeny

Primakov and Vice Premier Boris Nemtsov and new tycoons such as Boris Berezovsky, were important members of the Yeltsin administration. They were part of a larger group of accomplished Russians of Jewish heritage who stayed in Russia to work for progressive reform and who were able to hold high positions in the Yeltsin administration. His team recruitment process was inclusive not exclusive in terms of ethnic heritage in spite of his strategic decision to support ethno-Russian heritage revivalism. Thus the Yeltsin problem is not so much what the neo-imperial and neo-nationalist symbols mean in Yeltsin's hands but what they could turn into under a different president.

The Church and the Russian Military

The Russian Orthodox Church moved into the post-Soviet ideological vacuum and claimed a special, historic relationship between church and state without denying either the constitutional separation of Church and state or the existence of other religions with deep historic roots on the territory of the Russian Federation.

As soon as Gorbachev lifted the ban on religious freedom in 1988, the Church began expanding its work with the armed forces. In addition to opening chapels on military bases, placing icons in military institutions, and conducting weddings and funerals, the Church operates a department of military affairs and has sent politically astute clergy into political cauldrons such as the All-Union Officers Assembly meeting which took place in January 1992. At that meeting, Bishop Kirill made one of the best addresses and received a long ovation while Boris Yeltsin was treated to a much cooler reception. Patriarch Aleksy II sends clergy to every major military holiday event—everything from graduation and commissioning ceremonies to the fiftieth anniversary of the defeat of Nazi Germany. In connection with the fall and spring military drafts, he issues official statements to youth in which he advises them to do their military service with honor and dignity. In his fall 1995 draft message, Patriarch Aleksy reminded Russian youth to serve their country in the spirit of the holy princes Boris and Gleb and the sainted warriors Aleksander Nevsky and Dmitry Donskoi.

The Patriarch has endorsed the idea of reinstituting the office of military chaplains and would like to see every branch of the Russian military armed with its own patron saints and holiday liturgy services. In March 1994, Patriarch Aleksy II and Defense Minister Pavel Grachev signed formal agreements governing cooperation between the Ministry of Defense and the Patriarchy. However, at the signing ceremony, Defense Minister Grachev was politically correct and noted that the military was not embracing any particular faith. Grachev said, "It is appropriate to note that the Ministry of Defense is prepared to cooperate not only with the Orthodox Church but with other confessions since the personnel of the Russian army is multinational." The momentum favored the Church but at a Defense Ministry conference on patriotic education in the post-Soviet period, Bishop Kirill noted that some commanders had gone too far and ordered troops to celebrate religious holidays.[16]

On 1 December 1995, Patriarch Aleksy personally conducted the special rites to bless and dedicate the first, post-Soviet, Orthodox Christian chapel inside the military academy of the General Staff in Moscow, the Russian state's elite command school.[17] In summer 1997 he dedicated a new chapel in the park outside the main entrances to the Ministry of Defense. He has assigned saints to the service branches and has blessed key installations including the main command center for the Strategic Rocket Forces. Henceforth, the rockets would be under the protection of St. Barbara, the Paratroopers would be watched over by St. Michael the Archangel, and St. George the Dragon Slayer would be the overall protector of the Russian armed forces. The patriarch attended the celebrations marking the 36th Anniversary of the Strategic Rocket Forces (SRF) and gave several commanders Church awards for their service to national spiritual renewal. SRF Commander Colonel General Igor Sergeyev informed the patriarch that SRF military academy curricula would henceforth include materials to familiarize cadets with the history of the Russian Orthodox Church.[18]

The Church does not deny the existence of other religious confessions such as Buddhism, Islam, and Judaism in Russia; but it is openly hostile to new fashionable religious imports especially contemporary American-style fundamentalist evangelism and pseudo-Eastern cults. In 1997 Yeltsin signed into law a bill passed by the Duma and the Federal Council which grants greater legal protection to long-established religious congregations: Orthodox, Buddhist, Muslim, and Jewish, but limits the rights of newly formed religious communities.[19] The Orthodox Church assumes that it is the primary religious foundation for Russian statehood, period.

However, military sociologists reported that only 8 percent of the military personnel in the Strategic Rocket Forces considered themselves believers.[20] Surveys found a more positive attitude towards religion among younger servicemen but the believers were a still a minority in the military.[21] In Russian society as a whole—although it is still hard to define precisely what it means when respondents identify themselves as believers, surveys find that about 50 percent of respondents consider themselves definite believers in God these days and another 18.4 percent describe themselves as waverers.[22] Further, a majority of respondents regard religious institutional revival positively but both groups also agree that the constitutional provision that the state is secular should be maintained and only 18 percent of respondents endorse the development of religious political parties.

Boris Yeltsin has accepted Patriarch Aleksy II's blessings upon his presidential inaugurations with Aleksy serving as the official representative of all the confessions in Russia. The Church expects and gets the main attention in the news and its holidays are always mentioned. Islamic festivals receive less attention but they are covered by Russia's main television network and President Boris Yeltsin and Prime Minister Viktor Chernomyrdin sent congratulatory messages to be read in the main mosque in Moscow. Judaism and Buddhism appear only rarely in the main news.

The evidence suggests that the Yeltsin administration has decided to legitimize itself and its armed forces by drawing upon traditional Russian imperial and Orthodox symbolism. But this makes little sense since neither the empire nor the holy Orthodox tsar exist. The most important military memories are those associated with the Great Patriotic War, Afghanistan, and Chechnya. These veterans are real and these emotions are political facts in contemporary Russia.

On the one hand, it seems anachronistic for modern Russian military professionals to display imperial Russian regalia when they celebrate the fiftieth anniversary of military institutions created by Stalin. Thus, for example, Yeltsin's ministry of defense marked the April 1997 anniversary of a special artillery academy formed under Stalin in 1946–1947 with an imperial double-headed eagle from mid-nineteenth-century Russia bearing a "50." On the other hand, Stalin himself appropriated St. Aleksander Nevsky into the hierarchy of Soviet military awards series and created his own version of what had been a great imperial military honor.

Yeltsin's Russian Heritage Patriotism

Yeltsin consistently used ethnically neutral terms, the politically correct language which includes all the different ethnic groups in his discussions of Russian patriotism. His ministers of defense did the same. Thus, the name for the military is *Rossiiskiye vooruzhennye sily* not *Russkiye vooruzhennye sily*. The adjective *Rossiiskiye* includes all citizens and implies ethnic diversity and makes great sense since at least 20 percent of Yeltsin's citizens are primarily of non-Russian ethnic heritage and the group of mixed ethnicity is far larger. His own presidential leadership team included Russians of ethnic Russian, Ukrainian, Polish, Jewish, German, and Muslim heritage. They all worked under the imperial eagle and the democratic tricolor for a democratically elected president who ran the Kremlin by ukaz.

What post-Soviet Russia needs is its own *democratic* symbols to reinforce the idea that a *democratic* political transformation is underway. The revival of inappropriate symbols of autocracy and empire has not really solved the post-Soviet ideology gap problem. It does not serve modern Russian state national interests to fly the imperial double-headed eagle on diplomatic missions to states that are suspicious of Russian imperial ambitions. By adopting autocracy's emblem, Boris Yeltsin is sending the wrong message to the CIS and to the peoples within Russia who regard the double-headed eagle with hostility.

What makes 150,000,000 inhabitants of the Russian Federation into citizens who are ready to fight and to die for their country's territorial integrity? A democratic political system? What is the relationship between such political identification and one's sense of national history and general ideological orientation? Is the new Russia to have an ethno-national ideology rooted in Slavic, Orthodox, and imperial heritage and symbols or will it pull together around a common democratic ideology and a constitutional process? At this point, we do not have the answers to these important questions.

Conclusion

There are four key observations about Russian heritage revivalism that must be part of any book on the soldier in Russian politics. First, ethno-Russian nationalists are correct when they argue that the Russian state, armed forces, and church formed an organic whole through most of Russian history. This inevitably makes some citizens of modern Russia more Russian than others—the more authentic Russians are those of Orthodox religious and Eastern Slavic ethnic heritage. Second, the Russian state was always multinational, a conglomerate of Eurasian peoples, but it used dictatorship to hold them together. Third, there was a Bolshevik revolution and it provided formerly repressed minorities with new opportunities for education and advancement. This truth coexists with the persistence of ethnic prejudice and periodic repressions. Post-Soviet reality inherits that complex legacy. Fourth, post-Soviet Russia needs a democratic, internationalist ideology to give all citizens dignity, security, and a sense of belonging to one, civil society. This is especially important for the armed forces which must defend the interests of all the citizenry not just those of the dominant ethno-political heritage.

The Yeltsin administration has taken a wrong turn. Instead of filling the post-Soviet ideological gap with new democratic icons and building new, democratic, multiethnic and multiconfessional ideas into a post-Soviet, democratic patriotism, Yeltsin has revived symbols drawn from the imperial Russian heritage. He has an eclectic operating ideology. The double-headed eagle was back but the Kremlin's financial viability was not. He could not afford to replace all the old uniforms in a timely manner. As 1997 ended, some soldiers had uniforms with red stars and hammers and sickles others had the new neo-imperial regalia. Veterans continued to wear their Soviet medals and awards with honor and Soviet red flags of victory were still flown along side the new post-Soviet symbols. The eclecticism fit Russian reality.

In the final analysis for the military and the population at large these Russian heritage symbols did not satisfy the basic demand for effective political and economic reform. Neither did they move the military professional any closer to the best Western standards for modern military careers. Placing icons of St. Barbara in the central command for Russia's strategic rocket forces and building a new chapel outside the Defense Ministry's main entrance neither improved the military's budget nor the young Russian officer's confidence in the Yeltsin administration's ability to build a prosperous, modern, democratic Russia.

Notes

1. See G. Samoilov, "Glavnyi simvol prezidentskoi vlasti," *Krasnaya zvezda*, 12 May 1994.
2. See Ukaz Prezidenta Rossiiskoi Federatsii, "Ob uchrezhdenii voennogo geral'dicheskogo znaka—emblemy Vooruzhennykh Sil Rossiiskoi Federatsii," No. 46, 1997; Moscow, The Kremlin, 27 January 1997; *Krasnaya zvezda*, 4 February 1997.
3. See "Federal'nyi zakon, O dnyakh voinskoi slavy (pobednykh dnyakh) Rossii." The law was passed on 10 February 1995 and printed in *Krasnaya zvezda* on 16 March 1995.
4. The Germans: 1242 Teutonic Knights defeated by Aleksander Nevsky; 1918 Imperial Germany at war with Soviet Russia; 1941 Battle of Moscow: Hitler's Third Reich at war with Soviet Russia; 1943 Battle of Stalingrad: Hitler's Third Reich; 1943 Battle of Kursk: Hitler's Third Reich; 1944 Leningrad Liberated: Hitler's Third Reich; 1945 Victory in Europe. The Turks and Turkic Tatars: 1380 Dmitry Donskoi defeats Mongol-Tatar armies; 1790 Suvorov takes Turkish Fort at Ismail; 1790 Ushkov defeats Turkish naval squadron at Tendra; 1853 Nakhimov defeats Turkish naval squadron at Sinop.
5. See Colonel Yury Churkin's interview with Lebed, "Priority natsional'noi bezopasnosti," *Armeiskii Sbornik*, no. 9, 1996, pp. 2–9.
6. See Black Sea Fleet Commander, Admiral Viktor Kravchenko's review of the region's military history, "Proshloe, nastoyashchee, i budyshchee," *Armeiskii Sbornik*, no. 7, 1996, pp. 16 ff.
7. See Colonel General V. L. Manilov, "Ugrozy natsional'noi bezopasnosti Rossii," *Voennaya mysl*, no. 1, 1996, pp. 7ff.
8. See Robert V. Barylski, "Kazakhstan: Military Dimensions of State Formation over Central Asia's Civilizational Fault Lines," chapter 8 in C. P. Danopoulos and D. G. Zirker, eds., *Civil-Military Relations in the Soviet and Yugoslav Successor States* (Boulder, Colo.: Westview Press, 1996).
9. A good example of such advice and analysis is Nikolai Proskov's, "Shtoby ne voevat' potom pod Astrakhanu," *Krasnaya zvezda*, 9 June 1994.
10. Data from Robert Grigoryevich Landa, *Islam v istorii Rossii*; *Vostochnaya Literatura* (Moscow, 1995); see chapter X, "Postsovetskaya Rossiya i islam," pp. 260ff.
11. The dates celebrated are: 1709, Peter the Great's land victory over the Protestant Swedes, Catholic Poles, and Muslim Turks at Poltava; 1714, Peter the Great's naval victory over the Swedes at Gangut; 1612, Minin and Pozharsky's populist Russian rebellion against Catholic Polish occupation, the beginning of the end of Russia's Time of Troubles; 1812, Russians engage the Napoleonic armies at Borodino.
12. See Yury Rubtsov, "Ne znaya svoikh istoricheskikh kornei, nam bevozrodit' novuyu Rossiyu," *Krasnaya zvezda*, 16 March 1995.
13. See the preface's note on transliteration and translation.
14. See Dmitry Volkogonov's *Trotskii: Politicheskii portret* (Moscow: Novosti, 1992).

15. Some post-Soviet writing has started presenting data on Jewish accomplishments in the Soviet era, a neglected field of inquiry in Russia and the West. See for example, L. L. Mininberg's *Sovetskie evrei v nauke i promyshlennosti SSSR v period vtoroi mirovoi voiny (1941–1945)* (Soviet Jews in science and industry during the second world war), (Moscow: Its-Garant, 1995).
16. Reported by Captain Vladimir Chupakhin, "Obshchestvo bol'no bez dukhovnostyu" (Society ails without spirituality), *Krasnaya zvezda*, 12 April 1994.
17. Petr Karapetyan, "Armiya i tserkov' sdelali eshche odin shag navstrechu drug drugu," *Krasnaya zvezda*, 2 December 1995.
18. Lt. Colonel Sergei Popov, "Otchuzhdenie armii i tserkvi ushlo v proshloye" (Military-Church alienation has disappeared), *Krasnaya zvezda*, 16 November 1995.
19. The Orthodox Church argued that new cults threaten Russian religious life and should not have full protection until they demonstrate their wholesomeness. The Duma agreed and Yeltsin signed the bill (after vetoing the first version) in spite of strong American complaints.
20. Reported by Aleksandr Dolinin, "Sluzhba—delo svyatoe" (Service is holy), *Krasnaya zvezda*, 1 February 1995.
21. Source: Lt. General Sergei Zdornikov, chief of military-political education for the Ministry of Defense, interviewed by Vasily Semenov, "Kakaya zhe ideologiya nuzhna segodnya Rossiiskoi armii" (What type of ideology does the Russian Army need today?), *Krasnaya zvezda*, 8 September 1995.
22. See Mikhail Mchedlov's discussion of national survey data gathered in summer and fall 1995 on some 3,600 citizens of the Russian Federation in "Sovremennyi veryushchii," *Svobodnaya mysl*, no. 8, 1996, pp. 113–123.

19

Postscript: Civil-Military Relations in an Ukaz-Governed State

The Yeltsin record in civil-military relations is mixed. It blends democratic and authoritarian ideas and practices. In some ways Yeltsin operated more like a Soviet general secretary than a president serving under a democratic constitution. In others, Russia's first and twice democratically elected president is a liberal reformer. However, the new civil-military relations formed by the Russian Constitution of 1993 and the presidential ukazy promulgated by Boris Yeltsin from 1991–1997 fall short of the best international standards for democratic, balanced, constitutional control. Although Yeltsin had the power to appoint, promote, and fire the top military leadership, this power wasn't enough to guarantee military loyalty or compliance with his decrees. Military discontent increased and a loose military opposition began to emerge. The opposition argued that the Yeltsin administration had lost its mandate because it had repeatedly bungled the democratic revolution and had permitted it to be hijacked by a small, corrupt financial elite.

A detailed analysis of the events of spring and summer 1997 shows how civil-military relations operated in Yeltsin's ukaz-governed state and supports the book's contention that Yeltsin's architecture of power had more in common with Soviet than Western systems of checks and balances. The key events are Yeltsin's decision to humiliate and fire Defense Minister Igor Rodionov, Duma Defense Committee Chairman Rokhlin's open political attack on the Yeltsin administration, and the president's promulgation of a new powerful agency to monitor the armed forces. The chapter argues that good democratic political structures are more important in the long run than bold men at the helm. Poor structures—as the Yeltsin administration's record shows, encourage poor political behavior and breed tension in civil-military relations.

The Conflict Model's New Relevance

In the 1980's Western analysis of Soviet civil-military relations matured into a dialectical pattern which claimed that there were two competing models of Soviet reality which could be fused into a superior dynamic model that was closer to reality.[1] The conflict model emphasized that Communist Party civilian authorities feared the military professional even though all top military professionals were members of the Communist Party and formally participated in its system of elections and consultative meetings. It argued that modernization would produce military professionals who would inevitably demand a greater voice in military affairs. The congruity model made the necessary and logical criticism of the conflict school and explained that the top military officers were indeed part of the Soviet elite and that their policy disputes with civilians and with one another and their efforts to get a bigger share of the Soviet Union budget demonstrated that politics is alive and well even in the Soviet Union. The debate set things up for a fusion of the better points from the two competing schools into the participatory model. All three models were on target for a time but the target kept changing.

Gorbachev lost the Soviet military's support and Yeltsin captured it by demonstrating the type of bold action that officers hoped would quickly complete the transition from the collapsing Soviet to a viable post-Soviet defense system. The military supported Yeltsin's 1993 presidential putsch against the inherited constitutional structure because its system of checks and balances appeared to be blocking effective government. Yeltsin got his new presidential state and tried to reform Russia by issuing one ukaz after another from his Kremlin offices. But he lacked the type of disciplined public administrative system required to implement them and the new strong presidency seemed incapable of resolving Russia's most difficult economic and political problems. In keeping with the relationship between political effectiveness and political legitimacy pointed out by political sociologists, Yeltsin's political legitimacy began to suffer with each passing quarterly report on economic decline. Because his economic reform program failed to generate the revenue flows required to fund defense reform properly, Yeltsin moved into a negative relationship with the military. Rather than admit his mistakes, he preferred to attack the military for wasting funds and delaying reforms. This deepened military resentment and cynicism. Yeltsin responded by tightening presidential political control over the officer corps by instituting a new State Military Inspectorate—the president's eyes and ears inside the armed forces.

There were two main reasons for the rising tension between the military institution and the presidency. First, the president could not finance the military properly because the national economy was in decline and revenues shortfalls prevented the government from meeting its basic obligations. Second, the popular will as measured by the 1993 and 1995 Duma elections opposed the manner in which the elites surrounding the Yeltsin administration conducted economic and political reform.[2]

The Military Opposition Challenges Yeltsin's Policies

There are better and worse forms of democratic, law-governed control. The better engineered systems impose reasonable checks on presidential power without depriving the state of effective presidential control over the armed forces. The Yeltsin system was *ukaz-governed* and so heavily dominated by the presidency that it could not be considered nonpartisan. That architecture of power damages the Russian state's ability to produce national defense policies that have broad national support, solid input from the people's elected representatives in the Duma, and the benefit of military professional knowledge. It influences the political behavior of military officers negatively and tends to alienate and isolate military institutions from the presidency.

But what is worse for democratic development, too much power in the office of the presidency or too little? Is it better for the military professional to develop habits of suffering through and toughing it out even when the constitutional commander in chief appears to be making mistakes or to join a movement to force him either to change policies or resign from office? The answer is that the military in a democratic state should support due process and should not move into active political opposition. A civil-military conspiracy to dump an elected president would be a poor precedent for democratic development; so would a president who used armed forces to suspend the democratic process.

No conspiracy to remove Boris Yeltsin from office could be successful without the military's cooperation and participation. Similarly, military acquiescence would be necessary for any new Yeltsin assaults on Russia's basic law. In November 1990, when Soviet officers told Gorbachev in highly publicized meetings that they had initially supported him but were now turning against him, it was a sign that the president was in political danger. In spring and summer 1997 Boris Yeltsin began to note a similar shift in military sentiment. Instead of permitting the military to let off steam as if such antiadministration talk had no real significance, Yeltsin decided to take action to defend his authority, effectiveness, and legitimacy.

Minister of Defense Rodionov started speaking against what he considered the irresponsible management of national defense affairs. This led to a face-to-face session with Boris Yeltsin who had not been seeing Rodionov regularly. After that meeting on 17 February 1997, Rodionov thought that he had won Yeltsin's support. He told reporters that Yeltsin had endorsed his all-forces strategy: "I am leaving the Kremlin armed with the president's support.... And the first thing that I will do is gather my assistants and tell them: 'Continue boldly, roll up your sleeves, work on. The President is supporting us.'"[3] But the very next day something changed and Rodionov bluntly warned, "Unless timely concrete measures are taken, all could end catastrophically."[4] On Armed Forces Day—February 24, 1997 Defense Minister Igor Rodionov put on his general's uniform and told an elite Moscow meeting of top-ranking military veterans and heroes that those claiming that military reform is moving forward successfully under current conditions are deceiving the public.[5] He declared that unless things improve soon Strategic Rocket Forces commander Igor Sergeyev will no longer be able to report that the country's missile forces are reliable.[6] These statements directly contradicted the information the Yeltsin administration gave the national and international press after highly publicized visits by Prime Minister Chernomyrdin to the Strategic Rocket Forces.

Instead of firing Rodionov immediately, Yeltsin waited three months. When the ax fell, it came down mercilessly. Yeltsin staged the event and invited the press to show the world that he was fully capable of firing his top military officers even old friends in order to demonstrate that the armed forces must obey their constitutional commander in chief. Rodionov spent most of the first two weeks of May on foreign missions to the United States and China and on preparing his recommendations on comprehensive national defense reform which he expected to present to the forthcoming Defense Council meeting.

On 19 May 1997, Duma defense committee chairman, Lt. General Lev Rokhlin repeated and reinforced the same negative assessments that Defense Minister Rodionov had been making only more strongly. Yeltsin unilaterally cut the 1997 military budget by 20 percent. Instead of the 104.32 trillion rubles which the Duma passed and he signed, the military would only get 83.18 trillion. This amount would not even cover the cost of six months of the salaries and benefits mandated by Russian law. Rokhlin declared that the Russian Army was no longer capable of fulfilling its strategic tasks of defending the country against potential aggression. He then urged military officers to hold assembles, to pass resolutions, and to send them to the responsible political and governmental leaders. He warned "reformers" not to misinterpret military patience to mean that the armed forces were "compliant slaves." Rokhlin demanded an "authoritative voice" for the military in national defense affairs and issued a call to action.[7]

Yeltsin Fires Rodionov and Takes Command

Yeltsin staged a quick show trial at which he was political judge, jury, and executioner. On 22 May 1997, three days after the Rokhlin declaration, Defense Minister Igor Rodionov and Chief of General Staff Viktor Samsonov attended the important meeting of the Defense Council at which they expected President Yeltsin to approve their proposals for comprehensive all-forces reform. Yeltsin and his top aides came to the Ministry of Defense for that meeting. With the news cameras rolling, instead of praising his defense minister, Yeltsin launched into a harsh, growling attack on Rodionov and "the pack of do-nothing generals who were growing fat while soldiers wasted away." Rodionov stood at attention while Yeltsin accused the top brass of blocking reform to save their comfortable positions at Russia's expense. But the crafty Yeltsin was careful to isolate Rodionov for the political kill by praising the service commanders and the commanders of the military districts. The day before the big meeting, Yeltsin's representatives informed the elite paratroopers that he Yeltsin had personally ordered a halt to cuts in that branch which had a special relationship with the presidency.[8] Yeltsin's behavior was an affront to the standards of civilized statesmanship and his top aids bowed their heads in obvious embarrassment while Rodionov stood and took it in silence. Rodionov neither apologized nor refuted the president's thoroughly unprofessional display of anger. Chief of General Staff Samsonov likewise declined to present his report once Yeltsin had indicated that he would not give him the time required to explain it in detail. Yeltsin then fired them both. The cameras filmed him signing the ukazes.[9]

Yeltsin immediately named Strategic Rocket Forces commander Igor Sergeyev to serve as acting minister of defense. Yeltsin gave him the permanent appointment three days later after he passed the obligatory face-to-face interview. Col. General Chechevatov—the Far East military district commander whom Yeltsin had named acting chief of General Staff, did not pass the personal interview. Instead, Yeltsin appointed Col. General Anatoly Kvashnin. This was a controversial decision since Kvashnin was the overall commander of the armed forces in the North Caucasian Military District which includes Chechnya and had "lost" the war there.

On 22 May while Rodionov was being humiliated and purged, the presidential press service announced that federal military prosecutors had arrested Army General Konstantin Kobets, locked him in Moscow's infamous Lefortovo prison, and charged him with bribe taking and illegal arms possession. Kobets was the last of the original Yeltsin generals to fall from grace.[10] From 1990 on, Kobets had stood with Yeltsin through the various coups and putsches, yet now he was being sacked. Later that day Yeltsin boasted to visiting president Lukashenko of Belarus that he had finally put his generals in place. Although Lukashenko has a reputation for authoritarian behavior, he encouraged Yeltsin to change the subject.[11] There is significance in the fact that the set of leading officers and generals that had stood with Yeltsin in August 1991—Grachev, Gromov, Kobets, Korzhakov, Lebed, Rutskoi, and Shaposhnikov were no longer holding command positions in August 1997.

But there was still one talking general with a position of some public prominence, Lt. General Lev Rokhlin, chairman of the Duma's defense committee and a member of the ostensibly pro-Yeltsin political party Nash Dom Rossiya. Two weeks after Yeltsin fired Rodionov, Rokhlin sent 900 copies of a letter to Russia's top commanders and officers to protest against the government's failure to fund national defense properly and to urge them to organize and express their will to get policy changed. The letter repeated the same basic information and ideas that Rokhlin had already presented in his press conference of 19 May 1997 and which the Ministry of Defense daily had published on 20 May 1997. Minister of Defense Sergeyev ordered his commanders to seize the letters and to prevent any unauthorized "political" assemblies.[12] But Yeltsin also gave Sergeyev a new tool to fight corruption and to increase military discipline—special military police forces (Ukaz No. 669 of 4 June 1997).

In order to discourage soldiers from running for political office, Yeltsin fired off Ukaz No. 535 on 30 May 1997. This decree deprives any soldier who registers to run for any elective office of military pay and benefits from the moment of registration until the election results are in. Heretofore, people took a leave from military duty but kept receiving their pay. The new rule made it more difficult for soldiers to run for office. It was nonetheless a good rule since it made it more difficult for presidents and generals to deploy soldiers as candidates. Since Yeltsin was commander in chief, he believed that he had the right to issue such orders at will without any consultation with the Duma whatsoever.[13]

The officers maintained their professional cohesion and no significant renegade assemblies were reported. Instead, Boris Yeltsin began courting the military and supporting Sergeyev with promises of quick financial support to pay the officers and other military personnel their wages for the first half of the year. On 8 June 1997 Boris Yeltsin issued Ukaz No. 680—a presidential order requiring the federal government to pay the military its back pay and its current pay by 1 September 1997, and Ukaz No. 692 which shed the military of thousands of noncombat personnel. Yeltsin and Sergeyev assured the military that the first round of cuts—the trimming of some 200,000 positions from the Defense Ministry payroll over the next year, would primarily hit noncombat personnel.[14] Sergeyev invited officers to call or write immediately when and if the urgent salary transfers were being misappropriated or held back. He published the numbers and put staff on the hot lines.

By mid-June, the administration and the Ministry of Defense were singing from the same sheet of music—military reform was painful but it was underway and morale and combat readiness were both increasing. The administration scampered to raise cash to pay military salaries by selling blocks of stock in some of Russia's most attractive state-owned, energy and communications monopolies. Yeltsin's *molodaya kommanda*—Anatoly Chubais and Boris Nemtsov raised the 7.9 trillion rubles and got it to the military paymasters on time. The administration had made it through another military-financial and leadership crisis, the second within a year. Although the gambit had been successful and Yeltsin could boast that he had indeed gotten military reform off dead center, even Boris Nemtsov admitted that selling stock could not go on forever; and he warned that if the economy did not start to grow, the administration would have to rethink its basic policies.[15]

Modern Professionalism Still the Goal

The Yeltsin administration told the officer corps that higher salaries, better all-round support, and new, modern weapons were all in the grand plan. Those close to retirement were being written off in favor of the rising generation of officers. Less-essential military administrators would be cut through consolidation and downsizing. Outdated technology would be abandoned to make way for the new. The Ministry of Defense would either privatize or spin off many noncombat support services. It would also sell off surplus property. It would earn income overseas by providing training and other defense services to foreign states—all under careful governmental supervision. If all this worked, the Russian economy started growing, and the Kremlin treasury's tax receipts increased as projected, salaries and benefits could be increased. Defense Minister Sergeyev's reform plan included the following positive incentives: Military salaries and benefits would double and per-capita spending on new military equipment would triple by the year 2001. And combat training support would increase tenfold or more.[16] These projections fit the modern, military professional model better than late Soviet or early post-Soviet reality. The governing idea was to have a smaller, better trained, better paid professional military which concentrated on true national defense functions instead of a huge military payroll and hundreds of thousands of uniformed personnel engaged in everything form planting potatoes to testing strategic weapons.

Yeltsin sent a special presidential message to the officer corps which reinforced his commitment to improving military professionalism by removing nondefense and noncombat activities from the armed forces. Yeltsin said, "Military personnel should be military and should not have to concern themselves with all manner of non-military tasks and functions. Their high calling is to serve the Fatherland. My recent ukazes are just the beginning of an entire series. All questions related to the life and activities of the Armed Forces are and will remain at the center of my daily attention. Thank you for your dedicated service to the Fatherland. I believe that you will support the transformation and actively join in their implementation."[17]

The message fit the modern Western democratic paradigm but the manner in which Yeltsin staged Rodionov's firing was reminiscent of the Russo-Soviet authoritarian tradition. The democratically elected president made the key decisions and they included a definite effort to improve the military's professional focus as the country's experts at combat. The soldiers were to concentrate on soldiering while the politicians made the big allocation decisions and provided the rules and resources. In a weekly radio address, Yeltsin defended his behavior as personal intervention on behalf of the reforms necessitated because "some politicians and generals only accepted them at bayonet point."[18] But his gruff manners reflected the days when honest professionals could expect to be humiliated and bullied about by the likes of Nikita Sergeyevich Khrushchev. Yeltsin was a transitional figure.

The reform strategy's main outlines had been worked out by the General Staff under post-Soviet Russia's first and second former defense ministers Pavel Grachev and Igor Rodionov. Sergeyev completed the review and went over the plan with the military's top several dozen leaders before bringing it to Prime Minister Chernomyrdin, Vice Premier Anatoly Chubais, and President Boris Yeltsin. Sergeyev told fellow officers that he "defended our positions" and won the government's support for the plan which is now reinforced by presidential ukazy and government instructions and orders.[19]

Sergeyev presented this plan and reviewed the specific tasks and targets set for each major parts of the emerging new defense system architecture. He and his reform team visited all six military districts and the main fleet commands. At every stop the commanders had to show that they had already started making changes and that their troops were spending more time doing what the military is supposed to do—training for combat. He set the pace. They had to follow or get out of the way. The military profession had to bite the bullet and reform the military system. At every stop Sergeyev also met with regional civilian leaders and notables. The reform strategy could not be successfully implemented without good cooperation between Russia's civilian and military administrators.

Prime Minister Viktor Chernomyrdin and Vice Premier Anatoly Chubais announced that their plans for 1998 included an increase in defense spending and a bigger defense slice of what they expected to be a slightly bigger pie. They allowed that defense would be 4 percent of GDP rather than the 3.5 percent target the Kremlin had been demanding.[20] Yeltsin made several personal visits to defense installations and gave the impression that he supported the rising generation of military professionals and the scientific and technical teams that Russia was depending upon to create the new generation of defense systems. As if campaigning for office, Yeltsin listened to complaints and ordered his staff to get funds delivered immediately.

One hundred days after Yeltsin humiliated and fired Defense Minister Igor Rodionov and declared that he had taken military reform under his personal control, things were moving. Igor Sergeyev was pressing ahead and Yeltsin was backing him with better financial and political support than he had given Rodionov.

The Duma and the New Military Opposition

Lt. General Lev Rokhlin was elected to the Duma in the December 1995 elections on the pro-Yeltsin, Nash Dom Rossiya (NDR) party ticket.[21] Although the Communists (KPRF) had three times as many seats in the Duma as the NDR, political dealing about the distribution of powerful positions and chairmanships gave the important Defense and Security Committee chair to the NDR and to Lev Rokhlin. In June and July 1997, Lt. General Lev Rokhlin decided to break with the Yeltsin administration over the manner in which it treated military professionals such as Rodionov and its apparent disregard for the peoples elected representatives, the Duma. Rokhlin had always said that he had originally agreed to run for office and to take the Defense Committee for patriotic and military professional reasons. He wanted to work for a strong Russia and strong national defense. By summer 1997 Rokhlin concluded that the Yeltsin administration had failed the people on both counts and began mixing calls for strong defense with calls for Yeltsin's resignation.

On 9 July 1997 Lev Rokhlin began the public drive to build an All-Russia Movement to Support the Army. Igor Rodionov joined him for the press conference. In addition to Rokhlin and Rodionov, the controversial set of retired generals—active participants in the August 1991 coup such as Vladislav Achalov, Albert Makashov, and former KGB Chairman Kryuchkov quickly endorsed the movement. Rodionov commented that *now* the national political leadership will have to listen. The press immediately began to complain that hard-core authoritarians were involved. Rokhlin denied any authoritarian ambitions but he did not conceal his harsh political evaluation of Yeltsin's performance, a president who has failed to meet his constitutional obligations to provide for national defense.[22] By early September he was speaking openly about organizing to force Yeltsin into early retirement by political means within the law and the constitution.[23] He made a speaking of several key cities and delivered the same message. In Leningrad/St. Petersburg he declared, "We are organizing to change policy and to bring about the president's removal." At the new movement's first national meeting in Moscow on 20 September 1997, Rokhlin declared that Yeltsin must resign. This provoked harsh words from the Kremlin where Yeltsin growled that Rokhlin's movement had a "bandit leadership" that staged a performance "fit for a beer hall and not even a first class one."[24]

Rokhlin resigned from the NDR in order to avoid being tossed out but he refused to give up his important Defense Committee chairmanship. The NDR gave two main reasons for his removal. First, the position belonged to the NDR according to its gentlemen's agreement with the KPRF. Second, it made no sense to have the powerful Defense Committee in open opposition to the Kremlin at a time when everyone needed to pull together to make defense reform successful. Rokhlin countered that it was the Kremlin that turned a deaf ear to the peoples elected representatives in the Duma and ignored the Duma as a whole and the people's will. All this prompted Yeltsin to tighten his levers of control on the military.

Social scientists can stand back and comment on the spectacle. The Rokhlin movement was a typical example of military contestation which is more likely at a time when the civilian leadership is divided and there is a serious national financial crisis. If the economy were to improve and the government were able to fund national defense normally, the generals and colonels could be expected to tend to their primary duties as soldiers providing national security and to leave politics and public administration to fellow citizens who make that their profession. Yeltsin, Rokhlin, Rodionov, and Sergeyev all agreed that the military should not have to be actively involved in politics. Yeltsin and Sergeyev argued that the main economic and reform crisis had already subsided by the time Rokhlin's movement gathered in Moscow. However, as Vice Premier Boris Nemtsov pointed out, until the Russian economy revives and the Kremlin treasury begins to earn the revenue needed to pay federal salaries and benefits, it would be premature to announce that the general crisis was over.

The President's State Military Inspectorate

Yeltsin decided to tighten his political grip on all the armed forces on the Russian Federation. In summer 1997 there were at least fifteen departments and agencies in executive branch of the federal government that maintained armed forces of some type. The most important were:

Ministry of Defense,
Ministry of Internal Affairs (MVD),
Federal Security Service (FSB),
Federal Border Forces (FPS),
Railroad Armies,
Federal Tax Police,
Federal Communications Security Service (FAPSI),
Federal Civil Defense,
Federal Protection Service.

Former Defense Minister Rodionov and Chief of General Staff Samsonov consistently argued that Russia needed an all-forces reform not just military reform. They pointed out that the total number of authorized positions in the other armed forces was greater than the military's and that Russia could realize substantial savings by consolidating its diverse armed forces. Although Yeltsin recognized the waste, he preferred to keep the armed forces divided. He authorized the General Staff to prepare proposals for cost savings to be realized by combining some services but he kept the armed forces divided. Although fragmentation made him more secure in the Kremlin, it also created command and control problems. How could he be certain that all his generals were loyal, honest, and competent?

In the old days Soviet rulers used the KGB and special military intelligence services. They had special departments in the Central Committee where all high appointments were reviewed for political reliability. Instead of breaking with those Soviet models and sharing power over appointments and the tasks of supervising the military with the Duma, Yeltsin revived the Soviet model in which the Central Committee special department served the general secretary. More accurately, the old model never died. Yeltsin took over the Central Committee's office complex and renamed it the Presidential Administration. He created special departments within the Presidential Administration to monitor the armed forces and to control the promotions process.

On 28 August 1997, Yeltsin decided to give these functions better legal and administrative structure. Using his power to rule by ukaz, Yeltsin promulgated a powerful new State agency under his direct control, the State Military Inspectorate of the President of the Russian Federation (*Gosudarstvennaya voennaya inspektsiya Prezidenta Rossiiskoi Federatsii*). Yeltsin's ukaz gave the GVIP 100 full-time professional positions and empowered it to command the cooperation of other appropriate federal personnel as required. Acting on his own authority, Yeltsin named a civilian expert on Russian defense, Andrei Kokoshin, to serve as State Military Inspector. Kokoshin was quite well prepared having been both state counselor and first deputy minister of defense—Yeltsin's civilian eyes and ears in the Ministry of Defense. On 28 August 1997, Yeltsin relieved Kokoshin of those two positions but gave him a new, additional powerful assignment—Secretary of the Defense Council of the Russian Federation.[25] Thus, as State Military Inspector and Defense Council secretary, Andrei Kokoshin was Russia's top civilian overseer for national defense. These changes reduced the defense minister's scope of authority to narrower military ministerial affairs.

Yeltsin argued that his constitutional position as supreme commander of the armed forces empowered him to create any department required to exercise those vital functions. Accordingly he considered the Defense Council, the Security Council, and the State Military Inspectorate his patrimony, parts of the Presidential Administration not subject to legislative intervention and control.

The State Military Inspectorate of the President of Russia is an independent department within the Presidential Administration (*samostoyatelnoe podrazdelenie Administratsii Prezidenta*). It controls for legality, constitutionality, compliance with military reform orders, financial accountability, the proper use of resources, and other operations. The Inspectorate will also monitor and control new weapons systems planning, development, and production. It will even check on armed forces educational development. It will receive and respond to complaints from uniformed and civilian personnel working in all the Russian armed forces. All citizens are invited to turn to the GVIP with concerns about armed forces. In order to get the information needed to fulfill its mission, Yeltsin's ukaz empowered the State Military Inspectorate to demand any materials necessary, to obtain documents, and to solicit written reports. He gave its personnel the guaranteed right of access to all

buildings on the territory of the organizations, armies, and militarized formations under its inspection. Inspectors will be identified by special badges and
documents issued by the president. The state military inspector is to report to
the president and to make recommendations for the removal and disciplining
of personnel, changes in institutional structures, new legislation, and so on.[26]

The case for the new inspectorate is straightforward. The military cannot
be expected to police its internal operations objectively; therefore, an independent, civilian-led agency is a positive addition to the Russian political
system. But who inspects the new inspectorate to make certain that the president isn't abusing these new powers? The answer to this question is also
clear. There was no effective check on presidential power and Yeltsin wanted
not. The system needs checks and balances and the Duma and the Federal
Council are the natural choice for that role. However, when the Duma's
Defense Committee is led by a military officer who openly opposes the
president and demands his resignation, the president quite rightly will be
reluctant to share his authority to control the armed forces with it. And, as
long as the Federal Council is structured to be pro-administration, it cannot
serve as an independent check upon presidential power. Thus, the constitution and the laws governing military participation in politics would have to
be amended before Russia could gain a prudent system of checks and balances on presidential control.

Conclusion

The Russian president controls the armed forces but the control system
falls short of the democratic constitutional ideal where professional soldiers
are at least modestly shielded from manipulative and vengeful presidents by
a strong legislature and judiciary. Russia needs new constitutional provisions
and a new president before its military can enjoy the benefits of the Western
way of military life in a law-governed civil society. It also needs a viable
political economy. The Russia built by Boris Yeltsin lacked the constitutional
arrangements, laws, agencies, and commissions required to encourage the
military professional to make positive contributions to national policy development without engaging in partisan politics.

Post-Soviet Russia's third defense minister, Igor Sergeyev launched an
heroic effort to run the military as if it existed within such a law-governed
and economically viable state. His predecessor, Igor Rodionov began his tour
as defense minister with similar high goals as did Pavel Grachev. Although
Yeltsin accused the military of dragging its feet on reform, this book demonstrated that the military implemented enormous changes from 1985 to 1997,
a scale of military redeployment unprecedented in the peacetime history of
any major state. Some military officers made mistakes along the way as did
Russia's civilian leaders. But on the whole the military maintained its cohe-

sion and saved Eurasia from major civil war and protected Russia's political reform process.

What about the Russian revolution's citizen-soldier ideal? Should Russia return to the practices of 1989–1992 and give soldiers more political voice and direct involvement in national political life? The answer is negative. Given Russia's financial crisis—the state's inability to support a world-class military system properly, open political competition for military support would have created deep tensions within the armed forces. Unhappy soldiers and the political opposition would form political movements and alliances against the constitutional commander in chief, Boris Yeltsin. On the one hand, when a president—even a democratically inclined president, plays politics with military promotions and retirements and shows disrespect for top military leaders, he sets poor precedents. On the other hand, when prominent citizen soldiers such as Lev Rokhlin begin organizing a political campaign to intimidate their president and commander in chief into resigning, the soldier is crossing a dangerous line. This in turn reinforces the president's determination to impose political considerations on military appointments.

It is preferable for the military to express its concerns and to offer advice honestly through official channels than to remain silent when it believes the government is making a poor defense decision. However, once the advice has been given and legitimate constitutional authorities have made their decisions, the military officer's duty is to carry them out. This fundamental rule is necessary to protect the constitutional process and to prevent the militarization of politics. But there are circumstances during which even well-intentioned military leaders will find no easy answers.

Things began to unravel when Marshal Dmitry Yazov joined the conspiracy against president Mikhail Gorbachev. Yazov's betrayal damaged civilian trust in the military. Marshal Yevgeny Shaposhnikov tried to repair the relationship but soon had to make a choice between two competing leaders and two competing ideas for the Soviet Union's reconstruction. With Shaposhnikov's backing, Yeltsin emerged as the primary leader. But when Shaposhnikov vowed never to use the military against Soviet citizens, he made himself inappropriate to lead the military under Boris Yeltsin. His successor, Pavel Grachev was more flexible and loyal to Yeltsin; yet the press and the demokraty treated him harshly for using the military against Parliament, making war on the Chechens, and enjoying the comforts of membership in the national elite. However, Grachev obeyed his constitutional commander in chief and tried to make the best out of bad situations by insisting that Yeltsin put orders in writing and reaffirm presidential responsibility for the consequences of using military power in domestic politics.

National Security Adviser Lebed set a poor example by openly grabbing for power and influence and for making disparaging remarks about his constitutional superior, President Yeltsin. It was correct for Yeltsin to fire him.

Yeltsin was also correct to fire Defense Minister Rodionov after he began campaigning openly against the president's policy line. He should have resigned before making his disagreements with the presidential line public. Rokhlin's case was less clear since he had the right to speak as an elected deputy in the Duma. However, his active opposition to the president's defense record made it impossible for Yeltsin to give the Duma's defense committee a major voice in defense planning. He deliberately raised the level of tension between the president and the military, a political act that made it more difficult for Defense Minister Sergeyev to implement reform.

In the final analysis good political and military leaders are vitally important but not less important than good constitutional structures which over time shape even venal politicians into statesmen and can help nurture modern military professionalism. Today Russia's political structures fall short of the ideal but they do create situations in which the president and the opposition-dominated legislature can debate issues and make the political compromises required to conduct the nation's business responsibly. And the executive and legislative branches of government are held accountable to the people through competitive, democratic elections. There is certainly room to improve political structures and habits and to raise the quality of military professional life.

Social science has shown that societies in crisis tend to draw the military into politics. Conventional wisdom argues that the military will not retreat from politics until the Russian political economy achieves viability. Leading officers with progressive values have helped post-Soviet Russia to avoid civil war and nationalist dictatorship. The main point should not be whether the defense ministry is led by a civilian or a military professional. That person's values and the constitutional structure in which that person functions are what count. Russia needs a new understanding of patriotism based upon democratic values and constitutionalism rather than neo-imperial military history and symbols. It also needs changes in its political rules to create effective, responsible checks on presidential power.

This book has examined military dimensions of contemporary Russian politics and established the history of the military's role in the events that brought down the Soviet state and began Russia's political and economic reconstruction. It has demonstrated that military officers are necessarily part of the political reform process. The book was neither pro- nor antimilitary. Its main goal was to describe what actually happened and to place contemporary events in the context of Russia's century of change. To the extent that the analysis also clarified the relationship between political structures and political behavior it has wider implications for the theory and practice of democratic, constitutional control over the use of armed force in society.

Notes

1. See "Thinking About Civil-Military Relations in Russia," chapter 1 above.

2. See chapters 11, 13, and 15, above.
3. Cited by Aleksandr Pelts, "Obsuzhdeny samye vazhnye problemy," *Krasnaya zvezda,* 18 February 1997.
4. Cited by Aleksandr Pelts, "Vstrechi v Ministerstve oborony Rossii," *Krasnaya zvezda,* 19 February 1997.
5. Oleg Vladykin, "Ministr oborony RF Igor Rodionov: 'Sokhranit tot fundament, na kotorom postroim dostoinuyu Rossii armiyu,'" *Krasnaya zvezda,* 25 February 1997.
6. *Ibid.*
7. Interview by Col. Ivan Ivanyuk, "Ne dopustit' razrusheniya armii," *Krasnaya zvezda,* 20 May 1997.
8. Yeltsin's press secretary, Sergei Yastrzembski made this point when he announced the arrest of Army General Kobets to reporters on 21 May 1997, the day before Rodionov was purged. *Vremya,* 21 May 1997.
9. I monitored Russian news coverage of these events on the ORT's *Novosti* and *Vremya* evening news. *Krasnaya zvezda* also printed the president's harsh statements and described the events accurately for its military readers.
10. Charges reported in *Krasnaya zvezda,* 23 May 1997.
11. *Vremya,* 22 May 1997.
12. *Ibid.,* 4 June 1997.
13. Decree published in *Krasnaya zvezda,* 4 June 1997.
14. See *Krasnaya zvezda,* 18–19 July 1997.
15. Petr Karapetyan, "V rossiiskom pravitel'stve kazhdyi imeyet konkretnye obyazatel'stva pered armiei," *Krasnaya zvezda,* 10 September 1997.
16. Oleg Falichev, "Kontseptsiya stroitel'stva vooruzhennykh sil utverzhdena: S press-konferentsii ministra oborony RF generala armii I. D. Sergeyeva," *Krasnaya zvezda,* 9 August 1997.
17. President Boris Yeltsin, "Obrashchenie Prezidenta Rossiiskoi Federatsii, Verkhnogo Glavnokomanduyushchego B. N. El'tsina," *Krasnaya zvezda,* 30 July 1997.
18. Boris Yeltsin, "Reforma nachalas. Glavnoe seichas—ne teryat' tempa," *Krasnaya zvezda,* 26 July 1997.
19. Oleg Falichev, "Kontseptsiya stroitel'stva vooruzhennykh sil utverzhdena: S press-konferentsii ministra oborony RF generala armii I. D. Sergeyeva," *Krasnaya zvezda,* 9 August 1997.
20. Vladimir Ermolin, "Raskhody na oborony budut uvlicheny," *Krasnaya zvezda,* 27 August 1997.
21. See chapter 13 above.
22. *Vremya,* 9 July 1997.
23. *Ibid.,* 11 September 1997.
24. *Ibid.,* 22 September 1997.
25. Yeltsin removed Yury Baturin from that position. Baturin had been Defense Council secretary from 18 July 1996 to 28 August 1997.
26. Vladimir Gorev, "Effektivnyi kontrol'—svoevremmaya pomoshch," *Krasnaya zvezda,* 5 September 1997.

Bibliography

Akhromeev, Marshal Sergei F., ed., *Voennyi Entsiklopedicheskii Slovar'* (Military Encyclopedic Dictionary). Moscow: Voennoe izdatel'stvo (The Military Press), 1986.

Aksiutin, Yury V., ed., *Nikita Sergeevich Khrushchev: Materialy k biografii* (Nikita Sergeevich Khrushchev: Materials for a biography). Moscow: Politizdat, 1989.

Alexiev, Alexander R. and Robert C. Nurick, *The Soviet Military Under Gorbachev.* Santa Monica, Cal.: Rand Corporation, 1990.

Anishchenko, G., O. Krugusheva, O. Mramornov, A. Vasilevskaia, *Kommissiia Govorukhina* (The Govorukhin commission). Moscow: Laventa, 1995.

Apter, David E. *The Politics of Modernization.* Chicago: University of Chicago Press, 1965.

Arbatov, Georgi. *The System: An Insider's Life in Soviet Politics.* New York: Random House, 1993.

Azrael, Jeremy R. *The Soviet Civilian Leadership and the Military High Command, 1976–1986.* Santa Monica, Cal.: Rand Corporation, 1987.

Bakatin, Vadim. *Izbavlenie ot KGB* (Getting rid of the KGB). Moscow: Novosti, 1992.

Barylski, Robert V. "The Soviet Military Before and After the August Coup." *Armed Forces & Society,* vol. 19, no. 1, 1992: 27–45.

———. "Perestroika and Civil-Military Relations in the Soviet Union and the Peoples Republic of China," pp. 127–211 in Eberhard Sandschneider and Jurgen Kuhllmann, ed., *The Armed Forces in the USSR and the PRC. Forum International,* vol. 14, Munich, 1992.

———. "Central Asia and the Post-Soviet Military System in the Formative Year: 1992." *Central Asia Monitor,* vol. 1 (6), 992: 18–29.

———. "The Russian Federation and Eurasia's Islamic Crescent." *Europe-Asia Studies,* vol. 46 (3), 1994, 389–416.

———. "Kazakhstan: Military Dimensions of State Formation over Central Asia's Civilizational Fault Lines," chapter 8, pp. 123–51 in Constantin P. Danopolis and Daniel Zirker, eds., *Civil-Military Relations in the Soviet and Yugoslav Successor States.* Boulder, Colo.: Westview Press, 1996.

———. "Russian Domestic Politics, Military Power, and the Eurasian State System;" in Hafeez Malik, ed., *Roles of the United States, Russia, and China in the New World Order.* London: Macmillan, 1996.

Bialer, Seweryn and Michael Mandelbaum, eds. *Gorbachev's Russia and American Foreign Policy.* Boulder, Colo.: Westview Press, 1988.

Billington, James H. *Russia Transformed: Breakthrough to Hope.* New York: Macmillan, 1992.

Bluth, Christopher. *Soviet Strategic Arms Policy Before SALT.* Cambridge: Cambridge University Press, 1992.

Brezhnev, Leonid. *Pages from His Life.* New York: Simon and Schuster, 1978.

Browder, Paul Robert and Alexander F. Kerensky. *The Russian Provisional Government: 1917 (Documents),* 3 vols. Stanford, Cal.: Stanford University Press, 1961.

Brovkin, Vladimir N. *Behind the Front Lines of the Civil War.* Princeton, N.J.: Princeton University Press, 1994.

Bunich, Igor. *Khronika Chechenskoi boini: shest' dnei v Budennovske* (Chechen slaughterhouse chronicle: six days in Budyennovsk). St. Petersburg: Oblik, 1995.

Burlatskii, Fedor. *Russkiie gosudari epokha reformy* (Russian leaders of the reform era). Moscow: Shark, 1996.

Chaldymov N. A. and A.I. Cherkasenko, eds., *Armiia i obshchestvo* (Army and society). Moscow: Progress, 1990.

Cohen, Stephen. *Bukharin and the Bolshevik Revolution.* New York: Alfred A. Knopf, 1974.

Colton, Timothy J. *Commissars, Commanders, and Civilian Authority: The Structure of Soviet Military Politics.* Cambridge, Mass.: Harvard University Press, 1979.

Colton, Timothy J. and Thane Gustafson, eds. *Soldiers and the Soviet State: Civil-Military Relations from Brezhnev to Gorbachev.* Princeton, N.J.: Princeton University Press, 1990.

Conquest, Robert. *The Great Terror: A Reassessment.* New York: Oxford University Press, 1990.

Cooper, Julian. *The Soviet Defence Industry: Conversion and Economic Reform.* New York: Royal Institute of International Affairs and the Council on Foreign Relations Press, 1991.

Daniels, Robert V. *Red October: The Bolshevik Revolution of 1917.* New York: Charles Scribner's Sons, 1967.

Danopolis, Constantin P. and Daniel Zirker. *Civil-Military Relations in the Soviet and Yugoslav Successor States.* Boulder, Colo.: Westview Press, 1996.

Dokuchaev, General M. S. *Moskva. Kreml'. Okhrana* (Moscow, the Kremlin, the guards). Moscow: *Biznes-Press,* 1995.

Dolgoplatov, Yevgeny. *The Army and the Revolutionary Transformation of Society.* Moscow: Progress Publishers, 1981.

Epishev, Army General Aleksei. A., ed. *KPSS i voennoe stroitel'stvo* (The CPSU and military development). Moscow: Voennoe izdatel'stvo, 1982.

Erickson, John. *The Soviet High Command: A Military-Political History (1918–1941).* New York: St. Martin's Press, 1962.

Fainsod, Merle *How Russia is Ruled.* Cambridge, Mass.: Harvard University Press, 1963.

Fedotoff-White, D. *The Growth of the Red Army.* Princeton, N.J.: Princeton Univeristy Press, 1944.

Fitzpatrick, Sheila. *The Russian Revolution: 1917–1932.* New York: Oxford Univeristy Press, 1982.

Fleron, Frederick J., Jr. "Post-Soviet Political Culture in Russia: An Assessment of Recent Empirical Investigations. *Europe-Asia Studies*, vol. 48, no. 2, 1996, 225–60.

Friederich, Carl J. and Zbigniew K. Brzezinski. *Totalitarian Dictatorship and Autocracy*. New York: Praeger, 1977.

Gabrielov, L. V. and K.A. Korneenkova, eds. *Bor'ba KPSS za zavershenie stroitel'stva sotsializma, 1953–1958: Dokumenty i materialy* (CPSU's struggle to complete the building of socialism, 1953–1958: documents and materials). Moscow: Gosudarstvennoe izdatel'stvo politicheskoi literatury, 1961.

Gaidar, Yegor. *Gosudarstvo i evoliutsiia* (State and evolution). Moscow: Evrazia, 1995.

Galeotti, Mark. *The Age of Anxiety: Security and Politics in Soviet and Post-Soviet Russia*. New York: Longman Publishing, 1995.

Gareev, Col. Gen. Makhmut A. *M. V. Frunze, Military Theorist*. London: Permagon-Brassey's, 1988.

Gdlyan, Tel'man and Nikolai Ivanov. *Kremlevskoe delo* (The Kremlin affair). Rostov-na-Donu: "A-O Kniga," 1994.

Germani, Gino. *Authoritarianism, Fascism, and National Populism*. New Brunswick, N.J.: Transaction Publishers, 1978.

Goldgeiger, James M. *Leadership Style and Soviet Foreign Police: Stalin, Khrushchev, Brezhnev, Gorbachev*. Baltimore, Md.: Johns Hopkins University Press, 1994.

Golub, P. A. *The Bolsheviks and the Armed Forces in Three Revolutions*. Moscow, Progress Publishers, 1979.

Goncharov, V. *Nachalo* (The beginning). Minsk: Sovremennaia literatura, 1995.

Gorbachev, Mikhail. *Political Report of the CPSU Central Committee to the 27th Party Congress (February 25,1986)*. Moscow: Novosti, 1986.

———. *The August Coup: The Truth and the Lessons*. New York: Harper Colllins, 1991.

———. *Memoirs*. New York: Doubleday, 1996.

Gorshkov, M. K. and E.I. Zhuravlev, eds. *Nesokrushimaia i legendarnaia: v ogne politicheskikh batalii* (Undefeatable and legendary: in the fire of political battles). Moscow: Terra, 1994.

Gorlov, A. G. *Chechenskii krizis: ispytanie na gosudarstvennost'* (Chechen crisis: testing statehood). Moscvow: Kodeks, 1995.

———. *Kriminal'nyi rezhim: Chechnya, 1991–95* (Criminal regime: Chechnya, 1991–95). Moscow: Kodeks, 1995.

Grachev, Andrei. *Kremlevskaya khronika* (The Kremlin chronicle). Moscow: EKSMO, 1994.

Grechko, Marshal Andrei A. *The Armed Forces of the Soviet State*. Washington, D.C.: U.S. Government Printing Office, 1978. Translation of the 1975 Soviet edition: Moscow: Voenoe Izdatel'stvo, 1975.

Green, William C. and Theodore Karasik, eds. *Gorbachev and His Generals: The Reform of Soviet Military Doctrine*. Boulder, Colo.: Westview Press, 1990.

Gromov, Colonel General Boris V. *Ogranichennyi kontingent* (Limited contingent). Moscow: Progress, 1994.

Gul'binskii, Nikolai and Marina Shakina. *Afganistan, Kreml', Lefortovo: Epizody politicheskoi biografii Aleksandra Rutskogo* (Afghanistan, the Kremlin, Lefortovo: Episodes from Aleksandr Rutskoi's political biography). Moscow: Lada, 1994.

Herspring, Dale R. and Ivan Volgyes. *Civil-Military Relations in Communist Systems* Boulder, Colo.: Westview Press, 1978.

Herspring, Dale R. *The Soviet High Command, 1967–1989*. Princeton, N.J.: Princeton University Press, 1990.

Hough, Jerry F. *Soviet Leadership in Transition*. Washington, D.C.: Brookings Institute, 1980.

———. "Pluralism, Corporatism and the Soviet Union," in Susan G. Solomon, ed., *Pluralism in the Soviet Union*. London: Macmillan, 1983.

———. *How the Soviet Union is Governed*. Cambridge, Mass.: Harvard University Press, 1979.

Huntington, Samuel P. *The Soldier and the State*. New York: Vintage Books, 1957.

———. *Political Order in Changing Societies*. New Haven, Conn.: Yale Univeristy Press, 1968.

ITAR-TASS. *Konferentsiya: Problemy Voenno-Promyshlennogo Kompleksa (Vystupleniya uchastnikov), Moscow, 8–9 December 1993* (Conference: Military-Industrial Complex Problems). Moscow: ITAR-TASS, 1994.

Ivashov, Lt. General Leonid G. "Marshal Yazov: Avgust 1991-go." *Krasnaia zvezda*, August 20, 21, 22, and 25, 1992.

Jacobs, Walter Darnell. *Frunze: The Soviet Clausewitz, 1885–1925*. The Hague: Martinus Nuhoff, 1969.

Janowitz, Morris. *The Professional Soldier*. Glencoe, Ill.: The Free Press, 1961.

Jones, Ellen. *Red Army and Society: A Sociology of the Soviet Military*. Boston: Allen & Unwin, 1985.

Katkov, George. *Russia 1917: The February Revolution*. New York: Harper & Row, 1967.

Kerensky, Alexander F. *The Catastrophe*. New York: D, Appleton & Company, 1971.

Khasbulatov, Ruslan *The Struggle for Russia*. London: Routledge, 1993.

Khrushchev, Nikita S. *Khrushchev Remembers: The Last Testament*. Boston: Little, Brown and Company, 1974.

Knight, Amy W. *The KGB: Police and Politics in the Soviet Union*. Boston: Unwin Hyman, 1988.

Kolkowicz, Roman. *The Soviet Military and the Communist Party*. Princeton, N.J.: Princeton University Press, 1967.

Korablev, Yu. I., ed. *Voennye organizatsii partii bol'shevikov v 1917 godu* (The Bolshevik party's military organizations in 1917). Moscow: Nauka, 1986.

Krawciw, Nicholas S. H. "Ukrainian Perspectives on National Security and Ukrainian Military Doctrine," in Bruce Parrot, ed., *State Building and Military Power in Russia and the New States of Eurasia*. Armonk, N.Y.: M. E. Sharpe, 1995.

Kriuchkov, Vladimir. *Lichnoe Delo* (A Personal Affair), 2 vols. Moscow: Olimp, 1996.

Kuzio, Taras. "Ukrainian Civil-Military Relations and the Military Impact of the Ekrainian Economic Crisis," in Bruce Parrot, ed., *State Building and Military Power in Russia and the New States of Eurasia*. Armonk, N.Y.: M. E. Sharpe, 1995.

Lebed', Aleksandr. *Spektakl' Nazyvalsia Putsch* (The play called putsch). Tiraspol: Lada, 1993.

———. *Za derzhavu obidno* (Ashamed for the State). Moscow: Moskovskaia pravda, 1995.

Ligachev, Yegor. *Inside Gorbachev's Kremlin: The Memoirs of Yegor Lighachev*. New York: Pantheon Books, 1993.

Lipset, Seymour Martin. *Political Man: The Social Bases of Politics*. New York: Anchor Books, 1963.

Linz, Juan and Alfred Stepan, eds. *The Breakdown of Democratic Regimes*. Baltimore, Md.: Johns Hopkins University Press, 1978.

Lizichev, Aleksei D. *Put' peremen, vremya deistvii* (Road to Change, Time for Action). Moscow: Voenizdat, 1989.

Lukava, G. G. *V. I. Lenin o zashchite zavoevanii sotsializma* (V.I. Lenin on the defense of socialism's achievements). Moscow: Voennoye Izdatel'stvo, 1986.

Lysenko, Vladimir. *Ot Tatarstana do Chechni: stanovlenie novogo rossiiskogo federalizma* (From Tatarstan to chechnya: Establishing the new Russian federalism). Moscow: Institute of Contemporary Politics Press, 1995.

Malloy, James M. and Mitchell A. Seligson, eds. *Authoritarians and Democrats: Regime Transition in Latin America*. Pittsburgh, Pa.: University of Pittsburgh Press, 1987.

Mal'tsev, V. A. *G. A. Ziuganov i o G. A. Zyuganov* (G. A. Zyuganov and about G. A. Zyuganov). Perm: KPRF, 1995.

Maiorov, D. A., ed. *Neizvestnyi Rutskoi: politicheskii portrait* (The Unknown Rutskoi: a political portrait). Moscow: Obozrevatel', 1994.

MccGwire, Michael. *Military Objectives in Soviet Foreign Policy*. Washington. D.C.: Brookings Institute, 1987.

Medvedev, Roy. *Let History Judge: The Origins and Consequences of Stalinism*. Alfred A. Knopf: New York, 1971.

———. *The October Revolution*. New York: Columbia University Press, 1979.

———. *On Stalin and Stalinism._* New York: Oxford University Press, 1979.

———. *Khrushchev: A Biography;* New York: Anchor/Doubleday, 1983.

Menning, Bruce W. *Bayonets Before Bullets: The Imperial Russian Army, 1961–1914*. Bloomington: Indiana University Press, 1992.

Mishin, N., ed. *Lefortovskiye protokoly* (Lefortovo protocols). Moscow: Paleya, 1994. Aleksandr Rutskoi's testimony concerning the events of September-October 1993.

Moore, Barrington, Jr. *Soviet Politics—The Dilemma of Power: The Role of Ideas in Social Change*. Harper & Row: New York, 1965. (Reprint of 1950 edition.)

————. *Terror and Progress: USSR (Some Sources of Change and Stability in the Soviet Dictatorship)*. Cambridge, Mass.: Harvard University Press, 1954.

Nichols, Thomas M. *The Sacred Cause: Civil-Military Conflict Over Soviet National Security, 1917–1992*. Ithaca, N.Y.: Cornell University Press, 1993.

————. "An Electoral Mutiny? Zhirinovsky and the Russian Armed Forces." *Armed Forces & Society*, vol. 21, no. 3, 1995: 327–47.

Novychkov, N. N., et al. *Rossiiskiye Vooruzhennye Sily v Chechenskom Konflikte: Analiz, Itogi, Vyvody* (The Russian armed forces in the Chechen conflict: analysis, conclusions, and lessons). Paris-Moscow: Holveg-Infoglob-Trivola, 1995.

O'Donnell, Guillermo, Phillip C. Schmitter, and Laurence Whitehead. *Transitions from Authoritarian Rule: Prospects for Democracy*. Baltimore, Md.: Johns Hopkins University Press, 1986.

Odom, William E. "The Party-Military Connection: A Critique," in Dale R. Herspring and Ivan Volgyes, eds., *Civil-Military Relations in Communist Systems*. Boulder, Colo.: Westview Press, 1978.

Odom, William E. *Commonwealth of Empire? (Russia, Central Asia, and the Transcaucasus)*. Indianapolis, Ind.: Hudson Institute, 1995.

Ogarkov, Marshal Nikolai. *Vsegda v gotovnosti k zashchite otechestva* (Always Ready to Defend the Fatherland). Moscow: Voenizdat, 1982.

Ogarkov, Marshal Nikolai V., ed., *Voennyi Entsiklopedicheskii Slovar'*. Moscow: Voenizdat, 1983.

Ogarkov, Marshal Nikolai V. *Istoriya uchit bditel'nosti* (History Teaches Vigilence). Moscow: Voenizdat, 1985.

Osipov, G. V. *Reformirovanie Rossii: mify i real'nost* (Russia's reform: myths and reality). Moscow: Academia, 1994.

Parrot, Bruce. "Soviet National Security Under Gorbachev." *Problems of Communism*, 37 (November-December 1988): 1–36.

————. "Political Change and Civil-Military Relations," in Colton and Gustafson, 1990.

————, ed. *State Building and Military Power in Russia and the New States of Eurasia*. Armonk, N.Y.: M.E. Sharpe, 1995.

Perlmutter, Amos. *The Military and Politics in Modern Times*. New Haven, Conn.: Yale University Press, 1977.

Pipes, Richard. *Russia Under the Bolshevik Regime*. Alfred A .Knopf: New York, 1993.

Podberezkin, A. I. et al. *Kontseptsiia natsional'noi bezpasnotsi v 1995 godu_* (Russia's national security concept in 1995). Moscow: Obozrevatel', 1995.

Porter, Bruce D. *Red Armies in Crisis*. Washington, D.C.: Center for Strategic and International Studies, 1993.

————. *War and the Rise of the State: The Military Foundations of Modern Politics*. New York: Macmillan, 1994.

Proskurin, Aleksandr. *Vozvrashchennye imena* (Persons returned), 2 vols. Moscow: Novosti, 1989.

Redel, Colonel Carl W., ed. *Transformation in Russian and Soviet Military History*. Washington, D.C.: United States Air Force, 1990.

Rappaport Vitaly and Yuri Alexeev. *High Treason: Essays on the History of the Red Army, 1918–1938.* Durham, N.C.: Duke University Press, 1985.

Rashivalova, E. and N. Sergin, eds. *Putsch: Khronika trevozhnykh dnei* (Putsch: A chronicle of anxious days). Moscow: Progress Publishers, 1991.

Sakwa, Richard. "The Russian Elections of December 1993." *Europe-Asia Studies*, vol. 47, no. 2, 1995: 195–227.

Savinkin, N. I. and K.M. Bogolyubov, eds. *KPSS o Vooruzhennykh Silakh Sovetskogo Soiuza: Dokumenty 1917–1981* (CPSU on the Armed Forces of the Soviet Union: Documents 1917–1981). Moscow: Voennoye Izdatel'stvo, 1981.

Schapiro, Leonard *The Communist Party of the Soviet Union.* New York: Vintage, 1964.

Serov, Alexei, ed. *Leonid Brezhnev: The Period of Stagnation.* Moscow: Novosti, 1989.

Shaposhnikov, Marshal Evgeny I. *Vybor: Zapiski glavkomanduyushchego* (Choice: a supreme commander's diary). Moscow: Nezavisimoe Izdatel'stvo PIK, 1993.

Shevardnadze, Edvard. *Moi vybor: V zazhchitu demokratii i svobody* (My Choice: For the Defense of Democracy and Freedom). Moscow: Novosti, 1991.

Shul'govskii, A. F. *Armiia i politika v Latinskoi Amerike* (Army and politics in Latin America). Moscow: Nauka, 1979.

Shukman, Harold, ed. *Stalin's Generals.* New York: Grove Press, 1993.

Shultz, George P. *Turmoil and Triumph: My Years as Secretary of State.* New York: Charles Scribner's Sons, 1993.

Sobchak, Anatoly. *For a New Russia.* New York: The Free Press, 1992.

Solovyev, Vladimir and Elena Klepikova. *Boris Yeltsin: A Political Biography.* New York: G.P. Putnam's Sons, 1992.

Staar, Richard F. *The New Military In Russia: Ten Myths That Shape the Image.* Annapolis, Md.: Naval Institute Press, 1996.

Starr, S. Frederick, ed. *The Legacy of History in Russia and the New States of Eurasia.* Armonk, N.Y.: M. E. Sharpe, 1994.

Stepan, Alfred. *Rethinking Military Politics: Brazil and the Southern Cone.* Princeton, N.J.: Princeton University Press, 1988.

Stepankov, Valentin G. and Evgeny K. Lisov. *Kremlevskii zagovor* (Kremlin conspiracy). Moscow: Ogonek, 1992.

Suvorov, Viktor. *Inside the Soviet Army.* New York: Macmillan Publishing Co., Inc., 1982.

———. *Spetsnaz: The Story of the Soviet SAS.* London: Hamish Hamilton Ltd., 1987.

Trotsky, Leon D. *How the Revolution Armed,* 5 vols. London: New Park Publications, 1979. (English translation of *Kak vooruzhalas revoliutsiia,* Moscow: Supreme Council for Military Publications, 1923.)

———. *The History of the Russian Revolution.* New York: Simon and Schuster, 1932.

———. *Stalin: An Appraisal of the Man and His Influence.* New York: Harper & Brothers, 1941.

————. *Lenin: Notes for a Biographer.* New York: G. P. Putnam's Sons, 1971.

Tyushkevich, General Stepan Antonovich. *The Soviet Armed Forces: A History of Their Organizational Development.* Washington, D.C.: U.S. Government Printing Office, 1980. (Translation of *Sovetskiye vooruzhennye sily: Istoriya stroitel'stva.* Moscow: Voennoye Izdatel'stvo, 1978.)

Valenzuela, J. Samuel and Arturo Valenzuela, eds. *Military Rule in Chile.* Baltimore, Md.: Johns Hopkins University Press, 1986.

Vasilevsky, Marshal Aleksandr M. *Delo vsei zhizni* (A lifetime's work). Moscow: Izdatel'stvo politicheskoi literarury, 1974.

Volkogonov, Dmitry A. *Triumf i tragediia: Politicheskii portret I. V. Stalina* (Triumph and Tragedy: Political Portrait of I. V. Stalin), vol. 1, pt. 2. Moscow: Novosti, 1989.

————. *Trotskii* (Trotsky), 2 vols. Mosocw: Novosti, 1992.

Von Hagen, Mark. *Soldiers in the Proletarian Dictatorship.* Ithaca, N.Y.: Cornell University Press, 1990.

Voronin, Iurii. *Svinstom po Rossii* (Machine-gunning Russia). Moscow: Paleya, 1995

Welch, Jr., Claude E. *Civilian Control of the Military.* Albany: State University of New York Press, 1976.

————. "Military Disengagement from Politics: Paradigms, Processes, or Random Events." *The Armed Forces & Society,* vol. 18, no. 3, Spring 1992: 323–42.

Yazov, Army General Dmitry T. *Verny otchizne* (Loyal to the Fatherland). Moscow: Voennoe Izdatel'stvo, 1988.

Yeltsin, Boris. *Against the Grain: An Autobiography.* New York: Summit Books, 1990.

————. *The Struggle for Russia.* New York: Times Books/Random House, 1994. (Russian edition: *Zapiski prezidenta* [Presidential diary]. Moscow: Ogonek, 1994.)

Yergin, Daniel and Thane Gustafson. *Russia 2010 and What It Means for the World.* New York: Vintage Books, 1995.

Zakharov, M. V., ed. *50 Let vooruzhennykh sil SSSR* (50 Years of the Armed Forces of the USSR). Moscow: Voennoe Izdatel'stvo, 1968.

Zhukov, Marshal Georgyi K. *Memoirs.* New York: Delacorte Press, 1971.

Zhukov, V. I., V.M. Safronova, and V.V. Serebriannikov, eds. *Grazhdanskii mir i soglasie: Mirnoe rezreshenie konfliktov v obshchestve* (Civil Peace and Accord: The Peaceful Resolution of Societal Conflict). Moscow: Moscow Higher Party School Press, 1991.

Zisk, Kimberly Marten. *Engaging the Enemy: Organization Theory and Soviet Military Innovation, 1955–1991.* Princeton, N.J.: Princeton University Press, 1993.

Zyuganov, Gennady A. *Veriu v Rossiiu* (I believe in Russia). Voronezh: Voronezh, 1995.

Index